Business
and
Government

BUSINESS
AND
GOVERNMENT
SECOND EDITION

H. CRAIG PETERSEN
Utah State University

HARPER & ROW, PUBLISHERS, New York
Cambridge, Philadelphia, San Francisco, Washington,
London, Mexico City, São Paulo, Singapore, Sydney

1817.

Sponsoring Editor: David Forgione
Project Editor: Rhonda Roth
Cover Design: Michel Craig
Text Art: Fineline Illustrations, Inc.
Production: Debra Forrest Bochner
Compositor: ComCom Division of Haddon Craftsmen, Inc.
Printer and Binder: R. R. Donnelley & Sons Company

BUSINESS and GOVERNMENT, Second Edition
Copyright © 1985 by Harper & Row, Publishers, Inc.

Library of Congress Cataloging in Publication Data

Petersen, Harold Craig.
  Business and government.

  Includes index.
  1. Industry and state—United States.   2. Trade
regulation—United States.   I. Title.
HD3616.U47P44 1984   338.973   84-10803
ISBN 0-06-045149-1

87 9 8 7 6 5 4

To my parents

Contents

Preface

Although pleased with the success of *Business and Government,* I have become painfully aware of the frustration involved in writing such a book. Important changes in public policy have taken place since the first edition was published in 1981. These changes rendered certain parts of the book essentially obsolete. For example, the Justice Department's 1982 announcement regarding the IBM and AT&T antitrust cases required major modification of portions of the antitrust section and a complete rewriting of the telecommunications chapter. These changes and others have resulted in the second edition being a rather extensive revision of the first.

In addition to updating areas where major changes have occurred, the scope of the book has been expanded. For example, the second edition includes sections on airline deregulation and the Environmental Protection Agency. Discussions of conceptual points such as the public interest theory of regulation and decision rules for social regulation also have been added. Finally, as a concession to the beleaguered student, chapter length has been reduced by dividing several chapters.

In writing *Business and Government,* I have tried to avoid esoteric and peripheral points in order to concentrate on basic issues relating to public policy toward business. Where difficult concepts are encountered, examples and anecdotes have been used to ease the pain. However, the reader has not been spared an ample dose of economic theory when it was judged to be the best treatment.

Business and Government was written to suit a number of uses. For an undergraduate business and government course, the book could be used as the only text. As one of several books in an industrial organization course, it could serve as a self-contained survey of public policy toward business. At the graduate level (or for a more rigorous undergraduate course), *Business and Government* could be supplemented with journal articles and other readings.

Business and Government is intended primarily for students who have some familiarity with microeconomic theory. However, students without such preparation will find that the chapters on microeconomics and industrial organization provide sufficient background to prepare them for the remainder of the material in the text.

In treating each major topic, a theory-procedures-evaluation instructional approach is used. First, basic economic concepts relevant to the topic are presented. Second, institutions and procedures are discussed. Third, the consequences of these institutions and procedures are evaluated. For example, in dealing with public utility regulation, the concepts of natural monopoly and price discrimination are first introduced. Next, the regulatory process is described in some detail. Finally, conceptual and practical difficulties associated with public utility regulation are evaluated, and recommendations for reform are discussed.

I am indebted to Irving Morrisett and Garth Mangum for reviewing the second edition manuscript. The advent of microcomputers makes the traditional statement of gratitude to typists unnecessary. In its place I give praise to floppy disks, CRTs, and word-processing software. At the same time, any errors in the text (whether typographical, grammatical, factual, or conceptual), I ascribe to the same source.

H. Craig Petersen

Business
and
Government

one

BEGINNINGS

chapter 1

Preview

Chapter Outline

Introduction
The Visible Hand of Government
Text Objectives
Overview
  Beginnings
  Workable Competition and Antitrust Policy
  Regulation as an Alternative to Competition
  Social Regulation
  Selected Topics

The important thing for government is not to do things which individuals are doing already, and to do them a little better or a little worse; but to do those things which at present are not done at all.

JOHN MAYNARD KEYNES[1]

INTRODUCTION

The typical course in introductory or intermediate microeconomic theory serves to cloak the real world. The student is continually exposed to the wonders of the market as governed by the twin deities, supply and demand. The gospel of the market economy is that success is the product of a little capital, a lot of hard work, and a good idea. To these fundamentals, the economist adds the grand key of decision making—expand production until the cost of the last unit produced just equals the extra revenues that are generated ($MC = MR$ to the initiated).

Unfortunately, the fledgling entrepreneur soon learns that having built a better mousetrap, it is not the world that beats a path to her or his door, but rather a steady stream of bureaucrats with forms to be filled out and regulations to be satisfied. The economist sometimes presents simple economic concepts by resorting to a Robinson Crusoe model of a single individual alone on an island. An extension of the model includes the appearance of a man Friday who assists the hero in his daily chores. A more likely scenario would find Crusoe unable to employ Friday because of affirmative action restrictions or because the prevailing minimum wage rendered Friday's services unprofitable.

In today's world, the involvement of government in business activities is as much a reality as are the forces of supply and demand. There is little that the businessperson does that is not affected by actions or policies of some level of government. The scissors of supply and demand are still crucial factors in market outcomes, but to suppose they operate unaffected by social control is to be very naive.

Consider some of the problems faced by a hypothetical businessperson in the course of his work. In deciding to hire additional workers, the relevant factor is not just the market-determined wage and expected value of product produced, but also the current minimum wage, together with additional contributions that must be made for social security, worker's compensation, and unemployment insurance. In addition, workers can't be hired strictly on the basis of merit, but must be considered in light of how their employment would affect the racial and sexual mix of the firm's work force.

As the manager contemplates expanding the firm into a new product or geographical area, there are concerns beyond the ability to make a profit. If the project is to be a large one, it may be necessary to prepare an environmental impact statement to demonstrate that the proposed undertaking would not adversely affect the economic, social, and environmental conditions of the area. The peril of an endangered species of animal or plant life or the obstruction of a scenic view may be sufficient cause to delay or cancel the project. Even if the project is environmentally acceptable, it may be necessary to obtain a zoning variance before beginning operations. Also, for certain

---

[1]Keynes, J. M., *The End of Laissez-Faire* (London: Hogarth, 1926), pp. 46–47.

types of business activities the firm or individual may need to obtain a license showing that a minimal level of professional competence has been achieved.

Once the business is operational, the requirements of government don't go away, they just change. The entrepreneur may find that the unique idea that he has nurtured isn't really unique at all—in fact it is covered by an existing patent and he now faces a suit for patent infringement. In addition, the plant or office space may be determined by the visiting OSHA (Occupational Safety and Health Administration) representative to violate some section of that agency's regulations.

In marketing the product, care must be taken to assure that all claims are both accurate and documentable. What could be more galling than for a firm to be required to purchase advertising time to admit that its product really wasn't quite what was claimed? Even products that perform as advertised may be subject to challenge because of sharp edges, fire danger, or ostensibly cancer-causing components. Assuming that all the requirements for product and employee safety, advertising accuracy, employment fairness, and environmental protection are met, the businessperson is still faced with the day-to-day problems of collecting taxes and filling out the seemingly endless reports that are required by obscure regulations in voluminous policy manuals. Indeed, the reality of running a business is quite different from the neat and precise graphs and equations of economic pedagogy.

THE VISIBLE HAND OF GOVERNMENT

The average person is concerned about the interference of government in his or her life. There is a feeling that our lives are somehow less ours than they used to be; that the freedom of choice and action that we fancy we have always had is being usurped by faceless bureaucrats responding to jargonized regulations written in 50-pound books. Concerns about government involvement manifest themselves in different ways. One of the most common is the feeling that government is just too large. An organization such as the federal government, with over 2 million civilian employees and a 900 billion-dollar budget, must be a threat to the "little guy" trying to eke out a living by working long hours, driving a battered Ford, and buying margarine instead of butter. The sheer size of government conjures the impression of an unyielding, amorphous force devouring everything in its path.

FRANK AND ERNEST   by Bob Thaves

Cartoon by Bob Thaves. Copyright 1978 Newspaper Enterprise Association, Inc. Reprinted by permission.

Table 1.1. EMPLOYMENT AND EXPENDITURES BY 57 FEDERAL REGULATORY AGENCIES

Area	1970	1980	1982	1983	1984 (est.)	1985 (est.)
			Expenditures ($ billions)			
Social Regulation						
Consumer Safety & Health	$ 0.3	2.3	2.4	2.5	2.6	2.6
Job Safety & Other Working Conditions	$ 0.1	0.7	0.8	0.8	0.8	0.9
Energy & the Environment	$ 0.1	1.9	2.0	2.1	2.2	2.5
	$ 0.5	4.9	5.2	5.4	5.7	5.9
Economic Regulation						
Finance & Banking	$ 0.1	0.3	0.4	0.4	0.4	0.5
Other Industry-Specific	$ 0.1	0.4	0.4	0.3	0.4	0.3
General Business	$ 0.1	0.3	0.3	0.4	0.4	0.5
	$ 0.3	1.0	1.1	1.1	1.2	1.2
TOTAL	$ 0.8	5.9	6.3	6.5	6.9	7.2
TOTAL IN 1970 DOLLARS*	$ 0.8	3.0	2.7	2.7	2.8	2.7
			Permanent full-time positions (thousands)			
Social Regulation	9.7	66.4	57.6	55.3	55.4	55.9
Economic Regulation	18.0	24.1	22.2	21.6	21.6	21.6
TOTAL	27.7	90.5	79.7	76.9	77.0	77.5

*Adjusted by GNP deflator (actual and, for later years, estimated in budget).
Source: Center for the Study of American Business as reported in *Regulation,* March–April, 1984.

Table 1.1 reports employment and expenditures for federal regulatory agencies. In fiscal 1985 those agencies employed over 75,000 workers and spent $7.2 billion. This was a dramatic increase in comparison to 1970, when employment and expenditure totals were 27,700 workers and $0.8 billion, respectively. Part of the spending increase reflects inflation, but even in terms of 1970 dollars, expenditures more than tripled. However, it also should be noted that 1980 was the high point in terms of both employment and real dollar expenditures. This reversal reflects efforts by the Reagan administration to cut back on regulatory activities of the federal government. It remains to be seen whether the decline signals a long-term trend or is just a temporary abberration.

The dollar figures in Table 1.1 represent only the direct costs of government involvement. The compliance costs to firms of meeting government regulatory requirements are far greater. The Center for the Study of American Business estimates that total compliance costs may be as much as 20 times the federal budgetary expenditure.[2] Applying this multiplier to the fiscal 1985 regulatory budget results in an estimate of about $145 billion as the direct and indirect costs of federal government business regulation. This estimate is obviously a very rough calculation, but even if the "true" cost is only half, or even one-quarter of $145 billion, the total still is staggering.

A second, but related concern about government is that regulations and policies

[2]Weidenbaum, M.L., *Business, Government, and the Public,* 2nd ed., Prentice-Hall, Englewood Cliffs, N.J., 1981, pp. 343–344.

are not responsive to the needs and circumstances of individuals—that the need to formulate rules and procedures for large groups must necessarily assume priority over the desire to tailor programs for special conditions. This view suggests that if government is not the originator of the "Catch-22" syndrome, it is certainly the major proponent. The Catch-22 concept is illustrated by an event from the play of the same name.

In the play a pilot name Yossarian goes to a military doctor and claims that he is crazy and should be relieved from flying additional combat missions. The physician replies that no action can be taken unless a pilot makes a request to be grounded. Yossarian quickly makes such a request, but is then told by the doctor that he has proven himself to be perfectly sane and must continue to fly the missions.

As Yossarian talks with the doctor, the simple logic of this policy becomes clear. Only sane people are allowed to fly combat missions. But only a crazy person would want to risk his life on such a dangerous activity. Thus, anyone who wants to fly is crazy and shouldn't be allowed to go. Conversely, any pilot who tries to get out of flying the missions is sane and, therefore, qualified to fly. The paradox is that those who want to fly can't, and those who don't want to must.[3]

Disturbingly similar paradoxes sometimes occur when dealing with the government. *Money* magazine reported the following call for help:

> Bums, loafers, ne'er-do-wells: You're welcome in Hondo, Texas. That town of 6000 wants $700,000 in federal aid for a new civic center, but with only a 3% unemployment rate, it can't qualify. The mayor of the small town, Woodrow Glasscock, Jr., is looking for jobless people—180 of them. That would double the rate to 6% and make Hondo eligible for federal funds.[4]

Another anxiety about government regulations is that their costs often seem to exceed their benefits. The average person may have difficulty understanding why the habitat of an obscure fish or flower is given priority over a large industrial development providing jobs and higher wages for hundreds of people. An interesting example of a seemingly curious choice between costs and benefits was a proposed ban by the Food and Drug Administration (FDA) on the use of the sweetener saccharin in soft drinks and other uses. Medical research had provided some evidence that the consumption of saccharin might result in increased incidence of bladder cancer. Based on these findings, the FDA proposed that saccharin be banned. But, presumably, saccharin has some utility to people who desire to reduce their calorie consumption. The typical soft drink contains about 100 calories, while a can of Tab, Fresca, or some other diet drink may have less than a single calorie. A sound decision criterion would compare the risk of cancer from saccharin with the consequences of weight gain from drinking sugar-sweetened soft drinks. A study at the University of Pittsburgh made such a comparison. It was determined that the reduction in average life expectancy associated with the 100 calories in a nondiet soft drink is 100 times as great as the reduction attributed to the threat of cancer from saccharin in a diet drink.[5] The saccharin controversy represented

[3]Heller, J., *Catch 22: A Dramatization* (New York: Dell, Delacorte Press, 1973), p. 47.
[4]*Money* (Aug. 1977).
[5]Cohen, B. L., "Relative Risks of Saccharin Ingestion," *Science* (Mar. 3, 1978), p. 983.

an extreme and perhaps atypical example of the costs versus benefits of governmental involvement, but such instances have the effect of agitating and confusing the average person as to the propriety of government interference in market activities.[6]

TEXT OBJECTIVES

The discussion of the past few pages could easily give the impression that government involvement in business is typically irrational, unyielding, or ill-advised. Such is not the thesis of this text. While blanket denunciations of government seem to be politically popular, they ignore the many instances where government regulations and policies have saved lives, prevented injuries, preserved or rejuvenated natural resources, or assisted consumers in their struggle against concentrated economic or political power.

The purpose of this book is to provide a broad and balanced perspective of the government-business interface. In some cases it will be argued that the involvement of government in business activities serves a useful purpose. In other cases the actions of government are found to be based on rather questionable theoretical foundations. In still other circumstances it will be argued that, while the intent of certain government programs is sound, the costs of specific policies exceed the benefits that are obtained.

The general approach used in analyzing each area of government involvement is to begin by providing the theoretical and historical background for government actions. Once these underpinnings are understood, then the institutions and procedures used to implement the policies are described. Finally, the discussion focuses on existing data and research, in order to evaluate the merits of governmental activities.

This text is not intended to be an encyclopedia of government involvement in business and consumer activities. Indeed, it is doubtful that anyone could ever determine all the ways in which government programs and policies affect firms and individuals. Rather, the intent is to consider in detail selected areas of government involvement. Some important aspects of government policy are conspicuous omissions from the text, because they traditionally belong to other fields of economic study. For example, the regulation of the banking system is covered in great detail by courses and texts in money and banking. Similarly, government fiscal policy is reserved for courses in public finance and macroeconomics. Hence, these topics are not discussed here.

OVERVIEW
Beginnings

The point of departure for this text is an analysis of the relationships between market structure and industry performance. In evaluating government policy toward industry, the economist typically begins with the presumption that a competitive market structure generates results consistent with generally accepted objectives for the society. The outcomes associated with competition are then compared to those resulting from other market structures or other kinds of firm conduct. Once the ideals of industry performance have been identified, together with the deviations resulting from alternative situations, then policy recommendations are made to correct perceived problems.

[6]In this particular case, Congress also became agitated. Legislation was passed that postponed the FDA's proposed ban.

In Chapter 2 the theoretical relationships between market structure and economic performance are explored. Basically, the chapter is a brief review of the theory of the firm and welfare economics as taught in microeconomic theory courses. The discussion contrasts the efficiency implications of the extremes of market structure—perfect competition and monopoly. A simple model of oligopoly is also presented as a tool for demonstrating the tendency for oligopolists to engage in collusion.

Chapter 3 includes selected topics from the field of industrial organization. Barriers to entry and methods of measuring market structure are first considered. The remainder of the chapter describes the status and trends of industrial concentration in the United States.

The reader who is familiar with the material in Chapters 2 and 3 can skim over these chapters. However, students who have not yet been exposed to these topics or who are not yet expert in their application will find that a thorough study of the information is a high-yield investment. Chapters 2 and 3 are intended to provide the reader with the necessary background to understand the theoretical foundations of the policy measures discussed and analyzed in the remainder of the book.

Workable Competition and Antitrust Policy

If it is presumed that the best of all worlds is obtained from a competitive market structure, then a high priority for government would be to implement policies designed to favor or improve competition. Appropriately, the discussion of government action in this text begins with those policies intended to increase competition or produce competitive results. The primary political mechanism for improving competition in the United States is by application of antitrust laws. These laws give government the power to alter existing or proposed market structures and to impose civil or criminal penalties for certain types of business conduct deemed not to be in the public interest. Chapter 4 provides background on antitrust laws and procedures.

Chapters 5 and 6 focus on the use of antitrust policy to alter industry structure. The first section of Chapter 6 stresses the importance of correctly defining the product and geographic markets as a prelude to assessing market structure. The remainder of the chapter considers the application of antitrust law to firms that are alleged to already possess monopoly power. Chapter 6 deals with merger law. It was soon recognized by "trustbusters" that preventing the formation of a monopoly was easier than attempting to restructure firms once market power had been achieved. Accordingly, government is heavily involved in the evaluation of business merger activities.

Chapters 7 and 8 consider industry conduct. Next to his comments about the "invisible hand", the most frequently quoted statement of Adam Smith must surely be that "people of the same trade seldom meet together, even for merriment and diversion, but the conversation ends in a conspiracy against the public or in some contrivance to raise prices."[7] The realization of monopoly power does not require a formal alliance of firms, but can be achieved by ostensibly independent firms acting together to set prices or divide markets. Chapter 7 covers antitrust policies as they relate to such collusive activities. Chapter 8 looks at price discrimination and various types of restrictive practices. For example, firms with market power in one market may attempt to

[7]Smith, A., *The Wealth of Nations,* (New York: Random House, Modern Library, 1937), p. 128.

extend that power into more competitive markets by requiring a buyer to purchase the competitively produced product as a condition for obtaining the product over which they have market power. Such a policy is called a tied sale and may unfairly reduce opportunities for other businesses.

Chapter 9 is an evaluation of U.S. antitrust policies. Included are sections describing federal enforcement agencies, case selection, problems in litigating the "big case," and the use of alternative remedies and penalties. The chapter concludes with an evaluation of antitrust success in relation to monopoly, merger, collusion, price discrimination, and restrictive practices.

Regulation as an Alternative to Competition

Policies to enhance and extend competition are not possible or appropriate in all cases. The problem is not that competition is somehow less desirable than before, but that there are other considerations or objectives that are deemed to be of greater importance. These circumstances are considered in Part Three, Regulation as an Alternative to Competition.

For some technologies, efficiency requires that individual firms be large in relation to the size of the market. For example, the concept of the neighborhood electric generating plant has been discarded as being inefficient. Electricity is best provided by a single large firm, avoiding duplication of facilities and acting as a monopoly in a given area. To force a competitive market structure on such an industry would be to lose much more in efficiency than is gained from competition. At the same time, the potential abuses of monopoly must be considered. The solution that has been adopted in the United States is to provide the electric utility with a formal grant of monopoly power, while removing from the firm the right to make its own pricing and entry decisions. Quasi-administrative agencies have been established to assure that the publicly sanctioned monopoly power of the firm is not abused. Chapter 10 considers the theoretical basis for price regulation of public utilities. The historical evolution of regulation is also reviewed. In Chapter 11 the institutions and procedures of utility regulation are discussed.

Chapters 12 to 14 focus on current issues in economic regulation. Pricing topics such as the peak load problem and lifeline rates in the electric utility industry are considered in Chapter 12. In Chapter 13 the telecommunications industry is discussed to illustrate problems relating to competition in regulated markets. Details of the AT&T divestiture also are discussed. Chapter 14 discusses natural gas and airline passenger service as examples of the deregulation movement. Finally, Chapter 15 is an evaluation of economic regulation.

Social Regulation

In some cases, the perceived problem is not the price that is charged or the number of participants in the market, but the quality of the service or product that is sold. Government is extensively involved in protecting the health and safety of individuals and in assessing the quality of services and products. An individual desiring to be a pilot or a contractor soon learns that it takes more than just intent and effort. For many activities, a license certifying competency is required. The businessperson quickly learns that she or he had better follow the guidelines for work safety set up by OSHA or else expect problems. Products that are potentially dangerous or which are not exactly as claimed by their advertising are kept under careful scrutiny by various government agencies. Part Four deals with social regulation. In Chapter 16 the need for government is discussed together with basic decision-rules for government involvement. Efforts to protect consumers are the topic of Chapter 17. Occupational health and safety and environmental preservation are the foci of Chapter 18.

Selected Topics

Many of the problems that are dealt with in the United States by antitrust laws or by regulation are handled in other countries by government ownership of the enterprise. Regulation of telephone and electric utilities by administrative agencies is the norm in the United States, but is not the common arrangement in most other nations. Although there is a general presumption against public ownership in the United States, there are important examples of state enterprise. Chapter 19 considers the origins of public enterprise and suggests a theory of public enterprise performance. Case studies of municipal electric utilities, Amtrak, and the U.S. Postal Service are also presented.

Some government policies are specifically intended to limit competition. Patent rights are an example. Suppose a novel idea is developed after a great deal of thought and toil. The idea is marketed with the expectation that the inventor's extreme cleverness will result in his financial independence. The rude awakening is that a lazy and unethical competitor takes the idea and reaps the profits. The unfairness of this result may reduce the incentive to try again. Here competition may not be best, because it doesn't provide sufficient incentives for technological innovation. Some mechanism must be provided for the innovator to have assurance that he will capture the rewards for his effort. Considerations such as these led to development of patent rights. The theory and application of the patent process are considered in Chapter 20.

Wage and price controls are another important tool in the government arsenal for control over business. These may be applied to specific firms or levied on a broad basis. They may be voluntary or mandatory. Chapter 21 reviews the theory, uses, and evidence with respect to broadly applied incomes policies and also selective price controls.

chapter 2

Market Structure and Economic Efficiency

Chapter Outline

Here's the rule for bargains. "Do other men for they would do you." That's the true business precept.

CHARLES DICKENS

In this chapter basic concepts and methods of microeconomic analysis are presented. Some of the ideas may be new, but most will be at least vaguely familiar to students who have successfully completed a course in microeconomic theory. For those who have escaped micro, or for whom it did not "take," the material presented in the following pages will prove to be a useful aid to further study. A certain level of preparation is taken for granted in this and subsequent chapters. It is assumed that the reader is familiar with the operations of markets and the function of prices in clearing markets. It is also assumed that the reader understands demand and cost curves as used in traditional economic models. Finally, an acquaintance with marginal analysis is presupposed.[1]

This chapter is organized in the following manner. The first section considers the extremes of market structure—perfect competition and monopoly. The objective is to analyze and contrast the efficiency implications of these alternative structures. The second section uses the Cournot model as a simple example of oligopoly theory and to demonstrate the tendency of oligopolists to collude. A firm grasp of the concepts presented in this chapter is a prerequisite for understanding the issues and policies discussed in the remainder of the book.

THE EXTREMES: COMPETITION AND MONOPOLY

Over 60 years ago Frank Knight wrote, "In view of the fact that practically every business is a partial monopoly, it is remarkable that the theoretical treatment of economics has related so exclusively to complete monopoly and perfect competition."[2] Since that time important contributions have been made to the analysis of alternative market structures. However, classroom time is still heavily biased toward discussing the extremes of competition and monopoly. The reasons for such emphasis are considered later in this section, but at this point the standard economic models of these extreme market structures are presented, together with their virtues and vices.

Perfect Competition

Economics has been described as a discipline that takes simple ideas and makes them difficult. The economist's definition of competition supports that description. Perfect competition implies that there really is no competition in the sense that individual buyers and sellers, in making business decisions, do not have to take into account the impact of the actions of other economic units. This is because those units are so small in relation to the total market that their influence is imperceptible to other buyers and

---

[1]For students who feel the need for additional help, there are many good texts in microeconomics. For example, see Mansfield, E., *Microeconomics,* 4th ed. (New York: Norton, 1982).

[2]Knight, F., *Risk, Uncertainty and Profit* (Boston: Houghton Mifflin, 1921), p. 193, f.n.

sellers. Hence, economic units do not compete against one another, but rather operate in an economic environment that they perceive as fixed or given.

The traditional definition of *perfect competition* requires that four criteria be met. First, there must be a large number of buyers and sellers in the market. No single buyer or seller should be able to exert a significant influence over input or product prices. This criterion is sometimes described in terms of all buyers and sellers being "price takers" who assume that they can buy or sell all they want at the market-determined price. Graphically it is depicted as sellers facing a horizontal demand curve for their product and buyers being confronted by a horizontal supply curve for inputs.

The second assumption is perfect mobility of resources, which means that inputs such as labor and capital must be able to enter or leave the market with relative ease. It also implies that resources can be switched from one use to another. The third requirement is product homogeneity. For a given product, there should be no preference of consumers as to whom they purchase it from. The product of producer *A* should be indistinguishable from that of producer *B*. Finally, the assumption of perfect knowledge is imposed. Consumers, firms, and input suppliers must have complete information about prices and technologies.

Short-run Theory   The *short run* is defined as a period in which the use of at least one input is fixed. The discussion that follows assumes that the number of firms in an industry and the plant size of each firm is given, because the period being considered is too short to allow firms to enter or leave the industry or to change the basic nature of their production facilities. Obviously, the period of time that can properly be designated as the short run depends on the particular industry being discussed.

The firm in perfect competition faces a horizontal demand curve for its product, which implies that the firm can sell as much as it wants at the given price. The firm has no reason to price its product below the market price. Conversely, if it attempts to sell above the market price it will lose all its sales. The market price is determined by the interaction of the market supply and demand curves for the product. This demand curve is shown in Figure 2.1.

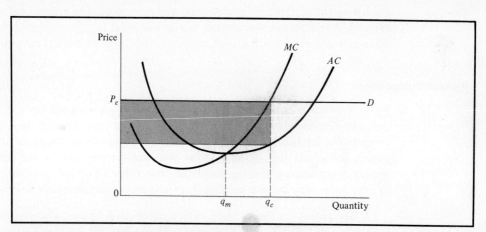

Figure 2.1.   Short-run equilibrium: competition.

The firm also has average- and marginal-cost curves, as depicted in Figure 2.1. These curves have the traditional shape, indicating that economies of scale allow the firm to reduce unit costs as it expands output from 0 to q_m, but beyond that point average costs increase. An important idea to remember is that the cost curves as shown in Figure 2.1 include a normal return to capital. That is, in addition to labor, materials, fuel, and other expenses, it is assumed that the firm is earning a return on the capital being employed that is comparable to the return on capital being earned in other markets. Thus, any time that the firm's average revenues are greater than its average costs, it is earning not only the normal return to capital included in the cost curves, but also additional profits. These often are referred to as excess or economic profits.

The traditional model of perfect competition also assumes that the objective of the firm is to maximize its profits. This is done by expanding production until the extra revenues generated by selling the last unit just equal the marginal cost of producing that unit. For an infinitely elastic demand curve, such as that depicted in Figure 2.1, this condition is met by expanding production to q_c where $P_e = MC$. If the firm increases sales beyond this point, the additional revenues, P_e, are less than the extra cost as shown by the marginal-cost curve. Similarly, if production is reduced below q_c, the loss of revenues is greater than the reduction in costs; hence, profits are decreased. Production at q_c represents the short-run equilibrium of the competitive firm in the sense that a profit-maximizing firm has no incentive to alter its output as long as the demand and cost curves remain as shown in Figure 2.1.

Long-run Theory   In the *long run* all inputs are variable. It is possible for firms to enter or leave the industry. It is also possible for firms to change their production facilities. Although the output q_c represents a short-run equilibrium, it is not the optimal choice in the long run. Producing at q_c, the firm is earning excess profits. Per unit excess profits are given by the vertical distance between the average-cost curve and the demand curve at the output q_c. Total excess profits are shown by the shaded area in Figure 2.1. Since the average cost curve already includes a normal rate of profit, the implication is that capital invested in the firm is earning substantially more in that use than is other capital in the economy. Thus, owners of capital have an incentive to withdraw their capital from uses that are producing only a normal return and to employ it where excess profits can be earned.

As additional capital flows into the industry, the industry supply curve, *SS,* is shifted to the right to $S'S'$, as shown in Figure 2.2. This shift may be interpreted as more firms operating in the industry or existing firms being expanded. It is useful to think of the supply-curve shift as depicting that more of the product will be produced at any given price than before the influx of capital. As the supply curve shifts to the right, the interaction of supply and demand generates a new equilibrium price, P'_e. As a result, the individual firm now faces a new horizontal demand curve, D', at that price. The output q_c no longer maximizes profits, because marginal costs are now greater than incremental revenues at q_c. Under these new conditions, the firm maximizes profits by cutting output back to q'_c, where price is again equal to marginal cost.

Although the individual firm is not as profitable as it was before, it is still earning excess profits. This can be seen by observing that the firm's average revenues, P'_e, are greater than average costs at the output q'_c. Thus, there is still an incentive for capital

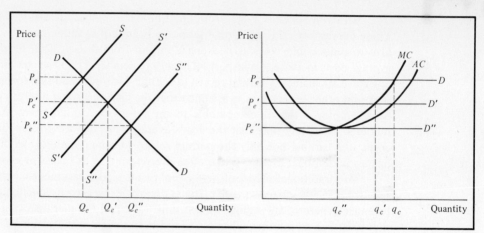

Figure 2.2. Long-run equilibrium: competition.

owners to channel capital into the industry. This causes further rightward shifts of the industry supply curve. The expansion of the industry continues until the supply curve is shifted to $S''S''$. With $S''S''$ as the industry supply curve, the equilibrium price is reduced to P_e'' and the individual firm now faces a horizontal demand curve at that price. Profits are maximized by producing q_c''. Notice that at q_c'' price is equal to marginal cost, but price is also equal to average cost. The firm's average revenues just equal average costs. Thus, the firm is earning a normal rate of profit (included in its average-cost curve), but there are no longer any excess profits. Because the return to capital in the industry is now no higher than the return earned in other segments of the economy, there is no further incentive for capital to flow into the industry. On the other hand, because capital is earning a normal return, there is no reason to expect capital to be withdrawn from the industry. The output q_c'' is the long-run equilibrium for the competitive firm.

"Virtues" of Competition   Perfect competition occupies a unique position in economic theory. Under some fairly restrictive assumptions it is possible to derive conditions for allocating resources to maximize social welfare. It can be shown that perfect competition meets these criteria for optimal resource allocation.[3] Such a demonstration is beyond the scope of this book, but the basic ideas can be presented here.

Prices play a central role in economic theory. The price that a person is willing to pay for a particular product is assumed to represent the value he attaches to having one more unit of that product. If a person is unwilling to buy the product at the offered price, it is because there are other things that could be obtained for the same expenditure and that provide greater satisfaction. Obviously, different people place different valuations on a particular product. Also, any given individual's valuation of a product is affected by how much of the product she or he already has. Traditional down-sloping demand curves depict these variations. When the price is high, some consumers drop out of the market. As price declines, there is additional demand. Normally, markets

[3]See, for example, Mansfield, op. cit., pp. 447–449.

charge a uniform price to all consumers. Purchasers are those who attach a value to the product greater than or equal to the cost of obtaining it. For those who value the product more than its purchase price, there is a windfall gain, which is often referred to as *consumer surplus.* Marginal consumers who value the product at its price can be thought of as getting just what they pay for. No one will voluntarily purchase the product if their valuation is less than the price.

The marginal-cost curves of Figures 2.1 and 2.2 represent the opportunity cost of producing one more unit of a product. For example, to produce an additional automobile, fuel, labor, and capital must be diverted from other uses. The value of these inputs in those other uses is given by their price. Thus their sum, as represented by marginal cost, is a measure of the opportunity cost of producing cars. In the model of perfect competition, increasing marginal costs result from decreasing marginal productivity of the inputs. Hence, the opportunity cost of producing additional output increases with the level of output.

The profit-maximizing firm will continue to expand its production as long as the additional revenues that it receives are at least as great as its marginal costs. Because the firm in perfect competition faces a horizontal demand curve, marginal revenue is just the market-determined price ($P = MR$). Thus, the firm expands until price equals marginal cost.

Concurrently, buyers purchase a product until price exceeds the relative value that they attach to the product. Because in perfect competition the price paid by buyers is just equal to the additional revenues received by sellers, production is expanded until the value that the last buyer attaches to the product is just equal to the opportunity cost of producing the product. It is often suggested that competition results in exactly the right amount of the product being produced. The preceding argument is the justification for that statement. If it costs more to produce the last unit of output than the value attached to that output by the last purchaser, then social welfare would be improved by shifting the resources used in producing that last unit to production of another good. Similarly, if there are potential customers who attach a value to the product greater than its marginal cost and who are not being served because of insufficient production, then welfare can be improved by expanding output. Another way of thinking about the result stems from the fact that perfect competition maximizes voluntary exchange. Production continues until there are no more consumers who will pay the opportunity cost of producing the product.

A second consequence of perfect competition is that inputs are efficiently allocated between alternative uses. Consider the allocation of capital as depicted by the long-run equilibrium of the competitive firm shown in Figure 2.2. In the long run, individual firms earn no more than a normal rate of profit. If returns to capital are a measure of the productivity of capital in a given use, then any time that capital is earning a higher return in one use than in another, productivity could be increased by shifting resources to the high-return use. This is what happens in the long-run model. Capital continues to flow into the competitive industry (entry) until excess profits are eliminated. Conversely, if the return in the competitive sector were less than the normal return, then capital would be taken from the industry (exit) until the productivity of the remaining capital had increased sufficiently to generate a normal return.

A third result of perfect competition in the long run is that production takes place at minimum cost. Notice that the equilibrium output in Figure 2.2 is at the minimum point on the average-cost curve. This does not suggest that a competitive firm necessarily is more efficient than a monopolist, but does imply that, given the technology available to the firm, it is minimizing unit costs of production.

Monopoly

The economic and legal definitions of monopoly differ. From the economist's point of view, *monopoly* exists when there is a single seller of a product. The legal interpretation is much less restrictive. As used in antitrust proceedings, a firm is viewed as having monopoly power when it has the ability to influence the market in which it operates. Often, firms that the economist would characterize as oligopolists are considered in court cases as firms with monopoly power. In this chapter the term *monopoly* is used in the narrow sense as being a single seller.

Theory   Demand and cost curves for a monopolist are shown in Figure 2.3. The cost curves again depict first increasing and then decreasing returns to scale. There may be some products that are produced under conditions of natural or technical monopoly with cost curves that are continually down sloping, but the analysis of these cases is deferred until Chapter 10.

A monopoly differs from the competitive firm in that it faces a downward-sloping demand curve. Because the firm is assumed to be the only seller of the product, the demand curve of the firm is the demand curve for the entire industry. Hence, the firm must recognize that its output decisions will influence price and vice versa. Because the selling price decreases with increased production, output increases cause the firm to sell its product at a lower price. The effect on total revenues depends on how the dollars gained from extra sales compare with the dollars lost from lower prices on sales that would have been made anyway. The net change in revenues associated with changes in output is given by the marginal-revenue curve shown in Figure 2.3.

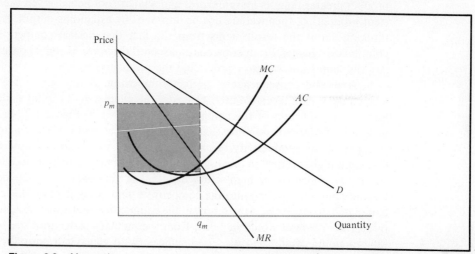

Figure 2.3. Monopoly.

The criterion for maximizing profits is the same for the monopolist as for the competitive firm—expand output until the additional revenues generated just equal the marginal cost. For the competitive firm the price was unaffected by output, so the decision criterion was to produce until price equals marginal cost. For the monopolist, the equivalent criterion is to produce at q_m, where marginal revenue equals marginal cost. At this level of output the monopolist charges what the market will bear, or P_m. Notice that the monopolist in equilibrium is earning excess profits, as indicated by the shaded area. If it were possible for resources to move into the industry, there would be an incentive for firms to try to enter and compete. Over time, the demand curve faced by the monopolist would become more elastic and excess profits would be dissipated. On the other hand, if the monopoly is the result of ownership of specialized inputs (e.g., oil reserves, patents, unique managerial talent, a choice location) or the result of government favor, then excess profits may persist. In such cases, Figure 2.3 depicts both the short-run and the long-run equilibrium for the firm.

"Vices" of Monopoly   To simplify the discussion of the effects of monopoly, it is assumed that the firm has constant average and marginal costs, as shown in Figure 2.4. To maximize profits the firm would produce q_m and charge P_m. As an alternative, suppose that a policymaker required the monopoly to use the competitive rule of equating price to marginal cost. In that case the price would be P_c. Those consumers who valued the product greater than or equal to P_c would be purchasers, resulting in total sales of q_c. Because all consumers are charged the same price, most buyers would receive a consumer surplus from their purchase. This surplus is represented by the difference between their valuation of the product (as depicted by the demand curve) and the market price P_c. For example, the consumer who places the highest valuation on the product has a surplus equal to the vertical distance AP_c. The marginal consumer, of course, has no surplus in that his valuation of the product is just equal to the price he must pay. The total consumer surplus when the price is set at

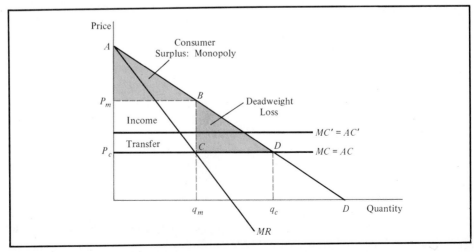

Figure 2.4.   Inefficiency of monopoly.

$P_c = MC$ is the area under the demand curve and above the marginal cost curve—the triangle ADP_c.

Now consider the choice of a profit-maximizing monopolist. As indicated, the price will be set at P_m and the quantity will be q_m. Although the price is much higher than under the competitive pricing rule, there is still an area of consumer surplus created by those individuals who place a value on the product that is greater than the price, P_m. The consumer surplus under monopoly is given by the area of the triangle ABP_m. This triangle is part of the consumer surplus under competition, ADP_c. The rectangle $P_m BCP_c$ was also a part of the consumer surplus under competition, but is now excess profit earned by the monopolist. The *excess profit* is a redistribution of income in relation to competitive pricing. The desirability of the shift depends on an evaluation of the relative needs of consumers versus owners of the firm, and cannot be answered on a strictly objective basis.

Finally, the last component of the consumer surplus under competition is the triangle *BCD*. This area is referred to as the *deadweight loss* or allocative inefficiency associated with monopoly. It represents a loss of value from monopoly pricing—a loss that is not gained by any group in the economy. It is a net loss to society. No assumptions about the relative worth of different groups are required to evaluate this impact of monopoly. It is a loss suffered by consumers that is not gained by anyone else. The source of this loss can be determined from Figure 2.4. The monopolist produces until marginal revenues are equal to marginal costs. To expand production beyond q_m would result in a loss of profits, because the incremental revenues are less than the extra costs that would be incurred. However, the consumer is charged a price, P_m, which is in excess of marginal cost. Only those consumers who value the product at or greater than P_m will enter the market. The last consumer will value the product at P_m, but the cost of producing is just $MC = P_c$. Hence, the value to the last user is much greater than the opportunity cost. Social welfare could be increased if more were produced. Specifically, expanding production by one unit would create a consumer surplus equal to the vertical distance between the demand curve and the marginal-cost curve. Additional output would create successively smaller incremental surpluses until the output q_c was reached, at which point there would be no additional consumer surplus. The triangle *BCD* represents the loss of consumer surplus stemming from the output-restricting tendencies of monopoly.

To summarize, monopoly produces too little output and sells at too high a price. While competition results in the lowest price consistent with the survival of the firm, the monopolist charges the highest price consistent with profit maximization. Resource allocation could be improved if more resources were channeled into the monopolized industry to expand production. There is also an income distribution effect associated with monopoly, but an evaluation of this transfer depends on judgments regarding the relative needs of consumers and producers. Although economic analysis provides little assistance in judging this income transfer, its importance in public policymaking should not be underestimated. In political debate, a legislator's call to take action against the abuses of monopoly is not commonly based on esoteric notions of allocative efficiency as found in economic textbooks, but usually on the unfairness of the income redistribution from consumers to shareholders.

One other possible effect of monopoly should be mentioned. The cost curves shown for both monopoly and competition assume that firms are attempting to minimize costs. For the competitor this is a reasonable position in that the entrepreneur may have no choice. Firms that are inefficient will not be able to survive. The monopolist, however, may not be under the same constraint. Earning excess profits, he has some discretion with respect to cost minimization. Rather than make the effort to keep costs down, he may pursue a utility-maximizing strategy of sacrificing some excess profits to ease his work burden. Graphically, this is depicted in Figure 2.4 as an upward shift of the monopolist's cost curves to $AC' = MC'$. For each unit of output, an additional cost of $MC' - MC$ is imposed on society. These costs represent an additional deadweight loss resulting from monopoly because they are resources that cannot be used elsewhere. This problem is often referred to as the *technical or x-inefficiency of monopoly.*

The ability of managers to ease their burden by becoming less cost conscious depends on the relationship between managers and owners of the firm. In most modern firms the managers are not the primary owners of the enterprise. Presumably, owners have the single objective of reaping as much profit from the firm as possible. If owners are unable to constrain the action of managers, then technical inefficiency is a possibility.[4]

Why All the Fuss about Competition and Monopoly?

The assumptions of the model of perfect competition are very restrictive. Few industries would meet the four requirements listed on page 14. Certain parts of the agricultural sector are the most likely candidates. In the Midwest there are many buyers and sellers of wheat. The wheat produced in a given location is relatively homogeneous. Compared to activities such as electricity production, resources can enter and leave agriculture without great difficulty. However, to claim that resources are perfectly mobile strains credibility. The assumption of perfect knowledge is even more difficult to satisfy. Rapid changes in technology, government policy, and market conditions make it extremely difficult for the average farmer to stay well informed. Large corporate farms can do a better job, but may violate the requirement that firms be price takers with respect to output and inputs. All in all, it is not easy to think of many circumstances where the requirements for a perfectly competitive industry are closely met.

It is also difficult to think of examples of pure monopoly. In a given community the local electric and telephone utilities usually fit the definition of being single sellers of their product. However, there may be substitutes that greatly reduce the monopoly power of these firms. For example, with an electric utility, consumers usually have the option of heating their homes, cooking, and washing and drying with gas instead of electricity. Large industries have the possibility of generating their own electricity if the rates of the local utility become too high. There are fewer substitutes for telephone service, although letter writing and telegrams are possibilities. Also, certain types of telecommunications services that had previously been provided exclusively by AT&T

[4]Alternative theories of the motivation of the firm and the question of the separation of ownership and control are important topics in modern economics. Indeed, Herbert Simon received a Nobel prize for his research in these areas. For a concise summary, see Koch, J. V., *Industrial Organization and Prices,* 2nd ed., (Englewood Cliffs, N.J.: Prentice-Hall, 1980), Chap. 3.

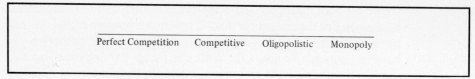

Figure 2.5. Spectrum of structures.

have recently been opened to other firms. The advent of competition in telecommunications is considered in Chapter 13.

If there are few, if any, examples of pure monopoly and perfect competition, then why spend days in economics courses and pages in this book talking about these extreme conditions? John Kenneth Galbraith takes a cynical view and argues that the focus on competition is an anachronism of bygone days when economics was developing and the world could be reasonably characterized as competitive. He further contends that economics provides a valuable service to powerful business interests by convincing the public that the economy really is competitive and that market forces effectively constrain the actions of big business.[5]

Milton Friedman disagrees with the premise that the model of perfect competition can be applied to only a few cases. He observes, "I have become increasingly impressed with how wide is the range of problems and industries for which it is appropriate to treat the economy as if it were competitive."[6] Friedman's view is not based on the belief that the strict requirements for perfect competition are frequently met, but rather that results similar to those generated from the competitive model are produced even if some of the assumptions are violated.

It is useful to think of perfect competition and pure monopoly as extremes on a spectrum such as depicted in Figure 2.5. Other market structures fall between these extremes.[7] Although there may be very few industries at the extremes, there are many that tend to one side or the other. The value of the models of competition and monopoly is that they bracket the actual results. Industries that are more like the perfectly competitive than the monopoly extreme are likely to behave more like perfectly competitive industries. Those that have many of the characteristics of monopolies will generate monopolylike results. In addition to providing information on the likely behavior and results of specific market structures, the extreme models of competition and monopoly provide guidance in making public policy. As a general rule, economists favor policies that move industries toward the competitive end of the spectrum. This justification for study of the extreme cases is highly simplistic, but it does provide a basis for appreciating well-developed and extensively stressed models of competition and monopoly.[8]

[5]Galbraith, J. K., *Economics and the Public Purpose* (Boston: Houghton Mifflin, 1973), Chap. 1.
[6]Friedman, M., *Capitalism and Freedom* (Chicago: University of Chicago Press, 1965), p. 120.
[7]The term *monopolistic competition* is sometimes used to describe firms near the competitive end of the spectrum. The concept developed because of dissatisfaction with the restrictive assumptions used to analyze monopoly and perfect competition. Monopolistic competition relaxes the requirement of product homogeneity and assumes that firms face competition from close substitutes called a product group. The theory of monopolistic competition is not explicitly developed in this text, but is well explained in Mansfield, op. cit., Chap. 11.
[8]Considerations other than the number of firms may influence the performance of an industry. For example, two firms vigorously competing in a market may produce results preferable to ten firms that have become adept at collusion. Factors affecting the ability of firms to collide are considered in Chapter 7.

IN BETWEEN: OLIGOPOLY

An *oligopoly* is an industry with few sellers. It is sometimes asserted that there is no economic model of oligopoly. This is true to the extent that there is no single model that is capable of analyzing the varied characteristics of oligopolistic industries. Oligopoly differs from both monopoly and perfect competition in one basic respect. In neither of the extreme market structures are individual firms required to take into account the impact of their actions on other firms and the impact of other firms on them. Under monopoly, by definition, there are no other firms to be considered. With perfect competition each firm is so small in relation to the total market that it has no perceptible effect on other firms. In contrast, firms in oligopolistic markets must constantly be concerned about the actions of their rivals. The difficulty in formulating models of oligopoly is the problem of depicting the ways in which firms interact and respond to one another. There are many factors—such as the maturity of the industry, the nature of the product, methods of doing business, and so forth—that affect firm interactions. It is not possible to develop a single model that effectively characterizes the strategies of all firms.

Cournot Model

There are, however, models that consider oligopoly under specific assumptions about firm interaction. One of the oldest and most useful is the *Cournot model,* developed by a French mathematician 20 years before the American Civil War. The Cournot model is briefly presented here to serve as a basis for discussing a fundamental characteristic of oligopolists: the tendency to collude.

Assume that there are only two firms in the market—a duopoly. Let marginal and average costs be zero.[9] The demand curve for the product is given by $P = 1000 - Q_T$ where Q_T is the sum of the output produced by the first firm, q_1, and the second firm, q_2. The marginal revenue equation associated with the demand curve is $MR = 1000 - 2Q_T$. First consider the results of monopoly and perfect competition. If the competitive pricing rule is invoked, then price is set to zero and the quantity is 1000. The zero price results from the assumption that marginal costs are zero. If there is a single seller, then the profit-maximizing price is $500 and the output is 500 units. The result is obtained by setting marginal revenue ($1000 - 2Q_T$) equal to marginal cost (zero) and solving for Q_T.

In analyzing the duopoly case an assumption must be made about the manner in which the two firms respond to one another. It is this assumption that differentiates the Cournot model from other duopoly models. Cournot assumed that each firm chooses an output to maximize its profits in the belief that the other firm will continue to produce the same output as it did in the previous period. Although the other firm will, in all probability, change its output from period to period, the firms are assumed to remain oblivious to this fact. As a starting point, suppose that only firm #1 is in the market in period #1. Thus, the firm acts as a monopolist in selecting its output. It produces 500 units and the price is $500. Table 2.1 depicts individual firm output, total output, and price during successive periods.

---

[9]These assumptions do not affect the basic results of the analysis, but they do make computations less cumbersome.

Table 2.1 COURNOT OUTPUTS AND PRICES

Period	q_1	+	q_2	=	Q_T	Price
1	500		0		500	500
2	500		250		750	250
3	375		250		625	275
4	375		312.50		687.50	312.50
5	343.75		312.50		656.25	343.75
6	343.75		328.13		671.88	328.12
—	—		—		—	—
n	333.33		333.33		666.67	333.33

In the second period firm #1 chooses its output assuming that firm #2 will continue to produce the same amount as it did in period #1, namely nothing. Thus, firm #1 again produces 500 units. Firm #2 selects a second-period output under the supposition that firm #1 will again produce 500 units. If the first firm produces 500, then the demand curve faced by the second firm is given by $P = 1000 - Q_T = 500 - q_2$. The associated marginal-revenue equation is $MR_2 = 500 - 2q_2$. The profit-maximizing output for the second firm is, hence, 250 units. Total output is 750 units and the price is $250.

In the third period firm #2 again produces 250 units, because it makes its decision on the assumption that the first firm will again produce 500 units. The first firm now selects its quantity presupposing that the second firm will produce 250 units, as it did in period #2. Thus, firm #1 faces the demand equation $P = 750 - q_1$, and the marginal-revenue equation $MR_1 = 750 - 2q_1$. Profits are maximized by producing 375 units. Total industry output is 625 and the price is $375.

The firms continue the same procedure period after period. Notice that the fluctuations in industry output and price become smaller as time goes on. Between periods #1 and #2 total output changes from 500 to 750 units. Between periods #5 and #6 the change is less than 16 units. In about ten periods the oscillations become very small, approaching the n period result, with each firm producing 333.33 units, total output being 666.67 units, and price equal to $333.33. At this point each firm behaves in the next period exactly as the other firm expected and there are no further changes. The n period results are the equilibrium solution of the Cournot model. Observe that industry output and price are between the monopoly and competitive results. Price is greater than with competition but less than for monopoly. Conversely, output is greater than under monopoly and less than for competition. The Cournot analysis can be extended to an industry with m firms. The equilibrium output is given by $Q_m = Q_c \cdot m/(m+1)$ where Q_c is the output using the competitive pricing rule and $m \geq 1$. For $m = 2$, the duopoly model just considered, the output is two-thirds the competitive output. As m becomes large, the ratio $m/(m + 1)$ approaches unity, indicating that the results approach those of competition.

Collusion

For each of the three market structures (monopoly, duopoly, and competition), individual firm profits can be calculated. Because costs are zero, profits equal revenues. In the monopoly case total profits are \$250,000 ($P \cdot Q_T = 500 \cdot 500$). Under competition there are no profits ($P \cdot Q_T = 0 \cdot 1000$). Under duopoly Table 2.1 shows that in equilibrium each of the firms earn \$111,109 ($P \cdot q_i = 333\frac{1}{3} \cdot 333\frac{1}{3}$) and total industry profits are \$222,218. Now suppose that instead of competing using the naive Cournot assumption, the firms are able to collude and set the monopoly price. Industry profits increase from \$222,218 to \$250,000. If the firms share equally in the profit pie, they will each get \$125,000. Obviously, the firms have an incentive to avoid competition and work together. There may be difficulties in dividing the profits and policing the agreement, but successful collusion has substantial rewards.

As a general proposition, oligopolists can always increase the size of total industry profits by colluding. Thus, there is an incentive for collusion in such industries. It is a maintained hypothesis that where there are industries with few enough sellers such that their actions impact on one another, firms will have a tendency to collude in the attempt to raise prices or otherwise reduce rivalry between firms. This tendency may take the form of overt price-fixing agreements, price leadership, or other stated or implied agreements to reduce competition. The exact nature of the collusion will be determined by the characteristics of the industry and by the impact of public policy.

Although successful collusion can improve the profitability of all the firms in an industry, any one firm can benefit still more by cheating on the agreement. If the decision of the group is to raise prices, the cheater can increase its share of the market and profits by setting a price below that charged by the rest of the firms. As long as the other firms adhere to the price-fixing agreement, the cheater will continue to prosper. Eventually, other firms may become aware of the cheater and reduce their prices. When this occurs the price-fixing agreement starts to fall apart. Unless there is a mechanism for restoring pricing discipline in the industry, the firms may revert to active price competition.

The success of collusive agreements depends on the costs of colluding and the ability of firms in the industry to detect and punish cheaters. If it is relatively easy to establish agreement among firms and if the actions of cheaters are quickly discerned and punished, then collusion may be common behavior in the industry. However, if the number of firms in the market, government policy, or other factors make coordination more difficult, then collusion is less likely. Similarly, if the actions of cheaters are difficult to detect, then the stability of collusive agreements is reduced. A primary goal of antitrust activities is to make collusion costly and unstable. By making price fixing and other types of industry coordination illegal, firms are forced to mask their activities or to rely on less formal agreements. Such agreements are costly to formulate and difficult to police. In Chapter 7 factors that affect the ability of firms to collude are considered in greater detail. Public policies to reduce the frequency and effectiveness of collusive behavior also are discussed in that chapter.

SUMMARY
The Extremes: Perfect Competition and Monopoly

Perfect Competition Firms maximize profits by expanding production until price equals marginal cost. In the long run, excess profits cause entry into the industry. Entry increases supply and drives down the market price. In long-run equilibrium no excess profits are earned.

By expanding production until price equals marginal costs, a competitive industry produces just the "right" amount of output. Mobility of resources assures efficient allocation of inputs between alternative uses. In the long run, production takes place at minimum average cost.

Monopoly   Firms maximize profits by equating marginal revenues and marginal costs. The monopoly price is greater than marginal cost. If entry is not possible, excess profits may persist.

In comparison to perfect competition, monopoly results in too little being produced and prices being set too high. Wealth is transferred from consumers to the owners of the firm. Monopoly also results in a deadweight loss to society. Finally, the absence of competitive pressures may allow the monopolist to be less efficient than competitive firms.

Why All the Fuss?   Few, if any, industries meet the restrictive assumptions for perfect competition or monopoly. However, the study of these structures is still a useful exercise. Industries that tend to either extreme probably exhibit performance characteristics similar to the polar cases. Also, perfect competition serves as a standard for evaluating the impacts and directions of public policy.

In-Between: Oligopoly

Cournot Model   An oligopoly is an industry with few sellers. Thus, each firm's decision making must take into account the reactions of its rivals. The Cournot model is a simple tool for analyzing the results of oligopoly. The model predicts that the equilibrium output (price) of an oligopolistic market structure is less (greater) than perfect competition, but greater (less) than monopoly.

Collusion   The Cournot model also demonstrates that if oligopolists can successfully collude to set the monopoly price, they can each increase their profits. The profitability of collusion depends on the costs of forming collusive agreements and the ability of firms to detect and punish cheaters.

DISCUSSION QUESTIONS

1. How is the duration of the short run determined by the nature of the industry being analyzed?

2. How might the "normal" rate of profit included in cost curves be estimated?

3. Suppose that one firm in an otherwise perfectly competitive industry has access to a more efficient production technique or a superior resource. What are the implications for long-run equilibrium in the industry?

4. How could the magnitude of the deadweight loss of monopoly be estimated?

5. What is the relationship between demand elasticity and deadweight loss?

6. Why is the number of sellers not a sufficient criterion for predicting industry performance?

7. Why is the behavioral assumption of the Cournot model rather unrealistic?
8. Collusion allows oligopolists to increase the total amount of profits earned in the industry. What methods could be used to divide the extra profits? What problems are there with each method?
9. How could "cheaters" conceal that fact that they are undercutting prices on a collusive agreement?

chapter **3**

Industrial Organization

Chapter Outline

If the facts do not conform to the theory, they must be disposed of.

MAIER'S LAW[1]

Industry performance is the ultimate concern of public policy. However, a major topic of public policy analysis is the investigation of industry structure and conduct. The rationale is the belief that somewhat predictable relationships exist between the structure and conduct of an industry and its performance. It is assumed that structure (e.g., number and size distribution of sellers) is an important determinant of conduct (e.g., pricing, marketing, and quality decisions). In turn, conduct affects industry performance (e.g., profits, product characteristics, efficiency).

The first section of this chapter focuses on barriers to entry as an important determinant of industry structure. Alternative views as to what constitutes a barrier to entry, sources of entry barriers, and the relationship between entry barriers and profit rates are all discussed. The second section is a brief description of the structure of U.S. industry. The Standard Industrial Classification and concentration indices are first introduced as tools for measurement. Data on aggregate concentration and concentration within industries are then presented. The chapter concludes with a short discussion of interlocking directorates and the concentration of stockholdings.

MARKET STRUCTURE: BARRIERS TO ENTRY

In the long run, barriers to entry may be the most important determinant of market structure. Although a given industry may be highly concentrated at any given time, the ability of firms in that industry to consistently implement policies that are not in the public interest is largely determined by the probability of new firms entering the industry. If entry is difficult, then firms are less constrained than if they must be concerned about a flock of new competitors.

Definition: Stigler Versus Bain

There is disagreement among economists as to what constitutes a barrier to entry. Joe Bain argues that entry barriers should be defined in terms of any advantage that existing firms hold over potential competitors.[2] In contrast, George Stigler contends that, for any given level of output, only those costs of producing that must be borne by new entrants but that are not borne by firms already in the industry should be considered in assessing entry barriers.[3]

Two examples illustrate the difference in philosophy. Suppose one firm had control over all the iron ore deposits in the United States. Hence, new entrants into the steel industry could get ore only by transporting it from Canada or some other foreign supplier. Transportation costs would cause potential competitors to have higher

---

[1]Block A., *Murphy's Law—and Other Reasons Why Things Go Wrong* (Los Angeles: Price/Stern/Sloan, 1977).

[2]Bain, J. S., *Barriers to New Competition* (Cambridge, Mass.: Harvard University Press, 1956), pp. 3–5.

[3]Stigler, G., *The Organization of Industry* (Homewood, Ill.: Irwin, 1968), pp. 67–70.

costs of producing steel than the existing firm. This disadvantage could prevent new firms from successfully entering the market. Both the Bain and the Stigler criteria for a barrier to entry are satisfied in this case. Alternatively, assume that iron ore deposits are equally available to the existing and the potential new firms, but that the existing firm is large enough to take advantage of highly efficient production technologies. If new entrants build plants of small scale, their costs may be so high that they cannot offer steel at a price competitive with the established firm. Thus, successful entry requires the construction of plants that are large enough to take advantage of economies of scale. Bain would consider this condition a barrier to entry because of the difficulties in coordinating and raising capital for large-scale entry. Stigler's definition would not recognize economies of scale as an entry barrier, because the old and the new firm both face the same cost conditions. For any given level of output that is produced, there is no cost disadvantage to the new entrants.

From a strictly conceptual point of view the Stigler position has appeal. Entry barriers are confined to problems faced by new, but not existing, firms. As a basis for public policy, the Bain definition seems to be more useful. Any condition that prevents firms from entering a concentrated industry should be of concern to policymakers.

Sources

Although there are many potential barriers to entry, four types are discussed here. The first is product differentiation. A firm that has been able to convince consumers that its product is significantly better than the product of new entrants has an advantage. The new firm may be forced to sell its product for a lower price that does not generate adequate profits. There is no requirement that the product really be superior, only that consumers perceive it as preferable. For example, aspirin manufacturers have been extolling the virtues of their product for years. The average person has a subjective feeling that Bayer and other well-advertised brands are better than unadvertised aspirin brands—in spite of the fact that they are often chemically identical. The result is that Bayer has a large share of the market and can sell its aspirin for a price much above the cost of production. Even if other manufacturers were to spend as much on advertising each year as does Bayer, it would be unlikely that they could ever catch up. Bayer's long tenure in the market has created a consumer loyalty that is difficult to overcome. Where established firms are benefiting from their past, a barrier to new entry exists.

A second restriction on entry is control of inputs by existing firms. If potential entrants cannot easily obtain the requirements for producing their product, then entry is deterred. Examples are scarcity of natural resources, locational advantages, and unavailability of managerial talent. Legal barriers are a third category. In some industries the maze of patents held by existing firms makes it virtually impossible for others to produce a comparable product. The alternatives are to invent around important patents, risk patent infringement suits, or agree to a licensing contract with the patent holder. Patents are discussed in detail in Chapter 20.[4] Another type of legal barrier is outright prohibition against entry. Public utilities, such as electric and gas companies,

[4]Situations in which technological information is not patented but still is not readily available are a related problem. For years Coca-Cola has guarded the ingredients of its syrup. There are many imitators in the market, but nothing exactly like a Coke.

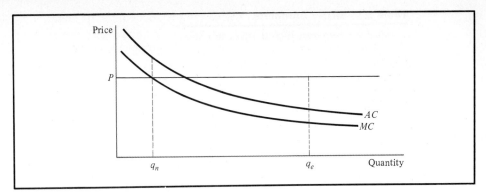

Figure 3.1. Economies of scale.

are given the right to operate in service areas without competition. Presumably, the disadvantages of granting monopoly rights are outweighed by other considerations. Chapters 10 through 15 consider public utility issues and problems.

Scale economies are another important deterrent to entry. Figure 3.1 shows the marginal- and average-cost curves for a firm producing a product under conditions of increasing returns to scale. As the firm expands, its marginal and average costs continually decline. New entrants operating at a small scale such as q_n may not be able to earn even a normal return on capital if they are forced to sell at a price, P, that allows the larger firm to cover its average costs and earn substantial excess profits by producing q_r units of output. Efforts to enter on a larger scale may be frustrated by the difficulties of obtaining capital and putting together the organization. The ability of the existing firm to grow gradually as compared to the requirement that the new entrant mature quickly may be a substantial advantage.

Evidence

Bain has provided interesting information on relative barriers to entry in different industries. His approach was to select 20 manufacturing industries and evaluate the conditions of entry. Each industry was rated with respect to factors such as economies of scale and product differentiation. They were then categorized as having very high entry barriers, substantial entry barriers, or moderate-to-low entry barriers. Bain's classification, first published in 1956, is shown in Table 3.1.

Several researchers have investigated the relationship between entry barriers and profit rates. Their findings suggest a positive relationship between profits and difficulty of entry.[5] For example, using data of the 1950s, Mann determined that the average profit rate of concentrated industries with very high entry barriers was 16.4 percent. For the same period, the percentage for concentrated industries with moderate-to-low barriers was 11.4. The evidence is far from conclusive, but does suggest that entry barriers can be an important determinant of industry performance.

[5]See Mann, H. M., "Seller Concentration, Barriers to Entry, and Rates of Return in Thirty Industries," *Review of Economics and Statistics*, Vol. 48 (Aug. 1966), pp. 296–307; and Shepherd, W. G., *The Treatment of Market Power*, (New York: Columbia University Press, 1975), pp. 96, 98.

Table 3.1 ENTRY BARRIERS

Industries with very high barriers to entry
Automobiles
Cigarettes
Fountain pens ("quality" grade)
Liquor
Tractors
Typewriters

Industries with substantial entry barriers
Copper
Farm machines (large, complex)
Petroleum refining
Shoes (high-priced men's and specialties)
Soap
Steel

Industries with moderate-to-low entry barriers
Canned fruits and vegetables
Cement
Farm machinery (small, simple)
Flour
Fountain pens (low priced)
Gypsum products
Meat packing
Metal containers
Rayon
Shoes (women's and low-priced men's)
Tires and tubes

Source: Reprinted by permission of the publishers. From Joe S. Bain, *Barriers to New Competition* (Cambridge, Mass.: Harvard University Press). Copyright 1956 by the President and Fellows of Harvard College.

THE STRUCTURE OF U.S. INDUSTRY

In this section evidence is presented as to the structure of U.S. industry. Specific questions to be answered relate to the actual degree of concentration of U.S. industry and whether concentration is increasing. Answering these questions requires the availability of a scheme for classifying industries and also a yardstick for measuring concentration. The usual classification method is based on the *Standard Industrial Classification Manual* (SIC) compiled by the Office of Management and Budget.[6] The most common techniques for measuring industrial structure are concentration ratios and the Herfindahl index.

Standard Industrial Classification

The SIC is by far the most common scheme for classifying industrial activity. It is used extensively by government, business, and academic researchers to present and analyze data. Its structure enables users to consider economic activity at different levels of detail as deemed necessary for the particular project. The most general category is at the division level, which includes 11 sectors: agriculture, forestry, and fishing; mining;

[6]*Standard Industrial Classification Manual* (Washington, D.C.: Government Printing Office, 1972).

construction; manufacturing; transportation, communications, electric, gas, and sanitary services; wholesale trade; retail trade; finance, insurance, and real estate; services; public administration; and nonclassifiable establishments. Industries are included in the division that is most characteristic of their activities.

Needs to present or analyze data in greater industry detail can use the two-, three-, or four-digit classifications of the SIC. The two-digit scheme subdivides industries by major group within a division. The three-digit breakdown divides the major groups into more specialized groups, and the four-digit classification subdivides by individual industry. Table 3.2 shows a sample page from the *Standard Industrial Classification Manual.*

The industries shown in Table 3.2 are part of Division D, Manufacturing. In that division there are 20 major groups, including Transportation Equipment, which is assigned the two-digit code, 37. There are seven groups or three-digit categories under major Group 37. Finally, under group number 371, Motor Vehicles and Motor Vehicle Equipment, two industries are shown. These are Motor Vehicles and Passenger Car Bodies, which has 3711 as its four-digit code, and Truck and Bus Bodies, which has been assigned the number 3713. Under each industry classification are specific products that are produced. Although the four-digit breakdown is the most specific provided in the SIC manual, the products listed under a particular industry can be rather diverse. For example, industry number 3711 includes both street flushers and hearses. Five-, six-, and seven-digit breakdowns are available from other sources, but are not often used.

Concentration Indices

Both empirical research and policymaking often require quantified measures of industrial concentration. The most commonly used measures are concentration ratios and the Herfindahl index.

Concentration Ratios   Assume that the objective is to quantify the concentration of sales in an industry. Let the market share of each firm be designated by X_i, where the firms have been ordered so that the largest market share is X_1, the next largest is X_2, and so on until the smallest, X_m, where m is the number of firms in the industry. The n-firm concentration ratio is the percentage of total industry sales made by the largest n firms and is computed by summing the market shares of the n largest firms. Thus:

$$CR_n = X_1 + X_2 + X_3 + \ldots + X_n$$

Industries are normally categorized according to their four-digit SIC code. The choice of n is arbitrary, but four-, eight-, and twenty-firm concentration ratios are the most common. However, in looking at aggregate concentration it would not be unusual to talk in terms of the proportion of sales of the largest 50, 100, or even 200 firms. In some cases the focus may be on assets, employment, or value added rather than sales. But the method of computing concentration ratios and their interpretation is not affected by the choice of data. Whatever the variable, the n-firm concentration ratios measures the proportion of activity by the n largest firms in the industry.

Table 3.2 SAMPLE PAGE FROM SIC MANUAL

STANDARD INDUSTRIAL CLASSIFICATION
Major Group 37.—TRANSPORTATION EQUIPMENT

The Major Group as a Whole

This major group includes establishments engaged in manufacturing equipment for transportation of passengers and cargo by land, air, and water. Important products produced by establishments classified in this major group include motor vehicles, aircraft, guided missiles and space vehicles, ships, boats, railroad equipment, and miscellaneous transportation equipment such as motorcycles, bicycles, and snowmobiles. Establishments primarily engaged in manufacturing mobile homes are classified in Industry 2451.

Group No.	Industry No.	
371		MOTOR VEHICLES AND MOTOR VEHICLE EQUIPMENT
	3711	Motor Vehicles and Passenger Car Bodies

Establishments primarily engaged in manufacturing or assembling complete passenger automobiles, trucks, commercial cars and buses (except trackless trolleys in Industry 3743), and special purpose motor vehicles. This industry also includes establishments primarily engaged in manufacturing chassis or passenger car bodies. Such establishments may also manufacture motor vehicle parts, but establishments primarily engaged in manufacturing motor vehicle parts except chassis and passenger bodies are classified in Industry 3714. Establishments primarily engaged in manufacturing truck and bus bodies and assembling them on purchased chassis are classified in Industry 3713; motorcycles in Industry 3751; wheel tractors, except contractors' off-highway types, in Industry 3523; tracklaying and contractors' off-highway tractors in Industry 3531; combat tanks in Industry 3795; and stamped body parts for passenger cars in Industry 3465.

Ambulances (motor vehicles)
Amphibian motor vehicles
Assembling complete automobiles, trucks, commercial cars, and buses
Automobiles
Bodies, passenger automobile
Brooms, powered (motor vehicles)
Cars, armored
Chassis, motor vehicle
Fire department vehicles (motor vehicles)
Flushers, street (motor vehicles)
Hearses (motor vehicles)
Mobile lounges (motor vehicle)
Motor buses, except trackless trolly

Motor trucks, except off-highway
Motor vehicles, including amphibian
Patrol wagons (motor vehicles)
Personnel carriers (motor vehicles)
Reconnaissance cars
Road oilers (motor vehicles)
Scout cars (motor vehicles)
Snowplows (motor vehicles)
Station wagons (motor vehicles)
Street sprinklers and sweepers (motor vehicles)
Taxicabs
Tractors, truck; for highway use
Universal carriers, military

	3713	Truck and Bus Bodies

Establishments primarily engaged in manufacturing truck and bus bodies, for sale separately or for assembly on purchased chassis. Establishments primarily engaged in manufacturing complete trucks and buses are classified in Industry 3711; stamped body parts for trucks and buses in Industry 3465; and truck trailers and demountable cargo containers in Industry 3715.

Ambulance bodies
Automobile wrecker-truck body
Bodies, dump
Bus bodies (motor vehicles)
Cabs, for agricultural tractors
Cabs, for industrial trucks

Hearse bodies
Truck beds
Truck bodies, motor vehicle
Truck cabs, for motor vehicles
Truck tops

Source: Office of Management and Budget, *Standard Industrial Classification Manual* (Washington, D.C.: Government Printing Office), 1972, p. 196.

To illustrate the computation and interpretation of concentration ratios, consider the following information. There are ten firms in an industry with market shares of 20, 30, 25, 3, 13, 3, 1, 1, 2, and 2 percent, respectively. The four largest firms make 88% of annual industry sales. Thus, the four-firm concentration ratio is $CR_4 = .88$. Similarly, the eight-firm concentration ratio shows the market share of the eight largest firms and is $CR_8 = .98$. Concentration ratios for four-digit SIC codes in manufacturing are published by the Department of Commerce in *Concentration Ratios in Manufacturing*.[7]

Concentration ratios are a useful measure of industry structure, but fall far short of indicating the degree of competition in the economy or within individual industries. One problem is the difficulty of correctly defining what constitutes an industry. Concentration ratios usually are based on somewhat arbitrary SIC classifications. While the SIC may be a good scheme for categorizing firms, it tells little about conditions of entry or product differentiation in the industry.

A second limitation of concentration ratios is their failure to reflect competition from foreign suppliers. For example, General Motors, Chrysler, Ford, and American Motors are the four largest manufacturers of automobiles in the United States. The four-firm concentration ratio for domestic production is over ninety percent. But to evaluate the auto industry on this basis would be nonsense. Firms such as Toyota, Honda, and Datsun have made significant inroads into the U.S. automobile market. The industry, considered in a world market perspective, is much less concentrated than the domestic four-firm concentration would suggest.

A third difficulty with concentration ratios is that they do not reflect the size distribution of firms in an industry. Consider two industries each consisting of four firms. In the first industry each firm has a market share of 25 percent. In the second, the respective market shares are 90, 4, 3, and 3 percent. In each case the four-firm concentration ratio is 1.00, but conduct of firms in the industry probably would be much different. In the first industry no firm has sufficient size to dominate the market. If firms are to engage in collusion, it must be accomplished using bargaining and compromise. However, in the second industry the large firm may be able to impose its will on its three small rivals. Prices will be set by the dominant firm and cheating can be effectively punished. A simple examination of concentration ratios would hide this potential difference in industry conduct.

The Herfindahl Index   The Herfindahl index is computed by summing the squares of each firm's market share. That is:

$$H = \sum_{i=1}^{m} x_i^2$$

For a perfectly competitive industry the index approaches 0. This is because each X_i is small and is further reduced by squaring. At the other extreme, the Herfindahl index for a monopoly would be 1.00.

---

[7]Department of Commerce, *Concentration Ratios in Manufacturing; 1977 Census of Manufacturing* (Washington, D.C.: Government Printing Office, 1981).

Table 3.3   THE TEN LARGEST INDUSTRIAL FIRMS IN THE U.S.: 1973 AND 1983

1983 rank	1973 rank	Firm	1983 sales (billions of dollars)	1973 sales* (billions of dollars)
1	2	Exxon	$88.6	$57.57
2	1	General Motors	74.6	80.19
3	7	Mobil Oil	54.6	25.5
4	3	Ford Motor	44.5	51.5
5	8	IBM	40.2	24.6
6	6	Texaco	40.1	25.5
7	16	du Pont	35.4	11.9
8	15	Standard Oil (Indiana)	27.6	12.1
9	11	Standard Oil (California)	27.3	17.5
10	5	Gulf Oil	26.6	18.8

*1983 dollars.
Source: Adapted from "The Fortune Directory of the 500 Largest Industrial Corporations," Fortune, Vol. 86 (May 1974), p. 232; and Vol. 106 (April 1984), p. 276.

The advantage of the Herfindahl index is that it takes into account the size distribution of firms in an industry. By squaring the market shares, the Herfindahl index gives greater weight to large firms. Consider the two industries just discussed. It has already been noted that the concentration ratio for each would be 1.00. However, the Herfindahl index for the first industry is 0.2500, while that of the second is 0.8134. This suggests that concentration is greater in the second industry.

Until recently, the Herfindahl index was primarily of theoretical interest. But in 1982, the Justice Department announced new guidelines for evaluating proposed mergers. These guidelines (discussed in Chapter 6) are based on industry concentration as measured by the Herfindahl index. As a result, the index now plays an important role in antitrust decisions.

Aggregate Concentration

Giant firms are an important and highly visible part of the U.S. economy. Alphabetical designations such as IBM and GM are as quickly recognized as PTA and UFO. The reigning queen of size (on the basis of sales) is Exxon. With sales of $89 billion, this giant oil company had 1983 revenues greater than the gross national product of all but 18 countries of the world. Nations such as Sweden, Saudi Arabia, Argentina, and Greece each had GNPs that were less than Exxon's sales.

Table 3.3 shows the 1983 sales rankings for the largest industrial firms in the United States. The ranking for 1973 is also provided together with 1983 and 1973 sales expressed in 1983 dollars.[8] It is interesting to observe that, of the top ten industrial firms in 1983, two are automobile manufacturers and six sell gasoline. Only two firms, IBM and du Pont, are not closely associated with automobile transportation, and du Pont made the top ten only because of its acquisition of Conoco, a large oil company. Americans truly have a love affair with their cars. The serious problems that occurred

[8]Public utilities are not included in the ranking.

in the 1970s as a result of shortages and high gasoline prices are not surprising in light of this dependency.

Trends in the structure of U.S. industry can be determined by examining aggregate concentration over time. Every five years the Bureau of Census conducts a comprehensive survey of manufacturing. In 1977 there were over 350,000 manufacturing establishments in the United States. The concentration of manufacturing activity can be evaluated by computing the proportion of total activity accounted for by the largest 50, 100, and 200 firms. These data are reported in Table 3.4. The measure of activity that is used is *value added*. Basically, value added is the dollar value of output minus the dollar value of inputs that are used to produce the output. It is used to indicate the net contribution a firm or industry makes to economic activity.

Table 3.4 shows that a relatively small number of firms generate a substantial share of value added in U.S. manufacturing. The 200 largest firms constitute less than 0.1 percent of total manufacturing establishments, but provide over 40 percent of value added. The data suggest that there has been an upward trend in the share of value added by large firms since 1947. The largest 50 firms increased their share from 17 to 24 percent and the 200 largest firms went from 30 to 44 percent. However, much of this increase took place in the ten years immediately following World War II. In recent years the tendency has been much less pronounced. Between 1963 and 1977 the share of the 50 largest firms remained essentially constant at 25 percent. The share of the largest 200 firms increased by only three percentage points from 41 to 44 percent during the same period.

Intra-industry Concentration

The aggregate concentration data of Table 3.4 indicate the importance of large firms, but provide little information about the amount of competition in U.S. manufacturing. Even though individual firms are large, it is possible that competitive pressures may exist if firms must compete with other firms that are sufficiently large to pose a viable threat. The structure of individual industries can be evaluated by using concentration ratios computed as part of the Survey of Manufacturing. Table 3.5 presents four- and twenty-firm concentration ratios for selected four-digit manufacturing industries. The measure of activity used to compute the ratio is sales.

The industries selected for Table 3.5 were chosen as illustrations of the market structure of important sectors of the U.S. economy. In the automobile industry, Gen-

Table 3.4 SHARE OF VALUE ADDED BY MANUFACTURE ACCOUNTED FOR BY THE 50, 100, AND 200 LARGEST MANUFACTURING COMPANIES: 1972 AND EARLIER YEARS

Grouping	Percentage of value added by manufacture					
	1947	1954	1963	1967	1972	1977
Largest 50 companies	17	23	25	25	25	24
Largest 100 companies	23	30	33	33	33	33
Largest 200 companies	30	37	41	42	43	44

Source: Dept. of Commerce, *Concentration Ratios in Manufacturing: 1977 Census of Manufacturing* (Washington, D.C.: Government Printing Office, 1981), Table 1.

Table 3.5   FOUR- AND TWENTY-FIRM CONCENTRATION RATIOS FOR SELECTED INDUSTRIES

Industry	Number of firms	1977 concentration ratios	
		Four firms	Twenty firms
Motor vehicle and car bodies	254	.93	.99+
Primary aluminum production	12	.76	1.00
Cereal	32	.89	1.00
Soap and other detergents	554	.59	.82
Tires and inner tubes	121	.70	.97
Petroleum refining	192	.30	.81
Newspapers	7,821	.19	.45
Soft drinks	1,758	.15	.36

Source: Computed from Department of Commerce, *Concentration Ratios in Manufacturing,* Table 7.

eral Motors, Ford, Chrysler, and American Motors dominate domestic production. Four firms also have a large share of sales in aluminum production, cereal, soap, and tire manufacture. The largest four firms make less than one-third of the sales in the petroleum refining industry, but the largest 20 firms make over 80 percent of sales. For newspapers and soft drinks the shares of even the largest twenty firms are relatively small. This is somewhat surprising in the soft-drink industry, because of the obvious domination of a few brands such as Coca-Cola and Pepsi. The reason is that favorites like Coke, which has a 27 percent share of the soft-drink market, are provided by multiple sellers, which are counted as separate firms in computing concentration ratios.

A more representative indication of the market structure of U.S. manufacturing is provided by Table 3.6. Within the SIC division, Manufacturing, there are 20 major industry groups. Table 3.6 shows the distribution of four-digit industries in each group by four-firm concentration ratio. Of 445 industries, 5 percent have four large firms that account for as much as 80 percent of the market. Concentration ratios for over 60 percent of the industries fall between .20 and .59. Less than 20 percent of industries have concentration ratios below .20. However, there are significant differences among major groups. Apparel and related products generally has low concentration ratios, while electrical machinery is much higher. These differences are explained primarily by barriers to entry. Competitors can enter apparel industries without great difficulty, but the size and capital requirements to manufacture electrical machinery are much more imposing.

Table 3.7 shows changes in market structure. It indicates that there was a slight increase in concentration in manufacturing between 1947 and 1977. In industries for which data are available, concentration ratios increased in about 40 percent of the cases, while about 30 percent of manufacturing industries experienced a decline in concentration over the period. Over the thirty-year interval, the unweighted average of concentration ratios increased, but only by 1.95 percentage points.

Although there was little change in overall manufacturing concentration, there were dramatic changes in certain areas. Concentration ratios changed by 21 percentage points or more in 14 of the 166 industries. These include a 43-point increase in the manufacture of malt beverages and a 38-point increase in the greeting card industry. At the other extreme, the four-firm concentration ratio for phonograph records and

Table 3.6   DISTRIBUTION OF CONCENTRATION RATIOS IN MANUFACTURING

Industry group	Number of industries	1977 Four-firm concentration ratio				
		0–19	20–39	40–59	60–79	80–100
Food and kindred products	47	4	17	16	8	2
Tobacco Manufacturing	3	0	0	1	1	1
Textile mill products	30	3	14	9	3	1
Apparel and related products	33	11	17	3	2	0
Lumber and wood products	17	9	7	1	0	0
Furniture and fixtures	13	6	4	3	0	0
Paper and allied products	17	3	7	5	1	1
Printing and publishing	17	7	7	2	1	0
Chemicals and allied products	27	1	11	8	7	0
Petroleum and coal products	5	1	2	1	1	0
Rubber and plastic products	6	2	0	2	2	0
Leather and leather products	11	2	7	2	0	0
Stone, clay and glass products	27	5	7	7	7	1
Primary metal industries	26	1	11	7	3	4
Fabricated metal products	36	13	10	10	2	1
Machinery, except electrical	44	13	11	17	2	1
Electrical machinery	35	0	12	15	1	7
Transportation machinery	18	1	3	6	6	2
Instruments and related products	13	0	8	3	2	0
Miscellaneous manufacturing	20	4	10	5	0	1
Total, all industries	445	86	165	123	49	22

Source: Computed from Department of Commerce, *Concentration Ratios in Manufacturing,* 1977, Table 5.

Table 3.7   CHANGES IN CONCENTRATION RATIOS: 1947–1977

Change in four-firm concentration ratio	Number of industries	Percentage of industries
+.21 or more	14	8
+.11 to +.20	31	19
+.06 to +.10	18	11
−.05 to +.05	51	31
−.06 to −.10	18	11
−.11 to −.20	25	15
−.21 or more	9	5
Total	166	100

Source: Computed from Department of Commerce, *Concentration Ratios in Manufacturing,* 1977, Table 7.

tapes declined by 31 percentage points and there was a 22-point decline in the computer equipment industry.

Interlocking Directorates and Stockholder Concentration

Concentration ratios and measures of industrial structure consider firms as legal entities and do not indicate the many, complex ways in which firms may be entangled other than by formal ownership. A common practice in the United States is for individuals to serve on the board of directors for several firms. Firms with at least one common director are said to have a *direct interlock*. Section VIII of the Clayton Act makes it illegal for a representative of one firm to sit on the board of a competitor, but direct interlocks are common between potential competitors, a firm and its suppliers, and firms in related areas. *Indirect interlocks* between firms are even more numerous. Suppose that Ms. Jones is a director of Aetna Life and Casualty and also a director of IBM. On the board of IBM is Mr. Hansen who is also a director of Prudential Insurance. Hence, Prudential and Aetna have an indirect interlock through IBM.

Interlocking directorates can reduce competition within an industry or between industries. A 1950 Federal Trade Commission report summarized the potential for abuse:

> An individual who is a member of more than one board of directors cannot divide his personality into unrelated segments. When sitting on one board he necessarily continues to know what he has found out on other boards, what he has recommended to those boards, and what action those boards have taken. He would be derelict to his responsibility if in two different boards of directors he supported policies each of which would tend to defeat the course of action he had recommended or seen adopted in the other company. . . . A director of two competing corporations cannot in good conscience recommend that either shall undertake a type of competition which is likely to injure the other. A director of two corporations that are respectively buyer and seller of the same commodities or services cannot in good conscience recommend that either concern prefer unrelated sources of supply or customers instead of the other company in which he is interested, nor that either concern press to the limits its ability to strike a good bargain at the expense of the other. A director who is on the board of an industrial company and a financial institution cannot in good conscience encourage the latter to finance expansion by competitors of the former which may jeopardize the former's prosperity; nor can he in good conscience encourage the industrial company to obtain its credit through other channels. Thus, the inherent tendency of interlocking directorates between companies that have dealings with each other as buyers and sellers, or that have relations to each other as competitors, is to blunt the edge of rivalry between corporations, to seek out ways of compromising opposing interests, and to develop alliances where the interest of one of the corporations is jeopardized by third parties. . . . [9]

A 1978 Senate subcommittee study collected data on direct and indirect interlocks among large corporations in the United States. [10] Data were collected for 130 of the largest firms in the country. A computer was used to trace the interrelationships between corporations. Excluding 7 investment advisory firms, the remaining 123 companies were, on average, interlocked with half of the other firms through a total of 530 direct and 12,193 indirect interlocks. For some firms, the interlocks were much more

[9]Federal Trade Commission, *Report of the Federal Trade Commission on "Interlocking Directorates,"* H. Doc. No. 652, 81st Cong., 2d sess. (June 30, 1950).
[10]Subcommittee on Reports, Accounting, and Managements, Committee on Governmental Affairs, United States Senate, *Interlocking Directorates Among the Major U.S. Corporations* (Washington, D.C.: Government Printing Office, 1978).

extensive. There were 9 firms that were directly or indirectly connected with over 90 other corporations. The 13 largest companies in the study reached an average of 70 percent of the other firms. The study notes that:

> The boardrooms of four of the largest banking companies (Citicorp, Chase Manhattan, Manufacturers Hanover, and J. P. Morgan), two of the largest insurance companies (Prudential and Metropolitan Life), and three of the largest nonfinancial companies (AT&T, Exxon, and General Motors) looked like virtual summits for American business. [11]

Traditional measures of industrial structure also fail to indicate the concentration of shareholdings among institutional investors in the United States. A 1978 Senate study found that voting power in 122 of the nation's largest companies is concentrated in the hands of a few institutional investors. [12] Twenty-one large investors were found to hold significant shareholdings in firms whose stock constitutes 41 percent of the market value of all stock outstanding. Morgan Guaranty Trust was revealed to be the most powerful stockholder. The bank was identified as the largest shareowner in 27 firms and among the top five in 56 companies. Morgan was also found to be the largest stockvoter in four of its large New York sister banks and also Bankamerica Corporation. In turn, these same banks are major shareholders in Morgan Guaranty's parent holding company, J. P. Morgan & Company. The intertwining of shareholdings would be expected to have an effect similar to interlocking directorates. A bank that has holdings in one of its competitors may not gain by competing so hard against the other firm that the firm's financial health is endangered. Similarly, an institution that has an interest in a potential supplier will have an incentive to make purchases from that firm rather than others. Such connections tend to foster coordination rather than competition. As such, they are inconsistent with government policies to promote competition. In spite of this fact, little control is exercised over the structure of corporate boards of directors and over stockholdings of institutional investors.

SUMMARY
Market Structure: Barriers to Entry

Barriers to entry may be the most important long-run determinant of industry structure. There is disagreement as to what constitutes an entry barrier, but the most useful definition for the analysis of public policy is probably Bain's position that a barrier to entry exists wherever an existing firm has an advantage over potential entrants.

Among the most important sources of barriers to entry are (1) product differentiation, (2) control over important inputs, (3) legal factors such as patents or monopoly grants, and (4) economies of scale. Empirical studies provide some evidence that high barriers to entry are associated with high profit rates earned by the existing firms in the industries.

[11]Ibid., p. 280.
[12]Subcommittee on Reports, Accounting, and Management, Committee on Governmental Affairs, United States Senate, *Voting Rights in Major Corporations* (Washington, D.C.: Government Printing Office, 1978).

The Structure of U.S. Industry

Standard Industrial Classification   The Standard Industrial Classification (SIC) is the most commonly used scheme for categorizing U.S. industry. Industries can be grouped broadly or more specifically, depending on the application.

Concentration Indices   Concentration ratios are used to describe market structures. Based on sales, employment, assets, or value added, an n firm concentration ratio indicates the proportion of industry activity generated by the largest n firms in the industry. A second measure is the Herfindahl index. Its advantage is that it reflects differences in the size distribution of firms in an industry.

Aggregate Concentration   U.S. industry is characterized by giant firms. Of the ten largest industrial firms (on the basis of sales), eight are either automobile manufacturers or in the oil business. The percent of total value added in manufacturing accounted for by the largest 200 firms in the United States was essentially unchanged between 1963 and 1977.

Intra-industry Concentration   Concentration within industries differs dramatically by industry. The top 20 firms are responsible for nearly 100 percent of sales in the automobile, primary aluminum, and cereal industries, but are relatively less important in newspaper publishing and soft-drink sales. For 60 percent of U.S. manufacturing industries the four-firm concentration ratio is between .20 and .59. The data indicate that intraindustry concentration increased slightly between 1947 and 1977.

Interlocking Directorates and Stockholder Concentration   Concentration ratios may understate the true concentration of U.S. industry. Studies indicate that large firms are extensively interconnected through the associations of their managers on corporate boards. In addition, stockholdings are concentrated in the hands of a few large firms. Twenty-one large firms have significant shareholdings in firms with market value equal to 41 percent of all stock outstanding.

DISCUSSION QUESTIONS

1. Stigler's concept of barriers to entry is conceptually appealing but not very useful as a standard for making and evaluating public policy. Do you agree or disagree? Why?
2. Are economies of scale more likely in manufacturing or service industries? Explain.
3. How might a researcher estimate barriers to entry in different industries?
4. Bain's work suggests very high barriers to entry for quality-grade fountain pens, but moderate to low barriers for low-priced pens. Explain his findings.
5. Does the Herfindahl index require more accurate data than the concentration ratio? Why?
6. The four-firm concentration ratio for the cereal industry was .89 in 1977. Are there significant economies of scale in the industry? What other factors might account for the high degree of concentration?
7. Should indirect interlocks involving large firms be prohibited?

two

WORKABLE COMPETITION AND ANTITRUST POLICY

chapter *4*

Antitrust: Background

Chapter Outline

"Now, let me state the present rules,"
The lawyer then went on,
"These very simple guidelines
You can rely upon:
You're gouging on your prices if
You charge more than the rest.
But it's unfair competition
If you think you can charge less.

"A second point that we could make
To help avoid confusion:
Don't try to charge the same amount:
That would be collusion!
You must compete. But not too much.
For if you do, you see,
Then the market would be yours—
And that's monopoly!"

RICHARD GRANT[1]

WORKABLE COMPETITION

Perfect competition is the standard of excellence for the economist. Almost any modern text in microeconomics includes a demonstration that markets characterized by a large number of buyers and sellers, a homogeneous product, complete mobility of resources, and perfect knowledge on the part of producers and consumers will generate a *pareto optimum* allocation of resources—that is, there is no other allocation that will make one party better off without hurting some other party. Unfortunately, perfect competition is little more than a gleam in the economist's eye. The highly restrictive assumptions of the model are rarely met in the real world. Moreover, the complexities of markets and politics of decision making make it unlikely that any reasonable set of public policies could establish the conditions for perfect competition. Thus, public policy must be content with seeking second-best objectives. J. M. Clark proposed that a realistic goal for policymakers is *workable competition.*[2] Clark argued that it is not necessary that all the requirements for perfect competition be strictly met in order to achieve results that approximate those of the competitive ideal. He suggested that markets may violate one or more of the criteria and still be acceptably or workably competitive.

Workable competition is not a precise standard. The basic criterion is that the power of firms to raise prices and to exclude competitors be limited. However, there is no objective measure to determine when that goal has been achieved. Still, there are some supplemental guidelines that suggest directions for public policy. These may be divided into structural, behavioral, and performance criteria.

---

[1]Grant, R. W., *The Incredible Bread Machine* (San Diego: World Research Inc., 1974), p. 174.
[2]Clark, J. M., "Toward a Concept of Workable Competition," *American Economic Review,* Vol. 30 (June 1940), pp. 241–256.

Structural

1. Although the number of sellers in a market may not be sufficient to eliminate all control over price by individual firms, there should be as many sellers as scale economies permit.
2. Firms should be relatively equal in size. No single firm or small group of firms should be able to dominate the market.
3. There should be no artificial barriers to entering or leaving the market.

Behavioral

1. Price, output, and marketing decisions of firms should be made independently, without collusion.
2. Firms should not be able to eliminate or weaken rivals except as a consequence of superior efficiency.

Performance

1. Profits should not be greatly in excess of those earned in other industries with comparable risk.
2. Selling costs and product differentiation should not be excessive.
3. Firms should operate efficiently. Inefficient firms should not be permanently protected from failure.
4. Firms in the market should be responsive to technological change.

In the United States the primary tool of public policy for promoting workable competition is through enforcement of the nation's antitrust statutes. These statutes acknowledge the existence of imperfections in the economy and are directed toward narrowing the gap between actual conditions and the competitive idea. The philosophy of antitrust is quite different from that of regulation. Regulation deals with market failures by continuously monitoring and specifying performance variables such as prices and profits. In contrast, antitrust operates on the premise that by modifying the structure of markets and the behavior of participants in markets, performance can be improved without direct government involvement in the decision-making of firms.

The term *antitrust* is a legacy from the past. In 1882, the stockholders of 50 oil refineries pooled their shares to create the Standard Oil Trust. In return they received certificates entitling them to a share of the earnings of the new organization. By substituting coordination for competition, the trust proved to be an effective vehicle for gaining control of markets and increasing profits. The initial agitation for legislation to protect competition was directed against the abuses of these trusts and, hence, the statutes became known as antitrust laws. Although the trust as a legal form has passed into history, the name has remained.

BEGINNINGS OF ANTITRUST
Rise of Big Business

The optimal form of business organization changed drastically during the nineteenth century. New techniques of production provided cost advantages to large enterprises.

The spread of the railroad reduced transportation costs and transformed local markets into regional and even national markets. Severe recessions in the 1870s and 1880s caused the collapse of thousands of small firms and concentrated market power in the hands of large producers. Finally, liberalization of incorporation laws made it easier to create large-scale organizations. New York was the first state to charter the corporation as a legal entity, but firms were limited to $100,000 in total capital and a life span of 20 years. As time passed, legislators realized that corporations could be an important source of revenues and they began to alter the standards for incorporation to induce new enterprises into their boundaries.

For many, the advent of the giant corporation and the increasing concentration of industry provided few benefits. Cost savings from production efficiencies were often dominated by the price-increasing effects of market power and consumers paid more, not less. The successes of capitalists were in stark contrast to farmers and industrial workers putting in long hours under poor conditions for low pay. In addition, some industrial leaders aggressively used prices, bribes, threats, and violence to eliminate competitors. Hamilton and Till paint a vivid picture of that era:

> The unruly times offered opportunity to the swashbuckling captains of industry, whose ways were direct, ruthless, and not yet covered over by the surface amenities of a later age. In sugar, nails, tobacco, copper, jute, cordage, borax, slate pencils, oilcloth, gutta percha, barbed fence wire, and castor oil they bluntly staked out their feudal domains. The little man caught in a squeeze play—the independent crowded to the wall by "the Octopus"—the farmer selling his wheat, corn, or tobacco under the tyranny of a market he did not understand—the craftsman stripped of his trade by the machine—the consumer forced to take the ware at an artificial price or go without—here were dramatic episodes. Industry was in the clutch of radical forces—and of iniquity. It was a period in which the ordinary man was confused, disturbed, and resentful. [3]

A potential source of redress against the abuses of big business was the judicial system through the common law. [4] The courts had previously held that business actions that had the effect of limiting the freedom to compete or of excluding competitors from the market were illegal. Theoretically, practices such as collusion to fix prices and selective price cuts designed to eliminate rivals could be successfully prosecuted. As a practical matter, the common law was essentially impotent as a restraint against business behavior. Court decisions were frequently inconsistent and poorly reasoned. Action could be taken only when a private party brought suit. Typically, the imbalance of resources between the plaintiff and the defendant made a fair hearing of the issues impossible. Also, the courts had no effective means of policing their decisions. As a result, the common law had not proven to be an adequate defense against the aggressive activities of big business.

The failure of the existing legal structure engendered the demand for new legislation to restrain business. In the 1880s the populist movement became a potent political

---

[3]Hamilton, W. H., and Till, I., *Antitrust in Action,* monograph no. 16, Temporary National Economic Committee (Washington, D.C.: Government Printing Office, 1941), p. 5.
[4]The common law is law based on precedents established by previous court decisions. In contrast, statutory law is created through legislation.

force. A coalition of farmers, laborers, and small businessmen, populism was an expression of resentment and frustration by the little guy against the "captains of industry" and their vast and oppressive organizations. Between 1880 and 1890 the populists were highly successful in electing representatives of their viewpoint to state legislatures and to Congress. In 1892 the Populist Party tallied over a million votes in the presidential election. At the state level, populist legislators spearheaded the passage of antitrust laws in 18 states between 1889 and 1891. Unfortunately, these state laws have been used very sparingly and with little effect. One problem has been the limited resources allocated by the states to investigate alleged violations. Another is that the scope of many cases reaches far beyond the confines of any single jurisdiction. It is only in the last few years that the states have become actively involved in antitrust litigation.

Sherman Act

The inadequacy of the common law and the limitations of legislation at the state level created a demand for federal antitrust legislation. In the 1888 presidential election the major political parties responded to the populist movement by avowing their intentions to enact federal legislation to curtail the evils of big business. Following the Republican victory, President Harrison urged the Congress to act on his campaign pledge. The response was a flurry of bills proposing a wide range of corrective and preventive measures. At one extreme were proposals for prison sentences for "malefactors of great wealth." At the other were cautious proposals for a constitutional amendment that would assure the legality of government action. The interest of the Republicans in antitrust legislation was partially a political ploy. The main issue of the day was the tariff, with the Republicans advocating a higher levy to protect developing American industries from external competition and the Democrats supporting a reduction in duties on the grounds that high tariffs aided monopolists in exploiting consumers. For the Republicans the support of antitrust legislation was a means of placating those who opposed higher tariffs. They could argue that the tariff prevented excessive foreign competition, while antitrust laws could be used to promote domestic competition.

Among the authors of antimonopoly bills was Senator John Sherman of Ohio. Sherman introduced "A bill to declare unlawful, trusts and combinations in restraint of trade and production." In spite of its ambitious title the provisions of the bill were rather weak and ambiguous. Some senators were unwilling to accept such a lukewarm measure and many proposals for strengthening were made. In debate, the record depicts Senator Sherman as confused and anxious to please. Repeatedly he acquiesced to objections and accepted amendments to his bill. The final product of the floor discussion was acceptable to almost no one and the measure was referred to the Senate Judiciary Committee for rewriting. Less than a week later the committee returned a proposal that bore little resemblance to the original effort of Senator Sherman. By the time the bill came back to the entire Senate, interest in further debate had largely been dissipated and the senators were anxious to get to the much weightier matter of the new tariff bill. With a minimum of debate and only one vote in opposition, the essentially rewritten bill passed the Senate. The measure was then sent to the House where a time limitation forced an early vote. The House approved the legislation by an unrecorded margin and it was signed into law by President Harrison in July 1890.

Senator Sherman claimed during the Senate debate that his bill was not really a new law, but rather an attempt to apply the resources of the federal government to enforcement of the existing common law. It is difficult to determine the real intent of Congress, because "the bill which was arduously debated was never passed, and ... the bill which was passed was never really discussed."[5] The prevailing feeling was that the act was a means of getting something on the books and that it would be amended on the basis of experience. In spite of the fact that the original bill was almost completely revised, the statute is commonly referred to as the Sherman Act. The act has remained essentially unchanged for 90 years. It is the model for most state antitrust legislation and the most important basis for federal antitrust activity.

The Sherman Act has two main sections:

Section 1. Every contract, combination in the form of a trust or otherwise, or conspiracy, in restraint of trade or commerce among the several states, or with foreign nations, is hereby declared to be illegal. Every person who shall make any such contract or engage in any such combination or conspiracy shall be deemed guilty of a misdemeanor. . . .

Section 2. Every person who shall monopolize, or attempt to monopolize, or combine or conspire with any other person or persons, to monopolize any part of the trade or commerce among the several states, or with foreign nations, shall be deemed guilty of a misdemeanor. . . .

These two sections focus on different types of undesirable business behavior. Section 1 was intended to prohibit firms from conspiring together to initiate and maintain practices against the public interest. Agreements to fix prices are an example of activities in violation of Section 1. Section 2 was designed to attack the problem of market dominance. Firms that aggressively move to gain control of their market may find themselves in violation of Section 2. The evolution of the law with respect to these two sections of the Sherman Act and also later antitrust legislation are considered in Chapters 5–8.

Clayton and Federal Trade Commission Acts

Enforcement experience with the Sherman Act from 1890 to World War I was less than a glowing success. The public perception was that industrial concentration had not been checked. Congressional hearings added to the public discontent by revealing new and continued abuses by business. There were at least three reasons for the initial ineffectiveness of the Sherman Act. First, although the Justice Department was given the responsibility for antitrust enforcement, it was not provided with the budget and personnel for the task. As a result, few suits were filed during this early period. Seven Sherman Act suits were filed during the Harrison administration, eight during Grover Cleveland's second term, and only three during the presidency of William McKinley. Many of these suits were directed against labor unions rather than business. The pace ac-

[5]Hamilton and Till, op cit., p. 11.

celerated during the terms of Roosevelt and Taft, but the supply of government action continued to be less than the public demand. In spite of his reputation as the "Great Trustbuster," Roosevelt has been described as a man who carried a big stick, but never hit anybody.[6]

A second reason for dissatisfaction with Sherman Act enforcement was the record of the courts in interpreting the act. The Supreme Court vacillated from one extreme to the other and finally settled on an interpretation that put the activities of all but the most blatant monopolists beyond the law. In *United States* v. *E. C. Knight Co.* (1895) the Court ruled that the Sherman Act did not apply to the sugar trust on the curious grounds that the law covered only commerce, and that manufacturing was not commerce. "Commerce succeeds to manufacture, and is not a part of it," was the phrase used in the opinion.[7] Just two years later in *United States* v. *Trans-Missouri Freight Assn.* (1897) the Court read Section 1 to prohibit all restraints of trade that were incidental to otherwise legitimate business activity, but business still remained uncertain as to what did and did not violate the law.[8] Surprisingly, one of the most significant blows to Sherman Act enforcement resulted from a successful government prosecution. In 1911 the Justice Department filed suit against Standard Oil of New Jersey, alleging that the firm had monopolized the oil refinery industry in violation of Sections 1 and 2 of the Sherman Act [*Standard Oil of N.J.* v. *United States* (1911)].[9] The Supreme Court ruled for the government and ordered the company dissolved into some 30 smaller firms. However, the Court also ruled that a violation of Section 2 required a showing, not only that the firm has a monopoly, but also that the monopoly was achieved by unlawful means. In the Standard Oil case both criteria were met and a conviction was obtained, but the new requirements announced by the Court imposed a difficult standard for successful future prosecutions.

A third explanation of the dissatisfaction with the Sherman Act stemmed from the government's inability to attack firms until they approached the status of monopolists. It was recognized that the time to deal with anticompetitive business practices was in the early stages and not after the firms had become entrenched in an industry. The language of the Sherman Act stressed the punishment of actions in restraint of trade rather than their prevention.

Tougher antitrust laws were a major issue in the 1912 election. Each of the three major political parties (Republican, Democrat, and Teddy Roosevelt's Progressive Party) favored new legislation. The winner, Democrat Woodrow Wilson, proposed that specific business acts be prohibited. He also favored the creation of a separate federal agency to administer the laws. This agency was to act as an investigative body and lend its expertise to the formulation of antitrust policy. Congress responded to the prodding of President Wilson by conducting extensive hearings, culminating in 1914 with the passage of the Clayton Act and the Federal Trade Commission Act.

[6]Assistant Attorney General Arnold Thurman as quoted in Green, M. J., ed., *The Closed Enterprise System* (New York: Grossman, 1972), p. 66.
[7]*United States* v. *E. C. Knight Co.,* 156 U.S. 1 (1895).
[8]*United States* v. *Trans-Missouri Freight Assn.,* 166 U.S. 290 (1897).
[9]*Standard Oil of N.J.* v. *United States,* 221 U.S. 1 (1911). Standard Oil and other important early Sherman Act monopoly cases are discussed in greater detail in Chapter 5.

Clayton Act   The Clayton Act was intended as a supplement to the Sherman Act. The intent of Congress was to provide legislation to check monopoly in its incipiency and to enumerate specific business practices that would be prohibited. The basic provisions of the act are contained in three sections:

> *Section 2.* It shall be unlawful for any person engaged in commerce, to discriminate in price between different purchasers of commodities, . . . where the effect of such discrimination may be to substantially lessen competition or tend to create a monopoly in any line of commerce. . . .
>
> *Section 3.* It shall be unlawful for any person engaged in commerce, to lease or make a sale or contract for sale of goods . . . on the condition, agreement, or understanding that the lessee or purchaser thereof shall not use or deal in the goods . . . of a competitor or competitors of the lessor or seller, where the effect of such lease, sale, or contract . . . may be to substantially lessen competition or tend to create a monopoly in any line of commerce.
>
> *Section 7.* No corporation engaged in commerce shall acquire, directly or indirectly, the whole or any part of the stock or other share capital of another corporation engaged also in commerce where the effect of such acquisition may be to substantially lessen competition between the corporation whose stock is so acquired and the corporation making the acquisition or to restrain such commerce in any section or community or tend to create a monopoly of any line of commerce.

These three sections each deal with a specific type of business practice. Section 2 is directed against price discrimination. Section 3 makes it illegal to tie the purchase of one product to the purchase of another product. Section 7 imposes restrictions on merger activity. Notice that the language of the Clayton Act is not absolute. In each case the practice is illegal only if it tends to substantially lessen competition or create a monopoly in any line of commerce.

Federal Trade Commission Act   The variability of court decisions left businessmen uncertain as to what constituted an antitrust violation. After 20 years with the Sherman Act, business desired a means of determining the propriety of their behavior without being drawn into an expensive and embarrassing court case. At that time the use of administrative agencies for regulation had become somewhat common at both the federal and state levels, and it was proposed that a similar agency be created to deal with antitrust matters. In 1914, Congress passed the Federal Trade Commission Act. This legislation established the Federal Trade Commission as an agency empowered to both investigate and enforce violations of antitrust laws. In 1903, Roosevelt had created a special unit in the Department of Justice to enforce the Sherman Act. Unlike the Justice Department, the FTC does not initiate prosecution of alleged violators through the federal court system. The five FTC commissioners have the right to issue cease-and-desist orders directly when they determine the law has been broken. The commission also is empowered to formulate trade regulations for specific industries. The organization and operation of the Federal Trade Commission and the Antitrust Division of the Department of Justice will be considered more fully in Chapter 9.

In addition to creating the FTC, the Federal Trade Commission Act has one substantive section:

Section 5. Unfair methods of competition in commerce are hereby declared unlawful.

The intent behind Section 5 was, like that of the Clayton Act, to provide the government with preventive, in addition to punitive, powers. Under Section 5 the FTC can attack unfair methods of competition before they reach the scope required for successful prosecution under the Sherman Act. The FTC has sole jurisdiction over enforcement of Section 5 and shares jurisdiction of the Clayton Act with the Antitrust Division of the Department of Justice.

REFINEMENTS IN ANTITRUST LEGISLATION

Passage of the Sherman, Clayton, and Federal Trade Commission Acts created the legal basis for federal antitrust activity. However, changes in economic conditions, interpretations of these laws by the courts, and the ingenuity of business in finding ways to circumvent the intent of the legislation have created the need for modifications to these basic statutes. Since 1914, the most important changes in the antitrust laws are the following.

Robinson-Patman Act

The Great Depression affected public thinking about business. The concern of the times was with keeping businesses operating and preventing prices from falling too low. Small businessmen were particularly pessimistic about their ability to compete against large chain stores. They complained that these multiple-outlet sellers were able to use their market power to extract price concessions from suppliers and, thus, undersell their smaller competitors. Food retailing was an oft-cited example. Small grocers complained that they couldn't survive against giants such as A&P, because A&P and similar firms could make purchases at discounts unrelated to the actual costs of supplying them.

Section 2 of the Clayton Act was intended to provide protection against price discrimination, but 20 years of experience had not created much confidence in its provisions. The government had often been unsuccessful in prosecuting alleged discriminators and new practices seemingly not covered by the act had appeared. The mood of the day was sufficient impetus for passage of an amendment to Section 2. The new legislation, commonly referred to as the Robinson-Patman Act, became law in 1936. The focus of the original Section 2 was against sellers who charged different prices to customers on the basis of geographic location and not cost. The Robinson-Patman Act retained the restriction on such practices, but also strengthened prohibitions against buyers receiving price concessions that enabled them to undersell their competitors in the same area. The use of quantity discounts was also restricted. In addition, practices such as granting advertising allowances to large buyers were prohibited. The specifics of the Robinson-Patman Act are considered in Chapter 8.

Wheeler-Lea Act

By the early 1930s, attempts by the FTC to prosecute under Section 5 of the Federal Trade Commission Act had been substantially limited by the interpretation of the act by the Supreme Court. The Court had read the legislation as applicable only to practices that had an adverse impact on a firm's competitors. The effect on consumers was not covered. In 1931, the FTC took action against a seller of patent medicine who was advertising that his product was a safe and effective way of eliminating "excess flesh off the human body" [*Federal Trade Commission* v. *Raladam Co.* (1931)].[10] The commission determined that the preparation was not harmless and issued a cease-and-desist order against the seller. The matter was ultimately appealed to the Supreme Court, which held that the commission had exceeded its powers. The Court ruled that the wording of Section 5 required a showing that a practice not only was unfair, but also that it caused injury to a competitor of the firm. The FTC's case was based on the finding that consumers might be harmed, but did not demonstrate that a competitor had been injured. As such, the advertisements were not considered unlawful. The difficulties that the FTC experienced in prosecuting "unfair methods of competition" led to the amendment of Section 5 by the Wheeler-Lea Act in 1938. Section 5 was rewritten to read:

> Unfair methods of competition in or affecting commerce, and unfair or deceptive acts or practices in or affecting commerce, are hereby declared unlawful.

The impact of the Wheeler-Lea revision was that the Federal Trade Commission could now move against unfair or deceptive acts that harm consumers, as well as unfair methods of competition that adversely affect a firm's rivals. This change is particularly important in allowing the FTC to perform its role of protecting consumers from false and misleading advertising claims. This function is further discussed in Chapter 17.

Celler-Kefauver Amendment

Section 7, the antimerger provision of the Clayton Act, was passed because the Sherman Act had proven inadequate to the task of preventing the spread of monopoly. It was possible to prevent mergers under the Sherman Act, but only when it could be shown that the consummation of the merger would cause the resultant firm to have monopoly or near-monopoly status. Combinations of firms of more modest size, even when the degree of competition in the industry was significantly reduced, could not effectively be restricted. Unfortunately, the first 35 years of experience with Section 7 revealed that it also had flaws. Like Section 5 of the Federal Trade Commission Act and Section 2 of the Clayton Act, the interpretations of the courts and the cleverness of business drastically reduced the effectiveness of the legislation.

Section 7 prohibited a firm from acquiring "the whole or any part of the stock or other share capital of another corporation" where the effect "may be to substantially lessen competition between the corporation whose stock is so acquired and the corpora-

---

[10]*Federal Trade Commission* v. *Raladam Co.,* 283 U.S. 643 (1931).

tion making the acquisition." It didn't take long for businesspeople to find ways around the language of the legislation. The act restricted mergers achieved by purchasing the stock of another firm, but said nothing about purchasing the assets of the firm directly. The Supreme Court paved the way for asset acquisitions by ruling that firms could initially make stock acquisitions, liquidate the stock, and then purchase the firm's assets. The Court ruled that as long as this was accomplished before the government issued a complaint, the merger was safe. [11] As a result, merger activity of large firms became heavily biased toward asset rather than stock acquisitions.

A second problem with Section 7 was its focus on eliminating competition between the merging firms rather than the broader perspective of a general lessening of competition. The act directed the courts to consider competition "between the corporation whose stock is so acquired and the corporation making the acquisition." This phrase greatly limited the government's ability to prevent mergers between firms who were not, at the time, direct competitors. For example, it was widely believed that a merger between the manufacturer of a product and the firm's distributors was beyond reach of the Clayton Act. Because of these limitations, Section 7 had little impact between 1914 and 1950. During that period only 15 mergers were dissolved, and 10 of those dissolutions were prosecuted under the Sherman Act. [12]

In the late 1940s several events provided the impetus for new legislation. First, there was a rash of mergers in the postwar period. Second, an FTC report warned that, in the absence of government action, "the giant corporations will ultimately take over the country." [13] Finally, in 1948, the government was unsuccessful in preventing a merger between two giants of the steel industry. The response of Congress to these events was the passage of the Celler-Kefauver Amendment in 1950, which amended Section 7 to read:

> That no corporation engaged in commerce shall acquire, directly or indirectly, the whole or any part of the stock or other share capital and no corporation subject to the jurisdiction of the Federal Trade Commission shall acquire the whole or any part of the assets of another corporation engaged also in commerce, where in any line of commerce in any section of the country, the effect of such acquisition may be substantially to lessen competition, or to tend to create a monopoly.

The new statute was designed to correct the weaknesses of the original. Asset, as well as stock, acquisitions were prohibited. The focus of reduced competition between merging firms was replaced by the provision that a showing of a lessening of competition "in any line of commerce in any section of the country" could be used to prevent a merger. The effect of the latter change was to bring mergers between firms in a buyer-seller relationship, firms in separate geographic locations, and perhaps even firms in essentially unrelated markets within the reach of antitrust law.

[11] *Arrow-Hart & Hegeman Electric Co.* v. *Federal Trade Commission,* 291 U.S. 587 (1934).

[12] Scherer, F. M., *Industrial Market Structure and Economic Performance,* (Chicago: Rand McNally, 1980), p. 548.

[13] Federal Trade Commission, *The Merger Movement: A Summary Report* (Washington, D.C.: Government Printing Office, 1948), p. 678.

INTRODUCTION TO ANTITRUST PROCEDURES AND ENFORCEMENT

Chapters 5 through 8 focus on the relationship between economic theory and the evolution of antitrust law. In the remainder of this chapter the reader is introduced to some basic concepts relating to antitrust procedures and enforcement. Chapter 9 provides greater detail on these topics and also evaluates the impacts of antitrust legislation.

Jurisdiction of Federal Antitrust Laws

The Interstate Commerce Clause of the Constitution gives the federal government jurisdiction over commerce "among the several states." The courts have interpreted this phrase very liberally with respect to the antitrust statutes. For example, in *Burke* v. *Ford* (1967), Oklahoma retailers were charged with geographically dividing the liquor market in that state. By segmenting the market each seller became, in effect, a little monopolist. The Supreme Court held that this purely *intra*state activity was a violation of federal antitrust laws based on the following reasoning. By dividing the market the sellers were able to raise liquor prices in Oklahoma. The price increase was assumed to cause a reduction in the demand for liquor within the state. Much of Oklahoma liquor was imported from other states, and so the Court concluded that market division had an impact on *inter*state commerce by reducing the sales of liquor from producing states into Oklahoma.[14]

In *United States* v. *Pennsylvania Refuse Removal Assn.* (1966) the Court refused to overturn the conviction of Pennsylvania garbage collectors who had been found guilty of conspiracy by the lower courts. The government had shown that some of the garbage was ultimately disposed of in New Jersey, and the Court accepted this as evidence that interstate commerce was affected.[15] More recently, the courts have ruled price-fixing agreements by local realtors to be a federal antitrust violation on the grounds that interstate commerce is indirectly affected. It would seem that the use of federal antitrust statutes to prosecute antitrust violations at the state and local levels is primarily limited by the resource constraints of the Department of Justice and the Federal Trade Commission and by the creativity of government and private attorneys in arguing the interstate commerce implications of the matters at hand.

Although federal antitrust activity is not severely restricted by state boundaries, there are some industries and activities that have partial exemption from antitrust laws. They include:

Export Associations. The Webb-Pomerene Act of 1918 allowed firms to combine to form export associations. The intent of the law was to give U.S. businesses the ability to successfully compete against foreign cartels. But approval for such associations must first be granted by the Federal Trade Commission.

Labor Unions. The Clayton Act specified that "nothing contained in the antitrust laws shall be construed to forbid the existence and operation of

[14]*Burke* v. *Ford,* 389 U.S. 320 (1967).
[15]*United States* v. *Pennsylvania Refuse Removal Assn.,* 384 U.S. 961 (1966).

labor . . . organizations. . . ." This was an important provision because the Sherman Act had previously been used to restrict the activities of labor unions. However, the Clayton Act does not protect unions who conspire to raise prices or to eliminate nonunion businesses from an industry.

Agricultural Cooperatives. The Capper-Volstead Act of 1922 authorized the creation of cooperatives for the purpose of marketing agricultural commodities. The objective was to provide farmers, ranchers, and dairymen with a means of matching the bargaining power of those on the buying side of the market.

Professional Sports. Owners of professional sports teams have been allowed to engage in activities that would be clear antitrust violations if practiced in other industries. An example is the draft system whereby negotiating rights to players are assigned to a single team. The draft clearly weakens the bargaining position of the athlete by giving the team a monopsony position. It is usually justified by the need to have balance in a sports league. The argument is that, without the draft system, the richer teams would soon have the best players and the league would no longer be competitive. However, recent experience in baseball and other sports suggests that "buying" a championship is not a sure thing.

Regulated Industries. Industries such as electric utilities, railroads, insurance, and banking are regulated by state or federal agencies. These agencies have a responsibility to protect the public interest. As a result, the regulated industries are treated somewhat more leniently under the antitrust laws than are other industries.

Complaints and Appeals

There are four ways by which antitrust proceedings are initiated. First, the Antitrust Division of the Department of Justice may, on the basis of a complaint that has been received or as a result of information that has been collected, initiate a suit. If the suit is continued to the point of formal litigation, it is first heard in the federal district courts. If either party wishes to contest the decision of the district court, the matter is taken to the circuit court of appeals and, ultimately, if the Court is willing to hear the case, to the Supreme Court. The Antitrust Division's responsibility is limited to initiating and prosecuting the case. The courts must determine guilt and remedies.

The second path of antitrust enforcement is through the Federal Trade Commission. When the commission staff decides to issue a formal complaint and the matter is contested by the defendant, the initial hearing is before an administrative law judge who is part of the FTC. If the decision in that hearing is in favor of the defendant, the matter is dropped. If the decision is to uphold the complaint, then the defendant has the right to appeal to the five FTC commissioners. If the decision is again against the defendant, then the matter may be appealed to the federal courts.

A third procedure involves state antitrust legislation. Most states have antitrust statutes. All but 4 states have laws similar to Section 1 of the Sherman Act and 37 states have some type of antimonopoly law corresponding to Section 2. Alabama is the only state lacking a statute similar to Section 5 of the Federal Trade Commission Act, which prohibits unfair practices; and 29 states have enacted legislation to deal with price discrimination.[16] Typically, complaints are prosecuted by the state attorney general and heard by the court system in the state. Appeals from decisions of the state supreme court may be taken to the federal courts. As previously noted, until the last few years enforcement of state laws was very lax. Recently, there has been renewed interest in enforcement of antitrust at the state level.

The fourth method for dealing with alleged antitrust violations is litigation by private parties. Individuals, groups, or firms may file suit in the federal district courts. Appeals are heard by the circuit courts of appeal and the U.S. Supreme Court. The use of antitrust suits by private parties has increased dramatically in recent years. From 1950 to 1959 about 2200 private suits were initiated. In the early 1960s the government obtained convictions against manufacturers of electrical equipment for conspiring to fix prices [*United States* v. *General Electric et al.* (1961)].[17] The government's success resulted in over 2200 private suits for damages in that case alone. Today, about 2000 private antitrust suits are filed in the United States each year—over 90 percent of all antitrust actions.

Disposition of Complaints

When a complaint is lodged by the Antitrust Division or the FTC, there are a number of options available to the defendant. In some cases the firm may voluntarily change its behavior to comply with the law. If the violation is not serious or appears not to be intentional, the government may simply drop the complaint. At the other extreme, the case may go to court, with the defendant pleading not guilty. In this circumstance there is a full-blown trial and the court must determine guilt or innocence. If the decision is guilty or if the defendant had initially pled guilty, then the court has the responsibility of affixing penalties and remedies.

Another option open to the defendants in some antitrust complaints is to plead *nolo contendere,* or "I do not wish to contend." If the court accepts this plea it is then treated as the equivalent of a guilty plea and the proceedings move directly to the consideration of penalties and remedies. Speeding the trial is beneficial to the government, but a nolo plea also has advantages for the defendant. A plea of nolo contendere does not constitute proof of guilt in other proceedings. As a result, private parties wishing to sue for damages are required to establish the guilt of the defendant before any award can be made. In contrast, a plea of guilty or a finding of guilt by the court after a not-guilty plea would be prima facie evidence of guilt in a private-party suit. The plaintiff would only be required to show the amount of damages resulting from the violation.

The most common resolution of federal antitrust complaints is by consent decrees or orders.[18] These are agreements worked out between the government's attorneys and

[16]Fellmeth, R. C., and Papageorge, T. A., "A Treatise on State Antitrust Law and Enforcement: With Models and Forms," *Antitrust & Trade Regulation Report,* Supp. no. 1 to Issue no. 892 (Washington, D.C.: Bureau of National Affairs, 1978), pp. 19–21.

[17]*United States* v. *General Electric et al.,* F. Supp. 197 (1961). This case is discussed in greater detail in Chapter 7.

[18]The agreement is referred to as a *consent decree* if negotiated by the Department of Justice and a *consent order* if the Federal Trade Commission is involved.

those of the defendant. They specify certain actions or procedures to which the firm must agree. In return, the government agrees to terminate further litigation. As with the nolo contendere plea, the consent decree must be approved by the courts. A consent decree is also similar to a nolo plea in that the firm accepts remedies without conceding that it has broken the law. In essence, the firm's officers say, "We didn't do it, but we won't do it again." Consent decrees do not constitute evidence of guilt in other proceedings, such as private antitrust suits.

Provisions negotiated by the Federal Trade Commission and the Xerox Corporation illustrate the nature of these agreements. The FTC charged Xerox with dominating the office-copier industry by engaging in unfair marketing and patent practices. In 1975 the commission and the firm announced that the suit had been settled by a consent order. The basic terms of the agreement were that Xerox was required to:

1. Stop the use of package pricing plans for large customers who required various types of copying machines. The government had argued that this practice made effective competition difficult for firms producing less than a full line of copiers.
2. Make its manufacturing expertise available to other firms (but not IBM) on a royalty-free basis.
3. License its competitors to use more than 1700 existing patents and also future patents issued during the six years following the agreement. Firms were not required to pay for the first three licenses, pay 0.5 percent of product revenues on the next three licenses, and receive additional licenses royalty free.
4. Forgive all liability for past patent infringements by firms taking licenses.
5. Pay reasonable royalties for patents and licenses from competitors.

At the time of the decree Xerox had about 85 percent of the market for plain-paper copying machines. The Xerox share is now considerably less than that figure, but it is difficult to determine how much of the decline is attributable to the agreement and how much is the result of intense competition in the industry.

Rule-of-Reason Versus Per se Offenses

The standard of proof in antitrust prosecutions differs with the nature of the alleged violation. Sometimes, while an act may have been committed, it is not obvious that there has been a net injury to society. Such cases are decided under a *rule-of-reason* standard. In rule-of-reason proceedings, successful prosecution requires not only the demonstration that the act has been committed, but also that society is best served by prohibiting, modifying, or punishing the act. Behind the rule-of-reason standard are several concepts. First, it has been recognized that some activities, while restraining trade, are necessary to the achievement of other legal and worthwhile objectives. For example, professional athletes have long been employed to extol the virtues of Wheaties —the "Breakfast of Champions." A clause in an athlete's contract that prohibits him from also doing advertisements for Rice Krispies may limit the marketing alternatives for Rice Krispies, but is a necessary restriction. The value of the Wheaties endorsement would be much reduced if it were known that the athlete imbibed in an occasional bowl of Rice Krispies as well.

A second basis for the rule-of-reason standard is the view that some activities that are technical violations of the antitrust laws are of such minor significance that they can safely be ignored. For example, the consequences of an agreement between two small retailers in Los Angeles to raise gasoline prices are not worth the resources required to prosecute the matter. Finally, sometimes the costs of an antitrust violation are exceeded by the benefits. Consider the case of a medium-sized manufacturer contemplating the acquisition of another firm of similar size. Assume that the industry is presently dominated by one firm about the size of the combined firm after the merger. The proposed acquisition would eliminate competition between the merging firms, but may increase competition in the industry by creating a countervailing force to the dominant firm. In this circumstance the courts may conclude that there would be net benefits to society if the merger were allowed.

On the other hand, certain activities are judged illegal without the requirement that the specific antisocial effects be shown. These acts are commonly referred to as *per se* offenses. Justice Black articulated this philosophy in *Northern Pacific Railway Co.* v. *United States* (1958):

> ... There are certain practices which because of their pernicious effect on competition and lack of any redeeming virtue are conclusively presumed to be unreasonable and therefore illegal without elaborate inquiry as to the precise harm they have caused or the business excuse for their use.[19]

The per se and rule-of-reason standards do not really represent a dichotomy, but rather different points along a continuum. The difference is in the volume and detail of economic evidence that must be presented for a successful prosecution. Rule-of-reason cases require extensive evidence showing the commission of the offense and its implications. Per se cases impose a much more limited showing only that the offense has been committed. In a sense, per se violations can be thought of as decided under an a priori rule of reason where the court has ruled that the nature of the offense automatically dictates that the social costs of the act are clearly greater than any possible benefits. Hence, there is no need to consider the evidence because the outcome is inevitable.

Not all antitrust violations fit into the tidy categories of being per se or rule-of-reason offenses. Still, there are some examples that can be cited as illustrations of each. Generally accepted as per se offenses are agreements to fix prices, divide markets between sellers, and to restrict, or pool, output. With some infrequent exceptions, group boycotts of other firms or individuals are also per se offenses. Offenses evaluated under a rule-of-reason standard are mergers and dominance or monopolization of a market by a large firm or firms. Certain activities are borderline cases and can be rationalized into either category. *Tying agreements* are an example. When a firm agrees to sell a product to another only on the condition that the buyer purchase a second product from the same firm, this is called a tied sale. Some authors consider tying contracts agreements to be per se violations of the law, while others find evidence that the courts have applied the rule of reason. The standard of proof for tying sales will be considered

[19]*Northern Pacific Railway Co.* v. *United States,* 356 U.S. 5 (1958).

in detail in Chapter 8. As a rough guide, violations involving business conduct for which there are no strong justifications are decided on a per se basis. Cases involving the existing or proposed structure of an industry usually are judged using the rule of reason.

The rule-of-reason and per se standards each have advantages and disadvantages. Under the rule of reason, alleged offenses are decided in terms of the facts of the individual case. It is possible to evaluate the particular circumstances in balancing the benefits versus the costs to society of the action. This case-specific analysis may result in decisions that are considered to be more fair. In contrast, the per se approach lumps individual situations into broad categories.

On the other hand, application of a rule-of-reason approach imposes a high resource cost on both the plaintiff and the defendant. The time of attorneys and the courts is tied up in the extensive presentation of evidence. The period from issuance of a complaint to final resolution may be so long as to make the final decision largely irrelevant. In addition, the case-by-case approach under the rule of reason increases the uncertainty of business as to what is and what is not a violation of antitrust laws. At the other extreme, the per se standard provides relatively clear notice to business as to the legality of specific acts. Another problem of the rule of reason is that it may push the courts and antitrust enforcement agencies in the direction of becoming regulatory bodies. In *United States* v. *Trenton Potteries Co., et al.* (1927) the Supreme Court made the following observation in condemning an agreement to fix prices:

> The reasonable price fixed today may through economic and business changes become the unreasonable price of tomorrow.[20]

The Court realized that the judicial system was not well suited to the requirement of continually monitoring the propriety of price fixing and other agreements. The only practical course for the courts was to act on the presumption that all such agreements are not in the interest of society and should be prohibited. A per se standard with respect to judging price-fixing cases achieves this objective.

Remedies and Penalties

Dissolution or Divestiture   Where the structure of the industry is an important element in the case, the courts may order dissolution or divestiture. In its 1911 decision, the Supreme Court ordered Standard Oil of New Jersey split into some 30 smaller firms. This was an example of *dissolution* and was considered necessary to eliminate Standard Oil's stranglehold of the oil refining industry. Dissolution is an extreme remedy, and has rarely been used in the last 60 years.

Divestiture is a less disruptive method of restructure in which a firm or firms may be required to sell off a specified part of their operations. Mergers that are successfully challenged by the Antitrust Division or the FTC are commonly dealt with by a divestiture order. For example, in 1960 Von's Grocery Company acquired Shopping

---

[20]*United States* v. *Trenton Potteries Co. et al.,* 273 U.S. 392 (1927).

Bag Food Stores. The government filed suit, charging that the merger would reduce retail grocery competition in the Los Angeles area. The Supreme Court upheld the government's complaint and ordered Von's to sell 35 of the 108 stores it had acquired in the merger [*United States* v. *Von's Grocery Co.* (1966)].[21] The firm was allowed to make the selection of the outlets to be sold. Not surprisingly, the least profitable 35 were chosen. The 1982 agreement between the government and AT&T that provided for the sale of local telephone operating companies is another example of a divestiture remedy stemming from an antitrust action.

Injunctions   In upholding a government or private complaint, the court may issue an injunction that prohibits or compels certain actions on the part of the firm. In merger cases the court may issue an injunction against a merger prior to its completion. In a tying case a firm may be enjoined from making the sale of one product conditional on the purchase of another. In a monopoly suit the corporation may be required to license its competitors who desire to use technology previously protected by the firm's patents. Where price fixing is the issue, a trade association may be prohibited from collecting and disseminating information that the court has found to be a central element in collusion between the firms. Violations of court injunctions can result in the firm's managers being held in contempt of court.

Fines   The original version of the Sherman Act provided for fines of up to $5,000. This amount was raised to $50,000 in 1955, but it was soon obvious that penalties of this magnitude provided little deterrent for large firms that stood to gain millions of dollars from violations. The limit was raised again in 1974 to $100,000 for individuals and $1,000,000 for corporations.

Prison Sentences   The original Sherman Act specified prison sentences of up to one year for violations. The 1974 revision changed criminal convictions under Section 1 from misdemeanor to felony offenses and lengthened the maximum sentence to three years. Until recently, prison sentences for Sherman Act violators were very rare. Even today long sentences are seldom imposed. Clayton and Federal Trade Commission Act convictions are civil rather than criminal offenses and do not involve prison sentences and fines.

Treble Damages   Both the Sherman and the Clayton Acts include provisions for the award of treble damages in private suits. If a private party can demonstrate that the antitrust laws have been broken and can prove the magnitude of damages sustained, the offending firm may be required to pay the plaintiff three times that amount. To illustrate, suppose that ABC, Inc., and Petersen Manufacturing are convicted of price fixing in a suit launched by the Justice Department. Firms that purchased ABC's (or Petersen's) product at inflated prices can now bring private damage suits. The successful government suit is prima facie evidence that ABC had violated the law and the task of the plaintiffs is to show the amount of damages. Suppose that it is determined that a particular firm purchased $1,000,000 in supplies from ABC during the price-fixing

---

[21]*United States* v. *Von's Grocery Co.,* 384 U.S. 270 (1966).

period and that the total price would have been $900,000 in the absence of collusion. Thus, the plaintiff has been overcharged by $100,000 and would be entitled to recover three times that amount, or $300,000. The prospect of huge awards for damages may be the most important deterrent to antitrust violations. In the electrical machinery conspiracy case previously mentioned, the manufacturers ended up paying total damages approaching half a billion dollars. These private damage suits were much more painful than the $2 million in fines and seven brief prison sentences (30 days) levied by the courts in the criminal proceeding.

SUMMARY
Workable Competition

The goal of antitrust policy is to promote workable competition. Structural objectives for workable competition are that there be as many sellers as economies of scale permit, that no one firm or group of firms be able to dominate the market, and that there be no artificial barriers to entry and exit. Behavioral objectives require that there should be no collusion between firms and that rival firms should not be eliminated unless they are less efficient than remaining firms. Finally, performance objectives include limiting excess profits, reducing selling costs, promoting efficiency, and encouraging technological change.

Beginnings of Antitrust

Rise of Big Business   Changes in production and marketing techniques in the 1800s provided advantages for large-scale business operations. However, aggressive actions on the part of entrepreneurs caused agitation for control of big business. The judicial system using the common law proved inadequate in limiting business abuses. As a result, public pressure increased for specific legislation to establish curbs on business.

Sherman Act   The Sherman Act has two main sections. Section 1 prohibits contracts, combinations, and conspiracies in restraint of trade. Collusion to fix prices is an example of a violation of Section 1. Monopolizing, attempting to monopolize, and combining or conspiring to monopolize are prohibited by Section 2. The intent was to prevent market dominance by giant corporations such as Standard Oil.

Clayton and Federal Trade Commission Acts   Disappointment with the Sherman Act led to passage of the Clayton and Federal Trade Commission Acts. The Clayton Act was designed to specify unlawful business practices and to check monopoly in its incipiency. The act restricts price discrimination, tied sales, and mergers where the effect is to substantially lessen competition.

The Federal Trade Commission Act created the Federal Trade Commission. One function of the commission is to advise businesspeople on the propriety of their actions prior to the issuance of a formal complaint. Section 5 of the act declares unfair methods of competition unlawful. This section is used to prosecute antitrust violations and also as the basis for the FTC's scrutiny of deceptive advertising.

Refinements in Antitrust Legislation

Robinson-Patman Act   The Clayton Act was judged inadequate in limiting price discrimination. The Robinson-Patman Act amended the Clayton Act price discrimination provisions. In particular, price concessions that could be offered to large buyers were limited.

Wheeler-Lea Act   The wording of Section 5 of the Federal Trade Commission Act focused on acts that injured competitors rather than the effect on competition and consumers. The Wheeler-Lea Act amended the FTC Act to allow prosecution of actions that have adverse impacts on consumers.

Celler-Kefauver Amendment   The Clayton Act prohibited firms from acquiring the stock of other firms if competition was substantially lessened. Court decisions held that asset acquisitions were not prohibited by the act. The courts also interpreted the act as applying only to firms engaged in direct competition with one another. As a result, few mergers were prevented by the Clayton Act. The Celler-Kefauver Amendment amended the Clayton Act to include asset mergers and also changed the wording such that a showing of a lessening of competition "in any line of commerce in any section of the country" is now sufficient grounds for preventing a merger.

Introduction to Antitrust Procedures and Enforcement

Jurisdiction of Federal Antitrust Laws   Federal antitrust laws have been broadly interpreted by the courts to cover even activities that are primarily intrastate in nature. However, certain industries and activities are partially exempt from antitrust action. For example, the Webb-Pomerene Act allows firms to form export associations. Agriculture, regulated industries, professional sports, and labor unions are all afforded special antitrust treatment.

Complaints and Appeals   Antitrust proceedings may be initiated in four different ways: (1) by the Antitrust Division of the Department of Justice, (2) by the Federal Trade Commission, (3) by state attorneys general under state antitrust statutes, and (4) by private parties. Appeals are heard through the federal court system.

Disposition of Complaints   Firms may plead guilty or not guilty to antitrust complaints. A nolo contendere plea may also be entered. A nolo contendere and a guilty plea are treated the same by the courts, but the former does not constitute prima facie evidence of guilt in private antitrust suits. Most antitrust complaints are settled by consent decrees or orders. These are negotiated agreements between the government and the parties involved. They normally stipulate some change in structure or behavior on the part of the firm.

Rule-of-Reason Versus Per se Offenses   Certain business activities, such as mergers, are evaluated on a rule-of-reason basis. The courts determine whether the costs of the action outweigh any possible benefits. For other actions, such as price fixing, a per se standard is used. No evaluation of costs and benefits is necessary. The mere commission of the act is deemed a violation of the law.

Remedies and Penalties   Firms convicted of antitrust violations may be dissolved into a number of smaller firms or required to divest themselves of parts of their operations. Injunctions may be issued that specify or prohibit certain courses of action. Sherman Act violations may result in fines or prison sentences. Both the Sherman and Clayton Acts provide for treble damage awards to private parties.

DISCUSSION QUESTIONS

1. One goal of workable competition is the elimination of artificial barriers to entry. What is meant by artificial barriers?
2. Is there ever justification for government action to prevent the demise of inefficient firms?
3. The common law was not an adequate basis for curbing business abuses. What are the shortcomings of statutory law intended for the same purpose?
4. Could private antitrust suits be part of a firm's strategy in dealing with its competitors?
5. One purpose of the Clayton Act was to specify unlawful business activities. Was this a realistic goal?
6. What is the difference between *injury to competitors* and *injury to competition?*
7. How would a firm go about making an asset acquisition of another firm?
8. What dangers are there in allowing firms to form export associations under the provisions of the Webb-Pomerene Act?
9. The Supreme Court is not obligated to hear all appeals of antitrust suits. What criteria should the Court use in deciding which cases to hear?
10. What are the advantages and disadvantages of resolving antitrust complaints by consent decrees or orders?
11. Price fixing is a per se violation of the law. Are there any circumstances that would justify price fixing?
12. Where divestiture is the ordered remedy in an antitrust suit, what are the advantages and disadvantages of requiring the firm to carry out the order quickly?
13. A firm convicted of price fixing can be fined. How could a judge fix the amount of the fine?

chapter 5

Antitrust: Market Definition and Monopoly

Chapter Outline

The price of monopoly is upon every occasion the highest which can be got. The natural price, or the price of free competition, on the contrary, is the lowest which can be taken, not upon every occasion indeed, but for any considerable time together. The one is upon every occasion the highest which can be squeezed out of the buyers, or which, it is supposed, they will consent to give: The other is the lowest which the sellers can commonly afford to take, and at the same time continue their business.

ADAM SMITH[1]

case by case basis approach

Regulation and nationalization are attempts to improve the performance of industry directly, while antitrust enforcement focuses on changing industrial structure and conduct as indirect means for improving performance. This chapter considers the structural approach to antitrust, which is based on the assumption that increasing the number and equalizing the size distribution of traders in a market yields net social benefits. Most advocates of using antitrust statutes to facilitate structural change rest their case on two propositions. The first is that highly concentrated industries and industries with one or more dominant firms are likely candidates for successful collusion. Deconcentration is a method of reducing the potential for collusion. The second assumption is that economies of scale in most industries are quickly exhausted and that leading firms often exceed the minimum optimal size required to realize any scale economies. Thus, a policy of deconcentration would not impose efficiency losses on most industries.

Another argument for deconcentration is the political power of giant firms. The excessive influence of the oil lobby in Congress, the meddling of International Telephone and Telegraph (ITT) in Chilean politics, and the common-law marriage between the leading weapons contractors and the Department of Defense are examples. Galbraith argues that the size of modern corporations is not primarily determined by the dictates of technology, but rather by the quest for power and influence. He observes:

> For any given level and use of technology there is, no doubt, a technically optimum size of firm. . . . But the need to control environment—to exclude untoward events —encourages much greater size. The larger the firm, the larger it will be in its industry. The greater, accordingly, will be its influence on setting prices and costs. And the greater, in general, will be its influence on consumers, and the community and the state—the greater, in short, will be its ability to influence, i.e., plan its environment.[2]

It may be in society's interest to allow firms to grow or to merge to realize technical economies of scale, but the social benefits of firms large enough to effectively exploit their political power are much less obvious. Antitrust enforcement is a possible method of reducing firms from privately optimal political size to socially optimal economic size.

This chapter is divided into three main parts. First, problems of defining markets and market shares are considered. It is not uncommon for antitrust cases to turn on

---

[1]Smith, A., *The Wealth of Nations* (New York: Random House, Modern Library, 1937), p. 61.
[2]Galbraith, J. K., *Economics and the Public Purpose* (Boston: Houghton Mifflin, 1973), p. 40.

the definition of the market accepted by the court. Second, the history and evolution of monopoly cases brought under Section 2 of the Sherman Act are discussed. The final section of the chapter evaluates recent developments in this area.

DEFINING THE MARKET
Need for Definition

Merger and monopoly cases require careful definition of market boundaries and market shares. Section 2 of the Sherman Act condemns "every person who shall monopolize, . . . or combine or conspire with any other person or persons, to monopolize any part of trade or commerce." To successfully prosecute, the government must convince the courts that a firm or firms have acquired a dominant position in some "part of trade or commerce." This requires that the market that is allegedly dominated be carefully and logically defined. A narrow definition that excludes other products and potential producers will show the defendants with a substantial market share and increase the probability of conviction. A more liberal definition of the products and suppliers that constitute the market reduces the computed market share and improves the prospects of the defendants.

The Clayton Act also imposes the need for defining markets in merger cases. Section 7 prohibits mergers where the effect "may be substantially to lessen competition" in "any line of commerce" and in "any section of the country." The phrase "in any line of commerce" implies the need to define the product market where competition is reduced, while "any section of the country" suggests the need to identify the geographic market being considered. Again, the choice by the court of broad rather than narrow product and geographic market definitions is often a crucial factor in the outcome of the case.

The determination of the relevant market can be expensive and time consuming. Participants in a suit involving IBM were asked to estimate the proportion of the three-year trial that was spent presenting evidence relating to the definition of the market [*United States* v. *International Business Machines Corp.* (1979)]. The consensus was that about half the trial involved this issue.[3] For two other monopolization suits the estimates ranged from 15 to 25 percent of total trial time.[4] The conflicting objectives of the litigants (the defense arguing for a broad definition and the plaintiff pushing for a narrow demarcation) is one explanation of the time spent in determining the relevant market. The inherent subjectivity of the problem is another. Market boundaries are not clear-cut and obvious. The choice of firms and products to be included or excluded must be based on incomplete evidence and judgment.

Consider a hypothetical Section 2 complaint in which Carter Enterprises is charged with monopolization of the U.S. market for chocolate-covered peanut butter cups. The government position is that chocolate-covered peanut butter cups represent a distinct market and that Carter's has a 95-percent share. Such a market definition

---

[3]*Report to the President and to the Attorney General of the National Commission for the Review of Antitrust Laws and Procedures,* Volume 2 (Washington, D.C., Government Printing Office, Jan. 22, 1979), p. 95; *United States* v. *International Business Machines Corp.,* 69 Civ. 200 (S.D.N.Y. 1969).

[4]*Report to the President,* p. 96; *SCM Corp.* v. *Xerox Corp.,* Civ. 15,807 (D. Conn. 1973); and *Berkey Photo, Inc.* v. *The Eastman Kodak Co., Inc.,* 73 Civ. 424 (S.D.N.Y. 1973).

may be too narrow, because there are other kinds of candy that can be purchased to alleviate one's craving for chocolate or for peanut butter (however, satisfying both with one purchase is more difficult). On the other hand, if the contention of the firm is that the market should be defined to include all types of candy, this is not very realistic either. The connoisseur of fine peanut butter cups may not be satisfied with cinnamon bears or lollipops. Somewhere between the extreme positions of the adversaries is the relevant market, but there are no hard and fast rules to fix its boundaries. Although hard candy is probably not an adequate substitute for peanut butter cups, what about M&Ms? If plain Hershey bars won't qualify, does the addition of almonds create an acceptable alternative? The choice is not obvious. Ultimately, the "correct" market definition in an antitrust proceeding is whatever the court decides it to be. One student of antitrust takes an even stronger position. He maintains that:

> . . . The courts have shown no real interest in developing objective criteria; rather, they fit the definitions to assure whatever decisions they wish to reach.[5]

This view is probably too cynical. However, it is clear that the determination of market boundaries by the courts is a highly subjective process.

Product Markets

At one extreme the product market could be defined to encompass all the alternative uses of an individual's income. At the other extreme is a definition that includes only a single, highly differentiated product. An interesting example of the struggle of the courts to delimit product markets is the so-called cellophane case [*United States* v. *E. I. du Pont de Nemours* (1956)].[6] The Justice Department charged that the du Pont corporation had illegally monopolized interstate commerce in cellophane. The decision turned on whether the Supreme Court would accept the government's or du Pont's definition of the products that effectively competed with cellophane and, thus, constituted the market.

The government contended that only those products that are "substantially fungible" and sell at "substantially the same price" should be included in the market with cellophane. Between 1937 and 1947 du Pont produced nearly 75 percent of all cellophane sold in the United States. Under the definition proposed by the government, du Pont's high market share was argued to represent prima facie evidence of monopolization. In contrast, du Pont took the position that, although cellophane had distinctive characteristics, it still faced significant competitive pressures from other products. The firm advocated a market defined as "flexible wrapping materials" and consisting of products such as wax paper and aluminum foil. Based on this broader definition, du Pont's share of the market was less than 20 percent.

The Court rejected the government's claim that only products that are essentially identical be included in the market. Instead, the test of "reasonable interchangeability" was imposed:

[5]Low, R. E., *Modern Economic Organization* (Homewood, Ill.: Irwin, 1970), p. 357.
[6]*United States* v. *E. I. du Pont de Nemours & Company*, 351 U.S. 377 (1956).

> The "market" which one must study to determine when a producer has monopoly power will vary with the part of commerce under consideration. The tests are constant. That market is composed of products that have reasonable interchangeability for the purposes for which they are produced—price, use and qualities considered.[7]

Speaking for the Court, Justice Reed went on to analyze how price, use, and qualities can be analyzed to determine those products that are part of the market by virtue of being reasonably interchangeable.

Price   The Court dipped into the economist's bag of tools to borrow the concept of cross elasticity of demand. *Cross elasticity* is defined as the percentage change in sales of one product resulting from a 1-percent change in price of another product—all other things held constant, of course. In the du Pont case the Court reasoned:

> If a slight decrease in the price of cellophane causes a considerable number of customers of other flexible wrappings to switch to cellophane, it would be an indication that a high cross-elasticity of demand exists between them; that the products compete in the same market.[8]

The trial record of the district court indicated that cellophane customers were very sensitive to price changes. As a result, the Supreme Court concluded that, on the basis of high cross elasticity of demand, cellophane should be considered as part of a broader market for flexible packaging materials.

Quality   Reasonably interchangeable products should have similar characteristics. Eighty percent of du Pont's cellophane was used for packaging of food. Suitable packaging materials have certain features. First, they must be transparent to allow the customer to inspect the purchase. Second, they must not easily transmit odors that could be picked up by the food. Finally, they must be moisture resistant to prevent spoilage. The Court determined that there were a number of products that qualified as acceptable substitutes for food packaging under these criteria.

Use   A highly pragmatic way of identifying products for inclusion in a market is by examining the uses of those products. Where products successfully compete with one another in actual use, they should logically be grouped together. The Court found that cellophane had competition from other materials in all of its major uses. The evidence indicated that cellophane furnished:

less than 7% of wrappings for bakery products

25% for candy

32% for snacks

35% for meats and poultry

[7]Ibid., p. 394.
[8]Ibid., p. 400.

27% for crackers and biscuits

47% for fresh products

34% for frozen foods.[9]

In summary, the Court determined that there were products whose demand was sensitive to the price of cellophane, that had characteristics similar to those of cellophane, and that successfully competed with cellophane in end use. Hence, it opted for the broader market definition proposed by the firm and exonerated du Pont of the charge of monopolization.

The continuing importance of the cellophane case stems from the criteria proposed to define markets. The test of reasonable interchangeability is still used to identify the relevant product market. However, the judicial system's application of the test is open to criticism. The focus on cross elasticity, qualities, and end use is deficient in several respects.[10] First, preoccupation with potential substitutes in use ignores substitutes in production. Even if there are no acceptable alternatives to a product, there may be other firms with production capabilities that could be adapted to produce the product. For example, Wham-O Manufacturing Co. has a 75-to-80 percent share of the retail Frisbee market. It is difficult to think of good substitutes for a Frisbee, but it doesn't follow that Wham-O necessarily possesses a high degree of market power because of the lack of alternatives.[11] Nothing about the production of a Frisbee is particularly complex or expensive. Hence, the ability of Wham-O to exploit its product is at least somewhat constrained by the threat of other producers expanding or initiating production. A correct definition of the product market should include close substitutes in production, as well as close substitutes in use.

A second criticism is that the concept of a "good" substitute, either in use or production, is meaningless without specifying the price of the product. Two products that could not be considered reasonably interchangeable because of a large difference in price may become acceptable alternatives as the price gap narrows. Slide rules and calculators are an example. Until recently, calculators were too expensive for the average college student. Universities around the nation taught courses in the use of the slide rule because the purchase of a calculator was not a feasible alternative. Dramatic improvements in calculator technology changed all that. At the present time it is possible to purchase a $30 hand-held calculator with all the capabilities of the most sophisticated slide rule. The consequence is that calculators have almost completely eliminated the demand for slide rules. A product that previously could not effectively compete eventually became the dominant technology because of the change in relative prices.

A third problem is that the existence of numerous reasonably interchangeable products can actually indicate a lack of competition. When the price of a product is near its cost of production, there may be few viable substitutes. As the seller increases

---

[9]Ibid., p. 395.

[10]For further discussion, see Posner, R. A., *Antitrust Law* (Chicago: University of Chicago, 1976), pp. 127–128.

[11]However, the firm does have considerable market power because of its control of the International Frisbee Disk Association, which promotes and regulates the competitive use of the product. See Koon, B., "How to Keep Sales of a Toy Up: Build a Sport Around It," *Wall Street Journal* (Aug. 17, 1979), p. 1.

the price, there are more and more acceptable alternatives. These alternatives can effectively compete only because of the high price that is now being charged for the product under consideration. This concept is especially relevant in evaluating the use of cross elasticities of demand as a tool of defining markets. The finding that demand for one product is highly sensitive to the price of another may simply reflect the fact that the price of the first is approaching the monopoly level. A more relevant comparison would be the cross elasticity at prices near costs of production. Recognizing the difficulties involved in using cross elasticities, the courts have stressed similar qualities and end uses in applying the reasonable interchangeability test.

Product market definitions should also consider costs of production and quality differentials. To illustrate, in the cellophane case the Court might have compared the quality and production costs of flexible wrapping materials to assess whether it was possible to produce materials of quality comparable to cellophane at nearly equal cost. If equal quality was not available at equal cost, then the Court could have considered whether the quality differentials between cellophane and other wrapping materials were offset by differences in production costs.[12] At least conceptually, this approach could be applied to all cases requiring definition of the relevant product market.

Geographic Markets

The choice of geographic market can be as important as the determination of the product market. Consider a proposed merger between two producers of cement. If the market is considered as being nationwide, then the industry will appear highly fragmented because the market share of the four largest cement companies is only about five percent.

But industry concentration on a national basis is irrelevant. Cement producers do not compete from coast to coast. Indeed, it would be unusual for a firm to transport cement more than about 100 miles. Thus, a more realistic market definition would consider individual metropolitan areas. In these smaller regions concentration ratios are much higher. One study estimated the average local or regional four-firm concentration ratio to be 0.52. Clearly, the designation of the geographic market makes a difference.[13] A merger in an industry where the top four firms control over half of the relevant geographical market should be viewed quite differently than if the top firms have only a five-percent share.

In *United States* v. *Philadelphia National Bank* (1963) the Supreme Court held that the relevant geographic market is "not where the parties to the merger do business or even where they compete, but where, within the area of competitive overlap, the effect of the merger on competition will be direct and immediate."[14] This analysis of the effects on competition must consider both the supply and demand sides of the market.

On the buyer side, the geographic market is limited to the area in which consum-

---

[12]See Turner, D. F., "Antitrust Policy and the Cellophane Case," *Harvard Law Review,* vol. 70 (1956) pp. 281, 302, 309, as noted in Posner, *Antitrust Law,* p. 128.

[13]Schwartzman, D. and Bodoff, J., "Concentration in Regional and Local Industries," *Southern Economic Journal* (Jan. 1971), pp. 343–348.

[14]*U.S.* v. *Philadelphia National Bank et al.,* 374 U.S. 321, 357 (1963).

ers can reasonably be expected to make purchases. That area varies dramatically with the nature of the product. For purchases of industrial machinery, corporations can afford to scour the entire nation looking for the most advantageous terms. To purchase an automobile a family may be willing to drive a considerable distance to get the best deal. In contrast, purchases of gas or groceries are usually made from vendors within a few miles of one's home.

In the Philadelphia National Bank case the Supreme Court judged that the relevant geographical market consisted of the four-county metropolitan Philadelphia area. In evaluating banking services the Court determined that:

> Convenience of location is essential to effective competition. Individuals and corporations typically confer the bulk of their patronage on banks in their local community; they find it impractical to conduct their banking business at a distance . . . the factor of inconvenience localizes banking competition as effectively as high transportation costs in other industries. [15]

For sellers, the geographic market is determined primarily by transportation costs. Sellers of heavy, bulky products such as cement tend to compete in local areas, while lighter, high-value products are shipped nationwide. In the latter case the large market is possible because freight costs represent only a small proportion of the total selling price. For example, in *United States* v. *Brown Shoe Co.* (1962) the issue was a proposed merger between the Brown and Kinney shoe companies. Each firm was engaged in both manufacturing and retailing operations. At the manufacturing level the Court held that the geographic market should be defined to include the entire nation: "The relationships of product value, bulk, weight and consumer demand enable manufacturers to distribute their shoes on a nation-wide basis, as Brown and Kinney, in fact, do." [16]

As a general rule, if a product is distributed nationwide and transportation costs are not significant, the courts are likely to define the geographic market to include the entire country. However, if transportation costs are important and buyers limit their search to a small region, then the market may be defined in terms of regions, states, or even individual cities.

Past court definitions of geographic markets exhibit some of the same deficiencies as product market definitions. A persistent problem has been the failure to recognize that historical evidence is biased by the existing degree of competition. If prices are held near the competitive level, then potential entrants in a region receive signals that entry is not profitable. Consequently, the market share of the existing firm or firms is computed to be relatively high. On the other hand, if the price is held substantially above production costs, then other firms may find it profitable to incur sizeable transportation costs to ship their product into the market. Thus, the exploitation of market power may result in the paradoxical finding that market power, as measured by market share, is not excessive. A proper definition of the geographic market requires that pricing and marketing policies of existing firms be examined. The simplistic focus on historical

[15]Ibid., p. 385.
[16]*Brown Shoe Co.* v. *United States,* 370 U.S. 294, 328 (1962).

patterns of buying and selling may be highly misleading unless evaluated in light of this broader perspective.

MONOPOLIZATION: STANDARD OIL TO ALCOA

Section 2 of the Sherman Act prohibits monopolizing, attempting to monopolize, and conspiring to monopolize. Since its enactment, the most controversial point with respect to Section 2 has been the standard of proof required for successful prosecution. The issue is whether the Sherman Act made monopoly power in and of itself an offense or whether the showing of industry dominance had to be accompanied by evidence of abusive practices. Over the past 90 years, the Supreme Court has positioned itself on both sides of this question and the particular side that the Court happened to take at any given time has had an overwhelming effect on the use of Section 2. When proof of antisocial acts or practices to achieve monopoly power has been required, there has been little Section 2 activity. When the Court has held that the government only had to show the existence of monopoly power, Section 2 cases have been more frequent and more successful.[17] The evolution of the standard for successful prosecution can be extracted from the leading Section 2 cases.

Standard Oil

Although a number of important monopoly cases were decided during the first 20 years after enactment of the Sherman Act, the first case of real significance was *Standard Oil Co. of New Jersey* v. *United States* decided in 1911.[18] John D. Rockefeller entered the oil business in 1862 by advancing money to improve an oil refinery in Cleveland. Ten years later Rockefeller controlled almost all of the 40 refineries in that city. By 1904 the holding company, Standard Oil of New Jersey, had an 85-percent share of refined oil sales in the United States. The firm also controlled the major pipelines used for transporting crude oil.

In 1906 the government brought suit under Sections 1 and 2 of the Sherman Act, alleging that Standard had conspired to restrain trade and commerce in crude oil, refined oil, and other petroleum products. The government contended that Standard had acquired control of these markets by resorting to an assortment of illegal practices that required 57 pages of the trial record just to enumerate. Standard's alleged abuses can be grouped into six general categories:

1. Rebates, preferences, and other discriminatory practices involving the railroads.
2. Control of pipelines and unfair practices against competing pipe lines.
3. Local price cutting to supress competition.
4. Industrial espionage and bribery.

---

[17]In recent years another factor has influenced Section 2 activity. Cases involving large firms have become so expensive, time consuming, and complex that the government must be very selective about initiating complaints. The problems of the "big case" are discussed in Chapter 9.

[18]*Standard Oil of N.J.* v. *United States,* 221 U.S. 1 (1911).

5. Operation of independent bogus companies.

6. Division of the market into geographic areas and limiting the operations of subsidiary companies. [19]

The Supreme Court ruled that Standard had monopolized the markets for crude and refined oil and that its position of dominance had indeed been achieved by illegal practices. The Court determined that Standard's intent to monopolize

> . . . was frequently manifested by acts and dealings wholly inconsistent with the theory that they were made with the single conception of advancing the development of business power by usual methods, but which on the contrary necessarily involved the intent to drive others from the field and to exclude them from their right to trade and thus accomplish the mastery which was the end in view. [20]

In 1913 Standard Oil of New Jersey was dissolved into 34 firms. However, the existing stockholders were given ownership in each of the new companies. As a result, the newly fragmented industry continued to be dominated by the same people. In addition, the new corporations each operated in their own geographic area with little interfirm competition. Several decades passed before any semblance of competition evolved in the industry.

The same year that the Standard Oil case was decided the Court also ordered the American Tobacco Company broken up. [21] In 1890 a trust had been organized by five cigarette manufacturers concerned about declining prices in the industry. In 1898 the organization spread its activities into chewing tobacco by purchasing five other manufacturers. A year later the facilities of 30 more manufacturers of plug tobacco were purchased and immediately closed. The trust also used selective price cutting and other practices to "encourage" competing firms to cooperate. Like Standard Oil, American Tobacco was found to have used illegal acts to acquire monopoly status.

U.S. Steel

In 1912 the government charged U.S. Steel with monopolizing the manufacture of iron and steel. [22] U.S. Steel had been formed in 1901 as a combination of previously independent firms. By 1911 the firm was responsible for about 50 percent of total U.S. iron and steel output. The government also charged that U.S. Steel had conspired to fix prices. The price-fixing charge was based on meetings with competitors such as the famous Gary Dinners, at which nationwide steel prices were agreed upon. In 1920 the Supreme Court rejected the government's contentions and found U.S. Steel not guilty. Technically the decision was based on the finding that U.S. Steel's market share had declined to the point that the firm had lost much of its monopoly power over the industry.

---

[19]See Einhorn, H. A., and Smith, W. P., *Economic Aspects of Antitrust: Readings and Cases* (New York: Random House, 1968), p. 38.

[20]221 U.S. 1, 76 (1911).

[21]*United States* v. *American Tobacco Co.,* 221 U.S. 106 (1911).

[22]*United States* v. *U.S. Steel Corp.,* 251 U.S. 417 (1920).

However, the Court also held that the earlier domination of the industry had been achieved without resorting to illegal acts against competitors. In fact, the record indicated that U.S. Steel had worked with and not against its competitors. Evidently, the Court's concern was focused on injury to competitors rather than injury to competition.

In Standard Oil and American Tobacco the government won the cases and was rewarded with dissolution. In U.S. Steel the company was acquitted. Although the outcomes of Standard and Tobacco differed from that of Steel, the reasoning of the Court was sufficiently consistent to put Section 2 prosecutions in limbo. In each case the Court held that illegal monopolization required a showing that the firm had a dominant position in the industry and that dominance had been achieved by abusive market practices. In Standard Oil and American Tobacco the government was able to convince the Court that both criteria had been met and the firms were found guilty. In U.S. Steel the government was unable to meet the dual standard of proof and lost the case. In its decision the Court explicitly rejected the government position that monopoly power was a per se violation of Section 2. Instead, the Court opted for a rule-of-reason interpretation based on the *abuse theory* of monopoly. Said the Court:

> The corporation is undoubtedly of impressive size, and it takes an effort of resolution not to be affected by it or to exaggerate its influence. But we must adhere to the law, and the law does not make mere size an offense or the existence of unexerted power an offense. It . . . requires overt acts, and trusts to its prohibition of them and its power to repress or punish them. It does not compel competition nor require all that is possible. [23]

The insistence of the Court in separating "bad trusts" and "good trusts" dealt a near fatal blow to prosecution of monopoly under Section 2 of the Sherman Act. Cases pending at the time the U.S. Steel decision was announced resulted in the defendant being exonerated or in ineffectual consent decrees. Twenty-five years passed before the government could again claim victory in a monopolization suit.

Alcoa

The Alcoa (Aluminum Company of America) case was viewed as representing a dramatic change in the standard of proof required in Section 2 prosecutions. Although recent developments suggest that the Alcoa precedent has been weakened, the case still occupies an important position in the evolution of antitrust law. It also serves as an excellent example of the importance of defining markets and market shares.

Alcoa was formed in 1888 and subsequently obtained a monopoly over the production of virgin (newly smelted) aluminum ingot by its control of important patents. When the patents expired in 1909 the firm attempted to maintain its position by entering into agreements with foreign producers to limit imports and by persuading

---

[23]Ibid., p. 451.

sellers of hydroelectric power not to sell electricity to potential competitors. A 1912 government suit against Alcoa resulted in a consent decree specifying that the firm would abandon its restrictive practices. However, the decree had little impact. By 1937 Alcoa was still the sole domestic producer of aluminum ingot with a market share of 90 percent, the remaining 10 percent coming from imports.

In 1937 the government brought suit charging that Alcoa had monopolized the markets for bauxite, water power, alumina, virgin aluminum ingot, castings, cooking utensils, pistons, extrusions and structural shapes, foil, miscellaneous fabricated articles, sheet, and cables. The district court ruled that the firm had monopolized none of these markets and dismissed the complaint. The government's appeal was heard by a three-member court of appeals, because four members of the Supreme Court had been involved in earlier litigation of the case and were obligated to disqualify themselves— leaving the Court with fewer than the six justices necessary for a quorum. As a result, the final verdict was rendered by a three-member panel of circuit court judges, the decision written by Judge Learned Hand [*United States* v. *Aluminum Co. of America* (1945)].[24]

Judge Hand organized his opinion around four questions. First, had Alcoa monopolized the market for virgin aluminum ingot?[25] Second, was the firm guilty of unlawful practices in the course of acquiring its monopoly? Third, had Alcoa been involved in a conspiracy with a Canadian producer, Aluminum Limited? Finally, what remedies would be appropriate if the firm were found guilty? With respect to the charge of using unlawful practices to secure a monopoly, the Court ruled that the government had failed to prove its case. Regarding the alleged conspiracy involving Aluminum Limited, it was determined that Section 1 of the Sherman Act had been violated. The crucial issue in the case, however, was whether Alcoa had monopolized the market for virgin aluminum ingot. This issue turned on the definition of the relevant market.

The geographic market was not a problem—aluminum is sold in a national market. The question of substitutes in production also was easily resolved. The facilities required to produce aluminum ingot are sufficiently specialized to limit the possibility that firms in other industries would convert existing plants to aluminum production. The focal point of the market definition issue was the determination of possible substitutes for virgin ingot. Judge Hand eliminated other metals such as steel and copper from consideration, concluding that aluminum has unique characteristics.

In the end, the most difficult question was whether secondary aluminum ingot was a viable substitute for virgin ingot and, thus, should be included in calculating Alcoa's market share. Secondary ingot is aluminum that has previously been used for some other purpose and then remelted to ingot form. It was used in some of the same applications as virgin ingot, but considered inferior as indicated by the fact that the price of secondary ingot was one or two cents a pound lower than virgin ingot.

In computing Alcoa's position in the market, three market share definitions were considered by Judge Hand:

---

[24] *United States* v. *Aluminum Co. of America,* 148 F. 2d 416 (2d Cir. 1945).
[25] The charge of monopolization of the other markets was not an important point of the decision.

$$MS_1 = \frac{\text{Alcoa's virgin ingot production minus aluminum used internally by Alcoa to fabricate products}}{\text{Total domestic virgin ingot production plus imports plus secondary ingot production}}$$

$$MS_2 = \frac{\text{Alcoa's virgin ingot production}}{\text{Total domestic virgin ingot production plus imports plus secondary ingot production}}$$

$$MS_3 = \frac{\text{Alcoa's virgin ingot production}}{\text{Total domestic virgin ingot production plus imports}}$$

The first definition was used by the district court in finding that Alcoa was not guilty of monopolization. Using this approach, Alcoa's market share was computed to be 33 percent. The second definition resulted in a 64-percent share. The third approach, accepted by the appeals court, set Alcoa's share at 90 percent of the relevant market.

Notice that the third definition is the only one of the three that does not include secondary ingot in the denominator. The Court's reasoning in making this choice is interesting, if somewhat suspect. Because Alcoa was the sole domestic producer of virgin ingot, the supply of secondary ingot was influenced by Alcoa's previous production decisions. Hence, the Court concluded:

> "Alcoa" always knew that the future supply of ingot would be made up in part of what it produced at the time, and, if it was as far sighted as it proclaims itself, that consideration must have had its share in determining how much to produce. . . . The competition of "secondary" must therefore be disregarded, as soon as we consider the position of "Alcoa" over a period of years; it was as much within "Alcoa's" control as was the production of the "virgin" from which it had been derived.[26]

The choice of the market share definition was crucial to the decision in the case. Judge Hand observed that 90 percent "is enough to constitute a monopoly; it is doubtful whether 60 or 64 percent would be enough; and certainly 33 percent is not."[27] Based on the finding that Alcoa had a 90-percent share of the market, the Court ruled that the firm had monopolized the market for virgin aluminum ingot.

Consider the findings of the Court. It was determined that Alcoa had monopolized the market, but that the monopoly had not been achieved by resorting to unlawful practices designed to deter entry. The precedent established by the Standard Oil, American Tobacco, and U.S. Steel cases suggests that the Court would find that Section 2 had not been violated. Instead, Judge Hand rejected the existing abuse theory and stressed a structural test for Section 2 cases. His interpretation of the Sherman Act was that "it did not condone 'good trusts' and condemn 'bad' ones; it forbade all."[28] Central to Judge Hand's analysis was his view that the existing rule of reason precedent was inconsistent with the treatment of firms involved in price fixing. Collusion to fix prices is a per se violation of the law. However, a firm with monopoly power has equal or greater power to fix prices. Why penalize a practice when undertaken by several firms

[26]148 F. 2d 416, 425.
[27]Ibid., p. 424.
[28]Ibid., p. 427.

while upholding the right of a single firm to do the same thing? Obviously, the monopolist "must sell at some price and the only price at which it could sell is a price which it itself fixed."[29]

Judge Hand did admit one possible defense for the firm found to have monopoly power. If monopoly is "thrust upon" a firm by virtue of the "superior skill, foresight, and industry" of its management, the firm may be absolved of the charge of unlawful conduct. For example, if rivals leave a market because changes in tastes, input prices, or technology cause it to be unprofitable, the remaining firm can hardly be held responsible. In the Alcoa case the Court found that industry dominance had not been thrust upon the firm, but rather had been achieved by Alcoa's aggressive, albeit lawful, practices. An important example was the firm's continual expansion of capacity beyond the needs of existing demand. This practice was viewed by the Court as a method for discouraging entry that might otherwise have occurred as the market expanded.

The remedies in the Alcoa case are much less important than the precedent it established. Judge Hand's decision came eight years after the original complaint was filed. His circuit court of appeals, in overturning the decision of the lower court, remanded the case to the district court to determine remedies. The district court's decision was finally handed down in 1950. By that time the composition of the industry had changed dramatically. During World War II the government had constructed additional aluminum manufacturing plants to meet the expanded demand. After the war those plants were sold to private industry under the proviso that Alcoa would not be allowed to bid. The result was the creation of a "big three" in the aluminum industry consisting of Alcoa, Kaiser, and Reynolds. Recognizing the change in industry structure, the district court determined that dissolution of Alcoa was not necessary. Thus, the government won the case but came away essentially empty handed.

Three years after Alcoa the Supreme Court seemed to confirm the shift in policy announced by the appeals court. Finding that motion picture distributors had monopolized the market for first-run films, the Court held that:

> monopoly power, whether lawfully or unlawfully acquired, may itself constitute an evil and stand condemned under Section 2 even though it remains unexercised.[30]

MONOPOLIZATION: A STEP BACK FROM ALCOA

The Griffith decision appears to be a rather clear statement that a per se standard would be used in evaluating cases brought under Section 2 of the Sherman Act. However, an examination of monopolization cases decided in the four decades since Alcoa indicates that the test has not been solely structural. Rather, it seems that Alcoa and subsequent decisions have had the effect of shifting the abuse theory to a different level.

The Double Standard

To prosecute successfully under Section 2, the government no longer is required to show that a firm has engaged in acts that, considered by themselves, represent antitrust

---

[29]Ibid., p. 424.
[30]*United States* v. *Griffith Amusement Co.*, 334 U.S. 100, 107 (1948).

violations. Instead, prosecutors can focus on patterns of business behavior that have the net effect of allowing a firm to gain and maintain a monopoly position. Under this interpretation, practices that would be legal when considered in isolation or when used by smaller firms, may be grounds for conviction if used by a firm judged to have dominance in an industry. That is, the standard used by the courts to judge the monopolist is more rigorous than that applied to smaller firms.

United States v. *Grinnell* is a good example of the double standard that the courts have used in evaluating the practices of firms with substantial market power. [31] Grinnell was a conglomerate with subsidiaries that provided "central station protective services" used to detect fires or burglaries. These automated systems were located on the premises of a business. When a problem was sensed, a signal was sent to a central station. In turn, guards were dispatched to the location and fire or police departments were also notified.

As in many Section 2 prosecutions, the relevant market was an important issue. Grinnell contended that there were close substitutes for central station protective services. For example, watchmen or alarms on the premises perform a similar function. The government argued that such alternatives were distinctly inferior and that the market should be narrowly defined to include only the central station services. In accepting the government's position, the court determined that Grinnell had an 87 percent share of the relevant market. This was judged to constitute a monopoly position.

Next the court considered the practices used by Grinnell to obtain and preserve its market share. The record indicated that the firm had reduced its prices in markets where it faced competition and increased rates in those areas where it was the only seller. Grinnell had also bought out several of its competitors. In addition, the firm had deterred new entrants by the threat of price retaliation.

None of these actions, viewed individually, are antitrust violations. Indeed, it could be argued that they are typical of the behavior of an aggressive firm. However, the court decided that, considered as a whole, the actions of Grinnell constituted a violation of Section 2. Writing for the court, Justice Douglas held that illegal monopolization requires "the willful acquisition or maintenance of that power as distinguished from growth or development as a consequence of a superior product, business acumen, or historic accident." [32]

A recent private action, *Berkey Photo* v. *Eastman Kodak,* suggests that there are limits to the higher standard of conduct required for firms with monopoly power. [33] Berkey was a major film processor and also manufactured cameras. The firm charged Kodak with using its market power in film manufacturing to expand its hold on the markets for amateur cameras and film processing. It was alleged that Kodak marketed new and improved types of film in cartridges that could only be used in Kodak cameras. This had the effect of excluding other camera manufacturers until they could develop a camera capable of using the Kodak format.

Berkey won the suit at the district court level, but the decision was partially

---

[31]*United States* v. *Grinnell Corp.,* 384 U.S. 563 (1966).
[32]Ibid.
[33]*Berkey Photo* v. *Eastman Kodak Co.,* 603 F2d 263 (2d Cir. 1979).

overturned by an appeals court in 1979. The appellate court determined that Kodak's actions were reasonable and acceptable behavior for an integrated firm producing both film and cameras.

IBM and AT&T

January 8, 1982 was a landmark in antitrust history. On that date the Justice Department announced (1) that it was dismissing a 13-year monopoly suit against International Business Machines and (2) that an eight-year suit involving the American Telephone and Telegraph Company had been settled by a consent decree. The IBM suit had been described as the "case of the century" and the AT&T action had been characterized as the "most important antitrust suit of all time."

IBM   In 1969 the Justice Department filed suit charging that IBM had illegally monopolized the market for general purpose digital computers.[34] The government took the position that the relevant market was general purpose computers and peripheral products such as tape and disk drives that could be used with IBM computers. Using this definition, IBM's market share was between 68 and 75 percent. An important component of the Justice Department's case was the allegation that the IBM monopoly had been perpetuated by pricing practices which unfairly restrained actual or potential competitors. One charge was that the firm was bundling the pricing of its computer systems. That is, that a single price was quoted for an entire system, without a breakdown of the prices of individual component parts. The intent of bundling was to encourage customers to purchase their entire system from IBM. The effect was to limit opportunities for competing companies selling only selected components of a system.

A second allegation was that computers sold in particularly competitive markets were priced to yield a profit rate much lower than the company average in the attempt to drive out competing firms. Also, reduced prices were offered to educational institutions. By quoting these lower prices, IBM had more in mind than increasing computer literacy. Computer science students who receive their training working on IBM equipment are likely to recommend purchase of such equipment when they move into the labor force. Thus, by making computers available at preferential prices to colleges and universities, the firm was able to enhance its position in other markets.

IBM argued that the government's market definition was too narrow. It contended that the market should be defined to include a wide variety of products associated with computers and data processing. Under such a definition, the firm's market share was only about 33 percent. IBM also asserted that market share really was irrelevant in that its position had been achieved as a result of superior skill and foresight.

The case proved to be a nightmare for all concerned. Millions of dollars were spent on litigation by IBM and by the government. Case preparation and the district court trial dragged on so long as to cast doubt as to whether monopolization suits against large firms are manageable under existing legal procedures. When President Reagan took office in 1981, he appointed William Baxter as the head of the Antitrust

[34] *United States* v. *International Business Machines Corp.,* 69 CIV 200 (S.D.N.Y.).

Division of the Department of Justice. Baxter initiated a review of the IBM case and concluded that the government was unlikely to be successful in the action. Further, his assessment was that if the government did win the case, market conditions had changed so much since 1969 that there was no obvious remedy. Even if the court decided that IBM had a monopoly during the 1960s, competition during the intervening years had substantially weakened the firm's position. As a result, Baxter ordered the suit dismissed as being "without merit." Although the district court judge was due to render his verdict within a few months, the action was effectively terminated as of the January 8, 1982 dismissal date.

AT&T   For decades the American Telephone and Telegraph Company was the reigning queen of size (on the basis of assets) in U.S. industry. It fact, it was the largest privately owned enterprise the world had ever known. The Bell System (AT&T, Bell Labs, and Western Electric) employed over one million workers. Alaska, Delaware, Hawaii, Idaho, Montana, New Hampshire, Nevada, North Dakota, South Dakota, Vermont, and Wyoming each had smaller populations than the number of people employed by this communications giant.

In 1974 the Justice Department filed suit seeking to break up the Bell System.[35] The action asked the courts to force the company to divest itself of its manufacturing arm (Western Electric) and its subsidiaries that provide local telephone service (such as Pacific Telephone and Telegraph and New York Telephone). The government charged that AT&T had engaged in various practices intended to exclude competitors.

It was alleged that the local telephone companies bought the bulk of their equipment from Western Electric even though other suppliers offered equipment that was less expensive and/or of higher quality. Because the Bell System was the major purchaser of telephone equipment, competing firms were unfairly foreclosed from the market. The government also contended that AT&T had used its market position to make it difficult for competing suppliers to connect their equipment to the telephone lines. Similarly, it was alleged that AT&T had refused to deal with or discriminated against firms attempting to provide long-distance service.

The company responded that it had been regulated for many years by state and federal commissions. As such, its policies had to be approved by these commissions and, hence, should be immune from antitrust scrutiny. AT&T also argued that many of the policies criticized by the government were necessary in order to maintain the quality of the telecommunications network.

The consent decree accepted by the Justice Department and the Bell System had advantages for both parties. A government victory was the specification that the local operating companies would be divested and that a separate subsidiary must be created to sell telephone equipment. To AT&T's benefit, the company was allowed to keep Western Electric. It also was allowed to compete in the rapidly growing market for computer services and data processing. Under terms of an earlier consent decree, the firm had agreed to stay out of these areas. The AT&T divestiture is considered in greater detail in Chapter 13.

[35] *United States* v. *American Telephone and Telegraph Co.,* Civil Action No. 74–1698.

SUMMARY
Defining the Market

Need for Definition   Monopolization and merger cases often turn on the definition of the market accepted by the court. Narrowly defined markets usually result in a higher computed market share and increase the chances for successful prosecution.

Product Markets   The courts have used the criteria of reasonable interchangeability to determine the relevant product market. The test is based on evidence relating to cross elasticity of demand, product characteristics, and the end uses of products. Frequently, product market definitions accepted by the courts have failed to consider substitutes in production and also the effects of historical pricing policies on the present degree of competition in the market.

Geographic Markets   The relevant geographic market must reflect transportation costs, the value of the product, and consumer buying patterns. When transportation costs are high relative to the value of the product and purchasers conduct their product search in a limited area, the geographic market may be defined to include a single state or even a community and its environs.

Monopolization: Standard Oil to Alcoa

Standard Oil   Standard Oil was charged with monopolizing the oil refining market. Finding that the firm had engaged in illegal acts such as predatory pricing, the court in 1911 ordered that Standard be split into 34 separate companies. In the same year the American Tobacco Company was broken up.

U.S. Steel   In 1920, U.S. Steel was acquitted of the charge of illegal monopolization. In this case the Supreme Court adopted a rule-of-reason approach requiring that the government show that a firm's monopoly position was achieved or maintained by illegal activities. The Court's position drastically impaired Section 2 prosecutions.

Alcoa   In 1945, Alcoa was successfully prosecuted under Section 2 of the Sherman Act even though the government failed to prove that the firm's monopoly position was the result of illegal acts. This case represented a change from the rule-of-reason approach used by the Supreme Court in the U.S. Steel case.

Monopolization: A Step Back From Alcoa

The Double Standard   The Alcoa decision did not represent acceptance of a per se standard in Section 2 cases. Rather, subsequent cases suggest that the court uses a double standard in evaluating the behavior of firms with a dominant market position. Policies that would be perfectly legal for a small firm may be viewed as antitrust violations when engaged in by a firm with monopoly power.

IBM and AT&T   In 1969, the Justice Department charged that IBM had monopolized the market for general purpose computers. The suit alleged that the firm's market share had been maintained by actions designed to unfairly exclude competitors. In 1982 the Justice Department dismissed the suit.

A 1974 suit against AT&T sought to divest the firm of its local operating companies and of Western Electric. The government contended that, like IBM, AT&T's policies were intended to limit competition. The suit was resolved by a consent decree, whereby the company would sell off its operating companies, but be allowed to compete in the computer and data processing markets.

DISCUSSION QUESTIONS

1. Could a narrowly defined product market ever decrease, rather than increase, the likelihood of a successful antitrust prosecution? How?
2. How could changes in technology affect the proper definition of the geographic market?
3. Have increases in petroleum prices over the last decade affected the product market for petroleum-based products such as plastics and heating oil? Explain.
4. One of the charges against Standard Oil was that the market areas of subsidiary companies had been divided geographically. Should such a practice be considered illegal?
5. Did Judge Hand select the appropriate market share definition in the Alcoa case? Is his reasoning sound for excluding scrap from the market share calculation?
6. What business practices may be acceptable when used by small firms, but not when used by large firms with market power?
7. Was it pure coincidence that the IBM and AT&T decisions were announced on the same day? What connection might there be between the two?
8. Many goods and services are now traded in world markets. How should the increased importance of international competition affect the interpretation of Section 2?

chapter *6*

Antitrust: Mergers

Chapter Outline

. . . the giant corporations will ultimately take over the country." [1]

The difficulty of dealing with firms that already have market power suggests the need to halt monopolization in its formative stages. Because industry dominance has frequently been achieved by acquisition, merger policy is an important tool for preventive action.

Antitrust provisions relating to mergers were discussed in Chapter 4. At this point, a quick review should suffice. The original Section 7 of the Clayton Act prohibited stock mergers where the effect was to substantially lessen competition between firms. The ingenuity of business quickly circumvented the intent of the law. Firms abandoned stock acquisitions in favor of purchases of assets. The courts judged this practice as beyond the reach of the Clayton Act and allowed considerable latitude in its application. Another limitation of the Clayton Act was the general perception that it could not be used to prosecute vertical and conglomerate mergers. The consequence of these weaknesses was that few mergers were prevented in the first 36 years after enactment of the Clayton Act.

The 1950 Celler-Kefauver Amendment to Section 7 was designed to plug the loopholes in the original legislation. The amendment allowed the government to prosecute asset acquisitions and also changed the emphasis of the act from a focus on injury to prospective competitors to the consideration of effects on competition. The 1976 Hart-Scott-Rodino Antitrust Improvements Act further aided merger prosecutions by requiring large firms to notify the government of the intent to merge. If a preliminary investigation suggests that the merger should be prevented, the government can seek a preliminary injunction from a federal district court to delay its consummation. The advantage of premerger notification requirements is that it is much easier to prevent a combination from taking place than to disentangle the firms after the merger has been completed.

The actual effect of a law ultimately is determined by the interpretation of the courts and the activities of enforcement agencies. This chapter focuses on the antitrust statutes as they relate to mergers. The first section considers incentives to merge. The second is an evaluation of the social benefits and costs of horizontal mergers and a discussion of important court cases in connection with such mergers. The final two sections of the chapter provide similar information with respect to vertical and conglomerate mergers.

INCENTIVES TO MERGE

The search for merger partners seems to have been high on the list of recreational activities for corporate executives during the last decade. Mergers involving large firms were frequently in the news. For example, in the soft drink industry, Coca-Cola acquired Columbia Pictures, Pepsi-Cola picked up Pizza Hut, and Seven-Up was acquired by Philip Morris. In the petroleum sector, U.S. Steel acquired Marathon Oil and Mobil Oil purchased Montgomery Ward. Representing the cigarette manufactur-

[1] Federal Trade Commission, *The Merger Movement: A Summary Report* (Washington, 1948), p. 68.

ers, Reynolds Industries took over Del Monte while the Liggett Group was acquired by a conglomerate, Grand Metropolitan.

All of these acquisitions involved sizeable sums of money. However, the largest merger of the period (indeed, the largest merger in history) was the wedding of du Pont and Conoco.[2] Consummated in August 1981, du Pont paid over $7 billion dollars for 55 percent of Conoco's stock. Although ultimately victorious, du Pont was far from being Conoco's only suitor. Mobil Oil, the nation's second largest firm was the first to make a bid. Seagram, the world's largest liquor producer was part of the contest. So was Texaco, the fourth-largest industrial corporation in the United States.

The du Pont-Conoco merger joined the ninth-largest oil company and seventeenth-largest industrial enterprise with the nation's most important chemical company and twenty-first-largest firm. The resulting company ranked just behind Ford as the seventh-largest industrial firm in terms of sales. The merger gave du Pont access to Conoco's oil reserves. In that some 80 percent of du Pont's chemical products are petroleum-based, this assures the parent company of a secure source of supply.

There are a number of reasons why firms decide to merge. In some cases the explanation may involve personalities or corporate politics. But most mergers take place because managers believe that there will be economic benefits resulting from the combination. However, incentives to merge for the acquiring firm may be quite different than the motives of managers of the acquired company.

The Acquired Firm

An acquired firm may be amalgamated into the parent firm and lose its identity. Even if the company remains as a separate division or subsidiary, its managers are likely to lose at least some of their control over the operations of the firm. Why then, would the managers or owners of such firms allow the merger to occur? Important explanations include the following.

Failing Firm   Due to changes in demand, costs, or technology, a firm may be facing bankruptcy. Other firms may have financial resources or management expertise that could improve the survival prospects of the company. In such circumstances, management of the failing firm may be forced to search for a merger partner.

Retirement   Where a business is owned by an individual who desires to retire or pursue other activities, a merger may be an attractive option. The owner can get his or her equity out of the business without crippling the firm. Tax considerations also favor this method of transferring ownership.

Risk Reduction   A small specialized firm may be vulnerable to changing economic conditions or competition from large corporations. By merging with a larger, more diversified company owners may be able to reduce their exposure to risk.

---

[2]At this writing, it appears as though a new record will be set. In February 1984, Texaco offered $128 per share for 79 million shares of Getty oil stock. Thus, the total purchase price will exceed $10 billion. The merger will benefit Texaco by doubling the firm's oil reserves. Getty shareholders benefit because of the increased value of their holdings. For example, Gordon Getty, already the richest man in the United States, stands to increase his wealth by nearly $1 billion as a result of the merger.

Lucrative Offer   An interested firm may offer to pay a premium price for the stock of a prospective merger partner. For example, suppose that a firm's common stock is selling for $50 per share. An acquisition-minded corporation offers to buy the stock for $70 a share on the condition that, by a specified date, it acquires over 50 percent of the total stock outstanding. Such an offer may be too attractive for shareholders to refuse.

Hostile Takeovers   In some cases, the management of the acquired firm may be opposed to the merger, but unable to prevent it. If the acquiring firm is able to purchase a majority of the voting stock, it can then use this position to elect a sympathetic board of directors and complete the merger.

The Acquiring Firm

The primary incentives for a merger from the standpoint of the acquiring firm are the following.

Market Power   Mergers between competing firms can have the effect of increasing the market power of the combined firm. The great trusts such as Standard Oil and American Tobacco, for example, were the result of mergers between competing firms. In each case the surviving company became the dominant force in its industry.

Technical Economies of Scale   If technology in an industry favors firms of large size, then smaller entities may be able to reduce average costs by merging with other companies in the same industry.

Pecuniary Economies of Scale   Merged firms may be able to exploit their monopsony power in the purchasing of inputs. Consider the case of mining operations seeking to ship coal. A combined firm requiring a significant proportion of railroad freight capacity in a region is in a better position to strike a good bargain with the railroads than would small firms acting independently.

Economies of Coordination   Cost savings may be possible by coordinating functions between different stages of production. For example, in a vertically integrated firm, product design at one stage of the production process may be modified to better suit facilities at a later stage.

Pooling of Risk   Hotels and resorts are adversely affected by increasing costs of travel and gasoline shortages. On the other hand, motion picture producers benefit from conditions that keep people close to home. A merger between Holiday Inns and Twentieth-Century Fox could serve to buffer the resulting corporation against changing economic conditions. By joining dissimilar firms, it may be possible to smooth out profit fluctuations.

Valuation Discrepancies   In some cases, the difference between the asking price of a firm and its value to a potential acquirer makes it a bargain. For example, a corporation may be able to pick up cheap production capacity by purchasing the facilities of another firm near bankruptcy; a firm may be undervalued because it has been operated inefficiently by poor management; a tired or elderly proprietor may be anxious to sell his operation and retire. In all of these situations there is a potential benefit to the acquiring firm, even though no scale economy, market power, coordination, or risk reduction advantages are expected.

Complementary Resources Sometimes the resources of individual firms can be meshed to form a more efficient single entity. In 1979, RCA agreed to acquire C.I.T. Financial Corp. for the modest sum of $1.35 billion. RCA is a major producer of electronic equipment. The firm needed a stable source of earnings to finance development of advanced electronic products and systems. C.I.T. was involved in financial services and could provide the necessary cash flow. The financial support of C.I.T. was used to complement the research and development capabilities of RCA.[3]

Stock Market Effects A rash of conglomerate mergers in the late 1960s was precipitated, at least in part, by entrepreneurs such as James Ling of Ling-Temco-Vaught. In 1960 LTV ranked as the three-hundred and thirty-fifth-largest firm in the United States on the basis of assets. After an eight-year flurry of acquisitions the firm leaped to twenty-second in 1968. The quest for growth was not irrational on the part of management—it was rewarded by increasing stock prices. In 1963 the price of LTV common stock was $9 per share. In 1967 the price peaked at $169.50 per share. Unfortunately, the bubble burst as cutbacks in defense spending and the antagonism of antitrust authorities to LTV merger activities caused the share price to plummet to just over $7 by 1970. In the last decade investors have been less willing to pay a premium for growth achieved by indiscriminate acquisitions.

HORIZONTAL MERGERS

Mergers are commonly divided into three broad categories—horizontal, vertical, and conglomerate. *Horizontal mergers* involve firms that compete for sales of similar products. For example, if General Motors were to acquire Chrysler, that would be a horizontal merger.

Benefits and Costs of Horizontal Integration

Horizontal mergers between large firms create the potential for abuse of the market power obtained by the combined firm. This abuse may take the form of higher prices, actions to deter entry or eliminate competitors, or the exercise of monopsony power over suppliers. The effects of merger are more serious than those of collusive agreements because of their permanence. An industry of ten firms colluding to fix prices is likely to experience periodic information breakdowns and cheating. A merger of all ten firms would eliminate such problems. Even if the merger involves only a part of the industry, the probability of successful collusion is increased. Suppose that eight

---

[3]The marriage didn't last. In 1983 RCA sold C.I.T. to Manufacturers Hanover for $1.51 billion.

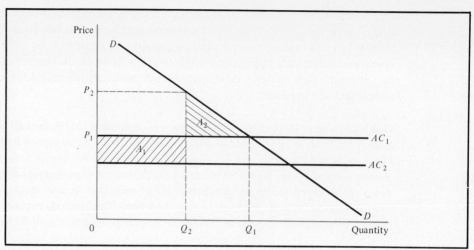

Figure 6.1. Welfare implications of horizontal mergers.

firms combine, leaving a total of only three competitors. If the merged firm is much larger than the other two, then its size allows it to dictate the terms of trade in the industry and also punish cheaters. Even if the three remaining firms are of nearly equal size, the chance of information lapses is reduced. Similarly, cheating is more easily detected.

The primary argument in support of horizontal mergers is the possibility of efficiency gains. These efficiency effects may result from several different factors. The merged firm may be able to reduce its cost of production and distribution by realizing economies of scale. Inefficient techniques may be abandoned as firms gain access to the patent rights and technical expertise of their new partners. Finally, mergers may concentrate assets in the hands of superior managers who have the ability to operate the firm more efficiently.

Although there may be other considerations, the basic decision to allow or prohibit a horizontal merger should rest on the evaluation of the costs of increased market power versus the social benefits of improved efficiency. Oliver Williamson has suggested a simple model for quantifying this trade-off.[4] Assume that a horizontal merger shifts the resulting firm's cost curve down from AC_1 to AC_2, while providing market power that is exercised by increasing prices from P_1 to P_2. The welfare trade-off is shown in Figure 6.1. The cross-hatched area A_1 represents the resource saving associated with producing Q_2 units at the reduced average cost, AC_2. The cross-hatched area A_2 is the deadweight loss stemming from increasing the price from P_1 to P_2. It represents the loss in consumer surplus as the higher price cuts demand from Q_1 to Q_2. The merger can be evaluated by comparing the cost saving and the deadweight loss. If the deadweight loss is greater than the efficiency gain, then the merger should not be allowed. On the other hand, if the resource saving more than

---

[4]See Williamson, O. E., "Economies as an Antitrust Defense: The Welfare Tradeoffs," *American Economic Review*, Vol. 58 (Mar. 1968), pp. 18–36.

offsets the loss in consumer surplus, then there may be a net benefit to society from the merger.

The actual use of the model to quantify the net impacts of mergers requires estimates of cost reductions, price increases, and demand elasticities. Based on some plausible estimates, Williamson concludes that "a merger which yields non-trivial real economies must produce substantial market power and result in relatively large price increases for the net allocative effects to be negative."[5] Other authors have severely criticized Williamson's conclusion. They contend that more sophisticated analysis implies that significant efficiency gains must be realized to outweigh the costs of increased market power.[6]

A number of limitations of the model are recognized by Williamson in his original analysis. For example, efficiency gains are often eventually realized by ordinary expansion of the independent firms. Thus, the cost savings from the merger are a temporary benefit. As such, they should be counted only until they would have been achieved by internal expansion. Another qualification considers the industry-wide impacts of a price increase. The increase in price may spread throughout the entire industry, while the cost reduction is limited to the merged firm. The consequence is that the deadweight loss in the entire industry must be compared to the resource saving in the combined firm. Other factors can also cloud the analysis. Costs and benefits are often highly speculative. Increased market power may dampen the rate of innovation of the merged firm. Political power and income distribution effects may also be important. Data limitations restrict the application of the Williamson model, but it still serves as a useful point of departure for evaluation of mergers. Although the discussion has focused on horizontal mergers, the approach is applicable to vertical and conglomerate mergers as well.

Evaluation of Horizontal Integration

If horizontal mergers result in efficiency gains, then the combined firm should earn a higher rate of return than its constituent parts. Similarly, if such mergers result in an increase in market power, then the resulting firm should be more profitable. Many researchers have studied the profit trends of firms involved in horizontal mergers. Studies of mergers in the United States tend to concentrate on the years before 1965, because antitrust activity has greatly limited horizontal mergers between large firms since that time. In other countries with less restrictive merger laws the research extends into the 1970s. Based on his review of these studies, Scherer finds that:

> . . . all reach essentially the same conclusion: that post-merger profitability experience of merger-prone companies was either less successful, or not significantly more successful, than the experience of otherwise comparable low-merger companies or the average of the merger-prone firms' home-base industries. The observed failure

[5]Ibid., pp. 22–23.

[6]Jackson, R., "The Consideration of Economies in Merger Cases," *Journal of Business,* Vol. 43 (Oct. 1970), pp. 439–47; and DePrano, M. E., and Nugent, J. B., "Economies as an Antitrust Defense: Comment," *American Economic Review,* Vol. 59 (Dec. 1969), pp. 947–53.

of active acquirers to achieve superior profit returns appears to persist over a wide range of comparison methodologies, company samples, and time frames.[7]

Research indicates that most horizontal mergers do not result in clear efficiency gains or substantial increases in market power. Indeed, it appears that the only consistent winners from horizontal mergers are stockholders of the acquired firm who were paid a premium for their shares. Stockholders of the acquiring firm may benefit if they sell their stock near the time the merger is completed, but their gains usually are offset by losses experienced by those who buy the stock and hold it during the postmerger period when share prices often decline.[8]

The Courts and Horizontal Mergers

Judicial interpretation of the Clayton Act shackled merger prosecutions for many years. However, the passage of the Celler-Kefauver Amendment in 1950 greatly changed the legal status of mergers.

Brown Shoe   The Supreme Court's first important merger decision under the Celler-Kefauver Amendment was *Brown Shoe Co.* v. *United States* (1962).[9] In 1955 the government brought suit against the Brown Shoe Company to prevent its acquisition of the G. R. Kinney Company. Both firms were important producers and retailers of shoes. At the time of the acquisition Brown was the third-largest retailer in the country with 2.1 percent of all outlets and the fourth-largest manufacturer with 4.0 percent of sales. Kinney was eighth in retailing with 1.6 percent of outlets and number twelve in manufacturing with a 0.5 percent share of the market.

The government charged that the merger was undesirable for at least three reasons. First, it would reduce competition in shoe manufacturing (a horizontal restraint). Second, competition would be affected in retailing (another horizontal restraint). Third, opportunities for sale of shoes by manufacturers to retailers would be foreclosed, because Brown would become an important supplier to Kinney (a vertical restraint). The challenge to the merger at the manufacturing level was rejected by the district court and not appealed by the government. The Supreme Court's deliberations focused on the vertical tie between a manufacturer and a retailer and on the horizontal combination of large retailers.

Fundamental to the Court's decision was the definition of geographic and product markets. Brown argued that the product market should be narrowly divided into subcategories specified by the price of the shoe and the sex and age of the purchaser. The Court opted for a three-category classification into men's, women's, and children's shoes. Brown maintained that the geographic market in retailing must be determined by a detailed analysis of buying patterns in specific areas. The Court ruled that the geographic market consisted of cities of ten thousand or greater and their environs. The

---

[7]Scherer, F.M., *Industrial Market Structure and Economic Performance,* 2nd ed., (Chicago: Rand McNally, 1980), p. 138.

[8]See Keenan, M. and White, L., *Mergers and Acquisitions* (Lexington, Mass.: Lexington Books, 1982) pp. 178–180.

[9]*Brown Shoe Co.* v. *United States,* 370 U.S. 294 (1962).

choice of geographic market was important, because Brown's retail outlets were concentrated in the inner cities, while those of Kinney were mostly in suburban shopping centers. By lumping cities and suburbs, Brown and Kinney were found to compete at the retail level.

On the basis of the Court's market definition, the evidence showed 32 cities in which Brown and Kinney's combined retail share was greater than 20 percent of women's shoes. In 31 cities the share of children's shoes exceeded 20 percent. In the 118 cities considered, the joint share of the two firms was at least 5 percent in one of the three lines. Although the merger made Brown and Kinney the second-largest shoe retailer in the nation, their combined share of less than 4 percent of retail outlets was light years away from the 90-percent share Judge Hand had specified as a clear indication of monopoly. It was also far below the 33 percent which he held as being insufficient to constitute a monopoly. However, the Court made it clear that the market share required to prevent a merger was much much less than that needed in monopoly cases. In ruling that the Brown-Kinney merger would not be allowed, the Supreme Court enunciated a case-specific rather than a broad structural standard.

> Congress indicated plainly that a merger had to be functionally viewed, in the context of its particular industry. That is, whether the consolidation was to take place in an industry that was fragmented rather than concentrated, that had seen a recent trend toward domination by a few leaders or had remained fairly consistent in its distribution of market shares among the participating companies . . . that had witnessed the ready entry of new competition or the erection of barriers to prospective entrants, all were aspects, varying in importance with the merger under consideration, which would properly be taken into account.[10]

Although the combined market share of the firms was small in most large cities, the Court held that the merger could still have significant adverse effects on the industry. In addition, the justices reasoned that by allowing the Brown-Kinney merger they would be hard pressed to prohibit future acquisitions in the industry. As a result, Brown was ordered to divest itself of Kinney. The issue was finally resolved by the sale of Kinney to F. W. Woolworth & Company.

Von's Grocery   The Court's willingness to prevent horizontal mergers even when relatively small market shares are involved was reaffirmed in *United States* v. *Von's Grocery Co. (1966)*.[11] In 1958 Von's acquired Shopping Bag Food Stores. At the time, Von's was the third-largest retail grocery chain in Los Angeles with 4.7 percent of total sales. Shopping Bag ranked sixth with 2.8 percent, and Safeway was the leader with about 8 percent. In 1966 the Supreme Court reversed the finding of a lower court and prohibited the merger.

There are important similarities in the Brown and Von's cases. In both situations the merged firms had small market shares in highly fragmented industries. Also, in both cases the Court expressed concern against a perceived trend to larger firms. In Brown the decision noted that "if a merger achieving 5 percent control were now approved,

[10]Ibid., p. 321, 322.
[11]*United States* v. *Von's Grocery Co.,* 384 U.S. 270 (1966).

we might be required to approve future merger efforts by Brown's competitors seeking similar market shares."[12] In Von's the Court was heavily influenced by the decline in independent single unit grocers—a 30-percent reduction between 1950 and 1961. The justices noted that:

> It is enough for us that Congress feared that a market marked at the same time by both a continuous decline in the number of small businesses and a large number of mergers would slowly but inevitably gravitate from a market of many small competitors to one dominated by one or a few giants, and competition would thereby be destroyed. Congress passed the Celler-Kefauver Act to prevent such a destruction of competition.[13]

Both mergers provided some prospect of lower prices for consumers through increased efficiency, but this defense could not be used to the benefit of the firms. On the contrary, the possible efficiency gains were seen as additional evidence of the threat to the viability of smaller firms. If the merged firms were more efficient, some smaller, less efficient firms would undoubtedly be forced out of business. Concern with injury to competitors, as opposed to effects on consumers and competition, has been a persistent theme of the courts. This bias may reflect the economic naiveté of judges or a conscious policy to not allow efficiency considerations to overwhelm equity effects.

General Dynamics   More recent cases hint that the Supreme Court will not continue to place such heavy emphasis on market shares and trends in concentration. In *United States* v. *General Dynamics* (1973), the merger of two large coal producers was upheld despite evidence showing a rapid decline in the number of firms in the industry.[14] The decision noted that firm-specific factors must be considered in addition to evidence on industry-wide structure and trends. In this instance, the acquired firm was determined to no longer be an important independent force in the industry because of its diminished reserves and long-term contracts.

The position of the courts in evaluating horizontal mergers and the policy of the antitrust agencies in challenging them has been a significant barrier to mergers between large firms with substantial market shares.[15] This suppression of horizontal mergers is one of the most dramatic effects of antitrust action. Most students of economics and public policy would applaud the tough stand taken by the government and the courts on this issue.

Merger Guidelines

Mergers between large corporations are a costly undertaking. Considerable expense is involved in finding a proper merger partner, structuring the merger proposal, com-

[12]370 U.S. 294, 333, 334.
[13]384 U.S. 270, 278.
[14]*United States* v. *General Dynamics Corp.,* 415 U.S. 486 (1973).
[15]To some, this statement may seem strange in light of Justice Department approval of actions such as the $10 billion merger between Texaco & Getty Oil. However, it must be remembered that market share, and not absolute size, is the key in evaluating horizontal merger. Although Getty & Texaco had combined 1982 revenues in excess of $60 billion, their market shares were small. For example, their combined share of U.S. oil refining was less than seven percent.

Table 6.1   HERFINDAHL INDICES FOR SELECTED INDUSTRIES

Industrial areas with the highest Herfindahl indices		Industrial areas with the lowest Herfindahl indices	
Military tanks	5823	Specialty dies and tools	11
Telephone and telegraph equipment	5026	Concrete blocks	27
		Metal plating and polishing	31
Sewing machines	4047	Commercial lithography	32
Cellulosic synthetic fibers	3189	Ready-mix concrete	32
Turbines	2443		

Source: Business Week, May 17, 1982, p. 120. Data: John E. Kwoka, using 1972 data from Economic Information Systems Inc.

municating information to shareholders, and, finally, integrating the acquired firm. This cost can be greatly increased if the merger is challenged by the government. The actual expense of litigation can be substantial, but even more important is the delay and uncertainty involved. To aid firms in evaluating the likelihood of government intervention, the Justice Department in 1968 announced guidelines to be used in deciding whether to challenge horizontal mergers. These guidelines involved overall industry concentration and also the market shares of the acquiring and acquired firms. However, during the 1970s the courts seemed to adopt a somewhat more lenient standard than was indicated by the guidelines.

In 1982, the Justice Department announced a new set of guidelines based on the Herfindahl index. As discussed in Chapter 3, this index is computed by summing the squared market shares of all the firms in an industry. As used in the guidelines, the index is computed by squaring market share percentages, not fractions. Thus, an industry with 10 firms each having a 10-percent market share would have a Herfindahl index of 1000. The index for an industry that has a dominant firm with a 50-percent market share and five smaller firms each with 10-percent shares would be 3000. Table 6.1 provides examples of industries with very high and very low Herfindahl indices.

Under the new guidelines, any merger that leaves the industry with a Herfindahl index of less than 1000 will not be challenged. Combinations resulting in a postmerger index greater than 1800 will almost always be challenged. Where the index falls between 1000 and 1800, the proposed merger will be carefully scrutinized to determine its competitive impact. In this region other factors such as efficiency impacts, trends in concentration, and barriers to entry are considered by the Justice Department.

VERTICAL MERGERS

Vertical mergers occur when firms operating at different stages of the production process combine. A vertical merger may involve a firm acquiring one or more of the sellers of its output, such as U.S. Steel merging with Ford. Alternatively, a vertical merger can involve the acquisition of a firm's suppliers. An example would be the purchase of Boeing by United Airlines.

The petroleum sector is an example of a highly integrated industry. Major oil firms hold significant reserves of crude oil, operate large refining facilities, control pipelines used for transporting crude and refined oil, and also own chains of retail gasoline stations. In contrast, the construction industry is much less integrated. Contractors purchase supplies from independent firms, subcontract specialty work, and often sell through realtors.

Despite seemingly obvious examples, vertical integration is not a well-defined concept. Theoretically, all the production stages of a firm could be divided into sub-processes and performed by independent firms. Hence, all businesses could be considered vertically integrated. As a working definition, a firm will be designated as vertically integrated if it "transmits from one of its departments to another a good or service which could, without major adaptation, be sold in the market."[16] This definition applies the pragmatic test of determining whether there is a market alternative to integration. A firm manufacturing transistors and using them to produce calculators would be labeled as integrated because a ready market exists for transistors. An automobile assembly line would not be an example of vertical integration because partially assembled cars are less easily salable.

The decision to perform a function internally as opposed to relying on markets is based primarily on considerations of efficiency and reliability. In the case of upstream integration, if a firm's needs for an input are insufficient to allow efficient internal production, and if the prospects for obtaining a stable supply of the input are good, then the firm will be unlikely to integrate that phase of its operation. However, if there is a possibility of disruption of supply or if the firm can operate at a scale large enough to produce the input at a competitive price, then vertical integration may be advantageous. Similar considerations affect the decision to become involved in downstream integration.

Benefits of Vertical Integration

For the firm, the benefits of vertical integration can come from several sources. The most commonly discussed is the technological interdependency of different stages of production. Sometimes production processes that occur one after another or that take place in close physical proximity can be performed more efficiently than if they are separated by time or space. Consider the smelting and fabrication of a metal by nonintegrated producers. The molten metal is first formed into ingots at the refinery. It is then cooled and shipped to the second firm for fabrication. The fabrication stage requires that the ingot again be heated. If the process were integrated, the metal could be fabricated directly from the hot ingot, saving the energy cost of the second heating. Additional savings in packing and handling are also likely. In an integrated facility the product does not have to be packed and loaded by the refinery and then unpacked and unloaded by the fabricator.

Another benefit of integration stems from the costs of using markets. Purchasing inputs from suppliers or selling to distributors may involve substantial search and negotiation expenses. First, suitable partners must be located. Changing prices or needs may dictate periodic reassessment of these partners. Next, the terms of the transaction must be established. Because the interests of the parties are divergent, skill and time may be required to reach agreement. When the trading partners have been satisfied, there is still the problem of monitoring performance. Dissatisfaction by one party may

[16]Adelman, M. A., "Integration and Antitrust Policy," *Harvard Law Review,* Vol. 63 (1949), p. 27.

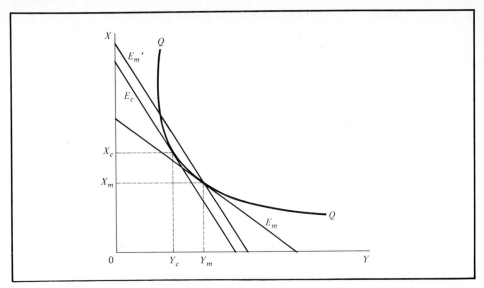

Figure 6.2. Resource allocation and vertical integration.

result in a disruption of supply or costly litigation. The difficulty of negotiating and maintaining the transaction is compounded by the imperfect flow of information. Each firm must use caution to avoid disclosing information that might allow competitors an advantage or permit the trading partner to better its relative position. Even the attempt to be completely open may be partially thwarted by differences in the training, procedures, or jargon of the personnel of each firm.[17]

A third benefit of integration is that it allows decision makers to seek global as compared to locally optimal allocations of resources. If two firms are independent, they are limited to maximizing their individual objectives. The vertically integrated firm can take an overall perspective in optimizing the allocation of resources of the combined entity. For example, consider a monopolist selling a product, Z, which can be produced using variable proportions of two inputs, X and Y. Initially, assume that X and Y are purchased in competitive markets at competitive prices, $P_{x,c}$ and $P_{y,c}$, which are equal to the opportunity costs of production. Technically feasible combinations of X and Y to produce Q units of Z are shown by the isoquant in Figure 6.2.

At prices $P_{x,c}$ and $P_{y,c}$ the least cost combination of inputs is (X_c, Y_c) and the total cost is given by $E_c = P_{x,c} X_c + P_{y,c} Y_c$. Now suppose that X is sold by a monopolist who charges a higher price, $P_{x,m}$. The least cost input bundle is now (X_m, Y_m). This input mix substitutes the relatively less costly Y for the more expensive X. At prices $P_{x,m}$ and $P_{y,c}$ the minimum expenditure necessary to produce Q is $E_m = P_{x,m} X_m + P_{y,c} Y_m$.

Remember that the competitive prices, $P_{x,c}$ and $P_{y,c}$, represent the opportunity cost of the inputs X and Y, respectively. Hence, the actual resource cost of using the

[17]For a more complete discussion of these points, see Williamson, O. E., "The Vertical Integration of Production: Market Failure Considerations," *American Economic Review,* Vol. 61 (May 1971), pp. 112–123.

bundle (X_m, Y_m) to produce Q is given by $E'_m = P_{x,c}X_m + P_{y,c}Y_m$. Because E'_m is greater than E_c, the pricing of X above its resource cost by the monopolist results in an inefficient use of resources. However, the two nonintegrated monopolists, each pursuing their own self-interest, will cause (X_m, Y_m) to be selected. The seller of X maximizes his profit by selling at $P_{x,m}$. The producer of Z minimizes his cost, given the prices $P_{x,m}$ and $P_{y,c}$ by using (X_m, Y_m) to produce Q.

Now assume that the supplier of X is acquired by the producer of Z. The producer of Z maximizes profits by minimizing the opportunity cost of production. Hence, the bundle (X_c, Y_c) will be selected. Thus, vertical integration encourages the firm to employ more efficient production methods because input prices are no longer distorted by monopoly pricing. Producing each level of output more efficiently, the profits of the integrated firm will be greater than the combined profits of the two firms prior to the merger. If the demand for Z is not completely inelastic, then consumers will also benefit as prices are reduced and output increases.

Costs of Vertical Integration

The attempt to restrict vertical integration stems from at least four basic concerns. First, it is alleged that vertical mergers foreclose the markets of independent suppliers and distributors. Consider the following hypothetical example. Suppose that integration of tire manufacturers and retailers has limited the sales of independent retailers to 30 percent of the market. Now assume that a nonintegrated tire manufacturer who is currently supplying 10 percent of the market proposes to acquire retailers with a total market share of 15 percent. Although neither the manufacturer nor the sellers involved in the acquisition has a large market share, the merger would have a significant effect on the remaining "free market." If the manufacturer's 10-percent market share is provided exclusively to the acquired retailers, then a full one-third of the supply sources of independent retailers has been eliminated. Similarly, the opportunities of nonintegrated manufacturers have also been reduced. Thus, the claim is made that the market would be foreclosed if the merger were permitted.

However, without further analysis the charge of foreclosure is not conclusive. It may be the case that retailers to be acquired were already selling the tires of their proposed merger partner. If so, then the major change is that the relationship becomes more stable and durable. If not, then the firm's previous set of retailers will now be in need of tire supplies. Although the vertical merger may disrupt existing patterns of sales, the markets of independent manufacturers and distributors have not really been foreclosed unless the manufacturer maintains its previous retail partners and expands to meet the needs of its new acquisitions. If this does happen, the problem is not so much vertical integration as it is the horizontal market power of the manufacturer. Although many economists are skeptical of the foreclosure argument against vertical integration, it remains an important judicial consideration in evaluating such mergers.

A second concern with vertical mergers is the ability of integrated firms to squeeze independent businesses. In the Alcoa case it was alleged that the firm had set a very high price for aluminum ingot while charging very little for rolling the ingots into sheets. As an integrated producer this practice presented no problems for Alcoa, because the profits from ingot operations could be used to subsidize the sheet aluminum rolling. The actual prices charged for the individual operations were little more than accounting entries and, in terms of overall profits, were meaningless. However, for nonintegrated producers of sheet aluminum, the price fixed by Alcoa for rolling was a matter of life and death. As the sole domestic producer, Alcoa determined the price of virgin aluminum ingot. Any profits made by independent sheet aluminum producers had to be made on the rolling operation after paying Alcoa's price for ingot. By setting an artificially low price for sheet rolling, Alcoa could eliminate its competition at that stage of the production process.

As was the case with foreclosure, the real problem was not vertical integration, but horizontal market power. Alcoa's ability to squeeze producers in the sheet aluminum market was created by the monopoly position in the ingot market. This suggests that the primary focus of public policy should be on limiting horizontal market power. If horizontal power is eliminated, then the basis for squeezing producers at another stage of production has also been removed.

A third objection to vertical integration is its potential effect on entry barriers. If the production of a product is highly integrated, it may be necessary for a new firm to attempt entry at more than a single stage of the process. For example, if tire manufacturers own all the retail outlets, then a new entrant in manufacturing must also enter at the retail level. Some potential competitors may be discouraged by the risk, capital requirements, and increased complexity required for entry at multiple stages. As a result, entry may be eliminated or at least delayed.

A fourth basis for restricting vertical integration is the desire to maintain potential competitors on the edge of the market. This argument rests on the assumption that the most likely entrants into a market are often firms that operate either upstream or downstream from the industry. Tire manufacturing and retailing can again be used to illustrate this point. If tire manufacturers are dissatisfied with the service being provided by retailers, they have the option of entering the market by opening their own retail outlets. Their resources and expertise improve the prospects for successful entry. The threat of entry by manufacturers may provide a strong incentive to existing retailers to compete vigorously for the favor of manufacturers.

If independent entry by manufacturers does occur, then new competitors are added to the retail industry. However, if entry occurs by acquisition of existing retailers, then the existing market becomes more concentrated. In addition, the competitive pressure exerted by tire manufacturers on the edge of the market is eliminated. The validity of the potential competition argument depends on industry-specific factors such as ease of entry, the relative bargaining power of firms at different stages in the production process, and existing concentration. For example, suppose that a retail industry has one large seller surrounded by numerous small firms. The acquisition of the small sellers by a manufacturer may improve competition in retailing by combining the small firms into an entity large enough to compete effectively with the dominant firm. In this case the positive effect of actual competition may far outweigh the alleged benefits of the manufacturer as a potential competitor threatening independent entry.

Evaluation of Vertical Integration

The decision to challenge a vertical merger should be based on the efficiency benefits of integration by acquisition as compared to any adverse effects on competition. In evaluating efficiency gains the possibility of internal expansion must be considered. A firm that independently enters a new market adds capacity. A firm that enters by merger simply formalizes control over existing capacity. If there is no efficiency loss associated with internal expansion, then that route is certainly preferable.

In determining the potential costs of vertical mergers, care must be taken to isolate the real cause of reduced competition. In some cases the anticompetitive effects that are ascribed to the vertical dimension of a merger are actually attributable to the horizontal market power of the firm. In such circumstances the proper focus of attack should be on reducing that horizontal market power. As a general proposition, the case against vertical mergers is not nearly as strong as the presumption against allowing horizontal combinations.

The Courts and Vertical Mergers

The legal status of vertical mergers is less definitive than that of horizontal combinations. However, some basic guidelines can be identified.

Du Pont–General Motors   In 1949, the government filed suit to require the du Pont Corporation to divest itself of a 23-percent holding in General Motors stock that had been acquired 30 years earlier [*United States* v. *E. I. du Pont de Nemours and Co.* (1957)].[18] The government charged that du Pont's position as the major supplier of finishes and fabrics to G.M. was based on the close relationship between the firms rather than on competitive merit. The end result was that a large portion of the market for fabrics and finishes was foreclosed to independent suppliers.

Three main issues faced the Supreme Court in the case. First, did the Clayton Act apply to vertical mergers? Because the alleged offense and the initial suit were prior to the Celler-Kefauver Amendment, the decision had to be based on the original act. Contradicting prevailing opinion, the Court held that vertical mergers were within reach of the 1914 Clayton Act. The second question was the relevant market. Du Pont argued for a broad definition that included all finishes and fabrics, but the Court ruled that automotive finishes and fabrics have "sufficient peculiar characteristics and uses" to constitute a "line of commerce" by themselves. The final question was whether the du Pont-G.M. tie had resulted in a substantial lessening of competition. Here the Court established two standards of proof: (1) the affected market must be significant and (2) the share of the market foreclosed must be substantial. The sheer size of the automobile industry met the first requirement and the 50-percent market share of G.M. satisfied the second. Accordingly, the Court determined that the stock acquisition had violated the Clayton Act and ruled that du Pont must divest itself of its holdings.

Brown Shoe   The Brown Shoe case is an important precedent for evaluating vertical mergers under the amended Clayton Act [*Brown Shoe Co.* v. *United States* (1962)].[19] The horizontal aspects of that merger have already been discussed. However, the vertical dimension of the merger was also judged unlawful. Prior to the merger Brown had not manufactured any of the shoes sold by Kinney. Subsequent to the acquisition Brown provided about 8 percent of Kinney's shoes. The Court's concern

[18] *United States* v. *E. I. du Pont de Nemours and Co. et al.,* 353 U.S. 586 (1957).
[19] *Brown Shoe Co.* v. *United States,* 370 U.S. 294 (1962).

with the vertical aspect of the merger was the fear that the retail market of independent manufacturers would be foreclosed. The Court feared foreclosure despite the fact that Kinney's share of retail outlets was only about 1.6 percent of the total. The Court also reacted against the trend towards vertical integration in the industry.

The Brown case suggested that the courts were willing to prevent vertical mergers even in relatively unconcentrated industries. However, present-day standards are somewhat less restrictive. Still, government challenges to vertical mergers will be upheld by the courts if it can be shown that the market shares of the merger partners are such that a substantial portion of the market could be foreclosed by the merger. Vertical mergers are particularly vulnerable if the evidence indicates that they have horizontal implications. That is, that they serve to augment the existing market power of either firm.

Although the legal constraints on vertical mergers are less restrictive than on horizontal acquisitions, the antitrust laws have limited this form of growth by large firms. In contrast, vertical integration by internal expansion has been essentially unaffected by antitrust policy.

CONGLOMERATE MERGERS

Conglomerate mergers can be divided into three subcategories. *Market-extension mergers* link firms selling similar products in different geographic areas. The purchase of a West Coast airline such as PSA by Eastern Airlines would meet that criterion. *Product-extension mergers* extend the operations of a firm into a related product market. If United Airlines acquired Greyhound Corporation, the merger would be of the product-extension type. Finally, *pure conglomerate mergers* involve combinations of firms operating in unrelated product markets. An example would be if Harper & Row, Publishers, and American Motors were to join.

Merger activity in the United States has occurred in waves. The first lasted from 1887 to 1904 and resulted in firms such as Standard Oil, American Tobacco, and U.S. Steel dominating their respective markets. The second wave extended from about the end of World War I to the Great Depression and involved combinations of smaller firms. The first flurry of activity has been characterized as "mergers for monopoly" and the second as "mergers for oligopoly."[20] A third wave of mergers began in the 1960s and has continued through the 1970s and early 1980s. It might be labeled as mergers for diversity or mergers for growth because a large proportion of acquisitions involve giant corporations purchasing firms in essentially unrelated markets. In the beginning most of these conglomerate mergers were made by thinly financed glamour firms such as Ling-Temco-Vaught, Litton, and Gulf & Western Industries. Today, diversification attempts are common among the largest and most stable corporations in American industry.

Costs of Conglomerate Mergers

There is no consensus as to the social costs of conglomerate mergers. However, the most frequently mentioned problems can be grouped into four main categories. First, it is often argued that the giant firm has an advantage over smaller corporations because

---

[20]Stigler, G. J., "Monopoly and Oligopoly by Merger," *American Economic Review,* Vol. 40 (May 1950), pp. 23–24.

of its superior resource base, or *deep pockets.* Such firms are not forced to continually earn a profit in each area of their operations, but can temporarily subsidize losses in one market with excess profits from another. Smaller firms operating in a single market may have greater difficulty in weathering economic setbacks. Deep pockets also give the conglomerate power to retaliate against aggressive behavior of small firms by selective price cuts or intensive advertising. It should be observed that, to the extent they exist, opportunities for *cross-subsidization* and *retaliation* are not limited to conglomerate firms, but are a general advantage stemming from large size.

The likelihood of reciprocal business dealings is a second objection to allowing conglomerate mergers. Diversified firms often interface with one another in many markets. *Reciprocity* occurs when a firm favors the buyers of its product in selecting suppliers of inputs for other phases of its operations. For example, suppose that a diversified firm manufactures both radios and automobiles. A second corporation makes transistors and rents automobiles. If the rental business uses the first firm's cars it may be rewarded with contracts to supply transistors. The alleged problem with such reciprocal arrangements is that markets of independent suppliers are foreclosed.

The social costs of reciprocity have been questioned by Stigler.[21] He argues that firms operating in competitive markets have nothing to gain from reciprocal arrangements because each firm can sell its total output at the going price and, thus, has no need to seek out special partners. If reciprocity occurs among oligopolists engaged in explicit or tacit collusion, deals to purchase inputs from a particular supplier may involve a price cut. Any practice that causes cheating on the collusive agreement should be viewed from society's perspective as a positive development. Finally, the only advantage of reciprocity to a monopolist is as a method for price discrimination. Although price discrimination increases the monopolist's profits, society benefits from increased output. Thus, Stigler suggests that reciprocity is unlikely in competitive markets, not necessarily harmful when practiced by the monopolist, and likely to increase competition in oligopoly situations.

Forbearance, or refraining from active competition, is a third supposed problem with conglomerate firms. Touching in so many markets, firms recognize that aggressive tactics in one area can precipitate retaliation in another field of their operations. The potential for widespread disruption of existing agreements and practices causes the firms to forego the immediate benefits of competition in a specific market for overall and long-term harmony. The likelihood of forbearance, reciprocity, and/or cross-subsidization by conglomerate firms depends critically on the way those firms are managed. Conglomerate management practices will be discussed later in this section.

A final concern with conglomerate mergers is the reduction in competition resulting from the disappearance of *potential competitors* positioned on the edge of the market. This argument assumes that giant firms with the resources to successfully enter an industry exert pressures that keep prices down and competition viable among the existing producers. The importance of potential competitors is an empirical (but probably nonquantifiable) question. It is not obvious that competition is better served by a

---

[21]As discussed in Allen, B. T., "Industrial Reciprocity: A Statistical Analysis," *Journal of Law and Economics,* Vol. 18 (Oct., 1975), pp. 507–520. See also Ferguson, J. M., "Tying Arrangements and Reciprocity," *Law and Contemporary Problems,* Vol. 30 (Summer 1965), pp. 552–580.

large firm that may enter a market or by that firm's actual entry into the fray. Also, the disappearance of one potential competitor may not be particularly significant. The number of potential entrants is a function of the actions of the firms in the market. If prices are increased and economic profits earned, then additional firms will find the prospect of entry desirable.

Benefits of Conglomerate Mergers

For the firm, diversification is supposed to bring about increased profitability and a reduction of risk. However, empirical studies provide support for neither of these assertions. Most studies have found conglomerates to have lower rates of return than nondiversified firms. The evidence on risk is less definitive, but does not support the hypothesis that conglomeration reduces the variability of returns. [22]

From the perspective of society, conglomerate mergers may be useful if they enable firms to use more efficient production, distribution, or management techniques. Once again, however, the evidence does not support the claim of superior conglomerate efficiency. This lack of evidence is not really surprising, given the nature of conglomerates. There are no compelling reasons for believing that fitting together a group of unrelated firms would create a new entity that performs better than the sum of its parts. In fact, it is likely that management control problems could reduce overall efficiency.

Evaluation of Conglomerate Mergers

Evidence showing that conglomerate mergers benefit society is less than overwhelming. However, the magnitude of the social costs created by such mergers is also largely speculative. Whether practices such as reciprocity, cross-subsidization, and forbearance are significant problems depends critically on the way in which conglomerate firms are managed. If most decisions are made at a central level, then the charges against conglomerates may have substance. On the other hand, if individual units are relatively autonomous, making their own decisions, then reciprocity and the like are much less probable. A 1972 Federal Trade Commission study investigated the management practices of the nine most active (in terms of acquisitions) conglomerates of the 1960s. [23] The report concludes that most operations of individual firms changed little after they were acquired by a conglomerate. Specifically, the administration of research and development, advertising and promotion, and purchasing were left to the operating units. The only functions that underwent much change were auditing, legal services, and borrowing. The need for coordination makes the centralization of these activities unsurprising. In addition, over one-half of the management of the acquired firms remained in their slots for at least three years after the merger. Another 40 percent were not immediately replaced, but left within three years. Only about 10 percent of top management were immediately replaced by the acquiring firm.

[22]Holzmann, O. F., Copeland, R. M., and Hayya, J., "Income Measures of Conglomerate Performance," *Quarterly Review of Economics and Business,* Vol. 15, No. 3 (Autumn 1975), pp. 67–78. The findings of these authors are consistent with those of other researchers.
[23]Staff Report to the Federal Trade Commission, *Conglomerate Merger Performance: An Empirical Analysis of Nine Corporations* (Washington, D.C.: U.S. Government Printing Office, 1972).

A study by Markham found that pricing and advertising decisions in conglomerates are commonly left to operating divisions, while investment choices are made centrally. Markham reports:

> ... There is little if any evidence that diversified companies, simply because of their diversification, present special problems beyond the reach of our antitrust policy as presently administered. As companies reach a threshold of diversification, such matters as pricing and related market activities increasingly are made a matter of divisional autonomy. This means that in day-to-day operations divisions of conglomerates function very much the same as undiversified companies. Moreover, the evidence is fairly persuasive that highly diversified companies are certainly no more, and may even be less, given to the practice of reciprocity than large corporations generally. Hence, the facts support the unspectacular conclusion that while conglomerates may organize themselves differently, their behavior in markets in which they operate is indistinguishable from other large companies.[24]

In summary, although there is no compelling evidence that conglomerate mergers provide significant benefits, there is also no reason to believe that they impose serious social costs. Unless bigness per se or the abuse of political power is an issue, there is no clear reason for taking a hard stand against conglomerate mergers.

Courts and Conglomerate Mergers

When the Justice Department or the FTC challenge conglomerate mergers, the charge is usually that a potential competitor has been eliminated or that the resources of the acquiring firm enable it to entrench the market position of its merger partner. The doctrine of potential competition was made necessary by the wording of the Clayton Act, which requires a showing that the merger must substantially lessen competition. In a pure conglomerate merger there is no prior interaction between the firms and, hence, no effect on competition. The government's solution has been to try and convince the courts of what might have been if the merger had not occurred and the acquiring firm had remained as a potential competitor. The entrenchment argument focuses on the ability of conglomerates to feed resources and expertise into acquired firms to enable them to improve their competitive position. Entrenchment may involve the practices of cross-subsidization, reciprocity, and forbearance discussed in the previous section.

Potential Competition   The Supreme Court first accepted potential competition as a basis for prohibiting mergers in a case involving El Paso Natural Gas Co. and Pacific Northwest Pipeline Corp. [*United States* v. *El Paso Natural Gas Co.* (1964)].[25] El Paso supplied natural gas to customers in California, while Pacific Northwest operated in Oregon. Although Pacific had no California operations, the evidence indicated that the firm had given serious consideration to moving into California and competing with El

[24]Markham, J. W., *Conglomerate Enterprise and Public Policy* (Boston: Division of Research, Graduate School of Business Administration, Harvard University, 1973), pp. 175–176.
[25]*United States* v. *El Paso Natural Gas Co. et al.,* 376 U.S. 651 (1964).

Paso. The Court ruled against the merger on the grounds that an important source of potential competition would be eliminated by the acquisition:

> We would have to wear blinders not to see that the mere efforts of Pacific Northwest to get into the California market, though unsuccessful, had a powerful influence on El Paso's business attitudes within the state.[26]

The elimination of a potential competitor was one of two central issues in *FTC* v. *Procter & Gamble Co.* (1967).[27] Procter & Gamble was the largest producer of detergents, soaps, toothpaste, and other household products. The firm had a 54-percent share of the detergent market, but was not involved in the manufacture or sale of bleach. Clorox held a 49-percent share of a bleach market in which the top six firms accounted for 80 percent of total sales. In ordering the merger dissolved, the Court determined that Procter & Gamble was the most likely entrant into the bleach market. By allowing Procter to acquire Clorox, the possibility of an additional, large-scale entrant would be eliminated.

More recently, the potential competition doctrine has had its ups and downs. In one case [*Bendix Corp.* v. *FTC* (1971)] the Federal Trade Commission ruled that, although a manufacturer of automotive components would not have entered the automobile filter manufacturing business by internal expansion, it was likely to enter by merging with a small firm to get a toehold in the industry. The result was that a merger with the third-largest producer of filters was not allowed.[28] On the other hand, the Supreme Court approved a merger between two brewers, Falstaff and Narragansett, when it was determined that Falstaff's management had decided against expanding, other than by merger, into Narragansett's market area. Hence, Falstaff was not considered a potential competitor [*United States* v. *Falstaff Brewing Corp.* (1973)].[29]

In *United States* v. *Marine Bancorporation, Inc.* (1974), the Supreme Court suggested three criteria that must be satisfied for successful application of the potential competition challenge.[30] First, the market in which the acquired firm operates must be concentrated. Second, the government must demonstrate that an alternative method of entry, such as internal expansion or acquisition of a small firm, exists for the acquiring firm. Finally, the alternative method of entry must carry a reasonable prospect of improving competition in the market of the acquired firm. Finding that the second and third conditions were not met, the Court allowed the merger.

Entrenchment   In the Procter & Gamble case the Court agreed with the government that a merger with Clorox would give the latter a substantial assist in enlarging its already dominant position in the bleach market. Procter & Gamble allegedly received discounts on advertising because of large volume purchases. A merger would transmit this promotional advantage to Clorox. Procter also had a vast network for distribution

---

[26]Ibid., p. 659.

[27]*FTC* v. *Procter & Gamble Co.*, 386 U.S. 568 (1967).

[28]*Bendix Corp.*, 77 FTC 73 (1970), vacated and remanded on other grounds, 450 F. 2d 534 (6th Cir. 1971).

[29]*United States* v. *Falstaff Brewing Corp.*, 410 U.S. 526 (1973).

[30]*United States* v. *Marine Bancorporation, Inc.*, 418 U.S. 602 (1974).

of merchandise to which Clorox would gain access. The Court also noted that the vast resources of Procter & Gamble allowed the possibility of selective price cutting to keep competitors in line in the bleach industry. Combining the entrenchment argument with the loss of potential competition, the merger was ordered dissolved.

The charge of entrenching the position of an acquired firm through reciprocal purchasing pressures was accepted by the Supreme Court in *Federal Trade Commission* v. *Consolidated Foods Corp. et al.* (1965).[31] Consolidated had diversified interests in food products, while the acquired firm, Gentry, Inc., specialized in the manufacture of dehydrated onion and garlic. The evidence indicated that Consolidated had pressured its suppliers of soups and similar goods to use Gentry products. Although the practice of reciprocity only slightly increased Gentry's market share, the Court's decision went against the firms.

Status of Conglomerate Mergers   Conglomerate mergers are one of the least-settled areas of antitrust law. During the 1960s, the government was quite successful in challenging conglomerate mergers. But during the 1970s and early 1980s few such mergers have been prohibited. The courts have not explicitly rejected the concepts of potential competition and entrenchment, but they now seem to require that the government present a much stronger case showing the anticompetitive effects of the merger. Also, the FTC and the Justice Department, particularly under the Reagan Administration, have shown little interest in preventing conglomerate mergers. Unless it appears that such mergers would increase horizontal market power, they are unlikely to be challenged by the antitrust agencies.

SUMMARY
Incentives to Merge

The Acquired Firm   A firm may be acquired to protect it from bankruptcy, because the owner wishes to retire, in the attempt to reduce risk, because a lucrative offer has been made, or as the result of a hostile takeover bid.

The Acquiring Firm   Incentives of the acquiring firm include (1) increased market power, (2) technical economies of scale, (3) pecuniary economies of scale, (4) economies of coordination, (5) pooling of risk, (6) valuation discrepancies, (7) complementary resources, and (8) stock market effects.

Horizontal Mergers

Benefits and Costs of Horizontal Integration   Horizontal mergers may result in efficiency gains that reduce production costs. However, increased market power may give firms the ability to raise prices. One method of evaluating such mergers is by comparing efficiency gains from scale economies to the loss of consumer surplus resulting from higher prices.

[31]*Federal Trade Commission* v. *Consolidated Foods Corp. et al.,* 380 U.S. 592 (1965).

Evaluation of Horizontal Integration   There is little evidence to indicate that merged firms are more efficient or more profitable than their premerger constituent parts. The only clear winners are the stockholders of the acquired firms.

The Courts and Horizontal Mergers   In the past, the courts have prevented horizontal mergers even when the market shares of the merger partners were relatively small. Although recent decisions have been somewhat more liberal, the courts continue to take a strong stand against such mergers.

Merger Guidelines   A merger is unlikely to be challenged by the Justice Department if the postmerger Herfindahl index is less than 1000. Challenge is likely if the index is greater than 1800.

Vertical Mergers

Benefits of Vertical Integration   Technological interdependency between different stages of production may create efficiency gains from vertical integration. Integration may also reduce costs of using markets by decreasing search and negotiation expenses. Also, vertically integrated firms can make resource allocation decisions on a global rather than a locally optimal basis.

Costs of Vertical Integration   Among the potential costs of vertical integration are (1) foreclosure of markets, (2) pricing policies that squeeze independent sellers, (3) increased entry barriers, and (4) elimination of potential competitors.

Evaluation of Vertical Integration   Costs that are ascribed to vertical integration often should be assessed to horizontal market power. The case against vertical mergers is less persuasive than the arguments against horizontal mergers.

The Courts and Vertical Mergers   Vertical mergers can be successfully challenged when the affected market is significant and the share of the market that would be foreclosed is substantial. However, such mergers are most likely to be prohibited where the combination augments horizontal market power.

Conglomerate Mergers

Costs of Conglomerate Mergers   The "deep pockets" of giant conglomerate firms may place smaller firms at a disadvantage. Reciprocal purchasing policies may foreclose markets for other firms. Another problem is that, fearing retaliation in other areas of their operations, conglomerates may refrain from aggressive competition. Finally, conglomerate mergers may eliminate potential competition.

Benefits of Conglomerate Mergers   Diversification can reduce risk. Conglomerate mergers may also improve efficiency in production, distribution, and/or management.

Evaluation of Conglomerate Mergers   The evidence does not support the view that conglomeration results in significant net social benefits or costs. Conglomerates organize differently than other large firms, but behave much the same.

The Courts and Conglomerate Mergers   Treatment of conglomerates is the least-settled area of merger law. In recent years, the courts have been less willing to accept potential competition and entrenchment as reasons for prohibiting conglomerate mergers. The best chance for preventing such a merger is by showing that it increases horizontal market power.

DISCUSSION QUESTIONS

1. Could a merger between PSA and Eastern Airlines be considered a conglomerate rather than a horizontal merger? Explain.

2. Consider an industry with a dominant firm. Is there a case for allowing smaller firms in the industry to merge? Explain.

3. Was it realistic for the Court to lump urban and suburban areas in defining the geographic market in the Brown case? Why?

4. Long-term contracts between firms are an alternative to vertical integration. From society's point of view, what are the advantages and disadvantages of such arrangements?

5. Should trends in concentration be a relevant consideration in deciding whether to prohibit a merger? Why?

6. From society's perspective, which is preferable, the entry of a firm into a new market by merger or by internal expansion? Explain.

7. How could a horizontal merger affect the distribution of income? Should these effects be considered by the courts in evaluating such mergers?

chapter 7

Antitrust: Collusion

Chapter Outline

Some in the business community view price-fixing sort of like jaywalking, you look around and you see if there's a policeman standing on the street corner. If he isn't there you jaywalk, even though you know it's illegal. [1]

Increases in oil prices by the Organization of Petroleum Exporting Countries (OPEC) were among the most important economic events of the 1970s. Between 1973 and 1980 the cartel raised the price of oil from $3 to $35 per barrel. The resulting strains were felt in developing and industrialized nations throughout the world. In the United States the highest rates of unemployment since the depression years and the most rapid increases in prices since the end of World War II were partially attributable to OPEC's economic muscle.

The Arab oil cartel is by no means the first successful agreement to fix prices of an important commodity. In 1301 the price of salt dropped because of competition between the mines of King Philip the Fair of France and those of Charles II, King of Naples. At the time salt played a vital role in the preservation of food. Florentine bankers who leased the mines proposed to the two kings that a single company be formed, which would sell the total output of both facilities at a higher price. The prospect of increased revenues to fill the royal treasuries was very attractive and the kings agreed.

Then as now, collusion can have religious or political overtones. For many years prior to 1461 the Turks had maintained control over the production of alum, an important ingredient used in cloth dyeing and leather tanning. In that year new alum deposits were discovered on land controlled by the Catholic church. To eliminate competition, Pope Pius II condemned the Turkish alum as heathen and prohibited its use by Christians. Nine years later an agreement was signed with Ferdinand, King of Naples, who owned another important source of alum. The express purpose of this agreement was to increase and stabilize the price of alum. Under its terms the price was fixed, and cartel members were left free to determine their output. Total profits were then divided among the members of the group.

Collusion to fix prices has continued into modern times. In the last century there have been copper cartels, sugar cartels, ice cartels, rubber cartels, and paper cartels. Some have been brief and ineffective, while others have imposed severe economic hardships on consumers. Some, such as OPEC, have been very open about their activities, while others have become involved in secret meetings and clandestine tactics that would be a credit to the CIA and KGB. The frequency of price-fixing agreements lends credibility to Adam Smith's observation that, "People in the same trade seldom meet together, even for merriment or diversion, but the conversation ends in a conspiracy against the public, or in some contrivance to raise prices." [2]

Chapters 5 and 6 focused on promoting competition by modifying the structure of industry. This chapter and the next consider antitrust policy designed to improve performance by altering industry conduct. The first section discusses factors affecting the decision to collude. The second examines explicit collusion such as price fixing

---

[1] Former Assistant Attorney General Thomas Kauper as quoted in Schellhardt, T. D., "The Rising Tide of Price Fixing," *Wall Street Journal* (July 30, 1975), p. 4.

[2] Smith, A., *The Wealth of Nations* (New York: Random House, Modern Library, 1937), p. 128.

agreements. The final section of the chapter deals with the problem of tacit collusion in oligopolistic industries.

THE DECISION TO COLLUDE

Firms in oligopolistic markets have an incentive to collude. Using the simple Cournot model, it was shown in Chapter 2 that two firms able to charge the monopoly price have a larger profit pie to divide than would result if they continued to act independently. If a mutually agreeable method for setting prices and sharing the spoils can be developed, then both firms benefit by avoiding competition.

Factors Affecting the Success of Collusion

Antitrust activities are intended to make collusive behavior less attractive by increasing the costs and reducing the benefits of industry coordination. An understanding of public policies designed to thwart collusion is facilitated by the following discussion of factors that affect the ability of firms to collude.[3]

Number and Size Distribution of Sellers   As a general proposition, the more sellers in a market the greater the difficulty of establishing and maintaining effective collusion. There are several reasons for this relationship. First is the problem of coordination. Successful collusion requires that all the parties to an agreement concur on the proper policy to be implemented and the means of its administration. Anyone who has served on a committee knows that the difficulty of getting agreements increases rapidly as more people are added to the group. Each person has a slightly different perspective of the problem and these views must be reconciled. Each person may interpret the statements and actions of others in a slightly different way. The same is true of firms that operate in different locations, with varying technologies, and under different pressures from stockholders. More firms imply greater diversity and increased possibilities for misunderstandings.

A second reason stems from the fact that, as the number of sellers increases, the market share and importance of any given seller decreases. Thus, the actions of a single firm have a reduced impact on the activities of the other firms. As a result, firms become less concerned about their interdependence and tend to view their economic environment as fixed or given. Finally, more sellers increase the probability that there will be at least one firm that chooses to operate outside the cartel in the attempt to increase its market share. If this firm succeeds in capturing a substantial share of the market, other firms will be tempted to withdraw from the agreement to capture a piece of the action. Industry coordination may eventually be destroyed and active competition will result.

The size distribution as well as the absolute number of sellers is an important determinant of the success of collusion. Consider two industries with four firms each. In the first industry the firms are of equal size, while in the second there is a giant firm

---

[3]A more detailed discussion of factors affecting the ability to collude is found in Scherer, F., *Industrial Market Structure and Economic Performance,* 2nd ed., (Chicago: Rand McNally, 1980), Chaps. 6 and 7.

with 90 percent of the market and three smaller firms that equally divide the remaining 10 percent. In the first industry any agreement must be reached by persuasion and compromise. No one firm is in the position to punish another that chooses to defect from the cartel. In contrast, in the second industry the large firm has the ability to inflict its will on the smaller firms. Pricing and other policies will overwhelmingly reflect the preferences of the industry leader. The small firms often have an incentive to accept the decisions of the dominant firm and operate under its umbrella. In many cases the small firms have no choice, knowing that the large firm has the ability to inflict serious economic harm on firms that do not follow its lead. To the extent that an industry is dominated by one or two large firms, the possibilities for effective collusion are enhanced.

Product Homogeneity   Homogeneous products are those that are considered perfect substitutes in the minds of consumers. For example, consider a family stopping along the roadside to purchase fresh vegetables. There are two stands, side by side, with identical appearance and service. The vegetables offered for sale are equivalent as judged by the potential purchasers. Under these conditions there is only one dimension in which the market owners can compete, and that is price. Consumers will tend to gravitate to the stand that offers the lower prices. This tendency will not come as a surprise to either owner. Hence, unless they can find some way of restricting competition, prices and profits will be low. The solution, of course, is to enter into an agreement to fix prices. If there are no other sellers in the area, it should not be difficult to formulate an effective cartel. Because there are only two sellers, there will be little problem with communication, and their locational proximity makes it easy to detect cheating. Consensus is further facilitated by the fact that the products they sell are identical. In their discussions there can be no effective claim that one owner's vegetables are better than the other. Previous experience indicates that consumers perceive them as equivalent and base their decision only on price. All that really has to be decided is the level of prices that will maximize their joint profits.

Now suppose that one of the owners discovers a way of growing larger, juicier, and redder tomatoes. These tomatoes are considered superior by customers as evidenced by increased sales when prices are the same. Even when the price of the better tomato is set above the common type, people seem willing to pay the differential. The seller of the inferior tomato is now forced to reduce the price of his product. As the differential increases, people again become willing to buy the cheaper brand and the other owner is forced to reduce the price of his obviously superior product. Again, profits and prices are low because of competition. The only difference is that there is now a price gap between the tomatoes with the larger tomatoes still commanding a premium.

The owners again realize the need for a pricing agreement. Now, however, the issues are not so simple. In addition to the general level of prices, the differential between the two types of tomatoes must be agreed upon. Each owner would be expected to have a different perspective on the size of that differential. Unless the price difference that puts consumers on the margin is the same for all price levels, it may be almost impossible for the two businesspeople to agree.

If there are other ways in which the products of one stand are differentiated from those of the other, the problems of collusion multiply. Suppose one owner takes more care in washing and displaying produce while the other tends to be more outgoing and personable. Suppose one has an attractive daughter and the other a surly spouse. Suppose one has drinks and candy for sale in addition to vegetables, while the other maintains only a narrow line of produce. All of these characteristics affect the propensity of consumers to go to one stand rather than the other. None of them can be evaluated in a straightforward, noncontroversial manner. Faced with these additional dimensions on which they can compete, the owners are much less likely to achieve a successful and stable collusive agreement.

Industries for which the products of individual firms are relatively homogeneous are usually better candidates for successful collusive behavior than are industries whose firms produce products that are perceived as being different by consumers. Where the product is homogeneous, the agreement is much less complex, focusing mainly on the single price, than for heterogeneous products that require firms to assess multiple product characteristics.

Size and Frequency of Orders   Industries in which orders received by firms tend to be small and frequent are more likely to be successful at collusion than if firms receive very large orders for their product at infrequent intervals. Consider the case of a duopoly selling books or some other low-price item by mail. The two firms agree to collude, set the monopoly price, and let profits be determined by the volume of orders received by each firm. In this circumstance there is little to be gained by surreptitiously offering lower prices to a few selected customers to obtain their business. The prospects for gain are outweighed by the likelihood of precipitating retaliatory actions from the other firm which would destroy the cartel and cause a general reduction in prices. Hence, the possibilities for successful collusion are relatively good.

Now consider the same two firms selling nuclear power plants. A single order may mean millions of dollars in profits to the firm. Given the uncertainties about nuclear reactors, orders may be very infrequent. Typically, an electric utility would put its reactor order out for bids with the lowest bidder likely to receive the contract. Again assume that the firms have agreed to collude on prices. The managements have adopted a policy of alternating on accepting bids. This is accomplished by having the firm whose turn it is to get the order submit the lower bid. Now suppose that a particularly large and profitable order comes to the attention of the two firms and that it has been many months since either has signed a new contract. Firm #1 should have the right to be the low bidder because firm #2 got the last order. Unfortunately, firm #2 knows that it may be many more months before a comparable order comes along. There is a strong incentive for firm #2 to defect from the cartel and submit a more competitive bid. The prospects of getting this lucrative contract may seem greater than the uncertain benefits of dividing future sales. Once the actions of firm #2 become known, its rival will be extremely reluctant to enter into future deals. The greater the stakes, the greater the incentive to cheat on a collusive agreement.

Selling Practices and Information Flows   The ability to collude is a function of the ease of detecting and punishing cheaters. Where there is little personal contact between buyers and sellers the possibilities for cheating are much less than when the parties negotiate face to face. This suggests that it would be easier for an industry that takes orders by mail to fix prices than for one that uses door-to-door salespeople. This is because it would be possible for each firm to make spot checks on the practices of its mail-order rivals.

The dissemination of information between firms can also be an important factor in industry behavior. Collusion is much easier to police when firms publish price lists than when price information is not widely distributed. Where industry trade associations collect detailed data on the operations of each firm the possibilities for collusion are further enhanced. Trade associations can play an important role by facilitating the flow of information between firms.

Industry Maturity   Agreements to restrict competition are made by people, not firms. Formulating these agreements requires that the participants develop effective methods of communicating with one another. They also require an understanding of the way in which individuals will react in given circumstances. This information does not come instantaneously, but is the product of previous social and business interactions. One of the main reasons for the so-called Gary Dinners was the development of a feeling of camaraderie among the leaders of the steel industry. Judge Elbert Gary, chairman of the board of U.S. Steel, regularly had his counterparts from other firms to his home between 1907 and 1911. He noted that the "close communication and contact" developed at these dinners generated much mutual "respect and affectionate regard" among steel industry leaders that all considered the obligation to cooperate and avoid destructive competition "more binding . . . than any written or verbal contract."[4] It is more than coincidence that the steel industry was controlled by an effective cartel during that period. As a general rule, industries where demand is stable, technology is not changing rapidly, and little turnover occurs among the top executives will have better luck in colluding than industries such as manufacturing pocket calculators, where firms are rapidly entering and leaving the market, the technology is changing on almost a monthly basis, and top executives are not well acquainted.

Cost Structure   Industries whose fixed costs are a high percentage of total costs may have special difficulties in maintaining price-fixing agreements during times of weak demand. Declining industry sales reduce revenues of individual firms much more than costs, because of the large overhead component that must be paid irrespective of the volume of sales. By reducing its price, any one firm can increase its market share. Because variable costs associated with expanding production are a relatively small part of the selling price, the firm can make a substantial contribution to its fixed costs by defecting from the agreement. This strategy will not go unnoticed by other firms, who will also reduce prices. Because marginal costs are low, it is possible that the breakdown in industry pricing discipline may precipitate a drastic reduction in prices that forces some of the firms out of the industry. The experience of the railroads during the late nineteenth century is a classic example of the tendency toward cut-throat competition of capital-intensive industries. Prices oscillated as cartels were established, broken apart

---

[4]From an antitrust brief cited by Fritz Machlup in *The Political Economy of Monopoly* (Baltimore: Johns Hopkins University Press, 1952), p. 87.

by cheaters and new entrants, and then reestablished. The early experience of the railroads is considered in Chapter 10.

Benefits and Costs of Collusion

The actual decision to collude is based on a benefit-cost calculation on the part of the firms involved. The potential benefit of price fixing is obvious—more profits. The costs fall into four interrelated categories. First, there is a cost associated with setting and changing the industry price structure. Each firm is in a different position, has different expectations, and varying economic clout in the cartel. In these circumstances it may not be easy to arrive at an agreement that every firm perceives as being beneficial. In addition, changing conditions will undoubtedly necessitate modifications to the agreement. All of these factors impose a resource cost on the participating firms.

A second cost of collusion is that imposed by the inevitable cheating that will occur from time to time. If prices are set in excess of marginal costs, then any one firm can increase its market share and total profits by selling at a price below that set by the cartel. The faithful members of the cartel are rewarded for their honesty with a loss of sales and profits. In the absence of preventive action, these firms will then cut their prices and industry cooperation will be replaced by price competition. Because there is always an advantage to cheating on a price-fixing agreement, the cartel must have some mechanism for detecting and punishing cheaters. Detection may require involved reporting of sales data, while punishment may take the form of selective price cuts designed to have a particularly severe effect on the cheater. Again, these activities are costly to the members of a collusive scheme and must be weighed against the expected benefits.

A third cost of cartelization stems from nonprice competition that may emerge in the industry. Having agreed to restrain from competing on the basis of price, firms may attempt to increase their market share by offering better service, upgrading the physical characteristics of their product, or providing consumers with a greater range of choice. None of these practices are costless. In fact, high profit rates are not really a good indication of the existence of price-fixing because, over time, nonprice competition tends to erode above-average profits of cartel members. It is possible that the most significant social cost of collusion is not the deadweight loss resulting from output not produced, but rather the higher costs that stem from nonprice rivalry.[5]

Legal penalties imposed on convicted colluders are the fourth cost of price fixing. These may take the form of fines, prison sentences, damage awards in private suits, or directives to change behavior (e.g., to abandon information dissemination practices, to license competitors to use patents, or to alter marketing methods). The threat of detection and punishment also increases costs in the other three categories. For example, if direct and open communication is impossible because of antitrust laws, then more covert means must be devised. These are typically more expensive and less reliable. Similarly, firms must use greater discretion in the punishment of cheaters if they know that the "feds" are monitoring their activities.

The decision to collude is not an either-or proposition. The magnitude of the

[5]See Posner, R. A., *Antitrust Law* (Chicago: University of Chicago Press, 1976), pp. 11–18.

markup over competitive prices and the mode of fixing prices depends on a number of factors, the most relevant for public policy being the magnitude of penalties and the probability of detection. If penalties are positively correlated to markups, then, for the firm, the optimal increase in prices is reduced if expected penalties are harsh. Also, as a general rule, if firms perceive that they are being actively scrutinized by antitrust authorities and that penalties from conviction will be severe, they will tend to adopt less easily detectable and less effective methods of collusion.

The most reliable method for setting prices is a joint sales agency whereby the firms in an industry establish an organization that sells all of their output at the specified price. Because the individual firms don't enter the market, there is no possibility of cheating and no incentive to initiate nonprice competition. However, such an agency would be immediately detected and successfully prosecuted under U.S. antitrust law. Thus, firms are forced to resort to methods that, although harder to detect, are also less effective. One alternative is bidding schemes. Where buyers select sellers on the basis of low bids, colluding firms can agree to inflate their bids while allowing each participant the opportunity to take its turn as low bidder. Carefully planned bidding rings can be very difficult to detect, but are also subject to cheating if cartel members independently reduce their bids to obtain a particularly lucrative contract.

EXPLICIT COLLUSION AND THE LAW

The Sherman Act prohibits "every contract, combination in the form of trust or otherwise, or conspiracy, in restraint of trade or commerce among the several States, or with foreign nations." Although the Supreme Court has authorized the FTC to prosecute price fixing, group boycotts, and other conspiratorial practices under Section 5 of the Federal Trade Commission Act, Section 1 is the primary legal weapon used for attacking collusive activities in the United States.[6]

Price Fixing

The first price-fixing case to come to the Supreme Court was *United States* v. *Trans-Missouri Freight Association* (1897).[7] Eighteen Midwestern railroads had entered into an agreement to fix prices in the attempt to eliminate ruinous rate wars. Challenged by the government, they claimed that their regulated status (by the Interstate Commerce Commission) made them exempt from Sherman Act prosecution. They also asserted that, regardless of the exemption claim, the rates that had been fixed were reasonable. A district court sustained the defendants on both counts, but the Supreme Court held that the Sherman Act condemned all restraints of trade, not just those that might be found unreasonable. The Court also recognized the practical problems that would have resulted had the judicial system been required to rule on the reasonableness of price-fixing agreements.

> The subject of what is a reasonable rate is attended with great uncertainty. What is a proper standard by which to judge the fact of reasonable rates? Must the rate be

---

[6]See *Fashion Originators' Guild of America, Inc.* v. *FTC,* 312 U.S. 457 (1941).
[7]*United States* v. *Trans-Missouri Freight Association,* 166 U.S. 290 (1897).

so high as to enable the return for the whole business done to amount to a sum sufficient to afford the shareholder a fair and reasonable profit upon his investment? If so, what is a fair and reasonable profit? That depends sometimes upon the risks incurred, and the rate itself differs in different localities: which is the one to which reference is to be made as the standard? Or is the reasonableness of the profit to be limited to a fair return upon the capital that would have been sufficient to build and equip the road, if honestly expended? Or is still another standard to be created, and the reasonableness of the charges tried by the cost of carriage of the article and a reasonable profit allowed on that? And in such case would contribution to a sinking fund to make repairs upon the roadbed and renewal of cars, etc., be assumed as a proper item. [8]

Trenton The per se standard announced in Trans-Missouri was strengthened by the Trenton Potteries decision [*United States* v. *Trenton Potteries Co., et al.* (1927)]. [9] In the attempt to get ahead, 23 manufacturers of bathroom fixtures conspired to fix prices. Through their trade association the manufacturers published standardized price lists, met to consider prices, and pressured one another to sell only at list prices. Brought to trial, the association claimed that the agreement had not injured the public. The trial record supported their contention, indicating that fixtures were frequently sold below the established prices. The Court again rejected the request for a rule-of-reason interpretation of Section 1. The justices argued that:

The reasonable price fixed today may through economic and business changes become the unreasonable price of tomorrow. . . . Agreements which create such potential power may well be held to be in themselves unreasonable or unlawful restraints, without the necessity of minute inquiry whether a particular price is reasonable or unreasonable. [10]

Socony The precedent established by Trenton was somewhat clouded by the substantial market share of the defendants. The 23 producers controlled over 80 percent of the market at the time. In the Socony-Vacuum Oil case the Court ruled that neither reasonableness of prices set nor lack of market power of the defendants was relevant [*United States* v. *Socony-Vacuum Oil Co. et al.* (1940)]. [11] Conditions in the petroleum industry in 1940 were quite different than during the 1970s. New oil supplies had depressed prices as independent refiners dumped gasoline in the Midwestern market. In the effort to prop prices, a group of major refiners conspired to purchase excess supplies from the independents. This gas was to be put on the market gradually to prevent depressing prices. There was no evidence that the defendants had fixed a specific price for the surplus supplies, but the Court still held that their actions constituted illegal collusion. Again rejecting the defense of reasonableness, the justices also held that the market power of the conspirators was not the issue. The Court indicated that the offense was the intent to fix prices, not the final outcome. The strong per se condemnation of price fixing established in Socony-Vacuum Oil has consistently been

[8]Ibid., p. 331.
[9]*United States* v. *Trenton Potteries Co. et al.,* 273 U.S. 392 (1927).
[10]Ibid., pp. 396–398.
[11]*United States* v. *Socony-Vacuum Oil Co. et al.,* 310 U.S. 150 (1940).

reaffirmed by the courts. Agreements to fix prices are a violation of the Sherman Act without regard to their effect. The prohibition applies not only to fixing minimum prices, but also to maximum prices and price differentials. Firms are simply not allowed to act in concert in determining prices.

Electric Machinery Conspiracy   In the early 1960s, 29 corporations were successfully prosecuted for fixing the prices of electrical equipment such as transformers, generators, and switchgear [*United States* v. *General Electric et al.* (1961)]. [12] The case established no important legal precedents, but is interesting because of the details of the conspiracy and the size of damage awards.

The manufacture of heavy electrical equipment is a highly concentrated industry that includes large firms such as General Electric, Westinghouse, and Allis-Chalmers. Firms in the industry had long been involved in collusive agreements and were frequent targets of antitrust investigations. In the late 1950s a major customer, the Tennessee Valley Authority, complained to the Justice Department that there had been an unusually rapid increase in the price of generating equipment. TVA also noted that sealed bids received from manufacturers were often identical. To obtain better terms the TVA investigated the possibility of purchasing from foreign manufacturers. Now it was the American manufacturers' turn to complain. They argued that TVA, as a part of the federal government, should "buy American." The government rejected the complaint and the firms responded by submitting lower bids to TVA. Unfortunately, the bids were again identical for some of the items. As a result, the Justice Department impaneled a grand jury to investigate the possibility of price fixing in the industry. In February 1960, the grand jury handed down the first 7 of 20 indictments against the firms.

The indictments alleged two primary types of conspiracies. For sales involving open bids the firms simply met to fix the prices that would be charged for different types of equipment. It was the sealed bid sales to the government that made the case intriguing. The intent of the conspiracy was to inflate prices while allowing firms to maintain a predetermined market share. For example, GE was allocated 42 percent of the market for switchgear, Westinghouse 38 percent, Allis-Chalmers 11 percent, and ITE Circuit Breakers 9 percent. Market shares were maintained by rotating bids so that each firm became the low bidder the requisite percentage of the time. This was accomplished by changing the order of bids about every two weeks or "with the phases of the moon." For example, on April 18, 1957, the TVA received the following bids for an oil circuit breaker:

General Electric	$7440 (Low)
Westinghouse	7445 (Middle)
Allis-Chalmers	7445 (Middle)
Federal Pacific	7610 (High)

Notice that while the bids are similar, one was high, one low, and the two middle bids identical. The next time a request for equipment went out, the bids ranked as follows:

---

[12] *United States* v. *General Electric et al.,* F. Supp. 197 (1961).

Westinghouse	$6465 (Low)
Allis-Chalmers	6470 (Middle)
General Electric	6470 (Middle)
Federal Pacific	6480 (High)

This time Westinghouse was the low bidder with Allis-Chalmers and General Electric submitting identical middle bids and Federal Pacific, allocated a small market share, still the high bidder. [13]

To avoid detection the conspirators engaged in elaborate precautions. Only first names were used and mail was always sent in plain envelopes to the homes of the executives. Calls were made from pay phones. Each firm was referred to by a code number. Expense-account vouchers were disguised by making them out for cities that were approximately as far from the firm's offices as the actual location of the conspiratorial gathering. The meetings themselves were often held in out of the way places —a favorite was Dirty Helen's Bar in Milwaukee. Above all, company lawyers were never told anything.

Luck played an important part in uncovering the agreements. As part of its investigation the Justice Department subpoenaed the records of the ITE Circuit Breaker Company. At ITE was an employee by the name of Nye Spencer who just happened to be acting as secretary for the switchgear conspiracy. A conscientious sort, Nye had kept detailed records of the conspiracy meetings to assist him in training his assistant. Confronted with the request for information, he turned over all his files to the government. Larger cracks in the dike appeared as lower-level executives turned state's evidence rather than further implicate themselves. Ultimately, the government was able to assemble a strong case, which the conspirators chose not to contest. Following sessions of plea bargaining an agreement was reached whereby the firms were allowed to enter nolo pleas to some of the indictments in return for pleading guilty to others.

The penalty phase of the case broke precedent as the judge sent seven defendents to jail for 30 days and granted suspended sentences to twenty others. Never before had business executives been sent to jail as a result of Sherman Act violations. The firms were also required to pay nearly $2 million in fines. However, the real penalty for the corporations was 1900 private suits resulting in damage payments of over $400 million. The lasting importance of the case probably stems from the realization of how painful treble damage suits can be.

Trade Association Activities   Most concentrated and many unconcentrated industries have a trade group. Auto makers have the Motor Vehicle Manufacturer's Association. The petroleum industry has the American Petroleum Institute. Lawyers have the American Bar Association and doctors the American Medical Association. There are also highly specialized organizations, such as the Catfish Farmers of America, the National Association of Pet Cemeteries, the International Frisbee Disc Association,

---

[13]For an interesting discussion of the case, see Fuller, J. G., *The Gentlemen Conspirators* (New York: Grove Press, 1962).

"Good Gracious, You Mean To Say Something's Been
Going On Here For Fifty Years?"

Straight Herblock. (New York: Simon & Schuster, 1964.)

and the Undergarment Accessories Association. The latter consists of manufacturers of trimmings, straps, and elastic for underwear.

When trade associations limit their activities to areas such as improving relations with labor and government, disseminating information on developments in technology, and providing general information about the industry to the public, they probably serve a useful purpose. Often, however, they are used to facilitate collusion in the industry. By supplying detailed data on prices, costs, and demand, they improve the flow of information necessary for effective price fixing. Operating as a common meeting place for executives, they also provide the opportunity for explicit discussions and ostracism of cheaters. Trade associations may be particularly useful in forming and maintaining agreements among relatively large numbers of conspirators. Case studies by Hay and Kelley found that of eight price-fixing cases including more than fifteen firms, a formal trade association was implicated in seven.[14] Nearly half of all criminal antitrust cases filed have involved trade associations.[15]

The courts have taken a rule of reason approach to trade association activities. When the association is disseminating information on proposed pricing in the industry, exerting pressure for industry discipline, or providing detailed information on the practices of individual firms, then the courts have usually ruled against the associa-

[14]Hay, G. A., and Kelley, D., "An Empirical Survey of Price Fixing Conspiracies," *Journal of Law and Economics,* Vol. 17 (Apr. 1974), pp. 13–38.

[15]Green, M. J., *The Closed Enterprise System,* (New York: Grossman, 1972), p. 161.

tions.[16] Where only past data is supplied, individual firms are not singled out, and there is no attempt to coerce members, the courts have been more favorable.[17]

Collusion and the Learned Professions

In the past, the legal system has not been completely impartial with respect to price fixing. The so-called learned professions, such as dentistry, medicine, and law, were treated in a much different way than the rest of business. Until recently, bar associations were allowed to establish suggested (but highly effective) minimum fee schedules. They also policed bans on lawyer advertising. Doctors and dentists adopted similar practices. Ethics codes prohibited advertising and relative value scales limited price competition. The latter assigned a numerical value to different services. These were then used to compute fees. For example, in California 5.8 units were assigned for an appendectomy, while a tonsillectomy for a child under 12 rated only 2.4. By multiplying the number of dollars per unit times the assigned number of units, the physician was able to determine his or her fee for each service.

In 1943 the Supreme Court held that the activities of medical groups were exempt from antitrust prosecution.[18] The basis for the exemption was the assumption that the medical profession was self-regulating. A supporting argument was that price competition and advertising in the medical profession would lead to a reduction in the quality of services offered and that the consumer often was not capable of differentiating between competent and incompetent practice. The same points have been made to support the exemption of other learned professions from antitrust restrictions.

Over the last decade the government and the courts have been less willing to accept the idea that the public was served by allowing special privileges to certain professions. An important case was *Goldfarb* v. *Virginia State Bar* (1975).[19] Goldfarb planned to build a house in Virginia and sought out a lawyer to make a title search as assurance that the property was not encumbered with the legal claims of others. Although the intended home site was part of a larger development carved out of a single parcel of land, the lawyer insisted on charging Goldfarb 1 percent of the value of the house for the search. Disgusted by the high price for work that had been done many times before, Goldfarb sought a more competitive rate from other attorneys. However, none would offer the service for a price lower than the 1 percent rate, which was suggested by the Virginia Bar Association. Goldfarb brought a price-fixing suit against the Bar Association. That suit ultimately was upheld by the Supreme Court.

Since the Goldfarb decision, other cracks in the wall of protection that surrounds the learned professions have begun to appear. The courts have held that lawyers have the right to advertise. The Federal Trade Commission has taken a similar position with the medical profession. Specialties within the medical profession have agreed to eliminate their use of relative value scales. Restrictions on the advertising of eyeglass and drug prices have been removed. In many cases formal changes in policy have not

[16]See, for example, *The Sugar Institute, Inc.* v. *United States,* 297 U.S. 553 (1936).
[17]See, for example, *Tag Manufacturers Institute* v. *FTC,* 174 F. 2nd 452 (1st Cir., 1949).
[18]*United States* v. *American Medical Association,* 317 U.S. 519 (1943).
[19]*Goldfarb* v. *Virginia State Bar,* 421 U.S. 773 (1975).

generated much change in actual practice, but in others consumers have undeniably benefited. To illustrate, before the ban on lawyer advertising was lifted, the going rate for an uncontested divorce in Phoenix was $350. Several years later the advertised rate was between $150 and $200. A legal change of name in New York, which used to cost as much as $200, dropped to $75. [20]

Other Collusive Activities

Price fixing is not the only collusive activity that can be prosecuted under the antitrust statutes. Other practices, such as allocation of markets and group boycotts, may also violate the law. *Market-allocation schemes* are agreements between firms to limit their sales to a specified market area or to a particular class of customers. The courts have held horizontal allocation of markets to be a per se violation of the law. From a theoretical point of view this makes good sense. Allocating markets makes each firm a monopolist in its own domain. As such, it has freedom to set prices and determine marketing practices without fear of competition. Market allocation may impose even greater social costs than price fixing in that cheating by selling across geographical or customer boundaries is more difficult to conceal than secret concessions on a fixed price. Thus, market-allocating schemes are likely to be more stable than price-fixing agreements.

The propriety of *group boycotts* is more difficult to evaluate. Usually, boycotts are employed to discipline firms that compete too aggressively or don't comply with traditional industry practices. A leading case is *Fashion Originator's Guild of America* v. *FTC* (1941). [21] The guild was an organization of firms engaged in designing and manufacturing women's dresses. A common practice was for other firms, not members of the guild, to copy the designs created by the guild and sell them at reduced prices. To prevent this practice, members of the guild agreed not to sell to retailers who carried the pirated styles. The guild's objective of preventing the theft of designs was laudable, but the Supreme Court ruled that the method, which involved an elaborate set of governing rules, was an illegal conspiracy under both the Federal Trade Commission and the Sherman Acts. The decision was based on a per se interpretation, which did not consider the potential benefits of the boycott or the unfairness of the style stealing.

It would be inaccurate, however, to conclude that all group boycotts are condemned under the antitrust laws. Reasonable actions taken to achieve lawful purposes may escape prosecution. A case in point is *Molinas* v. *National Basketball Association* (1961). [22] Molinas had been suspended from playing in the NBA for betting on the games of his team. He charged that his suspension by the association constituted an unlawful group boycott. The court ruled against Molinas, concluding that "a disciplinary rule invoked to prevent gambling seems to be about as reasonable a rule as could be imagined."

As a general rule, group boycotts designed to exclude or eliminate unruly or undesirable competitors are judged unlawful under a per se standard by the courts.

[20]Falk, C. H., "Lawyers Are Facing Surge in Competition as Courts Drop Curbs," *Wall Street Journal,* (Oct. 18, 1978), p. 1.
[21]*Fashion Originator's Guild of America* v. *FTC,* 312 U.S. 457 (1941).
[22]*Molinas* v. *National Basketball Association,* 190 F. Supp. 241 (S.D.N.Y., 1961).

Boycotts necessary to maintain the reputation of the industry or to improve (from society's perspective) trade practices are decided under the rule of reason. Boycotts directed to moral or social as opposed to business aims (such as the boycotts of lettuce and wine) have usually been left unchallenged.

TACIT COLLUSION AND THE LAW

The judicial system's strong condemnation of explicit agreements between firms is based on a legal concept of collusion that emphasizes evidence of the existence of conspiracy rather than the magnitude of its impact. This view has aided the prosecution of formal collusive agreements, but hampered the treatment of other undesirable business practices.

Dominant-Firm Price Leadership

There are several forms of price leadership, but the simplest involves an industry dominated by a single firm. This firm's size, location, or technology gives it power to dictate prices to the other firms in the industry. Marginal firms realize that they would be unable to survive in an atmosphere of intense price competition. Consequently, they are often perfectly willing to follow the pricing policies of the industry leader. By allowing the dominant firm to fix a high price, weaker firms become more profitable as they operate under the leader's umbrella. The result is uniformly high prices in the industry and an absence of price competition.

Dominant-firm price leadership poses a difficult problem for antitrust enforcement. If successful, it results in higher prices to the detriment of consumers. On the other hand, there has been no explicit agreement to fix prices and, hence, no conspiracy in the legal sense. Should the government prohibit large firms from selecting their prices or smaller firms from choosing to match those prices if such action is deemed advantageous? The status of dominant-firm price leadership was considered by the Supreme Court in a case involving the leading manufacturer of farm machinery, International Harvester [*United States* v. *International Harvester* (1927)].[23] The evidence indicated that Harvester set prices in the industry and other manufacturers usually followed suit. In rejecting a charge of illegal monopolization, the Court refused to penalize International Harvester for the practices of its competitors:

> The most that can be said to this, is that many of its competitors have been accustomed, independently and as a matter of business expediency, to follow approximately the prices at which it has sold its harvesting machines. . . . And the fact that competitors may see proper, in the exercise of their own judgment, to follow the prices of another manufacturer, does not establish any suppression of competition or show any sinister domination.[24]

As a general guide, if the leading firm does not use its market power to force smaller firms to follow its lead and if there is no evidence of an explicit agreement

[23]*United States* v. *International Harvester,* 274 U.S. 693 (1927).
[24]Ibid., pp. 708–709.

between the firms in the industry, then this form of price leadership will not be found to violate the antitrust laws. However, dominant firms may be prosecuted for monopolization under Section 2 of the Sherman Act. Prosecution for price discrimination under the Robinson-Patman Act also may be possible.

Oligopolistic Interdependence and Conscious Parallelism

The identifying characteristic of an oligopolistic market structure is that the individual firms must recognize their interdependence. Price changes initiated by one firm affect the sales and profitability of others and invite response. As previously noted, oligopolists can improve their lot if they can find a means of eliminating active price competition. Price leadership by a dominant firm may be effective, but most concentrated industries are not controlled by a single firm able to fix prices and discipline the other sellers. Formal agreements to set prices are a possibility, but the likelihood of successful antitrust prosecution may act as an effective deterrent. In many industries the dilemma has been resolved by resorting to informal rules and practices, which allow firms to change prices without their actions being regarded as competitive acts. For example, in the auto industry price and styling changes normally take place in the fall, accompanied by a great deal of fanfare. This practice is a well-understood tradition, which allows prices to be altered and new models introduced in an orderly way. No formal collusion is necessary among the auto executives. The needs of the industry are so well understood and the industry social structure sufficiently mature that the proper course is obvious to all without explicit agreement.

Second Tobacco Case   The tobacco industry provided an opportunity for the Supreme Court to consider the problem of tacit collusion among oligopolists [*American Tobacco Co. et al.,* v. *United States* (1946)].[25] For years the three leading firms in the industry, American Tobacco, Reynolds, and Ligget & Myers, had avoided overt price competition. At leaf tobacco auctions none of the firms bid unless all were present and the three producers always paid the same price. The firms used identical price lists and price changes were made simultaneously. On one occasion when leaf prices and labor costs were declining, the other two firms followed Reynolds in announcing a price increase. Despite the extreme uniformity of their behavior the government was unable to uncover any substantial evidence that the three firms had been involved in a conspiracy. Nevertheless, the Court found the defendants guilty on the wholly circumstantial evidence of parallel behavior. The Court announced that:

> No formal agreement is necessary to constitute an unlawful conspiracy. . . . The essential combination or conspiracy in violation of the Sherman Act may be found in a course of dealings or other circumstances as well as in an exchange of words.[26]

The tobacco case seemed to permit successful prosecution of tacit collusion by oligopolists. However, this conclusion is premature. In part, the Court in the tobacco

[25]*American Tobacco Co. et al.,* v. *United States,* 328 U.S. 781 (1946).
[26]Ibid., pp. 809–810.

case was reacting to the obviously antisocial behavior of the three firms. Although the government was unable to offer proof of formal conspiracy, it seemed highly unlikely that the firms could have played their game so well without meeting to specify the rules. The Court's willingness to convict on the basis of circumstantial evidence may not have been a condemnation of tacit collusion as much as it was an expression of belief that explicit price fixing was the real offense.

Theatre Enterprises Following the tobacco decision the courts ruled against tacit collusion—*conscious parallelism* was the phrase used to describe the practice—in several other cases. However, in *Theatre Enterprises, Inc.,* v. *Paramount Film Distributing Corp. et al. (1954)* the Supreme Court retreated from its earlier position.[27] The case was a treble damage suit brought by the owner of a theater located in a shopping center in the suburbs of Baltimore. The owner complained that nine film distributors had all refused to supply first-run films to his establishment. Instead, the new films were provided to downtown theaters. The trial produced no evidence that the distributors had jointly agreed to boycott the suburban movie house. A jury trial acquitted the defendants and the Supreme Court refused to overturn the jury's decision. The record indicated that the downtown theaters had a far greater drawing potential than that of the plaintiff and that they were much more active in advertising. Although the nine distributors had all refused first-run films to the suburban outlet, the Court determined that this was a rational business decision that could easily have been arrived at by the nine defendants acting independently. The justices qualified earlier decisions, noting that:

> . . . This Court has never held that proof of parallel business behavior . . . itself constitutes a Sherman Act offense. Circumstantial evidence of consciously parallel behavior may have made heavy inroads into the traditional judicial attitude toward conspiracy; but "conscious parallelism" has not yet read conspiracy out of the Sherman Act entirely.[28]

Subsequent decisions reaffirmed the policy that the simple existence of similar practices is not sufficient to convict firms of antitrust violations. If parallel behavior can reasonably be explained on the basis of other factors that would cause firms to independently come to like conclusions, then such behavior is beyond the reach of antitrust action. However, if similar actions result in prices or policies that cannot be convincingly explained by independent action, then lack of evidence of formal agreement may not ensure freedom from antitrust prosecution.

Recent Developments

Cereals Case In 1972, the Federal Trade Commission initiated a "shared monopoly" case involving the three largest manufacturers of breakfast cereal, Kellogg, General Mills, and General Foods [*FTC* v. *Kellogg et al.*].[29] The Commission's complaint

[27]*Theatre Enterprises, Inc.* v. *Paramount Film Distributing Corp. et al.,* 346 U.S. 537 (1954).
[28]Ibid., p. 541.
[29]*FTC* v. *Kellogg et al.,* Docket No. 8883, (1972).

alleged that "proliferating brands, differentiating similar products and promoting trademarks through intensive advertising result in high barriers to entry into the ready-to-eat cereal market." Between 1950 and 1972 the leading manufacturers introduced more than 80 new brands of cereal. The Commission contended that, although there were many kinds of cereal, small groups of brands might constitute oligopolistic markets, because they represented a product space or type of cereal that consumers viewed as different. The Commission argued that the leading manufacturers had introduced so many new brands that these product spaces were nearly filled, reducing the opportunities for new entrants. The FTC further argued that existing firms had a tacit understanding not to react with price cuts to the introduction of new brands by their leading rivals; however, the agreement did not necessarily apply to new entrants. It was also alleged that the cumulative effects of past advertising have differentiated the products of existing producers and further restricted the chances for new entry.

The FTC proposed that five new firms be created by requiring the three leading firms to divest themselves of certain brands and trademarks. In addition, the industry leaders would be forced to license other firms to use their trademarks on a royalty-free basis. The only restriction was that licensees be willing to meet quality-control standards. [30]

The case fits the tacit collusion category because there was no allegation that the firms had formed explicit agreements to promote their interests. Rather, the FTC explored the possibility that cereal manufacturers had created a shared monopoly by implicit understandings built up over years of operation. The case attracted considerable criticism. In fact, certain members of Congress threatened to introduce legislation forcing the Commission to drop the action. At the recommendation of one of their administrative law judges, the FTC commissioners dismissed the suit in early 1982.

Price Signaling   Some of the benefits of formal collusion can be achieved by "price signaling." This practice often involves press releases by firms about the need for price changes or announcements about impending changes. A recent Federal Trade Commission order involving the du Pont Co. and Ethyl Corp. is a good example. In 1983, the Commission ruled that the two companies had illegally signaled price changes for antiknock compounds used in gasoline.

Industry practice was to give purchasers 30 days notice of any change in prices. But du Pont and Ethyl began to announce new prices a few days in advance of the 30-day period. This allowed one firm to determine how the other would react to the change. If the competitor didn't follow suit, there was still time to adjust the price before it became binding. In this way, it was possible to achieve nearly uniform prices for the antiknock compounds.

The FTC ruling prohibited du Pont and Ethyl from announcing a price change before a date agreed upon between the companies and the purchasers. This provision was designed to prevent the firms from "testing the waters" with respect to their prices. The intent was to increase price competition in the industry.

---

[30]For an analysis of the cereals case, see Schmalensee, R., "Entry Deterrence in the Ready-to-Eat Cereal Industry," *Bell Journal of Economics,* Vol. 9, No. 2 (Autumn 1978), pp. 305–327.

Actions against price signaling are a recent development in antitrust enforcement. A potential legal problem of such actions is that prohibitions against the dissemination of information may violate the constitutional right of free speech. In February 1984, a Federal appeals court overturned the FTC's ruling. At this writing, the Supreme Court has not yet ruled on the issue.

SUMMARY
The Decision to Collude

Factors Affecting the Success of Collusion A number of factors affect the ability of firms to formulate and maintain successful collusive agreements. A small number of sellers, homogeneous products, observable selling practices, and well-established relationships between managers all facilitate collusion. In contrast, collusion is more difficult when firms are of near equal size, product orders are large and infrequent, information flows between firms are impeded, and fixed costs are large in relation to variable costs.

Benefits and Costs of Collusion The decisions to collude reflect a benefit-cost calculation by the firms involved. The potential benefit is increased profits. Costs of collusion include setting and changing prices, losses from cheating, nonprice competition, and legal penalties. The magnitude of price increases and the methods used to collude depend on the probability and consequences of getting caught.

Explicit Collusion and the Law

Price Fixing The courts have refused to accept the "reasonableness" of price fixing agreements as a defense in antitrust cases. Explicit collusion is a violation of the law without regard to its effects. One of the most important deterrents to collusion is the possibility of treble damage suits that may result.

A high percentage of price-fixing convictions involve trade associations. The courts have used a rule-of-reason standard in judging trade association activities. Unless there is evidence of coercion or if the information gathering and dissemination facilitates collusion, the courts usually have accepted trade association activities.

Collusion and the Learned Professions Professions such as law, medicine, and dentistry historically have received lenient treatment under antitrust laws. Recently, however, the courts have taken a much stronger stand against price fixing, advertising bans, and other restrictive practices by the learned professions.

Other Collusive Activities Geographical division of markets by independent firms is a per se violation of the law. Group boycotts intended to eliminate competition are also unlawful. Boycotts designed to improve trade practices are decided by a rule-of-reason standard. Boycotts for moral or social objectives are usually not challenged under antitrust statutes.

Tacit Collusion and the Law

Dominant-Firm Price Leadership   If a dominant firm does not use its market power to force smaller firms to follow its pricing practices and if there is no evidence of collusion between the firms in the industry, then price leadership by a dominant firm is not usually considered an antitrust violation.

Oligopolistic Interdependence and Conscious Parallelism   Similar pricing or other business practices by firms in a concentrated industry do not necessarily constitute illegal activity. A successful defense can be based on a demonstration that circumstances exist that would have caused the firms to come to the same decision acting independently.

Recent Developments   A much-criticized FTC case involving an alleged "shared monopoly" among cereal manufacturers was recently dismissed by the agency. In contrast, a 1983 Commission order prohibited "price signaling," which allowed firms to avoid price competition by announcing price changes before they became effective. However, the legal status of such signaling has not been finally determined.

DISCUSSION QUESTIONS

1. How does geographic proximity affect the ability of firms to collude?
2. When would firms be most likely to cheat on a price-fixing agreement, during a recession or during a time of general prosperity? Why?
3. What did the Supreme Court mean by the statement that "the reasonable price fixed today may through economic and business changes become the unreasonable price of tomorrow"?
4. Why are trade associations so often involved in collusive agreements?
5. Will allowing lawyers and doctors to advertise decrease the quality of their services? Should there be restrictions on the types of advertising permitted?
6. How might the number of defendants affect the court's decision in a case involving parallel behavior?
7. Suppose that collusion has effectively eliminated price competition. What types of nonprice competition may emerge as a substitute? Can collusion effectively suppress all forms of competition?

chapter *8*

Price Discrimination and Restrictive Practices

Chapter Outline

". . . to give the little business fellows a square deal." [1]

Monopoly and merger prosecutions are designed to prevent firms from charging too high a price. Laws against collusion make it difficult for all firms to charge the same price. But statutes dealing with price discrimination restrict firms from setting their prices too low. What is the poor corporate executive to do?

The theory and judicial treatment of price discrimination is the topic of the first section of this chapter. The remainder of the chapter considers restrictive practices that may have the effect of limiting competition. Three such practices are considered. They are:

1. Tying contracts—the requirement that a buyer purchase one product as a condition for obtaining another.
2. Exclusive dealing—an agreement to purchase some or all inputs from a single source.
3. Territorial limitations—exclusive market areas assigned by a firm to its distributors.

PRICE DISCRIMINATION

Price discrimination occurs when customers are charged different prices for a product or service and that difference cannot be accounted for by the variation in the cost of providing the product to the buyers. Three conditions are required for successful price discrimination. First, a firm must have market power that enables it to set prices. Second, there must be classes of consumers with different demand elasticities. Figure 8.1 illustrates a simple market with two classes of consumers. Assume for simplicity that the two classes represent different cities. Further assume that the unit cost of providing the product is constant and equal in both cities. Finally, assume that the demand for the product in the first city is more elastic than the demand in the second city.

If a single firm has a monopoly in both cities it will maximize its profits by equating marginal revenue and marginal cost and setting the monopoly price in each market. Notice that the price is much higher in the second city where demand is less elastic. Consumers in that city pay a higher price for the product even though it costs the firm no more to provide them with the product than it does those in the first city.

If it were possible for consumers in the first city to buy the product and sell it to residents of the second, then there would be no price discrimination. As long as there was a price differential it would pay people in the first city to buy the product at the low price and sell it in the second city at a price slightly lower than that offered by the monopolist. In the absence of transportation costs this process would continue until prices were the same in each city. Thus, the third condition for successful price discrimination is that the markets be separated in a way that prevents arbitrage.

[1]Representative Wright Patman commenting on the purpose of the legislation that bears his name. "Robinson-Patman: Dodo or Golden Rule?" *Business Week,* Nov. 12, 1966, p. 66.

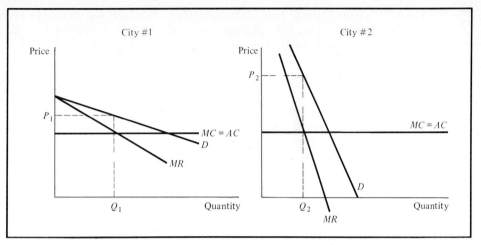

Figure 8.1. Price discrimination.

Benefits: Resource Allocation

The term *price discrimination* usually carries a purely negative connotation and is associated with greedy attempts to gouge the consumer for every extra cent. However, there are some aspects of price discrimination that may be beneficial to society. Consider a monopolist with cost and demand curves as shown in Figure 8.2.

If the monopolist maximizes profits by setting a single price, the optimum price is P_m and demand will be Q_m. Too little of the product is produced because the value of the last unit purchased (as measured by the price, P_m, paid by the final consumer) is considerably greater than the marginal cost of its production. Social welfare would be increased if production were expanded to Q_D, where marginal production costs are just equal to the price at which the last unit could be sold.

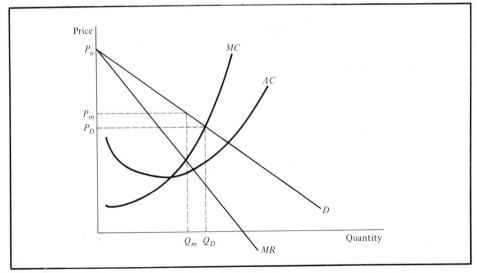

Figure 8.2. Resource allocation and price discrimination.

Now suppose that the monopolist is in a situation to charge every consumer a price equal to the full value that the buyer attaches to each unit of the product. The first unit will be sold at P_u and subsequent units at lower prices to buyers who value them less. The firm will continue to produce as long as there are buyers who will pay more than the marginal cost of production. Production stops at Q_D, where the demand and marginal-cost curves intersect. The firm is much better off than if it had charged a uniform price because it has sold Q_m units at prices greater than or equal to P_m, and additional units at prices greater than marginal cost. From the standpoint of overall resource allocation there has also been an improvement. Output of the product has been increased until the value of the last unit sold equals the marginal cost of its production. The optimal amount of output is now being produced.

The effect of price discrimination on individual consumers varies with the identity of the purchaser. The buyers of the first Q_m units have not benefited, because they have paid a price equal to or greater than the uniform price, P_m, which they would have paid without price discrimination. On the other hand, those buyers who value the product less than P_m but more than P_D are better off because they can purchase a product that previously was available only at a price greater than their individual valuations.

Discrimination can also be beneficial as a spur to competition. In industries where collusion (explicit or tacit) has blunted price competition, discrimination can be the wedge that opens the door to active competition. Firms that make selective price cuts to curry the favor of specific buyers may create an atmosphere where rivals respond with selective price cuts of their own. Ultimately, a general reduction in prices may result.

Costs: Predatory Pricing

On the other hand, price discrimination may be a means of discouraging entry and weakening existing competitors. Predatory pricing is an example. Consider the case of a large firm selling a single product in a number of distinct geographical markets. In some of the markets the firm has a monopoly, while in others it faces competition from smaller rivals operating only in a single area. The large firm can cut prices below cost in competitive markets and subsidize its losses from monopoly profits earned where the firm is the only seller. The smaller firms may be forced into bankruptcy or merger if the dominant firm keeps its prices down. When the smaller firms have either gone out of business or been acquired, prices are set at the monopoly level. Potential entrants to a market can also be deterred by the threat of predatory pricing. If the existing firm can create a credible threat that it will cut prices below cost to meet competition from new entrants, then all but the largest potential competitors may be frightened off. Used in this manner, predatory pricing may be a useful tactic to prevent entry in an industry where natural barriers are not effective.

The effectiveness of predatory pricing has been questioned.[2] One criticism is that

---

[2]See McGee, J. S., "Predatory Price Cutting: The Standard Oil (N.J.) Case," *Journal of Law and Economics,* Vol. 1 (Oct. 1958), pp. 137–169. See also Koller, R. H., "The Myth of Predatory Pricing: An Empirical Study," *Antitrust Law and Economics Review,* Vol. 4, No. 4 (Summer 1971), pp. 105–123.

merger is usually a superior alternative. Rather than absorb the initial losses resulting from predatory pricing, the large firm should merge with its competitors, set the monopoly price, and immediately share the spoils with its new partners. This is especially relevant, because the dominant firm, having a much larger market share, will suffer greater losses from sales below cost than will smaller firms. Another shortcoming of predatory pricing is that forcing other firms into bankruptcy may not be effective, because the physical capacity of the firms remains and can be purchased by other entrepreneurs who desire to enter the industry. Similarly, management talent will reappear if it is not co-opted through merger.

It may be true that a firm's immediate objectives are better served by merger than by predatory pricing. However, before dismissing the effectiveness of predatory pricing, the strategic benefits must be considered. Usually, mergers do not occur instantaneously with the acquired firm immediately accepting the first offer of the acquiring corporation. A period of bargaining takes place during which each firm attempts to strike the best deal. In some cases there may be no mutually acceptable price and, hence, no merger. The initiation or even the threat of below-cost pricing may accelerate the bargaining process and affect the price that the smaller firm is finally willing to accept. In general, a large firm with a reputation for predation will engender less aggressive competition from actual and potential rivals than will a firm known for its beneficence. Thus, the use or threatened use of predatory pricing may be strategically significant.

Price Discrimination and the Robinson-Patman Act

Provisions   The Clayton Act prohibited price discrimination where the effect "may be to substantially lessen competition." The restriction was qualified by the provision that price differentials stemming from differences in the quality of the product or the quantity sold were not unlawful. The quantity exemption was galling to small businesspeople who found themselves unable to compete with chain stores and other large enterprises. In 1936 the Robinson-Patman Act was passed as an amendment to Section 2 of the Clayton Act. The act has four main provisions:

1. Brokerage fees are illegal unless an independent broker is involved. A common practice of the 1930s was to give large purchasers a discount equal to the wholesaler's fee if they bought directly from the supplier rather than through a middleman.
2. Discounts, free advertising, promotional allowances, and the like cannot be provided to one buyer unless the same concessions are offered to all.
3. It is not lawful to sell at a lower price in one area than in another if the intent is to "destroy competition or eliminate a competitor."
4. Other forms of discrimination, such as quantity discounts, may be restricted if they have a substantial effect in lessening competition. The FTC is given power to set maximum quantity discounts.

The legislation also implies defenses that a firm charged with illegal price discrimination may use to exonerate itself. First, the firm may argue that price differences simply reflect variations in the cost of providing the product to individual buyers. Prices charged by a Los Angeles-based firm could be lower to a customer in Los Angeles than for a buyer in San Francisco. Second, price cutting to dispose of perishable or obsolescent goods or as part of an action by the firm to leave the industry is permitted. Selling last year's automobile models below cost is an example. Third, the defendant may assert that its prices were set "in good faith to meet an equally low price of a competitor." Faced with the potential loss of an important customer, a special deal could be offered to meet the competition. Fourth, price discrimination may be overlooked if it does not have a substantial effect in lessening competition. The courts typically do not deal in "trifles." Finally, a firm may contend that goods sold at different prices do not meet the statutory requirement of being "of like grade and quality." Lower prices can be charged for goods that are less desirable.

Judicial Interpretation   Price discrimination may be categorized in terms of primary-line and secondary-line discrimination. *Primary-line discrimination* involves harm to firms competing to sell the same product as the firm charged with discrimination. The most common example of primary-line discrimination occurs when a large seller sets different prices for its product in separate geographical markets, and the difference cannot be explained by variations in cost. *Predatory pricing* is an extreme example of primary-line discrimination whereby the price in some areas is actually set below cost. *Secondary-line discrimination* occurs when a buyer is granted a preferential price and, as a result, its competitors are injured. An illustration is a low price charged by a food distributor to a large grocery chain. Unable to purchase goods at a comparable price, small stores may not be competitive.

Primary-line discrimination   The Utah Pie case is an interesting and important illustration of the judicial system's treatment of primary-line discrimination [*Utah Pie* v. *Continental Baking* (1967)].[3] The Utah Pie Company had been selling fresh pies in the Salt Lake City area for many years. In 1956, Carnation Milk, Pet Milk, and Continental Baking began shipping frozen pies into the region. Utah Pie was a small, single-product firm with sales primarily in Utah, while the other three firms had broad product lines and sold in nationwide markets.

In 1958 Utah Pie's own frozen pie plant opened and the firm soon captured about two-thirds of the local market. Carnation, Pet, and Continental responded by drastically reducing their prices in the Salt Lake City area. In some cases the three large firms charged prices in Utah that were lower than those in markets closer to their points of manufacture. The immediate result was that Utah Pie's market share dropped to about one-third of the market in 1959. The Utah firm retaliated by filing a private antitrust suit requesting treble damages. The Supreme Court, hearing the case on appeal, found evidence of price discrimination with predatory intent and ordered the case remanded to a lower court for the determination of damages.

The Utah Pie decision has been criticized because of its failure to consider the

---

[3]*Utah Pie* v. *Continental Baking,* 386 U.S. 685 (1967). The consequences of the Utah Pie decision are considered by Elzinga, K. G., and Hogarty, T. F., "Utah Pie and the Consequences of Robinson-Patman," *Journal of Law and Economics,* Vol. 21, No. 2 (Oct. 1978), pp. 427–434.

dominance of Utah Pie in the market. Justice Stewart, in a dissenting opinion, argued that the Court had once again missed the distinction between injury to competition and injury to competitors. He contended that the case should have been decided on a single issue:

> Did the respondents' actions have the anticompetitive effect required by the statute as an element of a cause of action?

Stewart concluded that the anticompetitive effect was not demonstrated by the evidence:

> The Court's own description of the Salt Lake City frozen pie market from 1958 through 1961 shows that the answer to that question must be no. In 1958 Utah Pie had a quasi-monopolistic 66.5% of the market. In 1961—after the alleged predations of the respondents—Utah Pie still had a commanding 45.3%, Pet had 29.4%, and the remainder of the market was divided almost equally between Continental, Carnation, and other, small local bakers. Unless we disregard the lessons so laboriously learned in scores of Sherman and Clayton Act cases, the 1961 situation has to be considered more competitive than that of 1958. Thus, if we assume that the price discrimination proven against the respondents had any effect on competition, that effect must have been beneficent.

> The Court has fallen into the error of reading the Robinson-Patman Act as protecting competitors, instead of competition. . . . Lower prices are the hallmark of intensified competition. . . . I cannot hold that Utah Pie's monopolistic position was protected by the federal antitrust laws from effective price competition, and I therefore respectfully dissent. [4]

Ultimately, the parties agreed to a negotiated settlement. Although Utah Pie won the case, evidently the firm didn't strike a very good bargain, because it was forced into bankruptcy and out of business in five years. It should also be observed that none of the three defendants in the case has been able to achieve a high market share of frozen pie sales. The industry remains very competitive.

The *Utah Pie* case indicates that firms can be prosecuted for predatory pricing. The problem comes in defining what is meant by the term. There is general agreement that predatory pricing involves pricing below cost. But what is the relevant measure of cost? Does predation involve pricing below average total cost, average variable cost, or short-run marginal cost? The choice can be critical to the outcome of a case. A price set below average total cost may be above average variable cost. Conversely, a price that covers short-run marginal costs could be well below both average total and average variable cost. Figure 8.3 shows the relationship between these three measures of cost.

The courts have not been entirely consistent in defining predatory pricing. A number of decisions used average total cost as the lower limit for prices. Others have set average variable cost as the standard. Some opinions relied on profit rates rather than price-cost relationships. For example, an appeals court overturned a judgment

[4]386 U.S. 685, 705.

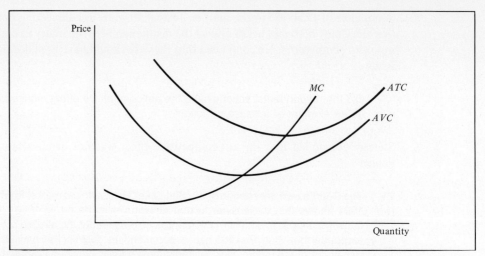

Figure 8.3.   Three measures of cost.

against IBM based on evidence that the firm had consistently earned over a 20-percent return on equipment that had allegedly been priced below cost.[5]

Many recent court decisions incorporate ideas contained in an important article by Areeda and Turner.[6] From a resource allocation perspective, these authors argue that short-run marginal costs are the appropriate standard. But from a practical point of view, they suggest the use of average variable costs.

Areeda and Turner give several reasons for preferring average variable costs. First, it is often impossible to obtain accurate marginal cost data. In many industries, average variable costs may be a reasonable approximation for marginal costs. Second, in the short run, average variable costs represent the threshold between continuing to produce and shutting down an operation. If price is below average variable cost, an entrepreneur can cut his losses by ceasing to produce. However, if price exceeds average variable cost, then it is better to continue producing even if price is below average total cost. The reason is that the excess can be used to pay a portion of the fixed costs. Thus, a price that is above average variable costs but below average total cost can be justified in its own right. In contrast, a firm that sets its price below average variable cost and continues to produce may be viewed as having other motives such as the exclusion of rivals.

The use of average variable costs as a price floor is not universally accepted. Some argue that if firms with "deep pockets" are allowed to set prices below average total costs, they may drive efficient, but smaller, rivals from the market. Because they can sustain losses for a long period of time, these large firms may be able to outlast their smaller competitors.

Average total cost is the most commonly suggested alternative to the Areeda-Turner position. Advocates argue that a firm with prices that cover average total cost

[5]*Telex Corp.* v. *International Business Machines Corp.,* 510 F. 2nd 894 (10th Cir. 1975).
[6]Areeda, P. and Turner, D.F., "Predatory Pricing and Related Practices Under Section 2 of the Sherman Act," 88 *Harvard Law Review* (1975), pp. 697–733.

is not in a position to eliminate equally efficient rivals. Frequently, they also suggest that the courts consider intent. That is, if price is found to be below average total cost, then the court should look for evidence indicating that the firm's pricing policies were designed to exclude competitors.

There seems to be a trend toward acceptance of the Areeda-Turner standard for defining predatory pricing. A number of decisions by appellate courts have defined predation in terms of pricing below average variable costs. However, the issue is far from resolved. Minority opinions in some of these cases have been sharply critical of the approach.[7]

Secondary-line discrimination   Historically, the courts have taken a tough stand against secondary-line discrimination. One reason may be that the legislative intent in passing the Robinson-Patman Act was to protect small retailers. A leading secondary-line case involved the pricing of salt [*FTC* v. *Morton Salt Co.* (1948)].[8] The Morton Salt Company is a major seller of salt. In the 1940s, the firm used the following pricing scale for high-grade salt:

Less-than-carload purchases	$1.60 per case
Carload purchases	1.50 per case
5,000-case purchase in any 12 consecutive months	1.40 per case
50,000-case purchase in any 12 consecutive months	1.35 per case

The schedule includes both quantity and volume discounts. The lower price for carload purchases is a quantity discount. The adjustments based on sales over a 12-month period are volume discounts reflecting cumulative purchases.

The Federal Trade Commission charged that the pricing scheme violated the Robinson-Patman Act. Morton countered that there was no discrimination because the discounts were available to all buyers on the same terms. The firm also argued that the competitive impact was insignificant because salt constitutes such a small proportion of sales in a grocery store.

The Supreme Court rejected Morton's contention that discounts were available to all customers. The Court found this to be true only in a theoretical sense. As a practical matter, only five major food chains bought enough salt in a year to qualify for the $1.35 per case price. Most customers bought less-than-carload quantities and did not receive any discount. The Court was also unwilling to accept the assertion that salt was such a trivial part of a store's purchases as to make the whole issue unimportant. The justices reasoned that a grocery store consists of many small items. Hence, the only way to protect the grocer is to assure that fair pricing practices be used for each item.

The Robinson-Patman Act does not prohibit all discounts. If the firm can demonstrate that its pricing schedule reflects differences in the cost of providing the good or service, this may be an acceptable defense against the charge of price discrimination.

---

[7]See, for example, "Laws Against Predatory Pricing Are Being Relaxed in Many Court Rulings," *Wall Street Journal,* July 14, 1982, p. 50.
[8]*Federal Trade Commission* v. *Morton Salt Co.,* 334 U.S. 3 (1948).

For example, in the Morton Case it is likely that the quantity discount for carload purchases could have been at least partially justified by reduced handling and shipping expenses. However, the volume discount based on cumulative purchases over a year's time is less defensible in terms of cost savings.

Impact   Most students of antitrust would agree that the Robinson-Patman Act has done more to retard than to promote competition. There have been many efforts to repeal or modify the law, but lobbying efforts by the owners of small businesses have so far been effective in preventing change. Over the years the Federal Trade Commission has initiated a large number of Robinson-Patman suits, but in recent times the agency has backed off. Today, most price discrimination cases are private actions.

RESTRICTIVE PRACTICES

Section 3 of the Clayton Act forbids the sale or lease of commodities on the condition that the buyer or lessee not use or deal in the products of competitors. Among the restrictive practices prohibited by this section are tied sales and exclusive dealing. Tied sales, or tying contracts, are arrangements whereby the purchaser of one product is required to buy a second product as well. Exclusive dealing involves agreements by firms to purchase one or more inputs from a single supplier.[9] Vertical territorial limitations are a third type of restrictive practice. The term refers to restrictions imposed by firms on the market areas in which their distributors may operate.

Tying Contracts

Broadly defined, most purchases involve tied sales. Go to a department store and try to buy just a right shoe. Get a car dealer to sell only the chassis of a new Chevrolet. Convince the school's ticket manager to sell a ticket for just the first quarter of the big football game. In each case the purchaser can get what he wants, but must pay for the entire package. Although thousands of everyday transactions are actually a forced combination of individual products, the legal treatment of tied sales ignores these conventional practices. Instead, the policy toward tying agreements focuses on products that are conventionally and conveniently sold separately.

Incentives for Tied Sales   There are a number of reasons why firms promote tying contracts. The most commonly suggested are:

1. *Leverage.* Suppose a firm has a monopoly over the sale of product *A* and that product *B* is marketed competitively. By tying the sale of product *A* to the purchase of product *B* it is alleged that the firm can leverage or extend its monopoly power into the second market. The analysis of this assertion is similar to that of vertical integration, as discussed in Chapter 6. First consider the case of products used in fixed proportions. If, for example, one unit of

[9]Tying contracts and exclusive dealing may also violate the Sherman Act.

A must always be used with one unit of *B,* then the tie will not create additional market power, because the producer can extract the full monopoly profit by its pricing of product *A.* There is no need to force buyers to purchase both products since *B* is not useful without *A.* The real problem is the firm's monopoly power in the market for product *A* and not the existence of the tying arrangement.

Where products can be combined in variable proportions, the analysis is more complex. If the firm sets a high price for *A,* purchasers may substitute some *B* for *A.* However, if the firm can somehow tie the sale of *A* and *B* together, there may be a pricing scheme that is more profitable than the unrestricted sale of *A* alone. Evaluation of the variable proportions case requires situation-specific consideration of independent versus tied sales to determine the implications of each.

2. *Price Discrimination.* Tying contracts may be a convenient method of increasing profits through price discrimination. A traditional example is copying paper and copying machines. Copiers are usually sold at a uniform price. However, an establishment that makes 10,000 copies per month will probably attach greater value to the machine than a firm that makes only 100 copies each month. If the firms are required to purchase all of their copying paper from the manufacturer of the copying machine, then it is possible to discriminate on the basis of intensity of use. Although each firm pays the same amount to obtain the machine, by charging a high price for paper the greater value of the copier to the high-use firm can be exploited and total profits increased. Price discrimination doesn't allow the seller to extend its market power to copying paper, but does increase the profitability of the existing degree of market power. Used as a method for price discrimination, tying contracts actually may improve resource allocation by increasing output as discussed earlier in the chapter.

3. *Quality Control.* To assure proper operations of machines, firms sometimes require that a purchaser of complex equipment use only supplies provided by the firm. If inferior or incompatible supplies are used, the machine may not function properly. Often, the failure of the equipment is blamed on the manufacturer rather than on poor supplies. To protect its good name a firm may require a tied sale to assure quality control. The need for tying contracts to assure quality depends on the feasibility of alternative arrangements. It may be possible to achieve the same results by specifying minimum standards for supplies or by recommending specific manufacturers. If reasonable alternatives exist, then the net social benefits of tying contracts are dubious.

4. *Efficiency Gains.* By selling products jointly, firms may realize savings on shipping, billing, handling, and so forth. If these savings result in prices lower than those offered by firms selling each of the products separately, then society is benefited.

5. *Avoidance of Price Controls.* Suppose that price controls have been imposed on product *A.* By tying *A* and *B* together it may be possible to charge a high price for *B* while staying below the price ceiling on *A.*

6. *Cheating on a Cartel.* Lumping the sale of two products together allows the individual prices to be concealed. If a cartel has fixed the price for one product, an effective mechanism for cheating is to shave the price of the tied product.

7. *Barriers to Entry.* If products are sold as a package, competitors may find it

difficult to enter the markets for either product individually. Forced to enter at both levels, entry may be prevented or delayed.

Tying Contracts and the Courts   An important early tying case involved IBM [*International Business Machines* v. *United States* (1936)].[10] In the 1930s, IBM was the dominant producer of mechanical data processing equipment, with a market share of over 90 percent. The firm had adopted the practice of requiring lessees to use only IBM tabulating cards. IBM argued that the restriction was necessary because the use of other cards might cause their machines to malfunction. The Supreme Court found that there were other manufacturers capable of producing high-quality cards. The Court also held that the market power of IBM resulted in a substantial share of the market for cards being foreclosed to other producers. IBM was required to modify its marketing practices, but the order was relatively ineffective, as the firm continued to dominate the market for both tabulating machines and tabulating cards.

Over the years the courts have taken an increasingly hard line against tying contracts. In 1949 the American Can Company was required to terminate its policy of forcing buyers of can-closing machines to use its cans [*United States* v. *American Can Co.* (1949)].[11] In *Northern Pacific Railway* v. *United States* (1958) the Sherman Act was used to prohibit the practice of selling and leasing railroad land on the condition that commodities produced on the land be shipped by Northern Pacific.[12] A 1962 decision prohibited the owners of a film library from selling films as a package without giving television networks the opportunity to select films individually [*United States* v. *Loew's* (1962)].[13] More recently, Twentieth Century-Fox pleaded no contest to a charge of violating a 1951 consent decree under which the firm agreed not to engage in block booking. In order to purchase the phenomenally popular *Star Wars,* theatre owners had been required to purchase a much less popular movie, *The Other Side of Midnight.*[14]

The Court's present treatment of tie-ins is not quite a strict per se interpretation of the law, but not really a full blown rule-of-reason inquiry either. When a tying contract involves a firm or firms with substantial market power or when a substantial share of the market is foreclosed by the agreement, then the practice is likely to be prohibited. However, there are possible defenses available to the firm. A corporation may be able to demonstrate that the tie-in is for the purpose of assuring quality control. This argument will be accepted only if there is no other feasible way of maintaining quality. A second defense is that the tied sale is designed to allow a small firm to establish its position in a new market. Although the courts may consider mitigating factors, the present tendency is to strike down tying contracts as serving no valid social purpose.

However, as with other aspects of antitrust, the status of tied sales depends not only on the position of the courts, but also on the frequency with which enforcement agencies file suit. Within the Reagan administration there has been little enthusiasm

[10]*International Business Machines* v. *United States,* 298 U.S. 131 (1936).
[11]*United States* v. *American Can Co.,* 87 F. Supp. 18 (N.D. Cal. 1949).
[12]*Northern Pacific Railway Co.* v. *United States,* 356 U.S. 1 (1958).
[13]*United States* v. *Loew's, Inc.,* 371 U.S. 38 (1962).
[14]*United States* v. *Twentieth Century-Fox Film Corp.,* 78 CR 641 (ELP), Sept. 12, 1978.

for prosecuting tying contracts. The view has been that this practice rarely results in significant harm to consumers. Under a different regime, the mood may be quite different.

Exclusive Dealing: Requirements Contracts and Franchising

Two forms of exclusive dealing are considered in this section—requirements contracts and franchise agreements. Firms that agree to purchase one or more of their inputs from a single supplier have entered into a *requirements contract.* An auto manufacturer who makes a long-term commitment to obtain aluminum only from Alcoa would fit this definition. Establishments with arrangements whereby they purchase all of their important supplies and use the trademark of a particular firm have entered into a *franchise agreement.* The local McDonald's is an example.

Effects of Requirements Contracts   Requirements contracts can benefit both the supplier and the purchaser. The supplier is guaranteed a market for his product. This facilitates long-term planning and allows a reduction in marketing expenditures. The buyer is protected against a disruption in supply and has some assurance of constant quality and stable price (depending on the terms of the agreement). However, requirements contracts may impose hardships on competing suppliers. If the agreement involves a large amount of the product or service, then other suppliers may find it difficult to compete. The possible foreclosure of markets is the primary objection to requirements contracts.

Effects of Franchising   Nearly 40 percent of retail sales in the United States are made by franchised businesses. Franchises are particularly common in fast foods, hotels and motels, and auto renting and sales. The franchise offers the greatest advantage when there are economies of scale in establishing and promoting a product that does not match economies of production and sales. The fast-foods industry meets these criteria. There are scale economies in convincing people to go to McDonald's, but not in slapping together a Big Mac. The same is true for hotels and motels and for auto sales and rentals. Local entrepreneurs benefit from franchise arrangements by being allowed to operate under a regionally or nationally known trademark that is promoted by an extensive advertising campaign. Usually, they also are guaranteed some degree of territorial protection against intrabrand competition (e.g., the right to be the only McDonalds's in a given geographical area). In return for these considerations, the local businessperson shares profits with the owner of the trademark. This is accomplished by payment of an original fee to obtain the franchise, royalty payments on sales, and, perhaps, being required to pay a surcharge on supplies obtained from the franchiser.

For the trademark owner, a franchise arrangement is an alternative to vertical integration. The franchise arrangement may be preferable, because of the quality of management skills that can be obtained. Because the local entrepreneur has a personal stake in the success of the enterprise, he or she may be willing to work longer and harder than a hired manager. Also, by delegating day-to-day operations to someone from the local area, the business becomes more responsive to the particular needs of the community in which it is located. In some cases franchising is simply a transitionary step between independent ownership and full vertical integration. Franchise owners are allowed to bear the initial risk and then the parent organization steps in later to purchase the most profitable outlets. [15]

Like requirements contracts, franchising forecloses market opportunities of independent suppliers. If the local Burger King is obligated to purchase its sauces and syrups from a single source, then independent wholesalers must look elsewhere to make sales. Franchise agreements also reduce *intra* brand competition if they guarantee each establishment its own territory. However, where *inter* brand competition is active, there may be little social harm. If Burger King is an effective competitor against McDonald's, then the fact that there is only one of each in a small town may not be too serious. It's true that multiple outlets in the town would compete against one another, but the parent firm could prevent this from occurring through vertical integration. Certainly, franchising does not restrict competition any more than would vertical integration.

Requirements Contracts and the Courts   During the 1940s, Standard Oil of California entered into contracts with independent gasoline retailers whereby Standard provided all of their gasoline and, under some of the contracts, other supplies such as tires, tubes, and batteries, as well. Standard produced nearly a quarter of all gasoline sold in the seven Western states, but the independent dealers involved had less than 7 percent of total sales. Although the market share of the independent dealers was not large in relative terms, it represented nearly $60 million in annual gasoline sales. Ruling that the requirements contracts had foreclosed a "substantial share of the line of commerce affected," the Supreme Court rule against the arrangements [*Standard Oil of Calif. et al.* v. *United States* (1949)]. [16]

In 1961 the Court was called upon to decide a breach of contract suit between Tampa Electric and Nashville Coal [*Tampa Electric Co.* v. *Nashville Coal Co.* (1961)]. [17] Tampa had agreed to purchase all of its coal requirements for a new generation site from Nashville. The contract was for 20 years, but an increase in the price of coal made the arrangement unprofitable for Nashville. The coal company attempted to break the contract on the grounds that it violated antitrust laws. The case turned on the definition of the market. Nashville argued that there was a substantial foreclosure of the market, because the volume of coal involved was equal to total coal sales in the Florida peninsula. Tampa proposed that the market be defined to include the production of coal in an eight-state area. The Supreme Court accepted the latter definition, which put the amount of coal sales foreclosed at about 1 percent of the total. Based on this market definition the contract was upheld.

Requirements contracts are judged on a rule-of-reason standard. The courts weigh the anticompetitive effect of market foreclosure versus the efficiency gains resulting from the arrangement. In general, if a contract involves a concentrated industry (especially where entry is difficult) and forecloses a substantial share of the market to other suppliers, it is likely to be held in violation of Section 3 of the Clayton Act or

[15]An excellent discussion of franchising is found in Caves, R. E., and Murphy, W. F., "Franchising: Firms, Markets, and Intangible Assets," *Southern Economic Journal,* Vol. 42, No. 4 (Apr. 1976), pp. 572–586.

[16]*Standard Oil Co. of California et al.,* v. *United States,* 293, 314 (1949).

[17]*Tampa Electric Co.* v. *Nashville Coal Co. et al.,* 365 U.S. 320 (1961).

Section 1 of the Sherman Act. The length of the agreement is also a factor. Requirements contracts of long duration are more likely to be prohibited than are short-term arrangements. If the agreement is for a relatively short period, then at the termination of the contract other suppliers have the opportunity to compete by offering better terms.

Franchising and the Courts   As witnessed by their popularity, franchise arrangements usually are legal. However, they may run afoul of the law if the local franchises are required to purchase supplies or equipment only from the parent organization. An important case involved a fast-food chain, Chicken Delight [*Siegel* v. *Chicken Delight, Inc.* (1972)]. [18] The firm had licensed several hundred franchisees to operate under its trademark. There was no franchise fee and the local outlets did not have to pay royalties based on their sales. However, Chicken Delight did require its franchise holders to purchase cookers and fryers and certain packaging supplies from the parent firm. These purchases were made at prices above those charged by competing suppliers of the products. A private suit by one of the local outlets charged that this practice illegally tied the sale of the Chicken Delight trademark to the purchase of supplies.

Basic issues in the case were whether the firm had sufficient market power in the tying product to restrain trade in the tied product, whether a substantial volume of commerce was foreclosed, and whether there were any justifications for the scheme. With respect to the first two issues, the Court held the trademark conferred market power and that competition was restrained. On the third, Chicken Delight argued that its policy was necessary to assure that the quality of food turned out by the franchises would guarantee the good name of the parent firm. Disagreeing, the Court ruled that the equipment and supplies were not so specialized as to preclude their purchase from other sources. Hence, the tying arrangement was found to violate the law, in this case the Sherman Act. However, the Court did admit that there may be supplies and equipment that are sufficiently important for quality control and for which there are no good alternative sources of supply so as to justify the requirement that they be purchased only from the franchiser. In general, recent decisions have attempted to limit excessively restrictive practices of franchisers, while recognizing the importance of the franchise as a business form.

Territorial Limitations

Coca-Cola has a 27-percent market share of soft-drink sales. Pepsi is not far distant with a 19-percent share. But the four-firm concentration ratio for the soft-drink industry is only .15. As mentioned in Chapter 3, the explanation is that the actual sellers of soft drinks are hundreds of bottling companies around the country who have been granted licenses to use the trademarks and syrups of the parent companies. Standard industry practice is for each of these bottlers to be allocated a specific geographic market area within which they may market soft drinks.

Effect of Territorial Limitations   Territorial limitations reduce *intra* brand competition. Consider the system used by the soft-drink industry. A grocery store in New York

---

[18]*Siegel* v. *Chicken Delight, Inc.,* 448 F. 2d 43 (9th Cir. 1971), cert. denied 405 U.S. 955 (1972).

can buy Coke only from the supplier who has the New York franchise. With no alternative source, the price is likely to be higher than if competition were present. In 1973, Federal Trade Commission economists estimated that territorial limitations imposed by firms such as Coca-Cola and Pepsi cost soft-drink consumers an extra $250 million. The Commission was prepared to abolish the practice. But in response to an effective lobbying campaign, Congress passed a law that exempts the soft-drink industry from prosecution.

The issue of *intra*brand versus *inter*brand competition was first mentioned in connection with exclusive dealing. It is even more important in evaluating territorial limitations. Although such restrictions clearly limit competition for the sale of a single brand, they may increase competition between brands. A firm that guarantees an exclusive market area has a right to expect that its distributors will do a superior job in marketing the product. As the only seller, a distributor will be willing to advertise, knowing that other firms will not benefit from that advertising. Also, the prospect of an adequate profit margin should encourage distributors to provide prompt and high-quality service. These attributes all work to improve the competitive position of the product vis-à-vis other brands.

Territorial Limitations and the Courts   In judging territorial limitations, the undesirable effects of reduced *intra*brand competition should be weighed against the possible social benefits stemming from increased *inter*brand competition. However, the courts have not always been willing to use this approach. Instead, on at least one occasion, they focused on legal questions relating to property rights.

In *United States* v. *Arnold, Schwinn & Co. et al.* (1967) the Court struck down a bicycle manufacturer's marketing scheme.[19] The firm had allowed its distributors to sell only to franchised retailers within the distributor's authorized territory. The retailers were permitted to sell bicycles to the general public, but not to unfranchised retailers. An important consideration of the Court was who held legal title to the goods. If a manufacturer retained title and supplied dealers with goods on consignment, then the supplying firm had some latitude in specifying sales conditions. On the other hand, if the goods were actually sold to the dealer, then the manufacturer lost control and any restrictions imposed were considered vulnerable to antitrust challenge. In the Schwinn case, the court held that

> once the manufacturer has parted with title and risk . . . his effort thereafter to restrict territory or persons to whom the product may be transferred . . . is a per se violation of Section 1 of the Sherman Act.[20]

From an economic point of view, the Schwinn decision is difficult to defend. The anticompetitive effects of territorial limitations have nothing to do with whether goods are sold or consigned to distributors. The problem with Schwinn was recognized in a number of lower court decisions that interpreted the case very narrowly so as to limit its importance. Finally, in 1977, the Supreme court overturned the Schwinn precedent

[19] *United States* v. *Arnold, Schwinn & Co. et al.,* 388 U.S. 365 (1967).
[20] Ibid., p. 382.

with its decision in the Sylvania case [*Continental T.V., Inc., et al.* v. *GTE Sylvania* (1977)].[21]

During the early 1960s, Sylvania saw its market share for the sale of televisions drop below 2 percent. The industry is one in which marketing and servicing are extremely important. Hence, to improve the quality and commitment of its distributors, the company embarked on a policy of limiting franchised dealers to a specified market area. There is evidence that the strategy was successful. In the space of just three years Sylvania's share of the market more than doubled.

The origin of the antitrust case was a dispute with Continental, a franchisee operating out of San Francisco. Continental sought to open an outlet in Sacramento, but Sylvania refused on the grounds that the city was adequately served by existing Sylvania retailers. Continental then filed a suit charging that Sylvania's territorial limitations were an illegal restraint of trade in violation of the Sherman Act.

Writing for the Court, Justice Powell argued that the issues in Sylvania and Schwinn were very similar. His decision essentially overturned the Schwinn precedent, calling it "an abrupt and largely unexplained departure" from earlier decisions of the Court. Powell's opinion stressed the need to consider the benefits of increased interbrand competition versus the costs of reduced intrabrand competition. Basically, the Sylvania precedent establishes that territorial limitations will be judged under a rule-of-reason standard.

SUMMARY
Price Discrimination

Price discrimination occurs when differences in prices cannot be accounted for by differences in costs. Three conditions must be met for successful price discrimination —the firm must have power over price, there must be classes of consumers with different demand elasticities, and markets must be separable.

Benefits: Resource Allocation   Price discrimination may result in a more efficient allocation of resources. By expanding production until price equals marginal cost, the price discriminating monopolist produces the optimum amount of output. However, there are income distribution effects to be considered. Additional consumers benefit, but some purchasers who previously bought at a uniform price must now pay more.

Costs: Predatory Pricing   Firms operating in multiple markets can cut prices in markets where they face competition and subsidize their losses from other markets. When competition is eliminated, prices can be set at the monopoly level. Merger may be a better alternative for the firm than predatory pricing. However, the threat of predation can be an effective strategic tool for improving the terms of a merger.

Price Discrimination and the Robinson-Patman Act
Provisions   The Robinson-Patman Act amends Section 2 of the Clayton Act. It restricts the use of brokerage fees, promotional allowances, and quantity discounts.

[21]*Continental T.V., Inc., et al.* v. *GTE Sylvania Inc,* 433 U.S. 36 (1977).

Cost differentials, disposal of perishable or obsolescent goods, response to competition, and quality differences are possible defenses to the charge of price discrimination under the act.

Judicial interpretation   Primary line discrimination occurs when price differentials in different markets do not reflect variations in costs. Predatory pricing is an example, but there is disagreement as to how to define the practice. Several recent appellate court decisions have adopted the Areeda-Turner position that predatory pricing can be inferred if prices are set below average variable cost.

Secondary-line discrimination involves a lower price being granted to one buyer than to other purchasers. The courts have taken a tough stand on secondary-line discrimination when the injury to competitors has been shown to be significant. Overall, the Robinson-Patman Act has probably done more to retard than to promote competition. Presently, most cases are private suits filed by the owners of small businesses.

Restrictive Practices

Tying Contracts
Incentives for tied sales   Firms use tying contracts to (1) extend leverage in monopoly markets, (2) increase profits through price discrimination, (3) control quality, (4) reduce costs, (5) avoid price controls, (6) cheat on a cartel agreement, and (7) create barriers to entry.

Tying contracts and the courts   When a tying contract involves a firm or firms with market power or when a substantial share of the market will be foreclosed by the agreement, the practice is likely to be prohibited by the courts.

Exclusive Dealing: Requirements Contracts and Franchising
Effects of requirements contracts   Requirements contracts facilitate long-term planning, reduce marketing expenditures, guarantee supplies, and assist in assuring constant quality and stable price. However, they may foreclose markets to independent suppliers.

Effects of franchising   Local entrepreneurs benefit from a franchise by receiving the benefits of a large-scale advertising campaign and protection from intrabrand competition. The franchise owner benefits by receiving a higher quality of management with a personal stake in the success of the business. Franchises foreclose markets and restrict intrabrand competition.

Requirements contracts and the courts   Requirements contracts are judged under a rule-of-reason standard. If the contract involves a concentrated industry or forecloses a substantial share of the market, it is likely to be held illegal.

Franchising and the courts   In general, franchise agreements are legal. However, attempts to require franchises to purchase supplies only from the parent organization may violate the law. As with requirements contracts, a relevant consideration is the size of the market foreclosed to other suppliers.

Territorial Limitations

Effects of territorial limitations   Territorial restrictions reduce intrabrand competition. However, they may increase competition between brands by allowing parent firms to sell their products through more efficient and responsive distributors.

Territorial limitations and the courts   The Schwinn case focused on property rights and held that a manufacturer who actually sold goods to a dealer could not impose territorial restrictions. This precedent was overturned by the Sylvania decision, which established a rule-of-reason standard.

DISCUSSION QUESTIONS

1. Does the pricing of children's and adults' theater tickets meet the three criteria for price discrimination?
2. How would the value of a product relative to its transportation cost affect the ability of a large multimarket firm to practice predatory pricing?
3. How could treble damages be calculated in a case like Utah Pie?
4. How might a service station involved in a price fixing cartel use tied sales to cheat on the established price?
5. In the Schwinn case, the Supreme Court distinguished between goods sold to dealers and goods sent on consignment. Does this distinction make any difference with respect to the economic impact of the alternative arrangements? Explain.
6. Why should the courts prohibit requirements contracts between a parent firm and its franchises, but allow the same arrangement within a firm that is vertically integrated?
7. Why is franchising more common in fast foods than in manufacturing?
8. If the courts were to require a showing of intent in predatory pricing cases, what kinds of evidence should a prosecutor look for?

chapter **9**

Antitrust: Evaluation

Chapter Outline

. . . A higher percentage of persons convicted of violating (federal) migratory bird laws were sentenced to prison, for longer terms, than those who violated the antitrust laws.[1]

After 90 years with the Sherman Act there are still large firms with substantial market power and smaller firms combining to acquire market power. Also, collusion, price discrimination, and restrictive practices have not been eliminated. Still, it would be a mistake to conclude that antitrust efforts have not affected the development of U.S. industry. This chapter evaluates the impacts of antitrust. The first section provides additional background on the activities of the Federal Trade Commission and the Antitrust Division of the Department of Justice. The second describes the case selection process of the Antitrust Division. The third section focuses on litigation and the problem of prosecuting the "big case." In the fourth section alternative penalties and remedies are analyzed. The final section summarizes the effects of specific areas of antitrust activity.

FEDERAL ANTITRUST ENFORCEMENT AGENCIES
Antitrust Division of the Department of Justice

From 1890 to 1904 the government averaged fewer than two antitrust cases per year. One explanation for the lack of activity is that antitrust added yet another burden to already busy attorneys in the Department of Justice. In 1904 Congress appropriated funds to establish a special antitrust section. Initially, the new agency was staffed by only five attorneys. But by 1983 the Antitrust Division had grown to include over 300 lawyers and about 40 economists. Between 1973 and 1982 an average of 74 cases were filed each year.[2]

The composition of cases filed by the the Justice Department has changed substantially in recent years. Between 1890 and 1969 about one-third of all cases involved the charge of horizontal conspiracy (primarily price fixing). Allegations of monopolization were about 14 percent and merger cases represented a little over 7 percent.[3] In contrast, Table 9.1 shows the composition of cases filed between 1973 and 1982. Over that ten-year period more than two-thirds of all cases dealt with price fixing. Monopoly suits dropped to less than 5 percent of the total and merger actions increased to about 11 percent. The remaining cases involved price discrimination and various types of restrictive practices.

Federal Trade Commission

The FTC was established by the Federal Trade Commission Act of 1914. The Commission is divided into three bureaus. The Bureau of Economics is a support unit providing

[1] Assistant Attorney General Donald Baker, as quoted in "Antitrust Unit to Ask $1\frac{1}{2}$ Year Jail Terms for Most Found Guilty of Fixing Prices," *Wall Street Journal* (Nov. 22, 1976), p. 25.

[2] Department of Justice, *Comparative Analysis of Antitrust Cases Filed by Fiscal Years,* Washington, D.C.

[3] Computed from Posner, R.A., "A Statistical Study of Antitrust Enforcement," *Journal of Law and Economics* (Oct. 1970), p. 398.

**Table 9.1 COMPOSITION OF CASES FILED
BY THE DEPARTMENT OF
JUSTICE: 1973–1982**

Allegation	Number	Percent
Price fixing	515	69.2
Monopolization	34	4.5
Mergers	83	11.2
Other	112	15.1
Total	744	100.0

Source: Department of Justice, *Comparative Analysis of Antitrust Cases Filed by Fiscal Years,* Washington, D.C.

**Table 9.2 FEDERAL TRADE COMMISSION
ANTITRUST ACTIVITY:
1973–1982.**

Allegation	Number	Percent
Horizontal restraints	45	16.8
Monopolization	10	3.7
Mergers	86	32.1
Vertical restrictions	71	26.5
Price discrimination	24	9.0
Other	32	11.9
Total	268	100.0

Source: Federal Trade Commission, *FTC Unfair Competition Complaints,* Washington, D.C.

analysis and statistics. The Bureau of Consumer Protection deals with unfair business practices, such as deceptive advertising. Its activities are discussed in Chapter 17. The Bureau of Competition is the antitrust arm of the commission and is charged with the responsibility of relieving "anticompetitive pressures and restrictions on the prices and supply of goods and services to consumers."

The FTC has statutory responsibility for enforcement of the Federal Trade Commission Act and, with the Department of Justice, the Clayton Act. However, the Supreme Court has approved the use of Section 5 of the Federal Trade Commission Act in prosecuting violations (such as price fixing and group boycotts) that are covered by the Sherman Act.[4] Thus, the Commission effectively has been granted joint jurisdiction over the Sherman Act as well.

Between 1915 and 1969, over half of all Federal Trade Commission antitrust complaints involved price discrimination. During that same time period, mergers represented less than 10 percent of total actions.[5] Like the Antitrust Division, the FTC has changed its focus in recent years. Table 9.2 shows the composition of FTC suits from 1973 to 1982. During that period, Robinson-Patman violations made up only 9 percent of complaints, while merger investigations constituted almost one-third of FTC antitrust activity.

[4]See *Fashion Originator's Guild of America, Inc.* v. *FTC,* 312 U.S. 457 (1941).
[5]Computed from Posner, op. cit., pp. 370, 398.

An important difference between the Federal Trade Commission and the Department of Justice is the FTC's nonadjudicatory activities.[6] Most of the Antitrust Division's output is the product of formal litigation through the federal court system. The FTC does file suits (which are initially heard within the Commission, as described in Chapter 4), but the agency provides advisory opinions as well. These opinions give advance information as to whether a proposed course of business action violates any of the laws administered by the Commission. For example, a trade association might obtain an opinion on the legality of a contemplated information and dissemination program.

The Federal Trade Commission also issues *Trade Regulation Rules*. One limitation of formal litigation is that the precedents developed by individual cases may not be broad or conclusive enough to redirect the practices of an industry without filing additional suits. Trade regulation rules allow the Commission to act against pervasive patterns of undesirable business behavior by setting industrywide standards of conduct. An example is the rule on eyeglasses. In the past, the sale of eyeglasses and contact lenses was often tied to eye examinations. When a person had an eye examination, it was expected that glasses or contacts would be purchased from the same establishment. Since the individual was not provided with the results of the examination, he or she could do little if dissatisfied with the prices, quality, or selection of products offered. The Commission established a trade regulation rule that gave consumers the legal right to obtain their prescription immediately after an eye examination and without additional charge. In this way the FTC hoped to eliminate the industry practice of tie-ins and to increase competition in the sale of eyeglasses and contact lenses.

In recent years, the broad powers of the Federal Trade Commission have been the object of intense criticism by business and the Congress. The promulgation of industrywide trade regulations has been a particular focus of discontent. Critics claim that the rules often are unrealistic and that FTC officials are not responsive to the circumstances of individual businesses.

In 1980, the Federal Trade Commission Improvements Act gave Congress authority to overturn trade regulation rules adopted by the FTC. However, in a 1983 case involving immigration proceedings, the Supreme Court ruled that the legislative veto is unconstitutional. The justices noted that the function of Congress is to pass legislation that is then sent to the president. The president has the option of signing or vetoing the bill. The Court held that if Congress wants to block the action of an executive agency, it must follow normal procedures by enacting legislation and submitting it to the president. Because the legislative veto does not involve presidential approval, its use was prohibited. The Court's decision should have far-reaching consequences. The veto provision had been incorporated into 57 different laws.

Interagency Coordination (Competition?)

In the past the FTC and the Antitrust Division have maintained areas of special emphasis, but have also overlapped in broad areas of their antitrust activities. The public posture of the agencies is that the allocation of cases is made on the basis of the

[6]Nonadjudicatory activities are legal proceedings that do not formally involve the judicial system.

agency best suited to perform the investigation and litigation. The reality is that
interagency coordination is often haphazard and the search for "good" cases is sometimes highly competitive. A high-ranking official in the Antitrust Division relates the
following example:

> We sent over the cats and dogs which we really didn't want, keeping the good stuff.
> Generally relations were remote and competitive. At one point during the merger
> wave, the FTC offices opened at 8:30 and the Division's at 9:00. We found that they
> were calling up by 9:00 saying which mergers they wanted. So we arranged to
> . . . get the *Wall Street Journal* delivered before 8:30 to spot the good mergers
> first. [7]

Periodically there are proposals to merge the antitrust functions of the FTC and
the Antitrust Division into a single agency that would have complete responsibility for
federal antitrust activity. None of these proposals has gotten very far. It is perhaps
fitting that the governmental agencies charged with maintaining competition in the
American economy also are required to compete in the performance of that function.

CASE SELECTION

Suzanne Weaver's *Decision to Prosecute* provides an interesting account of the workings
of the Antitrust Division. [8] Weaver interviewed staff lawyers and front office personnel
from the division, congressional staff members, representatives of the private antitrust
bar, journalists, and others in her investigation of the antitrust case selection process
in the Justice Department. The discussion that follows is based on her research.

The division receives information regarding possible antitrust violations from a
number of sources. Citizens or businesspeople may write to complain about specific
business practices. Publications such as the *Wall Street Journal* or an industry trade
magazine sometimes report activities of interest. Relevant data may be contained in
reports that firms are required to file with government agencies. Division lawyers
occasionally receive tips from personal contacts in business or government. Finally, the
division periodically conducts studies of specific industries.

Like all bureaucracies, the Antitrust Division has a well-developed hierarchy. At
the top is the Assistant Attorney General for Antitrust (AAG). Beneath the AAG are
the director of operations, the section chiefs, and the staff lawyers. When information
is received by the division it is filtered down to the appropriate section chief. Each
section typically deals with a certain group of industries or type of commerce. On
receiving information the section chief makes an initial evaluation of its value (useless
information is discarded) and transmits it to a staff lawyer. The recipient is allocated
information on the basis of experience, case load, capabilities, and special interests.

[7]Green, M. J., *The Closed Enterprise System* (New York: Grossman, 1972), p. 428.
[8]Weaver, S., *Decision to Prosecute: Organization and Public Policy in the Antitrust Division* (Cam-
bridge, Mass.: MIT Press, 1977). Similar studies of the Federal Trade Commission include Katzmann, R.A.,
Regulatory Bureaucracy: The Federal Trade Commission and Antitrust Policy, (Cambridge, Mass.: MIT
Press, 1980) and Clarkson, K.W. and Muris, T. J., *The Federal Trade Commission Since 1970,* (London:
Cambridge University Press, 1981).

The staff lawyer must decide whether a particular item has any potential as the basis for filing a complaint. More than 90 percent of all information is not factual, doesn't deal with illegal activities, or is of so little importance as to warrant no further attention. However, if the staff lawyer's initial investigation determines that there may be an antitrust violation, then a request is made to the section chief to proceed with a formal investigation. A persuasive case for an investigation made by a staff lawyer would rarely be denied at the section level.

Formal investigation often requires a substantial investment of time and resources. It is not uncommon for an investigation to run for six months or a year. During that period the staff member collects and evaluates additional information. Of the cases that are seriously investigated, about half are finally recommended to the section chief for prosecution. During the investigation the function of the section chief is to provide guidance and technical expertise. Although the chief must approve all cases that are recommended, the decision is normally an agreement between the section chief and the staff lawyer. The chief is more likely to suggest changes to a proposed complaint than to make an initial yes-no decision.

Cases that are recommended for prosecution by the section chief must then be approved by the director of operations. A high percentage of cases recommended by the section chiefs are ultimately approved by the director. The main criterion seems to be the prospect for a successful prosecution. At this level, decisions still reflect the desire to maintain the reputation of the agency rather than the influence of political factors.

Finally, cases proposed for prosecution must be accepted by the AAG. About 60 percent of all recommended cases are accepted without change. Another 30 percent are questioned solely on the basis of relatively small details of the case. Thus, about 90 percent of all recommended cases are approved by the AAG with little or no change. When the AAG does question or reject a proposed case, it is normally because of concern with short-run economic conditions, such as stock market effects, national defense, or foreign relations. Although critics have often alleged that Congress and the White House exert a strong influence over the selection of antitrust cases by the division, Weaver discounts the importance of such external influences.[9] She argues that for most examples of cases allegedly suppressed on the basis of political considerations, the division staff had already arrived at a consensus decision not to prosecute based on evidentiary reasons.

Although the AAG ultimately approves a very high percentage of the cases that are recommended at lower levels, it should not be concluded that the AAG exerts no influence on the directions of antitrust policy in the division. One source of influence from the top is the establishment of new units with specialized missions. For example, an energy section was created in response to the "energy crisis" of the 1970s. The mere fact that such a group exists and receives resources means that energy problems are given greater emphasis than in the past.

The AAG may also shape the direction of division activities by announcing the need to act against specific acts, to investigate certain industries more carefully, or to

[9]Ibid., pp. 137–163.

test new theories. Even without an actual reallocation of resources, these areas will be investigated more actively as the staff realizes that they are more likely to receive approval if they get on the bandwagon. Conversely, the AAG can discourage investigations by letting it be known that he or she does not consider certain areas to be important. For example, in the Reagan administration, Assistant Attorney General Baxter expressed the opinion that restrictive practices such as tying contracts usually are not anticompetitive. Under Baxter, the division gave much less attention to such practices.

Another important factor affecting case selection in the Antitrust Division is the nature of information received and processed by staff lawyers. Ideally, the division would select cases on the basis of a complete knowledge of business activities in the U.S. economy. The reality is that the staff is highly constrained by the data it receives. Weaver describes the position of staff lawyers:

> They do not see themselves working in an environment of plentiful prosecution opportunities among which discretionary choices must be made. Instead, they see their environment as marked by scarcity of such information.[10]

Historically, the estimated magnitude of potential economic benefits from a successful antitrust prosecution seems to have been a relatively unimportant factor in the decision to file a complaint. Rather, the division staff has responded to the organization's internal incentives. This incentive structure was such that it was "probably more important to win cases than to reduce economic losses or inequities in order to move up the success ladder in the Justice Department."[11] Thus, the prospect of victory has been the most important single factor in explaining the choice of cases to be prosecuted. Recently, the division has attempted to base case selection more on the economic impact of industry practices, but it is likely that maintaining an impressive won/lost record will continue to be an important goal.

LITIGATION: THE "BIG CASE"
Background

In January 1969, the Justice Department filed suit against IBM charging that the firm had violated the Sherman Act by monopolizing the market for general-purpose computers. The government proposed that the company be split into several competing firms. The suit was the culmination of an investigation that began in 1966.

Under judicial rules of discovery, the government and IBM each had the right to obtain evidence from the other side. During six years of pretrial activity:

> The government produced approximately 26 million pages of documents; IBM selected approximately 890,000 for copying.

[10]Ibid., pp. 60–61.
[11]Siegfried, J. J., "The Determinants of Antitrust Activity," *Journal of Law and Economics* (October 1975), p. 573.

> IBM produced approximately 65 million pages of documents to various plaintiffs. . . .
>
> The parties took 1,309 depositions. . . .[12]

The suit came to trial in a district court in May 1975. The Justice Department spent three years and over 500 trial days in the presentation of its case. By the time IBM had finished its defense, the trial transcript had run beyond 100,000 pages with additional exhibits totaling over 200,000 pages. Among the decisions faced by the district court judge was a government subpoena for additional documents that IBM claimed would require 62,000 person-years and $1 billion to satisfy. Although the firm had an incentive to overstate the costs of compliance, there is no doubt that the resources required to prosecute and defend a protracted antitrust case are staggering. When the Justice Department dismissed the suit in January 1982, the government had already spent over $12 million. The cost to IBM was several times that amount.

One of the major causes of decade-long antitrust suits such as the IBM case is the discovery process. Until the late 1930s it was difficult for one party in a proceeding to obtain the necessary information about the other. Liberalized discovery rules have greatly increased the flow of information between litigants. However, improved access to information has been a mixed blessing. Discovery can be an effective means of harassing the opposition. By requesting large numbers of documents, a large firm may severely tax the abilities of a smaller company. One judge described the changed rules on discovery as shifting proceedings from "trial by ambush" to "trial by avalanche."[13] While the discovery process may be an effective tool of private firms in antitrust litigation, its use by government can also be troublesome, as division or FTC attorneys try to collect every shred of evidence necessary to assure victory. As part of the Justice Department's divestiture suit against AT&T, the government asked for all Bell System documents "prepared, sent, or received since Jan. 1, 1930, which relate or refer in whole or in part to, or which constitute, instructions, directives or suggestions regarding the purchase by AT&T or any Bell Company of telecommunication equipment from Western Electric." Because Western Electric was the sole supplier of equipment to the Bell System during most of that period, the request is not the kind of activity that can be completed on a leisurely Saturday afternoon.

Another problem with the litigation of large antitrust suits is the complexity of the issues involved. Cases such as IBM and AT&T deal with highly sophisticated technologies and difficult economic questions. The average juror simply does not have the background to understand and evaluate the issues in such cases. In a suit filed by Memorex against IBM, the jury was required to evaluate IBM designs for connecting computers and data storage machines. Convinced that the jurors were unable to grasp the details of the case, the judge questioned them to determine their level of understanding. One juror was asked to give an example of an interface (the connection between the computer and a peripheral device). Her response, "Well, if you take a blivet, turn

---

[12]National Commission for the Review of Antitrust Laws and Procedures, *Report to the President and the Attorney General,* Vol. 2 (1979), p. 22.

[13]Judge Charles Renfrew, as quoted in "Why Those Big Cases Drag On," *Time* (Jan. 8, 1979), p. 62.

it off one thing and drop it down, it's an interface change, right?" Another, asked to explain a method of copying a competitor's product called "reverse engineering," said, "That's when you would take a product and you would alter it, or modify it for your own purpose, that is, you would reverse its function and use it in your own method."[14] Even if jurors had the technical preparation to understand the individual issues in a large antitrust case, it's not clear that they have the ability to coordinate and synthesize the incredible volume of evidence presented.

Recommendations for Change

Protracted and complex antitrust cases greatly limit the impact of the antitrust statutes. One of the reasons for the government's relative inactivity in Section 2 Sherman Act cases is the substantial resource cost of such proceedings. Limited in budget and personnel, the Justice Department (as well as the FTC) must select its cases carefully. In 1978, President Carter established a prestigious commission to consider the need for procedural changes in antitrust litigation. Six months later the National Commission for the Review of Antitrust Laws and Procedures presented its report.[15] The report identifies the major problems involved in processing large antitrust suits. Among those problems were:

1. **Scope.** Many cases relate to the development of an industry over long periods of time. Recreating these histories is a laborious and complex task.
2. **Technical Issues.** Complaints against IBM, AT&T, and other large firms often involve their most sophisticated products. The technology may strain the capabilities of the industry's best scientists, let alone jurors with a high school education.
3. **High Stakes.** In a suit against AT&T, Microwave Communications Inc. sought $3.0 billion in damages. With the potential gains and losses so great, firms are willing to invest a great deal of time and money to assure that no claim or defense has been overlooked.
4. **Discovery Process.** The discovery phase of a proceeding may drag on for years because one side views delay as an advantage. Among the available strategies are delaying the production of documents, denying the existence of evidence, flooding the opposition with irrelevant information, and making frivolous claims.
5. **Inexperience and Turnover of Government Lawyers.** The commission found that Justice Department lawyers sometimes compensate for a lack of experience by being overly cautious. The high turnover rate of personnel within the government was also determined to be a cause of delay.

Having identified the major problems, the commission suggested changes in the judicial system designed to improve litigation of the "big case." At the heart of these recommendations is the view that judges must take a much more active role. Traditionally, judges have functioned to assure that each side is given a fair opportunity to

[14]Shaffer, R. A., "Those Complex Antitrust Cases," *Wall Street Journal* (Aug. 29, 1978), p. 16.
[15]National Commission for the Review of Antitrust Laws and Procedures, op. cit.

present its case, but have been reluctant to aggressively alter the rate and the direction of the proceedings. The commission suggested that judges should exercise early and continuous control. Especially important is the control of discovery. Litigants must not be allowed to harass, overwhelm, or dally with one another.

The commission recommended that judges set timetables for completion of the phases of a proceeding. Attorneys who engage in dilatory tactics would do so at the risk of receiving judicial sanctions. To reduce the incentives for delay on the part of defendants, it was suggested that interest be added on to any judgment. For example, if a firm was found guilty of price fixing that occurred five years previously, the plaintiffs would be entitled to interest from the date of the offense to the date of conviction.

The commission also recognized that the adversary system is not particularly well suited for the analysis of complex technology, esoteric economic theory, and reams of statistics. It was suggested that trials could be simplified by use of pretrial stipulations whereby the opposing parties agree to certain facts, which are then no longer in dispute. The commission also proposed that a large case should sometimes be divided into a number of separate trials. In this way a judge or jury could concentrate on a specific issue rather than be overwhelmed by masses of largely irrelevant facts.

Often, the efforts of blue ribbon commissions receive momentary attention in the media and then are largely forgotten. In this case, some of the commission's recommendations were translated into legislation. The Antitrust Procedural Improvements Act of 1980 gave judges the authority to fine attorneys who engage in dilatory practices. It also allowed the courts to award interest on damages if there is "undue delay" resulting from actions by parties involved in the suit. These changes should help, but many problems still remain in litigating the "big case."

REMEDIES AND PENALTIES

Often the remedies and penalties imposed on convicted antitrust violators are too weak to serve as an effective deterrent to future violations. There is a marked contrast between the courts' treatment of those convicted of antitrust offenses and individuals found guilty of street crimes. In the electric machinery conspiracy, 7 businessmen were given 30-day jail terms and 20 more got off with suspended sentences. At about the same time, a New Jersey man found guilty of stealing a pair of sunglasses and a box of soap was put in jail for four months. Another man, on conviction of his third minor offense (this one for stealing $70 from a gas station), got ten years to life. Students caught with marijuana in their possession have been sentenced to as much as ten years in jail, while their elders receive a minor fine and a tongue lashing for milking the public of $10 million in a price-fixing conspiracy.[16] Considered as a benefit-cost calculation, antitrust crimes probably do pay. Many violations go undetected. Complaints often end in innocuous consent decrees. Even a conviction may carry penalties that are far less costly than the accrued benefits of the unlawful activity. The oft-cited adage that the government wins the cases and loses the remedies is an accurate assessment of many proceedings.

[16]Green, op. cit., pp. 168–169.

Dissolution and Divestiture

Dissolution and divestiture are potentially potent remedies in antitrust proceedings. However, the reality is that the judicial system has been very reluctant to order substantial divestiture or dissolution of firms convicted of antitrust violations. Between 1890 and 1974, 118 single-firm monopolization cases were decided. The government obtained some relief in over 80 percent of those cases, but an order for substantial divestiture occurred in only 23 percent. For 82 cases decided between 1940 and 1974, the government achieved a significant restructuring of the firms only 15 percent of the time. [17] With the exception of the 1982 AT&T consent decree, the track record since 1974 is no better.

There are several reasons to explain the reluctance of the courts to order drastic structural changes. Justices may be convinced that breaking up a firm would result in efficiency losses or that the pace of innovation in the industry would be slowed. Also, by the time a case has been decided, the circumstances that led to the decision have sometimes changed dramatically. The Alcoa case is an example. In the remedy phase of the proceedings the court determined there was no need to divide Alcoa because the sale of wartime aluminum plants had greatly reduced the firm's market share. Finally, dissolution may also be resisted on equity grounds. The beneficiaries of a monopoly are often early entrepreneurs who have long since sold out. Splitting up the firm would not penalize the real culprits, but only impose costs on innocent present-day stockholders.

Even where the courts have ordered substantial divestiture, the effect is often cosmetic. Posner investigated the consequences of 11 national-market monopolization cases in which the courts ordered a significant restructuring of the firm. The case-by-case results were as follows:

1. Standard Oil of New Jersey (1911)—Regional monopolies were substituted for a national monopoly.
2. American Tobacco (1911)—American was carved into three new companies. These firms continued to collude for many years.
3. du Pont (1912)—The firm was ordered to divest itself of explosive plants, many of which produced black powder. This form of explosives became obsolete shortly after the sale.
4. International Harvester (1918)—The firm still had a two-thirds market share of the manufacture of agricultural machinery even after the divestiture.
5. Corn Products (1919)—A glucose manufacturer was required to sell six plants. The consensus was that the firm was strengthened by the sale. Two of the divested plants subsequently went bankrupt.
6. Eastman Kodak (1920)—Kodak was ordered to divest itself of certain assets, but the firm continues to be the leading producer of photographic equipment.
7. Pullman (1947)—The firm was required to choose between manufacturing and operating railroad sleeping cars. By shedding its money-losing operating division, the firm was actually strengthened.
8. Grinnell (1968)—Grinnell was required to sell its central-station protection

[17]Posner, R. A., *Antitrust Law* (Chicago: University of Chicago Press, 1976), pp. 82–83.

businesses in 27 cities. The divestiture represented only a small part of the firm's business and the firm's profits and sales increased dramatically during the period after divestiture.

9. United Fruit (1958)—It took 14 years for the firm to rid itself of the required proportion (35 percent) of its banana operations. By that time the divested operations represented only about 10 percent of United's banana output.

10. IBM (1956)—IBM was required to limit its market share of tabulating card manufacturing to 50 percent. This operation was a trivial part of IBM's total business.

11. MCA, Inc. (1962)—MCA was required to get out of the talent-agency business. By the time of the divestiture the firm had already moved heavily into television production. One of the terms of the consent decree under which this case was settled allowed MCA to purchase Decca Records.[18]

A serious problem with large cases proposing dissolution and divestiture is the length of time required for their resolution. Posner's study of litigated national market monopolization cases revealed that the average time between the initiation of the case and the final degree was over six years.[19] Often, several more years elapse from the time of final judgment to the completion of the required sales. The passage of time can make the remedy ordered by the courts unnecessary or ineffective.

The probability that an antitrust proceeding will result in dissolution or substantial divestiture is not very great. Still, the AT&T case shows that it can happen. Although the government got most of what it asked in that case, it remains to be seen who will be the ultimate beneficiary. One interpretation of the consent decree is that AT&T really was the winner. Allowed to shed marginally profitable operations and given the right to enter rapidly growing computer and data processing markets, the firm may be in an ideal position to take advantage of future opportunities. The AT&T breakup will be discussed in greater detail in Chapter 13.

Fines and Damages

In considering whether to embark on a course of unlawful activity, corporate executives compare the expected benefits and the expected costs. As a highly simplified example, assume that fines are the only penalties that the courts impose on convicted antitrust offenders. Further assume that two firms are contemplating a price-fixing conspiracy. The expected benefits of the conspiracy are the increase in profits resulting from the agreement. Abstracting from the costs of establishing and maintaining conspiracy itself, publicity effects, and litigation expenses, the expected costs are fines levied by the courts if the arrangement is detected and successfully prosecuted. Specifically, the expected cost is the fine that would be imposed times the probability of being convicted. For example, if the expected present value of price fixing is $10 million in additional profits to the firm, the fine that could be anticipated on conviction is $15 million, and the probability of being fined 20 percent, then proceeding with the conspiracy makes economic sense because the expected benefit of $10 million far exceeds the expected cost

[18]Ibid., pp. 85–87.
[19]Ibid., p. 88.

of $3 million. To dissuade the firm from colluding, the fine times the probability of being convicted must increase.

At present, the maximum fine for antitrust violations is $100,000 for individuals and $1 million for firms. As a practical matter, the average fine is well below those limits. For example, between 1957 and 1976 in 18 criminal cases involving price fixing of bread, the average fine paid by individuals was about $4,000 and the average fine imposed on each firm was just over $20,000. The average fine as a percent of the defendant's annual sales was 0.31 percent. The maximum was about 1.0 percent of annual sales. [20]

Recently, however, the courts have been imposing much tougher financial penalties on antitrust offenders. During fiscal 1982, total corporate fines in Justice Department cases were nearly $37 million. This is over 20 times the 1973 total of $1.4 million. [21] The Antitrust Division has issued guidelines for assessing fines. For individuals, the recommended base fine is $50,000. This may be adjusted upward or downward depending on the offense and the net worth of the person. For corporations, the guidelines call for a minimum fine of $100,000 or an amount equal to 10 percent of corporate sales in affected line of commerce.

The impact of treble damages in antitrust cases must not be forgotten. The real importance of the electrical machinery cases of the 1960s was the staggering total of damages (over $400 million) that the firms ultimately paid. More recently, in 1983 Litton Industries was awarded nearly $300 million in treble damages as a result of a successful suit against AT&T. A pending suit by MCI against AT&T may generate an even larger award. In 1980 a jury fixed treble damages at $1.8 billion in the case. A federal appeals court later overturned the decision and returned it to the district court for reconsideration.

A proposal by the Justice Department may limit treble damage awards. The Antitrust Division has suggested that treble damages be awarded only in cases, such as price fixing, where the antitrust violation is judged under a per se standard; that is, where the defendent should have known that the act was illegal. Under this proposal, the plaintiff in a rule-of-reason action could only sue for actual damages.

Imprisonment

In 1974, the maximum prison sentence for antitrust violations was increased from one to three years, but prison sentences have been imposed sparingly. The electrical machinery case marked the first time that antitrust violators, other than union officials or perpetrators of violence, had been sent to jail. When offenders have been incarcerated, the terms usually have been very short. As with fines, there is some indication that the courts are becoming less lenient. During fiscal 1978, jail sentences for antitrust offenders totaled 1561 days. But during 1981, the total climbed to over 7000 days. [22] More

[20]Block, M. K., Nold, F. C., and Sidak, J. G., "The Deterrent Effect of Antitrust Enforcement," *Journal of Political Economy* (Vol. 89, No. 3, 1981), pp. 429–440.
[21]Department of Justice, *Comparative Analysis of Antitrust Cases Filed by Fiscal Years,* Washington, D.C.
[22]Department of Justice, *Annual Report* (Government Printing Office: Washington, D.C.).

jail sentences were imposed during the first three years of the Reagan administration than during the previous 90 years of antitrust history.

Justice Department guidelines recommend a sentence of 18 months for criminal antitrust violations, but suspended sentences are common. Typically, the amount of time actually served is from 30 to 120 days. There are several reasons why prison sentences have been light and imposed infrequently in antitrust cases.

First, the guilty parties usually are respectable members of the community and judges seem reluctant to throw them in with unwashed pimps, drug dealers, and joint smokers. Second, recidivism is uncommon in antitrust matters, and there is no compelling need to protect society from convicted violators. Third, while violations such as price fixing are relatively obvious, in some circumstances a corporate executive may have simply interpreted the facts differently than a judge or jury. Many issues in antitrust are still unsettled, and the line between lawful and illegal activity is not well defined. Finally, if fines can be structured to provide an equal level of deterrence, they are preferable. Imprisonment imposes a deadweight loss on society, because of the high cost of the confinement. Also, there is a loss of productivity as corporate executives are taken from their jobs and placed in jail.

Injunctions

Injunctions can be used to terminate current actions or prevent certain courses of behavior in the future. Although injunctions may be useful in eliminating specific restrictive practices, collusion, price discrimination, and the like, they have little value as a deterrent to other firms. An injunction specifies what a firm can and cannot do, but usually imposes no penalty for previous illegal actions. Unless other penalties are used, firms have an incentive to violate the law until they are prohibited from doing so.

Consent Decrees

Eighty to ninety percent of all federal antitrust complaints end in consent decrees.[23] Although such arrangements provide benefits to both the firm and the government, they are subject to abuse. In the past, deliberations leading to a consent decree were conducted in secret and interested parties other than the potential litigants had little to say about the outcome. The dangers of a decision made on the basis of political pressures were much greater than in a courtroom setting. Consent decrees also provide overburdened FTC and Antitrust Division lawyers with an opportunity to claim victory with a minimum expenditure of resources. These victories may be purchased at the expense of striking a poor bargain with the firm.

The Antitrust Procedures and Penalties Act of 1974 was intended as a check on the abuse of consent decrees. It requires the Justice Department to make public proposed decrees and to prepare a statement that considers the predicted effects. The court that affirms the decree must then hold a hearing in which interested parties are allowed to present their positions on the proposed agreement. Based on the evidence presented,

[23]Consent *orders* when negotiated by the Federal Trade Commission.

the court must then make an assessment of the impact of the decree and determine whether it is in the public interest.

EVALUATION OF U.S. ANTITRUST ACTIVITY

Has U.S. antitrust activity been effective in promoting workable competition, or has the primary effect of antitrust been to enrich lawyers and economists? In this section the impact and present status of each of the major areas of antitrust are evaluated.

Monopolization

The courts have retreated from the view articulated in the Alcoa case that the mere existence of monopoly power is sufficient to constitute a violation of Section 2 of the Sherman Act. Successful prosecution now requires a showing of market power together with evidence of the intent to monopolize. While the limits of lawful activity may be tighter for dominant firms, it would appear that at least some indication of abuse must be shown.

One of the most serious problems faced by the government in bringing Section 2 cases is the resource cost and long duration of such proceedings. Because of budget limitations, only a few cases can be brought and the outcomes are highly uncertain. On the rare occasions when the government has won an order for substantial restructuring of a firm, the changes have usually had little real impact on the firm or industry involved. Typically, by the time divestiture is accomplished, the evolution of the industry has greatly blunted the impact of the reforms.

In spite of its many limitations and problems, Section 2 has probably been a "modest deterrent to high concentration."[24] The primary impact may come not from the results of litigation, but as firms modify their plans to take account of the costs and uncertainties of Section 2 prosecutions. It is sometimes suggested that the "ghost of Senator Sherman sits in every corporate boardroom."

Mergers

Although the total number of mergers has not declined since passage of the Celler-Kefauver Act, there has been a dramatic change in the composition of merger types. Government merger policy has been most effective in preventing horizontal acquisitions between large firms. The outcomes of suits to prohibit vertical and conglomerate mergers have been less certain. Table 9.3 indicates that since the early 1950s merger activity has clearly shifted from horizontal to conglomerate acquisitions.

During 1978 to 1979, nearly 80 percent of all large mergers involved firms with unrelated product lines. Only about 13 percent of all large mergers were between firms competing for the sale of the same product—down from about 40 percent in 1951 to 1954. It is generally agreed that the anticompetitive effects of horizontal mergers are greater than those of conglomerate mergers. In fact, it is sometimes argued that a pure

[24]Stigler, G. J., "The Economic Effects of the Antitrust Laws," *Journal of Law and Economics,* Vol. 9 (Oct. 1966), p. 232.

Table 9.3 **LARGE ACQUISITIONS IN MINING AND**
MANUFACTURING BY TYPE OF ACQUISITION:
1951–1979*

Type of acquisition	Percentage of all assets acquired		
	1951–54	1963–66	1978–79
Horizontal	40%	14%	13%
Vertical	9	15	9
Conglomerate	52	72	78
Product extension	43	43	37
Market extension	4	13	1
Pure	5%	16%	40%

*Acquired firms with assets of $10 million or more. Percentages may not
sum to 100 because of rounding.
Source: Mueller, W. F., *The Celler-Kefauver Act: Sixteen Years of Enforcement,* Staff Report to the Antitrust Subcommittee, Committee on the Judiciary,
U.S. House of Representatives (Washington, D.C.: Government Printing Office,
1967), p. 110; and Federal Trade Commission, *Statistical Report on Mergers and
Acquisitions* (1979), p. 109.

conglomerate acquisition, by definition, does not have an adverse effect on competition.
To the extent that conglomerate mergers cause less social harm than horizontal combinations, the trend since the amendment of the Clayton Act in 1950 has been beneficial.
Although it is impossible to determine exactly how much of the change in the composition of merger types is attributable to antitrust efforts, the government's successes in
prohibiting large mergers between direct competitors must be regarded as an important
factor.

However, enforcement of antimerger laws slackened under the Reagan administration. In the first year after announcing its 1982 guidelines, the Justice Department
challenged only three mergers. In early 1984, the FTC approved a $10 billion merger
between Texaco and Getty Oil—the largest merger in history. Merger activity in 1983
reached a nine year high with over 2500 combinations taking place.

Collusion

Illegal price fixing costs Americans billions of dollars each year in higher prices. Certain
industries are chronic offenders. The electrical machinery manufacturers had a long
history of conflicts with the government prior to the big cases of the 1960s. Paper
manufacturers have repeatedly been brought to court. Between 1975 and 1978, 36
companies were found guilty of or pleaded no contest to charges that they had fixed
prices of products such as coffee and pet food bags, labels, and folding cartons. More
recently, the Justice Department has found evidence that bid-rigging in highway construction is at near epidemic proportions. In fiscal 1982, 80 of the 112 suits filed by the
Antitrust Division involved this practice.[25] By mid-1983 bid-rigging probes had resulted in successful prosecution of 410 companies. Fines of $52 million and jail sentences totaling 50 years had been imposed.[26]

[25]Department of Justice, *Comparative Analysis of Antitrust Cases Filed by Fiscal Years,* Washington,
D.C.
[26]"New Twist in Antitrust," *Wall Street Journal* (Sept. 16, 1983), p. 26.

Although explicit collusion has not been eliminated by antitrust efforts, the per se stand of the courts has had a significant impact in reducing the most effective forms of price fixing, group boycotts, market allocation, and so forth. Conspirators have been forced to abandon overt methods such as the joint sales agency and to settle for less easily detectable and less efficient methods. With respect to price fixing, former Solicitor General Robert Bork maintains that such cases "deliver more consumer welfare for the enforcement dollar than any other kind of prosecution."[27]

While overt collusion is severely condemned by the courts, the problem of tacit collusion remains unresolved. Only rarely have the courts been willing to apply the doctrine of the 1946 American Tobacco case and convict firms without evidence of an explicit agreement. As long as the judicial system continues to focus on evidence of the existence of conspiracy rather than the results of joint action, much of the behavior of firms in oligopolistic industries will continue to be beyond the reach of antitrust.

Price Discrimination

The total compliance and litigation costs associated with the Robinson-Patman Act between 1936 and 1974 have been estimated to be about $1.4 billion.[28] During that period the Federal Trade Commission issued some 1,400 complaints and over 8,000 private suits were filed. The intent of the Robinson-Patman Act was to protect small businesses, but many of the complaints have been against small firms. The act is widely regarded as poorly worded and ill conceived. Because it has been used to restrict active price competition, its net effect has probably been to reduce rather than to promote competition.

Restrictive Practices

The courts have taken a hard line against tying contracts. Unless a firm is a new entrant into an industry or a very small share of the market is involved, such agreements usually are judged to be illegal. The result is that the most flagrant examples of tying contracts have been eliminated.

Generally, the argument accepted by the courts in ruling against tying arrangements is that they foreclose the market to competitors. In Chapter 8 it was suggested that tied sales often serve as a method of price discrimination. The implication is such practices should be judged under the more flexible rule-of-reason standard used for price discrimination, rather than the near per se standard now used by the courts.

Exclusive dealing and territorial limitations are evaluated using a rule-of-reason standard. In recent decisions the courts have shown a willingness to evaluate the economic impact of alleged violations. It is difficult to assess the impact of antitrust policy in these areas, but it is likely that the net effect has been to alter the terms of agreements in such a way as to reduce the advantage of the parent firm.

[27]Bork, R. H., *The Antitrust Paradox: A Policy at War with Itself* (New York: Basic Books, 1978), p. 406.

[28]Elzinga, K. G., and Hogarty, T. F., "Utah Pie and the Consequences of Robinson-Patman," *Journal of Law and Economics,* Vol. 21 (Oct. 1978), p. 433.

SUMMARY
Federal Antitrust Enforcement Agencies

Antitrust Division of the Department of Justice   The Antitrust Division files about 74 cases each year. Historically, price-fixing allegations have been the most frequent subject of Justice Department cases.

Federal Trade Commission   From 1915 to 1969, over 50 percent of all FTC antitrust cases involved price discrimination, but this area now represents only a small proportion of total complaints. The FTC also issues advisory opinions and industrywide trade regulations.

Interagency Coordination (Competition?)   Antitrust cases are supposedly handled by the agency best equipped for the task. In reality, there is some competition for cases between the FTC and the Antitrust Division.

Case Selection

Information on possible antitrust violations is received by the Justice Department from a number of sources. Individual staff lawyers receive responsibility for a case based on their interest and case load. Before formal filing, a case must be approved by the section chief, director of operations, and the assistant attorney general for antitrust. An important criterion in deciding whether to prosecute a case is the probability of success.

Litigation: The "Big Case"

Background   Major antitrust suits require much time and money. Discovery rules allow the defendant to delay and the plaintiff to harass. The complex issues involved in large cases such as IBM may be too difficult for jurors to understand.

Recommendations for Change   The National Commission for the Review of Antitrust Laws and Procedures recommended that judges take a more active role in streamlining complex antitrust litigation. The commission suggested that judges set deadlines, penalize dilatory tactics, and control the discovery process. Some of these recommendations were implemented by the Antitrust Procedural Improvements Act of 1980.

Remedies and Penalties

Dissolution and Divestiture   With the AT&T case as an important exception, dissolution or substantial divestiture has not frequently been used in antitrust proceedings. Where such remedies have been applied the effects have been largely cosmetic. One reason is that large suits typically take so long to complete that conditions can drastically change by the time the decision is reached.

Fines and Damages   In the past, fines levied on antitrust offenders have been nominal in comparison to the benefits of certain types of activity, such as price fixing. More recently, the courts have begun to impose heavier fines. A more potent deterrent, however, is the prospect of treble-damage suits by private parties.

Imprisonment   The courts have been reluctant to impose prison sentences for antitrust violations, but the frequency and duration of prison sentences has increased in the last few years. From an efficiency standpoint imprisonment is less desirable than fines, because of the deadweight loss imposed on society.

Injunctions   Injunctions can be used to terminate, modify, or prevent undesirable business activities. However, unless firms believe that other penalties will be imposed, they have an incentive to violate the law until formally restrained.

Consent Decrees   Most antitrust complaints are resolved through consent decrees. In the past, the secrecy of negotiations excluded other interested parties from affecting the outcome. The Antitrust Procedures and Penalties Act of 1974 now requires that third parties be given an opportunity to state their case in such proceedings.

Evaluation of U.S. Antitrust Policy

Monopolization   Section 2 cases are limited by the costs and uncertainty of the proceedings. However, the costs and uncertainty are borne by the firm, as well as the government. The possibility of antitrust action probably acts as a restraint on the behavior of large firms.

Merger   Merger policy has altered the composition, if not the number, of mergers. Presently, only about 20 percent of all mergers are horizontal or vertical combinations. Thirty years ago nearly half of all mergers were horizontal or vertical. Such mergers probably had greater social costs than the conglomerate acquisitions that dominate merger activity today.

Collusion   Explicit collusion has not been eliminated by antitrust activity, but the most effective forms have been greatly restricted. The legal status of tacit collusion is still unsettled. Thus, subtle forms of collusion by oligopolists probably remain beyond the reach of antitrust.

Price Discrimination   Most price-discrimination suits are now initiated by private parties. The Robinson-Patman Act is generally considered to be a poor law that has restricted rather than promoted competition.

Restrictive Practices   Where a substantial share of the market is foreclosed, tying contracts have been severely restricted by the courts. Antitrust laws probably have altered vertical agreements in such a way as to benefit small firms.

DISCUSSION QUESTIONS

1. Should Congress have the authority to veto trade regulations proposed by the Federal Trade Commission? How might this precedent affect other independent regulatory agencies?

2. What are the advantages and disadvantages of having two agencies with overlapping antitrust responsibilities?

3. Is the probability of obtaining a conviction an inappropriate criterion for deciding which alleged antitrust violations to prosecute?

4. Is it possible to impose deadlines and streamline antitrust procedures while still giving each party a fair hearing?

5. Compared to crimes such as robbery or assault, would long prison terms for antitrust offenders be an effective deterrent?

6. What could be done about industries where price-fixing violations are common?

7. In deciding antitrust cases, why have the courts so often focused on property rights rather than competition?

8. What would be the effects of eliminating consent decrees as a possible outcome of antitrust complaints?

three

REGULATION AS AN ALTERNATIVE TO COMPETITION

chapter **10**

Economic Regulation:
Background and Theory

Chapter Outline

Regulation is a peculiarly American institution. . . . (It) is a reflection of the democratic and egalitarian principles held by the Founding Fathers, especially their fear of centralized government power. Its organizing principle is that decisions should be based upon objective analysis in a process that allows people who are likely to be affected by the decision to have their views heard and considered. [1]

The antitrust approach to public policy focuses on structure and conduct in an industry. It is based on the presumption that society is best served by government actions designed to increase competition between firms. In contrast, the regulatory approach concentrates on industry performance. It is based on the assumption that there are circumstances where competition either is not possible or not desirable. To prevent adverse consequences from the lack of competition, government steps in and "assists" firms to perform in a socially acceptable way. This assistance may take the form of requiring approval of price changes, regulating the entry or exit of firms in a market, or prescribing standards for a product or service.

In modern society, government regulation is a pervasive force. However, there was a time when government involvement in the economic decisions of firms was minimal. The first section of this chapter reviews the historical evolution of the "visible" hand of regulation. The next three sections consider theories of regulation. Discussed first is the traditional view that regulation serves to protect consumers against the economic power of producers. Second is a discussion of regulation as a method of taxation. The chapter concludes by presenting a theory which asserts that the results of regulation can best be explained as responses to pressures from various interest groups.

THE EXPANDING SCOPE OF REGULATION
Beginnings

Regulation of commerce dates from antiquity. The rulers of ancient Babylonia decreed restrictions on wages and prices that lasted for a thousand years. During the rule of the Caesars, privately owned water supply, garbage disposal, and fire-fighting enterprises were allowed to exist in Rome, but were restricted in their operations so as to serve the public interest. In the Middle Ages religious views tempered the avarice of businesspeople. The influence of the Church was strongly felt in encouraging businesspeople to charge no more than the "just price." In *The Worldly Philosophers*, Heilbroner relates the fiery condemnation of an unfortunate merchant by a seventeenth-century minister. The unscrupulous businessman had been found guilty of the heinous crime of making a sixpence profit on a shilling. The minister's subsequent Sunday sermon was intended to save his flock from the practice of false principles of trade. Among the heresies identified were the notions that:

I. A man might sell as dear as he can, and buy as cheap as he can.
II. If a man lose by casualty of sea, etc., in some of his commodities, he may raise the price on the rest.
III. He may sell as he bought, though he paid too dear. [2]

[1]Noll, R.G., and Owen, B.M., eds., *The Political Economy of Regulation: Interest Groups in the Regulatory Process,* (Washington, D.C.: American Enterprise Institute, 1983), p. 1.
[2]Heilbroner, R., *The Worldly Philosophers* (New York: Simon & Schuster, 1967), p. 20.

The most direct antecedent of regulation in the United States was the concept of enterprises "affected with a public interest," which comes from the English common law. In England, certain occupations—such as baker, brewer, cab driver, ferryman, innkeeper, miller, smith, surgeon, and tailor—came to be viewed as closely connected with the well being of society. Practitioners of these professions were not allowed to act solely in their self-interest, but were required to set prices and render service in a socially responsible manner. For example, an innkeeper whose establishment was far from the next resting spot was expected to refrain from exploiting his monopoly position and to keep rates at a reasonable level. This common-law tradition of social responsibility was successfully exported to the United States.

Constitutional Basis for Regulation

In the United States the authority to regulate has been granted to the states and also to the federal government. The constitutional authorization for state regulation is the Tenth Amendment, which specifies that those powers that are not delegated to the federal government and not specifically prohibited to the states may be exercised by the states. Also, the courts have long recognized the police powers of the states—the right to enact legislation to safeguard the health, safety, morals, and general welfare of their citizens.

Federal regulation is based on Article I, Section 8, of the Constitution. The Interstate Commerce Clause of this section gives Congress the right "to regulate Commerce . . . among the several States." The ambiguous term "among" has been interpreted broadly by the courts. The current interpretation of the Interstate Commerce Clause is that it provides the Congress with a right to regulate business that is "as broad as the economic needs of the nation."[3] The final clause of Article I, Section 8, buttresses the Interstate Commerce Clause by authorizing Congress "to make all laws which shall be necessary and proper for carrying into Execution the foregoing Powers, and all other Powers vested by this Constitution in the Government of the United States." This clause also has been interpreted broadly by the courts. Under the existing interpretation, the federal government is permitted to exercise implied powers that allow it to do not only those things that are explicitly specified, but also those which the courts view as implicitly sanctioned by the Constitution.

Development of Regulation in the United States

Railroads   One of the great developments of the nineteenth century was the coming of the railroad. Certainly no innovation changed the shape of the nation more than did the advent of a widespread rail network. The importance of the railroad was not lost to local, state, and federal officials. Although U.S. railroads were built by private firms, the contributions of the various levels of government were substantial. Competition between communities for a rail line was often fierce. In 1880 the Northern Pacific offered to extend a line to Superior, Wisconsin, in return for one-third of the city's land, premises, and real estate. The community accepted the offer.

[3]*American Power and Light Company v. Securities and Exchange Commission,* 329 U.S. 90, 104 (1946).

States often provided cash donations or subscribed to railroad securities. The amount of debt incurred to finance this assistance sometimes became very burdensome. For example, in 1870 in Virginia the interest on railroad associated debt was about $2,000,000, while the state's total income was less than $3,000,000.[4] In some cases the burden became so great that the states repudiated their debts, justifying their action by the claim of illegality or fraud in the issuance of the bonds.

The federal government also was extensively involved in helping the railroads. Federal assistance often took the form of land grants. Over 130 million acres were given to the railroads by the federal government—an area equivalent to the states of Michigan, Wisconsin, Illinois, Indiana, and nearly half of Ohio. The government also aided the railroads by remitting tariffs on iron used for rails and by providing millions of dollars in loans. It is estimated that the total amount of public aid for railroad construction was well over $1 billion.[5]

Early Regulation   Financial aid given to the railroads was not provided out of a sense of compassion and brotherhood. The government, particularly municipalities competing for new rail lines, expected substantial economic benefits. In addition to increases in land values, it was anticipated that the railroads would provide cheap transportation of agricultural and other products to growing Eastern markets. Public aid was often provided in the belief that the economic growth of the community would more than compensate for the initial costs of bringing in the railroad. In many cases sleepy towns were indeed transformed into thriving commercial centers with the coming of the railroad. For many, however, the railroad was not the panacea that had been promised. The railroads often showed their gratitude for public assistance in strange ways. Shippers on monopoly routes were treated in a high-handed manner and their shipments were sometimes ignored. Special rates and treatment were provided for favored customers. An infamous example involves the Standard Oil Company, which established an arrangement with the Cincinnati and Marietta Railroad to ship its oil for 10 cents per barrel, while its competitors were charged 35 cents per barrel. The most disturbing part of the agreement was that Standard Oil got the 25-cent differential paid by the independent shippers.[6]

In addition to discriminating between customers, the railroads also practiced discrimination between locations. Small towns that had made substantial financial sacrifices to bring in the railroad found themselves paying rates far higher than shippers in large cities, where there was more competition for freight traffic. For example, in the fall of 1868 the cost of shipping grain from Chicago to the Eastern seaboard was $1.88 per hundred pounds. By the summer of 1869 competition had driven the price down to 25 cents per hundred. Rates for grain shipments from outlying areas where the railroads had a monopoly showed no such change.[7] An economist might argue that as long as the low rates from Chicago covered variable costs and made some contribu-

[4]Scott, W. A., *The Repudiation of State Debts* (New York: Crowell, 1893), p. 216.
[5]Federal Coordinator of Transportation, *Public Aids to Transportation,* Vol. 1 (Washington, D.C.: Government Printing Office, 1940), p. 19.
[6]Fair, M. L., and Williams, E. W., *Economics of Transportation and Logistics* (Dallas: Business Publications, 1975), p. 425.
[7]Jones, E., *Principles of Railroad Transportation* (New York: Macmillan, 1924), p. 94.

tion to overhead the rural shipper was not being unfairly treated. This insight was somehow lost to farmers who were paying rates to ship their grain that were four or five times those of Chicago shippers.

The financial manipulations involved in railroad construction also created public dissatisfaction. Unscrupulous financiers issued securities valued at three or four times the cost of railroad construction and took the difference as personal profits. As a result, instead of receiving large dividends, many owners of railroad securities found themselves holding stock of firms that had been forced into bankruptcy. A prime example was the Erie Railroad, which came to be known as the "scarlet woman of Wall Street." Chartered in 1832 at an estimated cost of $3 million, the firm twice went bankrupt and finally began operation on its main road 36 years later, at a total cost of $16.5 million.[8]

The final straw and proximate cause of widespread railroad regulation was an agricultural depression in the early 1870s.[9] A large expansion of domestic agriculture and a decrease in demand for grain in foreign markets caused agricultural prices to tumble. Farmers were caught in the pinch between low prices and high freight rates. The result was an agrarian revolt called the Granger Movement. The Grange gained control of a number of Midwestern legislatures and responded to antirailroad feeling by passing laws creating commissions and attempting to regulate the abuses of the railroads. Many of these laws were later repealed or changed, but they primed the fitful drive for regulation in the United States.

The railroads and other industries affected by the new legislation challenged the constitutionality of the acts. In 1877, six disputes, which have collectively become known as the Grange cases, came to the Supreme Court. The most important of these was *Munn* v. *Illinois,* in which the Court made its first significant attempt to designate those industries "affected with a public interest" and, thus, candidates for regulation. The Munn case did not directly concern railroads at all, but was triggered by a law passed by the Illinois legislature that regulated maximum prices and required licenses for grain elevators and warehouses. Two partners in a Chicago grain elevator business, Munn and Scott, were sued for failure to comply with the legislation. Munn and Scott argued that the law was unconstitutional because it deprived them of property without due process and because they were engaged in a private business that should not be subject to regulation. The Court upheld the convictions of Munn and Scott, noting that their business stands "in the very 'gateway of commerce,' and takes toll from all who pass," and that it "most certainly 'tends to a common charge, and is become a thing of public interest and use.' "[10] Although there were nine different grain storage companies in Chicago, it was shown that they met periodically to set prices. The Court viewed these firms as holding a "virtual monopoly" and held that the state could legitimately regulate their operations.

Over the next six decades the Supreme Court attempted to differentiate between those industries that were in the public interest and, hence, subject to regulation and those that were strictly private concerns. It is somewhat difficult to discern a clear

[8]Phillips, C. F., *The Economics of Regulation* (Homewood, Ill.: Irwin, 1969), p. 446.
[9]Eight states established regulatory commissions prior to 1870, but these agencies were primarily advisory and fact-finding bodies.
[10]*Munn* v. *Illinois,* 94 U.S. 131 (1877).

pattern in the decisions. A North Dakota law fixing prices for grain storage was upheld even though the market was highly fragmented (125 different owners within the state).[11] The unloading and weighing of grain from ships in New York was deemed within the public interest.[12] A requirement of fire insurance firms in Kansas to reduce premiums was also considered acceptable.[13] On the other hand, regulation of theater ticket prices in New York[14] and gasoline prices in Tennessee[15] was not permitted. State requirements that employment agencies in New Jersey[16] and ice sellers in Oklahoma[17] obtain licenses were also invalidated.

The difficult task of defining those industries that are "affected with a public interest" was finally abandoned by the Court in the Nebbia case [*Nebbia* v. *New York* (1934)]. A 1933 New York law had created a board empowered to fix minimum prices for milk. A price of 9 cents per quart was set. An enterprising Rochester grocer named Nebbia attempted to beat the system by offering two quarts of milk plus a 5-cent loaf of bread for 18 cents. Brought to the bar of justice, Nebbia argued that the retailing of milk was a highly competitive business, in which the state had no business interfering. Nebbia lost a 5 to 4 decision, and the Court went on to establish the current precedent as to the class of firms that can be regulated. The essence of the decision was that:

> It is clear that there is no closed class or category of business affected with a public interest. . . . [A] state is free to adopt whatever economic policy may reasonably be deemed to promote public welfare, and to enforce that policy by legislation adopted to its purpose. The courts are without authority either to declare such policy, or, when it is declared by the legislature, to override it. If the laws passed are seen to have a reasonable relation to a proper legislative purpose, and are neither arbitrary nor discriminatory, the requirements of due process are satisfied.[18]

Simply stated, the effect of the Nebbia decision was to bring virtually all industries within the potential domain of regulatory power. No longer would the courts sort industries to determine if they were sufficiently in the public interest to warrant regulation. The legislative branches of government were assumed to have the power to regulate any industry as long as that authority was not exercised in an arbitrary or discriminatory manner. Henceforth, the courts would focus their attention on how regulatory powers were used rather than what was being regulated. The proliferation of governmental regulatory activities over the last 40 years is a partial legacy of the Nebbia decision.

Even before Nebbia, it had become clear that one type of business was an acceptable candidate for regulation—the public utility. It is difficult to define precisely what makes a business a public utility. Indeed, there is no definition that could neatly

---

[11]*Brass* v. *North Dakota ex. rel.,* Stoeser, 153 U.S. 391 (1894).
[12]*Budd* v. *New York,* 143 U.S. 517 (1892).
[13]*German Alliance Insurance Co.* v. *Lewis,* 233 U.S. 389 (1914).
[14]*Tyson and Brother* v. *Banton,* 273 U.S. 418 (1927).
[15]*Williams* v. *Standard Oil Co.,* 278 U.S. 235 (1929).
[16]*Ribnik* v. *McBride,* 277 U.S. 350 (1928).
[17]*New State Ice Co.* v. *Liebmann,* 285 U.S. 262 (1932).
[18]*Nebbia* v. *New York,* 291 U.S. 531, 536 (1934).

describe all the industries that the courts have designated as public utilities. However, as a rough working definition, there seem to be two general characteristics. First, the industry provides a product or service of particular importance. Either the day-to-day livelihood or the future growth of the society depends on the continued and reasonable provision of the product or service. Second, the nature of the production process of the product or service is such that competition is seen as yielding undesirable results. The public utility designation is applied to firms providing electric power; natural gas; local water and sewerage supply; telephone, telegraph, and cable communications; and urban and interurban passenger and freight transportation. Although other enterprises such as warehouses, docks, stockyards, taxis, and stock exchanges are sometimes spoken of as public utilities, the use of the term here will be confined to the narrower, more common set of industries enumerated above.

Public utility regulation was an accepted fact long before the Nebbia case. Railroad regulation at the federal level began with the establishment of the Interstate Commerce Commission in 1887. By that date 25 states had already established commissions to regulate railroads. In the first decade of the twentieth century state commissions began to expand their jurisdiction to include the other public utilities. By the 1930s the great majority of states had established some sort of regulatory agency. The operation of these state agencies is discussed in Chapter 11.

Federal Regulation   Some federal involvement in regulatory activities goes well back into the nineteenth century, but the major thrust is a product of the Depression years of the 1930s. Never before had the United States experienced an economic calamity of the magnitude of the Great Depression. At its peak, one-quarter of the nation's work force was unemployed. In real terms, the gross national product shrank by nearly one-third between 1929 and 1933.

Although certain industries were regulated, the prevailing public mood just prior to the Depression was supportive of a laissez-faire business environment. Business was booming, expectations were high, and government was relatively small and unobtrusive. Fortunes were being made by financial speculation and the captains of industry engineered their giant corporations upward and onward. The agony of the Depression radically changed attitudes toward business. The collapse of the stock market shattered the dreams of many Americans. Prolonged unemployment tarnished the shining image of the free enterprise system. People began to look more and more to government to help them in their plight. Government responded by establishing programs that encroached further into the realms of business than ever before.

The nature of the times is indicated by the passage of the National Industrial Recovery Act (NIRA) in 1933. The thrust of the NIRA was dramatically different than the procompetitive policies that had previously been pursued. The theme of the NIRA was cooperation rather than competition. For example, trade associations were encouraged to establish codes of fair conduct. Many of these codes included explicit provisions for fixing minimum prices and slowing the rate of changes in price. The undesirability of allowing collusion in normal times was well recognized, but it was felt that such extreme measures were justified to bring the economy back to a more healthy condition. Although the NIRA was declared unconstitutional by the Supreme Court in 1935, the fact that the legislation passed at all indicates a change in philosophy.

Most of the major federal regulatory agencies were created during the 1930s. Only the Federal Power Commission (now the Federal Energy Regulatory Commission), the Interstate Commerce Commission, and the Federal Trade Commission existed prior to this time, and the jurisdiction and powers of these agencies were significantly expanded during this period.

In addition to the activist mood of the times, the intrusion of the federal government into regulation reflects changing technological and business conditions. Originally, regulation of electricity, telephone, and natural gas was left primarily to the states. Over time the firms providing these services began to overlap state boundaries. With the advent of regional firms, the state agencies designated to regulate them found themselves in a difficult position. The states could only regulate operations within their boundaries, but the firms were making decisions on a broader scope. Federal regulation was seen as necessary to regulate interstate operations. The Federal Communications Commission was created, and the Federal Power and Interstate Commerce Commissions were substantially altered to deal with such problems.

A second aspect of changing technology was the emergence of new industries in transportation and communications. One charge of the new Federal Communications Commission was to maintain order and decency in radio and television. The Civil Aeronautics Board was created to regulate a fledgling airlines industry. The Interstate Commerce Commission was expanded to recognize the growing importance of trucking as an alternative mode of freight transportation.

The powers and duties of federal commissions have expanded over time as new problems or changes in technology created the demand for additional regulation. Only in the last few years has there been an indication that the operations of these agencies might level off or be curtailed. Recent efforts to deregulate airlines, trucking, natural gas, and telecommunications are a dramatic reversal of the trend toward more regulation.

CONSUMER PROTECTION THEORY OF REGULATION

The traditional view of economic regulation is that it serves the "public interest" by protecting consumers against high prices or unreliable service. The need for economic regulation to protect consumers is alleged to occur when one or more of the following conditions exists:

- natural monopoly
- undue price discrimination
- destructive competition

Natural Monopoly

Certain industries are sometimes referred to as natural monopolies. The term is used to describe situations where technology provides substantial cost advantages to larger firms and, hence, the only stable market structure is that of a single firm serving the entire market. Smaller firms are either forced into bankruptcy or acquired by the dominant firm. Consumers in the market are then left to the whims of the resulting monopolist.

Figure 10.1 illustrates the cost characteristics of a natural monopoly. The short-run average-cost curves for plants of different sizes are designated *SRAC*. Remember that in economics the short run is defined as a period brief enough so that some costs must be considered as fixed. In this case it is the basic size of the production facility that cannot be varied in the short run. As the level of production is increased for any given plant size, the fixed costs of the facility are spread over more units, and average costs decline. The upward-sloping portion of the short-run average-costs curve reflects the high cost of expanding production as the capacity of the plant is approached. It should also be observed that the cost curves of Figure 10.1 include a normal return to capital. Thus, a firm that is just covering its average costs is earning a return on capital comparable to that earned by capital employed in other uses with similar risk.

Suppose that four firms, each with a plant of size *A,* are competing in the market and each is producing 100 units of the product. For the firms to earn a normal return on capital the price can fall no lower than P_A. However, if two firms of plant size *B* were to share the market, they could supply the same 400 units of total product by each producing 200 units and the price could drop as low as P_B. Finally, a single firm could produce the 400 units of output and reduce the price to P_C by building a plant of size *C.* If this single firm were in the market, there is no level of production that could be chosen by firms with either plant size *A* or *B* that would allow these firms to cover their costs at the price P_C. The cost advantages of the larger firm are so great that the other firms cannot compete. In the long run the smaller firms will be forced from the market and only the larger firm will remain. The single firm is referred to as a natural monopolist, because the natural result of competitive forces ends with the survival of the fittest or most efficient firm.

There are several sources of the cost advantages of the larger firm. First, technologies that are cost effective at high levels of production may actually increase unit costs at lower levels of output. For example, million-dollar machinery used for cutting and stamping auto bodies by General Motors would make little sense for the backyard car manufacturer. Geometric relations are another factor causing decreasing average costs. A gas company using 12-inch pipe has 3 cubic inches of pipe volume per square inch

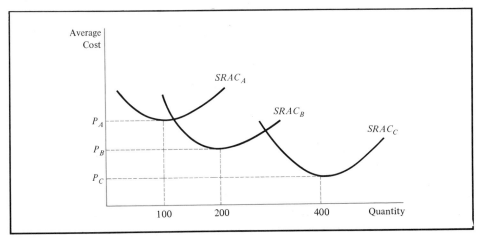

Figure 10.1. Natural monopoly.

of pipe surface, while a firm with output sufficient to justify 24-inch pipe will have 6 cubic inches of volume per square inch of surface. The reduced cost per unit of pipe volume occurs because the materials requirement varies with the diameter of the pipe, while the volume varies with the square of the radius of the pipe. Thus, the larger firm using bigger pipelines will have lower unit costs.

Two other causes of decreasing costs are specialization of labor and inventory economies. As a firm becomes larger, the demand for employee expertise in specific areas grows. Instead of being generalists, workers can concentrate on learning all the aspects of particular segments of the production process. Size also affects unit costs, because larger firms may not have to increase inventories or replacement parts proportionately with size. For example, suppose that a small firm uses a machine that is critical to the firm's operations. Let the probability that the machine will break down during a month be 10 percent. If a replacement is not readily obtainable from a nearby supplier, the firm may be forced to keep a backup on the premises. Suppose that a larger firm uses ten of the same machines, each with a 10-percent probability of malfunctioning. The probablity that two of those machines will break down in a month is 0.1×0.1, or 1 percent. The likelihood that five of the machines will become inoperative is $.1^5$, which is essentially zero. Thus, while the small firm may be required to have one backup machine for each operating machine, the larger firm may have a high degree of reliability with a much lower ratio of backup to operating machines and, hence, a lower per-unit cost.

It is doubtful that there is any industry that exhibits continuously decreasing costs. Beyond some level of output, cost-reducing forces are probably exhausted and problems of coordination start to drive average costs up. However, even if there are no pure cases of natural monopoly, demand conditions may produce equivalent results. Figure 10.2 illustrates the long-run average-cost curve for a product that has decreasing average costs up to some level of output and increasing average costs thereafter. The long-run average-cost curve in Figure 10.2 is generated by selecting the most efficient

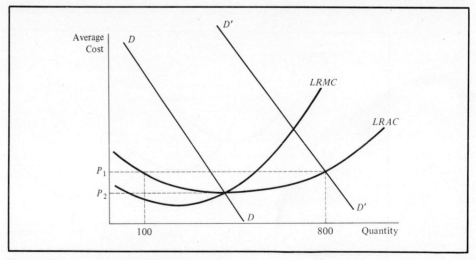

Figure 10.2. Demand-created natural monopoly.

plant size for any given level of output. It is the envelope of the short-run average-cost curves of Figure 10.1 and represents the cost conditions faced by firms in the industry when they have sufficient time to make whatever changes in plant size they deem necessary.

If the demand curve for the product is given by $D'D'$, then it may be possible for the market to support more than a single firm. For example, if a single firm were to attempt to supply the entire market and produce 800 units, it would have to charge at least P_1. But it would be possible for a small firm to enter the market and produce 100 units or more, which it could sell at P_1 and still make a profit. In this case the larger firm does not have a clear-cut cost advantage and an oligopolistic market structure would probably result.

On the other hand, if the market demand was given by DD, then the portion of the long-run average-cost curve that turns upward is irrelevant. A single firm charging at least P_2 would be the most efficient supplier. No smaller firm could exist in the market at that price. A single firm would evolve to serve the market, not because of unending cost advantages associated with size, but because of the limited demand for the product. Notice, however, that if the single firm exploits its market power by setting price substantially above P_2, then successful entry may be possible.

The existence of a natural monopoly poses something of a dilemma for public policy. One alternative is to let the firm operate as a monopoly. If the firm faced the demand curve DD as shown in Figure 10.3, the monopoly price would be P_m and the quantity Q_m. The firm would then earn an excess or economic profit given by the area of the rectangle $P_m ABC$. Compared to marginal-cost pricing, the monopoly-pricing scheme would result in a welfare loss and also a transfer of consumer surplus from consumer to producers.

If the firm is not to be allowed to act as an unconstrained monopolist, there are several alternatives open to the policy maker. One is to invoke antitrust laws and split the firm up into smaller competing firms. It is not clear that the public would be made better off by this action. The inefficiency of these small firms requires that they charge a high price just to earn a normal return on capital. There is no guarantee that the price

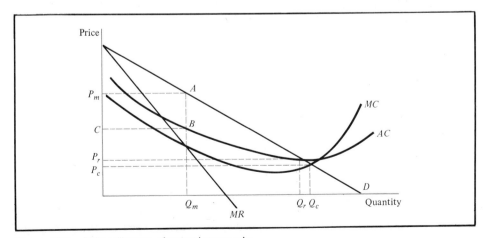

Figure 10.3. Policy dilemma of natural monopoly.

required by such firms to earn a normal return would not be higher than the price that the more efficient monopolist would charge to maximize profits. Thus, unless competition is desired for its own sake, the antitrust approach may not be a desirable solution.

A third solution is to allow the firm to maintain its monopoly position, but require it to price at marginal cost. For the demand and cost curves in Figure 10.3, this would result in a price of P_c and a quantity of Q_c. At this level of production there is no welfare loss, because production is expanded until the cost of producing the last unit is equated to the value of that unit. There is also no transfer of surplus from consumers to producers. In fact, the problem is quite the reverse. Because the monopolist is producing in a region of decreasing costs, its marginal cost is less than its average cost. Being required to price at marginal cost, the monopolist is unable to earn a normal return on capital. This is easily seen by observing that, at the output Q_c, the average revenue as given by the demand curve is less than the average cost.

If a policymaker requires a firm with decreasing costs to price at marginal cost over a long period of time, then some provision must be made to compensate the investors in the firm for the losses that must be sustained. One way of doing this is to provide a subsidy to the firm. This approach is sometimes used with publicly owned bridges. The marginal cost of allowing another car over the bridge is almost zero. Cars are allowed to pass without charge or at nominal cost, and the cost of building and operating the bridge is paid from tax revenues. In the United States the policy of providing subsidy from public funds has never been very popular. There have been exceptions, such as subsidies for airlines, urban transportation, and rural electricity and gas, but the general philosophy has been that public utility services should be largely self-sustaining.

Another possibility is public ownership of natural monopolies. If efficient resource allocation requires pricing at marginal cost and if subsidy to a private enterprise is not considered acceptable, then a "simple" solution is for the government to nationalize the industry. This is the approach to natural monopolies that has been taken in most other nations. Telephone service, electric power, natural gas, and railroad transportation are provided by the state. The evaluation of this approach is a complex question. Past experience with public ownership is discussed in Chapter 19. Although there is some precedent for government ownership of utilities in the United States (the Tennessee Valley Authority and numerous municipal electric utilities, for example), this approach has been the exception rather than the rule.

The actual scheme for dealing with pricing of the product of a natural monopoly in the United States may best be thought of as a compromise solution. The nature of the compromise is illustrated by Figure 10.3. A simple description of public utility price regulation is that price is set equal to average cost. That is, the firm is allowed to charge a price that allows it to earn no more than a normal return on its capital. This is shown in Figure 10.3 by the price, P_r, and the quantity, Q_r. It is a compromise because the price that is set is less than the monopoly price, but higher than marginal cost. There is some welfare loss, because price is not equated to marginal cost, but far less than if the firm were allowed to act as a monopolist. On the other hand, the firm is self-sustaining—there is no need for the subsidy that would be required with marginal-cost pricing. Thus, this mechanism achieves some of the gains from marginal-cost pricing without requiring public subsidy.

As in all microeconomics, it is a great deal easier to draw diagrams than to translate theory into actual practice. Although every author knows exactly what the demand and cost curves of a firm look like, managers and regulators are not so fortunate. In the absence of exact information some workable procedures have been developed to set prices in regulated industries. For most public utilities the mechanism used is the rate case. In this proceeding the firm and the government present evidence as to what prices would allow the firm to earn a normal return on capital. This determination requires estimating what the firm's revenues would be under different prices, what the firm's expenses will be, and what amount of profit constitutes a normal return for the firm. The public utility rate case will be considered in detail in Chapter 11.

Undue Price Discrimination

Price discrimination occurs when consumers are charged different prices for a product and the differences in price cannot be accounted for by cost differentials. The three requirements for successful price discrimination are that consumers have different demand elasticities, that markets be separable, and that the firm has power over price.

The telephone industry provides good examples of successful price discrimination policies. Rates for basic telephone service are higher for business users than they are for residential users. There is no particular reason to assume that the cost of installing and maintaining a phone in an office is different than putting one in a kitchen. There are, however, possible differences in demand elasticity for business versus home phone customers. Consider the extreme example of a stockbroker. The vast majority of orders for the purchase or sale of stock come to the broker by phone. There is no way the business could be conducted without a phone. By way of contrast, if there is a neighbor's phone that can be used in an emergency, it is quite possible to get along without a telephone in one's home. In economic terms, the stockbroker has a more inelastic demand for telephone service than the residential customer.

The other conditions for price discrimination are also met in the telephone industry. There is really no way that a low-cost home phone can be resold to a business customer. There is a physical connection between the customer and the phone company in each case. If the stockbroker doesn't hook up to the local phone company, there is no practical way for him or her to have access to customers calling in orders.

Residential customers looking at the price they have to pay for telephone service in relation to the commercial user are delighted. Commercial users are less ecstatic. They probably view the differential as being unfair. If the phone company were allowed to determine its rate structure without interference, then businesspeople's only recourse would be to try to persuade the company to lower their rates. If the residential-commercial differential is not reduced, there is little else they can do except complain long and loud about the inequity of the matter.

The plight of the victim of price discrimination may provide an argument for regulation. Perhaps government should intervene to protect the commercial user from a truly unfair situation. The issue is not one of efficiency, but of fairness. The presumption is that the monopolist should not be allowed to use its power to "unduly discriminate" against some consumers. Some discrimination may be acceptable and, as will be shown in the next chapter, actually represents the best alternative to marginal-cost pricing. The argument for regulation is that help is needed when that discrimination becomes undue. There is no clear definition of the distinction between due and undue discrimination. In the end, *undue discrimination* is whatever the regulatory commissions or the courts say is undue discrimination.

Destructive Competition

The problem requiring public intervention in the case of natural monopoly is that there is too little competition. It is sometimes argued that in other industries there is actually too much competition and that the steadying hand of government is required to protect the industry from itself, and consumers from the industry. There are at least two circumstances where regulation has been advocated to prevent "destructive competition."

The first case is that of industries with a large and highly specialized fixed investment and relatively low operating costs. The railroads are a good example. The major expense in starting a railroad is for the roadbed and terminal facilities. Once these are constructed, they have few uses other than transporting freight or passengers. Compared to the cost of building the line, the expense involved in carrying a few more passengers or a few additional tons of freight is very small. Thus, if a railroad were to find itself with excess capacity in terms of its fixed investment and faced with competition from other lines, there would be a strong incentive to cut costs to capture a larger share of the market. Any extra business that can be acquired that pays enough to cover operating costs and still provides some contribution to overhead is desirable to the railroad, because the return on its investment will increase.

During the late 1800s competition often resulted in excess capacity and the railroads did respond by cutting prices. However, competing railroads often faced the same problem and retaliated with further price cuts. The history of American railroads is replete with examples of price wars between competing lines. A case in point is the dramatic reductions in rates for shipping grain from Chicago to the East Coast that were mentioned earlier in the chapter.

At first blush it would seem that such price cutting would be a boon to shippers, but this was not always true. Railroad managers were all too aware of the tendency toward rate wars. When all competing lines cut rates, none of the firms gain unless total market demand is expanded considerably. Rather than exist with prices only slightly above marginal costs, the railroads often engaged in price cooperation in order to restore higher prices. One of the many forms of cooperation was simple price-fixing agreements. A related form was the traffic pool. Firms involved in traffic pools would agree to serve only a predetermined part or proportion of the market. Alternatively, firms would take whatever traffic came their way and then divide profits in an agreed manner. In any of these cases the final result was that price competition was restrained.

A second problem was that service tended to deteriorate as prices went down. When firms cut rates they also had to cut expenditures on maintenance and improvements. In addition, firms with greater financial strength were often able to survive rate wars, while other firms were either forced into bankruptcy or acquired by the larger firm. The final result was a monopoly, with the remaining firm able to set prices without fear of retaliation from other firms. In this case the short-run benefit to the consumer

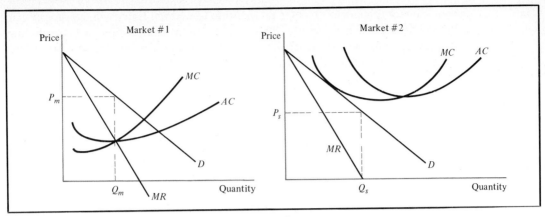

Figure 10.4. Initial demand and cost curves: unregulated firm.

of the price war may have been outweighed by the long-term costs of being served by a monopolist.

Where destructive competition among firms results in collusion, poor service, or the demise of other firms, there is often a demand for regulation to moderate the excesses of the market. In this case the objective of regulation is not usually to determine maximum prices, but to put a floor under rates. In this role the regulatory agency functions as a cartel manager for the industry. Hopefully, however, the level of prices set by the agency would be considerably less than that of an industry cartel.

TAXATION BY REGULATION

Some students of the regulatory process argue that the regulation sometimes serves as a substitute for direct taxation.[19] The contention is that certain regulatory institutions have economic or social objectives that could not be achieved in unregulated markets. The regulatory process can be used to achieve these objectives by compelling a regulated firm to provide a service that would not otherwise be provided or to provide the service at a price so low as to require a subsidy. To the extent that other prices of the regulated firm must be high enough to support the low-priced or unprofitable service, some users are being required to support the social objectives of the regulators. Where the regulated firm has been guaranteed a monopoly, it may be said that some consumers are experiencing *taxation by regulation*.

Consider the following hypothetical example. An unregulated firm is providing service in two markets. The original demand and cost curves are shown in Figure 10.4. Initially, assume that the firm has a monopoly in the first market and charges the monopoly price, P_m. Note that the second market is much different from the first. Indeed, no price can be charged that will allow the firm to cover its costs. However, because of good will or whatever, assume that the firm charges P_s in the second market and subsidizes the losses with the monopoly profit that it earns in the first market.

This firm will always remain a monopolist in the second market, because there

---

[19]The most articulate exposition of this position is by Richard Posner. See "Taxation by Regulation," *Bell Journal of Economics and Management Science*, Vol. 2, No. 1 (Spring 1971), pp. 22–50.

is no reason for other firms to enter an unprofitable market. Entry will, however, occur in the first market. The excess profits act as a lure for competition. If not prevented by regulation, entry will continue until all of the firm's excess profits have been eliminated. At this point the firm is no longer able to support its "hobby" in the second market. With no excess profits in market #1 and a loss in market #2, the firm will sustain an overall loss unless it discontinues its unprofitable operations in the second market. Thus, entry in one market results in the firm's exiting the other market.

Now, suppose that the firm is regulated by an agency with the power to prevent entry in market #1. Further suppose that the agency considers it socially desirable to maintain the service provided in market #2. The regulatory authority may strike a bargain with the firm that it will not allow entry in the profitable market if the firm will continue to provide subsidized service in the other market. The net effect is that the agency has achieved its social goals and the firm continues to earn at least a normal return on its overall operations. The burden of this policy falls on consumers in market #1. Instead of reaping the benefits of lower prices resulting from competition, they continue to face the monopoly price. This additional cost may be thought of as a tax that they are compelled (if they want the service) to pay to support the provision of the service in the other market.

There are many examples that illustrate the taxation-by-regulation concept. Historically, airlines and railroads were required to provide service, however unprofitable it may have been, to sparsely populated areas. Evidently, the regulatory agencies attached a positive social value to rural life and acted to reduce some of its costs. The provision of high-cost telephone service to isolated areas is another manifestation of the same philosophy.

Sometimes certain social groups are singled out for special treatment. Several state commissions have allowed special lower rates on electricity and telephone for senior citizens. Lifeline rates have been proposed to provide minimum blocks of electricity for low-income groups. To the extent that such tariffs earn less than the overall return allowed by the commission, they must be subsidized by other customers.

In the radio and television industry, stations are normally expected to provide part of their air time for public service or documentary programming. With a few notable exceptions, such programs are notoriously unprofitable. The stations are granted their licenses and permitted to charge what the market will bear with the expectation that some of the excess profits that are earned will be used for these public edification efforts. Similarly, cable television franchises are sometimes granted by municipalities on the condition that certain channels be made available for use by the city or by educational institutions.

There is always a cost involved when a regulatory agency pursues social objectives. This cost is borne by some set of customers if internal subsidization is involved. It is paid by the stockholders if some markets are maintained and there is no internal subsidy. It is paid by future generations if low prices result in excessive resource use or in outdated technology because entry is not allowed. The tendency of legislative bodies to allow taxation by regulation is great, because of the ease with which it may be accomplished. The budget of a state legislature or the Congress is a subject of examination. Expenditures on specific programs are a matter of public record. However, it is much more difficult to determine when one market or service of a regulated firm is subsidizing another. Thus, it may be possible to achieve social goals in a more covert manner through the regulatory process than through the legislative path.

INTEREST GROUP THEORY OF REGULATION

Many scholars do not subscribe to the view that regulation effectively protects the public interest. Instead, they argue that the effects of regulation can best be explained in terms of regulators responding to information and pressures from various groups who have an interest in the outcome of a decision. This "interest group" theory of regulation has been presented in several different ways.

Industry Capture Theory

One theory of regulation posits that regulatory agencies are "captured" by the industry that they are charged with regulating. Under this view, policies of the agency are designed primarily to benefit the needs of existing firms in the industry. This capture can occur in several ways. Sometimes the initial push for regulation is alleged to come from the industry. For example, Kolko contends that the early regulation of the railroads was the result of efforts by railroad owners. He uses Marxist analysis to argue that regulation was used to protect capitalists from consumers and workers.[20]

A different explanation is offered by Bernstein.[21] He suggests that regulatory commissions evolve through four stages. The first is the *incipiency* stage, during which the commission seeks to identify its mission and to establish procedures. Next is the *youth* phase, which is characterized by aggressive attempts to carry out the commission's legislative mandate. Third is a *mature* stage, in which public support has waned and conflicts with the industry being regulated are less frequent. Finally, in *old age* policymakers and the staff of the commission see their interests as closely connected with those of the industry. At this point, the commission has been captured and most of its actions are designed to protect and promote the interests of the industry.

A third variation of the capture theory comes from Stigler.[22] His model considers regulation as a means for the redistribution of wealth. This redistribution occurs as commissions make rules that favor one group over another. In principle, the powers of regulatory commissions could be used to confer benefits on any segment of society. In practice, Stigler argues that industry is far more effective than consumers in winning the political game. Thus, the net result is that the regulatory process usually favors industry at the expense of consumers.

Modern Interest Group Theory

The main contribution of Stigler is not his conclusion that regulation will benefit industry, but rather his analysis that suggests that some groups are more likely to be

[20]Kolko, G., *Railroads and Regulation, 1877–1916* (Princeton, N.J.: Princeton University Press, 1965).
[21]Bernstein, M., *Regulating Business by Independent Commission* (Princeton, N.J.: Princeton University Press, 1955), pp. 74–102.
[22]Stigler, G.J., "The Theory of Economic Regulation," *Bell Journal of Economics and Management Science,* Vol. 2, No. 1 (Spring 1971), pp. 3–21.

well represented in the regulatory process than others. Stigler's work has evolved into a more general theory of how interest groups affect the outcomes of regulation.

Modern interest group theory starts from the premise that regulation can have important effects on the distribution of wealth. As a result, those who will be affected by regulatory decisions have an incentive to try and influence those decisions. This can be accomplished by means such as lobbying, providing data, hiring expert witnesses, and conducting publicity campaigns. The responsibility of regulators is to sift through the information received and differentiate between arguments that reflect only special interests and those that support the public interest as the policymakers perceive it.

Limited budgets and staff force regulators to make decisions at least partially on the basis of information that is supplied by various interest groups. Thus, those groups that do the best job of representing their interests are most likely to receive favorable treatment by the regulatory body. But such representation can be a time-consuming and expensive process. As a result, certain types of special interest groups may have an advantage in regulatory proceedings. Factors affecting the degree to which a group will be well represented in a regulatory decision include degree of self-interest, size, homogeneity, and uncertainty.

Degree of Self-Interest   The more important a decision is to a group, the more effort the members of that group will expend to influence the decision. For example, an electric utility that is requesting a $100-million rate increase has a much greater stake in the decision of the regulatory commission than does the consumer whose monthly electricity bill will increase by $3.50 if the rate increase is approved. As a result, the utility will spend a great deal of time and effort trying to sway the commission, while an individual consumer may do little more than grumble when the higher bill comes.

Size of the Group   All other things being equal, a smaller group is better able to promote its views than a group consisting of many people or firms. The reason is that organizational problems increase with size. Also, large groups tend to have more serious problems with free riders. A single consumer, asked to contribute to a fund to lobby for reduced electricity rates, may rationalize that his or her failure to contribute will have no noticeable effect on the effectiveness of the group. In contrast, in a consortium of three or four firms, one defector might spell the difference between success and defeat.

Group Homogeneity   If all of the members of a group are in a similar position and have similar objectives, then the group does not have to spend time and money hammering out compromise positions for presentation before the regulatory body. All of the resources of the group can be marshaled to achieve the common goal.

Uncertainty   If the results of a particular decision are predictable, then members of a group will be more willing to make contributions than if the results are uncertain. For example, if there is a lack of information as to whether deregulation of an industry will lead to higher or lower prices for consumers, then consumer groups may have little impact on the decision process.

Stigler's early formulation of interest group theory predicted that regulation is biased toward producers. The modern theory is roughly consistent, but somewhat more general. Existing firms in an industry are likely to have a high stake in regulatory decisions, be relatively few in number, hold similar objectives, and have a good idea about the outcome of regulatory decisions. Thus, the views of those firms are likely to be well represented in the regulatory process. In contrast, consumers, small firms attempting to enter a regulated industry, and those advocating the use of new technologies are likely to be poorly represented. As a result, the theory predicts that there will be a tendency for regulatory decisions to favor the existing firms in a regulated industry. The theory also suggests that small, one-issue consumer groups such as environmentalists and senior citizens can have an important impact on the outcomes of decisions.

PUBLIC INTEREST OR PRIVATE INTEREST?

Does regulation protect the public interest or is it a tool for protecting special interests? In most cases, the clear intent in setting up a regulatory body is to protect the public interest. But there are many examples of the use of regulation for the benefit of established firms and industries. The broadcast industry for several years was able to convince the Federal Communications Commission to impose standards that greatly restricted the growth of cable television. Similarly, the railroads used their influence to limit the growth of trucking. Regulations were imposed that attempted to preserve market shares of railroads in markets where trucking had economic advantages. The financial ill health of the railroads may be partially explained by the attempts of the Interstate Commerce Commission to artificially prop up an industry that technology had bypassed.

Interest group theory presents a convincing case for the proposition that such examples are likely to be the rule rather than the exception. However, the industry bias of regulation should be considered as a tendency, not an inevitable result. There are important factors that work to promote the public interest in the regulatory process.

Political Entrepreneurs

The interests of consumers often are too diffuse and the impacts of a regulatory decision on the individual consumer too small to guarantee effective participation by consumers. But the cause of consumers may be championed by political entrepreneurs. Such persons are only too willing to exploit the misdeeds of a regulatory commission as a means of furthering their own ambitions. Often, these entrepreneurs are politicians trying to get elected or reelected. In the presidential election of 1976, President Carter used the need for deregulation as an effective issue. Ironically, President Reagan used the same tactic against Carter in the 1980 campaign.

In other cases, the political entrepreneurs may be authors using their writing skills to agitate for reform. For example, a book by Upton Sinclair was an important force behind food and drug regulation in the United States. Similarly, Ralph Nader's writings called attention to the need for safer automobiles.

Scholarly Criticism

In recent years, economic and legal scholars have given a great deal of attention to the regulatory process. Much of their work has been extremely critical of the effects of regulation. The analysis of such scholars has provided a reputable foundation for those who advocate change. In particular, political entrepreneurs often team with academics who support their views. The appointment by President Reagan of William Baxter as head of the Antitrust Division of the Department of Justice was a good example. While on the faculty of the Stanford Law School, Baxter had written extensively on the need for antitrust reform.

Financial Incentives of Regulators

Regulators seldom have a financial incentive for favoring the interests of a regulated firm or industry over those of the general public. Undoubtedly, there are regulators who have received money or other compensation for tilting decisions to the benefit of a particular firm or group, but such occurences are rare.

It is sometimes suggested that members of commissions make decisions with an eye to eventually getting a lucrative job with one of the firms that they regulate. However, many regulators move, not to industry, but to another job in government. Those that do go into industry are unlikely to land a high-paying executive position by virtue of building a reputation as a patsy.

Conclusion

These mitigating factors work against the tendency of regulation to serve special interests. But their influence is felt with different strengths, at different times, in different regulatory bodies. The regulatory process deserves neither blanket praise nor blanket condemnation. It must be examined on a case-by-case basis to determine its effects. The next eight chapters take a closer look at regulation in the United States.

SUMMARY
The Expanding Scope of Regulation

Beginnings   Regulation of business dates back to ancient times. However, the immediate precursor of regulation in the United States was the concept from English common law of enterprises "affected with a public interest." These enterprises were expected to operate in a socially responsible manner.

Constitutional Basis for Regulation   The Constitution gives the states those powers not specifically delegated to the federal government nor forbidden to the states. The police powers of the states are also recognized by the Constitution. The constitutional basis for federal regulation is the Interstate Commerce Clause.

Development of Regulation in the United States
Railroads   Nineteenth-century municipalities competed vigorously for railroad lines by promising financial assistance. The federal government also contributed large

sums of money to railroad development. In total, over $1 billion in public assistance was provided.

Early regulation   In many cases the railroads proved ungrateful for the aid they had received. Service was poor and rates excessive in many areas. The Granger movement was partially a response to the abuses of the railroads. During the 1870s Granger-dominated legislatures established commissions to regulate railroads in a number of states. Over the next 60 years regulation was extended to other industries. In the Nebbia case the Supreme Court held that any industry could be regulated, and that the future concern of the courts would be the process rather than the existence of regulation.

Federal regulation   The Great Depression ushered in an era of federal regulation. Most of the federal agencies with authority to regulate prices and entry were either created or strengthened during the 1930s. Only in the last few years has there been any indication that the growth of federal regulation might slow.

Consumer Protection Theory of Regulation

Natural Monopoly   If industry technology is characterized by continuously declining costs, then the result of market competition may be a single firm supplying the entire market. Unless constrained, this monopolist can exploit consumers by charging high prices. There are several alternatives for public policy. The first is to use antitrust laws to break up the firm. However, the efficiency benefits of large size will be lost. The second is to force the firm to price at marginal cost. Because marginal costs are less than average costs, this alternative would require a subsidy. Public ownership is a third possibility, but is often opposed on philosophical grounds.

The solution that has been widely accepted in the United States is to regulate prices charged by the firm. Regulation is best thought of as a compromise whereby prices are set equal to average cost. Average-cost pricing limits the firm to a normal, or "fair," return on its capital.

Undue Price Discrimination   Many services provided by regulated firms meet the criteria for successful price discrimination. Regulation is a method for curbing undue price discrimination. The determination of what constitutes undue discrimination is an equity consideration and cannot be answered on an objective basis.

Destructive Competition   Industries with high fixed and low variable costs often engage in bouts of periodic and severe price cutting. As firms are forced from the industry, service may deteriorate. Also, there is a strong tendency for firms in the industry to form cartels to stabilize prices. In the airline and railroad industries regulatory agencies have acted as cartel managers by establishing minimum prices.

Taxation by Regulation

Regulation can be used as a vehicle for achieving the social objectives of policymakers. By preventing entry in some markets, regulators guarantee firms excess profits. In return for their monopoly position the firms may be required to provide services in markets that are unprofitable or at prices that are insufficient to yield a normal return on capital. The excess profits from the entry-controlled markets are used to subsidize the unprofitable services. Thus, purchasers in these markets are "taxed" by regulation. Low electric rates for senior citizens and airline and rail service to small communities may be examples of taxation by regulation.

Interest Group Theory of Regulation

An alternative view of regulation is that the process responds to pressures from interest groups. Those groups that can best represent their interests are those most likely to receive favorable treatment. Groups with a large stake in the outcome, small size, homogeneity, and certainty about the outcome of a decision are likely to be well represented. Producers and single-interest groups frequently meet these criteria. As a result, the regulatory process may favor such groups.

Public or Private Interest?

The bias of regulation should be considered a tendency and not an inevitable result. Certain factors serve to protect the public interest. They include political entrepreneurs who exploit agency misdeeds, scrutiny by scholars, and the lack of financial incentive for regulators to help special interest groups. The actual effect of regulation must be considered on a case-by-case basis.

DISCUSSION QUESTIONS

1. Why would the work of a blacksmith have been considered as "affected with a public interest" under English common law? What about a baker?
2. Has the intended meaning of the Interstate Commerce Clause been changed by the broad interpretations of the Supreme Court? Is a broad interpretation desirable?
3. Government subsidies may be desirable when externalities are involved. What externalities would justify the federal government's support of the railroads in the nineteenth century?
4. What was the purpose of the price floor on milk that was at issue in the Nebbia case? Could the state's objectives have been achieved in other ways?
5. What impact would a modern-day depression have on the scope of federal regulation?
6. Can a monopoly persist in an industry that does not have declining costs?
7. Why do public utility services often meet the three criteria for successful price discrimination?
8. Given the choice, would an industry prefer to form its own price-setting cartel or have the cartel managed by a regulatory agency?
9. Is direct taxation preferable to taxation by regulation? Why?
10. What legal strategies can an industry employ in using the regulatory process to promote its interests?
11. How could interest group theory be used to predict which professions would have licensing requirements and which would not?

Economic Regulation: Institutions and Procedures

Chapter Outline

Regulation is like growing old: we would rather not do it—but consider the alternative.

William G. Shepherd

This chapter is an introduction to the basic institutions and procedures of economic regulation as practiced in the United States. It begins with a discussion of the history, functions, and organization of state and federal regulatory commissions. The last two sections of the chapter focus on public utility price setting by these commissions. The modern rate case often is divided into two phases. In the first, the total revenue to which the regulated firm is entitled is determined. This is the revenue requirement portion of the proceeding. The second phase of the rate case deals with rate structure. Its purpose is to determine how the revenue requirement is to be apportioned among various customers and services and to determine the structure of individual rates.

INSTITUTIONS

State and federal government in the United States sometimes is described as consisting of three independent branches—executive, legislative, and judicial. However, many regulatory activities involve organizations that do not fit neatly into any of the three branches. Often, the responsibility for regulation is given to administrative commissions. These commissions may be sufficiently independent to constitute almost a fourth branch of government.

Administrative Commissions

History   Each of the traditional branches of government has had its fling with regulation. Under the common law there were those firms "affected with a public interest" that were expected to provide adequate and nondiscriminatory service at reasonable rates. Individuals believing they had been treated unjustly could initiate court action. Until the mid-1800s the court system was about the only means of redress available to the consumer.

Judicial regulation was not very satisfactory. Getting a judgment against a firm was a slow and costly procedure. Decisions tended to be rendered on narrow legal precedents rather than existing economic realities. Also, the courts confined themselves primarily to providing compensation for past abuses. Instead of taking the initiative to prevent undesirable business practices, judicial action responded to complaints as they were presented.

Dissatisfaction with the courts led state legislatures to become involved in the regulation of business. Legislative action took three forms. First, general laws for incorporation were enacted. Intended for hundreds of different types of business, these laws often were too broad to regulate the behavior of specific industries. Second, individual firms were granted special charters specifying their duties and rights in considerable detail. Changes in economic conditions reduced the effectiveness of these charters, because of their inflexibility. Altering the charter usually required the action of the legislature, and most legislatures were in session only a brief time during the year.

The third type of legislative activity was laws enumerating the acceptable behavior for certain types of firms. These suffered from the same deficiencies as the charters. An additional defect of both was that legislators ordinarily lacked the expertise to formulate rules for the operation of specific industries. In some cases, good economics was buried under politics, bribes, and graft. Even sound legislation could be thwarted by the problem of enforcement. There was no method of continuously monitoring a firm's activities. Violations of the law were the responsibility of the court system. Although the existence of specific legislation made it somewhat easier for consumers to prove their case, most of the problems discussed in connection with judicial regulation were still present.

During the late 1800s and early 1900s, franchise regulation was a common method of business control. The local franchise became popular because of the inadequacies of the other attempts at regulation and because most of the firms that were to be regulated operated within a single community. Franchises were based on agreements between a firm and a city, whereby the city would grant the firm the privilege (often the exclusive privilege) of operating in the community and using its streets, tracks, underground conduits, and so forth. In return, the firm would agree to provide service of a specified kind at specified rates. Up until the end of World War I, public-utility regulation was usually by local franchise.

Court rulings and changing economic conditions caused the franchise to become a much less effective regulatory technique after World War I. Court decisions held that the franchise had the status of a contract and, hence, could be changed only by the agreement of both parties. Because changes in the provisions of the agreement normally benefited one party at the expense of the other, agreement was difficult to obtain and the franchise contract proved to be unresponsive to the need for change. Changing technology also had an impact on the franchise concept. Technology for telephone, electricity, and other services gave advantages to large firms. When firms operated only within municipal boundaries, the cities could potentially exert effective control, but as firms expanded to serve states and regions, control became much more difficult. Thus, state and federal regulatory bodies with broader geographical authority became necessary to deal with these giant firms.

In addition to being able to deal with the entire firm, the state and federal commissions were more efficient by avoiding needless duplication. Small cities seldom were able to afford the kind of expertise that could be marshaled by the firm. It was more practical to have a single state or federal commission than to rely on small and relatively uninformed staffs in each community. As a result, regulation by municipalities has almost entirely been replaced by commission regulation at the state and federal levels. Cities still grant franchises to firms, but these franchises are usually limited to authorizing the firm to operate and do not involve rates and other matters.

At the state level, administrative commissions date back to the Rhode Island commission of 1839. However, these early commissions had little real power and confined themselves primarily to making recommendations to their legislatures. Although many states established commissions for railroad regulation in the last quarter of the nineteenth century, the beginning of modern state regulatory commissions was in New York, Wisconsin, and Georgia in 1907. The Wisconsin commission served as a model for similar agencies in other states. The commission was granted jurisdiction

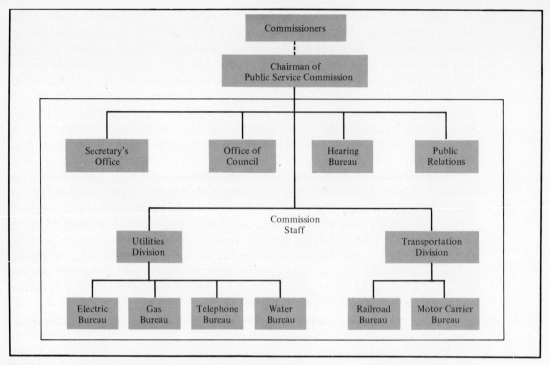

Figure 11.1. Public service commission organization chart.

over companies providing light, power, heat, water, gas, telephone, telegraph, and rail transportation. Among its powers were the right to investigate the rates and service of the firms under its jurisdiction. If investigation revealed the service in question to be substandard or the rates to be unreasonable or unfairly discriminatory, the commission could prescribe new rates and standards of service. By 1920, two-thirds of the states had some form of commission. Today, every state has a regulatory commission. Although there are some variations, the powers and jurisdiction are similar to those of the early Wisconsin commission.[1]

Organization   State commissions usually are called public service or public utilities commissions. Figure 11.1 is an organization chart for a typical commission. It shows the commission as consisting of two basic parts—the commission staff and the commissioners. The commission staff is one of the regulated firm's adversaries in hearings before the commissioners. The staff must evaluate the evidence presented by the firm and make its own recommendations. While consumer groups are becoming increasingly important in regulatory proceedings, it is still the commission staff that has the major responsibility for presenting the public's case to the commissioners. In terms of dollars and number of people, the match between the firm and the staff often is very one sided. Although larger states such as New York have commission staffs that consist of several

[1]Details regarding commission jurisdiction and procedures can be found in National Association of Regulatory Utility Commissioners, *Annual Report on Utility and Carrier Regulation* (Washington, D.C.).

hundred people, in smaller states the staff may have less than a dozen professionals. Most of the professionals on the staff are accountants, lawyers, or engineers. Compared to their counterparts in industry they are usually underpaid. The turnover of commission staff is high and it is not uncommon for an employee to leave the staff to take a better paying job with one of the firms that he or she has been involved in regulating.

The commissioners are the second basic part of the commission. They consider the evidence and recommendations of the staff, of firms, and of other groups and then formulate the commission's policies. Most state commissions have three commissioners, but the range is from one in Oregon and Rhode Island to seven in Massachusetts and South Carolina. Commissioners serve for terms of four to ten years. They may be elected to the position, appointed by the governor of the state, or appointed by the governor with the consent of the legislature. Most states do not have specific qualifications for regulatory commissioners. The typical commissioner has a legal background and some involvement in politics. Critics of the regulatory process allege that commissioners usually are either aspiring young politicians attempting to stage a political career from a commissioner's job or else unsuccessful political operatives who have obtained the job as a reward for services rendered.

Independence   At the beginning of this section, regulatory commissions were described as almost a fourth branch of government. Their independence is by design. Legislative bodies recognized that it would be tempting for presidents, governors, and legislatures to try to tamper with regulatory authorities in the attempt to further their own political fortunes. Thus, commissions were structured to provide a certain degree of freedom from such tampering. Commissioners are usually appointed for fairly long terms and their tenure is staggered to prevent an executive from replacing an entire commission in one fell swoop. Most commissions are structured by law so that no more than a simple majority of the commissioners can represent a single political party. The removal of commissioners is difficult, requiring evidence of malfeasance in office, neglect, or inefficiency. Also, commissions usually act on the basis of fairly explicit rules and precedents. Adherence to these rules and precedents tends to restrict interference from outside sources by forcing the commission to act in a more patterned manner.

The independence of commissions varies greatly from commission to commission. Although nominally independent, the commissions still are tightly interconnected with the other branches of government. Commissioners aspiring to higher office cannot afford to offend members of the executive branch. Individuals looking at the commission as a long-term position must concern themselves with their reappointment. Legislatures have great potential influence on commission operations through their control of the budget. A commission that operates contrary to the will of the legislature may find its scope of operations curtailed.

The courts also can exert control over regulatory commissions through the appeals process. In the early days of regulation, judges often took it upon themselves to review in detail the findings of commissions. The Supreme Court's findings in *ICC* v. *Alabama Midland Ry. Co.* (1894) suggests why the courts chose to become involved.[2] The case dealt with setting rail rates in Alabama. The Interstate Commerce

---

[2]*Interstate Commerce Commission* v. *Alabama Midland Ry. Co.,* 1968 U.S. 144 (1894).

Commission had jurisdiction in the matter and based its decision on the finding that there was effective competition by water for the freight traffic on the rail route in question. As the Supreme Court examined the case, it was shown that the presence of water competition was questionable at best. The river on which freight could supposedly be transported was dry half the year, only three feet deep, and so overhung with trees as to make boat passage impossible. As a result, the court modified the ICC's decision. With improvement in the quality of commission regulation, the courts have shown more restraint in overturning commission decisions. Although decisions are often appealed to the courts, the courts now usually restrict themselves to instances where commissions have violated the law or their own procedures.

The actual independence of commissions from other forces (including the firms they regulate) is a function of the economic conditions of the times and the personalities involved. Where commissioners are ill prepared or disinterested or where they have strong political allegiances, the commission may do little more than rubber stamp the recommendations of a strong governor or president. In other cases a close and long-standing relationship with the regulated industry may result in an implicit or explicit bias toward that industry. The following dialogue from a recent state commission hearing illustrates the frustration of an attorney who believed a commissioner had lost his objectivity and become a sponsor for the position of an electric utility.

> Mr. ———: "Madam Chairman, I ask to have the questioning of Commissioner X stricken from this record."
>
> Chairman: "On what basis, Mr. ———?"
>
> Mr. ———: "On the basis that it was what has generally been termed before this Commission as friendly cross-examination. And in my opinion it shows a prejudice by the Commissioner on behalf of Utah Power and Light. I don't think a Commissioner should assume an advocate position and attempt to benefit one party to these proceedings. He shouldn't engage in questioning that is clearly friendly cross-examination."
>
> Commissioner X: "Well, Mr. ———, I think you're insulting the Commission. I think you've done it many times and gotten away with it, and I'll just put for the record I think you're insulting the Commission and I think it's out of order."[3]

On the other hand, some state and federal commissions take a strong stand and attempt decisive and innovative actions. The appointment of Alfred Kahn as chairman of the Civil Aeronautics Board resulted in drastic change. The objective of typical bureaucrats is to protect their jobs and expand their kingdoms, but Kahn took the CAB position with the announced intention of deregulating the airline industry and eliminating the agency. Although he was head of the agency for only a short time, most of his goals have been accomplished.

Federal Regulatory Commissions

Because of similarities in the jurisdiction and operation of state commissions, they were discussed as a group in the previous section. However, commissions at the federal level

---

[3]Re *Utah Power and Light,* case no. 78-035-03, Utah Public Service Commission (1978), pp. 386, 387, 390.

are sufficiently different to require individual description. Although there are many federal agencies that have regulatory authority, only three are discussed here—the Interstate Commerce Commission, the Federal Energy Regulatory Commission, and the Federal Communications Commission. Other federal regulatory agencies are discussed in Chapters 17 and 18.

Interstate Commerce Commission   The oldest of the federal commissions is the ICC, which was created in 1887. Initially formed to regulate the railroads, the agency was granted authority over oil pipelines in 1906, motor carriers in 1935, and water carriers in 1940. Its main functions include setting rates and approving changes in routes. However, the recent trend toward deregulation has touched the ICC, and its authority to regulate the trucking and railroad industries has been curtailed.

Federal Energy Regulatory Commission   The Federal Power Commission was created in 1920 to oversee hydroelectric power projects. In 1935 it was given the responsibility for regulating interstate wholesale transactions of electric energy. In 1938 it assumed the responsibility for wholesale interstate sales of natural gas.[4] The need for federal intervention in interstate wholesale electricity and gas transactions stemmed from the *cost-plus* nature of state regulation. In setting rates, the states take the firm's expenses essentially as provided by the utility and add on a "fair" sum for profit. As the firm's expenses increase, commissions typically allow the increase to be passed on to consumers. Thus, price regulation by state commissions can be described as cost plus profit.

When electric and gas utilities operate within a single state, commissions can (at least in theory) effectively limit prices. When firm operations overlap state boundaries, the degree of control is greatly reduced. Consider the following hypothetical example. Yosemite Electric serves customers in California by purchasing power from Casino Power in Nevada, and both firms are controlled by a parent, or *holding,* company, Hughes Inc. Power purchased from Casino is a cost to Yosemite. (See Figure 11.2.) In determining the price that Yosemite may charge consumers for electricity, the California Public Utilities Commission takes all of Yosemite's costs and adds on the appropriate profit. If by accident or design Yosemite pays a high price for power from Casino, the extra cost will be passed on to Yosemite consumers as higher electricity prices. Although consumers may complain that their electric rates are too high, Yosemite will be able to counter that its profits are not excessive.

Casino Power is regulated by the Nevada Public Service Commission. The commission is charged with the responsibility of seeing that Casino does not make excessive profits on its Nevada operations. However, it has no authority over transactions that cross state boundaries. If the Nevada PSC and the California PUC do their job, neither firm will earn above average profits on their intra- (within) state operations. However, Casino may be very profitable on its overall (interstate and intrastate) operations if it obtains an excessive price for power sold to Yosemite. From Yosemite's point of view, as long as it is allowed to pass on the cost of purchased power and to earn a normal rate of return, there is little incentive to try to strike a better bargain with Casino. Because the two companies are part of a single holding company, it is actually desirable

---

[4]In 1954 the commission unwillingly accepted responsibility for the regulation of the wellhead price of natural gas. Chapter 14 discusses recent developments in this area.

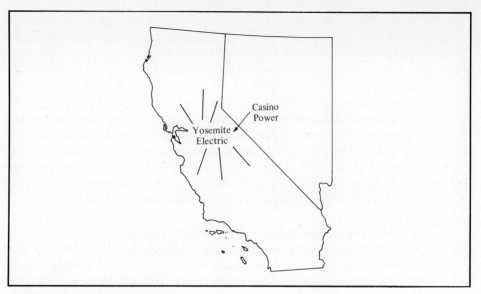

Figure 11.2. Interstate transactions.

not to limit the price. Because the higher price to Yosemite may be passed on to consumers, there is no loss on California operations. The gain to Casino becomes additional profit for the holding company. It is obtainable because neither the California PUC nor the Nevada PSC has authority to regulate the interstate wholesale transactions.

Granting authority to the Federal Power Commission over interstate wholesale sales of electricity and natural gas was an attempt to plug this loophole in the regulatory process. The commission was charged with the responsibility of making sure that interstate operations of companies do not yield excessive profits. In the example, the FPC would have acted to limit Casino to a normal rate of profit on the power sale to Yosemite. By reducing the cost to Yosemite, the California consumers should see lower electric rates.

In 1977 the Federal Power Commission was abolished and its activities transferred to the newly created Federal Energy Regulatory Commission in the Department of Energy. FERC was established to provide a broader and better coordinated approach to energy regulation. In addition to its other responsibilities, the new agency performs the basic functions of the old Federal Power Commission.

Federal Communications Commission The FCC was created in 1934 and operates in two main areas. First, it has jurisdiction over interstate and foreign telephone and telegraph service. The need for a federal agency to control interstate telephone and telegraph rates stems from the same problem with cost-plus regulation that led to the FPC's regulation of interstate electricity and natural gas prices. Second, it has responsibility for regulation of radio and television. The FCC allocates the electromagnetic spectrum and issues licenses. There is no federal or state price regulation over the broadcast industry.

THE RATE CASE: REVENUE REQUIREMENT

Probably the most visible function of the state and federal regulatory commissions is setting prices for the products and services of the industries that they regulate. The procedure used for price determination is a quasijudicial exercise called the rate case. There are two basic objectives in the rate case. The first is to find a general level of rates or prices under which the firm will earn no more than a fair or normal return on its capital. This occurs in the revenue requirement phase of the proceeding. The second takes place in the rate structure phase and involves determining rates that do not unduly discriminate against any class of consumers.

The rate case is primarily concerned with equity or fairness. If prices are raised, then stockholders of the firm benefit at the expense of consumers. If the firm is not allowed to raise prices or if the increase is small, then the consumer's benefits from lower rates are obtained at the expense of lower returns to investors. If a general increase in profits to the firm is granted while keeping prices to some groups low, then higher prices must be paid by other groups. The rate case is basically a *zero sum game.* One group can benefit only at the expense of others. Thus, it becomes an adversary proceeding with each of the involved parties trying to get a bigger share of the pie.

The procedure for determining the general level of rates in a rate case is easily described in theory if not in practice. The firm is to be granted overall revenues sufficient to allow it to earn just a fair return on its capital. The concept can be reduced to the following simple equation:

$$RR = E + s \cdot (RB - DEP) \qquad (11.1)$$

where RR = Revenue requirement
E = Expenses
s = Fair return on capital
RB = Capital, or rate base
DEP = Depreciation

Total revenue allowed by the regulatory commission is to be sufficient to allow the firm to cover its expenses plus earn the fair return on the depreciated value of its capital base. The rate case is a cost-plus form of price setting. Revenues are geared to cover the firm's costs of operating plus an add-on as a return to capital. In the rate case it is necessary that each of the components of equation 11.1 be determined. The commission must decide on the firm's allowable expenses, what constitutes a fair rate of return on capital, what is the depreciated capital or rate base to which the fair rate is to be applied, and, finally, the revenue requirement necessary to cover the sum of expenses plus return to capital. Once the general level of revenues is determined, the commission must then determine how those revenues are to be apportioned among the various classes of consumers. The commission's intent in this portion of the proceeding is to avoid undue discrimination.

The basics of the rate case are discussed in the pages that follow. First, the initiation and basic procedures of the rate case are considered. Next, the methods of determining expenses, the fair return, the rate base, and required revenues are examined. Finally, in the next section, methods for structuring rates are analyzed.

Getting Started

The rate case is usually initiated by the firm or by the commission staff. If changes in technology reduce the cost of providing the product or service, then the staff may initiate action for a reduction in rates.[5] Much more common in present inflationary times is the request by the firm for a rate increase to compensate for increases in cost. Normally, the firm will come to the commission with a specific request for an overall increase in revenues and a breakdown of how the increased revenues are to be apportioned among the different classes of consumers. Once the request is made, the commission may suspend the proposed rates pending the outcome of the rate case or may allow the firm to charge the new prices with the provision that any excess dollars collected will be refunded if the commission fails to approve the full request of the firm.

The rate case itself is similar to a courtroom proceeding. Witnesses are sworn in, questioned by their attorneys, and then required to submit to cross-examination by other attorneys. Evidence that is presented must conform to rules specified by the commission and a complete transcript is kept of the proceedings. An attempt is made to allow all interested parties the opportunity to voice their opinions. It is not uncommon for the commission to hold hearings in different cities to assure that opinions are received from a broad spectrum of the population. Often, however, these hearings do little more than fulfill the legal responsibilities of the commission and have little impact on the actual outcome of the issue.

The first substantive issue in the rate case is that of selecting the test year. The test year is the source of the data to be used in fixing expenses, the rate base, revenues, and the fair return. Often it is the last 12-month period for which data are available. Sometimes it is the last calendar year. In other cases commissions have recognized that the rates they are setting are for the future and have required a future test year. In this circumstance the rate case is based on projections of the firm's costs and revenues over the next 12-month period. The future test year has the advantage of coinciding with the period for which rates are being set, but the disadvantage of being more speculative than a test year based on historic data.

Operating Expenses

Operating costs include materials and supplies, fuel, wages and salaries, maintenance, depreciation charges, and taxes. In terms of absolute dollar size, they are far more important than profits as a determination of prices. Operating costs may represent from three-fourths to four-fifths of the total revenues for electric and gas utilities and between two-thirds to four-fifths in the case of airlines and railroads. A breakdown of revenue uses by one utility, Utah Power and Light, is shown in Figure 11.3.

In spite of the relative importance of operating costs, relatively little time is spent in evaluating them during the rate case. Typically, the estimate of costs provided by the firm is accepted by the commission staff and the commissioners with little dissent or debate. Only when there is clear evidence of poor judgment or an obvious padding

---

[5]However, it would not be uncommon for the firm to request a rate reduction if it had excess capacity, viewed the demand for its product to be very elastic, or wanted to gain goodwill and head off a potentially larger rate reduction request made by the commission staff.

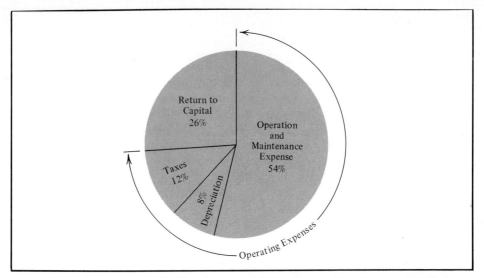

Figure 11.3. Use of revenues by Utah Power and Light. (*Source:* Utah Power and Light. *Annual Report.* Salt Lake City, Utah: 1983.)

of expenses will the commission act to reduce the level of allowable operating costs. Traditionally, the evaluation of operating expenses is viewed as a function of the management of the firm. Commissions rarely have the resources or expertise to become intimately involved in the day-to-day decisions of management. Managers, in the absence of gross abuses, are assumed to be able to make these specific determinations.

Disallowance of expenses involves an evaluation of the interests of consumers versus those of investors. If imprudent or excessive expenditures are allowed by the regulatory commission, then prices charged to consumers will be higher. On the other hand, if the commission disallows such expenses, then the firm may not be able to earn a fair or normal profit rate and may have difficulty raising capital.

Depreciation Allowances   Allowances for depreciation are considered to be a part of the firm's operating expenses. As the firm operates, capital equipment such as electrical generators, locomotives, and telephone switching gear wears out. This consumption of capital is an expense of producing the product or service that the firm must be allowed to cover if it is to maintain its financial health. Obviously, it is far easier to determine the cost of fuel that has been burned in a year or the amount that has been paid for wages and salaries than it is to specify the correct allowance for capital consumed. Usually, the depreciation allowance is computed using standardized accounting procedures. For example, if the accepted useful life of an electric generator is 40 years and a linear, or *straight-line,* method of depreciation is being used, then the depreciation allowance for that piece of equipment will be 2.5 percent of its original cost each year. For purposes of computing depreciation as a component of operating expenses, most commissions have adopted straight-line depreciation on original cost. Tax laws allow the use of accelerated depreciation in computing tax liabilities of the firm, but a discussion of these provisions is beyond the scope of this text.

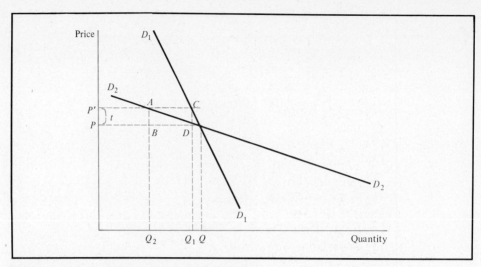

Figure 11.4. Tax collections and demand elasticity.

Taxes Taxes are a major component of utility operating costs. For telephone and electric companies they average about one-fifth of total revenues. Utilities, as a group, are taxed much more heavily than other firms. There are several aspects of these industries that make them "tax collectors par excellence." [6] First, they are normally of sufficient size to make tax administration and collection efficient. Second, the large investment in plant and equipment generates substantial revenues from the property tax. Third, because they produce goods and services for which the public has relatively inelastic demand, the increases in prices triggered by higher taxes are unlikely to have much effect on demand. Thus, a lower rate of tax will produce more tax revenues than would be required if a product with more elastic demand were taxed. This point is illustrated by Figure 11.4.

Let D_1D_1 be the demand curve for a good or service provided by a public utility and D_2D_2 a product or service with more elastic demand from some other industry. Initially the price for both is set at P and the quantity demanded is Q. Suppose a tax equal to t is placed on the product so that the new price is P'. There is now Q_1 of the utility's product demanded and Q_2 of the other firm's product. The price increase has caused little change in the demand for the utility's product, but a substantial change in the demand for the other product. The tax on the utility's product yields PP' CD in tax revenues, while the tax on the product of the other firm brings in only $PP'AB$. That is, a given rate of tax yields a greater tax revenue when applied to the product with more inelastic demand.

Although regulated firms may have some characteristics that make them good candidates for heavy taxation, they also have features that argue for a lighter tax load. First, although heavy taxing of firms with inelastic demand may be an efficient way of collecting tax revenues, it may be objectionable on equity grounds. Typically, consumption of the goods and services of public utilities do not increase proportionately with

[6]Clemens, E. W., *Economics and Public Utilities* (Englewood Cliffs, N.J.: Prentice-Hall, 1950), pp. 526–527.

income. Households have minimum requirements for electricity, natural gas, tele-phone, and water that must be purchased even at very-low-income levels. If utility rates increase because of taxes, it may be difficult for low-income groups to reduce the burden by cutting consumption.

A second problem in taxing public utilities occurs if such firms are really declin-ing-cost industries. Where costs go down with expansions in output, a given tax may cause the price of the product to increase by more than the amount of the tax change. This result is shown by Figure 11.5.

Suppose a tax of t dollars per unit is imposed on the product. Hence, the average-cost curve can be thought of as shifting up (from AC to AC_T) by the amount of the tax. If the regulatory commission sets price equal to average cost, then the price will be P before the tax and P_T after the tax. Notice that the increase in price is greater than the amount of the tax. As the tax is imposed, the demand for the product is reduced. Thus, as the firm reduces its level of production, some of the advantages of scale are lost and the unit production costs increase. The higher production costs dictate a price that is still higher and that causes a further reduction in demand. This cycle continues until price reaches P_r and output is reduced to Q_r.

It is entirely possible that losses in the efficiency of large-scale production may overwhelm the advantages of taxing a product with relatively inelastic demand. The price increase may actually be greater than would be required to generate the same amount of revenue from a firm with more elastic demand. Thus, the desirability of heavy taxation of public utilities is an empirical question relating to the nature of the demand curve and the extent of scale economics.

Rate Base

Valuation   The profit allowed the firm is the product of the permissible rate of return on capital and the amount of capital (or the rate base) to which the rate is to be applied. In the early days of regulation the calculation of the rate base was a time-consuming

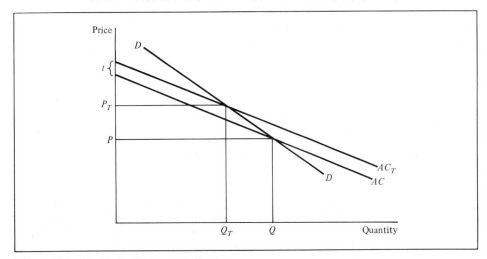

Figure 11.5.   Taxing declining-cost industries.

and hotly disputed issue. The primary problem was the question of how the firm's capital should be valued. There were two basic points of view. On one side were those who contended that capital should be valued at its original cost. If a firm paid $10 million for an electric generator, then that should be the amount on which the firm was allowed to earn a return.

The opposition came from proponents of reproduction-cost valuation. When prices are not stable, the cost of replacing capital is not equal to the cost of obtaining it. Today the problem is rapidly increasing costs of capital equipment. For example, in 1960 the average cost per kilowatt-hour (kwh) of installed electric generating capacity was $200. By 1984 the average cost was over $1000 per kwh. Reproduction-cost advocates argue that the firm should be allowed to earn a fair return on the present value of its capital.

The controversy over valuation soon came to the courts. In 1893 the state of Nebraska created a Board of Transportation with authority to set maximum rates for hauling freight. One of the board's first orders determined rail rates by valuing railroad property at the current reproduction cost. Normally a firm would be delighted to have a commission adopt a reproduction-cost valuation because there has been a general upward trend in prices over the last hundred years. Unfortunately, much of the railroad property had been purchased during the Civil War, when prices were higher than in the 1890s. Hence, the railroads contested the issue and argued for a valuation on original cost.

In 1898 in the case of *Smyth* v. *Ames* (1898) the court ruled that the rates set by the board were too low.[7] The importance of the decision, however, was the court's directive that commissions must determine the *fair value* of the firm's property and the enumeration of the factors that must be taken into account in computing fair value. The court listed six specific measures of fair value, but only two—reproduction cost and original cost—were of any lasting importance. Under the doctrine of *Smyth* v. *Ames,* commissions must take into account both the reproduction cost and the original cost of the firm's capital in determining the fair value of the rate base. The court did not specify the relative weights that should be given to the two factors. During times of rising prices, original cost and reproduction cost can be thought of as the extreme points on the valuation spectrum shown below.

Original |————————— Fair value —————————| Reproduction
  cost | | cost

The lowest valuation of the rate base considered in a rate case is based on the original cost of the assets. The highest is computed by valuing assets at their current value or reproduction cost. The so-called fair value of the rate base is somewhere between the two extremes. The commissions (and sometimes the courts) must determine what constitutes fair value. In some cases fair value may be interpreted to mean simply original cost. In other cases commissions have held that reproduction cost is the proper fair value. Usually fair value means a value for the rate base somewhat, but not greatly, in excess of original cost.

[7]*Smyth* v. *Ames,* 169 U.S. 466 (1898).

The determination of the fair value of the rate base gives the commission considerable discretion in setting rates. By its valuation of the rate base, the commission may be able to justify its own preconceptions about the proper level of rates. A reading of the rate orders of some commissions stirs the strong suspicion that setting the fair value is sometimes a ruse. An interesting example is found in a rate order of the Pennsylvania Public Utility Commission.[8] The commission had previously denied a proposed rate increase by the firm (Pennsylvania Power and Light) and directed the utility to file a modified increase in electric rates. The commission then used the evidence of the rate case to justify the increase that it had directed. In the proceedings the commission found that the fair rate of return was 7 percent and that, under existing rates, the firm had earned $60.5 million in profits over the last year. The original cost of the firm's capital was fixed at $768 million and the reproduction cost accepted by the commission was $1.4 billion. In order to justify the new rates, the commission had to determine that the firm would earn just a fair return (7 percent) on the fair value of its rate base. What valuation of the rate base would show the firm earning the fair return under the new rates? The answer is the solution to the equation:

$$\text{Profit} = s \cdot RB \qquad (11.2)$$

where Profit = $60.5 million and s = 7 percent. The necessary valuation is $864 million dollars. Without any evidence in the rate order to document its finding, the commission found that $864 million was a reasonable fair value of the rate base. Because it was determined that the firm would earn no more than a fair return on the fair value of its capital, the modified rate increase was approved. With the range of valuation from $768 million for original cost to $1400 million for reproduction cost, the commission probably could have justified almost any decision that it wanted to make.

The determination of the fair value of the rate base greatly increased the time, cost, and complexity of the rate case. In the 1944 Hope Natural Gas Case the Supreme Court relaxed the rules for valuation of the rate base.[9] The Federal Power Commission had forced the Hope Natural Gas Company to reduce its wholesale gas rates under an order based on an original cost valuation. The firm contested the decision, arguing that the commission had not taken reproduction cost into account. In upholding the commission, the court set down the *end-result* criterion for rate making. The court argued:

> . . . [i]t is the result reached not the method employed which is controlling. It is not theory but the impact of the rate order which counts. . . . Rates which enable the company to operate successfully, to maintain its financial integrity, to attract capital, and to compensate its investors for the risks assumed certainly cannot be condemned as invalid, even though they might produce only a meager return on the so-called "fair value" rate base.[10]

The Hope decision greatly simplified the rate case. It stipulated that the basic criterion which the courts would use in reviewing commission decisions was the impact

[8]Public Utilities Reports, 3d Series, Vol. 87, pp. 450–468.
[9]*Federal Power Commission* v. *Hope Natural Gas Co.,* 320 U.S. 591 (1944).
[10]Ibid., pp. 602, 605.

of those decisions on the firm and not whether the commission had adhered to particular methods or formulas in making the decision.

Although the Hope decision freed the commissions from use of the fair-value rate-base valuation concept as far as the courts were concerned, there are still some states that use the fair-value method. The general trend, however, is for commissions to use the much simpler original-cost valuation. One of the results of the Hope decision was to shift much of the emphasis and controversy in the rate case from the rate-base valuation to that of the fair return and the rate structure.

There have been thousands of pages devoted to the proper method of rate-base valuation. The debate is of little importance if the focus of a rate order is on the impact, or end result, of that order. Perhaps the most crucial argument against fair value is its lack of precision. There is no objective criterion for assigning relative weights to original and reproduction cost. Also, because the commission can award the firm larger or smaller amounts of profit by varying the allowed or fair return, there is really little need to become involved in unanswerable questions of rate-base valuation. A higher return applied to an original cost rate base can generate the same profits for the firm as a lower return on a higher fair-value rate base.

In actual practice, there is some evidence that firms operating in jurisdictions where commissions use fair-value rate base valuation are allowed higher profits than those in original-cost states. A study by the author examined 50 electric-utility rate cases between January 1969, and December 1971.[11] In 32 of these cases the rate base was valued at original cost and in 18 fair value was used. In the 18 fair-value cases the commissions also indicated their findings as to the original-cost rate base. The ratio of the fair value to the original-cost rate base ranged from 1.03 to 1.41.

In each of the cases examined the commission specified the fair return that the firm would be allowed to earn. For the fair-value cases, this return was to be applied to the fair-value rate base. Using the ratios of fair value to original cost, it was possible to compute the allowed return on a comparable rate base (original cost) for all the observations.[12] Multiple regression analysis was used to investigate the relationship between the allowed return on original cost and the valuation of the rate base. It was found that a higher return on original cost was allowed in the fair-value jurisdictions. For example, a rate base valued at 30 percent above original cost was associated, statistically, with about a one percentage point increase in the allowed return in comparison to an original cost valuation. Similar results were obtained using rates of return actually earned by the utilities subsequent to the rate case.[13]

One explanation for these findings is that it is politically more acceptable to inflate the rate base than it is to increase the allowed return. A 12-percent allowed return when other commissions are allowing only 10 percent is highly visible. In contrast, determining the rate base is an issue specific to a particular rate case and much less subject to

[11]Petersen, H.C., "The Effect of 'Fair Value' Rate Base Valuation in Electric Utility Regulation," *Journal of Finance,* Vol. 31, No. 5 (Dec. 1976), pp. 1487–1490.

[12]For example, if a rate of return of 8 percent on the fair-value rate base is allowed and if the fair-value rate base is 25 percent greater than original cost, then the allowed return on original cost is 10 percent.

[13]Other studies generally are consistent with these results. See Petersen, H.C., "The Effect of 'Fair Value' Rate Base Valuation in Telephone Regulation," *The Engineering Economist,* Vol. 22, No. 1 (Jan. 1977) and Edelman, R.B., "Rate Base Valuation and Its Effect on Rate of Return for Utilities," *Public Utilities Fortnightly* (September 2, 1982), pp. 40–44. One exception is Primeaux, W.J., "Rate Base Methods and Realized Rates of Return," *Economic Inquiry* (Jan. 1978), pp. 95–107.

comparison and criticism. Table 11.1 shows rate base valuation methods of the various state regulatory commissions.

Depreciation The firm is typically allowed to earn a fair return only on the undepreciated value of its rate base. The discussion of expenses pointed out that part of the capital stock of the firm is considered to be used up in the process of producing the firm's product. Thus, an allowance for depreciation is included as a part of operating expenses. To allow the firm to earn a return on capital that has already been deducted as an expense would be to allow earnings on capital that has already been paid for by the consumer. Hence, the rate base to which the fair return is applied is a total sum from which accrued depreciation allowances have been deducted. For example, if a firm had capital with original cost of $1 million and a useful life of ten years, the firm would be allowed to claim a depreciation deduction of 10 percent, or $100,000 each year. At the same time, the depreciation allowances would be subtracted from the original sum to compute the rate base. After five years the fair return would be applied to a rate base of only $500,000.

Rate of Return

A central issue in a modern rate case is the proper rate of profit, or fair return, that the firm should be allowed to earn on its rate base. Profits serve a critical economic function by determining the amount of new capital that will flow into an industry. If the allowed rate of return is set too low the utility may be unable to finance the expansion of facilities necessary to meet a growing demand for its services. On the other hand, if the allowed rate of return is greater than the minimum needed to attract capital, then consumers will pay unnecessarily high prices.

In competitive industries the forces of the market determine the rate of profit. If profits are excessive, then additional investment flows into the industry, supply is increased, and prices and profits are reduced. If profits are considered deficient by investors, then capital leaves the industry, supply is decreased, and prices and profits increase. However, for the regulated firm competition in product markets either does not exist or is greatly limited. Hence, in the rate case the judgment of the regulators must be substituted for the forces of competition.

A number of methods are used to determine the fair rate of return. The firm may present evidence on the profit rates of comparable firms and ask that it be allowed to earn a similar return. The firm may argue that its profits must be high enough to assure that its common stock sells above book value. The issue of being able to cover fixed-interest obligations may also be raised. However, the most common method for determining the fair rate of return in a modern rate case is the *cost-of-capital approach.*

Regulated firms typically have three primary sources of external capital—bonds, preferred stock, and common stock or equity capital. There is a cost associated with each of the three. The cost of selling bonds is the interest that must be paid. Because bond interest is a legal obligation of the firm, the risk of the bond buyer is reduced. Hence, the cost of obtaining capital through bonds is usually lower than the other two forms of financing.

The cost of selling preferred stock is the fixed dividend that must be paid. The payment of this dividend has preference over any payment of dividends to the holders

**Table 11.1 RATES OF RETURN PRESCRIBED OR FOUND
REASONABLE BY STATE COMMISSIONS, 1981**

State	Electric	Gas	Telephone	Rate-base valuation
Alabama	9.97%	8.09%	9.70%	Original cost
Alaska	13.36	11.07	12.28	Original cost
Arizona	9.28	9.05	—	Fair value
Arkansas	10.51	12.21	10.11	Original cost
California	12.20	12.20	12.91	Original cost
Colorado	10.75	10.75	10.07	Original cost
Connecticut	12.14	12.21	13.55	Original cost
Delaware	—	—	—	Original cost
D.C.	10.09	9.60	10.66	Other
Florida	10.44	10.46	10.24	Original cost
Georgia	11.21	11.60	11.57	Original cost
Hawaii	10.25	10.90	7.09	Original cost
Idaho	11.49	10.48	9.33	Original cost
Illinois	8.50	10.20	11.79	Original cost and fair value
Indiana	7.50	7.00	7.35	Fair value
Iowa	9.42	9.32	8.81	Original cost
Kansas	9.98	9.53	9.68	Original cost
Kentucky	11.44	11.80	11.34	Original cost
Louisiana	11.78	11.52	10.89	Original cost
Maine	10.78	12.09	9.24	Original cost
Maryland	10.96	12.00	11.70	Fair value
Massachusetts	—	—	—	Original cost
Michigan	9.31	9.34	9.14	Original cost
Minnesota	9.73	10.03	11.10	Original cost
Mississippi	9.88	8.80	9.86	Original cost
Missouri	10.67	11.36	11.92	Original cost
Montana	9.90	10.50	10.90	Original cost
Nebraska	—	—	9.25	Original cost
Nevada	11.16	11.56	8.60	Original cost
New Hampshire	14.26	11.33	10.12	Original cost
New Jersey	10.69	12.02	9.49	Other
New Mexico	—	10.76	—	Fair value
New York	10.12	12.88	11.94	Original cost
North Carolina	10.88	10.30	10.19	Original cost
North Dakota	10.71	10.65	11.49	Original cost
Ohio	11.15	11.24	12.13	Original cost
Oklahoma	10.52	11.57	10.22	Fair value
Oregon	12.65	12.04	11.10	Original cost
Pennsylvania	11.53	11.72	12.10	Fair value
Rhode Island	9.60	10.58	10.40	Original cost
South Carolina	10.61	11.91	10.26	Original cost
South Dakota	10.60	9.85	—	Original cost
Tennessee	12.48	14.70	11.90	Original cost
Texas	11.94	—	11.79	Original cost
Utah	11.87	11.51	10.03	Original cost
Vermont	10.80	13.74	—	Original cost
Virginia	10.65	9.76	9.26	Original cost
Washington	11.71	12.55	10.82	Original cost
West Virginia	10.60	10.90	10.25	Original cost
Wisconsin	11.16	12.33	11.00	Original cost
Wyoming	10.00	11.34	10.50	Original cost

Source: National Association of Regulatory Utility Commissioners, *1982 Annual Report on Utility and Carrier Regulation* (Washington, D.C.: 1982), p. 460.

of common stock. The cost of capital from preferred stock is usually higher than for bonds, but less than for common equity.

The basic cost of selling common stock is any dividends that might be paid. Unlike bond holders or preferred stock owners, purchasers of common stock are not guaranteed any particular return on their money. The firm determines the dividend that is to be paid and this may change from time to time. During the 1970s, the giant New York electric utility, Consolidated Edison, omitted its dividend because of poor earnings. Thousands of stockholders who had bought shares as a steady source of income with little risk were surprised and hurt. Because of the attendant risk of common stock, it has a higher cost than the other forms of external financing.

In determining the firm's cost of capital, the commission must estimate the cost of each method of financing. The cost of debt and preferred stock are fairly straightforward. Debt cost is usually computed by dividing total interest obligations by total debt. The dividend yield is the common measure of the cost of preferred stock. This is computed by dividing the annual dividend of a share of preferred stock by the current price of the stock.

The most difficult part of the cost of capital computation is the determination of the cost of equity capital. In fact, it may require a major portion of the total time and expense in a modern rate case. The problem is that there is no simple, noncontroversial way of estimating the cost of equity capital. With preferred stock the cost is taken to be the dividend yield, but for preferred stockholders the dividend is fixed and unchanging over time. Shareholders of common stock know that the dividend may be changed by the company at any time. Usually, shareholders expect that there will be an increase in dividends if they continue to hold the stock. As a result, they may be willing to purchase a stock that has a dividend yield somewhat lower than they could have gotten by buying bonds. For example, at this writing the dividend yield of Utah Power and Light common stock is 10.0 percent, but the firm has bonds outstanding that yield 13.0 percent. A rational investor would accept the risk of the common stock only if there was some other component to the return. One possibility is the likelihood that the dividend will be increased over time and the investor's return on his original investment will increase.

It may seem as though the discussion has overlooked the obvious reason for buying stock—the possibility of increase in the share price itself. That is, the investor would accept the lower dividend yield because of expected price appreciation. The basic question is, why would the price of the stock increase? As the price increases, the dividend yield for any given dividend decreases. But why would an investor buy stock that had increased in price and had a current yield of, say, 7.0 percent? Behind the increase in utility stock prices is the belief that, as the firm's earnings increase over time, dividends will also increase. The higher price is paid in the expectation of higher future dividends.

If the cost of equity capital is computed using the current dividend yield of the stock, then the true cost is underestimated. Some consideration needs to be given to the prospect of increased future dividends that the firm will pay. If it is assumed that the present value of those future dividends determines the price of the firm's stock and that the rate of dividend growth will be less than the cost of equity capital, then it can be shown that the cost of equity capital is given by the following equation:

$$r_e = \frac{DVD}{P} + g \qquad (11.3)$$

where r_e is the cost of equity, DVD is the current dividend, P is the current price of common stock, and g is the expected annual growth rate of dividends. This approach is referred to as the *discounted-cash-flow method.*

Equation 11.3 makes the computation of the cost of equity appear straightforward. Unfortunately, there is one major problem. Although it is easy to determine DVD and P, the proper value of g is highly subjective. No one knows how rapidly the firm's dividends will grow or how fast investors expect them to grow. A common practice is for g to be computed based on the recent history of earnings per share of dividends for the firm or industry. But, if industry experience is selected, which firms should be included? If either the individual firm or industry data are used, what is the proper number of years? Too few years may provide data that are not representative. Too many years include ancient history that is no longer relevant.

By a judicious selection of data, a utility official, commission staff member, or hired consultant can produce almost any desired growth rate and, hence, estimated cost of equity capital. It is not uncommon for expert opinion on the cost of equity to differ substantially. For example, in a case before the Tennessee Public Service Commission, an expert witness for South Central Bell Telephone Company used the discounted-cash-flow method to estimate the cost of equity at about 14 percent. A witness for the commission staff used the same technique to compute an estimate of slightly over 11 percent. The choice by the commissioners was of some importance. Using the recommendations of the company witness, the firm would have been allowed $20 million more in profits than if the reasoning of the staff witness were accepted. The commission actually adopted costs of capital just slightly in excess of those presented by the staff witness. [14]

Once each component of the cost of capital has been determined, then the overall or weighted cost of capital must be computed. This is done by multiplying each capital cost by its relative weight in the firm's capital structure. For example, suppose that a firm had 50-percent debt, 10-percent preferred stock, and 40-percent common equity capital, and that the costs were 8, 10, and 16 percent, respectively. The weighted cost of capital used in specifying the fair rate of return is computed as follows:

Debt	50% @ 8% = .040
Preferred	10% @ 10% = .010
Common	40% @ 16% = .064
Weighted Cost of Capital	.114 or 11.4%

Although a commission may choose to make small adjustments to the weighted cost of capital, the fair return is usually based primarily on this computation. Other data such as earnings of comparable firms, interest coverage, and stock prices in relation to book value are used as supporting evidence. Table 11.1 shows rates of returns prescribed by state commissions for electric, gas, and telephone utilities.

[14] *Public Utilities Reports,* 4th Series, Vol. 22, pp. 257–280.

Revenue Requirement

The final objective in the first phase of a rate case is to determine the firm's revenue requirement. The revenue requirement is just the sum of allowable expenses and allowable profit. For example, if a regulatory commission determined that an electric utility's expenses were $800 million and that the firm should be allowed to earn a 10-percent return on a rate base of $2 billion, then the revenue requirement would be $1 billion. Coming into a rate case, the firm has existing prices that generate a certain amount of revenue. If those revenues are less than the revenue requirement, then the firm has demonstrated a need for a rate adjustment.

Firms typically propose a new set of rates in a rate case. Associated with the new rates is a projection of the expected revenues that they will generate. In evaluating the proposed rates, the commission compares the projected revenues to the revenue requirement. If the total is less than the revenue requirement, then the proposed rates may be accepted. If the analysis indicates that the proposed rates would yield revenues in excess of the revenue requirement, but that revenues are inadequate based on existing rates, then a modified set of new rates will be ordered based on the revenue requirement.

THE RATE CASE: RATE STRUCTURE

The emphasis of the public-utility rate case has shifted over time. Before the 1944 Hope decision the major area of controversy was the valuation of the rate base. After Hope, attention shifted to the fair rate of return—especially the return on equity. Until recent years commissions paid relatively little attention to the rate structure. The need for increases in total revenue was often met by adjusting all rates on a nearly proportionate basis. Commissions got involved in the structure of rates primarily in response to complaints received from specific groups of consumers. It was the firm that took the lead in determining what the structure of rates should be.

Prices as Signals

In recent years, more attention has been paid to the structure of rates. As electricity, natural gas, telephone, and other regulated prices have risen, consumers have become more vocal in calling for rate reform. Also, commissions have begun to realize that rate structure adjustments provide signals that can be used to improve the allocation of resources in regulated industries. If the price of a particular good or service is increased, consumers are signaled that they should reduce consumption. In contrast, if prices are reduced, then consumers are signaled to increase their use of the good or service.

Potential competitors in an industry also are responsive to the signals they receive from rate structures. If the price for a good or service is set well above cost, alternative suppliers may have an incentive, if allowed by the regulatory body, to compete with the regulated firm. The rapid growth of long-distance telephone companies such as MCI is a good example. Conversely, if commissions allow monopoly services of a regulated firm to subsidize the prices of potentially competitive services, then competitors are signaled that entry into the subsidized market would not be profitable.

Design of the rate structure is extremely important. Any set of prices chosen by a regulatory commission generates signals that affect the actions of consumers and potential competitors. If the rate structure is arbitrary or ill conceived, then the price signals may cause utility consumers and competitors to allocate their resources in an inefficient manner.

Some excellent examples of prices as signals can be found in the telephone industry. Off-peak discounts for long-distance calling immediately come to mind. The heaviest calling load tends to occur between 8 A.M. and 5 P.M., while few calls are made late at night or early in the morning. The result is that the telephone system must be designed to meet the peak demand while much of the network remains idle during the off-peak hours.

Regulatory commissions have helped telephone companies improve resource use by approving rate structures that provide substantial discounts for calls placed during low-use periods such as evenings and weekends. These discounts signal telephone users to change their calling behavior. To the extent that they induce more off-peak and less peak period calling, resource use can be improved. Requirements for capital expenditures to meet peak load can be postponed and previously idle facilities will be utilized at very low cost. The cost savings can be shared by all of the firm's customers.

The telephone industry also provides an example of a pricing policy that results in an inefficient allocation of resources. Most telephone subscribers pay a fixed monthly fee for the right to receive telephone calls and to make calls in the local area. Under this "flat-rate" pricing scheme, the monthly bill is the same whether the person makes one or a thousand local calls.

Consider the signals that are provided to the customer under flat-rate pricing. The marginal cost of an extra local call is zero. However, the extra expense incurred by the phone company is not zero. While it is true that the cost of a call made during the dead of night may be very low, those calls that are made during the busiest periods of the day can impose a rather substantial cost on the company.

When customers contemplate making a local call, they implicitly calculate whether the value of the call is at least as great as the opportunity cost of making it. Only those calls for which the customer perceives that the benefits exceed the costs will be made. Now, if the extra expenditure required to make the call is zero, then the customer will make calls of very low value. But those calls may impose a substantial cost on the phone company and ultimately on the general body of ratepayers.

The result is that the company is providing a service for which the benefit to the customer is less than the cost to the firm. Clearly, this is not desirable allocation of resources. Flat-rate pricing of basic telephone service is a poor pricing policy because it causes overuse of the telephone system. The telephone company's customers are not to be blamed for this misallocation of resources. The problem is the signals that are generated by flat-rate pricing. Since an unlimited number of additional calls can be made for nothing, there is no incentive for subscribers to cut back on their calling.

Cost-of-Service Pricing

As commissions have become more involved in determining the structure as well as the level of rates, they have required that firms provide additional information about the cost of serving individual categories of consumers. Often, the commission will request that the firm compute the rate of return being earned for each category of service or for each product that is provided. These data are then used by the commission in making rate adjustments. This is called cost-of-service pricing. For example, if a particular service or product is shown to be earning a very low rate of return under existing rates, then the commission may approve a larger rate increase than for a service or product that is earning a higher rate of return. The commission's attempt to equalize rates of return is consistent with its mandate to prevent "undue discrimination."[15]

A general proposition of rate-making is that no service or product should be subsidized by another. However, the question of what constitutes a subsidy may prove difficult to define. It is generally accepted that if the revenues from a product or service exceed the costs, then there is no subsidy involved. Unfortunately, there is no consensus as to which costs should be included in the comparison.

Fully Distributed Costs Some costs obviously are related to providing a particular service or product. For example, meters on homes have the sole purpose of measuring the amount of electricity used by residential customers. There is little doubt that the cost of such equipment should be counted as part of the cost of providing residential electric service. Other costs cannot be clearly identified with a particular service or product. High voltage transmission lines are a good example. Electricity for industrial and commercial, as well as residential, users is transmitted through these lines. There is no clear-cut way of assigning transmission expenses to any single type of service. Depending on how such *common costs* are allocated, particular services or products may or may not appear to be subsidized.

Some judicial and regulatory bodies have adopted the concept of *fully distributed costs* in examining subsidy in the rate structure. Using this approach, those costs that are clearly related to a particular service or product are assigned to that service or product. All other costs are distributed to categories on the basis of some relative measure of physical output such as kilowatt-hours of electricity or million cubic feet of gas or on the basis of maximum demand. For example, suppose that common costs are allocated on the basis of consumption. If residential users consume 60 percent of the electricity sold by a utility in a given year, then 60 percent of those costs that were not directly assignable to a specific category of service would be apportioned to residential customers. Any method of fully allocating common costs must be arbitrary. There is no conceptually correct method for making the allocation. The best that can be hoped for is that the assignment will prove to be useful or acceptable for the purpose at hand.

Incremental Costs Most economists would be more comfortable with a subsidy test based on incremental costs. Incremental costs are the added costs to the firm of providing a service or product over and above the costs of providing the remaining services or products. The advantage of this approach is that it avoids arbitrary allocations of essentially unallocatable costs. The use of the incremental-cost approach to determine whether a subsidy is involved in a particular rate structure can be illustrated

---

[15]However, if the commission has social goals in relation to a service or product it may not require that all rates of return be nearly equal. For example, electricity used for street lighting may be allowed to earn a less than average return, because of perceived community benefits from well-lit streets.

using a simple example. A railroad provides passenger service between San Francisco and Chicago. An intermediate stop along the way is Denver. The fare from San Francisco to Denver is sufficient to generate revenues in excess of the marginal cost of the Denver stop such as ticketing, station facilities, and extra fuel, but not sufficient to cover its proportion of fully distributed joint costs (however apportioned) such as tracks, engines, and train yards.

Using fully distributed costs the San Francisco-Denver route would appear to be subsidized; using incremental costs it would not. In fact, based on the point of view of incremental costs, the addition of the San Francisco-Denver route may actually lead to reduced fares between San Francisco and Chicago. If the Denver fare can cover the incremental costs plus a little bit more, then the excess can be used to pay part of the fixed costs of the longer route. In doing so, it may be possible to reduce the San Francisco-Chicago fare. The basic philosophy behind the incremental-cost-subsidy test is that any action that makes everyone at least as well off as they would have been without the action cannot involve a subsidy. Because travelers to Denver can now go by rail if they choose, they are better off. Because travelers to Chicago may have lower fares because the Denver fare makes a contribution to fixed costs, they are also better off.

The following example illustrates the importance of the choice of fully distributed versus incremental costs. In the case of *Ingot Molds, Pa., to Steelton, Ky.,* (1965), the Louisville and Nashville Railroad filed with the Interstate Commerce Commission to lower its freight rates from $11.86 to $5.11 per ton to meet price competition from a combined truck-barge operation. [16] The railroad had substantial fixed costs, not all of which could be unambiguously allocated to the route in question. The railroad's fully distributed costs were $7.59 per ton, but the incremental costs of freight transportation on this route were only $4.69 per ton. Because the truck-barge operation had few fixed costs, its fully distributed and incremental costs were approximately equal, about $5.19 per ton.

The railroad argued that a rate of $5.11 per ton did not involve a subsidy from other routes, because it more than covered incremental costs. The competing truck-barge firm contended that the proposed lower rail rates would be subsidized and, hence, represent unfair competition. Their argument was that the proper test was in terms of fully distributed costs and that the proposed rates were considerably less than the $7.59 cost. The decision of the ICC turned on whether the appropriate test was incremental or fully distributed costs. The ICC rejected the proposed freight rate as being unfair based on fully distributed costs as the relevant criterion.

Both incremental and fully distributed costs are used in modern rate proceedings. The selection of method depends on the commission and the issue at hand. Although the ICC was granted court approval to use fully distributed costs, recent congressional legislation directed the agency to move to the incremental-cost standard. [17] The Bell System has argued strongly for incremental costs in telephone matters and commissions seem increasingly receptive. Electric utility rates have long been evaluated in terms of fully distributed costs, but incremental analysis in connection with time-of-day rates

[16] *Ingot Molds, Pa., to Steelton, Ky.,* 326 ICC 77 (1965).
[17] *Railroad Revitalization and Reform Act of 1976,* PL94-2C, 94th Cong., 2nd Session (1976).

is now being considered by many commissions. The trend is slow, but seems to be moving in the direction of incremental cost as the test for subsidies.

Ramsey Pricing

Most regulatory commissions rely heavily on cost of service studies as a basis for structuring rates. An alternative method is Ramsey pricing, which incorporates both cost and demand conditions.[18] This approach will become increasingly important as competition erodes the monopoly position of regulated firms.

In Chapter 2 it was argued that marginal cost pricing is the prescription for optimal resource allocation. However, if marginal costs are declining or if some services are subsidized, the price-equals-marginal-cost rule will not allow the regulated firm to achieve its revenue requirement. Hence, a "second-best rule" is required. This rule must specify how prices should be set to allocate resources efficiently, subject to the constraint that the firm meet its revenue requirement. The solution to this problem has spawned an extensive economic literature.[19]

If a natural monopoly is providing its product to a number of different customers, Ramsey prices provide guidelines on the prices that these customers should be charged. It is known that the price to all consumers cannot be set at marginal cost, so the question is how far to set the price above or below marginal cost for different categories of consumers. In its most simple form, the Ramsey pricing rule argues that welfare will be maximized if the deviation from marginal cost is inversely related to the consumer's elasticity of demand. That is, for consumers with very elastic demand the price should not deviate very far from marginal cost. For customers with inelastic demand the price should be higher in relation to marginal cost. Intuitively, if a consumer has an elastic demand for a product, then raising the price causes a substantial change in his behavior as he makes a large reduction in consumption. If demand is highly inelastic, then large changes in price are accompanied by little change in consumption. At the extreme, if demand were totally inelastic (a vertical demand curve), then there would be no change in consumption as price increased.

Following is a simple example of Ramsey pricing. Suppose that a firm sells two products, A and B. The marginal cost of each is constant and equal to $10. The firm has common costs of $99. Further suppose that if prices are equated to marginal costs, then 10 units of each product will be sold. However, since neither product makes any contribution to common costs, the firm would be $99 short of meeting its revenue requirement.

The question is how to increase prices to meet the revenue requirement while minimizing the effect on consumption patterns. Assume that demand elasticity for A is −0.1 and that it is −1.0 for B. The Ramsey principle specifies that, because demand is more inelastic, product A should be priced further above marginal cost than product B. One simple formulation of Ramsey pricing uses the inverse elasticity rule. This specifies that departures from marginal cost should be inversely proportional to

---

[18]In recognition of an early statement of the concept. See Ramsey, F. P., "A Contribution to the Theory of Taxation," *The Economic Journal,* Vol. 37 (Mar. 1927), pp. 27–61.

[19]An excellent explanation is found in Baumol, W. J., and Bradford, O. F., "Optimal Departures from Marginal Cost Pricing," *American Economic Review,* Vol. 60 (June 1970), pp. 265–283.

demand elasticity. In this case, since elasticity for *A* is one-tenth that of *B*, the deviation of the price of *A* from marginal cost should be ten times what it is for *B*.

Using this rule, the solution can be shown to be pricing product *A* at $20 and B at $11. The 100-percent increase in the price of *A* will decrease demand by 10 percent (because elasticity = −0.1) to 9 units. The 10-percent increase in the price of *B* will decrease demand by 10 percent (because elasticity = −1.0), also to 9 units. Each unit of *A* sold make a $10 contribution to common cost for a total of $90. Each unit of *B* makes a $1 contribution for a total of $9. Together, they allow the firm to meet its revenue requirement by covering the $99 in common costs. Note that this objective is achieved with minimal impact on patterns of consumer demand.

Ramsey pricing is sometimes criticized on the grounds that the largest price increases are imposed on those with the fewest alternatives. While this is true, the more important point is that there really is no alternative to using some variant of the Ramsey pricing rule. There is a limit to the contribution to common costs that can be extracted from services with elastic demand. If large price increases are imposed on these services, consumption will decline as consumers shift to other services or suppliers. The net result is that the regulated firm's remaining customers are left to meet the revenue requirement by themselves.

Although a manager would be very unlikely to be familiar with the intricacies of Ramsey pricing, most firms approximate its application in their policy decisions. Where it is possible to separate consumers of different demand elasticities, higher prices are often charged to those with more inelastic demand. For example, movie theaters charge higher rates for adults than they do for children, in spite of the fact that the marginal cost of serving them is essentially equal. Children may have narrower posteriors than the average adult, but the typical chair is of standard width. The pricing differential is based on the belief that many parents would not bring their children to movies if they had to pay full price (elastic demand). Of course, such naïveté presumes that parents really have a choice in the matter.

It would be conceptually possible for regulators to rigidly apply the Ramsey pricing rule. As a practical matter, the amount of data required to make a precise determination and the dissatisfaction of consumers charged the higher price impose severe constraints on the full application of this rule. However, the pricing of telephone service at a higher rate to commercial than to residential users and the lower prices for electricity to large industrial users represent attempts to incorporate the Ramsey principle.

SUMMARY
Institutions

Administrative Commissions

History   Judicial, legislative, and municipal franchise regulation proved unsatisfactory in the United States. As a result, regulation today is primarily the responsibility of administrative commissions. Every state has a regulatory commission. Most state commissions have jurisdiction over companies providing electricity, water, gas, telephone, and some forms of transportation.

Organization State commissions are usually called public service or public utilities commissions. The typical commission consists of two parts. The commission staff evaluates industry and consumer proposals and makes recommendations to the commissioners. The commissioners judge the merits of the issues and render decisions. The size and quality of commissions varies dramatically from state to state.

Independence Regulatory commissions are structured to be somewhat independent of the judicial, legislative, and executive branches of government. By staggering the terms of commissioners, making their removal difficult, and adhering to prescribed procedures, commissions are protected from political influences. However, the isolation is far from complete and regulatory decisions are often affected by politics.

Federal Regulatory Commissions The Interstate Commerce Commission (ICC) deals mainly with prices and entry for trucking and railroads. The Federal Energy Regulation Commission (FERC) sets prices for interstate wholesale sales of electricity and natural gas. The Federal Communications Commission (FCC) has jurisdiction over interstate operations of telephone and telegraph companies. It also is charged with the allocation of the electromagnetic spectrum to radio, television, and other uses.

The Rate Case: Revenue Requirement

Introduction The rate case is used to determine the level and structure of rates. The rate level is set such that the firm is able to recover its expenses and earn a "fair" return on its capital. The structure of rates is adjusted to avoid "undue discrimination."

Getting Started Requests for price increases are generally initiated by the firm, and proposals for price reductions are initiated by the commission staff or by consumers. The rate case is similar to a courtroom proceeding. Witnesses are sworn in, provide testimony, and are cross-examined. An attempt is made to allow all interested parties the opportunity to voice their opinions.

Operating Expenses Operating expenses include materials and supplies, fuel, wages, maintenance, depreciation, and taxes. Normally a high percentage of the expenses proposed by the firm is allowed. When expenses are disallowed, the return earned by the firm's stockholders is reduced.

Depreciation allowances Depreciation is considered a part of the firm's operating expenses. As the product or service is produced, the firm's capital stock wears out. The firm is allowed to set rates to recover the allowance for depreciation.

Taxes Regulated firms are efficient tax collectors because of their large size, capital-intensive technology, and inelastic demand. However, if the firm has declining average costs, the attempt to increase taxes may increase the price of the product by more than the amount of the tax.

Rate Base   The value of the firm's capital stock or rate base as determined by the commission can have a significant effect on prices and profits. Original-cost valuation is based on the original cost of acquiring capital. Reproduction cost considers the cost of reproducing capital at present prices. Fair value is a subjective measure of value between original and reproduction cost. In the Hope Natural Gas case the Supreme Court held that the end result of a rate case and not the method employed is the important consideration.

Rate of Return   The fair rate of return is a controversial issue in modern rate cases. The firm must be allowed to earn a sufficient return on its investment to attract capital. However, an excessive return results in high prices to consumers. Frequently, the fair return is based on the firm's cost of capital, which is computed as a weighted average of debt, preferred stock, and common equity capital costs. The most difficult computation is the cost of common equity. A widely used approach estimates the cost of common equity as the dividend yield of common stock plus the expected rate of dividend growth.

Revenue Requirement   The firm's revenue requirement is the sum of its expenses and allowed profits. If the revenue requirement is greater than current revenues, then the firm will be granted a rate increase. If the requested increase provides revenues in excess of the revenue requirement, only a portion of the requested increase will be granted.

The Rate Case: Rate Structure

Prices as Signals   In recent years, increased attention has been paid to the structure of rates. Commissions have come to recognize that prices generate signals that can be used to improve resource allocation.

Cost of Service Pricing   A generally accepted proposition is that no service or product should subsidize another. However, the existence of a subsidy depends on the definition of costs that is used. Prices that appear to be subsidized based on fully distributed costs may not involve a subsidy when judged on the basis of incremental costs.

Ramsey Pricing   Ramsey prices consider both costs and demand conditions. The Ramsey principle dictates that departures from marginal cost pricing be inversely related to the elasticity of demand. It is based on the premise that the firm's revenue requirement should be achieved while minimizing the effect on consumption patterns.

DISCUSSION QUESTIONS

1. Should regulatory commissioners be elected or appointed?
2. Should regulatory commissions be completely independent of political influences?
3. Should the standards of evidence be as strict in a rate case as in a court of law?
4. From a resource allocation perspective, what types of taxes should be imposed on public utilities?

5. How should depreciation be determined when a commission sets the rate base on the basis of fair value?

6. Sometimes a regulatory commission will accept a hypothetical rather than the actual capital structure of the firm in computing the cost of capital. What purpose would be served by this choice?

7. What is the difference between incremental and marginal costs?

8. Suppose a regulated firm has increasing marginal costs. Could Ramsey pricing be used to allocate resources efficiently while assuring that the firm doesn't *exceed* its revenue requirement?

chapter 12

A Regulated Monopoly: Electricity

Chapter Outline

During the past decade, the lives of few people have been more harried than those of state commissioners charged with the responsibility of regulating electric utilities. (The) commissions have been asked to mediate some of the most rancorous of recent domestic political disputes. . . .[1]

Once virtually ignored, the electric power industry has become an object of concern and controversy in recent years. On one side, the utilities have pressed for large rate increases to offset high fuel costs and interest rates. On the other side, consumers, particularly those with electric heating, have argued that rates must be held down because their budgets are already stretched to the limit. Environmentalists have further complicated the issue by calling attention to pollution resulting from conventionally generated electricity and radiation hazards associated with nuclear power plants.

In response to these pressures, state and federal regulatory commissions are being forced to reexamine their policies. Rate structures are an important example. Until the late 1960s, technological advances and scale economies permitted continual reductions in the price of electric power. Commissions responded by approving tariffs designed to encourage the use of electricity. Today, circumstances have changed for many utilities. The present need is to provide consumers with price signals that hold down costs and promote conservation.

This chapter focuses on the electric utilities as an example of a regulated monopoly. The first two sections describe the structure and regulation of the industry. The last two consider current issues in rate structure design. Discussed first is the important topic of time-of-use pricing. The chapter concludes with an analysis of lifeline rates as a means of helping the poor meet the burden of rising electricity prices.

THE ELECTRIC POWER INDUSTRY

In 1879 Thomas A. Edison perfected the incandescent light bulb. Three years later the Edison Electric Illuminating Company opened its Pearl Street station in downtown New York City. At first, individual utilities served only a small area because electricity was supplied as direct current and efficiency losses limited transmission to distances of less than a mile. A few years later the invention of the transformer allowed the voltage of alternating current to be "stepped up" and "stepped down." Increasing the voltage level reduced efficiency losses and permitted electricity to be profitably transmitted over long distances. This new development made the use of giant centralized generating facilities possible and propelled the electric power industry to a position of importance in the modern economy.

Importance

Today, electricity is a vital ingredient in almost every phase of economic activity. The generation, transmission, and distribution of electric power is one of the nation's largest

[1]Anderson, D. D., in Wilson, J. Q., ed., *The Politics of Regulation* (New York: Basic Books, 1980), p. 3.

industries. In 1982, revenues from sales of electricity in the United States exceeded $120 billion. Since World War II, consumption has increased nearly ten times—from 256 billion kilowatt-hours in 1947 to nearly 2,300 billion kilowatt-hours in 1982.

The nation's dependence on electric power has several times been demonstrated by the virtual paralyses that accompanied blackouts in giant metropolitan areas of the northeastern United States. All but the most intimate human activity essentially stopped when the lights went out, the refrigerator quit, the heating system no longer functioned, and the television ceased its babbling. It is difficult to overestimate the importance of the electric power industry to the United States and other industrialized nations. Although it is a relatively inefficient form of energy (only about one-third of the energy in fuels burned to generate electricity is transformed into usable electric power), the convenience and versatility of electricity suggest that the future will bring a further move toward the all-electric society. The silent, nonpolluting electric car is being actively investigated as the replacement for noisy, dirty automobiles using the internal combustion engine. Electricity is already the most common heating source in new residential construction in the United States. Microprocessors for computers and fiber optics in telecommunications suggest a vastly expanded future role for electricity-based technologies.

Market Structure

In most nations, electricity is provided by publicly owned enterprises. However, in the United States about 80 percent of all electricity is generated by investor-owned utilities. Federal projects such as the Tennessee Valley Authority provide another 10 percent, and the remainder comes from power districts, municipal utilities, and consumer-owned cooperatives. One exception to this pattern is Nebraska, where electricity is provided by a statewide public power system. Although the vast majority of electric utilities have a designated market area in which they are the sole supplier, there are about 50 cities in the United States in which private and public enterprises compete for electricity sales.

Three stages of operation are involved in the electric power industry. First is the generation of electricity from fossil fuels, nuclear energy, or hydroelectric facilities. Second is the transmission of power from the generating facilities to population centers. The third stage is the distribution of electricity to final users. Although many small private and public utilities operate only in the distribution stage, most large investor-owned utilities are vertically integrated. For example, Utah Power and Light generates electricity at various coal-burning plants in the state, owns lines used to transmit electricity at high voltages to cities such as Salt Lake City, and also operates a distribution system capable of reducing voltages and providing power to individual homes and businesses.

Scale economies have caused the private electric utility industry to be characterized by large firms. In 1982, operating companies had revenues in excess of $1 billion from the sale of electricity. Consolidated Edison (New York City), Pacific Gas and Electric (Northern California), Commonwealth Edison (Northern Illinois), and Southern California Edison all surpassed $4 billion in electric revenues for that year. In addition, several holding companies such as the Southern Company (Alabama,

Georgia, Mississippi, and Florida) and American Electric Power (Ohio, West Virginia, and Indiana) also exceeded the $4 billion mark.

REGULATION
Rate Levels

Regulation of retail prices of electricity really began just after the turn of the century with the establishment of state regulatory commissions. By 1930, most states had agencies responsible for performing this function. The need for price regulation of declining cost industries such as electric power is presented in Chapter 10. The mechanics of state regulation are considered in detail in the discussion of the rate case in Chapter 11. That chapter also presents the case for regulation of wholesale electricity prices by the Federal Energy Regulatory Commission. The effects of rate of return regulation on prices and efficiency in the electric utility industry are evaluated in Chapter 15. Hence, these topics are not discussed here.

Although state and federal regulatory agencies were charged with the responsibility for determining electricity prices, until the 1960s many of these commissions played a relatively passive role in formulating policy and regulating prices in the industry. An important reason for the lack of direction provided by the commissions was the impact of technology. New developments in generation and transmission resulted in reductions in the cost of supplying electric power. Also, scale economies provided producers with incentives to reduce rates in the attempt to expand consumption. Table 12.1 indicates that the price of electricity decreased continually from 1931 to 1970. It was not until

Table 12.1   ELECTRICITY PRICES: 1931–1982

Year	Revenues per kilowatt-hour
1931	5.78¢
1937	4.30
1947	3.09
1957	2.56
1967	2.17
1970	2.10
1971	2.19
1972	2.29
1973	2.38
1974	2.83
1975	3.21
1976	3.45
1977	3.78
1978	4.03
1979	4.33
1980	5.36
1981	6.19
1982	6.81

Source: Moody's Public Utilities Manual, 1983 (New York: Moody's Investor Services, 1983), p. a22.

the 1970s that high interest rates, environmental restrictions, and soaring fuel costs began to dominate the influence of technology and drive up the cost of electric power. Between 1970 and 1982, the average price of a kilowatt-hour of electricity more than tripled. In comparison, the Consumer Price Index increased by about 145 percent over the same period.

Commissions that, prior to 1970, had not been faced with a request for a rate increase in decades now are forced to deal with frequent filings—often on an annual basis. The Federal Energy Regulatory Commission in the exercise of its responsibility to set prices for interstate sales of electricity for resale has experienced similar pressures to approve price increases. As a result, consumers who have been accustomed to an abundant supply of low-cost energy are accusing electric utilities of piling up profits at the expense of human misery and commissions of being pawns of the industry. In turn, power producers are complaining that rates are being adjusted too slowly and too little to generate funds needed to finance construction of generating plants necessary to meet future demands.

Rate Structures

During the infancy of the electric power industry, it was not uncommon for consumers to be charged a fixed price, regardless of the amount of electricity they used. Because this pricing scheme encouraged wasteful consumption, it was soon replaced by a uniform price per kilowatt-hour purchased. As the industry matured, more complex rate structures evolved. Customers were classified according to end use, demand elasticities, and the cost of providing service. There were many subgroups, but the primary classifications were into residential, commercial, and industrial users. Commissions allowed firms to charge residential consumers—who typically have a relatively inelastic demand for electricity—higher rates than industrial users—who often have alternative sources of energy and, by virtue of their ability to take electricity at high voltages and in large quantities, could be served at lower cost.

Electricity rates within a category often vary with the volume of usage. For example, residential rates can be broken into three broad categories—declining block, level block, and inverted block. Examples of each are shown in Table 12.2.

Table 12.2 DECLINING, LEVEL, AND INVERTED BLOCK TARIFFS

Declining block	
First 100 kwh	$.08 per kwh
Next 300 kwh	.05 per kwh
All additional kwh	.04 per kwh
Level block	
All kwh	$.06 per kwh
Inverted block	
First 200 kwh	$.05 per kwh
Next 600 kwh	.07 per kwh
All additional kwh	.09 per kwh

Declining Block   Declining block tariffs incorporate a high price per kilowatt-hour (kwh) for the initial block of power purchased and then reduced rates for one or more additional blocks of consumption. This structure is the basis for winter residential rates for nearly one-half of all privately owned electric utilities in the United States. During the summer months, about one-fourth of investor-owned utilities bill residential customers under a declining block tariff.

Declining block rates are a remnant of the time when utilities promoted electricity consumption to take advantage of efficiencies of large-scale generation. By offering low rates for additional consumption, consumers were encouraged to use their electric appliances more intensively and also to purchase additional electricity-consuming devices. This strategy, combined with a general decline in electricity prices, was highly effective. Residential electricity usage increased from an average of 80 kwh per month in 1940 to 675 kwh per month in 1973. Since 1973, rapidly increasing prices have kept average consumption essentially unchanged.

Level Block   The level block tariff has the virtue of simplicity. It involves a fixed cost per kilowatt-hour regardless of the amount of electricity used during the month. There has been a gradual shift from declining block to level block residential tariffs in the United States. Currently, the level block rate structure is used by almost half of privately owned utilities in the winter and nearly two-thirds for summer rates.

Inverted Block   Inverted block rates have higher per kilowatt-hour prices for additional blocks of consumption. They are intended to track the utility's costs more closely. For most companies, additions to generating capacity cost far more per kilowatt than the average cost of existing capacity. The inverted block tariff is designed to promote efficient resource allocation by providing proper price signals to the large volume electricity user. To date, however, only a small proportion of investor-owned utilities have adopted the inverted block tariff for residential customers.

Industrial Tariffs   Rate structures for large industrial customers are somewhat more complex than those used for residential electricity consumers. Often, they include a charge, not only for the total amount of electricity used during the billing period (measured in kilowatt-hours), but also for the maximum rate of consumption at any instant during the period (measured in kilowatts). Table 12.3 shows a sample rate schedule for large industrial customers.

Traditionally, regulated public utilities have been required to provide adequate service to all customers in their service area. Hence, an electric utility must have

Table 12.3   DECLINING-BLOCK INDUSTRIAL TARIFF

First 100 kw	$4.07 per kw
Next 200 kw	$3.86 kw
All additional kw	$3.32 per kw
First 1,000,000 kwh	1.52¢ per kwh
All additional kwh	1.33¢ per kwh

sufficient generating capacity to meet the maximum electricity demand of its customers. Obviously, there is a cost to providing that capacity. It is appropriate that customers who create the need for generating capacity be charged for that expense. This is the rationale behind the kilowatt or demand charge levied on industrial users. Normally, demand charges are imposed only on large-quantity purchasers. Serving the requirements of residential customers also forces the firm to maintain generating capacity, but the cost of special meters required to monitor the maximum demand of small residential consumers has been considered to be greater that the benefits that could be derived from metering. The same is true for all but the largest commercial customers. Hence, the difference in industrial, as compared to residential and commercial, tariffs reflects practical rather than theoretical differences in pricing policy. All three categories of consumers impose a capacity cost on the utility, but this cost can economically be separated out only for industrial users. For commercial and residential users the capacity-related expense is included as a customer charge or as part of the per-kilowatt-hour price of electricity in the initial blocks of the tariff.

CURRENT ISSUES: TIME-OF-USE PRICING
Generating Technology and Peak Loads

The demand for electricity by a utility's customers varies with the season of the year. Utilities with service areas in cold climates may have substantial numbers of electric heating customers. On cold winter days these customers all require large amounts of electricity at the same time. Over the course of a year the maximum amount of electricity that the utility is required to supply at any given time occurs during these days. Consequently the firm is referred to as a *winter-peaking utility.* The amount of generating capacity that the firm maintains is based on the anticipated peak winter demand. During the summer months much of this capacity sits idle. In contrast, if the utility's customers are in an area that has hot summers, the maximum demand probably occurs when air conditioning systems are turned up on a particularly hot day. Such utilities are designated as *summer peaking.* Capacity is planned to meet the summer peak and the firm may have excess capacity during the winter. [2]

Utilities also experience substantial variations in demand during each 24-hour period. Usually, demand is low during the night, increases as individuals prepare for their day's activities and factories begin operations, builds to a daily peak during the afternoon, and tails off in the evenings. Figure 12.1 shows a simplified daily-load curve for a typical utility.

Utilities use a mix of technologies to meet variations in daily electricity demand. Figure 12.1 indicates that the firm has to meet a demand of at least 800,000 kilowatts throughout the day. This constant requirement is referred to as the *baseload demand.* The baseload is usually supplied using generating technologies that have a high capital cost but relatively low operating costs. Nuclear power is a prime example. Nuclear plants are very expensive to build (capital cost), but once constructed the continuing expenditure for nuclear fuel is much less than the cost of coal, oil, or natural

---

[2]This discussion is much simplified and neglects many factors, such as sales and purchases to or from other utilities, maintenance, and outages.

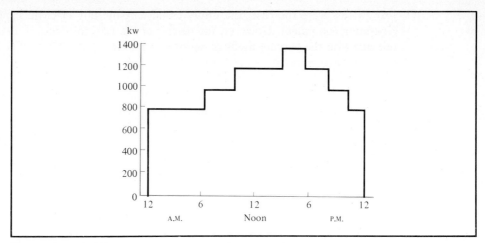

Figure 12.1. Daily-load curve of a typical electric utility.

gas required to produce the same amount of electricity in a nonnuclear facility. Because the nuclear plant is kept in operation at or near capacity throughout the year (barring mishaps), the fixed cost incurred to build the plant is spread over a large number of kilowatt-hours and the cost per kilowatt-hour is kept low.

For about 16 hours a day the utility depicted in Figure 12.1 must supply at least 1 million kilowatts of electricity. The intermediate demand between 1 million and 1.2 million kilowatts is provided using generating technologies that involve a lower capital cost but somewhat higher operating costs than the baseload method. Because the generators are not in use a good deal of the time, the fixed cost is spread over a smaller number of kilowatt-hours. This results in a high fixed cost per kilowatt-hour. However, by selecting a technology that conserves on fixed costs, the total cost of producing to meet intermediate demand is reduced.

Finally, for a few hours in the late afternoon, demand peaks at 1.4 million kilowatts. To meet the requirements of its peak the utility uses diesel turbines or some other method of generation that has a relatively low capital cost per unit of capacity, but is less efficient than the baseload or intermediate load technologies in its use of fuel. Because the generating units are in use only a small portion of the time, the optimal technology to provide the peak load is one that minimizes the fixed capital cost.

When the sum of fixed and operating costs are considered, the baseload generating technology is the most efficient and the peaking equipment is least efficient. Thus, for any given total amount of electricity to be produced during the year, the utility is better off if more is generated using baseload and less using peaking capacity. Shaving the peaks of demand allows the firm to save on fuel expenditures, while more complete utilization of base and intermediate-load capacity causes fixed costs to be spread over additional units of production, with a relatively small increase in operating costs. Thus, if demand can be shifted from peak to off-peak periods, the firm can reduce its expenses and, for any specified set of prices, increase its profits.

From an efficiency standpoint, electric utilities should have a constant demand for electric power—a demand that does not vary with the time of day or season of the year. If this were the case, the utility could employ only efficient, capital-intensive generating equipment. However, the desires of the firm for constant demand do not coincide with the varying needs of consumers for electricity. The reality is that when the weather gets hot and sticky, the air conditioner goes on. If that event occurs at the same time for 100,000 other people and creates a peak demand for the utility, the firm's problem is of no immediate concern to the individual consumer. Under traditional declining-block tariffs, the cost of electricity is determined by the amount and not the time of use. The marginal kilowatt-hour costs the customer the same whether it is consumed at 3 P.M. on a hot July afternoon or at 3 A.M. the next morning.

Theory of Peak-Load Pricing

Traditional Pricing Theory   Faced with high interest rates, decade-long delays in the construction of new plants, and skyrocketing fuel prices, utilities and their regulators have become increasingly interested in the use of innovative rate structures as a means of curbing and shifting electricity consumption. By providing the proper financial incentives to consumers, costly additions to generating capacity can be postponed, and existing facilities used more efficiently. If this can be accomplished, both the firm and the electricity consumer can benefit. The firm will be able to avoid periods of low profitability while awaiting regulatory approval of rate adjustments. Customers can be spared increases in rates stemming from new construction or inefficient generation necessary to meet sharp system peaks.

Basic to most current proposals for rate structure revision is the principle that prices should reflect the costs of providing electricity. If electricity is consumed at times of peak demand, then the contributors to the peak should stand the bulk of the cost of the required capacity rather than those whose consumption is concentrated during off-peak periods. This concept is referred to as peak-load or time-of-use pricing. The basic principles underlying peak-load pricing are discussed in this section. The following section describes time-of-use pricing experiments in the United States (where the practice has not been extensively used) and in France (where peak-load pricing has been used for many years).

A peak-load problem may occur when three conditions are encountered in the production of a product. First, the product is not easily storable. In the case of electric power the economic and technical problems associated with storing electricity require that production must take place at the time of demand. Second, the same physical plant is used to produce the commodity during different periods. For electricity, a firm's generating facilities are used to meet demand during each 24-hour day and throughout the year. Finally, different periods have different demand characteristics. With electricity, demand is a function of the period being considered. Daytime demand is greater than nighttime. Winter demand is usually greater than summer or vice versa, depending on the firm's service area.

To illustrate the concept of peak-load pricing, assume that demand for electricity during a day can be divided into three periods of equal length.[3] Period 1 is a time of

---

[3]This discussion follows that suggested in an important paper: Steiner, P. O., "Peak Loads and Efficient Pricing," *Quarterly Journal of Economics,* Vol. 71 (Nov. 1957) pp. 585–610.

low demand and occurs at night. Period 2 has moderate demand and occurs in the morning and early evening. Period 3 occupies the middle of the day and is the time of peak demand. Let the demand curve for electricity in period 3 be at all prices greater than the demand curve for period 2, which, in turn, is at all prices greater than the demand in period 1. Alternatively stated, at any given price the demand is greater in period 3 than in period 2, and the demand in period 2 is greater than the demand in period 1.

Further consider that there are only two kinds of costs involved in the production of electricity. Let b represent fuel costs per unit of output, with b assumed not to vary with the period or the level of output. Let B be the cost of a unit of generating capacity, with B assumed to be constant with respect to the amount of capacity required.

The price that electricity consumers pay is the sum of the fuel cost and the capacity cost (which includes a reasonable rate of return on capital). Because the fuel cost per unit of output is assumed constant, it can be subtracted from the price in each period without altering the results of the analysis. Figure 12.2 depicts the three demand curves, D_1, D_2, and D_3, after the fuel cost has been subtracted. As a result, the vertical scale starts with b (the fuel cost) instead of zero. Because fuel costs have been netted out, Figure 12.2 can be considered a graph of the demand for production capacity. Hence, each point on the three demand curves indicates the amount of capacity that the firm's customers want in a period at a given price of capacity.

The D_T curve in Figure 12.2 is the result of vertically summing the three individual demand curves (i.e., adding the vertical distances above the horizontal axis at each point along the horizontal axis). Remember that the same generating capacity is used

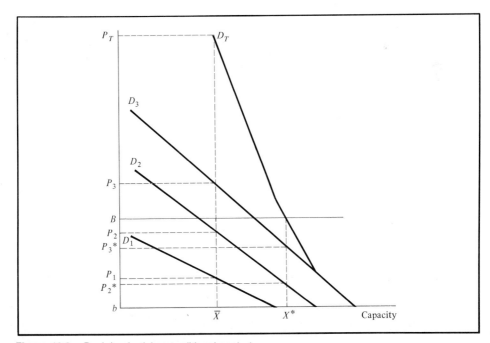

Figure 12.2. Peak-load pricing: traditional analysis.

to produce electricity in each of the three periods. The individual demand curves indicate the willingness of consumers to pay for capacity during each period. For example, consumers in period 1 will pay P_1 per unit for $\overline{X}$ units of capacity. Consumers in period 2 will pay P_2, and those in period 3 will pay P_3. Because the capacity is usable to serve consumers in each period, the total value or demand for $\overline{X}$ units of capacity is $P_T = P_1 + P_2 + P_3$.

The cost of a unit of capacity is B. Efficient allocation of resources suggests that capacity should continue to be added until the value of the last unit is just equal to the cost of obtaining it. The total value of capacity is read off the D_T curve and suggests that, at a cost of B, X^* units of capacity should be employed. The peak-load pricing problem is to determine who should pay for the X^* units of capacity. Notice that even if the cost of capacity were zero, less than X^* units of capacity would be required to meet the demand in period 1. Thus, the selection of X^* units provides no benefits to the consumers in period 1. The implication is that they should not be required to pay a capacity charge. Users in that period would properly be charged only the energy cost, b, per unit of electricity consumed.

In contrast, because period 2 and 3 users attach a positive value to X^* units of capacity, they should be assessed part of the cost. Specifically, the value attached in period 2 is P_2^* and in period 3 it is P_3^*. The sum of P_2^* and P_3^* just equals the unit cost of capacity, B. By apportioning P_2^* of capacity cost to period 2 and P_3^* to period 3, the cost of capacity is recovered. Thus, the total price of electricity to period 2 users should be $P_2^* + b$ and to period 3 users, $P_3^* + b$.

Notice the basic principles involved in this scheme of peak-load pricing. Because the off-peak users place no value on the marginal units of capacity, they pay only an energy charge. The capacity charge is shared by the users who value the capacity, and the capacity charge is assessed in proportion to value. Because the peak users (period 3) attach more value to the capacity, they pay a higher price than do the period 2 customers.

This pricing philosophy has been incorporated into public utility rate cases for many years, but on a limited and questionable basis. In deciding how to apportion rate increases, commissions must face the question of how to allocate the cost of capacity. This has usually been done according to the class of consumer rather than the time of consumption. For simplicity, assume that there are only three categories—residential, commercial, and industrial. Also assume that during the test period used in the rate case the utility experiences its annual system peak at 3 P.M. on July 24 and that the peak is 2 million kilowatts. At the time of that peak, residential customers are estimated to have required 1 million kilowatts and commercial and industrial users 500,000 kilowatts each. A common method of capacity cost allocation is to apportion costs to the user categories in proportion to the demand at the time of system peak. Using this *single-coincident-peak* method of demand cost allocation, residential users would be apportioned one-half the capacity cost and the other two categories one-quarter each.

The problem with this procedure is that customers may be unfairly charged capacity costs for which they are not responsible. The grouping "residential customers" is arbitrary and used primarily out of convenience. Granted, residential electricity consumers have many similar demand characteristics, but there are also great variations. One customer may have an air conditioner that he turns up on a hot day, thus

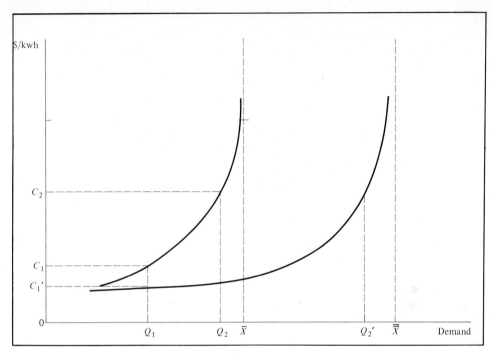

Figure 12.3. Peak-load pricing: revised analysis.

contributing to the peak. Another may be a couple who work and won't turn the unit on until early evening. Still another may be too poor to have an air conditioner at all. However, because they all consume electricity in their homes, they are classified in the residential category and are required to pay the higher prices stemming from the peak demand that only some of them create. Further, under a traditional declining-block tariff, the price is the same regardless of the time of consumption. In fact, the only way to reduce the per-unit cost of electricity is to use more. The declining block tariff produces the paradoxical result that the customer who contributes to the need for capacity by turning up his air conditioner and using a large amount of electricity will pay less per unit of consumption than the elderly person who suffers through the heat in the attempt to save money.

Revised Pricing Theory   The analysis of peak-load pricing of the previous pages is much simplified. The conclusion that off-peak users should pay none of the costs of capacity has been widely promoted by economists, but requires a slight modification to fit the realities of actual production technologies.[4] Figure 12.3 depicts the unit energy costs of producing different quantities of electricity with a fixed amount of capacity. At this point the assumption of constant energy costs is abandoned for the more realistic view that energy costs increase as a system's generating capacity is approached. This result is a simple manifestation of diminishing marginal returns that occur when

[4]The following discussion is the author's diagrammatic exposition of Panzar, J. C., "A Neoclassical Approach to Peak Load Pricing," *Bell Journal of Economics,* Vol. 7, No. 2 (Autumn 1976), pp. 521–530.

additional variable inputs (fuel) are applied to a fixed input (capacity). Let capacity at any given time be $\overline{X}$. It has already been noted that utilities use different types of generating technology to meet different demand situations. As capacity is approached the firm shifts to less-fuel-efficient peak-load technologies. Thus, the per-unit energy cost increases as shown in Figure 12.3. If the peak demand experienced by the firm is Q_2, then the unit energy cost at the time of peak is C_2. If the off-peak demand is Q_1, then the unit off-peak energy cost is C_1. Because the peak demand is near the system's capability, C_2 is much greater than C_1.

Now suppose that the peak demand increases to Q'_2, which necessitates an increase in generating capacity to $\overline{\overline{X}}$. The traditional analysis would suggest that the addition to capacity benefits only peak-load users and, hence, they should be assessed the full cost. However, notice that off-peak users may benefit from the capacity addition. By expanding the size of the system, it is possible to incorporate generating units that are more fuel efficient. This may be the result of economies of scale, new equipment, or better use of facilities. The important point is that the expansion of capacity can reduce the unit fuel cost of producing at off-peak. Figure 12.3 shows a reduction from C_1 to C'_1. Hence, the off-peak users have benefited from the addition to capacity and, accordingly, should be required to pay part of the cost.

The amount of capacity costs that should be apportioned to off-peak consumers depends on the amount of benefit they receive. It is possible to envision situations in which they don't benefit at all. Specifically, if capacity expansion does not create lower costs at the off-peak level of demand, then there would be no benefit, and off-peak users should not be expected to share capacity costs. This could occur if economies of scale in production had already been exhausted or if only peaking equipment was added with no change in the facilities used to meet the off-peak demand.

Although economists have long advocated apportioning capacity costs only to peak users, regulators have been somewhat reluctant to apply the principle rigorously. The foregoing analysis suggests that the traditional solution proposed by economists was overly simplistic and that policymakers may have been well justified in their foot-dragging. The revised formulation of peak-load pricing argues that capacity costs should be borne most heavily by those who make the heaviest demands on the system, but that the benefits to off-peak users of additional capacity must also be considered. To the extent that off-peak customers benefit, they should pay a portion of the cost. The exact apportionment cannot be determined on the basis of any simple formula, but requires extensive and complex analysis.

Applications of Time-of-Use Pricing

Utilities experience both daily and seasonal peaks. Accordingly, applications of time-of-use pricing have focused on rates that differentiate electricity prices by the time of day (TOD) and by the season of the year (seasonal). Although the simple models of the last section suggest that rates should be unequal whenever the marginal costs of providing electricity differ, such a prescription is impractical. The value of time-of-use pricing is that consumers are provided signals that allow them to alter their consumption patterns. If the rates are too complex, consumers may be unable to respond in a rational manner and the new rate structure will serve no useful purpose. The actual implementation of time-of-use pricing requires a compromise between the basic principle that users should pay the full cost of the electricity that they consume and the practical constraint that consumers be able to understand and adjust to the pricing scheme.

With respect to seasonal rates, the most frequent compromise is to adopt winter and summer tariffs. If the utility is summer peaking, then summer rates are higher, and vice versa for winter-peaking utility. Table 12.4 is an example of seasonal rates. Notice that the rate structure for each season incorporates the declining-block form, but that there are only two blocks.

For time-of-day rates the usual practice is to divide the 24-hour day into two or three periods. A two-period tariff might specify a peak rate charged from 7 A.M. to 7 P.M. and an off-peak rate from 7 P.M. to 7 A.M. A three-period division might also add an afternoon block between 2 and 5 P.M. These designations would apply Monday through Friday only. During the low-demand weekend, the off-peak rate would prevail at all times or, at least, the weekday afternoon peak-period rate would not be charged. Table 12.5 shows a three-period TOD tariff for a hypothetical electric utility.

In Table 12.5, the customer charge allows the utility to recover its costs of billing, hookup, and administration from all customers. The implicit assumption in this flat-rate tariff is that the cost of providing electricity varies with the time of consumption and not with the volume of consumption.

The ratio between the peak and off-peak price of electricity in Table 12.5 is 4:1. One of the objectives of time-of-use pricing is to induce consumers to shift their patterns of electricity consumption to off-peak hours, allowing the utility to use its generating facilities more efficiently. Without time differentiated rates, consumers concentrate their consumption during certain hours. This choice suggests that electricity has greater value during those times. Obviously, in Houston, turning on the air conditioner during the middle of the night brings less relief than cooling the house on a July afternoon. For air conditioning the peak rate probably results in air conditioners being turned

Table 12.4 SEASONAL RATES FOR A SUMMER-PEAKING UTILITY

May through October	
Customer charge	$4.00
First 500 kwh	$ .09 per kwh
Additional kwh	$ .07 per kwh

November through April	
Customer charge	$4.00
First 500 kwh	$ .07 per kwh
Additional kwh	$ .05 per kwh

Table 12.5 TIME-OF-DAY TARIFF

Customer charge	$4.00
Weekdays 7 P.M.–7 A.M.	$ .03 per kwh for all kwh consumed
Weekdays 7 A.M.–2 P.M. 5 P.M.–7 P.M.	$ .06 per kwh for all kwh consumed
Weekdays 2 P.M.–5 P.M.	$ .12 per kwh for all kwh consumed
Weekends 7 P.M.–7 A.M.	$ .03 per kwh for all kwh consumed
Weekends 7 A.M.–7 P.M.	$ .06 per kwh for all kwh consumed

down or off and less electricity being used rather than consumption being shifted to another time. In order to have much impact on the peak load caused by air conditioning, the peak-period price must be high enough so that substantial numbers of customers prefer the discomfort of a muggy room to the discomfort of high electric bills.

For other electricity users, the peak/off-peak differential may simply shift the time of consumption. Housewives who normally do their washing in the late afternoon will be induced to wait until evening. Dinner may be postponed long enough to put the cooking period into the time of lower evening rates. Industries that are large consumers of electricity may alter production schedules. Instead of concentrating production during the traditional 8 to 5 working day, firms will schedule production runs at night. In all of these examples individuals change their patterns of activity in response to changes in relative prices. As with air conditioning, the savings from altering consumption patterns must exceed the inconvenience involved in making the change.

Time-of-use pricing schemes have both an efficiency and an equity effect. If the utility's demand can be leveled over the course of a day and over the seasons of the year, then costly additions to capacity may be postponed. A more immediate impact is that generation can be concentrated more heavily on fuel-efficient baseload facilities. These efficiency gains may retard an otherwise rapid escalation of electricity prices. Potentially, all of the firm's customers can share in the gains.

On the other hand, the burden of a large peak/off-peak differential may be imposed unequally on individual consumers. While some purchasers may be able to shift or reduce consumption in response to peak-load pricing, others may have much less flexibility. A beautician can hardly ask her customers to return in the middle of the night so that she can reduce the cost of operating hair dryers. Senior citizens may be unable to tolerate the high temperatures that result from shutting off their air conditioners. Although cost data may indicate that a very large peak/off-peak price differential is warranted, regulatory commissions sometimes find that the political pressures stemming from equity effects impose a significant constraint on their flexibility in implementing cost-based rate structures.

United States   Seasonal rates are quite common in the United States. Commissions in 40 of the 50 states have approved summer/winter differentials. In states where such rates have not been authorized, the explanation often is that the utilities operating in those areas have no distinct seasonal peak. Thus, there is no need for separate summer and winter rates.

Time-of-day rates have been approved in 35 states, but this total is somewhat misleading. In many jurisdictions the tariffs authorized by the commissions are optional or experimental. There are only a few utilities that have been allowed to implement permanent, mandatory time-of-day rates. However, such tariffs are likely to become more common in the future. In 1978, Congress passed the Public Utilities Regulatory Policies Act (PURPA).[5] This legislation directed state regulatory commissions to hold hearings and adopt a stance on a number of issues relating to rate structure design.

---

[5]Public Law 05-617, 95th Congress.

Relevant to the discussion of peak-load pricing are three positions ennunciated by Congress in the act:

1. *Declining-Block Rates.* The energy component of a rate may not decrease as consumption increases unless the utility can demonstrate that the cost of the energy component decreases as consumption increases.
2. *Time-of-Day Rates.* Unless determined not to be cost effective, rates shall be on a time-of-day basis that reflects the cost of providing service at different times during the day.
3. *Seasonal Rates.* The rates charged by an electric utility shall be on a seasonal basis that reflects variations in providing service at different times during the year.

Basically, the act opposes declining-block tariffs unless they can be cost justified, directs the use of TOD rates except when the costs of implementation exceed the benefits, and supports without qualification the use of seasonal rates. Each state commission was given the option of deciding for itself whether to adopt any or all of the standards. But the commissions were all required to consider the matter. If a commission decided against adoption of any of the standards, it was required to make public the reasons for its decision. Many of the experimental time-of-day rates approved by state commissions were established in response to PURPA deliberations.

To date, there is only a limited amount of information regarding the effects of time-of-use rates in the United States. During the 1970s, the Department of Energy funded a number of experiments to collect data on this topic. One of the most informative studies was conducted in Wisconsin.

The Wisconsin experiment involved mandatory time-of-day rates for 700 randomly selected families in the northeastern portion of the state.[6] Data on electricity consumption of the families were collected at 15-minute intervals for an entire year prior to the study. During the experiment, similar data were collected for a three-year period.

The experimental tariffs incorporated a peak period and an off-peak price. Three different peak/off-peak ratios were used, varying from 2:1 to 8:1. That is, the most extreme form of time-of-day rates used had a peak period price that was eight times the off-peak rate. Peak periods were designated as weekdays and off-peak times were evenings and weekends. In every case the time-of-day tariffs were designed such that, if the average family made no changes in its consumption habits, the total bill under the experimental rate structure would have been the same as under the existing rate structure.

Results of the study revealed that time-of-day rates can cause consumers to significantly alter their patterns of electricity usage. As expected, consumption shifted from peak to off-peak hours. Most of the consumers in the sample benefited because their total electricity bills were lower than they would have been under the existing

---

[6]For a nontechnical presentation of the results, see Caves, D.W. and Christensen, L. R., "Time-of-Use Rates for Residential Electric Service: Results from the Wisconsin Experiment," *Public Utilities Fortnightly* (March 17, 1983), pp. 30–35.

rates. The results suggested that the utility could also benefit in that electricity use declined significantly during times of peak demand on its facilities. Projected to all of its customers, this decline in peak demand could allow the utility to reduce costs by economizing on the use of inefficient peak-load generating equipment and also by postponing additions to capacity.

France   Time-of-use pricing is much more common in Europe than in the United States. European practices are illustrated using France as an example. Electricity in France is generated and distributed by a single, government-owned utility. The system has a winter seasonal peak and daily peaks around eight in the morning and five in the afternoon. Time-of-use pricing has been used with industrial customers for 30 years and peak-load tariffs for residential consumers have been available for over 20 years.

Industrial users are billed under the so-called green tariff. Each day is divided into three pricing periods:

Peak Hours: 7 A.M. to 9 A.M. and 5 P.M. to 7 P.M., Monday through Saturday.

Shoulder Hours: 6 A.M. to 10 P.M., except Sunday and peak hours.

Off-Peak Hours: 10 P.M. to 6 A.M., and all day Sunday.

The shoulder periods correspond to the times of intermediate demand discussed earlier in the chapter. The year is also divided into peak, shoulder, and off-peak seasons. The peak period runs from November to February, the shoulders are October and March, and the off-peak goes from April to September. Thus, the price of electricity is determined by both the time of the day and the season of the year when it is consumed. Figure 12.4 shows the energy charges per kilowatt-hour for the different time periods.

In addition to TOD and seasonal rates, French industrial customers also pay for *subscribed power.* Each firm contracts for a maximum demand (kilowatts) during each of the tariff periods. Part of a company's electric bill is this charge for demand. Firms with greater maximum demand (especially during the peak periods) are required to pay a greater demand charge. If a firm's demand during any period exceeds that for which it has contracted, then an extra charge is levied. The subscribed demand fee is used to meet much of the capital cost of new generating equipment in the system. Table 12.6 indicates the subscribed demand for industrial users taking power at high voltages. Notice that the demand charge differential between winter peak and summer off-peak is almost 30:1. This reflects the fact that the French system is winter peaking and, hence, that peak users should be apportioned the major portion of the capacity cost. Rates for October and March are not included in Table 12.6. However, they are the same as those for the winter season, except that the daily peak rate is not used. The table also shows energy charges. These charges correspond to those that are depicted graphically in Figure 12.4. They are levied at a constant rate without regard to the total volume of consumption.

For residential customers a demand charge would require a meter capable of measuring demand in each time period. The cost of such meters is a small fraction of the revenues collected from an industrial user, but may be a significant amount in compari-

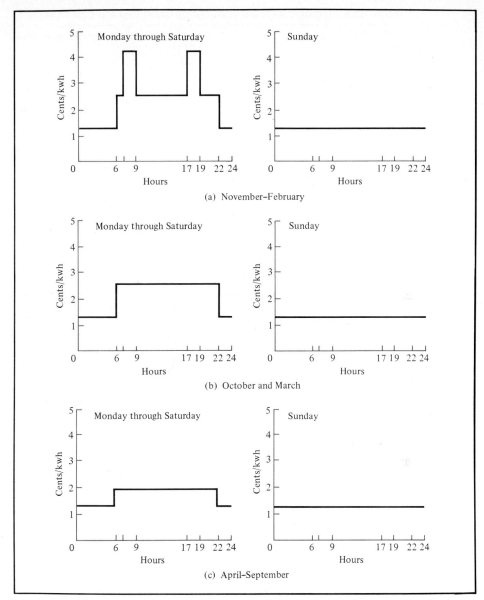

Figure 12.4. French industrial rates under the green tariff. *Source:* Mitchell, B. M., Manning, W. G., and Acton, J. P. *Electricity Pricing and Load Management: Foreign Experience and California Opportunities.* (Santa Monica: Rand Corporation, March 1977), p. 19.

son to the annual bills of residential customers. French utility managers have solved this problem by imposing a fuse or circuit-breaker charge. Customers purchase from the utility a circuit breaker of a specified rating. For example, a customer might purchase a 3-kilowatt circuit breaker. If, at any time, the demand for electricity in the residence exceeds 3 kilowatts, the breaker trips. The circuit breaker may be reset, but to avoid

Table 12.6   ENERGY AND SUBSCRIBED DEMAND CHARGES IN FRANCE

| | Prices for supply at 60 to 90 kv | | | | |
| | Winter | | | Summer | |
Type of Charge	Peak	Shoulder	Off-peak	Shoulder	Off-peak
Subscribed-demand charge					
($/kw/yr)	12.18	4.06	1.01	2.64	0.41
Energy charge (¢/kwh)	4.30	2.58	1.33	1.96	1.27

Source: Mitchell, B. M., Manning, W. G., and Acton, J. P., *Electricity Pricing and Load Management: Foreign Experience and California Opportunities* (Santa Monica: Rand Corporation, March 1977), p. 20.

tripping it again, the customer must cut back on the demand for electricity by turning off a television, dishwasher, or some other electricity-using devise. A customer who has a greater demand for power may purchase a larger fuse, but the price goes up with capacity. For example, the cost of a 3-kilowatt fuse is about 5 percent of the cost of an 18-kilowatt fuse. Hence, customers who impose a greater demand on the system are assessed a greater share of the cost. However, notice that there is nothing in this scheme that takes into account when the maximum demand of a customer occurs. A consumer who has maximum demand in the evening would pay the same as one with a maximum at the time of system peak. This is a compromise dictated by the conflicting goals of using time-of-use pricing and keeping metering costs within reason.

Off-peak residential customers in France can achieve some savings by choosing the optional *double tariff.* Under this rate schedule the monthly fixed charge is increased to cover the cost of a meter that totals daytime and nighttime consumption of electricity separately. The advantage to the customer is that electricity used between 10 P.M. and 6 A.M. is billed at about one-half the standard rate. This tariff is particularly advantageous for those who have electric water heaters. The storage tank can be heated with cheap electricity at night and then used as necessary.

Time-of-use pricing in France has helped that nation's electric system operate more efficiently. Since the tariffs were adopted, off-peak demands have grown more rapidly than peak demands. This has allowed the enterprise to postpone additions to generating capacity and to spread the fixed costs of baseload capacity over a greater volume of output. The discussion in this section has focused on France, but most other European countries use some variant of peak-load pricing. Their experience suggests that implementation of time-of-use pricing is not without problems, but there seem to be some gains—especially with large industrial customers where the volume of consumption can justify expensive metering devices and detailed tariffs.

CURRENT ISSUES: "LIFELINE" ELECTRICITY RATES[7]

The declining block rate structure used by many utilities may be especially burdensome for low-income groups. If low-income consumers tend to be low-volume users of electricity, then a declining block tariff, because it recovers a large portion of the utility's total revenues from the initial consumption blocks, will result in a high cost per kwh used.

[7]This section is based on Petersen, H. C., "Gainers and Losers with Lifeline Electricity Rates," *Public Utilities Fortnightly,* Nov. 25, 1982, pp. 33–35.

"Lifeline" electric rates are frequently suggested as a means of mitigating the impact on the poor of high electricity prices. Although many forms of lifeline rates have been proposed, a typical tariff would provide for the first 300 to 400 kwh of electricity per month to be provided at a low rate, with a higher price per kwh for consumption in excess of 300 to 400 kwh. The philosophy behind lifeline rates is that electricity is a necessity in modern society and every family should be able to purchase enough electricity to meet its minimum needs without undue budgetary stress. The 300 to 400 kwh block is chosen because it represents an amount sufficient to supply basic lighting, refrigeration, and cooking needs of the average family.

Utility regulation is based on the premise that public utilities should be allowed to charge rates high enough to provide a fair return on invested capital. Normally, individual rates are set to cover the cost of providing service to each class of customers. However, the lifeline concept requires that the initial block of consumption be priced below cost. The consequence is that the deficiency must be recouped by increasing rates for subsequent usage blocks or for other classes of customers. Thus, lifeline rates are an example of taxation by regulation as discussed in Chapter 10. Some lifeline proposals limit the required increase to higher-volume residential customers, while others spread it more broadly by increasing electric rates for commercial and industrial customers in addition to high-volume residential users.

Pros and Cons of Lifeline Rates

Advocates of lifeline rates are primarily concerned with providing rate relief for the poor. They assert that low-income groups are low-volume users and, hence, will have their electric bills reduced. Lifeline advocates also argue that their proposals will promote conservation. Under declining block tariffs additional consumption is encouraged by low rates. In contrast, the lifeline concept tends to produce an inverted block rate structure. Since additional kwhs are more expensive, consumers are provided with an incentive to conserve on their use of electricity.

Opponents of lifeline rates suggest that such tariffs may not promote conservation. They argue that the impact of lifeline depends on whether consumers make electricity consumption decisions on the basis of the charge for incremental kwhs of consumption or on the basis of their total electric bills. If the total monthly bill is the determining factor, then a lifeline tariff that reduces the electric bills of many customers may actually promote the use of electricity.

Lifeline critics also cast doubt on the assertion that such tariffs would be effective in providing financial assistance to the poor. The lifeline concept is based on the premise that low-income groups use less electricity. While this is true in aggregate, it is not true in every case. There are low-income customers who use relatively large amounts of electricity. Conversely, many high-income customers are low-volume electricity consumers. Since the availability of a subsidized initial block of electricity requires that the deficiency be made up by increasing the charge for subsequent blocks, it is possible that the total bills of some high-income customers may be decreased and those of some low-income customers may actually be increased by lifeline proposals.

A related problem with lifeline rates is that of renters whose electric bills are included in their rental payments. Landlords are often classified as commercial users or in a residential tariff for which a lifeline block has not been authorized. Hence, these renters will not receive the benefits of the lifeline tariff. In fact, since the rates to other user classes must be increased to recover the lifeline deficiency, they may find their monthly rental rates increased as landlords pass on the change in electricity costs. Unfortunately, the proportion of low-income households in rental units is considerably greater than in other types of housing. The consequence is that lifeline rates may injure many of those in greatest need.

Evidence and Evaluation of the Effects of Lifeline Rates

A number of studies have considered the effects of lifeline rates as a mechanism for helping the poor.[8] The approach of these studies is to compare monthly electric bills under traditional tariffs to those that would result from a hypothetical or actual lifeline rate structure. A calculation is then made of the break-even point. That is, the monthly usage is computed beyond which the consumer pays a higher bill under lifeline rates than under the alternative tariff. Finally, customers are examined by income levels to determine the proportions better and worse off under lifeline rates.

These studies are consistent in their findings that lifeline rates are a relatively inefficient method for redistributing income. They reveal that from one-tenth to one-third of low-income electricity consumers would pay higher bills under lifeline rates. They also estimate that about one-third of upper-income families would pay less under such tariffs.

The problem is that conventional lifeline proposals are not targeted specifically at those who are in greatest need of help. An improved lifeline concept would establish some kind of need criteria for eligibility. One possibility would be to require customers to certify that their incomes are below a certain level. Another approach would tie eligibility to various forms of welfare assistance.

Although basic lifeline proposals can be refined and improved, it is not clear that lifeline electricity rates are the best method of providing assistance to the deserving poor. It is possible to achieve the same results at a lower cost by providing direct subsidies to low-income groups. The advantage of subsidies is twofold. First, a general subsidy does not distort relative prices. In contrast, lifeline rates may make the use of electricity more attractive in comparison to other energy forms and, hence, alter patterns of consumer choice. Second, the subsidy decision is traditionally a prerogative of the legislature. It is preferable that an elected body make decisions relating to the redistribution of income and that the (in most cases) appointed members of state regulatory commissions interpret their rate setting function more narrowly.

SUMMARY
Electric Power Industry

Importance   The U.S. economy is highly dependent on the electric power industry. Electricity consumption has increased nearly tenfold since the end of World War II. It is likely that the importance of electricity will continue to increase over time.

---

[8]Findings of a number of lifeline studies have been reported in *Public Utilities Fortnightly*. For example, see Petersen, op. cit. *and* Canan P., and Hennessy, M., "In Defense of Lifeline Rates: An Empirical Analysis," Nov. 5, 1981, pp. 31–35.

Market Structure   Three stages are involved in getting electricity to consumers—production, transmission, and distribution. Most firms in the industry operate at all three levels. The industry is characterized by large firms, but there is very little direct competition because most firms have an exclusive market area.

Regulation

Rate Levels   Technological advances resulted in continually declining electricity prices until 1970. Since 1970, high interest rates, increasing fuel costs, and environmental requirements have caused electricity prices to climb rapidly. As a result, state and federal commissions have been besieged with requests for rate increases.

Rate Structures   In the early days of the electric power industry, customers were often charged a flat rate regardless of their actual consumption. Today, most utilities use declining- or level-block tariffs. Industrial tariffs usually impose a demand charge in addition to the quantity charge.

Current Issues: Time-of-Use Pricing

Generating Technology and Peak Loads   The demand for electricity varies with the time of day and season of the year. Daily-peak demands are met using fuel-intensive generating technology, while the baseload demand is met using more efficient capital-intensive technology. Costs decrease if demand can be shifted from peak to off-peak periods.

Theory of Peak-Load Pricing   Economic theory suggests that costs should be allocated to consumers on the basis of causality. The traditional theory of peak-load pricing assumes that off-peak users derive no benefits from generating capacity and, hence, that all capacity costs should be assessed to peak users.

A revised theory of peak-load pricing notes that off-peak users may also benefit from generating capacity. If an expansion of capacity results in more efficient production during the off-peak period (because of economies of scale or technological change), then prices to off-peak users should reflect the benefits received from the expansion.

Applications of Peak-Load Pricing   In practice, peak-load pricing usually takes the form of seasonal and/or time-of-day rates. Seasonal rates specify a winter/summer differential. Time-of-day rates typically divide each 24-hour day into two or three blocks.

Time-of-day pricing has not been widely used in the United States. However, the Public Utility Regulatory Policies Act of 1978 has accelerated rate structure reform. PURPA required that each state commission hold hearings to consider the use of seasonal and time-of-day rates. The act also discourages the use of the declining-block rate structure.

Seasonal and time-of-day rates have been used in France for many years. Industrial users are also assessed a demand charge for "subscribed" power. For residential consumers the demand charge takes the form of a circuit-breaker fee. Residential customers expecting to have a high maximum demand for electricity must pay a higher price to purchase a circuit breaker with greater capacity.

Current Issues: Lifeline Rates

Lifeline rates are an example of taxation by regulation. Typically, they provide a low-cost initial block of electricity that is subsidized by high-volume customers.

Pros and Cons of Lifeline Rates   Advocates of lifeline rates argue that they can be used to promote conservation and to assist the poor. Critics charge that low-income groups are not always low-volume electricity users.

Evidence and Evaluation of the Effects of Lifeline Rates   Research indicates that some of the poor pay more and many of the rich pay less under lifeline rates. The problem is that such rates frequently are not restricted to those that they are designed to benefit.

DISCUSSION QUESTIONS

1. Why is vertical integration common in the electric power industry but not in the natural gas industry?
2. Under a declining-block tariff, prices go down as consumption increases. Would the marginal cost of providing electricity to a particular residential customer really decrease with increased consumption?
3. Since electric utilities don't compete for sales to consumers, is there any reason why they should not be allowed to form close interfirm ties, such as a strong trade association?
4. Does a utility's peak demand always determine the amount of capacity that the firm must have? Why?
5. Could peak-load pricing change a utility's peak and off-peak periods? How should this possibility be taken into account in setting rates?
6. Should the federal government mandate the use of peak-load pricing for all utilities?
7. Is the French experience with peak-load pricing relevant for the United States? Why?
8. Why are seasonal rates more common than time-of-day rates?
9. The chapter suggests that income redistribution should be left to legislative bodies rather than attempted by regulatory commissions. Do you agree?

chapter 13

Regulation and Competition: Telecommunications

Chapter Outline

Telephones are rented only to persons of good breeding and refinement. There is nothing to be feared from your conversation being overheard. Our subscribers are too well-bred to listen to other people's conversations. [1]

Even in the most favorable circumstances, economic regulation is a difficult task. Commissions typically are hampered by inadequate information, limited resources, and changing economic and technological conditions. The task becomes even more complicated if the regulated firm faces competition from other, unregulated suppliers. In this circumstance, the ability of regulators to implement policy is constrained by the discipline imposed by market forces.

The telecommunications industry is an excellent example. For nearly three-quarters of a century the Bell System, aided by its regulators, maintained a monopoly over much of the telecommunications market. But technological changes in recent years generated intense competitive pressures from unregulated firms. Originally, state and federal regulatory bodies used their power over entry to resist these pressures. But ultimately policymakers were forced to recognize that the Bell monopoly could not continue in its present form. The result was a complete restructuring of the telecommunications industry—a change that could be compared to taking a 747 airliner apart in midair while making sure that it continues to fly.

This chapter takes a close look at the telecommunications industry in the United States. The specific focus is on how public policy has responded to pressures to open the industry to competition. The first section describes the operation of the telephone network and the second considers optimal pricing of telephone services. Sections three and four examine the evolution of the industry over time. Finally, section five outlines present industry structure and discusses prospects for the future.

THE TELEPHONE NETWORK

In 1876, Alexander Graham Bell received patent number 174,465 for an "improvement in telegraphy"—the telephone. Bell's patent was probably the most valuable ever issued. Nearly abandoned by its inventors as an economic failure, the telephone has revolutionized modern life. Table 13.1 shows the increase in the number of telephones in use in the United States between 1882 and 1981. At the present time over 96 percent of all U.S. households have at least one telephone. In 1982 over 300 billion calls were made—an average of about 1,600 per phone. Prior to discussing pricing and current issues in the telephone industry, a brief, nontechnical introduction to the telephone network will be useful. Figure 13.1 depicts a simple telephone system. The two rectangles represent local exchanges, which are served by separate central offices. The central office can be thought of as consisting of switching facilities that allow subscribers in a given exchange to place and receive calls. If customer *A* wishes to call customer *B,* the call goes over the *local loop* to the central office. The central office connects the

[1] Telephone company advertisement as quoted in Todd, K.P., ed., *A Capsule History of the Bell System* (New York: American Telephone and Telegraph Co., n.d.).

Table 13.1 TELEPHONES IN THE
UNITED STATES:
1882–1981

Year	Number
1882	97,700
1890	227,900
1900	1,355,900
1910	7,635,400
1920	13,411,400
1930	20,201,600
1940	21,928,000
1950	43,003,800
1960	74,341,100
1970	120,221,000
1980	180,000,000
1981	182,000,000

Source: Federal Communications Commission, *Statistics of Communications Common Carriers* (Washington, D.C.: Government Printing Office, (annual).

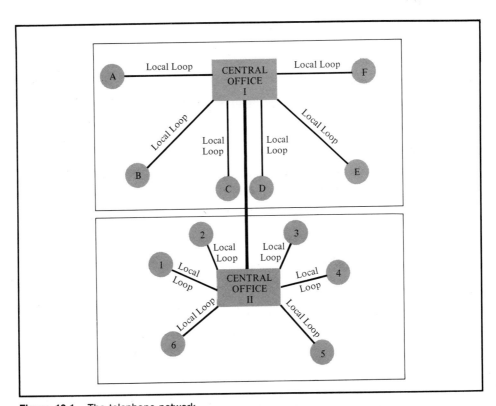

Figure 13.1. The telephone network.

call to customer *B* using the office's switching facilities and the call goes out over another portion of the local loop.

If a subscriber in exchange I desires to talk to someone in exchange II, then the trunk lines that connect the exchanges must be used in addition to the local loops and switching facilities of central offices. When customer *B* places a call to customer 2, the call goes over the local loop of exchange I to that central office. The central office switches the call through the trunk lines to the central office of exchange II, which sends the call over exchange II's local loop to the location of customer 2. Calls between separate exchanges are referred to as toll calls, because the customer is assessed a charge based on the distance between the exchanges, the duration of the call, and the time of day of the call. [2]

The equipment necessary to make telephone calls can be divided into usage- and nonusage-sensitive facilities. *Usage-sensitive facilities* are those for which the amount of equipment needed depends on the number of calls made. For example, trunk lines between exchanges are usage sensitive. If more calls are made or if people talk longer, then additional trunk lines may be necessary. Some of the switching facilities of central offices are also usage sensitive, because an increase in the number or duration of calls may require more switching capacity.

Nonusage-sensitive facilities include the telephone, structure wiring at a subscriber's location, the local loop, and dedicated switching equipment (those switching devices that are used only to serve a particular customer). These are necessary to provide access to the telephone network, but are not affected by an increase in telephone calling. For example, the local loop connecting a customer with the central office must be in place to give the user access to the phone network, but an increase in calling affects only the proportion of time that the loop is in use. The distinction between usage- and nonusage-sensitive costs is important for the pricing of different telephone services. This topic is considered in the next section.

OPTIMAL PRICING OF TELEPHONE SERVICES
Time-of-Use Pricing

Pricing of telephone services is a complex issue. First, all the difficulties associated with peak-load problems in electricity pricing also are present in the telephone industry. As a public utility, telephone companies must stand ready to meet the maximum demand of their customers. For most areas this peak demand occurs in the early afternoons on weekdays and is caused by a high volume of business usage. However, the facilities constructed to meet the peak demand are idle for much of the remainder of the time. The volume of calls at the system peak is many times the usage during the early morning hours. Telephone companies are far ahead of their electric counterparts in instigating time-of-use pricing to deal with this phenomenon. For years, long-distance rates have been lower in the evenings and on weekends than during weekday business hours. Figure 13.2 shows dial-direct discounts for toll calls at different times during the week.

---

[2] Calls within an exchange (local calls) are billed separately in some areas, but the norm in the United States is to provide the customer with an area within which he or she can make an unlimited amount of calls for a set monthly charge. In some locations the monthly rate may allow customers to call between exchanges. Where such "extended area service" exists, calls between exchanges are not properly classified as toll calls.

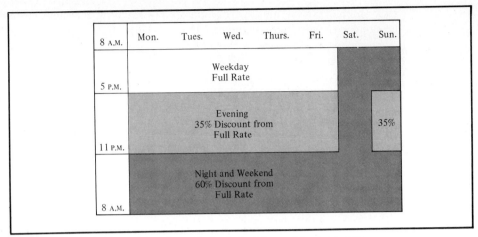

Figure 13.2.   AT&T time-of-day discounts for long-distance telephone calls.

Externalities

A second complicating factor in pricing telephone services involves externalities.[3] Two externalities are commonly identified. First, when a person initiates a phone conversation, it is because the expected benefits of the call exceed the time and money costs of making the call. However, the recipient usually also benefits. True, there are nuisance calls, obscene calls, and boring calls, but the fact that people continue to answer their phones is evidence that they attach a positive expected value to receiving a phone call. An externality arises if the caller cannot capture the benefits received by the party being called. Thus, the caller makes the call because its value exceeds the cost, but the caller does not take into account the benefits to the party called. Hence, the demand for making calls understates the true value of the activity. The result is that fewer calls are made than if their full value was taken into account by the caller.

The second externality arises when a new telephone subscriber joins the network. The decision by an individual to hook up to the system is based, like the decision to make a phone call, on an assessment of the benefits versus the costs. Benefits include the ability to make calls and the utility of receiving calls from others. Costs are the expense of adding another user to the system. But, again, the new customer is unable to capture all of the benefits of his action. When a new subscriber is added to the network, existing customers benefit in two ways. First, they may receive calls from a person who could not have called them before. Second, they can make calls to someone who previously was not part of the network. Because the potential customer, in deciding whether to purchase access to the phone system, cannot capture these external benefits, they are not included in his calculations. The result is that the demand for access is understated and fewer people join the system than if the full social benefits were considered.

Even assuming that the true marginal costs of gaining access to the telephone network and of making a call could be determined, the presence of externalities suggests

---

[3]The analysis of telephone externalities is formally presented by Taylor, L.D., *Telecommunications Demand: A Survey and Critique* (Cambridge, Mass.: Ballinger, 1980).

that optimal pricing must go beyond simply equating marginal costs to price. The economist's traditional recommendation for setting prices equal to marginal cost assumes no externalities and is based on the following arguments. First, that individuals maximize their welfare by purchasing a service until the value of the last unit is just equal to the price that is paid. Second, that optimal resource allocation on the producer side requires that firms continue to produce until the cost of producing the last unit just equals the price at which it can be sold. In competitive markets this decision rule allows the firm to maximize profits. From the perspective of society, setting price equal to marginal cost maximizes voluntary exchange. No other price will result in as much mutually beneficial exchange of the service. In terms of simple supply-and-demand analysis, a competitive market generates this result by tending to an equilibrium with price at P_e and quantity at q_e as shown in Figure 13.3.

However, the simple $P = MC$ rule does not take into account the presence of externalities. Individuals make their purchase decisions on the basis of personal benefits that are implicitly incorporated into the demand curve, DD. Since others receive benefits from the telephone that cannot be captured by the individual making a call or choosing to hook onto the network, the full social value of those activities is shown by the demand curve, $D'D'$. The intersection of $D'D'$ and SS yields a price of P_e' and a quantity of q_e'. But, to cause individuals to increase their purchases to q_e', the price would have to drop to P_e''. However, at that price the firm would have an incentive to cut its production below even q_e. To cause the optimum quantity, q_e', to be purchased the customer must face the price P_e''. To induce firms to produce that amount they must receive at least P_e'. One solution is to subsidize the price by the amount $P_e' - P_e''$. If this occurs then the price to the consumer is set below marginal cost, but the optimal amount, q_e' is exchanged.

The foregoing analysis is applicable to the pricing of access to the telephone network and also pricing of telephone calls. It suggests that prices of both access and

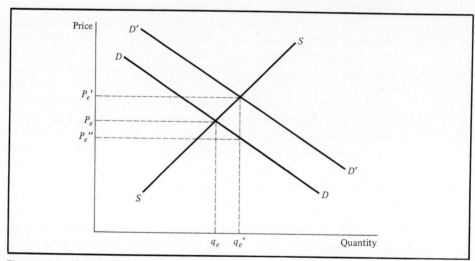

Figure 13.3. Optimal pricing with externalities.

usage should be set below their marginal costs to take account of the externalities associated with those activities.

Although the externalities argument applies to usage as well as access, the usage externality is invariably ignored in discussions of rate structure design. One justification for this practice is the assumption that the benefits of receiving calls balance out among telephone users. A second is that the calling party can capture most of the benefits received by the person being called. For example, if the call is made by a business soliciting sales, a successful transaction will compensate the firm for making the call.

Unbundling

For years, charges for various products and services provided by the local telephone company were lumped together. Each month the customer received a bill that aggregated the cost of the basic telephone unit, access to the telephone network, unlimited local calling, and various other services such as directory assistance. Only the amounts for specialized equipment and for long-distance calling were broken out on the monthly billing. Recently, there has been a rapid movement toward "unbundling" of prices in the telephone industry. Unbundling involves charging separate prices for individual products and services. For example, an unbundled bill might itemize charges for each piece of equipment leased from the phone company; directory assistance requests beyond some monthly minimum; local and long-distance usage measured in terms of the number, distance, duration, and timing of local calls; and basic access to the telephone network.

Unbundling of prices represents an important step toward efficient resource allocation in the telecommunications industry. With aggregated prices, customers often were unaware of the cost of specific products and services. As such, they were unable to make intelligent decisions as to whether such items were necessary. With unbundled prices, consumers are able to tailor phone service to meet their specific needs. Also, the use of aggregated prices made it difficult for other firms to compete for sales of telephone equipment. When the customer's monthly bill already included the cost of the telephone unit, there was little incentive to buy a telephone from someone else. However, once the payment to the local phone company was unbundled and based on actual products and services being used, then the customer had reason to shop for better prices.

Although unbundling has increased competition and improved consumer decision making in telecommunications, the process is not yet complete. Most telephone subscribers still pay a flat monthly rate that lumps access and unlimited local calling. As discussed in Chapter 11, this results in inefficient resource allocation because telephone customers have no reason to limit their calling. Since there is no additional charge for using the local phone network, facilities may be used for low-value calls even though such calling imposes a substantial cost on the phone company.

For example, two computer chess fanatics may decide to leave their terminals connected via the phone system while they meet for an afternoon round of golf. Under a flat-rate pricing scheme there is no direct cost to them of doing so. But because this connection occurs during the telephone company's afternoon busy period, it adds to peak demand. In the long run, failure to conserve on calling requires the purchase of additional equipment by the phone company and drives up costs.

In the past, the cost of measuring and billing local calls made flat-rate pricing a necessity. Today, electronic switching systems have greatly reduced these measurement costs. They will allow a gradual unbundling of access and usage. The access charge will be based on the nonusage-sensitive costs of joining the telephone network. The usage charge will reflect the usage-sensitive costs of making telephone calls. Ultimately, there should be no need to distinguish between local and long-distance calling. Every call will be billed on the basis of time of day, duration, and distance.

FROM COMPETITION TO REGULATED MONOPOLY

Initially, Bell and his associates exploited their patent rights by renting telephone units. Potential users were left to install the connecting wires. However, the firm's services were quickly expanded. The first local telephone network began operations in New Haven in 1878, and the first switchboard was used in Boston in 1888. The demand for telephone service increased rapidly from these beginnings. Entrepreneurs interested in providing service to new areas were granted licenses in return for stock interests in the venture.

Between 1876 and 1894 Alexander Graham Bell's American Telephone Company parlayed its patent privileges into a virtual monopoly over telephone service in the United States. There were some early skirmishes with Western Union over the validity of patent rights, but these were resolved under the terms of a compromise whereby Western Union was to serve the market for telegraph services, while the Bell System specialized in voice communications.[4]

The Early Competitive Years

When the Bell patents expired in 1894, many small telephone companies entered the market. Sometimes these independent firms simply moved in to offer service where it did not previously exist, but often they entered in direct competition with existing Bell operations. As new competitors, their tactic was to make the claim of lower rates and better service. In 1902, 1,002 cities with population greater than 4,000 had telephone service. Of these, Bell had a monopoly position in 414, independent telephone companies provided the only service in 137, and competition between two or more firms existed in 451 cities. In total, over 3,000 commercial and nearly 1,000 cooperative telephone companies were in operation at that time.[5]

The flurry of competition that followed the expiration of patent rights had a dramatic effect on Bell's market share. During the patent years the company had almost total control over telephone service in the United States. However, by 1902 the firm's market share had dropped to just over 50 percent. Competition also resulted in a rapid

[4]An interesting historical aside is that Western Union was offered the Bell patents for $100,000 but refused to buy on the grounds that the "electrical toy" had no future.
[5]Gabel, R., "The Early Competitive Era in Telecommunications, 1893–1920," *Law and Contemporary Problems,* Vol. 34 (Spring 1969), pp. 340–359.

drop in prices. Table 13.2 shows the average annual rates per customer for Bell subscribers and for customers of independent telephone companies. The table indicates that rates declined substantially between 1894 and 1907. Some of the decline must be attributed to cost-reducing effects of technological change. However, competition undoubtedly spurred Bell to share these gains with its customers.

Notice that the rate reductions occurred both in locations without competition from independent telephone companies and in those areas with competition. One explanation is the threat of potential competition. Bell recognized that prices needed to be reduced to deter entry in its monopoly markets, as well as to meet competition in areas where competitors were already established.

The conventional view of telecommunications technology is that local telephone service is characterized by declining average costs. As such, competition would result in an inefficient duplication of facilities. The competitive era of telephone service (1894 to about 1910) calls this assumption into question. Table 13.2 indicates that competition resulted in a dramatic reduction in rates. There are also indications that innovation was stimulated by competition. For example, the dial telephone was developed and first used by independent phone companies. For a number of years the Bell System strongly resisted its use. Important innovations in switching and transmission technology also came from non-Bell sources.

On the other hand, there were some serious problems stemming from telephone competition. Many of the independent firms were awarded franchises on the basis of rate promises they couldn't keep. One illustration is the Atlanta Telephone and Telegraph Company. The firm was given its market area on the basis of a proposal to charge annual rates to business customers of $36 and to residential customers of $24. In operation, Atlanta's actual rates were 50 percent higher at $48 and $36, respectively.

In other cases independent phone companies proved to be technically or financially unsound. In the former circumstance the quality of service was unacceptable and in the latter the firms were unable to survive changes in general economic conditions. Between 1903 and 1906, 85 independent telephone companies went bankrupt. Most of

Table 13.2 ANNUAL RATES FOR BELL AND INDEPENDENT TELEPHONE COMPANIES: 1894 AND 1907

	Bell rates		Independent rates
	1894	1907	1907
Exchanges without Competition			
Business	$68.10	$36.00	Not available
Residential	56.00	23.75	Not available
Exchanges with competition			
Business	78.65	41.25	$37.15
Residential	65.00	22.80	23.25

Source: Gable, R., "The Early Competitive Era in Telecommunications: 1893–1920." Reprinted with permission from a symposium entitled "Communication," Part I, appearing in *Law and Contemporary Problems*, Vol. 34, No. 2, p. 340 (Durham, North Carolina: Duke University School of Law, Spring 1969). Copyright 1969 by Duke University School of Law.

these were small firms, but phone companies in Kansas City, Augusta, and Richmond were among the casualties. [6]

In assessing the competitive era of telephone development, it is not obvious that the benefits of competition exceeded the costs. However, the view that telephone service is a natural monopoly with no role for competition was not clearly demonstrated either. The demise of telephone competition was a result of factors other than just the superior efficiency of the dominant firm.

State and Federal Regulation

The Bell System responded to competition in two ways. First, the company embarked on an aggressive program of acquisition. Hundreds of small independent telephone companies were purchased between 1894 and 1913, when the company agreed to abide by the so-called *Kingsbury Commitment*. Taking its name from the Bell vice-president who authored it, the Kingsbury Commitment was the firm's response to an antitrust suit initiated by the Justice Department. Under this agreement the Bell System agreed to interconnect with independent telephone companies and to terminate its policy of acquiring competitors. Even after the 1913 commitment, Bell sometimes got involved in acquisition activities. Usually, however, the company has followed a policy of only acquiring firms in financial difficulty.

State Regulation.   The second Bell response to competition was to promote regulation of the industry. Initially, the company's management had opposed regulation. However, as competition became more intense, regulation was viewed more favorably. In 1907 only five states had commissions with authority over telephone operations, but the number grew rapidly over the next 20 years. As commissions were established, Bell magnanimously provided legal and technical assistance in their formation. The company also aided independents with their rate cases. The motive was that if the competing firms were allowed to increase their rates, then commissions would find it difficult to deny rate relief to Bell.

Whether because of the influence of the Bell System or for other reasons, the initial decisions of state commissions tended to favor exclusive service areas for telephone companies. The combination of Bell's aggressive acquisition activities and regulatory support of monopoly greatly diminished the importance of competition in the industry. Today, there are hundreds of independent telephone companies, but none compete directly in providing local telephone service. Each firm has its own exclusive area of operation.

Federal Regulation   The Mann-Elkins Act of 1910 gave the Interstate Commerce Commission authority to set minimum and maximum rates for telecommunications services. However, because of railroad regulatory functions and inadequate budgets, the commission never assumed a very active role in telephone regulation. Between 1910 and

---

[6]Stehman, J. W., *The Financial History of the American Telephone and Telegraph Company.* Reprints of Economic Classics (New York: A. M. Kelly, 1967). The high incidence of bankruptcy is not necessarily evidence of failure in telephone competition. An efficient economic system must always include provision for the exit of failing firms, as well as the entry of new competitors.

1934 only four telephone cases were decided and those did not involve important issues. In August 1918, the government took over telephone operations as a war measure, but the system was returned to private management in July 1919.

Acting on the recommendation of a committee of experts that federal communications regulation should be concentrated in a single agency, Congress passed the Communications Act of 1934. The act created the Federal Communications Commission for the purpose of regulating interstate and foreign communications by wire and radio. The avowed purpose of the legislation was to "make available, so far as possible, to all the people of the United States a rapid, efficient, nationwide and world-wide wire, and radio communication service." The philosophy of promoting universal radio and wire communications has had an important impact on the development of the telephone industry.

The FCC was given the standard powers of federal regulatory commissions—to assure that rates are just and reasonable, to prevent unreasonable discrimination, and to require that firms acquire certificates of convenience and necessity before operating new services. In its early years the commission limited its activities to making studies and recommendations regarding the firms it regulated. On issues relating to the Bell System the firm was generally allowed to broaden and solidify its monopoly positions. However, since the late 1950s the FCC has taken a much more active role in setting policy in the communications industry. Specifically, during the last two decades the FCC has had an important impact in expanding the degree of competition in telecommunications.

Pricing in a Regulated Monopoly

During the monopoly era (and, to a lesser degree, in today's more competitive telephone industry) pricing of telephone services involved a substantial dose of taxation by regulation. Rates for certain services were increased to provide excess profits so that other services, deemed to have special worth to society, could be provided at lower cost to encourage their use. Universal access and uniform rates are two aspects of telecommunications pricing policy that illustrate this principle.

Universal Access   An efficient and widespread communications network was a congressional goal expressed in the Communications Act of 1934. The intent of Congress was that the telephone system should be easily accessible to all citizens. This policy has been implemented by holding down the price of basic telephone service in order to increase the number of subscribers to the system. The evidence suggests that the policy has been very successful. In 1934 only about one-third of American homes had a telephone. At present, 96 percent of homes have at least one phone. Although every father of a teenager is convinced that the nation faces an acute telephone shortage, the reality is that there are three phones for every four people in the United States.

Historically, the mechanism for promoting universal service has involved subsidizing the flat-rate monthly phone bill with revenues obtained from other services such as interstate and intrastate toll calls and sales of telephone equipment. However, as regulated firms, the phone companies could not make this decision unilaterally. The subsidy had to be approved by the regulatory bodies having jurisdiction—the state

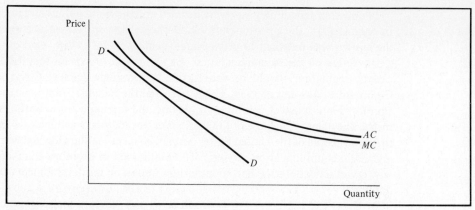

Figure 13.4.   Toll calls between rural locations.

commissions with respect to the monthly flat rate and for intrastate toll calls and the FCC for interstate toll tariffs. Over the years, these commissions consistently accepted the principle of subsidizing the price of basic telephone service. In so doing, they used the regulatory process as a means of redistributing income. Heavy toll users were charged more, with the benefits accruing to those who make few toll calls. The restructuring of the telephone industry will make it difficult to continue the subsidy for basic service. This issue will be discussed later in the chapter.

Uniform Rates   Rates for long-distance calls are based primarily on the distance, time of day, and duration of the call. Other factors affecting the actual cost of making the call usually are subjugated in the attempt to set uniform, easily understood rates and to subsidize long-distance calling between points where low-call volume and high costs would not allow the service to stand on its own.

To illustrate, consider telephone traffic between San Jose and San Francisco and between two rural locations that are separated by a similar distance (about 60 miles).[7] Scale economies stemming from the high volume of telephone calls between San Jose and San Francisco allow the cost per call on this route to be quite low. In contrast, infrequent conversations between the two rural points result in a very high cost per call. If customers in the rural areas were required to pay the full cost of their calls, few calls would be made. In all likelihood the demand would be so small as to preclude the telephone company from earning a reasonable return on the investment required to provide the service. If the firm were to make its investment decisions on a piecemeal basis, or if the company did not have other operations on which to make up the loss, the service would not be provided at all. The situation is illustrated by Figure 13.4. There is no price that could be set for calls that would allow the firm to earn a normal return on its investment in the rural areas. Insufficient demand makes the market a losing proposition.

In determining telephone policy, regulators typically have viewed the provision of telephone communications between rural points to have social benefits in addition

[7]This example was discussed in Chapter 10, but is presented here in greater detail.

to those that are captured by the calling parties as embodied in the demand curve. Hence, the demand curve understates the true value of the service, and the market will underallocate resources to this area. As previously noted, the policy prescription is to subsidize the rates for these calls. This is accomplished by allowing telephone companies to earn an excess return on other parts of their operations, which compensates for losses in markets such as that depicted in Figure 13.4.

For the moment, assume that a phone company has only two routes. One is between the two rural points and the other is San Francisco to San Jose. To subsidize rates between the rural points, the rates between San Francisco and San Jose must be priced to yield excess profits. This policy is shown in Figure 13.5. The regulatory commission allows the utility to charge P for calls between San Francisco and San Jose. Because the price is greater than average cost at Q the price is sufficient to yield a normal return on that operation and also to make a contribution to the loss sustained in serving the rural route.

In practice, this objective is achieved by authorizing the firm to charge the same price for calls between both sets of points. Between San Jose and San Francisco the price more than covers the firm's costs, and between the rural points the price is somewhat less than the cost of providing service. Overall, the price is set to just allow the utility to earn a "fair" rate of return on its total investment in serving the two markets.

The concept of uniform rates also applies to the pricing of basic telephone service. Within a given local area the price that telephone subscribers pay for access to the system is not closely correlated to the actual cost of providing them service. For the phone company the lowest-cost users are those who arc located in close proximity to the central office. The cost of serving those who are on the periphery of the exchange is much higher. The social goal of providing wide access is used as a rationale for disregarding these cost differences. Typically, subscribers in a given telephone exchange are all charged the same monthly rate for equivalent service.

As with uniform rates for long-distance calling, uniform pricing of basic access can be achieved only by requiring low-cost users to subsidize high-cost subscribers. The magnitude of the required subsidy can be substantial. In Hope Hull, Alabama, the

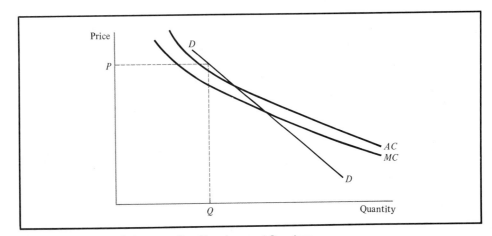

Figure 13.5. Toll calls between San Francisco and San Jose.

telephone company recently made an investment of $357,000 to serve 73 new customers. This investment would have justified a monthly charge of $102 per customer. The actual rate for Hope Hull customers was $13.75 per month.[8] The difference was made up in the form of higher rates paid by other Alabama telephone users.

The powers of the regulatory commissions play a crucial role in implementing uniform pricing of telephone services. The obvious impact is their willingness to approve such rate structures. However, an equally important role is their ability to exclude competition. Figure 13.5 depicts a price that allows the firm to earn an excess return on its investment. Economic theory predicts that whenever an above-average return on capital is being earned, entry will take place. As new entrants come into the industry they drive down prices and, hence, the rate of return on capital. Entry continues until excess profits in the industry have disappeared.

If regulatory commissions allowed existing firms to earn excess profits in some markets as a means of subsidizing others, and if there were no restrictions on entry, then new firms would quickly enter the profitable markets. Competition would eventually drive prices down and excess profits to zero. At this point the existing firms would no longer be in a position to subsidize high-cost services. Earning just a normal return in the competitive market and sustaining a loss in their unprofitable rural markets, the firms would no longer be able to earn a fair return on their total investment.

The presence of competition in the markets that had previously provided the subsidy prevents prices from being raised there and, as shown in Figure 13.4, no price would make the rural markets profitable. If the firm is to earn a fair return, only two alternatives are viable. The first is to terminate service in the unprofitable market. However, such service is deemed to have external benefits by regulators. The second possibility is to prevent entry into the profitable market. By legally preventing new firms from entering, the existing firm's monopoly profits are protected and the company retains its ability to subsidize unprofitable operations.

Historically, restriction on entry is the solution that has been used by regulatory commissions in the United States. By protecting excess profits in some markets, uniform pricing of toll calls was made possible. Promotion of universal service by subsidizing basic exchange rates also required entry restrictions in markets where excess profits were being earned.

LEAKS IN THE DIKE: DEFINING THE BOUNDARIES
BETWEEN MONOPOLY AND COMPETITIVE SERVICES

Over the last two decades the most important issues in telephone regulation have involved policies with respect to entry. The debate has centered on the proper boundaries between the regulated monopolies and unregulated competitors. Changes in technology and philosophy have repeatedly forced regulators to draw and redraw these boundaries. This section traces the evolution of entry policy with respect to (1) special-

---

[8]deButts, J. D., "Telecommunications Policy for the Future—A Balance of Interests," testimony before the Senate Subcommittee on Communications (New York: American Telephone and Telegraph, Mar. 21, 1977). While potential customers on the perimeters of an established service area may be served at the same price as existing subscribers, this principle has its limits. To extend service to remote points, a resident or business may be charged a much higher price.

ized carriers of long-distance telephone communications and (2) the sale of terminal equipment (e.g., switchboards and telephones).

Specialized Carriers

Microwave Transmission   Long-distance telephone calls usually are made with little thought of the technology required to complete the call. To the extent that the process is considered, the typical view is of a set of electrical impulses being transmitted by wire from one point to another. Today, however, most telephone conversations are not carried by wire. The majority of calls rely on microwave relay stations spaced within line of sight of one another throughout the nation. The principle is the same as for radio broadcasting, except that the microwave band of the electromagnetic spectrum is at a higher frequency and has a more limited transmission range than the band allocated to AM and FM radio.

Microwave technology was demonstrated as early as 1915, but the applied research to make it practical was not completed until World War II. Between 1945 and 1950 a number of firms constructed commercial microwave facilities to transmit television signals. The first was Western Union, which opened a network between New York and Philadelphia in 1945. The Bell System entered the field two years later. Originally, the industry was highly competitive, but a series of actions by the Federal Communications Commission effectively thwarted competition. First, the commission set aside certain portions of the microwave spectrum for use by common carriers only.[9] Second, the commission implicitly accepted the Bell System's existing policy of refusing to interconnect with the facilities of other companies. Third, the FCC determined that only common carriers could furnish service over the so-called video frequencies. Other firms were required to abandon their systems when common carrier service became available.

Although hundreds of private microwave systems were constructed during the 1950s, the Bell System and the other common carriers achieved an overwhelming dominance in the field. A major reason was that the private systems were all licensed for a one-year period and faced the prospect of losing their license if common-carrier service developed to meet their needs. This uncertainty limited investment in private microwave systems and caused potential users to look toward the common carriers for service.

Above-890 Decision   In 1954, two North Dakota television stations requested that the FCC change its policies to permit businesses to construct microwave facilities for their own use without regard to the availability of common-carrier service. The common carriers (with Bell the most vocal and influential combatant) argued against the policy revision. They based their position on three points. First, the proliferation of systems might cause interference with existing facilities and reduce the quality of service. Second, the needs of national defense required that the communications system be developed under a coordinated plan, which could best be achieved by large-scale firms.

---

[9]Common carriers are firms that offer facilities and services to all users willing to pay the price. This is in contrast to specialized carriers, whose facilities and services are restricted to specified users.

Finally, the common carriers argued that easing entry restrictions would cause "cream skimming" and thwart the goals of universal access and uniform rates. The cream-skimming argument has historically been the most important and durable objection of the common carriers to competition. As such, it deserves further discussion.

Previous sections stressed that low monthly charges for basic telephone service and nominal rates for calls over low-volume routes are made possible by pricing other services to yield excess profits. These excess profits are guaranteed by the powers of the regulatory commissions to prevent entry. If entry were allowed, new firms would concentrate in the most profitable markets of the existing firms in the attempt to skim the cream (profits) from these areas. The consequence would be that the prices of the subsidized services would have to be increased to compensate for the loss. Thus, Bell and the other common carriers argued that removing entry restrictions would impede the achievement of social objectives such as uniform rates and universal access.

In its historic 1959 Above-890 decision, the Federal Communications Commission rejected the arguments of the common carriers. [10] The commission determined that sufficient frequencies exist above 890 megacycles to meet present and future needs of private users and the common carriers. The FCC also concluded that the restriction on entry would not significantly impair the ability of the common carriers to provide service to the general public—a denial of the importance of the cream-skimming argument. The commission implemented its decision by removing the significant regulatory barriers to operation of private microwave systems by businesses and governmental agencies.

Faced with competition in microwave communications, the Bell System filed new tariffs proposing lower rates for selected services. The objective was to discourage entry by reducing the profit potential. The next issue to face the FCC was how low the rates of common carriers would be permitted to go. The commission agreed that carriers should be allowed to compete, but not engage in predatory pricing to prevent entry. Bell and the other common carriers argued that they should be allowed to reduce rates down to the incremental costs of providing the service. In contrast, potential competitors took the position that prices should not be allowed to fall below fully allocated costs, which included a "fair share" of the system's overhead costs. The FCC opted for fully allocated costs and required the carriers to refile tariffs at a higher level to meet this criterion.

At this point the commission's position with respect to competition was as follows. First, restrictions on entry were to be eased. Second, the common carriers were allowed to compete on price with new entrants. But, third, price competition was limited by the requirement that any tariff must fully cover distributed costs of the service. In effect, the carriers were told that they could compete—but not too much.

MCI   The above-890 decision permitted private firms to operate microwave facilities for their own use, but not to provide the service for others. In the 1960s a small firm, Microwave Communications, Inc., (MCI) sought FCC permission to provide business

---

[10]*Allocation of Microwave Frequencies Above 890 Mc.,* 27 FCC 359 (1959). Eight-hundred-ninety megacycles is the beginning of the microwave portion of the electromagnetic spectrum.

users with private-line service between St. Louis and Chicago. In most cases the service offered would have connected branch offices of businesses located in the two cities. Customers were to be allowed to share lines and contract for specific periods when they would take service. MCI proposed to provide the microwave network between the two points and its subscribers were to use the facilities of existing carriers (essentially the Bell System) to connect their offices with MCI. The proposed service would have been similar to the system already offered by Bell and Western Union, but was to be less expensive—about half the price charged by the existing firms.

The Bell System opposed the MCI application and refused to provide interconnection with the MCI network. The argument of cream skimming was again raised. Bell contended that competition would occur only in lucrative markets, and the existing firms would be left with the burden of serving unsubsidized, unprofitable markets, while competing in more profitable markets. Bell also claimed that high-quality service in telecommunications could be assured only if a single firm was given the right to provide end-to-end service. Forcing interconnection with MCI and similar firms would cause the quality of common-carrier service to be dependent on the linkages offered by competitors.

The FCC's decision again eased entry restrictions.[11] MCI was permitted to provide the service and the Bell System was required to interconnect. In deciding the issues, the commission went beyond the question of MCI's application and established a new category of "specialized common carriers," who would be allowed to operate microwave facilities in competition with existing services. A long sequence of appeals by Bell ensued, but in 1978 the Supreme Court finally upheld the actions of the commission.

During the appeals process the survival of MCI was highly uncertain. Litigation was costly and time consuming. Facilities for MCI's first route cost $2 million and took 7 months to build. In contrast, the company's legal battles were drawn out over ten years and cost the firm over $10 million. Today, however, the firm is a profitable enterprise. MCI's 1983 revenues were over one billion dollars and profits were about $200 million. Over time, the firm has moved aggressively into the broader market for long-distance communications and now has about 3 percent of the total market.[12] Other firms have followed MCI's lead by entering into new markets with an expanded menu of offerings. Although AT&T is still the dominant supplier, the service has become very competitive.

Terminal Equipment

Early Bell System Policy   Terminal equipment allows users of telecommunications services to interface with the network. The most common example is the telephone

---

[11] *In the Matter of Microwave Communications, Inc.,* 18 FCC 953 (1969).

[12] Unsatisfied, MCI filed a $900 million (treble damages on this amount would total $2.7 billion) antitrust suit against AT&T. The firm claimed that AT&T illegally prevented it from entering the market for private line, long-distance telephone service. A jury awarded MCI $1.8 billion in damages—the largest antitrust judgement in history. However, the jury verdict was overturned by an appeals court. Final resolution is pending.

itself. Switchboards and computer terminals also fit the definition. Historically, the Bell System took a very rigid stance against the use of terminal equipment not provided by the company. For years the firm's policy was:

> No equipment, apparatus, circuit or device not furnished by the Telephone Company shall be attached to or connected with the facilities furnished by the Telephone Company, whether physically, by induction or otherwise. . . . In case any such unauthorized attachment or connection is made, the Telephone Company shall have the right to remove or disconnect the same; or to suspend the continuance of said attachment or connection; or to terminate the service. [13]

Bell's position was based on the argument of system technical integrity. The company maintained that, unless a single firm had end-to-end responsibility for the telecommunications system, there would be no way to determine who was responsible for disruptions in service. With no means of assessing blame, the incentive to prevent disruptions would be reduced. Because the Bell System was viewed essentially synonymously with telephone communications, any problems would be blamed on Bell, whether the firm was the guilty party or not.

Bell went to extremes in enforcing its policy against non-Bell terminal equipment and supplies. In North Carolina the company opposed the activities of a firm that was selling advertising space on a plastic phone book cover, which was then distributed throughout the state. Although the state supreme court ultimately upheld the right of consumers to put whatever they wanted on their phone books, the North Carolina Utility Commission had initially upheld Bell in its objections.

On another occasion Bell objected to the sale of a device called the Hush-A-Phone. A cuplike instrument that was snapped over the mouthpiece of the telephone, the Hush-A-Phone was designed to give the user some degree of privacy in his conversations and to reduce the amount of room noise being transmitted over the telephone lines. The telephone company contended that the device impaired telephone service because the listener heard a softer and somewhat distorted sound. Although the manufacturers of the Hush-A-Phone sold over 125,000 instruments between 1921 and 1946, Bell also argued that there was no real demand for the product.

The FCC sustained Bell, but a 1956 federal appeals court decision ultimately determined that the Hush-A-Phone posed no real threat to the quality of the network. The court also found that Bell's restrictions on terminal equipment represented an "unwarranted interference with the telephone subscriber's right reasonably to use his telephone in ways which are privately beneficial without being publicly detrimental." [14] The result of the decision was an easing of the FCC's policy regarding the use of non-Bell terminal equipment. The commission modified its stance and gave approval for the use of devices that show no indication of being dangerous or impairing the quality of telecommunications services.

[13] *In the Matter of Use of the Carterfone Device in Message Toll Telephone Service,* 13 FCC 2.d 420, 427 (1968).
[14] *Hush-A-Phone Corporation et al.* v. *United States of America and Federal Communications Commission et al.,* 238 F. 2d 266, 269 (1956).

Carterfone   Although the FCC relaxed its rules for "alien attachments," the Bell System's reaction was to construe the policy very narrowly. The matter came to a head with a dispute over the use of the Carterfone. The Carterfone was a product that allowed operators of private radio systems to connect directly to the telephone network. Like the Hush-A-Phone, it required no electrical connection to the telephone network. The handset of an ordinary telephone was placed in a cradle, and the Carterfone amplified signals coming to and emanating from the radio system.

In deciding the Carterfone question, the FCC determined existing policies were inadequate in that they still failed to distinguish between devices that have a potentially adverse affect on the telecommunications network and those that are harmless. [15] The result was that Bell was required to propose new policies for dealing with terminal equipment. The company's response was to allow interconnection with equipment manufactured by other firms, as long as the user first acquired an "interface" device from Bell. These interface devices were designed to cause malfunctioning terminal equipment to disconnect from the system before any damage was caused. Ostensibly, the intent was to guarantee that system integrity would not be compromised by the presence of the alien attachments.

In actual use the interface devices were effectively used by the Bell System not only to protect the technical dimensions of the network, but also the market share of the firm. By charging a high price for the interface mechanism and by not rushing to install it, the benefits of using non-Bell terminal equipment were greatly reduced. Although 960,000 of the devices were purchased between 1968 and 1977, the impact of competition in terminal equipment sales was still greatly reduced by the strategies of the Bell System.

Registration and Competition   By the mid-1970s the Federal Communications Commission had shifted from being a protector of telephone monopolies to serving as an advocate of increased competition. Recognizing that Bell was using the interface device requirement to deter competition, in 1975 the commission opted for a program whereby terminal equipment could be connected to the network once it has been registered with the FCC and certified as not harmful to the system. Once again the Bell System challenged the FCC's decision in the federal courts, but in 1977 the Supreme Court validated the commission's order by refusing to review the case. Under current standards all that manufactures of terminal equipment must do is obtain from the FCC a registration number for devices to be connected to the network.

Although the registration program was slow to gain momentum, it effectively promoted competition in the market for terminal equipment. Literally hundreds of firms responded by offering products. Not too many years ago the local phone company was the only source of telephone equipment. Those telephone companies were quite similar to Henry Ford and his Model T—customers could have any color they wanted, as long as they wanted black. Today, more than 1,000 different models of telephones are mass marketed through mail-order houses, electronics stores, discount outlets, and department stores.

[15]Carterfone, op. cit.

CURRENT ISSUES: OPENING THE FLOODGATES OF COMPETITION

Federal Communications Commission policies with respect to competition from specialized carriers and terminal equipment manufacturers resulted in a gradual, but continual, erosion of the monopoly position of existing telephone companies. However, this trend toward competition was time consuming, costly, and uncertain. Problems associated with this piecemeal approach led the FCC to explore the need for basic structural change in the telecommunications industry.

In 1980 the commission took the bold step of ordering the American Telephone and Telegraph Company to form a separate subsidiary for the purpose of marketing terminal equipment and other services such as data processing and storage.[16] Products and services offered by the new subsidiary were to be free from regulation. The premise of the FCC order was that competition would keep prices down and eliminate the need for regulation. At the same time, forcing AT&T to operate through a separate subsidiary would prevent the firm from subsidizing its competitive operations with revenues derived from monopoly services.

During the period that the FCC was pushing back the boundaries between competition and monopoly, the Justice Department was also seeking structural change in the telecommunications industry. In 1974, a Sherman Act suit was filed seeking to force the firm to divest itself of a substantial portion of its operations. In January 1982, the case was settled by a consent decree that gave the government most of the structural changes requested.

The combination of actions by the FCC and implementation of the consent decree brought about one of the most important industrial reorganizations in American economic history. These bold strokes transformed the industry from a near monopoly dominated by AT&T into an increasingly competitive oligopoly. The remainder of this section considers the specifics and implications of these changes. First is a brief review of the telecommunications industry before divestiture. Next comes a discussion of the industry after divestiture. Finally, prospects and problems for the future are considered.

The Telephone Industry Before Divestiture

For almost a century the telephone industry in the United States was dominated by the Bell System. During the latter part of that period the system consisted of three parts. Figure 13.6 is an organization chart for the Bell System at that time. The parent firm was the American Telephone and Telegraph Company. It was both a holding and an operating company. It was an operating company in that its Long Lines Department was responsible for long-distance telephone service. It was a holding company because of its stock interests in 22 operating companies that provided local and intrastate telephone service throughout the United States.

The second part of the Bell System was Western Electric. One hundred percent owned by AT&T, this firm's responsibility was to manufacture and distribute telephone equipment used by AT&T and its operating companies. Western Electric was a gigantic

[16]Federal Communications Commission, *Second Computer Inquiry,* docket no. 20828, Apr. 7, 1980.

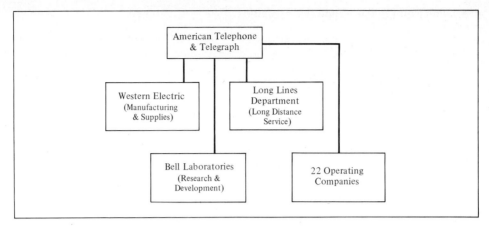

Figure 13.6. The predivestiture Bell System.

concern. In 1983, it was the nineteenth-largest industrial enterprise in the United States, with sales of over $13 billion.

On several occasions the Justice Department attempted to force AT&T to divest Western Electric. The Antitrust Division based its case on two alleged problems stemming from vertical integration. First, it argued that, because AT&T and its operating companies purchased almost all of their telephone equipment from Western Electric, the market was essentially foreclosed to other manufacturers of telephone equipment. Second, in that the local operating companies were regulated on a cost-plus basis, the lack of arm's-length bargaining between the divisions of the Bell System allowed Western Electric to charge high prices for equipment. These high prices could then be passed on as an expense by the regulated operating companies. On every occasion, AT&T was able to defend itself successfully against these charges by showing that Western Electric had not been more profitable than comparable manufacturing firms. The parent organization also claimed that Western's superior efficiency allowed it to provide telephone equipment at lower prices than could have been obtained by alternative suppliers.

Bell Telephone Laboratories was the third part of the Bell System. It was the research and development arm of the organization and was jointly owned by AT&T and Western Electric. Many of the most significant technological developments in electronics and telecommunications have come from Bell Labs. Perhaps the most important example is the transistor, which has played such a crucial role in communications, data processing, space exploration, and defense. Bell Labs also had a hand in the development of the laser and of fiber optics.

Although the Bell System was the undisputed leader in the predivestiture telephone industry, there were other large holding and operating companies such as General Telephone and Telegraph, United Telecommunications, and Continental Telephone Corporation. At the other end of the size spectrum were about two thousand small, independent telephone companies. Many served rural areas with only a few hundred firms. Each of these firms had an exclusive service area for local service, but tied into the Bell network for long-distance calling.

Divestiture and Present Industry Structure

The Justice Department's 1974 antitrust suit against AT&T sought to force the company to divest itself of Western Electric and its local operating companies. The suit alleged that AT&T had violated the Sherman Act by the use of unfair business practices designed to exclude competitors. By the beginning of 1982 both parties had presented their case in a federal district court and were awaiting the judge's decision.

The Consent Decree Those who had followed the proceedings closely were in general agreement that the government was likely to be granted at least some of the structural changes that were sought. Thus, it came as somewhat of a surprise when, on January 8, 1982, AT&T and the Justice Department announced the signing of a consent decree to end the case. Under federal law the decree had to be subjected to public comment and approved by the judge in the case. After receiving nearly 10,000 pages of comments and making some changes in the original agreement, the consent decree was approved in final form in June 1983.

The resolution of the case was widely viewed as victory for the Justice Department. Under its terms AT&T agreed to divest itself of its operating companies, form a separate subsidiary for the sale of telephone equipment, and no longer use the Bell name or logo. The general philosophy behind the agreement was that the operating companies, as regulated monopolies, should be severed from the more competitive parts of the telephone business, such as sale of terminal equipment and long-distance communications.

In spite of the dramatic reorganization required, the argument can be made that AT&T shrewdly positioned itself to take advantage of future opportunities.[17] First, the firm maintained ownership of Western Electric and Bell Labs.[18] Second, the agreement frees AT&T from the terms of a 1956 consent decree that prohibited the company from moving into the market for computers and data processing. Finally, in divesting the local operating companies, the parent organization got rid of the least profitable portions of its operations, while remaining involved in those areas that present the brightest profit prospects for the future.

Implementation of the Consent Decree Figure 13.7 is an organization chart for AT&T after divestiture. The company designated the unregulated subsidiary as AT&T Technologies. Its function is to market telecommunications and computer equipment to end users. It also assumed ownership of installed phones and other equipment that previously had been owned by the local telephone companies.

As a result of the reorganization, Western Electric became a part of AT&T Technologies. Previously, Western Electric had a quasicaptive market in the form of

---

[17]An excellent exposition of this point of view is MacAvoy, P. W., and Robinson, K., "Winning By Losing: The AT&T Settlement and Its Impact on Telecommunications," Vol. 1., No. 1, *Yale Journal on Regulation,* 1983, pp. 1–42.

[18]Although AT&T was ordered to give the local companies exclusive use of the Bell name, Bell Laboratories was allowed to retain its name.

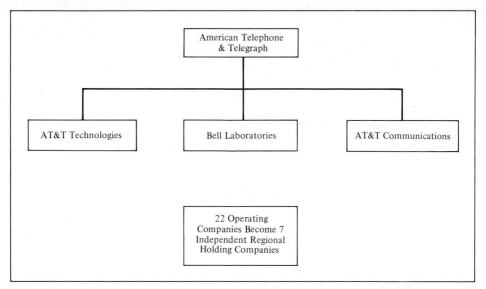

Figure 13.7. AT&T after divestiture.

the local operating companies. Now it must market its products in a competitive environment. Products for end users will be sold by another division of AT&T Technologies, but Western will have the responsibility for selling equipment to telephone companies and other business customers. Research and development assistance will continue to be provided to Western Electric by Bell Labs.

AT&T's Communications Division assumes an expanded role in the reorganized system. The divested operating companies will be responsible for the local telephone network and some intrastate toll calling, but most long-distance facilities will be taken over by AT&T. In providing long-distance communications services, AT&T Communications faces competition from other firms such as MCI and Sprint. In the past, AT&T had an advantage because of the integrated nature of the Bell System. Calls were routed over Bell facilities and customers of other firms were required to punch in additional numbers in order to link up with those systems. By 1987, the local telephone companies will be required to provide access to long-distance carriers on an equal basis. Customers will simply indicate which firm they wish to do business with, and the operating company will route calls through that firm's facilities.

With respect to divestiture of the local telephone companies, AT&T was given some latitude in determining the specific form of the reorganization. The firm chose to consolidate the 22 operating companies into seven regional holding companies as shown in Figure 13.8. As of their January 1, 1984, creation date, each of these firms ranked in the top fifty in the United States in terms of assets. An important question was the treatment of AT&T's 3.2 million shareholders. It was determined that owners of 10 or more shares of stock would receive 10 shares in the parent company and one share in each of seven holding companies. Holders of fewer than ten shares received cash in lieu of stock in the local telephone companies.

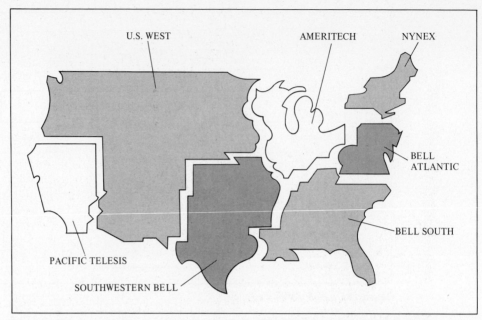

Figure 13.8. Consolidation of operating companies into seven regional holding companies.

Basically the local operating companies are to function as a connecting bridge between telephone equipment purchased in competitive markets at one end of the local network and communications services provided by competing firms at the other end. Although the philosophy of the telecommunications reorganization was to separate monopoly and competitive services, this distinction was blurred by two changes in the original consent decree. First, the local operating companies are permitted to continue publishing and selling advertising for the Yellow Pages. In some locations there are competing publishers of directories, but the intent is that profits from this activity can be used to subsidize basic service rates. Second, the local telephone companies are allowed to sell telephone equipment. The rationale is that increased competition will benefit the consumer.

Prospects for the Future

The far-reaching structural changes mandated for the telephone industry will have significant impacts on consumers. Some customers, primarily high-volume users, will be better off as competition forces prices down. Others are likely to see their phone bills increase. Three areas of particular concern for the future involve the loss of end-to-end responsibility, increasing basic exchange rates, and the potential for bypass of the local telephone network.

End-to-End Responsibility   Historically, the Bell System maintained end-to-end responsibility for the telephone network. If a problem arose, it was Bell's job to find and correct it. With a nonintegrated system no single entity has overall responsibility. This fragmentation is likely to cause problems and consumer dissatisfaction. To cite a simple example, suppose a residential customer buys a phone from Sears and attaches it to the local telephone network. After a year something goes wrong and the person can no longer make calls. He calls the phone company and requests repair service. When the repairperson arrives, she determines that the problem is in the Sears phone. Not only will the phone company not make the repair, but the customer will be charged for the service call.

Increases in Local Telephone Rates.   In the past, cross-subsidization from other telephone services allowed regulators to keep rates for local service low. However, this required that entry be prohibited to eliminate cream skimming in profitable markets. A main source of local service subsidies was the Bell System's highly lucrative long-distance toll monopoly. Long-distance calls were priced above cost and the excess used to keep local telephone rates low. But divestiture and competition will eventually eliminate the subsidy that local phone companies receive from this source.

In its place, the Federal Communications Commission proposed that a monthly access charge be paid to the local phone companies by residential and business customers. This charge was intended to reimburse the local companies for providing telephone subscribers access to the long distance network. Imposition of the access charge, together with cost increases resulting from inflation and the need to modernize facilities, would have caused a significant increase in local telephone service rates. At the time of divestiture (January 1984), many analysts were predicting that rates would double or triple within the next few years.

The prospect of large rate increases generated fierce opposition to the FCC access charge proposal. In late 1983, a bill was passed by the House of Representatives that banned imposition of the charge on residential and small business customers. It also mandated that long-distance rates be set so as to provide a continued subsidy to local telephone service. At the same time, the Senate was considering legislation with similar provisions. Faced with the prospect of hostile action by Congress, the FCC capitulated and postponed implementation of the residential and small business access charge until mid-1985.

Even without the access charge, local service telephone rates are likely to increase rapidly in the next few years. A major concern is that price increases will undermine the goal of universal access. In particular, the poor and the elderly may be forced to give up phone service. A partial solution is to offer a lifeline rate which provides access to the network and a limited number of local calls each month. Alternatively, the subsidy for basic service could be targeted at low-income customers who are likely to terminate service if required to pay substantially higher rates.[19]

Bypass of the Local Network.   Technological change is rapidly reducing communication costs. An equivalent change in the airline industry would have allowed the supersonic transport Concorde to carry a half million passengers at a speed of 20 million

---

[19]The actual rate of attrition resulting from higher rates might be quite low. Taylor estimated that the elasticity of demand for telephone service is less than -0.1. That is, a doubling of rates would reduce the number of subscribers by less than ten percent. Taylor, L.D., *op. cit.,* p. 80.

miles per hour at an average cost of one cent per trip. In the future, these advances may eliminate cost advantages of the local operating companies. If this occurs, high volume customers may bypass the local network and establish their own direct communication links using satellites, fiber optics, or other means.

The likelihood of bypass will increase if regulators set rates for high-volume users that are substantially above the cost of obtaining the services using alternative suppliers or technologies. If many large users bypass the local network, the financial health of the local phone companies may be impaired, and basic service rates could be forced even higher.

SUMMARY
The Telephone Network

The local loop is used to connect the subscriber with a central office. Calls between central offices are routed over trunk lines. Usage-sensitive equipment includes trunk lines and some switching facilities. Nonusage-sensitive equipment, such as the local loop, are required to provide basic access to the network.

Optimal Pricing of Telephone Services

Time-of-Use Pricing Telephone companies typically experience peak loads on weekday afternoons. For many years telephone tariffs have incorporated discounts for calls made during the evenings and on weekends.

Externalities Two externalities complicate the pricing of telephone services. First, callers confer benefits on the recipients of calls. Second, existing subscribers benefit when a new customer joins the network. The usage externality usually is ignored, but the subscriber externality dictates that access should be priced below its marginal cost.

Unbundling Unbundling involves disaggregating the prices charged for goods and services used by the telephone customer. Unbundled prices allow the consumer to make informed choices. A logical part of the unbundling of prices is to assess separate charges for access and local calling.

From Competition to Regulated Monopoly

The Early Competitive Years Many small telephone companies entered the market when the Bell patents expired in 1894. By 1902, direct competition between phone companies existed in over 400 cities.

State and Federal Regulation Initially, the regulatory process was used by the Bell System to limit competition in the industry. In 1934 the Federal Communications Commission was established to regulate broadcast and wire communications. The FCC was given authority to set interstate toll rates and to regulate entry.

Pricing in a Regulated Monopoly   Historically, universal access and uniform rates have been fundamental objectives of telecommunications policy. Both have been implemented through taxation by regulation. Some services have been priced above cost to yield excess profits that could then be used to subsidize other services. This practice required limitations on entry.

Leaks in the Dike: Defining the Boundaries Between Monopoly and Competitive Services

Over the last two decades, technological changes have repeatedly forced the FCC to redraw the boundaries between regulated telecommunications monopolies and unregulated competitors.

Specialized Carriers   Until 1959, FCC policies suppressed competition in microwave communications by providing advantages to Bell and a few other common carriers. In its Above-890 decision the commission opened the microwave portion of the spectrum to business and governmental users. In the 1960s, MCI sought FCC permission to provide business users with private-line services. After ten years of litigation, MCI's entry was finally approved. Today, there are many firms offering long-distance services.

Terminal Equipment   Historically, the Bell System opposed the use of terminal equipment not sold or leased by its local phone companies. In 1956 the FCC and the courts ordered Bell to interconnect with equipment that posed no technical threat to the telephone network. But Bell construed the meaning of "technical threat" very narrowly so as to exclude much of the equipment offered by competitors.

In response to the FCC's 1968 Carterfone decision, Bell agreed to allow interconnection if users would purchase an "interface" device designed to prevent harm to the telephone network. The interface concept was soon abandoned, and the FCC now requires only that terminal equipment be registered with the commission. The registration program had a significant impact in stimulating competition in the market for terminal equipment.

Current Issues: Opening the Floodgates of Competition

The Telephone Industry Before Divestiture   In its predivestiture form, AT&T provided long-distance telephone service and held controlling stock interest in 22 operating companies. The firm also owned a manufacturing company, Western Electric. Together, AT&T and Western Electric jointly owned Bell Labs.

Divestiture and Present Industry Structure   The basic philosophy underlying the required structural changes in the telecommunications industry was that monopoly services should be separated from those provided in competition with other firms. Under terms of FCC rulings and a 1982 consent decree, AT&T set up AT&T Technologies to manufacture and sell products and services to end users. The 22 operating companies were spun off as seven regional holding companies. These holding companies provide a bridge between telephone equipment at one end of the line and various communications services at the other. The consent decree guarantees that competing long-distance carriers will have equal access to the local telephone network by 1987.

Prospects for the Future   AT&T no longer has end-to-end responsibility for the telephone network. This change may cause problems as consumers are unable to identify the source of difficulties. Another concern is the likelihood of substantial increases in basic service rates as competition limits the subsidies that can be derived from other services. A related problem is the possibility that high-volume users may use new technologies to bypass the local telephone network. This could impair the financial health of the operating companies.

DISCUSSION QUESTIONS

1. Is measured service always a more efficient pricing scheme than flat-rate pricing?
2. Why is the telephone industry so far ahead of the electric utilities in the application of time-of-use pricing?
3. How should the FCC determine which applicants are granted licenses to use specific portions of the electromagnetic spectrum?
4. From an efficiency point of view, what are the advantages and disadvantages of uniform rates?
5. How could the access externality be quantified?
6. For services provided in competition with other firms, should local phone companies be required to set rates based on fully distributed costs?
7. Technological change may weaken the natural monopoly argument for regulating local telephone companies. If this occurs, should this market be opened to competition?
8. How could Ramsey pricing be used in pricing the services of regulated telephone companies?

chapter *14*

Deregulation: Natural Gas and the Airlines

Chapter Outline

Conviction has been gathering that the regulatory systems do not realize, but even operate to defeat the aims for which they were designed.

Felix Frankfurter[1]

The above quotation was written by Supreme Court Justice Felix Frankfurter over fifty years ago. Since that time, concern has continued to mount about the ability of the "regulatory systems" to achieve the "aims for which they were designed." In recent years, critics of regulation have been successful in getting legislation passed to partially deregulate certain industries. This chapter focuses on the natural gas and airline industries as examples of the trend toward deregulation.

The case studies of natural gas and the airlines are organized in a parallel manner. First, the structure of the industry is discussed. Next comes a review of past and present regulatory policies. Finally, the discussion concludes with an evaluation of the effects of deregulation.

NATURAL GAS

Natural gas is a hydrocarbon that is extracted from porous rock formations. When these formations are tapped, natural pressures cause the gas to flow toward the well bore. Often, natural gas is found as a byproduct of oil exploration. Until the 1920s, this "associated gas" was used primarily as a source of pressure to drive the oil to the surface. Once recovered, it was often burned off or blown off at the well site.

The Natural Gas Industry

Two events led to the present status of natural gas as a highly valued national resource. First, vast new gas fields were discovered in the Southwest during the late 1920s and early 1930s. Second, the development of seamless pipe allowed natural gas to be transported over long distances without serious problems of leakage. Today, gas is a critically important component of the U.S. energy supply. In 1982 over one-fourth of the nation's energy consumption came from natural gas. Figure 14.1 depicts the relative importance of the major classes of gas users. Industrial consumers take the largest share of natural gas—about 41 percent. Residential customers and electric utilities are next with 24 and 19 percent, respectively. Imports currently represent less than 5 percent of total consumption, but have been increasing over time.

Industry Structure There are three stages involved in getting natural gas to final consumers. First is the production and gathering of gas from wells. Second is the transmission by pipelines from the region of production to the location of use. The third stage is the distribution of gas by utilities to final users. Vertical integration is less common in the natural gas than in the electric power industry. Although some companies have joint ownership of either production-pipeline or pipeline-distribution facilities, independent operation is the norm.

[1]Frankfurter, F., and Hart, H. M., "Rate Regulation," *Encyclopedia of the Social Sciences,* Vol. 13 (New York: Macmillan, 1934), pp. 104–112.

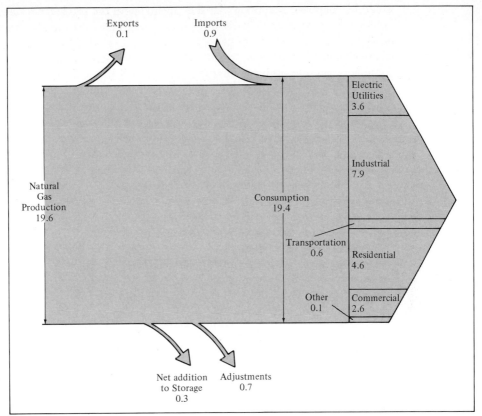

Figure 14.1. Use of natural gas, 1981 (trillion cubic feet). (Energy Information Agency, *Annual Report to Congress, 1982,* Vol. 2. Washington, D.C.: Government Printing Office, 1982, p. 101.)

At the production stage there are hundreds of independent producers, but the major oil companies play an important role. Together, they account for nearly one-half of total natural gas product. Although a pipeline company in a given region may have several sources from which it can purchase gas, the large market shares of the oil companies and their entanglements in other sectors of the economy enhance the possibilities for collusion in dealing with pipelines and for effective lobbying at the political level.

At the transportation stage the number of firms is less than at the production level, but some degree of competition still exists in most markets. A pipeline might be in a monopsony position in some production regions or have a monopoly in supplying gas to certain cities, but scale economies are not sufficient to exclude competitors in the more profitable markets. In contrast, at the distribution level, substantial economies of scale do exist and most communities are served by a single utility.

Regulation at Wholesale and Retail Levels   If firms are not vertically integrated, three market transactions take place in getting natural gas from the ground to the final user. First, contracts between producers and pipelines usually specify that the producer will provide a certain quantity of gas over a long period of time. A 20-year commitment would be common. The price that the pipeline pays the producer is referred to as the *wellhead* or *field price*. Distributor-pipeline contracts also involve an agreement to provide a specified volume of gas for an extended period. The price paid by the utility to the pipeline is designated as the *wholesale* or *city-gate price*. Finally, the rate that consumers pay the utility for natural gas is called the *retail price*.

Regulation of natural gas at the retail level is based on the premise that the distribution of gas is an activity characterized by declining average costs. As such, the most efficient form of market organization is that of a single firm serving a given market area. In the United States, the retail price of natural gas is regulated by state commissions on a rate of return on capital basis. Specific procedures of the utility rate case were discussed in Chapter 11.

Experience with regulation at the retail level soon made obvious the need for control of the wholesale price. Because state regulation was on a cost-plus basis, utilities that paid an excessive price for gas purchased from interstate pipelines could pass these costs on to final consumers. To plug this gap in the regulatory process Congress passed the Natural Gas Act of 1938. The act gave the Federal Power Commission (now the Federal Energy Regulatory Commission) the right to establish "just and reasonable" rates for interstate sales of natural gas for resale. It also gave the commission the right to require that pipelines obtain FPC approval before constructing, altering, or abandoning interstate pipelines and other facilities.

Regulation of the Wellhead Price of Natural Gas

Until 1954 the FPC took the position that it did not have responsibility for regulating the wellhead price negotiated between independent gas producers and pipeline companies.[2] The commission's stance was based on the view that such transactions took place at arm's length and, hence, forces of competition provided adequate protection for consumers. The commission also argued that it lacked the resources to perform such a function.

Phillips Decision   The responsibilities of the commission were changed dramatically by the Phillips Petroleum case of 1954.[3] At the time Phillips was the largest of the independent gas producers. When the company raised its wellhead price for natural gas, the state of Wisconsin, as well as the cities of Milwaukee, Detroit, and Kansas City, complained to the FPC. The commission's response was to reaffirm its position that it had no jurisdiction in the matter. Wisconsin and the three municipalities took the matter to the federal court system, with the final decision being rendered by the Supreme Court.

A major controversy in the case was the balance of power between producers and pipelines. Wisconsin argued that Phillips had monopoly power and, thus, was able to charge excessively high prices at wellhead. Phillips rebutted by pointing out that the producer market was highly fragmented with some 2300 independent producers sup-

---

[2]Where the producer and the pipeline are affiliated, the intent of regulation may be thwarted in the same manner as when a pipeline and utility are legally connected. In 1945 the Supreme Court upheld the FPC's contention that its mandate to regulate interstate wholesale transactions gave it the right to regulate wellhead transactions between affiliated firms. See *Colorado Interstate Gas Co.*, 324 U.S. 581 (1945).

[3]*Phillips Petroleum Co.* v. *Wisconsin*, 347 U.S. 672 (1954).

plying gas to the pipelines. Hence, the competitive market structure on the sellers side made it unlikely that producers could exploit consumers. The company also contended that the intent of Congress in passing the Natural Gas Act of 1938 was to exempt production and gathering activities from federal regulation.

The Court's decision went against the company. Although agreeing that the actual production and gathering of natural gas was, indeed, exempted by the 1938 act, it was determined that the sale of gas to pipelines was a necessary part of the intent of the legislation to provide "protection of consumers against exploitation at the hands of natural gas companies."[4] Prior to the decision the FPC had jurisdiction over 157 pipelines. After Phillips, the commission found itself in the position of attempting to regulate over 4000 independent producers of natural gas.

The Court's decision was highly controversial. In 1955 identical bills were introduced into the House of Representatives and the Senate. These bills would have exempted independent gas producers from federal regulation. Both bills passed and were sent to President Eisenhower to be signed into law. The president had previously indicated his support for the bills. However, on the day of the proposed signing a member of the Senate revealed that an oil company lawyer had offered a $2,500 donation to his campaign fund as an inducement for his vote. Eisenhower responded by vetoing the bill on the grounds that the tactics of its supporters needed further investigation.

In 1958 a number of exemption bills were again introduced with the support of President Eisenhower. While they were being considered by Congress, it became known that a Texas politician, involved in the preparations for a $100-a-plate dinner for the House minority leader, had indiscreetly suggested on the invitations that attendance was important because the representative's influence was critical to the passage of an exemption measure. Again stung by a blatant attempt to promote legislation, the matter was dropped by Congress. It was not until the late 1970s that an act to deregulate the wellhead price of natural gas was finally approved. If either of the two events just described had not occurred, it is likely that wellhead regulation of natural gas would have ended prior to 1960. As the effects of regulation are discussed later in the section, it is interesting to consider how different the current energy picture might be if the backlash from these lobbying efforts had not stymied legislation in the 1950s.

Area Rates and the "Interim" Freeze   Inundated with requests for approval of price changes, the FPC first attempted to apply traditional regulatory procedures and determine the price for each producer on the basis of cost plus return on capital. This policy proved unworkable for a number of reasons. First, the number of necessary proceedings was far greater than the commission had resources to handle. By 1960 there were 3,278 requests for rate increases pending. It was estimated that just processing existing requests would have taken until the year 2043.[5] Second, many of the independent producers were very small, with records insufficient for a full rate of return proceeding. Finally, the method simply was not suitable for natural gas producers. Much of the natural gas in production is obtained jointly with oil. There is no nonarbitrary way of allocating the joint costs involved. In addition, the relationship between natural gas

[4]Ibid., p. 684.
[5]See *In re Phillips Petroleum Company*, 24 FPC 537 (1960).

investment and output is not predictable, as it is with electricity. A small investment may result in a rich well in one case, while a large investment may yield only a trickle of natural gas in another.

In the attempt to expedite its responsibilities, the FPC abandoned the idea of determining a price for each firm. Instead, it divided the country into 23 geographic areas and initiated a determination of uniform ceiling prices for each area. These area prices were based on the average costs of firms in each region. In 1960 the first area rate proceeding began. It involved an area of west Texas and southeastern New Mexico called the Permian Basin. Setting area rates proved to be a slow process. The rate determination for the Permian Basin took five years to be completed and three more years before it was finally approved by the Supreme Court. By 1974, area rates had been completed for only 7 of the 23 areas and changing conditions had already necessitated a review of the findings for the Permian Basin.

During the 14 years of area-rate investigations the commission was forced to establish an interim method of price regulation. Its solution was essentially to freeze the wellhead price of natural gas at its 1959-to-1960 level. Between 1960 and 1973 the wellhead price of natural gas increased from 14.0 to 21.6 cents per thousand cubic feet. The increase was due primarily to unregulated intrastate sales. In terms of constant 1972 dollars the price was virtually unchanged over the period. The result of the freeze was even more dramatic in terms of its impact on residential prices. In real dollars, the price of natural gas to residential customers actually declined by nearly 20 percent from 1960 to 1973.

Nationwide Rates   In the early 1970s it became obvious that the area rate procedures were much too cumbersome and slow to deal with rapidly changing economic conditions. Another problem was that the interim rates were so low that the price of gas was far out of line with other energy sources. Thus, in 1974 the FPC opted for a nationwide ceiling on the wellhead price of natural gas. One of the features of this nationwide rate was that reserves of natural gas already under contract to pipelines (old gas) were priced differently than newly discovered natural gas (new gas). The reasons for the different prices was the recognition that higher prices were a necessity to stimulate exploration for new supplies on one hand, and a reluctance to confer a windfall on owners of gas that had already been discovered and developed on the other.

The commission's first attempts at nationwide rates were too niggardly and had to be adjusted upward. With these adjustments came additional definitions of gas categories with their associated prices. By 1976 the FPC was policing a five-tiered pricing scheme with prices as high as $1.42 per thousand cubic feet (Mcf) for gas produced after January 1, 1975, and as low as $0.295 per Mcf for gas contracted for sale before January 1, 1973. Gas produced between those two dates could be sold at a maximum of $0.93 per Mcf.

Effects of Wellhead Regulation

Nationwide rates were set by the Federal Power Commission from 1974 to 1978. In 1978, Congress acted to gradually decontrol the wellhead price of natural gas. Before discussing the era of deregulation, the effects of the period of price controls are first considered.

Resource Allocation   Regulation of the wellhead price of natural gas had an important impact on resource allocation. Both supply and demand were affected. The supply-side consequences are considered first.

The supply of natural gas means different things to different people. Often, energy discussions focus on the fact that there is a fixed amount of natural gas. Once consumed, this gas is gone forever. Although this view is technically correct, it may not be very relevant as a basis for formulating energy policy. In specifying the nation's natural gas resources, the concept of "proven reserves" is used. Proven reserves refer to the amount of natural gas that could be extracted from the earth under existing technological and economic conditions. If improved methods for recovering natural gas are employed, then the amount of proven gas reserves increases. If the price of natural gas increases, then there are natural gas supplies that previously were too expensive to recover but may now be profitably developed. Again, the amount of proven reserves increases.

The notion of proven reserves meshes very nicely with the economist's concept of the supply curve. Shown in Figure 14.2, the supply curve *SS* indicates the available quantity of natural gas as a function of price. As price increases, it becomes economically feasible to produce from gas supplies that were too costly to tap at lower prices.

Both opponents and proponents of deregulation generally concede that higher prices will have an effect on gas supplies. A major issue in the debate over deregulation centers on the slope of the supply curve. If the supply curve is relatively horizontal, like *SS*, then relatively small increases in the price will result in substantial additions to the supply of natural gas. However, if the supply curve is inelastic (more vertical) such as *S'S'*, then higher prices will do little to elicit additional gas supplies. The slope of the supply curve is highly dependent on the time period being considered. In the short run (e.g., less than a year) supplies cannot be very responsive to price changes. Existing reserves can be depleted more rapidly, but the rate of extraction is limited by technical factors. If a given reservoir is emptied too fast, the total amount of recoverable gas is reduced. Another possibility is to drill new wells or reopen old wells. The availability of drilling equipment and the inventory of existing wells limits the amount of additional gas that can be produced from these attempts.

Over a longer period of time the supply curve is considerably more elastic. If the

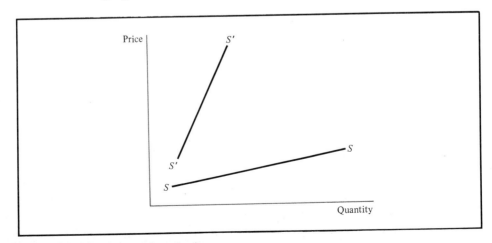

Figure 14.2.   Supply curve for natural gas.

period being considered is five or ten years, then research and development efforts may result in improved methods of detecting and drilling for gas. Exploration activities can be stepped up. New equipment can be produced to meet the demand for more wells. However, the incentive to expand production is tied to the profitability of such efforts.

Table 14.1 shows the changes in exploratory wells drilled for natural gas between 1948 and 1981. These numbers track changes in federal price regulation policy with remarkable accuracy. Beginning in 1948 the number of gas wells drilled increased steadily until 1955 (the year after the Phillips decision). Between 1955 and 1959 there

**Table 14.1   EXPLORATORY WELLS
DRILLED FOR NATURAL
GAS: 1948–1978**

Year	Gas wells drilled
1948	370
1949	420
1950	430
1951	450
1952	560
1953	700
1954	720
1955	870
1956	820
1957	870
1958	820
1959	910
1960	870
1961	810
1962	770
1963	660
1964	580
1965	520
1966	700
1967	530
1968	490
1969	620
1970	480
1971	440
1972	600
1973	900
1974	1200
1975	1170
1976	1400
1977	1480
1978	1600
1979	1780
1980	1970
1981	2380

Source: Energy Information Agency, *Annual Report to the Congress, 1981,* Vol. 2 (Washington, D.C.: Government Printing Office, 1982), p. 37.

was little change (the period during which the FPC was groping for a solution to its unwanted jurisdiction over wellhead prices). From 1960 to 1971 there was a steady decline in the number of wells drilled (the period of the freeze). Beginning in 1972 (as prices began to rise) the number of exploratory wells started to increase—from a low of 440 in 1971 to 1,600 in 1978 and up to 2,380 by 1981. During this period the OPEC cartel greatly increased petroleum prices and adjustments in the nationwide natural gas price ceiling substantially raised the selling price of newly discovered natural gas.

Next, the effects of wellhead regulation on demand are considered. Relative to other forms of energy, natural gas has been rather inexpensive—especially during the early 1970s when the price of oil rose so quickly. The result is that natural gas is extensively used for home heating, generating electricity, and many industrial processes. The law of demand suggests that, *ceteris paribus,* as natural gas prices increase, the quantity of gas consumed will decline. However, the rate of adjustment is constrained to be much slower than with other commodities such as beef or movies. To use natural gas the consumer must first make an investment in equipment. The expenditure may be a heating system for a residential user, a generator for an electric utility, or a furnace for heavy industry. Once this equipment is in place, the natural gas customer must incur substantial expense to convert to another form of fuel. Unless the price of natural gas increases very rapidly in relation to other fuel prices, the most economical decision is to stick with natural gas. Although the intensity of use of the gas-consuming apparatus may be reduced, the ability to reduce natural gas demand is limited by the stock of gas-using equipment already purchased. In terms of the jargon of economics, the demand for natural gas in the short run is quite inelastic. In the long run, users can convert to other energy sources, and so the demand is more elastic. However, as long as natural gas prices remain below the energy equivalent costs of other energy forms, gas consumption may not be very responsive to price even in the long run.

Low prices for natural gas also affected the space conditioning efficiency of American homes. In a given climate there is an optimum energy conservation expenditure (insulation, weather stripping, double-glazed windows, and so on) associated with any given level of fuel prices. At low prices for heating fuels, it didn't pay to insulate heavily. Millions of homes were constructed during the era of cheap natural gas. As prices have risen, homeowners have found these structures to be energy inefficient. However, the cost of weatherizing older homes can be rather high. Thus, the high demand for natural gas that existed during times of low prices further retarded the adjustment to higher prices.

To summarize, controlled prices for natural gas reduced the quantity supplied of gas and increased the quantity demanded. Without regulation, prices perform the important rationing function of equating supply and demand. During the period when the price of natural gas was constrained by the FPC to be below the market-clearing price, shortages of natural gas were experienced as quantity demanded exceeded the quantity producers were willing to supply. During the late 1960s these shortages were somewhat camouflaged. By drawing more rapidly on existing reserves, it was possible to meet the annual consumption demands. However, these gas reserves represented the future supply of natural gas. One measure of the drawdown in reserves is the reserve-production ratio. It represents the number of years that the existing rate of consumption can be sustained without additional reserves being found and developed. Figure 14.3 shows that this ratio declined dramatically for interstate pipelines during the period of wellhead regulation. In 1963 there were over 20 years of reserves in terms of that year's consumption. By 1978 the backup was just over 8 years.

In the 1970s the shortage became more obvious. As previously noted, the rate of withdrawal from a gas reservoir is limited by the losses that result from excessively rapid extraction. As the reserve-production ratio declined, the point was finally reached where the demands for consumption could no longer be met. Unable to ration on the basis of price, pipelines and utilities had to resort to more arbitrary rationing schemes. Many natural gas distribution utilities were forced to declare a moratorium on hookups to new homes. Some industrial customers found it necessary to convert to more expensive fuel sources. The same was true of electric utilities that switched from nonpolluting gas to polluting coal or from domestic natural gas to imported oil for generating electricity.

Income Distribution   Controls on the wellhead price of natural gas had distributional, as well as allocative effects. When prices were held below market-clearing levels, customers still able to purchase natural gas benefited because they paid a lower price. However, these gains were achieved at the expense of producers whose incomes were reduced. In addition, some consumers were hurt because they were unable to obtain gas that would have been available (and that they would have voluntarily purchased) at a higher price. Producers were also affected by the loss of these marginal sales because they were profitable at the higher unregulated price. Figure 14.4 illustrates these impacts.

Let P_e and q_e be the market-determined price and quantity of natural gas in the absence of regulation. P_c and q_c are the controlled price and associated quantity supplied. Notice that q_c is less than the quantity demanded at P_c. When prices are reduced from P_e to P_c consumers of the q_c units of natural gas that is supplied gave an amount equal to the rectangle, $P_e P_c BA$ on their purchases. This sum represents a redistribution of income from producers to consumers.

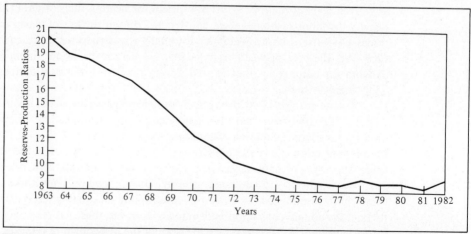

Figure 14.3. Reserves-production ratios of interstate natural gas pipeline companies. (Department of Energy, *Gas Supplies of Interstate Natural Gas Pipeline Companies—1982.* Washington D.C.: Government Printing Office 1983, p. 13.)

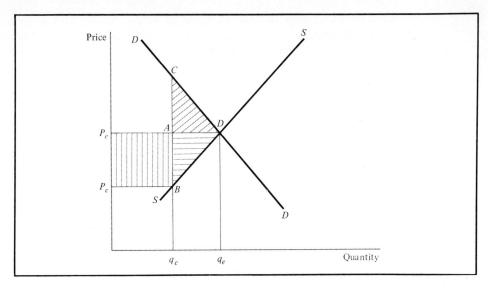

Figure 14.4. Distributional impacts of price controls.

Because the supply curve indicates the marginal costs of supplying additional units of output, the triangle *ABD* represents another loss of profits to producers as a result of regulation. Finally, the triangle *ACD* represents the loss of consumer surplus to customers who would have purchased $q_e - q_c$ extra units at the market-determined price, P_e, but are now unable to do so because the lower price has reduced the quantity supplied.

An evaluation of wellhead price controls on natural gas must weigh the impacts on the different groups involved. Are the benefits of lower prices to purchasers of q_c units more important than the reduction in producer profits and the loss of consumer surplus to customers unable to purchase $q_e - q_c$? These are equity questions that must be answered by the political process. Implicitly, during the period of regulation the evaluation considered the benefits to existing consumers as more important.

Market Power   Opponents of price controls argue that regulation of the wellhead price of natural gas is unnecessary because there are a relatively large number of producers in each market. In fact, they contend that pipelines often have monopsony power in determining wellhead prices. Hence, the real danger is that producers rather than consumers will be exploited.

Although the structure of the natural gas production industry may suggest competition or monopsony, a detailed study of the firms involved indicates that the dominant firms may be able to collude and set prices above competitive levels. About half of all interstate sales of natural gas are made by ten of the largest oil companies. These firms interact in many other phases of the economy and may be able to coordinate natural gas prices. If collusion does exist, then price controls may be justified as a means of restricting producer profits.

Another problem with a gas production industry dominated by giant, diversified firms is that they are able to time the flow of gas to the market so as to maximize their profits. Small, independent producers may have little choice but to provide gas at a relatively steady rate. In contrast, giant oil firms can hold back gas supplies in order to take advantage of anticipated increases in regulated prices. There have been repeated claims that oil companies have held back on both gas and oil in the expectation of more liberal pricing policies by the federal government. It is impossible to know how much energy has been withheld, but the prospect of higher future prices can provide an incentive for waiting.

Current Issues: Deregulation of the Wellhead Price

Several factors led to legislation approving gradual decontrol of the wellhead price of natural gas. Among the most important were concern about the declining reserve-production ratio, shortages caused by an extremely cold winter in 1977, and a general sentiment that new approaches were needed in energy regulation.

Natural Gas Policy Act of 1978.   Like most important and controversial pieces of legislation, the Natural Gas Policy Act of 1978 (NGPA) represented the results of political compromise. On one side of the issue were those who favored immediate deregulation as a means of increasing supplies and encouraging conservation. Opposing deregulation were those who were unwilling to provide the natural gas industry with windfall profits and also those who were skeptical of the magnitude of the increase in supply that would be forthcoming as a result of removing price controls. Agreement was finally reached by specifying a program of gradual decontrol that focused primarily on "new" gas. The legislation was extremely complex (covering more than 200 pages and identifying 28 separate categories of natural gas), but the main provisions of the NGPA were as follows:

1. The price of newly discovered natural gas (both in interstate and intrastate markets) will be decontrolled as of January 1, 1985. The price of hard-to-get gas (defined as gas found in wells over 5000 feet deep drilled after 1977) will also be decontrolled in 1985.
2. After price controls are off for at least six months (after July, 1985), either the president or both houses of Congress (by concurrent resolution) can reimpose controls for an 18-month period. Without passage of additional legislation, all controls will terminate December 31, 1988.
3. At the time of enactment, the ceiling price on newly discovered gas was set at $2.09 per thousand cubic feet. Until April, 1981, that price was allowed to climb at a rate of 3.7 percent plus the rate of inflation. From 1981 until the time of decontrol, the rate of increase is limited to 4.2 percent plus the inflation rate.
4. To qualify as newly discovered, gas must come from a well $2\frac{1}{2}$ miles from an existing well, 1000 feet deeper than a nearby existing well, or from a well that had not previously provided natural gas in commercial quantities.
5. When the contracts on old gas expire, the new price that can be charged depends on whether the sale is interstate or intrastate. Interstate contracts were allowed to rise to $.55 per Mcf plus the rate of inflation since April, 1977. Intrastate contracts can go to $1.00 per Mcf plus the inflation rate since that date. [6]

---

[6]Public Law 95–621 (Nov. 9, 1978).

Notice that the provisions of the act mandated decontrol, but not immediately. Also, if the results of decontrol are deemed unsatisfactory by the president or the Congress, a mechanism for returning to regulation is provided. The potential windfall to producers is limited by restricting rapid price increases to newly discovered gas. An important part of the legislation was the extension of regulation to intrastate transactions. A glaring deficiency with the previous two decades of natural gas policy was that higher prices for sales within state boundaries caused large volumes of natural gas to be excluded from interstate markets.

Effects of Deregulation   The relatively short interval of time since passage of the 1978 NGPA makes it difficult to assess the effects of decontrol. Also, since the act specified that decontrol would be gradual, the process is not complete at this writing. Still, it is possible to make some preliminary observations about the effects of partial deregulation of the wellhead price of natural gas.

Increased supplies of natural gas   As shown in Figure 14.5, the wellhead price of natural gas has risen rapidly since the FPC first embarked on the setting of nationwide rates in 1974. As the price increased, producers were signaled that sources of gas that previously could not be economically developed could now be profitable. By the early 1980s, there was a glut of natural gas in the United States. In some cases, gas produced as a byproduct of oil was actually burned off at the wellhead because of the

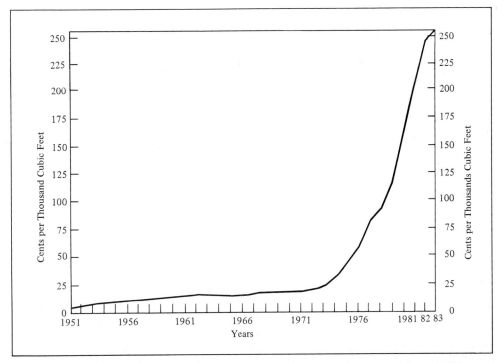

Figure 14.5.   The wellhead price of natural gas. (Energy Information Agency, op. cit., p. 114.)

difficulty of finding a market. However, deregulation was not the only cause of the surplus. The supply/demand balance also was affected by two mild winters and a serious recession.

In addition to adding to total supply, partial decontrol also had a positive effect on the geographic flow of natural gas. Under controls, the price of interstate gas was regulated, but the intrastate price was not. As a result, the intrastate price was often much higher. Sometimes the ratio was as much as 4:1. The result was that natural-gas-producing states such as Louisiana, Oklahoma, and Texas had plenty of gas during times of scarcity in states such as New Jersey and New York. Under the provisions of the NGPA, price differentials have been reduced, and the distribution of gas between states has improved.

Higher prices to consumers   The steep increase in the wellhead price has been painful to final consumers. In some states the residential price of natural gas increased by 20 to 40 percent in a single year. The Department of Energy publishes data showing comparable residential natural gas prices in various major cities. Table 14.2 shows the price per million BTU for 1980 and 1983. Two points stand out. First, there is a wide disparity in prices between cities. The 1983 price in Boston was $8.17 per million BTU, but only $4.30 in San Francisco. Second, the price increases have been unevenly distributed. The average percentage increase between 1980 and 1983 was 66 percent, but the change was more than 100 percent in some cities such as Kansas City and Minneapolis/St. Paul.

Deregulation of the wellhead price of natural gas is not the only explanation for the large price increases experienced by residential customers. Another component of the change reflects the use of *take-or-pay* contracts by gas pipelines. It has already been mentioned that low prices caused shortages of natural gas in the mid-1970s. These shortages were highlighted during an especially severe winter in 1976-7. Gas companies were scrambling to find adequate supplies in a tight market. Take-or-pay contracts were a solution designed to lock in supplies of gas. They specified that the pipeline companies were required to purchase a certain amount of gas each year for, perhaps, 20 years. If the companies chose not to take the gas, the contracts required that they still had to pay for it.

The laws of supply and demand dictate that with a glut of natural gas, the price should drop. This did occur for some new gas brought to the market. The problem was that, locked into take-or-pay contracts, the pipeline companies had to continue to use more expensive gas. Thus, many consumers received little benefit from the surplus of natural gas.

Resource allocation problems   Decontrol increased supplies and equalized the flow of gas between geographic areas. However, specific provisions of the NGPA also caused resources to be inefficiently allocated in some cases. A major source of difficulty was the multitiered pricing scheme specified by the legislation. Based on NGPA provisions, a pipeline might buy gas from a producer under one price category (perhaps old gas under contract) for $.25 per million cubic feet and from another producer (say newly discovered gas from deep wells) for $10.00. These numbers are not misprints—in some cases the price of gas from one source was 40 to 50 times that of another source of supply.

**Table 14.2 AVERAGE RESIDENTIAL PRICE OF
NATURAL GAS FOR SELECTED CITIES**

Metropolitan area	Price per million BTU		
	March 1983	March 1980	Percent increase
Atlanta	$6.07	$3.67	65
Baltimore	6.89	4.01	72
Boston	8.17	5.14	59
Buffalo	7.05	4.15	70
Chicago	5.45	3.77	45
Cincinnati	6.15	3.40	81
Cleveland	5.37	3.43	57
Dallas-Fort Worth	5.22	2.82	85
Denver-Boulder	6.04	3.52	72
Detroit	5.32	3.52	51
Houston	5.57	3.57	56
Kansas City	5.77	2.57	125
Los Angeles	4.83	2.83	71
Miami	4.52	4.39	03
Milwaukee	6.59	3.60	83
Minneapolis-St. Paul	5.94	2.36	152
New York	8.11	5.43	49
Philadelphia	7.34	4.37	68
Pittsburgh	5.72	3.21	78
Portland (Ore.)	6.73	4.94	36
St. Louis	6.74	3.50	93
San Diego	5.67	2.96	92
San Francisco-Oakland	4.30	2.91	48
Seattle	6.75	4.83	40
Washington, D.C.	7.69	4.48	71
U.S. City Average	6.02	3.62	66

Source: Department of Energy, *Natural Gas Monthly* (Washington, D.C.: U.S. Government Printing Office, monthly).

Normally, buyers search for the lowest price. But the pipelines often faced circumstances that did not cause them to seek to minimize costs. First, regulated on a cost-plus basis, they had no real need to cut costs. Higher prices paid for gas could be passed on to buyers. Second, the take-or-pay contract provisions often required them to take high-cost gas even though less expensive sources were readily available. Third, many pipelines were also producers of natural gas. The Natural Gas Policies Act specified that they could charge the highest price for their own gas that they had paid for another source of gas. Thus, they benefited from buying at least some high-priced gas.

Problems caused by the multitiered pricing scheme of the NGPA were especially serious for small producers. Take-or-pay contracts typically involved large producers. Thus, small producers found themselves foreclosed from the market. In some cases they decided that it was profitable to reduce their output until they could be classified as *stripper* wells. Stripper wells are those that have a daily output below some specified level. The act provided that gas from stripper wells could be sold for a substantially higher price than for comparable gas produced from higher volume wells. The intent was to encourage pumping residual gas from wells that were essentially empty. This was to be a way of increasing the total supply of gas. But in some cases, the owners of wells could make more money by cutting back below the stripper level, than by producing at the higher level of output.

Prospects for the Future   Deregulation is too new and too incomplete to be able to make accurate predictions about its ultimate effects. However, the first few years experience with decontrol have led to varied and sometimes inconsistent proposals for change.

Change the pace of deregulation   There are those who argue that decontrol of the wellhead price of natural gas should be accelerated. Based on essentially the same body of evidence, others are equally insistent that deregulation should be slowed or abandoned. Much of the argument stems from disagreement as to the long-run effect on prices of complete decontrol. Advocates of free-market prices contend that prices would actually be lower under deregulation because of the vast increase in supplies that would result. In contrast, control proponents see huge increases in price as the legacy of complete deregulation.

Increased state role   State regulatory commissions have felt most of the heat stemming from large jumps in the residential price of natural gas. In many cases, commissions have had little choice because they were simply approving a pass-through of higher prices paid by gas utilities. Recently, some of these state commissions have requested that they be able to participate in decisions about wellhead and wholesale rates.

Closer scrutiny by the FERC   Presently, the FERC's examination of wholesale rates is based primarily on the notion that there should be no fraud involved in the price negotiations between pipelines and producers. It has been proposed that "prudence" be included in the FERC's charge. That is, higher wellhead prices would be approved only if the pipeline company could demonstrate that it had been prudent in its contract negotiations.

Contract renegotiation   Take-or-pay contracts have been a source of considerable dissatisfaction. One option would be for Congress to declare such contracts void. Another is for pipelines to simply ignore take-or-pay clauses and force producers to renegotiate or litigate for breach of contract. In some instances producers have been willing to reconsider the terms of the original contract. By late 1983, there was evidence that natural gas prices were leveling off. In 1982, the average retail price of natural gas increased by more than 25 percent. In 1983, the average increase was only about 5 percent. However, it is too early to determine whether this represents a long-term trend or just a temporary aberration.

AIR PASSENGER SERVICE

Airline passenger service has experienced rapid growth and substantial technological change. Air travel now accounts for about four times the combined total of intercity passenger-miles generated by buses and railroads. Equipment has evolved from open cockpit biplanes with little more than a prayer book for the timid to wide-body jets with sleeping berths, movies, gourmet meals, and telephone service.

During most of this period of growth and change, the airlines were subject to regulatory policies that caused the industry to operate inefficiently. In most cases, problems with the existing scheme of regulation simply led to more extensive regulation. However, the airline industry represents a break with tradition, in that the recent response to defective regulation has been greater reliance on market forces. This portion of the chapter traces the history and effects of the transition from regulation to deregulation.

The Economics of Air Travel

Demand for Air Travel The demand for air travel is a *derived demand*.[7] That is, travel is a means of getting from one point to another to accomplish some purpose such as selling a product, vacationing in another city, or visiting a friend.

Once the decision to travel has been made, the individual must then decide what mode to use (e.g., air, train, bus, car) and when to travel. Although some people obtain utility from the trip itself, most travelers act to minimize the "full cost" of their trips. This full cost includes the price of the ticket, the total time in route, discomfort during travel, and any inconvenience caused by the schedule of the selected mode.

There are trade-offs between these components of the full cost of travel. For example, suppose a businessperson is considering driving a car or flying from San Francisco to Sacramento (a distance of about 120 miles). In terms of out-of-pocket costs, driving is probably the cheapest way to go. This mode also affords the maximum flexibility because departure time can be determined by the traveler. However, automobile travel is slow and tiring. Air travel has the advantage of requiring less time in route and being more restful, but it is more costly. Also, travelers are bound by flight schedules. They may want to leave at 9 A.M., but find that there is no available flight until noon.

The demand for air travel can be thought of as a function of air fares, prices of other modes of travel, airplane speed, quality of service, and scheduling frequency. Demand decreases with higher prices and increases as other forms of travel become more expensive, planes fly faster, additional flights are scheduled, and quality of service such as meals, leg room, and baggage handling improves.

Supply Conditions Capacity costs represent about three-fourths of total airline costs. Capacity costs are basically the expenditures on the airplanes themselves. They are not fixed costs. Unlike dollars spent on telephone cable or electric generators, airplanes can be easily transferred from one use to another. A company with excess capacity on its St. Louis-to-Chicago route can quickly move planes to a Houston-to-Denver route that needs extra flights. Similarly, there are lease and used aircraft markets that allow equipment to be shifted between prosperous firms and those in financial difficulty. The

---

[7]For an indepth discussion of the economics of air travel, see Douglas, G.W., and Miller, J.C., *Economic Regulation of Domestic Air Transport* (Washington, D.C.: Brookings, 1974).

important implication of this point is that barriers to entry and exit in the airlines industry are not high. The substantial mobility of capital makes it relatively easy for firms to come and go.

Once the aircraft is available, several factors influence the cost of serving a particular passenger. One important determinant is the distance flown. A substantial proportion of the fuel used during a flight is required while the plane is taking off and climbing to its cruising altitude. This fuel cost is independent of the distance involved. Other distance-independent costs of a particular flight include ticketing, baggage handling, and meals. Since these costs do not vary with the length of the trip, the cost per mile declines with increasing distance.

The degree of utilization of the aircraft is another factor affecting costs. Until a plane reaches its seating capacity, the marginal cost of adding another passenger is very small—the extra fuel required because of extra weight and, perhaps, a meal. The standard measure of aircraft utilization is the load factor. The load factor is just the percentage of seats filled divided by total seating capacity. Higher load factors mean lower costs per passenger-mile.

A third possible determinant of costs is the size of the firm. If there are economies of scale, then larger firms will have an advantage because of their lower costs. A number of researchers have investigated scale economies in the airline industry. Their findings suggest that costs do not vary appreciably with firm size.[8]

The supply conditions in the airline industry have important implications. First, since costs decrease with distance, long-haul trips will tend to be more profitable than shorter flights. Second, high load factors decrease costs. However, the fact that demand is not totally predictable implies that the airlines must always operate with some degree of excess capacity. Third, since the industry has constant returns to scale, there should be little concern about natural monopolies that require regulation. Finally, since fixed costs are relatively low, economic theory suggests that the industry is not particularly susceptible to destructive competition such as was experienced by the railroads during the late 1800s.

Forty Years of Regulation

Air passenger service in the United States began in 1914 with a flying boat carrying travelers between Tampa and St. Petersburg. Like most early "airlines," the service was not financially viable. To promote civilian aviation, Congress in 1926 transferred the task of carrying mail from the army to private air carriers. This financial support from the government gave the carriers a financial base from which to expand their passenger operations. Between 1926 and 1930, the number of passenger-miles increased from 1.3 to 85 million.

The Civil Aeronautics Act of 1938   Initially, mail contracts were assigned somewhat arbitrarily. In 1934 Congress required that awards be based on sealed bids, but the airlines responded by submitting extremely low bids in the hope that they would be allowed to raise rates once route authority was received. When the rate increases

[8]Ibid., pp. 14–18.

weren't granted, many firms were brought to the brink of financial disaster. This crisis in the airline industry set the stage for legislation authorizing greater government control.

To promote safety and to restrain perceived destructive competition in the airline industry, Congress passed the Civil Aeronautics Act of 1938. The Act created the Civil Aeronautics Board (CAB) as an independent regulatory agency with broad powers for regulating the airlines. The most important of these powers were complete control over entry and exit and the right to set minimum and maximum air fares.

Entry and exit The Civil Aeronautics Act specified that an airline must obtain a *certificate of convenience and necessity* from the CAB before providing service on a route. It also specified that 16 existing airlines would automatically be granted authorization to continue operations between city pairs already being served. These airlines (such as United, American, and TWA) became the so-called trunk lines that dominated the industry during the period of regulation. Mergers reduced the number of trunks to 11, but as late as 1978 they provided almost 90 percent of total passenger miles.[9]

Initially, most city pairs were served by a single carrier. Over time, the CAB allowed additional entrants in most markets, but route authority for dense, lucrative markets was almost always given to one of the trunk lines. A number of smaller firms were granted authority to operate in certain regions of the country, but none of these airlines achieved the status of the trunk lines. The explanation was not that there were no requests for such expansion. On the contrary, between 1938 and 1978, the CAB received many applications from firms wanting to serve as trunk lines. All were denied.

CAB policy with respect to exit usually was quite lenient for the trunk lines. Where another carrier remained to serve a city pair, a firm typically was allowed to terminate service if the operation was unprofitable. In contrast, regional airlines providing the only service to smaller cities usually found exit much more difficult.

Air fares Until the late 1960s, CAB price regulation was perfunctory. First-class rail fares were the most important determinant of airline tickets. Price changes usually were proposed collectively by the carriers serving a market. Indeed, by use of its powers to establish minimum rates and prevent entry, the agency functioned rather effectively as a cartel manager for the airline industry.

Throughout most of its existence, the CAB did little to establish rate structures that promoted efficient utilization of resources. Although there is substantial fluctuation in air travel demand over the course of a day, few applications of peak-load pricing were approved until the late 1970s. However, rate structures did incorporate the concept of taxation by regulation. Rates for long flights were set above cost in order to generate excess profits that could be used to subsidize unprofitable service between smaller cities. The objective was to assure at least a minimal level of service to such communities. However, for reasons discussed in the next section, the profits available for cross-subsidization were much less than the CAB intended.

---

[9]Civil Aeronautics Board, *Air Carrier Traffic Statistics* (Washington, D.C.: Government Printing Office, monthly).

**Table 14.3 COMPARISON BETWEEN INTERSTATE AND
INTRASTATE FARES, 1975**

City pair	Fare	Miles
Los Angeles-San Francisco (intra)	$18.75	338
Chicago-Minneapolis (inter)	38.89	339
Los Angeles-Sacramento (intra)	20.47	373
Boston-Washington (inter)	41.67	399
San Francisco-San Diego (intra)	26.21	456
Detroit-Philadelphia (inter)	45.37	454

Source: Civil Aeronautics Board Practices and Procedures, Report of
the Subcommittee on Administrative Practice and Procedures, U.S. Senate
(1975), p. 41.

Effects of Regulation The CAB had authority to set air fares for trips crossing state
boundaries, but intrastate fares were either unregulated or regulated by state commissions. Table 14.3 compares 1975 interstate and intrastate fares for city pairs of comparable distance. It indicates that the CAB-exempt intrastate fares were considerably lower.
For example, the distance between Los Angeles and San Francisco (intrastate) is almost
exactly the same as between Chicago and Minneapolis (interstate), but the fare was less
than half.

The primary reason for higher prices on the interstate routes was that costs were
pushed up by excessive nonprice competition. The CAB effectively eliminated price
rivalry between the interstate carriers, so they turned to service competition in the
attempt to increase their market shares. Some of this competition took the form of
upgrading meals, providing inflight entertainment, and mounting expensive advertising
campaigns. But, the most significant form of service competition involved scheduling
additional flights between city pairs.

As more flights were added, the load factors of the interstate carriers decreased.
For example, in late 1950s and early 1960s, the average load factor for the regulated
interstate carriers was 59 percent. This compared with a 71-percent load factor for the
intrastate California airlines. [10] On any given route, there is a break-even point represented by the load factor below which the airline loses money by serving the route. The
effect of CAB regulation was to drive load factors toward this break-even point. When
the agency allowed price increases, the break-even load factor was reduced. Frequently,
the airlines responded by adding additional flights until they approached the new
break-even point. Thus, fare increases did not increase profits, just costs. That is, under
CAB regulation, prices determined costs rather than costs determining the level of
prices.

This nonoptimal price/quality mix prevented the CAB's scheme of cross-subsidization from working. Prices were set above costs and new entrants prohibited in dense
routes. But because the CAB did not have legal authority to limit the number of flights
by a carrier granted the right to serve a particular route, the differential soon was
eliminated as scheduling rivalry drove up costs and ate up the potential profits available
to subsidize service to smaller communities.

[10]Jorden, W.A., *Airline Regulation in America* (Baltimore: Johns Hopkins, 1970), p. 203.

Current Issues: Deregulation of Air Passenger Service

For many years students of the regulatory process had been critical of the CAB. In the mid-1970s they were joined by several influential congressional representatives and by President Carter. Perhaps the most significant event leading to deregulation was the appointment in 1977 of Alfred Kahn as the chairman of the agency. In his new position, Kahn advocated that the airlines be allowed greater discretion in setting fares and restructuring the routes they serve. The CAB took steps to implement this philosophy, but there was some doubt as to whether the agency had the legal right to effect such a radical change.

The Airline Deregulation Act of 1978   In 1978, Congress gave explicit approval to the CAB's actions by passing the Airline Deregulation Act.[11] The legislation authorized the CAB to permit the airlines greater flexibility in setting fares and eased requirements for entry and exit. With respect to fares, the act directed the CAB to determine a "standard industry fare level" based on costs. Without CAB approval, the airlines were permitted to set prices 5 percent above or 50 percent below the standard level. This "zone of reasonableness" was later expanded.

With respect to entry, the legislation effectively changed the criteria for obtaining route authority. Whereas the CAB had for many years looked at the impact of entry on existing carriers serving a market, under deregulation the agency's main task is to make sure that new applicants are financially and technically qualified. Exit was also simplified. A firm desiring to abandon service was allowed to do so after a short transition period.

One of the most striking features of the Airline Deregulation Act of 1978 was a provision that will eliminate the CAB. The act specified that all CAB control over fares and routes was to end in 1983 and that, unless the agency can justify its continued existence, it is to be abolished in 1985. Such action is virtually without precedent. Many federal regulatory agencies have been established over the last 50 years, but few have been terminated.

The Effects of Airline Deregulation   It is still too early to make a definitive assessment of the effects of airline deregulation, but some preliminary observations can be offered. Various critics of decontrol suggested that deregulation would cause (1) higher prices on many routes, (2) loss of service to small communities, and/or (3) destructive competition resulting in an industry dominated by a few large firms. Most of these fears were not substantiated by the first five years of deregulation.

Higher prices   Although extremely low fares have been offered on some routes, the overall level of prices has risen substantially since 1978. But the primary cause was not deregulation. Between 1979 and 1982 the cost of jet fuel increased by 150 percent. Every one cent increase in the price of fuel adds about $100 million to airline expenses.[12] Although the airlines sustained losses in excess of one billion dollars during

[11]Public Law 95–504, 92 Stat. 1705.
[12]*Wall Street Journal,* May 2, 1983, p. 29.

Table 14.4   AVERAGE 1981 FARES AS A PERCENTAGE OF CAB STANDARD FARE

Distance	Percent of standard fare		
	Top 100 markets	Second 100 markets	Sample of smaller markets
0–500 miles	89	97	113
501–1000 miles	98	96	101
1001–1500 miles	82	89	97
1500+ miles	66	84	91
Average of all distances	86	94	108

Source: Graham, D.R., Kaplan, D.P., and Sibley, D.S., "Efficiency and Competition in the Airline Industry, *Bell Journal of Economics,* Vol. 14, No. 1 (Spring, 1983), p. 122.

this period, it can be argued that their plight would have been even worse if they had not been able to adjust fares rapidly in response to fuel price increases.

A more meaningful evaluation of the effects of deregulation on air fares can be made using the standard industry fare method mentioned earlier. Essentially, this is a price computed from a formula that takes into account changes in fuel and other costs. Under regulation, this procedure was used by the CAB as a guide for price setting. Table 14.4 compares prices as determined for 1981 using this formula with actual 1981 prices charged in various types of markets and for various distances. The table indicates that prices in the top 200 markets were less than they would have been based on the standard formula. However it also shows that fares in a sample of smaller markets were somewhat higher. This is not surprising because new entrants have concentrated on high-density markets. The table also depicts relative prices as declining with distance. This result is also explained by greater competition in long-haul routes.

In addition to fare levels, deregulation also has had a significant effect on the structure of rates. During most of the years of CAB regulation, few pricing innovations were allowed. In contrast, decontrol has resulted in many fare experiments. During 1982, 80 percent of airline passengers flew using tickets with discounts averaging 50 percent off full fare.[13] Although the proliferation of fares caused some confusion for customers and travel agents, it did allow travelers to tailor trips to meet their budget and timing needs. For example, most flights set aside a number of seats for travelers needing a specific flight, while tourists can get bargains if they are willing to make reservations far in advance or fly during off-peak periods.

Service to small communities   Under provisions of the Airline Deregulation Act large airlines quickly dropped at least some jet service from 170 smaller cities. Almost 100 of these cities lost all jet service.[14] However, it would be a mistake to conclude that smaller cities necessarily are worse off as a result of decontrol. Commuter airlines have more than filled the void. The number of commuter lines has doubled in the last ten years. Although they usually use slower and less comfortable planes, the small size of their aircraft allows more frequent flights. In many cases two departures per day on a large jet have been replaced by five or six flights on a

[13]*Time,* Feb. 21, 1983, p. 53.
[14]*Wall Street Journal,* Aug. 23, 1982, p. 19.

smaller, prop-driven plane. Thus, the loss of comfort and speed must be weighed against greater scheduling convenience.

Destructive competition and dominance by large firms   Although fares on some dense, long-haul routes were driven far below their previous levels, the primary reasons were a depressed economy and a temporary glut of wide-body aircraft. There is no clear indication that destructive competition will cause collapse of small firms and eventual dominance by a few large firms. In fact, the evidence indicates that the largest airlines have actually lost market shares since deregulation. The share of the trunks was 90 percent in 1978, but had dropped to 84 percent by late 1983.[15] This loss was picked up by regional carriers expanding their operations and, in many cases, by new airlines entering the market.

Although there has been no strong concentration trend in the industry, there has been a restructuring of routes resulting in more efficient operation of the system. An important component of this restructuring has been the expansion of regional carriers into nationwide markets. In many cases, this has allowed airline passengers to travel from point-to-point with less inconvenience. One of the least pleasant parts of air travel is connecting with different airlines. Problems with lost baggage, late flights, and long terminal walks all contribute to the aggravation. The process is much more pleasant if the customer can remain on the same plane, or at least with the same airline from start to finish.

One explanation for the success of the regional airlines is that they had already established feeder networks bringing passengers from smaller to larger cities. As they extended their routes to other large cities, passengers found it convenient to stay with the same airline. The consequence of this restructuring has been a reduction airlines switching. Since 1978 the proportion of passengers forced to change airlines over the course of a trip has decreased by nearly 40 percent.[16]

Expansion by regional carriers has had a positive influence on airline passenger service, but entry by new firms has been equally important. These new carriers have forced the larger airlines to be more cost conscious. Operating their equipment more intensively, providing fewer frills, and using mostly nonunion labor, their presence has greatly stimulated price competition in the industry.

SUMMARY
Natural Gas

Discovery of vast supplies and improved methods of transportation transformed natural gas from an unwanted by-product of oil drilling to a valuable national resource.

The Natural Gas Industry   Hundreds of firms are engaged in the production of natural gas. However, the importance of the major oil firms at this stage of operation makes collusion possible. Some competition exists at the transmission level, but the distribu-

---

[15]CAB, *op. cit.,* Oct. 1983, pp. 2, 5.
[16]Graham, D.R., Kaplan, D.P., and Sibley, D.S., "Efficiency and Competition in the Airline Industry," *Bell Journal of Economics,* Vol. 14, No. 1 (Spring 1983), p. 119.

tion of natural gas usually is provided by a single utility with an exclusive market area.

The wellhead price of natural gas is the price paid to producers. The wholesale price is the amount charged by pipelines to utilities. The retail price is the cost to final consumers.

Regulation of the retail price is the responsibility of state regulatory commissions. Wholesale price regulation is under the auspices of the Federal Energy Regulatory Commission. It is necessary because of the cost-plus nature of regulation, which allows high prices paid by pipelines to be passed on as higher retail prices.

Regulation of the Wellhead Price of Natural Gas   In 1954 the Supreme Court held that the Federal Power Commission had the responsibility for regulating the wellhead price of natural gas. The decision was highly controversial and several unsuccessful attempts were made to pass legislation that would have overturned the Court's decision.

In response, the FPC first attempted to set individual wellhead prices, but this proved impractical. Next, the commission divided the country into 23 geographic regions and tried to determine area rates. As an interim solution, the price of natural gas at the wellhead was essentially frozen between 1960 and 1973. In 1974 the FPC set nationwide rates for natural gas. These rates allowed a higher price for newly discovered gas than for existing reserves. Ultimately, the nationwide rates evolved into a five-tiered system of prices.

Effects of Wellhead Regulation   Controls on the wellhead price of natural gas had adverse impacts on resource allocation. Low prices reduced the incentive of firms to produce, while signaling consumers that there was little need to economize on the use of natural gas. The result was shortages.

Regulation also affected the distribution of income. Controls favored those consumers who were able to purchase natural gas at reduced prices. On the other hand, producers and those consumers unable to obtain natural gas were adversely affected.

Current Issues: Deregulation of the Wellhead Price   The Natural Gas Policy Act of 1978 provided for gradual deregulation of the wellhead price by 1985. If the results are considered unsatisfactory, the act provided for temporary reinstatement of controls. Without further legislation, all controls are to expire in 1988.

Effects of deregulation   Partial deregulation contributed to a surplus of natural gas in the early 1980s. It also improved the distribution of gas supplies between states. However, stiff price increases were levied on consumers in many cities. One cause of the price jumps was take-or-pay contracts that required pipelines to pay for gas even if it was not needed. The multitiered pricing scheme of the NGPA also caused problems. In some cases, the price of gas from one source was as much as 40 times that from another source of supply.

Prospects for the future   Some suggest that the pace of decontrol should be accelerated, while others call for it to slow. Other proposals include a greater role for the state commissions and closer examination of contract negotiations by FERC. There have also been calls for Congress to void take-or-pay contracts.

Airline Passenger Service

The Economics of Air Travel The demand for air travel is a derived demand. In making travel decisions an individual seeks to minimize the full cost of the trip. The demand for air travel is a function of air fares, prices of other modes of travel, airplane speed, quality of service, and scheduling frequency.

Costs per passenger-mile decrease with distance and increasing load factors. Studies suggest that the industry is characterized by constant returns to scale. Since fixed costs are relatively low, there is no clear tendency toward destructive competition.

Forty Years of Regulation A 1938 act created the Civil Aeronautics Board and gave it power to set fares and determine conditions of entry and exit. Until the late 1960s, price supervision was perfunctory. In contrast, the CAB's control over entry was used to restrict competition.

Under regulation, fares in unregulated intrastate routes were considerably lower than those subject to the CAB. The explanation was that regulation led to excessive service competition. The main form of this nonprice competition was increased scheduling frequency, which led to low load factors and higher costs per passenger-mile.

Current Issues: Deregulation of Air Passenger Service The Airline Deregulation Act of 1978 allowed the airlines to vary fares within a zone of reasonableness and made entry and exit easier. One of its most notable features was a provision that required the CAB to justify its continued existence beyond 1985.

Air fares have increased during the first five years of deregulation, but much of the change can be accounted for by higher fuel prices. On many routes prices are lower and rate structure innovations have benefited air travelers. Some small communities have lost service from the major airlines, but in most cases this service has been replaced by commuter lines offering more frequent flights. Predictions of an industry dominated by a few large firms have not materialized. In fact, the expansion of regional airlines and the entry of new firms have greatly increased competition and improved resource allocation in the industry.

DISCUSSION QUESTIONS

1. What are the advantages of natural gas as an energy source?
2. Assume that market power is on the buyer's side for natural gas at the wellhead. What does economic theory predict about prices? About the need for regulation?
3. What effect might the FPC's natural gas freeze have had on the influence of OPEC?
4. If gas producers anticipate that price controls are temporary, how might their production decisions be affected? How would consumers be affected?
5. What problems are associated with making energy policy on a piecemeal basis (i.e., one industry at a time)?
6. Should Congress act to void existing take-or-pay contracts? What effect might such action have on future contract negotiations?
7. Suppose the government were to develop a rationing scheme for allocating scarce supplies of natural gas. What criteria should be used to determine which users receive priority?

8. Five or six hundred miles usually is considered to be the break-even point beyond which air travel has a clear advantage over driving. Why would this be so?
9. Could scale economies in aircraft maintenance provide a cost advantage for larger carriers? Are there alternative arrangements for smaller firms?
10. How might the use of computers have affected the proliferation of air fares in recent years?
11. What problems might the CAB, scheduled to be abolished in 1985, have experienced in functioning during the early 1980s?
12. Fares often are lower on routes to vacation spots than for those connecting other points. Why?

chapter **15**

Economic Regulation: Evaluation

Chapter Outline

[Said] an aged West Coast Indian, sitting on a rock and looking out to sea, . . . "Lighthouse, him no good for fog. Lighthouse, him whistle, him blow, him ring bell, him flash light, him raise hell; but fog come in just the same."

The most basic question one can ask about economic regulation is whether it makes a difference in the behaviour of the regulated industry. . . . The net effect of the busy humming of the regulatory machinery may be only to irritate entrepreneurs and to enrich their lawyers, without effecting a fundamental alteration in the state of affairs that would have existed in the absence of regulation.

Roger C. Cramton[1]

The goals specified by legislatures in creating regulatory commissions were rather explicit. The primary responsibilities of the commissions were to assure adequate service, keep prices at a reasonable level, and prevent undue price discrimination. With such clear-cut objectives it would seem that evaluating regulation would be a fairly simple task. Is service adequate? Are prices reasonable? Do rate structures avoid excessive discrimination? Unfortunately, these are the very questions that make rate cases so complex, costly, and time consuming. There is no consensus as to what constitutes adequate service, reasonable rates, and undue discrimination.

An alternative method of evaluation would compare results with regulation to those that would have occurred if firms had been left to their own devices. Is service better, are prices lower, are rate structures less discriminatory than if market forces had shaped the industries? Again, these questions are difficult to answer. Almost all public utilities are regulated in the United States, so there is really no way of knowing what results unregulated firms would produce. Similarly, there is no basis for comparison in other nations, because such firms usually are owned by the government.

These rather formidable difficulties notwithstanding, this chapter is an attempt to evaluate economic regulation. The first section considers the most basic question— what effect has regulation had on prices? The next section discusses efficiency problems associated with the regulatory process. Various procedural problems, together with recommendations for change, are considered in the third section. Finally, the chapter concludes with a discussion of the recent trend toward deregulation.

REGULATION AND PRICES

Important changes in government policy have made the airlines and the telecommunications industry much more competitive. These changes allow some preliminary assessments to be made regarding the effect of regulation on prices of those services.

As discussed in Chapter 14, one method of analyzing air fares is to compare actual prices under deregulation with those that could have been justified using the CAB's standard airfare formula. Such comparisons indicate that consumers traveling over dense routes, especially for long distances, are paying substantially less than the formula would dictate. However, prices for passengers traveling between smaller cities are higher.

[1]Cramton, R. C., "The Effectiveness of Economic Regulation: A Legal View," *The American Economic Review,* Vol. 53 (May 1963), p. 182.

With respect to telecommunications, hundreds of firms entered the market once the FCC began allowing competition for long-distance telephone service. The fact that they were able to make a profit while offering rates considerably below those of AT&T suggests that regulation artificially inflated the price of toll calls as a means of subsidizing local service. As competition eats away the subsidy by driving long-distance rates down, regulators are being forced to increase local telephone rates.

Evaluating the effects of regulation is more difficult in industries such as natural gas and electricity, which have not been opened to competition. Some evidence is provided by Figure 15.1. The graphs show trends in the prices of natural gas and electricity relative to all other consumer purchases. The relative price of natural gas climbed from 1950 to 1960 and then declined until about 1970. Since 1970, natural gas prices have increased much faster than prices of other consumer purchases. A large part of the fluctuations in the relative price of natural gas can be explained by federal regulatory policy. The decline between 1960 and 1970 reflects the period when wellhead prices were essentially frozen. The run-up since 1970 is the consequence of gradual deregulation at the wellhead.

Turning to electricity, Figure 15.1 indicates that the relative price declined between 1947 and 1970. But the cause of the decrease is unclear. Regulation may have been a major force, or the drop may simply reflect improvements in generation and transmission technology. Since 1970, high fuel prices and pollution control requirements have caused the relative price of electricity to increase. Once again, however,

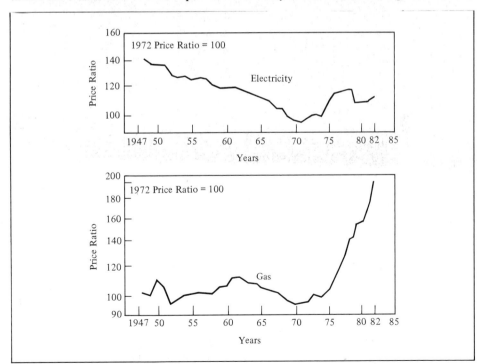

Figure 15.1. Ratio of electricity and natural gas prices to prices of all other consumer items. (Federal Energy Regulatory Commission, Washington, D.C.)

there is no simple way of determining how relative prices would have varied if electricity prices had not been subject to regulation by state and federal commissions.

A number of studies have used analytical and statistical tools to investigate the effects of regulation on electricity prices. These studies are of two types. The first approach is historical and compares prices in states with regulation to prices in states that had not yet established regulatory commissions. The second technique attempts to compute the profit-maximizing price of an unregulated firm and compare it to the regulated price.

Regulated Versus Unregulated Prices

The best known historical study is that of Stigler and Friedland.[2] It is presented here in some detail to illustrate how such a study might be approached and to point out the difficulties involved in evaluating the effects of regulation.

The basis for the Stigler-Friedland (SF) study was the fact that during the first third of this century there were a number of states that had not yet established regulatory commissions. Stigler and Friedland evaluated the effects of regulation by comparing electricity rates in states with commissions to those without commissions. Initially, they observed that in 1917 the average revenue per kilowatt-hour of electricity sold was 1.88 cents in 31 regulated states and 3.20 cents in 16 unregulated states. At first glance it would seem that regulation was effective in reducing rates. However, an examination of rates in 1912 suggests that there may have been other factors involved. In 1912 there were only 6 states with commissions and 42 without. For the 25 states instituting regulation between 1912 and 1917 the average revenue per kilowatt-hour was 2.30 cents in 1912. For the 16 states not regulated by 1917 the average was 4.07 cents in 1912. Evidently, rates were lower in the regulating states before as well as after regulation. Based on this evidence, it is not possible to determine the effects of regulation in moderating electricity prices.

Stigler and Friedland attempted to net out the effects of regulation from other factors by use of statistical techniques. They hypothesized that variations in electricity prices are the result of a number of factors. Specifically, they assumed that electric rates could be explained by variations in population density (an economies-of-scale argument), fuel prices, method of electricity generation (fossil fuel versus hydroelectric), income, and whether or not a state had a regulatory commission. The basic question was, "When the effects of all the other factors have been accounted for, is there any residual difference in electricity prices that might be explained by the existence or absence of a regulatory commission?"

Stigler and Friedland interpreted their results as showing that regulation had no conclusive effect in reducing electricity rates. Looking at data for 1912, 1922, 1932, and 1937, they found rates essentially the same in regulated and unregulated states in 1912, and from 4 to 10 percent lower in 1922, 1932, and 1937. To the uninitiated it seems very strange that those figures were argued to imply no effect of regulation. For the lower regulated rates in 1922 and 1932, the SF contention was based on the statistical nonsignificance of the estimated effects of regulation. Statistical tests involve a degree

[2]Stigler, G. J., and Friedland, C., "What Can the Regulators Regulate? The Case of Electricity," *Journal of Law and Economics* (Oct. 1962), pp. 1–16.

of uncertainty. It is possible that findings may stem from chance rather than depicting a real relationship. Traditionally, statisticians require that the probability that a result is not a statistical quirk be rather high. Stigler and Friedland used a fairly standard 95-percent confidence level. This means that there was only a 5-percent chance that the finding of lower rates in regulated states is a statistical aberration. The SF findings for 1922 and 1932 do not pass this test. However, the 1937 findings do pass the test and the 1922 and 1932 pass a 90-percent test.

Using the strict 95-percent test and noting that the 1937 result came about mainly because of lower rates to commercial and industrial customers, SF concluded that "the individual utility system is not possessed of any large amount of long run monopoly power," and that "the possibility becomes large that the commission will proudly win each battlefield that its protagonist has abandoned, except for a squad of lawyers."[3]

The SF study is subject to criticism on a number of grounds. First, it tells us little about the present effect of regulation. The study period of 1912 to 1937 was a time when regulation was just feeling its way. Commissions were new and inexperienced. Regulation was bogged down in the controversy over the proper method of valuation. For all their faults, modern commissions are much better staffed and more knowledgeable than the commissions studied by SF. The methodology of their study dictated that the data be old. To compare states with and without regulation required that there be enough observations in each category. After 1940 almost all states had established regulatory commissions.

A second problem with the SF study is that it ignored the threat of regulation. To the extent that their findings show that regulation had little effect, the explanation may be that commissions were first created in states where they were perceived as most needed. States where the monopoly power of electric utilities had not been exploited had not yet felt the need for a regulatory commission. Similarly, the threat of regulation may have acted as a deterrent to the firms' increasing prices. A third criticism of SF is that their own data may be used to infer that regulation did have an effect on prices. By relaxing the confidence level to 90 percent, the data suggest that the hypothesis that regulation reduces electricity rates cannot be rejected.[4]

There have been other attempts to determine the effectiveness of regulation in reducing prices. A study by Jackson tried to use the SF method for 1940 to 1960.[5] Although most states regulated electricity prices during that period, there were a few, such as Texas, that did not. Jackson found that the effect of regulation in reducing electricity prices was statistically significant for commercial and industrial, but not residential, users in 1940 and 1950. The effect in 1960 was statistically significant for all classes of users. A possible explanation of Jackson's findings is that, during periods when technological change was reducing the costs of producing electricity, regulation was not very effective in assuring that the cost savings were passed on to consumers. However, when upward pressure on rates began in 1960, regulation had an effect in limiting the increases. However, Jackson's results are somewhat suspect, because of the small number of unregulated states in his sample.

[3]Ibid., pp. 15–16.
[4]Alternatively, if the prior hypothesis is that regulation reduces electric rates, then a one-tailed test at 95 percent would be appropriate. Using this test, the hypothesis could not be rejected.
[5]Jackson, R., "Regulation and Electric Utility Rate Levels," *Land Economics,* Vol. 45 (Aug. 1969), pp. 372–376.

Profit-Maximizing Versus Regulated Prices

A study by Moore represents an early attempt to use economic theory to estimate the effect of regulation on prices.[6] Using 1962 data for a cross section of firms, Moore estimated a demand function. This demand information was then combined with cost data to compute the price that unregulated, profit-maximizing firms would charge their residential customers. These prices were then compared with the actual prices that state regulatory commissions had approved for the electric utilities in the sample. Moore interpreted his results as indicating that the benefits of regulation were not very great. He estimated the average regulated price to be less than 5 percent below the profit-maximizing level.

A later, more sophisticated version of Moore's approach was used by Meyer and Leland.[7] Based on data from 1969 and 1974, their models allowed for variations in the effect of regulation between states and customer classes. Although they do not quantify their findings, they conclude that regulation, on average, results in prices that are significantly different from those that would be charged by the profit-maximizing monopolist. However, their analysis also suggests that the effectiveness of regulation varies substantially from state to state. In addition, Meyer and Leland found evidence of cross-subsidization between customer classes. Their 1969 data was interpreted as showing that regulation favored commercial and industrial customers, but the results for 1974 indicated that the bias had shifted to the benefit of residential consumers. This change may be explained by the increasing attention that regulatory commissions began to give to rate-structure design during the 1970s.

The method used by Moore and by Meyer and Leland is appealing because of its ties to economic theory. Also, in contrast to the approach of Stigler and Friedland, it can be applied to current data. Unfortunately, the validity of the findings are dependent on the ability of the researcher to estimate accurately the demand and cost curves of electric utilities. This task is not an easy one.

REGULATION AND EFFICIENCY

As discussed in Chapter 11, regulation of electric, gas, and telephone utilities is a cost-plus procedure that uses the rate of return on capital as a basis for evaluating proposed price changes. There are predictable efficiency problems stemming from the use of this approach. They involve the incentive for the utility to be efficient at any point in time (static efficiency) and also the incentive to be efficient over time (dynamic efficiency).

Static Efficiency

In setting rates, the expenses of a public utility are accepted with little controversy in a rate case. The firm can be reasonably certain that most of the expenses it incures can

---

[6]Moore, T., "The Effectiveness of Regulation on Electric Utility Prices," *Southern Economic Journal*, Vol. 36, No. 4 (April 1970), pp. 365–375.

[7]Meyer, R. A. and Leland, H. E., "The Effectiveness of Price Regulation," *Review of Economics and Statistics* (Nov. 1980), pp. 555–566.

be passed on to the consumer in the form of higher prices. Why then should utility managers worry about being cost conscious? Keeping wages down and dismissing unproductive workers causes altercations with unions. Hard negotiations to get the best buy on fuel or equipment involve a psychic and time cost to management. Spartan offices and tight expense accounts reduce the "fun" of being a high-powered executive. If the firm is to be allowed a fair rate of return even if expenses are a bit excessive, then management can meet its obligations to stockholders and, at the same time, make life just a little bit easier for itself.

Obviously, there are some constraints on a utility's expenses. At some point the regulatory commission might disallow certain excessive expenditures. Also, if regulation is not instantaneous, the firm may have to pay extra expenses out of potential profits until it gets rate relief. The point, however, is that the public utility, regulated on a cost-plus basis, does not have the same incentives to cut costs that an unregulated firm does. For the unregulated firm there is a trade-off between costs and profits. If the managers can cut costs, then those savings show up on the bottom line as an increase in profits. To the extent that management must be responsive to the wishes of stockholders, there is an incentive to increase profits by reducing costs. For the regulated firm that incentive is somewhat reduced. Because the firm is not allowed to achieve its maximum profit potential (which assumes that regulation is at least somewhat effective), the profit loss from higher costs is reduced. Thus, regulated firms may be more inefficient than firms that are constrained only by market forces. One possible explanation of the findings of Stigler-Friedland and the other researchers is that the inefficiency resulting from regulation offsets the reduction in profit rates and, hence, there is no net reduction in prices.

The cost-plus nature of regulation may cause a general increase in the utility's costs. However, the rate-of-return-on-capital basis of regulation may dictate the nature of the inefficiency. It has long been suggested that public utilities increase their total profits by overuse of capital. Because profits are determined by the fair rate of return times the rate base, the more capital the firm uses the greater are its profits. This idea became important to economists after it was stated mathematically by Averch and Johnson (AJ). Beginning with the assumptions that firms attempt to maximize profits, that there is no delay in the regulatory process, and that the allowed rate of return granted by commissions is greater than the firm's cost of capital, Averch and Johnson argue that the regulated firm will use more capital to produce any given level of output than would be required for cost-minimizing production.[8]

The mathematics of the AJ proposition are beyond the scope of this text, but the basic idea is shown by Figure 15.2. Assume that the firm's product is produced using capital *(K)* and labor *(L)*. The cost of capital is r and the wage rate is w. The regulatory commission allows the firm a return on its capital *(s)* that is greater than the cost of that capital. The convex isoquant in Figure 15.2 shows all the technically feasible ways of producing some given level of output, $\overline{Q}$.

The cost-minimizing combination of labor and capital occurs where the ratio of input prices equals the slope of the isoquant. Intuitively, this is the point where the

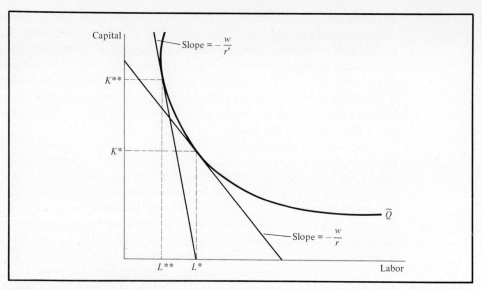

Figure 15.2. Averch-Johnson effect.

relative cost of obtaining labor and capital is equal to the relative contribution that they make in the production process. If capital costs more relative to labor than it contributes, then costs can be reduced by using more labor; similarly for capital. Only when relative costs are equal to relative productivities are costs minimized. The most efficient combination of inputs to produce $\overline{Q}$ is *(L*, K*)*. If an unregulated firm is to maximize profits, a necessary condition is that it first minimize the cost of producing $\overline{Q}$ or whatever level of output is selected.

The regulated firm chooses the optimal input combination in the same way as the unregulated firm, but the choice is based on different data. AJ assume that the regulated firm is allowed to earn more on each unit of capital employed than the cost of obtaining that capital. Thus, the net cost of that capital to the firm might be thought of as being somewhat less than the market price, because the firm increases its net profits with each unit employed. Let the firm's perceived cost of capital be $r' < r$. The optimal input bundle for the regulated firm is chosen by equating the ratio of input costs to the ratio of marginal products of the inputs (the slope of the isoquent). However, the regulated firm uses the ratio w/r' rather than w/r. The optimal bundle is *(K**, L**)*, which involves more capital and less labor than the cost-minimizing bundle. Although the regulated firm can increase the profits that it is allowed to earn by overutilizing capital, the actual cost of its production is increased. Thus, the rate of return on capital basis of regulation causes production inefficiency.

Public utilities argue that they do not attempt to increase their profits by increasing, or "gold planting," the rate base. Critics are equally vocal in claiming that they do. A number of researchers have attempted to put the Averch-Johnson thesis to empirical test. Focusing on electric utilities, they investigated whether regulation causes inefficiency through the excessive substitution of capital for other inputs. Advocates on either side can find evidence to support their position.[9] Although the question is far from closed, these results suggest that the focus of regulation on profit rates alone is not enough. Restraints imposed on the rate of return may be offset by other inefficiencies, which make the net effect on prices uncertain.

Dynamic Efficiency

For any product or service there is an optimal rate of innovation. Cost-saving technologies should be introduced when the unit total cost of producing using the new technology is less than the unit variable cost using the existing technology. For example, consider electricity generation. Suppose that an older generator requires 3 cents per kilowatt-hour in fuel, labor, and maintenance costs. A newly developed generator has fuel, labor, and maintenance costs of $1\frac{1}{2}$ cents per kilowatt-hour and an initial cost of 1 cent per kilowatt-hour (computed by dividing the intial cost of the machine by the projected number of kilowatt-hours that will be produced). The unit variable cost of the existing generator is 3 cents per kilowatt-hour.. The unit total cost of the new generator is only $2\frac{1}{2}$ cents per kilowatt-hour. Hence, the new equipment should be installed, because the firm can reduce its costs of producing electricity.

Regulation may change the rate at which firms introduce new technologies. To the extent that innovation is too rapid or too slow, the firm will be producing inefficiently. There are aspects of the regulatory process that both accelerate and retard the rate of innovation. To illustrate, firms incorporate new technologies to reduce production costs. An unregulated firm reaps the benefits of the cost savings in the form of extra profits. The regulated firm may not be able to retain the rewards of innovation. If new technologies reduce its costs, the regulatory commission may deem its profit rate excessive and force a rate reduction. To the extent that the firm is not allowed to retain cost savings from innovation, the incentive to innovate is reduced.

Restrictions on entry into regulated markets also can have an adverse impact on dynamic efficiency. One of the virtues of competition is that it forces existing firms to improve the products and services that they currently offer and also to expand their menu of offerings. Where firms are protected from competition, the incentive for change is diminished. Even if competition is allowed, the push to innovate may be dulled. If competitors are required to gain approval for new offerings, then the element of surprise is lost and the other firms in the market have time to posture themselves to minimize the impact of change. This posturing may take the form of urging the regulatory commission not to allow the new offering, suggesting that it be priced so as to be less competitive, or disparaging its usefulness.

On the other hand, there are features of regulation that may encourage innova-

---

[9]These who detected overcapitalization include Petersen, H.C., "An Empirical Test of Regulatory Effects," *Bell Journal of Economics and Management Science,* Vol. 6, No. 1 (Spring, 1975), pp. 111–126; Courville, L., "Regulation and Efficiency in the Electric Utility Industry," *Bell Journal of Economics and Management Science,* Vol. 5, No. 1 (Spring, 1974), pp. 53–74; Spann, R. M., "Rate of Return Regulation and Efficiency in Production: An Empirical Test of the Averch-Johnson Thesis," *Bell Journal of Economics and Management Science,* Vol. 5, No. 1 (Spring, 1974), pp. 38–52. Doubters include Boyes, W.J., "An Empirical Examination of the Averch-Johnson Effect," *Economic Inquiry,* Vol. 14 (Mar., 1976), pp. 25–35.

tion. First, the regulated firm is somewhat sheltered from risk. The cost of unsuccessful innovation may be passed on to the consumer in the form of higher prices. Second, the capital bias of regulated industries may induce additional innovation. For the regulated industries most technological change involves the substitution of capital for other inputs. In the electric-utility industry, nuclear and solar generation require more capital and less labor and fuel than conventional fossil fuel generation. In the telephone industry change has taken the form of automated switching equipment that requires fewer operators and less maintenance. Because the firm can increase its total allowed profits by expanding its rate base, it has an incentive to incorporate such capital-using techniques.

The net effect of regulation on the rate of innovation of public utilities is uncertain. There is no way in which it can be predicted on a theoretical basis and no conclusive empirical findings. It can be observed, however, that technological change and innovation has been very important in the regulated industries. Although electricity costs seem high to the average person, they are much lower than they were in the development days of electric energy. The same is true in other regulated industries. Technological breakthroughs have drastically reduced the costs of providing service. However, observation that change has been important in the regulated industries does not necessarily imply that regulation hasn't retarded the rate of innovation. It is possible that the rate of change would have been much more rapid if the firms had been unregulated. Unfortunately, there is no way of knowing what the rate of innovation would have been in the absence of regulation.

PROBLEMS WITH THE REGULATORY PROCESS

There is a wide divergence of views regarding the regulatory process. Some consider it a prime example of American genius in steering a path between the abuses of unconstrained monopoly and the inefficiency and political undesirability of public enterprise. Others are highly critical of what they perceive to be a proindustry bias. Most observers, however, see value in some aspects of regulation, but also recognize deficiencies that need to be corrected.

Regulatory Lag

The regulatory process is something less than instantaneous. From three months to a year may elapse from a firm's request for a rate adjustment to the commission's final decision. If the decision is appealed through the judicial system, it may be several years before the outcome is known. As long as the rate case remains an adversary proceeding with all interested parties being given the opportunity to present their case, then *regulatory lag* will be an integral part of regulation.

During inflationary times regulatory lag can result in a utility filing a request for a rate increase even before the last case has been decided by the commission. In some states regulatory commissions are required by law to render a decision on a rate increase within a certain time period. If they fail to do so, the increase becomes effective immediately. However, such provisions usually produce only marginal improvement because the time limits are long—typically from six months to a year.

The immediate effects of regulatory lag depend on whether there is upward or downward pressure on the regulated firm's costs. If technology is reducing costs, then the delay may allow firms to increase their profits for a period of time by retaining the cost of saving. If inflationary pressures are increasing costs, then the firm will find its profit margins squeezed while it awaits rate relief. Although regulatory lag is generally considered to be a defect in the regulatory process, it may actually moderate some of the incentive problems created by regulation. If the firm knows that it will not immediately be able to pass on all increases in cost, then there is an incentive to keep costs down. Lag may also affect the rate of innovation. If cost savings from the introduction of new technology are not immediately skimmed off by the regulatory commission, then the firm may perceive greater benefits from innovation. In a sense, one defect in the regulatory process (lag) may serve to moderate another defect (lack of incentives).

Expertise of Commissioners

Utility commissioner's have a difficult job. The issues involved are extremely complex and the hours in hearings can be excruciatingly boring. In the end, it is a thankless task, because some groups are going to be angered regardless of what decision is reached. As a result, it is sometimes difficult to pursuade competent and interested people to take and remain in these positions. Where the job is a political appointment, it is often awarded to a crony seeking a secure spot or to an individual who views it as a brief interlude on his or her way up the political ladder.[10] Some of these people turn out to be fine public servants, but others never take the time or have the skills to function effectively. For example, the following excerpt from the *Wall Street Journal* describes the qualifications and behavior of a past member of one of the federal regulatory commissions:

> Mrs. X, who sang on a morning radio show from 1936 to 1939, spent nearly 10 years in Congress (she is probably best remembered as the first woman to wear a pantsuit on the House floor). Then, in 1971, President Nixon picked her—mainly because she was a friend, a Republican, and a woman—to be one of the FCC's Commissioners.
>
> Even during the Senate hearing to confirm her nomination to the FCC, that brief and distant singing career emerged repeatedly as a key qualification. Illinois Republican Sen. Charles Percy told his colleagues, "Having had a career as a radio vocalist, she is familiar with many of the operations of the broadcast industry from her own unique experience."
>
> Probably the most notable thing Mrs. X has done so far in her seven-year FCC term is to spend $4,600 of government money installing in her office a private bathroom with a large goldframed mirror.
>
> Mrs. X acknowledges her lack of expertise. "I came on with the idea of not getting too involved with any one issue," she says. . . . Her legal assistant is almost a shadow commissioner. He writes Mrs. X's speeches and her rare written opinions.

[10]Regulatory commissioners are elected in about a dozen states. There is some evidence that elected commissions are more likely to hold down rates, but this short-run objective may be achieved at the expense of the long-term financial health of the firms being regulated.

In commission meetings he frequently jumps up to explain her views on complicated issues or walks up to the commission bar to advise her on a vote.[11]

Even commissioners who have some training for their jobs may find themselves overwhelmed by their task. They must develop an understanding of the specific problems of each industry that they regulate. Often important issues in the rate case turn on situations unique to a particular industry. Becoming an expert on any one industry is difficult enough, but commissioners are expected to be experts on all the industries that they regulate. A typical state commission might have jurisdiction over electric, natural gas, telephone, water, trucking, taxi, airline, and railroad operations within a state. Each of these industries have their own special problems and, perhaps even more serious, their own jargon that must be mastered. Obtaining the necessary expertise is a very difficult task.

To leave the impression that regulatory commissioners are never qualified for their positions would be unfair. Sometimes persons with impeccable credentials have been chosen. An excellent example was the appointment of Alfred Kahn as chairman of the Civil Aeronautics Board. Dr. Kahn was one of the nation's foremost authorities on regulation and had previously been a progressive and effective chairman of the New York Public Service Commission. One also has to be careful of making the assumption that training in economics or work in the industry to be regulated is a necessary condition for being an effective commissioner. It may be that the legalistic and political nature of the commissions dictates that persons with well-developed political instincts will be the most effective commissioners.

Resource Imbalance

The public interest in a rate case is presented by the commission staff and, sometimes, by various public or private groups. The advantage of superior resources is almost always with the firm. The utility typically has more and bigger guns to present its case. A small state commission may have one or two staff members working on a particular issue, while the preparation of the firm's case may involve dozens or even hundreds of employees. Also, the firm has the advantage of being the source of data used in the decision process. Although it is obligated to comply with reasonable requests for information, the firm is in a position to provide and format data to further its own interests. In some circumstances the firm may argue that requests for information cannot be filled because the data are not available. In other cases it may choose to inundate the regulatory commission with more facts and figures than could ever be evaluated.

To the extent that firms dominate regulatory proceedings because of superior resources, better results may be obtained by increasing the budgets of commissions to allow larger and better-qualified staffs. Unfortunately, regulatory commissions are often not the first priority for legislatures besieged with requests for additional money.

[11]Elliot, K. J., "Mrs. X Wanted Only to Sing, but She Ended Up on the FCC," *Wall Street Journal* (Oct. 25, 1974), p. 15. Reprinted by permission of the *Wall Street Journal,* © Dow Jones & Company, Inc. (1974). All rights reserved.

In some states the operations of regulatory commissions are financed by funds collected directly from the firms that are regulated. Obviously, such moneys are ultimately paid by the customer in the form of higher prices, but this may be a more politically acceptable way of increasing commission budgets than the more visible mechanism of a line appropriation from the legislature.

Too Much Law and Accounting, Too Little Economics

Much of the emphasis in the rate case has been on legal definitions and accounting conventions. Submerged in the requirement to correctly value the rate base, account for depreciation properly, provide all parties with a fair chance to state their case, and so on, principles of efficient resource allocation have often been ignored or rejected. For example, in the past, commissions have become involved in examining the structure of rates primarily to fulfill their legal requirement of preventing undue discrimination. But, economists have long argued that the rate structure is an important tool that can be used to reduce costs in an industry. By adjusting relative prices, consumption can be shifted from times when heavy demand imposes the need for additional capacity to other times when there is excess capacity. By postponing the need for additional investment in capacity, such shifts reduce costs and, ultimately, prices.

Many commissions continue to rely primarily on legal and accounting concepts in rate making. Economists maintain (not surprisingly) that the regulatory process would provide much better results if commissioners would use more economics and less law and accounting in their decision making. The general trend is toward greater reliance on economic principles, but the march is very slow.

Lack of Incentives

The lack of incentives for regulated firms to cut costs has already been discussed. The regulatory process could be improved if commissions had tools to encourage efficiency. One suggestion is to award efficient firms a slightly higher rate of return or to penalize inefficient firms with a lower rate of return. The biggest problem with such an approach is determining and measuring efficiency or inefficiency. Consider the case of electric utilities. How are the operations of a hydroelectric utility in Oregon to be compared to those of an oil-burning company in New York or a firm using primarily nuclear generation in Michigan? There are so many determinants of cost and efficiency that it is doubtful that the decisions of commissions could consistently withstand the court challenges of firms that had been penalized or consumer groups paying higher prices because of efficiency bonuses.

DEREGULATION

Over the past ten years there has been a continuing trend toward deregulation. Some aspects of this trend were discussed in previous chapters. Much of the telephone industry has been opened to competition. The wellhead price of natural gas is gradually being decontrolled. Restrictions on pricing, entry, and exit in the airline industry are being phased out. But the movement is much broader than these three industries. A number of other sectors are in various stages of deregulation.

Deregulation of Transportation Industries

Trucking companies and railroads compete for shipper's dollars. Trucking tends to have an advantage in transporting high-value goods over relatively short distances, while railroads are better suited for moving bulk goods over long hauls. However, past regulatory policies sometimes ignored these natural advantages.

Railroads   The Interstate Commerce Commission was established in 1887 to regulate the nation's railroads. Until the late 1970s, the commission maintained tight control over pricing, entry, and exit. These policies frequently were cited as an important reason for the loss of market share and low profits of the railroads.

Congressional legislation in 1976 and 1980 made it easier for the railroads to enter new markets and abandon unprofitable routes. The acts also gave the railroads the right to increase or decrease prices within a "zone of reasonableness" without commission approval. Further, the ICC was empowered to exempt certain commodities from all rate regulation. In 1979 the commission used this authority to give the railroads complete autonomy over rates for shipping fresh fruits and vegetables. The results were dramatic. Between 1979 and 1982, the railroads more than doubled the amount of perishable products carried. [12]

Trucking   Interstate Commerce Commission regulation of trucking dates back to 1935. As with the railroads, poorly conceived regulatory policies caused inefficiencies in the industry. For example, a trucking company might have received authorization to transport goods from Atlanta to Philadelphia, but not from Philadelphia to Atlanta. As a result, the firm's trucks would have to return empty. In another situation, a company might be granted the Atlanta-to-Philadelphia route, but be required to make the trip via Pittsburgh.

During the 1970s, the ICC gradually loosened its control over trucking. Later, the commission received a formal mandate for its actions in the form of the Motor Carriers Act of 1980. This legislation eased entry and exit restrictions and provided for flexibility in pricing. Shippers clearly have benefited from trucking deregulation. Between 1978 and 1983, the real (inflation-adjusted) price for truckload shipments dropped an average of 26 percent, while for smaller loads the average price decreased by 15 percent. During the same period, the number of carriers increased from 17,000 to 25,000. [13]

A survey by Moore of shipper's views regarding service suggests that deregulation has not resulted in a deterioration in the quality of service provided by trucking firms. Seventy-one large shippers were asked to assess changes in the quality of service

---

[12] American Railway Association, *Freight Commodity Statistics,* 1970–1982. Also see German, H. W., and Babcock, M. W., "The Impact of Rail Deregulation on the Movement of Fresh Fruit and Vegetables," *The Logistics and Transportation Review,* Vol. 18, No. 4 (December 1982), pp. 373–384.

[13] Moore, T. G., "It's a Success, but Truck Deregulation Remains a Long Haul," *Wall Street Journal* (July 26, 1983), p. 32.

between 1980 and 1982. About 35 percent responded that the quality of service had improved, 51 percent thought it was unchanged, and 14 percent said it was worse. With respect to rural areas, an ICC study concluded that service to most small communities was either unchanged or improved since deregulation.[14]

Deregulation of Broadcasting

The electromagnetic spectrum is a scarce resource. It can accommodate only a limited number of users and some portions of the spectrum are more valuable than others. For example, the higher the frequency, the more the signal takes on the characteristics of visible light. As a result, high-frequency transmissions, such as by microwave, require that sending and receiving stations be in line of sight. This is much more expensive than if the stations could be widely spaced.

Since demand for spectrum far exceeds supply, unregulated access to this resource probably would result in chaos as users vied for frequency space. In 1934, the Federal Communications Commission was given the responsibility for allocating the electromagnetic spectrum. The commission performed this function by splitting it into segments reserved for various uses. For example, the band from 535 kHz to 1600 kHz was set aside for AM radio.

Under FCC rules, radio and television station owners do not have to pay for their spot on the spectrum. They are simply required to obtain a license that must periodically be renewed. The FCC also does not engage in price regulation. Networks and station owners are free to charge advertisers whatever the market will bear. For example, the cost of a minute of advertising time during the Superbowl is approaching $1,000,000. However, broadcasters are expected to function in the public interest. This includes providing public interest programming such as documentaries and fair coverage of controversial issues. This requirement can be thought of as an example of taxation by regulation. That is, broadcasters are allowed to earn excess profits, but then are expected to use some of this money on programming deemed by the FCC to be in the public interest.

Recently, the FCC has allowed additional entry into radio and television broadcasting. In particular, it has authorized a large number of low-power television stations. The limitation on broadcasting power restricts these stations to serving a small geographic area. One of the Federal Communications Commission's primary concerns always has been that network-affiliated stations would dominate small markets and that local views would not be expressed adequately. In authorizing additional low-power entrants, the intent is to create stations that will be locally oriented and provide an expanded range of programming.

Since 1977, the number of radio stations has increased by nearly 20 percent and the number of television stations by almost 40 percent. With additional stations competing for listeners and viewers, the need for the FCC to monitor the activities of broadcasters is reduced. Consequently, the commission has moved to cut back on its oversight functions. The result will be stations that are less responsible to the FCC for their programming decisions.

[14]Moore, T. G., "The Record on Rail and Truck Reform," *Regulation,* (Nov./Dec., 1983), pp. 33–42.

Deregulation of Natural Monopolies

Conditions resulting in a natural monopoly were cited in Chapter 10 as one justification for economic regulation. But the "naturalness" of natural monopoly is not a universally accepted idea. Some economists see every monopoly as the product of government interference. To quote a disbeliever:

> One of the most unfortunate phrases ever introduced into law or economics was the phrase "natural monopoly." Every monopoly is a product of public policy. No present monopoly, public or private, can be traced back through history in a pure form. . . . "Natural monopolies" in fact originated in response to a belief that some goal, or goals, of public policy would be advanced by encouraging or permitting a monopoly to be formed, and discouraging or forbidding future competition with this monopoly.[15]

Natural Monopoly and Potential Competition   It is possible to accept the premise that a single supplier may most efficiently serve a market, but reject the conclusion that the natural monopolist will be able to set the monopoly price. A leading exponent of this position is Demsetz, who argues that if there are no legal barriers to entry and if the cost of forming contracts with prospective customers is low, then potential competition will restrain the monopolist.[16] If the single supplier sets prices too high, then rivals will appear and capture a share of the market. The telephone industry provides an example. State and federal regulatory decisions forced AT&T to charge prices for long-distance service that were substantially in excess of marginal costs. When the FCC finally allowed entry, MCI and other firms successfully entered under the price umbrella created by public policy.

Natural Monopoly and Contract Carriers   The distribution networks of electric and gas companies traditionally have been considered to be natural monopolies. Even so, there may be alternatives to regulation. One proposal would restructure these distribution systems as contract carriers. These carriers would carry electricity and gas for others on a space-available basis. The basic requirement imposed by regulators would be that the prices set by the distribution companies clear the market. That is, that they result in the use of all available distribution capacity.

Under this proposal, final users of electricity and gas would no longer be forced to deal with a single utility. They could contract for service with any firm supplying energy through the distribution system. Competition between these firms would eliminate the need for regulation of the retail price. Because electricity and gas are fungible commodities, it wouldn't matter that the product received by a particular customer wasn't the same as was supplied to the network by his or her company. All that is necessary is that the total quantity paid for by a company's customers be equal to the total amount supplied by the firm.

---

[15]Nelson, J. R., "The Role of Competition in the Regulated Industries," *The Antitrust Bulletin* (Jan.–Apr., 1966).

[16]Demsetz, H., "Why Regulate Utilities?" *Journal of Law and Economics,* Vol. 11 (April 1968), pp. 55–65.

The contract carrier concept as applied to gas and electric distribution systems is now in the idea stage, and has not yet been implemented in any community. Still, it suggests that there are additional options for deregulation.[17]

SUMMARY
Regulation and Prices

Determining the effect of regulation on prices is a difficult task. One approach compares prices in states with regulation to those without regulatory commissions. However, this method cannot be used to investigate the current effect of regulation. A second approach compares regulated prices with those that would be charged by a profit-maximizing monopolist.

Regulation and Efficiency

Static Efficiency   The cost-plus nature of regulation may reduce incentives for managerial efficiency. Specifically, the Averch and Johnson thesis suggests that regulation can create a bias toward using relatively more capital than would be required for efficient production.

Dynamic Efficiency   Regulation can affect the rate of innovation. The Averch-Johnson effect may accelerate innovation because capital-using technological change will be profitable to the firm. However, if the benefits of cost-saving innovation are quickly stripped from the firm by a rate adjustment, then the incentive to innovate is reduced. The net impact of these two forces is uncertain.

Problems with the Regulatory Process

There are several problems with public utility regulation. First, long periods of time may elapse from the initiation of a rate case until its completion. However, commissions in some states are required by law to render a decision within a specified time period. Second, regulatory commissioners often are appointed on the basis of political connections. Even commissioners who have experience may find themselves overwhelmed by the details and jargon of the issues that they must decide. Third, in a rate case, the firm usually has the advantage of superior resources. Commissions typically are understaffed and their employees underpaid. This resource imbalance can bias the rate case in the firm's favor.

A fourth problem is that the rate case is based heavily on legal and accounting concepts. However, there is a slow trend toward greater reliance on principles of economics. A final problem is that the regulatory process does not incorporate rewards for efficiency or penalties for inefficiency.

[17]However, the Federal Energy Regulatory Commission has approved a two-year experiment that essentially deregulates wholesale electricity rates of six utilities in the Southwestern United States. Under this plan, the utilities can raise or lower wholesale prices and swap power without advance approval.

Deregulation

Deregulation of Transportation Industries Historically, the Interstate Commerce Commission has regulated trucking and the railroads. Recent legislation gave firms in these industries greater freedom over entry, exit, and pricing decisions. One result has been lower rates for most shippers.

Deregulation of Broadcasting The Federal Communications Commission is responsible for allocating the electromagnetic spectrum. In return for the right to use a portion of the spectrum, broadcasters are expected to provide public interest programming. However, the FCC is now in the process of authorizing more stations and cutting back on its oversight functions.

Deregulation of Natural Monopolies Some economists believe that potential competition may prevent natural monopolists from setting high prices. One alternative to regulating gas and electricity distribution companies would be to restructure them as contract carriers. Under this proposal, final users would contract with competing firms who supply energy through the distribution system.

DISCUSSION QUESTIONS

1. Can the philosophical bias of a researcher affect the interpretation of empirical results? Explain.

2. Are the assumptions of the Averch-Johnson model realistic? Under what economic conditions would an AJ effect be most likely?

3. Could the period over which a regulated firm was allowed to depreciate its equipment affect the rate of innovation? Explain.

4. Should regulatory commissioners be required to have certain qualifications or experience? What kinds of background would be most relevant?

5. Should utility commissioners be elected? Why or why not?

6. How has deregulation of telecommunications and the airlines affected innovation in those industries?

7. Is there a need to regulate the generation of electricity? Explain.

8. How has the growth of cable television affected the need to regulate broadcast television?

four

SOCIAL REGULATION

Social Regulation: Background and Theory

The code of the ancient Babylonian ruler Hammurabi dealt with shoddy products in a simple and forceful way: "If a builder builds a house for a man and does not make its construction firm, and the house which he has built collapses and causes the death of the owner of the house, the builder shall be put to death." Babylonian homes were noted for their sturdy construction.

The previous part considered economic regulation of industry. It focused primarily on government's role in setting prices and controlling entry and exit. But in recent years the scope of regulation has greatly broadened. Today, government regulation extends not only to prices and the number of firms allowed in a market, but also to the safety and quality of goods and services purchased, the accuracy of information provided by sellers, and the human and environmental impacts associated with production. The extension of the hand of government into these areas often is referred to as social regulation.

Social regulation is the topic of the three chapters in this section. In Chapter 16 the need for social regulation is considered. Alternative decision-rules for government involvement also are discussed. The next chapter deals with consumer protection regulation. Finally, Chapter 18 describes and evaluates efforts to protect workers and the environment.

THE EXPANDING SCOPE OF SOCIAL REGULATION

There are several reasons for the recent surge in regulatory activities. Advocates charge that a basic cause has been a growing feeling of manipulation and exploitation of consumers by business. As products have become more complex, as advertising has become more sophisticated, and as business and employment dealings have become more impersonal, the average citizen (at least in the eyes of the average politician) has become less able to cope with his or her economic environment. Another cause is a general change in society's view of the legitimate role of government. Over the last half century, government has encroached more and more into the traditional domain of business. Starting with the New Deal spawned by the Great Depression and gaining momentum from the activist mood of the Vietnam era, the scope of government has steadily increased. The trend may have been arrested by recent moves toward deregulation, but a significant retreat is unlikely.

Probably the strongest forces behind the new wave of social regulation have been specific events that mobilized public demand for change. The thalidomide tragedy of the early 1960s is a prime example. Evidence that the substance was responsible for thousands of birth defects precipitated a drastic strengthening of U.S. drug laws. Certainly the last 20 years have not brought tragedies or revelations any more compelling than in previous times, but the willingness of Congress to act and the ability of the mass media to publicize problems quickly and effectively have caused a more dramatic response to such events.

Finally, the impact of individual crusades should be mentioned. In 1965 a young lawyer named Ralph Nader published *Unsafe at Any Speed,* in which he claimed that General Motors' rear-engined Corvair had a disconcerting tendency to roll while cornering. Nader's book attracted national attention because of its detailed case studies and impressive engineering data. General Motors responded with an intensive attack on the credibility of both Nader and his book, but the damage was done and the Corvair was eventually discontinued.[1] Since that time Nader has established the Center for the Study of Responsive Law and organized his "Nader's Raiders" to continue the quest against unsafe products and working conditions. His efforts have been a major factor in passage of at least five federal laws: the Motor Vehicle Safety Act (1966), the Wholesome Meat Act (1967), the Natural Gas Pipeline Safety Act (1968), the Coal Mine Health and Safety Act (1969), and the Occupational Safety and Health Act (1970). In addition, he and his group have forced changes in the operations of the Federal Trade Commission and other federal agencies. Although many would disagree with the goals and the results of Ralph Nader's efforts, his experience is proof positive that individuals can have a significant influence on public policy.

Whereas the older federal regulatory agencies such as the ICC, FCC, and FPC (now FERC) primarily are concerned with prices, entry, and exit in specific industries, the new agencies charged with social regulation have a much broader scope of operations. Agencies such as the Consumer Product Safety Commission (CPSC), and the Occupational Safety and Health Administration (OSHA), and the Environmental Protection Agency (EPA) have powers that stretch across industry boundaries. The same is true for other agencies such as the Food and Drug Administration (FDA) and the Federal Trade Commission (FTC), which have been given additional powers under recent legislation. At the present time there are over 400 units in 40 different federal government agencies that have some responsibility for protecting consumers, workers, or the environment. At the state level there are hundreds more. The activities of these state and federal agencies can be classified into three broad areas. First, they may be charged with providing the public with improved information and assuring that information coming from the private sector is accurate. Second, some have the right to set standards for products and services, working conditions, or the environment. Finally, certain agencies have the power to prohibit the use or sale of certain products or substances that are deemed to present a substantial risk to safety or health.

The objectives of these regulatory agencies would seem to be relatively noncontroversial. Their general purpose is to protect individuals from situations that might be detrimental to their health or safety or to assist them in evaluating the usefulness of products. Ralph Nader said it this way: "The upshot . . . is simply to hold industry to higher standards of excellence, and I can't see why they should object to that kind of incentive."[2]

The reality is that social regulation is a highly controversial issue. OSHA, for example, probably has been the most frequently criticized regulatory agency in the nation. The other agencies also have their share of critics. Some complain that they do too little, while others argue that they are far too much involved and in the wrong ways. The basic issue is one of individual choice versus government protection. Should citizens be left to make their own decisions with government playing a minor role in

---

[1] Part of the G.M. plan was to hire a private detective to follow Nader to expose dimensions of his personal life that would be embarrassing. Unfortunately for G.M., Nader's idea of a good time was to spend a weekend working in his office and the company ended up paying a $280,000 judgment from a lawsuit brought by Nader. Much of this money was used to finance future crusades.

[2] As quoted in Carson, R. B., *Economic Issues Today* (New York: St. Martin's Press, 1978), p. 40.

providing information, or should government intervene to protect people from their own folly and from the actions of unscrupulous businesspeople?

ROLE OF THE MARKET

Traditional economic theory argues that the characteristics of goods and services are effectively determined by the dollar votes of consumers—consumer sovereignty. As consumers make known by their purchases that they want safer or more durable products, businesses respond to satisfy those preferences. Consumers who desire to protect themselves further against the economic hazards of certain products or situations may be able to purchase insurance to meet their specific objectives.

One of the virtues of markets is that they provide for diversity of consumer preferences. Some consumers may demand extremely safe or very high-quality products, for which they are willing to pay a premium. Others, because of income constraints or different tastes, prefer lower-quality products that are less expensive. For example, one buyer may choose a big-screen television complete with remote tuner and four-year warranty. Another may select a 4-inch black-and-white set. An affluent doctor might buy his Mercedes diesel with air bags and safety bumpers, while the struggling college professor orders his Honda stripped and accepts the increased risk of injury. As long as there is sufficient demand to justify meeting the preferences of different groups of consumers, the market has an incentive to respond with a variety of products and services.

Sometimes consumers encounter dishonest or incompetent individuals in their business dealings. Almost everyone has a horror story to relate about a friend or relative who was victimized by an auto repair shop, a real estate salesperson, or a shaky handed dentist. Defenders of the free market argue that there are corrective forces that tend to weed out shoddy performances. Specifically, as word gets around that a person or establishment is a rip-off joint, consumers in the area begin to take their business to firms that have a better reputation. Travelers who are unable to benefit from word-of-mouth information also have ways of protecting themselves against shysters. They can rely on travel guides that provide information for a price. They can also take their business to operations that are part of regional or national chains. The need to maintain a good reputation causes these chains to police the operations of their franchises. Fast-food establishments are a good example. You may not rate a Big Mac with Mom's home cooking, but at least you can be sure of what you're getting whether you visit the golden arches in Maine or in California.

Market forces also have an impact on health and safety conditions for workers. If employees are considering jobs that involve substantial risk to their health or personal safety, they will require extra compensation to work there. They may ask for higher wages or bargain for various types of protection. Both of these alternatives increase the cost of labor to the firm. The firm may either continue to pay the higher wage rate or take steps to reduce the risk to which its employees are subjected. If the firm chooses to improve working conditions, then the employee's risk is reduced. If the decision is to pay the higher wage rate, then workers are compensated for the risk. One of the virtues of the market is that it allows both employers and employees to reveal and exercise their diverse personal preferences. Workers who are highly adverse to risk will accept lower wages in safer professions, while those who attach a lower cost to the prospect of injury or illness will be paid a higher wage or receive attractive benefits of other sorts. Just as workers are allowed to determine the risk-compensation trade-off that fits their personal preferences, the employer is also able to select the safety-wage premium package that he or she finds most profitable. Hazards that are very costly to eliminate will remain, with workers receiving compensation in the form of higher wages, while easily correctable hazards will be eliminated to make working in the establishment more desirable.

Finally, the market also operates to provide information about the products, services, and employment choices people must make. Each person can make better decisions if she or he has more information. However, the cost of information is not zero. Time and effort must be expended to acquire knowledge. Initial bits of information may be highly useful, but continued search ultimately yields reduced marginal returns. For each person and for each decision there is an optimal amount of information search that should be undertaken. Like other allocation decisions, the search for information should be continued until the marginal cost of the next fact is just equal to the marginal benefit. Obviously, it is impossible to know how useful a piece of information will be until it has been obtained and evaluated. Hence, the decision-rule must be modified in terms of expected or anticipated benefits. That is, search for information until the expected usefulness of the last item is equal to the marginal cost of obtaining it.

There are many sources of information available to consumers. Advertising is an obvious example. Personal examination of goods in the store is another method, as is the evaluation of products already purchased. The recommendation of friends or experts is yet another possibility. In addition, there are organizations that specialize in providing information about product characteristics. Consumer's Union, Consumer Reports, and Underwriter's Laboratory all market information. Workers also have sources of information about employment opportunities. Current and past employees of a firm, employment agencies, and libraries all can provide useful clues.

NEED FOR GOVERNMENT

Advocates of legislation to protect consumers, workers, or the environment typically have serious questions about the ability of market forces to assure proper standards for health, safety, and quality. They argue either that there are imperfections in markets that yield undesirable results or that economic criteria are not broad enough to use as a basis for decision making. The following discussion considers the most common and important justifications for government involvement.

Ignorance

Obtaining Adequate Information   Several private organizations specialize in selling information to consumers. For example, every issue of *Consumer Reports* contains evaluations of dozens of different products. The publisher provides the information for the price of the magazine.[3] But only the original purchaser is required to pay that price. Anyone can go to a library and obtain the same information for nothing. Theoretically, hundreds of people could peruse a single issue without the publisher getting a cent beyond the purchase price of the one copy. The fact that *Consumer Reports* continues to be published is evidence that it is at least marginally profitable, but the public-good nature of information suggests that it may be undersupplied by the market.

The acquisition and evaluation of information can be a very expensive process. It is not uncommon for *Consumer Reports* to conduct extensive tests on the products evaluated. However, once the information has been processed and published, the marginal cost of transmitting it is very small. Additional persons can become informed at very low cost, and those who have already been informed do not have the quality of their knowledge diminished by the existence of new users. In this circumstance the market does not function effectively. Those who produce information are unable to capture the full value of the service they provide. Thus, the amount of information that is forthcoming from market sources is less than is socially optimal. In economic terms, producers maximize profit when the marginal revenue resulting from the provision of an additional unit of information equals the marginal cost. The optimal amount of information from society's perspective involves equating the value of the last unit of information to its total cost. Since producers can't capture the full value of the marginal information unit, the market undersupplies. Hence, government action may be appropriate to provide additional information.

Information costs may be especially high when the use of a product involves the risk of death. One source of information is through the use of a product. As people gain experience, their ability to make good decisions increases. However, use of this "learning by doing" method of acquiring information is not very practical when the choice of a product or occupation causes death or serious injury. A similar problem occurs when it is the cumulative use of a product or the long-term exposure to a substance on a job that represents the hazard. By the time the individual is aware of the risk, the damage has already been done. Again, government regulation may be an acceptable alternative to search.

Even if the market did provide the appropriate amount of information, there is still the problem of the consumer staying informed. For some products change is very rapid. The hand calculator market is a good example. Calculators are purchased relatively infrequently. A consumer may reenter the market when his needs change, when his old model is lost or broken, or perhaps, to make a purchase as a gift. During the interval since his last purchase, he is likely to find that prices and characteristics have changed dramatically. He must retool in order to make an intelligent purchase —his search for information at the time of his original purchase may be nearly useless under current conditions. Although the calculator decision may be one of the more difficult, the consumer is faced with hundreds of decisions about products and services that are increasingly complex. In modern society the number and technical sophistication of the products that are purchased dictates that people will be less familiar with any given part of their world than they would have been in times past.

---

[3]To avoid conflicts, *Consumer Reports* accepts no advertising.

Processing Information   Consumers may have difficulties processing information. The average person simply does not have the background to assess accurately many of the complicated products he uses. The modern automobile, high-technology electronic equipment, and new drugs involve concepts and expertise with which the average person is not comfortable. The sophisticated marketing techniques of firms through the mass media compound the problem. Individuals are bombarded with conflicting information and claims about products. Although the most discerning of people may realize that athletes have no special qualifications to help judge orange juice and cereals, it is more difficult to know whether product comparison experiments reported on television are valid or the result of research chicanery. Inundated with raw data, it is sometimes hard to get out from under the pile to make an informed and logical decision.

Externalities

Externalities are the primary rationale for government action to protect the environment. Costs are an important component in the decision process of the managers of a firm. But the costs used in decision making usually include only actual dollars paid out by the business. Typically, social costs such as air and water pollution are not taken into account. Because these resources are considered to be free goods, the firm has no incentive to conserve on their use. Thus, it may be necessary for government to intervene to force managers to consider all of the costs associated with their actions. Externalities and environmental pollution will be considered in greater detail in Chapter 18.

The externality problem is not limited to business decisions. It also can be used to justify government regulation of consumer decisions. The smoking controversy provides an interesting example. It is increasingly clear that cigarette smoking is correlated with a high incidence of lung cancer. Government publicity campaigns, warnings on labels, and the position of the medical profession have provided consumers with a considerable volume of information to evaluate the risk of smoking. In spite of these efforts, cigarette consumption continues to increase. Presumably, people who make the decision to smoke compare the risks of cancer against the enjoyment they receive from smoking and conclude the latter outweighs the former. If there were no other factors involved, it could be argued that the market, through the vehicle of consumer preferences, had determined the optimal amount of cigarette smoking.

However, in the case of cigarettes the smoker is not the only person affected. Any nonsmoker trapped in a long meeting in a small room with smokers knows the agony of that confinement. The actions of smokers impose significant costs on other people. It has been claimed that inhaling the exhausts of others substantially increases the risk of disease or illness to nonsmokers. Typically, nonsmokers have no way of avoiding the cost that is imposed on them. They must either bear the externality stoically or relocate. If the cost of smoking to nonsmokers was included as part of smokers' decisions, then the optimal amount of smoking would be reduced in comparison to a decision based only on the effects of smoking on smokers. Because there is no market mechanism to force smokers to incorporate the external effects of their actions in their decision making, there are too many people smoking too many cigarettes.

It is not difficult to think of other examples where external effects cause a nonoptimal amount of safety or quality to be selected. The teenager who speeds through a school zone may be capable of evaluating the personal risks involved, but not those of potential victims. Although it is possible to sue for compensation in the event of an accident, it would be rare for an award to provide full compensation to a grieving parent for the loss of a child. Also, the existence of insurance means that the driver is not required to pay the full cost of a judgment. Thus, the cost of an accident is under-estimated by the driver, who assumes a greater amount of risk than is optimal from the point of view of society.

Demand Manipulation

A cornerstone of traditional economic theory is the concept of consumer sovereignty. Firms are assumed to base their production decisions on the revealed preferences of consumers. As purchasing decisions indicate a change in those preferences, firms respond by altering the attributes and amounts of the goods they produce. The role of the firm is considered to be primarily passive. It makes little attempt to alter the preferences of consumers, but reacts rapidly to take advantage of changes. Advertising is viewed as a means of providing information.

Galbraith and others argue that consumer sovereignty has been replaced by producer sovereignty.[4] They contend that large firms effectively manipulate consumer wants. An interesting, but somewhat suspect example from the 1920s involved the tobacco industry:

> George Washington Hill, a manic, boisterous, authoritarian salesman, president of the American Tobacco Company, was an exciting client for many years. Lucky Strikes were his dominating theme. Cigarettes had not yet been proven carcinogenic. Opera stars endorsed Luckies as "kind to your throat" in huge newspaper advertisements. "Reach for a Lucky, instead of a sweet" and other slogans swept the country. Lucky Strikes became the number one cigarette. Mr. Hill wanted more women to smoke Lucky Strikes; research showed that sales to them were down because the green-packaged cigarettes clashed with their costumes. "Change the color of the package," I suggested. Mr. Hill was outraged. I then suggested we try to make green the dominant color of women's fashions. "What will it cost?" he asked. For want of a better figure, I said, "$25,000." He quickly rejoindered, "Spend it." For a year we worked with the New York Infirmary for Women and Mrs. Frank A. Vanderlip, its president, to hold a Green Ball, with tableaux of socialites dressed in green based on paintings of the Malmaison masters in the Luxembourg Museum in Paris. We worked with manufacturers of accessories for dresses and textiles to ensure that gloves, stockings, shoes, and other accessories would also be green. *Harper's Bazaar* and *Vogue* featured green covers of fashions on the date of the Green Ball. Green became fashion's color.[5]

The above is an extreme case of demand manipulation by firms, but it is clear that firms do have an effect on consumer demands. The millions of dollars spent by McDon-

---

[4]This is a basic concept in Galbraith's writings. See, for example, *Economics and the Public Purpose*, Chap. 14.

[5]Bernays, E. L., "Emergence of the Public Relations Counsel: Principles and Recollections," *Business History Revue*, Vol. 45, No. 3 (Autumn 1971), p. 304.

ald's are designed to do more than inform the individual that the local franchise is there with a hot Big Mac. Football players in panty hose, Olympic gold-medal winners sitting down to heaping bowls of Wheaties, and well-tanned young women provocatively clothed on the pages of dozens of magazines can hardly be described as merely informational.

Under the assumption of consumer sovereignty, if automobiles guzzled gas and were unsafe, manufacturers could claim that they were simply responding to the wants of consumers. If children's toys stressed violence or sexuality (look at a Barbie doll sometime), then the onus was on parents for not buying the proper kinds of toys. The producer is innocent. His role is much like Pavlov's dogs responding to stimuli. Unless regulators are assumed to have some superior wisdom, there is no reason why producers should not be allowed to provide consumers with what they want.

However, if the manipulation of wants by producers is admitted, then there may be a case for government intervention. If the plethora of shoddy and unsafe products reflects the sophisticated efforts of producers to shape consumer preferences to the needs of the firm rather than the intrinsic desires of individuals, perhaps there is a need to protect consumers against risks and low-quality products. In this case it may be argued that, although consumers are apparently allowed to choose, in reality, they have already been deprived of the right to make their own decisions by the machinations of producers. Here, the need for government is to protect the individual against the most serious problems created by producer want-manipulation.

Inadequate Insurance

Consumers and employees can avoid unnecessary risk by selecting relatively safe products and by seeking low-hazard employment. Additional economic protection against risk can be obtained by purchasing insurance. Firms are able to provide insurance profitably because most people are risk averse. Suppose that a doctor faces a 1-percent chance of a successful malpractice suit each year and that the estimated cost of a suit is $1 million. Hence, the expected cost of malpractice suits is $10,000 per year. Now assume the doctor has the opportunity to purchase malpractice insurance that will pay the full cost of any suit. If the doctor is risk averse, she will be willing to pay more as an insurance premium than the expected yearly cost of malpractice suits. The reason is fairly clear. She can pay the, say, $11,000 annual premium without much disruption of her normal activities. On the other hand, a $1 million judgment, although unlikely, would wipe her out. The insurance company is able to provide the protection for $11,000 because the premium exceeds the expected cost and because it is able to spread the risks over a large number of customers. This pooling of risk reduces the probability that the firm will be called upon to pay out a large proportion of its resources to meet claims in any given year.

It should be possible to purchase insurance as protection against almost any kind of risk. Indeed, the famous English firm, Lloyd's of London, has specialized in unusual insurance policies. They have issued policies covering athletes' feet, singers' voices, and actresses' bosoms. Unfortunately, Lloyd's is not the typical insurance company, and there is reason to believe that the private insurance market does not provide the level of insurance protection that consumers and employees desire.

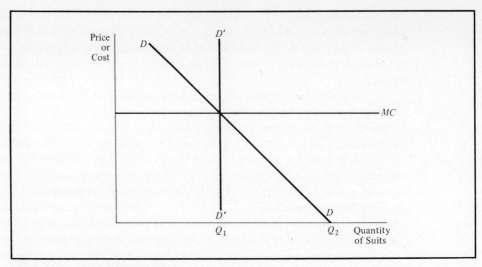

Figure 16.1. Malpractice insurance.

Part of the problem stems from the impact that insurance may have on individual behavior. The physician and her malpractice problem can be used to illustrate this concept. A doctor can be thought of as having a demand for malpractice suits. It is possible to reduce the probability of a malpractice suit almost to zero by getting second opinions, taking more time on procedures, running extra tests, and so forth. These activities have a cost to the doctor in the form of fewer patients that can be seen and reduced patient satisfaction stemming from higher bills. *Ceteris paribus,* the efforts of physicians in avoiding malpractice suits will be inversely related to the cost of such suits.[6] If a successful suit costs the doctor only a few thousand dollars, then less care will be exercised than if an action results in a crippling multimillion-dollar judgment. In Figure 16.1, the curve *DD* depicts an annual demand for malpractice suits that is sensitive to the expected cost of such suits. The demand curve *D'D'* represents a demand curve that is not price sensitive. The price or marginal cost of malpractice suits, *MC,* is assumed constant and indicates the probable cost of a successful suit. For any given type of occurrence, this cost is determined by the willingness of juries to make awards.

Without insurance, a physician would adopt practices expected to result in Q_1 malpractice suits. This is true whether the demand curve is *DD* or *D'D'*. Now suppose that insurance companies will provide malpractice insurance for a total premium equal to the annual expected cost of suits. If the cost per suit is *MC,* then the total premium will be set at $Q_1 \cdot MC$. Notice that the payment of this premium is not tied to the occurrence or nonoccurrence of a suit—the premium must be paid in either case.

For doctors who have purchased malpractice insurance, the effective cost of a

---

[6]Among those things ignored in this analysis are the physician's desires to help patients, his or her reputation, and so on.

malpractice suit is zero.[7] The insurance company takes care of the judgment and the premium is a sunk cost. Now the true nature of the demand curve becomes crucial. The insurance company has set the premium on the assumption that the number of suits it will be required to pay for is Q_1. If the demand curve of physicians is $D'D'$, their behavior will not change once they are insured and the insurance company should be able to make a profit. On the other hand, if malpractice suit demand is sensitive to price, the annual number of malpractice suits will be Q_2. Because the cost of a suit has declined to zero, doctors have less incentive to exercise care than before. Presumably, by being a little less precise they can see more patients and increase their income. For the demand curve DD, one of the results of insurance is a decrease in the quality of medical care and an increase in the number of malpractice suits.

The insurance company faces special problems if DD is the demand curve. They have set the premium to yield a fair return on the assumption that the number of suits will be Q_1. However, once insured, the physician's change in behavior increases the number to Q_2. As a result the premiums no longer cover the costs of suits and the firm cannot operate profitably. The insurance company will continue to offer insurance only if it can raise the premium enough to take in $Q_2 \cdot MC$. But this amount is greater than the expected total cost of malpractice suits $(Q_1 \cdot MC)$ in the absence of insurance. Although risk-adverse consumers are willing to pay premiums greater than the expected cost of the events insured against, there is certainly a limit to this willingness. If that limit is less than the required premium of $Q_2 \cdot MC$, then doctors will choose to bear the risk of judgments from malpractice suits rather than purchase insurance. In this situation there will be no private market for insurance.

The dilemma just described is caused by the natural tendency of people to demand more as the price is reduced. Because insurance has the effect of reducing the price or cost of certain types of behavior to zero, the demand is increased. The problem can arise in many contexts. Workers who have insurance against job-related injuries may be less cautious. Drivers may be less worried about damaging an expensive new car. A business, protected by liability insurance, may devote fewer resources to improving product safety.

Private insurance is least likely to be offered (1) where the quantity demanded at zero price is much greater than the demand at the price the individual would pay in the absence of insurance, (2) where events are nonrandom and it is difficult to spread risks, and (3) where individuals are not highly risk-averse. If any of these conditions are met, there may be a case for government intervention.

Philosophical Reasons

Some supporters of regulation argue that the criteria used by economists to evaluate the need for and effects of regulation are simply too narrow. They contend that it is neither possible nor desirable to put a price on everything. Speaking of job safety, Representative Phillip Burton argued that workers have an "inalienable right to earn

---

[7]There may be a serious effect on the doctor's reputation, but this is neglected to simplify the discussion. The basic conclusion is unchanged by this assumption.

their living free from the ravages of job-caused death, disease, and injury." In his view, bodily integrity is not a commodity appropriate for trade on the market, any more than one's vote or freedom is.[8] Although there is considerable merit in the idea that a person's life is intrinsically different than a piece of machinery, it will be shown later in the chapter that life really is not priceless. Embedded in every policy dealing with safety or health is an implicit value of the individual's life and well-being.

Another basis for government intervention involves equity considerations. Typically, those who are forced to purchase lower-priced, riskier products; accept lower-quality health care; and work under significant hazards are the poor, the unskilled, and members of minority groups. Although their choices may represent a rational selection for their circumstance, there should be little comfort in their ability to make the best of a very bad situation. A strong motive behind many government programs designed to improve the lot of consumers and employees has been the desire to provide special helps for disadvantaged groups.

Finally, although rarely stated explicitly, there is often an element of paternalism embedded in attempts to improve health, safety, and quality. Some, by virtue of education, political success, or economic means, claim to know better what people should have than do the people themselves. Government intervention is a mechanism for imposing the values of the "wise" on producers, employees, and consumers.

DECISION-RULES FOR GOVERNMENT INVOLVEMENT

The previous section discussed possible justifications for social regulation. This section goes one step further and evaluates alternative decision-rules for government action. Four rules are considered. They are (1) no-risk society, (2) lowest feasible risk level, (3) benefit-cost analysis, and (4) cost-effectiveness.

No-Risk Society

Suppose that government action could bring about a no-risk society by eliminating all health, safety, and quality problems. Consumers would never have to worry about shoddy or dangerous products. Workers could go about their jobs knowing that there was no possibility of being injured or exposed to dangerous substances. The environment would forever remain unsullied by pollution.

Total elimination of risk is a noble, but not a very practical goal. Although many health, safety, and quality concerns can be eliminated at nominal cost, there are other problems that would be prohibitively expensive to correct. For example, chlorination is an effective and relatively inexpensive technique for purifying water. Still, there are illnesses each year caused by contamination of water supplies. Preventing all such illnesses would require safeguards that are much too costly for the typical municipality. Thus, residents continue to be exposed to some level of risk from their drinking water.

The Environmental Protection Agency has taken a similar position in dealing

---

[8]As quoted in Nichols, A. L., and Zeckhauser, R., "Government Comes to the Workplace: an Assessment of OSHA," *Public Interest* (Fall 1977), p. 46.

with atmospheric pollution. With respect to the emission of cancer-causing substances into the air, the agency has recognized that:

> A requirement that the risk from atmospheric carcinogen emissions be reduced to zero would produce massive social dislocations, given the pervasiveness of at least minimal levels of carcinogenic emissions in key American industries. Since few such industries would soon operate in compliance with zero-emission standards, closure would be the only legal alternative. Among the important activities affected would be the generation of electricity from either coal-burning or nuclear energy; the manufacturing of steel; the mining, smelting, or refining of virtually any mineral (e.g., copper, iron, lead, zinc, and limestone); the manufacture of synthetic organic chemicals; and the refining, storage, or dispensing of any petroleum product.[9]

The vast majority of regulatory activities reflect the idea that economic factors must be considered in setting health, safety, or quality standards. However, some forms of social regulation have imposed an absolute standard that requires the elimination of all risk. The so-called Delaney Clause is the most notorious example. This amendment to the Food, Drug, and Cosmetic Act specifies that "no additive shall be deemed to be safe . . . if it is found, after tests which are appropriate for the evaluation of the safety of food additives, to induce cancer in man or animal."

The Delaney Clause sets a no-risk standard. No substance that is added during the growing, processing, or packaging of food will be permitted if there is evidence that it causes cancer in man or beast. There is no provision for evaluating the amount of risk or the impact of prohibiting the use of the substance. Essentially, the language of the legislation implies that no measurable risk is too small and no impact of removal is too great. The saccharin controversy mentioned in Chapter 1 is a consequence of the Delaney Clause. Because there was evidence that the substance caused cancer in test animals, the Food and Drug Administration prepared to ban saccharin from the marketplace. Only a special exemption granted by Congress prevented the FDA from carrying out its intentions. This exemption allowed the addition of saccharin to food products, but required a label indicating the dangers of its use.

Theoretically, the Delaney Clause could become more restrictive with advances in research technology. Scientific instruments now have the capability of detecting concentrations as small as one part in a billion. Experiments have been devised that are much more sophisticated in isolating cancer-causing substances. Thus, the absolute standard specified by the Delaney Clause represents a wider net than it did a few years ago. Many additives may now qualify for which the associated risks are extremely low. To ban them all would not necessarily be in the public interest.

While bound by the conditions of the Delaney Clause, the FDA's solution has been to define some risk levels as zero for regulatory purposes. Specifically, if an additive is estimated to cause less than one case of cancer per million lifetimes, the risk is considered negligible. The Environmental Protection Agency uses a similar procedure, but has set the standard of negligible risk at one cancer in 100,000 lifetimes.

[9]"National Emission Standards for Identifying, Assessing, and Regulating Airborne Substances Posing a Risk of Cancer," *Federal Register,* Vol. 42 (Oct. 10, 1979), pp. 58, 660.

Lowest Feasible Risk Level

In some cases the decision-rule used by regulatory bodies has been to set standards that reduce risks to their *lowest feasible level*. Generally, the interpretation of the term *feasible* is based on technological and financial considerations. That is, given the existing technology for risk reduction, the objective is to reduce risk to the lowest level that is consistent with the survival of the businesses involved.

By recognizing that serious problems can be caused by business failures, this approach does give some consideration to the economic impact of regulatory actions. However, it is deficient in several respects. First, determining the lowest feasible level is dependent on the regulator's ability to assess the overall financial condition of an industry. This is a difficult task at best, but it is further complicated by variations in the financial impact on individual firms within the industry. For example, installing pollution-control equipment in a plant during construction usually is much less expensive than retrofitting an existing plant. Thus, a standard that could be met by a firm with a new plant might be ruinous to a firm using older production facilities. Second, there is no consideration of the optimal level of risk reduction. In a profitable industry, the costs imposed by the standard might far exceed the benefits. For a struggling industry, a standard based on feasibility might do little to correct a serious problem.

Benefit-Cost Analysis

Many of the benefits of social regulation can be obtained only at the expense of higher prices and restricted choice of goods and services. Consider the case of DES, a growth stimulant for steers. Tests showed that this substance could cause cancer in humans. However, its use was tolerated as long as no residuals could be detected in edible beef. But by the mid-1970s, sophisticated instruments became available that could detect minute amounts of DES, and the substance was banned. One effect was an increase in beef prices—perhaps by as much as 10 percent. On the benefit side, the banning of DES was estimated to reduce the incidence of cancer by considerably less than one case per year.

Is society better off without DES? One way of answering this question is to compare the benefits of cancer prevention with the increased cost of beef. This approach is called benefit-cost analysis. Focusing on the efficient allocation of resources, it is based on the premise that benefits and costs can be quantified in terms of common units —usually dollars. With respect to social regulation, benefit-cost analysis can be used to determine if government involvement is warranted and the proper extent of government action. The prescriptions are that government should intervene only when the total benefits to be realized are greater than the total costs imposed and that the extent of government action should not go beyond the point where marginal benefits equal marginal costs.

Automobile Safety: An Example of Benefit-Cost Analysis   Consider an automobile model that has multiple engineering defects which have been determined to pose a potential hazard to those who ride in the car. Assume that the car is no longer being sold by the manufacturer, but that accidents involving vehicles already on the road are expected to cause an average of 10 deaths per year. This death total can be reduced if the auto maker recalls the cars and corrects at least some of the defects. The annualized costs of reducing deaths to various levels are shown in Table 16.1. The table indicates an increasing marginal cost of death prevention. The annualized cost of moving from ten to nine deaths per year is $200,000, but the marginal cost of reducing the number of deaths each year from one to zero is $3,000,000 and the total annual cost of getting to the zero death level is $11,000,000. This reflects the fact that some defects are easily corrected, while fixing others may require expensive modifications to the vehicle.

The National Highway Traffic Safety Administration (NHTSA) is the federal government agency charged with regulating automobile safety. This agency has the power to force recalls and repairs of defective vehicles. Assume that the NHTSA makes its decisions on the basis of benefit-cost analysis (an assumption that is not strictly true). Further suppose that policy makers at the agency have set the value of saving a life at $800,000 (assessing the value of life is considered later in this section).

By examining marginal benefits and marginal costs it is now possible to formulate a policy with respect to the automobile in question. The marginal cost of saving the first life is $200,000. Thus, there is a net benefit involved in requiring the manufacturer to take at least some action. On the other hand, the marginal cost of reducing the annual death total from one to zero is $3,000,000. This amount is greater than the assigned value of $800,000 for saving a life. Hence, benefit-cost analysis would suggest that the NHTSA agency not go that far in mandating repairs.

Proceeding until marginal benefits equal marginal costs would dictate that sufficient repairs be required to reduce the number of lives lost to six. Beyond that point, marginal costs exceed marginal benefits. Note also that in reducing annual loss of life to six, the total benefit of $3,200,000 is greater than the total cost of $2,000,000. Thus, benefit-cost analysis suggests that there is a net benefit associated with the recall action.

The Value of Life   Critics of benefit-cost analysis argue that it is not possible to assign a dollar value to human life. They are undoubtedly right if they mean that there is no consensus as to what that valuation should be. However, they err if they suggest that

Table 16.1   ANNUALIZED MARGINAL COST OF
FIXING AUTOMOBILE SAFETY DEFECTS

Deaths per year	Annual marginal cost of death prevention	Value of one life saved
10	$ 0	
9	200,000	$ 800,000
8	400,000	800,000
7	600,000	800,000
6	800,000	800,000
5	1,000,000	800,000
4	1,200,000	800,000
3	1,400,000	800,000
2	1,600,000	800,000
1	1,800,000	800,000
0	2,000,000	800,000

such valuations can be avoided. Every decision involving health or safety implicitly makes an assumption about the valuation of human misfortune.

As an example, consider the 55-mile-per-hour speed limit. A main argument of its proponents is that it saves lives. Supporters judge the saving of those lives (together with fuel savings) as being more important than the loss of time resulting from slower travel. Advocates of increasing the speed limit (to the extent that they evaluate the data in the same way) implicitly attach a greater value to the time savings than they do to the reduction in fatalities.

Proponents of the lower speed limit put a high value on saving lives, but this does not imply that they view life as priceless. If additional lives can be saved by limiting driving speed to 55 miles per hour, then more lives would probably be spared by reducing the limit to forty, thirty, or twenty miles per hour. Actually, if the only goal is to reduce traffic deaths, the optimal policy would be a nationwide ban on automobile driving. As long as people are allowed to drive cars, some are going to be killed. Why is there no clamor for such drastically reduced speed limits? Primarily because it is recognized that a twenty- or thirty-mile-per-hour limit would cripple the nation's distribution system, greatly increase the cost of goods, make commuting by car virtually impossible, and spoil almost everyone's recreation. The cost of these events is deemed to be too great. Society is willing to accept a certain number of injuries and deaths to gain the benefits of a reasonable driving speed. In choosing a nonzero speed limit, a value has implicitly been placed on human life.

The same is true for hundreds of other activities. Miners would not be allowed in coal mines if society really placed an infinite price on their lives. Amusement parks would not be permitted to operate roller coasters. DelMonte and S&W would not be allowed to sell canned food. Children would be kept off bicycles. The question is not, "Can a value be put on human life or suffering." Every policy or action of society involves some implicit valuation. The question is whether that value is acceptable and whether it is consistently used as a basis for resource allocation decisions.

Several approaches have been used for assigning a dollar value to life. In liability suits involving death or disability, awards often are based on the discounted value of future earnings. Some researchers have suggested using data on how much people are willing to pay for accidental death or injury insurance. But the most commonly used research technique is based on workers' "willingness to pay" for safety as revealed by their employment decisions.

This method is best illustrated using a simple example. In order to induce people to work at risky jobs, employers must pay higher wages. These wage premiums compensate the workers for the greater chance of injury or death that they bear in comparison to working at other jobs. Studies of the magnitude of risk differentials are reviewed in the next chapter. Assume for now that for every 0.1-percent increase in the probability of death, workers demand $500 annually in additional wages. This means that the extra wages paid by the employer amount to $500,000 for every job-related death. Thus, in a statistical sense, the value of life is estimated to be $500,000.

A wide range of estimates have been generated using this approach. One of the problems has been the types of workers surveyed. Some studies have concentrated on those in high-risk jobs. In such studies, the estimated value of life has been as low as $200,000. Studies using a random sample of workers have produced estimates as high as $10,000,000. There is an explanation for this discrepency. Workers in high-risk jobs are likely to be less risk averse than the general population of workers. Thus, they require lower wage premiums. The result is a lower calculated value of life for such workers.

After a thorough review of existing studies, Viscusi recommends that:

> For purposes of policy evaluation, . . . estimates of $500,000 seem most reasonable for workers in high-risk jobs (about $\frac{1}{1,000}$ annually). For workers facing less severe risks (about $\frac{1}{10,000}$ annually), an estimate of $2,000,000 appears more reasonable. [10]

Benefits and Individual Behavior   Earlier in the chapter, inadequate private insurance was cited as a reason for government intervention. The difficulty was that insurance lowers the price of certain activities and thus encourages the insured to "consume" more of that activity.

A similar problem can complicate the valuation of benefits in benefit-cost analysis. Government regulation may change the relative costs of certain actions. These changes can cause individuals to behave differently than they did before government intervention. One consequence is that the estimate of benefits may, ex post, not prove to have been very accurate.

Auto safety equipment is an interesting example. Since 1968 the NHTSA has required special safety equipment on new automobiles. Among the initial requirements were seat belts, energy-absorbing steering columns, penetration-resistant windshields, dual braking systems, and padded instrument panels. All of this equipment was intended to reduce traffic injuries and fatalities. Estimates based on field studies and accident data indicated that the 1968 NHTSA standards would reduce the occupant death rate substantially. These estimates were based on technological considerations alone. That is, they took the probability of an accident as given and assessed how the probability of surviving the accident was affected by safety equipment.

Peltzman has argued that technological assessments greatly overestimate the benefits of mandated auto safety equipment, because they fail to take account of changes in driving behavior. [11] He points out that the typical driver may be thought of as facing a choice involving the probability of death or injury from accident and what Peltzman refers to as "driving intensity." The latter involves more speed, thrills, and so on, and requires the sacrifice of some safety. Each driver makes a choice of intensity versus safety, depending on his or her personal values. Those who put a premium on excitement will select a safety-intensity mix quite different than the timid souls who hug the right-hand lane. Figure 16.2 depicts this choice. The ray OA represents possible trade-offs between driving intensity and probability of death to the driver. The positive slope of OA implies that increased driving intensity is associated with a higher probability of death. Assume that, with no safety equipment required on automobiles, a particular individual chooses the safety-intensity combination represented by point C.

Now assume that the government requires automobiles to be made safer by installing various types of safety equipment. This decree changes the safety-intensity

---

[10]Viscusi, W. K., *Risk by Choice* (Cambridge: Harvard University Press, 1983), p. 106.
[11]Peltzman, S., "The Effects of Automobile Safety Regulation," *Journal of Political Economy,* Vol. 83, No. 4 (July–Aug. 1975), pp. 667–725.

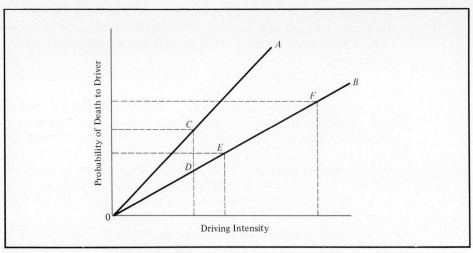

Figure 16.2. Safety-intensity trade-off.

trade-off. With seat belts, safety windshields, and so on, the probability of death is reduced for any given level of driving intensity. The new trade-off is shown by the ray *OB* in Figure 16.2. The vertical distance *CD* represents the effect of the safety requirements at the initially chosen level of driving intensity. It corresponds roughly to the technical estimates previously mentioned. Notice, however, that the choice of *C* as the optimal safety-intensity trade-off was based on the driver's evaluation of the excitement of fast driving in comparison to the expected probability of death. With safer autos, the probability of death has been reduced, and hence, reckless driving becomes less costly. It would be expected that the new safety-intensity choice would involve more speed and thrills. Suppose the new selection is point *E*. The effect of the safety regulations is now the vertical distance between *C* and *E*—a smaller safety gain than is predicted by technological studies. Indeed, it is possible that the demand for driving intensity is so elastic that the driver of the safer car will select point *F,* which actually results in a higher probability of death than before the government got involved. In this case the safety standards make no positive contribution, but simply impose a cost on the purchaser of the car in the form of higher prices for the mandated equipment.

It is unlikely that government-mandated auto safety equipment would actually cause an increase in driver deaths, but there are other undesirable possibilities. Although the probability of driver death is likely to decrease, greater driving intensity may increase the total number of accidents. There may be an increase in property damage and injuries. It is also possible that pedestrian deaths may jump as drivers increase their driving intensity. Peltzman tested these hypotheses using U.S. data before and after the imposition of auto safety standards by the NHTSA. Although his data are crude, the results are generally consistent with the above hypotheses and raise questions about the efficacy of mandated auto safety equipment. Peltzman found that mandated safety equipment reduced driver deaths much less than technological studies would have predicted. He also found evidence that safety standards had shifted the burden of accidents from drivers to pedestrians, and that increases in property damage and total accidents had resulted.

Cost-Effectiveness

Cost-effectiveness is a decision-rule that avoids the need to attach a dollar value to both the benefits and costs of a policy option. It can be thought of as solving a constrained optimization problem. When cost is the constraint, the goal is to obtain the maximum benefit for a given number of dollars. If a fixed level or amount of benefit has been specified, then the objective is to minimize the cost of achieving the benefit level. In either case, the solution to the problem is essentially the same. Resources should be allocated among various activities such that the extra benefit per dollar spent is equal for all activities.

Automobile Safety Revisited: An Example of Cost-Effectiveness   The defective automobile example discussed earlier in the chapter can be used to illustrate the concept of cost-effective resource allocation. Suppose that the NHTSA comes up with the novel idea of reducing the required repairs if the manufacturer of a defective vehicle will agree to spend money to improve highway safety in other ways. For example, the firm might hire people to drive drunks home from bars. Dollars could be spent on this program in lieu of repairing some of the problems with the company's automobile. Assume that the NHTSA has estimated the marginal cost of saving lives using this "drunk-chauffeur" concept and that the numbers are as shown in Table 16.2. As before, the table implies an increasing marginal cost of saving lives. This might reflect the fact that some drunks are much easier to assist than others. The costs of saving lives by repair of the defective automobile also are shown in the table.

Under this hypothetical proposal, the objective of the NHTSA is to assure that the auto manufacturer allocates its resources between the two life-saving schemes in a cost-effective manner. One approach would be to specify a reduction in lives and let the firm determine the amount and distribution of dollars to be spent. Suppose that the

Table 16.2   ANNUALIZED MARGINAL COST OF TWO METHODS OF SAVING LIVES

Reduction in deaths per year	Annual marginal cost of death prevention	
	Drunk-chauffeur	Automobile repair
1	$ 100,000	$ 200,000
2	200,000	400,000
3	300,000	600,000
4	400,000	800,000
5	500,000	1,000,000
6	600,000	1,200,000
7	700,000	1,400,000
8	800,000	1,600,000
9	900,000	1,800,000
10	1,000,000	2,000,000

company is required to take action that will result in an annual saving of six lives. Table 16.2 indicates that, with an annual cost of $100,000, the chauffeur program is the most effective way of saving the first life. The best strategy for saving the second and third lives involves spending $200,000 for each alternative. The chauffeur program is the least cost option for life number four. Finally, the last two lives can most efficiently be saved by the expenditure of $400,000 on the next level of repairs and another $400,000 on getting drunks safely home from bars. Note that, at the margin, the benefit per dollar spent is equal for each life-saving option.

Under this scheme, action by the NHTSA saves six lives each year and the annual cost to the auto manufacturer is $1,600,000. In contrast, mandating repairs would have required an annual total expenditure of $4,200,000. Using only the chauffeur program would have cost $2,100,000.

An alternative method would be to stipulate the total number of dollars to be spent and direct the firm to maximize the number of lives saved. Suppose that the company is required to spend a total of $3,300,000 each year. By repeatedly selecting the lowest-cost option for saving an additional life, a total of nine highway deaths can be prevented. Again, the cost-effective solution requires that the benefit per dollar spent be equal for each alternative. The marginal cost of saving the sixth life with the drunk-chauffeur program is the same $600,000 that is necessary to save the third life by repairing a defect in the vehicle. Using Table 16.2, it can easily be shown that this is the most effective means of spending $3,300,000.

Estimates of the Cost of Life-Saving Options   Some government agencies use cost-effectiveness as a tool in decision making, but there is no evidence that overall government regulatory efforts are guided by the principle. Some policies require the expenditure of millions of dollars per life saved, while other options that could save lives at a much lower cost are ignored. Table 16.3 provides estimates of the cost-effectiveness of various alternatives. It shows a huge variation in the benefit per dollar spent. For

Table 16.3   COST PER LIFE SAVED OF VARIOUS LIFE-SAVING OPTIONS

Life-saving option	Cost per life saved
Immunization programs in less-developed countries	$ 100
Mandatory seat belt usage	500
Food to less-developed countries	5,000
Mobile intensive care units in large cities	12,000
Pap tests	45,000
Smoke alarms	60,000
Breakaway signs on highways	100,000
Air bags	300,000
Removal of radium from drinking water	2,500,000
Emission of radioiodine from nuclear reactors	100,000,000

Source: Cohen, B. L., "How Much Should We Spend to Save a Life," *Public Utilities Fortnightly* (November 19, 1981), pp. 22–25.

example, the Nuclear Regulatory Commission has set standards for emission of a highly dangerous substance, radioiodine, from nuclear reactors. One hundred million dollars is the estimated cost of each death prevented. In contrast, an immunization program in Indonesia has been implemented at a cost of $100 per life saved.

The failure of government to make policy decisions in a more cost-effective manner can be at least partially explained by political considerations. While there is broad popular support for mandating high levels of safety for nuclear reactors, seat belts and pap tests are viewed as matters of personal choice. Although they can save lives at low cost, a government policy requiring their use would be very unpopular.

Problems with the Cost-Effectiveness Decision-Rule   The cost-effectiveness standard avoids the necessity of assigning dollar values to benefits, but there still are problems with its use. One is the difficulty of estimating costs. Often, a new technology is to be used for which there is no good cost data. Where existing techniques are involved, much of the cost information may have to be obtained from the firms involved. If the companies oppose the proposed regulation, they may be able to prevent its implementation by overstating costs.

Another problem is determining the appropriate goal. As mentioned earlier, the resource allocation problem may be stated in terms of maximizing benefits subject to a cost constraint or minimizing cost subject to a benefit constraint. But what level of costs or benefits should be specified? When has enough money been spent and how many lives should a policy try to save? Without a method of comparing benefits and costs, any decision must be essentially arbitrary.

SUMMARY
The Expanding Scope of Social Regulation

In recent years, government has become much more involved in social regulation. Specific events, individual and group crusades, and general public discontent have fueled this expansion of regulatory activity.

Role of the Market

Traditional economic theory suggests that characteristics of goods and services are largely determined by the dollar votes of consumers. Hence, the presence of low-quality products reflects consumer preferences. Similarly, dangerous occupations may exist because some workers are willing to assume job-related risks in return for higher wages.

Need for Government

Ignorance   The public-good nature of information dissemination may cause markets to undersupply data on product and employment characteristics. Even when adequate information is available, rapid changes in technology and the complex nature of many choices can cause decision making to be difficult.

Externalities   Producer and consumer decisions sometimes impose costs or benefits on other people. Because these decisions are often made without taking into account the associated externalities, too many or too few resources may be allocated to an activity.

Demand Manipulation   Galbraith and others argue that consumer wants are manipulated by advertising and other marketing techniques. They contend that consumer demands do not accurately reflect the preferences of individuals.

Inadequate Insurance   Individuals can protect themselves against risk by purchasing insurance. However, insurance has the effect of reducing the cost and increasing the demand for risky activities. In some cases, the result may be that private firms cannot profitably offer insurance.

Philosophical Reasons   Some argue that health and safety are not appropriate commodities to be traded in markets. They also contend that the poor usually bear a disproportionate share of the risks of shoddy products and unsafe working conditions.

Decision-Rules for Government Involvement

No-Risk Society   One approach to social regulation is for the government to mandate the total elimination of certain risks, regardless of the cost. The Delaney Clause, which prohibits the use of food additives that cause cancer, is an example.

Lowest Risk Feasible Level   Another decision-rule is to require that risks be reduced to their lowest feasible level. Usually, this level is determined by considering the available technology and the financial impact on the firms involved.

Benefit-Cost Analysis   Efficient allocation of resources requires that regulatory activities should not proceed beyond the point where the marginal cost exceeds the marginal benefit. One difficulty in using benefit-cost analysis is assigning a dollar value to preventing injuries and death. Value of life estimates range from $200,000 to several million dollars.

A second problem with benefit-cost analysis is that users of safer products or workers in less risky job situations may exercise less care than before. This can cause the actual benefits of safety improvements to be less than estimated.

Cost-Effectiveness   The cost-effectiveness decision-rule avoids the necessity of putting a dollar value on preventing injuries or deaths. It specifies that resources should be allocated such that their marginal benefit in different uses is equal. In practice, government regulatory activities do not reflect this principle. Many options for saving lives at low cost are ignored, while other regulations cost millions of dollars per life saved.

DISCUSSION QUESTIONS

1. Would consumer groups be more effective in lobbying for price limitations or quality standards? Why?

2. Are workers able to assess risks accurately in bargaining for wage premiums? What types of risks would be most difficult to evaluate?

3. If all producers have equal opportunities to advertise their products, is it still possible for firms to manipulate consumer wants?

4. Should firms actually be required to meet minimum quality standards or just required to indicate plainly when the standards are not met? Explain.

5. How do deductible clauses in insurance policies reduce the problem of under-provision of insurance?

6. If studies estimate that the value of life in risky occupations is about $500,000, then why are mining companies willing to spend millions of dollars to save the life of a trapped worker?

7. Is the discounted value of future earnings a good measure of the value of life? Why or why not?

8. Table 16.3 shows that the cost of saving a life in less-developed countries can be relatively low. Why aren't more resources of nations such as the United States devoted to such purposes?

chapter 17

Social Regulation: Consumer Goods and Services

If I knew for a certainty that a man was coming to my house with the conscious design of doing me good, I should run for my life.

Henry David Thoreau

The old adage that the consumer is king is not just sexist, it is also a highly debatable proposition. Too often, consumers are victimized by unsafe products, misleading advertising, or incompetent practitioners. In this chapter, institutions and procedures used in the United States for protecting the consumer are discussed. Topics include efforts by occupational licensing boards to assure competent and ethical practices in specific professions; activities of the Food and Drug Administration and the Consumer Product Safety Commission to upgrade product safety; and the role of the Federal Trade Commission in regulating deceptive advertising, labeling, and packaging.

PROFESSIONAL COMPETENCY: OCCUPATIONAL LICENSING
Background

In Illinois a would-be blacksmith can be fined or put in jail for shoeing a horse without first having obtained a license. Employment restrictions of this type are not uncommon in the United States. In each of the 50 states there are boards empowered to establish and enforce standards of professional competency for specific professions. Twenty-three states license midwives, 19 license bug exterminators, and 13 license well-diggers. There are states that require licenses for threshing-machine operators, scrap-tobacco dealers, egg graders, guide-dog trainers, yacht salesmen, tree surgeons, tattoo artists, tile layers, potato growers, and lightning-rod salesmen. Since 1952 the number of occupations licensed in one or more states has increased from 70 to 500.

Ostensibly, the need for licensing stems from the difficulty faced by consumers in differentiating qualified and competent practitioners from quacks and charlatans. The case for regulation is particularly strong when a service is so technical as to render the average person unable to make an a priori judgment or when the consumer's decision making is hindered because the service is used infrequently. Neurosurgeons and heart specialists would fit both of these criteria. The need for licensing is further strengthened if there is considerable variation in the quality of service offered by the members of a profession and if variations in service quality are of great importance. Again, medical care is a good example. Hundreds who could have been treated by a competent doctor are injured or killed by their reliance on miracle remedies of "healers." Potential externalities are another basis for licensing. Conceivably, an ignorant layperson could start an epidemic by inappropriate or careless use of dangerous drugs. The cost would be borne, not only by the willing patient, but also by unsuspecting third parties.

In most states the power to regulate individual professions is granted by the legislature to state boards. Usually, these boards consist primarily of members of the profession to be regulated. Thus, the professions are often in the enviable position of being able to set and enforce their own standards and procedures. Specific rule-making authority varies from profession to profession and from state to state. Some boards may

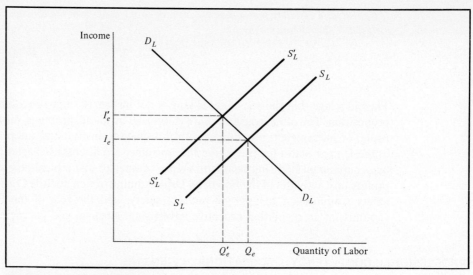

Figure 17.1. Entry restrictions.

be largely advisory, while others are granted almost complete power to establish standards of practice and ethics. The right to set minimum standards for entry into the profession is a common privilege granted to these boards. These entry standards may include specific educational background, examinations to demonstrate competency, proof of good character, demonstration of financial responsibility, and any number of other requirements. Sometimes the relationship between the service to be performed and the criteria for obtaining the license is not obvious. In the past, there were states where a person could not fill a drug prescription, tune a piano, or spay a dog without that person certifying that he or she was not a communist.[1]

Evaluation

Occupational licensing may confer benefits on consumers by protecting them from unscrupulous and incompetent practitioners. However, there may be substantial costs associated with licensing. If the standards imposed by licensing boards make it more costly for an individual to enter an occupation, then the supply of labor in the field will be reduced and the cost of the service will increase. This result is shown in Figure 17.1. The decision to work in an occupation depends on the expected returns from the job in relation to the costs of entry, such as obtaining education and purchasing equipment. The supply curve shown in Figure 17.1 indicates the number of individuals who will enter the occupation at different income levels. As the expected income increases, more people judge that the returns from employment in the field justify the costs of entry. The equilibrium income and quantity are determined by the interaction of supply and demand.

[1]Gellhorn, W., *Individual Freedom and Government Restraints* (Baton Rouge: Louisiana State University Press, 1956), pp. 129–130.

Now assume that a licensing board requires that significantly higher standards be met by prospective entrants into the occupation. A college degree might be required where only two years of college were necessary before. The examination necessary to obtain a license could be made more difficult or graded more rigorously. Periods of apprenticeship might be lengthened. All of these changes have the effect of increasing the cost of entry into the occupation. Some individuals who previously assessed the expected returns as sufficient to justify the costs of entry will now conclude that the increased costs are too great. As a result, the supply curve shifts to the left as shown by the curve $S_L'S_L'$ in Figure 17.1. At equilibrium there are fewer people in the occupation and expected income is greater. Those who are in the field benefit because they are better paid. On the other hand, consumers pay a higher price for a reduced volume of services.

Empirical evidence supports the conclusion that strict licensing standards increase compensation to members of an occupation. One study investigated the impact of licensing requirements on clinical laboratory personnel.[2] Members of this occupation perform laboratory tests in hospitals and clinics. There are three main types of non-supervisory personnel who work in these laboratories—technologists, technicians, and aides. Technologists are the most highly skilled. Technicians are somewhat less trained, but are relatively good substitutes for technologists. Aides are used to perform routine tasks under close supervision. In some states the technician category is not recognized. Without a college degree and formal training at the technologist level, no one is permitted to work above the level of aide. By eliminating the technician classification, the number of persons allowed to do more than routine operations is reduced. Hospitals and clinics are forced to substitute the more highly qualified technologists for technicians. It would be expected that the wages of technologists should be higher in such states. The data are consistent with this view and indicate that restrictive entry requirements increased the wages of technologists by over 16 percent.

Another cost of occupational licensing is reduced geographic mobility. In a free market, workers tend to leave locations with low labor demand and migrate toward fast-growing areas where incomes are highest. Over time, this movement has the effect of reducing income differentials between regions. But licensing can perpetuate these differentials by creating barriers that restrict movement between states. For example, in a majority of states, regulatory authorities will not accept a license obtained by a dentist practicing in another state. Consequently, dentists seeking to work in states without reciprocity agreements must pass an examination and meet local standards regardless of their previous experience. These requirements limit the interstate mobility of dentists.

Kleiner, Gay, and Greene tested the hypothesis that licensing represents a significant barrier to occupational mobility.[3] Focusing on 14 occupations licensed in all states, they derived an index of restrictiveness for each occupation. They found that interstate mobility was inversely related to licensing barriers. For example, only three

[2]White, W. D., "The Impact of Occupational Licensure of Clinical Laboratory Personnel," *The Journal of Human Resources*, Vol. 13, No. 1 (Winter 1978), pp. 91–102.
[3]Kleiner, M. M., Gay, R. S., and Greene, K, "Licensing, Migration and Earnings: Some Empirical Insights," *Policy Studies Review* (February 1982), pp. 510–522.

states had unrestricted reciprocity for barbering. Significantly, barbers had the lowest interstate migration rate of the 14 occupations studied. Mobility also was especially low for dentists and optometrists.

In addition, Kleiner, Gay, and Greene evaluated the effect of licensing on earnings. They estimated that incomes of persons in licensed occupations would be 7 to 18 percent lower if all states followed a practice of unrestricted reciprocity.

Some increase in the price of a service might be justified as payment for the improved consumer protection that results from licensing requirements. However, it is not always true that licensing guarantees a better quality of service. A Federal Trade Commission study focused on the fact that television repairpersons were licensed in Louisiana, but not in the District of Columbia. The report found the incidence of poor service was about equal, but that repair prices were 20 percent higher in Louisiana.[4]

Occasionally, entry standards seem to be much higher than needed to protect consumers. Barbering in Arizona is a case in point. Aspiring barbers in that state must complete 1250 hours of instruction at a certified barber college. This total is 50 hours more than is required at most law schools. On finishing school, an 18-month apprenticeship is required before the candidate is eligible to take the state's qualifying examination. Failing the examination means another six months of apprenticeship before another attempt can be made.

Clearly, licensing can be a potent tool for restricting entry and driving up compensation in an occupation. Thus, it is not surprising the members of a profession usually are very active in the licensing process. Friedman and Stigler argue that the pressure to set minimum standards for entry almost always has come from the practitioners of an occupation and not from consumers in need of protection.[5] The reason is easy to understand. Consumers are involved in the evaluation and purchase of thousands of goods and services. The gains of protection from shoddy or dishonest service to any one consumer are relatively small. In contrast, the advantages to the members of an occupation of being able to restrict entry may be substantial. Thus, it is the practitioners who exert the political pressure for licensing.

Another cost of occupational licensing is restricted consumer choice. Consumers who can afford to pay the higher prices may get a better quality of service because of licensing provisions, but others may be forced to forego the service because of its high cost. Consider the licensing of doctors. Ostensibly, there should be no argument about the desirability of requiring minimum qualifications for doctors and health care. The services provided by physicians and hospitals simply are too important to be left to unqualified individuals. It is possible, however, that standards may be so strict as to expose consumers to greater risk than if less restrictive provisions were imposed.

In most states there are many medical services that only a licensed physician is allowed to provide. Although some of these services could be provided equally well by nurses or paramedics, the law prevents them from doing so. By restricting the supply of medical care, the price is driven up. Although the demand for medical care is

---

[4]Federal Trade Commission, *Regulation of the Television Repair Industry,* Staff Report (1978).

[5]See Friedman, M., *Capitalism and Freedom* (Chicago: University of Chicago Press, 1962), p. 143 and Stigler, G., "Theory of Regulation," *Bell Journal of Management Science* (Spring 1971), pp. 3–21.

relatively inelastic, there is some sensitivity to price. Cuts that should be stitched can be bandaged and allowed to heal even though they leave unsightly scars. Pain can be endured by resorting to a heavy dose of aspirin or other (stronger) drugs. Children can be doctored using home remedies. Women can avoid the spiraling cost of hospitals by having their babies at home. Hence, as the price of health care increases, the consumption of traditional medical services diminishes.

The net effect of strict health care standards is an empirical question. On the one hand, if standards are effective, then those who go to physicians and hospitals should get better care and be exposed to a reduced risk of incompetent practice. On the other hand, if restrictions drive up the price of medical care by reducing the supply of doctors or by increasing the cost of doing business, there will be a decrease in the quantity of health care demanded. For any given person, the degree of risk in comparison to less restrictive standards is determined by the reduction in risk associated with medical care consumed versus the increase in risk resulting from medical care that is foregone because of high prices.

It is possible that an individual could end up assuming greater risk as a result of high medical standards. This is especially likely for the poor, because their demand for medical care is relatively elastic. Low-income groups might actually be better off if they were allowed to seek out lower-priced, more risky health care. Optimal standards for medical care require an assessment of the benefits of reducing the risk of shoddy practice versus the consequences of higher prices.

In spite of the problems, there is general agreement that occupational licensing is desirable for doctors, dentists, and other occupations where consumers find it difficult to evaluate the service or where the consequences of poor service are serious. However, for many other occupations there are alternatives to licensing. If the main goal is to provide information to the consumer, that objective can often be accomplished by certification. Certification indicates that a practitioner has certain skills, but does not prohibit others from offering the service. The title of certified public accountant is an example. Anyone can function as an accountant, but only those who have met certain criteria are allowed to represent themselves as CPAs. Consumers who want protection against incompetent accountants can pay a premium price to obtain the services of a CPA. Others, who prefer lower-priced services with less assurance of quality, can hire an accountant who has not been certified. The advantage of the certification procedure is that it fulfills the need for consumer information without restricting consumer choice. Presumably, there would always be a price differential between practitioners who have been certified and those who are not, but the existence of alternatives reduces the power of a profession to artificially increase the compensation of its members. As the premium required to hire a certified practitioner increases, more and more consumers will be willing to bear the risk of employing an uncertified person. This alternative is an effective check on prices charged by certified members of the profession.

PRODUCT SAFETY: FOOD AND DRUG ADMINISTRATION (FDA)
Background

Some scientists believe that the widespread incidence of gout among the aristocrats of ancient Rome was the result of lead poisoning. The source of the problem probably was wine made in lead pots. It is estimated that wealthy Romans absorbed as much as 1500 micrograms of lead per day—about 30 times the average for a city dweller in the United States. Researchers speculate that chronic lead poisoning may account for the degenerative behavior of emperors such as Nero and Caligula.[6]

Although there were no Food and Drug Administrations in the ancient world, there were attempts to protect consumers. Hebrew and Egyptian laws dealt with the handling of meat. Greek and Roman statutes prohibited adding water to wine. In the homes of royalty, the "king's taster" protected the monarch from poisoned food.

In modern times, the push for consumer protection regulation first gained momentum in the late 1800s. The growth of large-scale food processing industries greatly diminished the ability of consumers to judge the products that they were buying. Purchasers of canned and otherwise processed foods had no way of knowing the ingredients and methods used to produce the final product. Often, they were better off not knowing. Unsanitary facilities and adulteration of foods were not uncommon in that era. Writing in his highly influential book, *The Jungle,* Upton Sinclair describes the making of sausage from spoiled meat, sawdust, poison bread, rat carcasses and dung.[7]

The case for government regulation of the food and drug industry is particularly strong. Few people have the competence to evaluate the thousands of drugs that are on the market. The average consumer can never know what went into the jar of peanut butter that he purchased at the supermarket. Also, the price of an error in selection may be very high—death or serious illness. In spite of the apparent need for legislation, Congress and the general public were apathetic. It was not until writers such as Sinclair dramatized the problem that Congress was finally induced to act.

Origins and Procedures

In 1906 Congress passed the Food and Drugs Act, which prohibited the adulteration and misbranding of goods sold in interstate commerce. The act also created the Food and Drug Administration as an enforcement agency. The law provided that adulterated or misbranded foods and drugs could be seized by the FDA and that offenses were punishable by fine or imprisonment. Although the 1906 statute probably helped in preventing extreme abuses, it had some serious limitations. First, it did not cover cosmetics or therapeutic devices such as muscle developers, weight-reducing equipment, and sun lamps. These areas soon proved to be particularly susceptible to problems. Second, because there was no provision for inspection of food-processing facilities, FDA actions were primarily after the fact. Third, the act did not allow for control of false advertising claims. Only statements made on packages or labels could be regulated. Fourth, enforcement was made difficult by the small staff of the FDA and its inability to obtain strong penalties for violations. Prison sentences resulting from infrequent convictions under the act were uncommon, and fines rarely provided much of a disincentive to firms.

Problems with adulterated and misbranded foods and drugs continued through

---

[6]"Ancient Rome's Ills and Illnesses Linked in Scientist's Study," *Wall Street Journal* (March 17, 1983), p. 17.

[7]Sinclair, U., *The Jungle* (New York: Doubleday, 1906), p. 321.

the 1920s and 1930s. The media continued to call attention to the most flagrant abuses. The FDA did its best to arouse public sentiment for stronger legislation. The agency set up a museum that became known as the Chamber of Horrors. Its contents were hardly suitable for an after-dinner conversation:

> Samples seized from foods on public sale—filthy candy, decayed fruit, worm-eaten nuts, butter full of maggots, and raisins infested with insects; samples of patent medicines to cure every known disease, with testimonials from their users, accompanied by copies of their death certificates; and samples of cosmetics—eye-lash beautifiers containing poisonous aniline dyes, hair removers containing thallium acetate, and hair tonics, freckle removers, ointments, and salves containing mercury or other dangerous ingredients—together with photographs of women who had been blinded, paralyzed, or permanently disfigured by their use.[8]

Like much of the legislation designed to protect consumers, the final catalyst for stronger food and drug laws came from a tragedy. In 1937 a drug manufacturer marketed a product containing a deadly poison. The initial sales of the product were determined to be the certain cause of over 70 deaths. The FDA moved to seize the unsold portion of the product and to prosecute the manufacturer, but did not have the power to have prevented the tragedy. The next year Congress passed the Food, Drug, and Cosmetic Act of 1938.

The 1938 statute strengthened the definitions of adulteration and misbranding. In particular, the concept of misbranding was changed to cover statements that are "false or misleading in any particular." Also, the FDA was empowered to require additional information on the packages or labels of foods and drugs. The coverage of the original 1906 statute was extended to include cosmetics and therapeutic devices. In addition, the FDA was given the right to conduct inspections of factories producing foods, drugs, and cosmetics and to license manufacturers and set standards of sanitation. An important provision of the act was the requirement imposed on drug manufacturers to obtain FDA approval before putting new drugs on the market. The agency was authorized to deny approval for those drugs that were found to be unsafe. Finally, penalties for violation of the act were increased.

The 1938 statute required manufacturers to present evidence that new drugs were safe. This evidence was usually based on animal tests and then, if the animal tests indicated no health hazards, limited tests on humans. The FDA had little to do with the planning and monitoring of these tests. Moreover, firms only had to demonstrate that the new drugs were safe—not that they were effective. During the late 1950s, Senator Estes Kefauver's Antitrust and Monopoly Subcommittee conducted hearings on the drug industry. The subcommittee's report argued that drug manufacturers were earning excessive profits and that new drugs introduced were often ineffective. The report also contended that a major cause of the high cost of drugs was expenditures by drug manufacturers to differentiate their products. By developing a new drug slightly different from existing products, firms could broaden and lengthen patent protection and maintain their market shares.

Kefauver introduced legislation to correct the problems found by his committee,

---

[8]Wilcox, C., *Public Policy Towards Business,* 4th ed. (Homewood, Ill.: Irwin, 1971), p. 589.

but opposition from drug manufacturers and the American Medical Association blocked his efforts. At this juncture another tragedy spurred Congress to action. A sleeping pill called thalidomide caused over 7,000 babies in West Germany to be born without arms and legs. The FDA had resisted approving thalidomide for use in the United States, but the manufacturer, as part of the required testing program, sent the pills to U.S. physicians. The inability of the FDA to regulate the testing program provided the impetus for the Drug Amendments of 1962.

The 1962 amendments gave the FDA authority to regulate the testing of new drugs. They also required that manufacturers must demonstrate that new drugs are not only safe, but effective. "Effective" was defined to mean that the drug must be shown capable of meeting all the claims that are made for it. Another important provision was the right granted to the FDA to remove from the market immediately any drug that the agency deemed to represent a substantial risk to public health.[9]

Much of the present effort of the FDA focuses on two areas—misbranding and adulteration. A drug is considered to be *misbranded* if its label does not show the name of the manufacturer and an accurate statement of the quantity of the contents. Also, its label must provide adequate directions for its use and any warnings necessary to protect its users. The label is defined to include information attached to the product container and also any other written material that accompanies the article. Accompanying materials have been defined very broadly to include promotional materials sent to distributors as long as a year after the original shipment of the drugs.

Proper branding of food requires that the name and place of business of the manufacturer be on the package, along with an accurate statement of the contents. There are some foods for which standards of identity have been established. Hence, to carry the name of the particular food, the product must meet certain standards. For example, to qualify as "beef with gravy" a product must contain at least 50 percent beef. "Poultry chop suey" must have at least 4 percent chicken. However, "chop suey with poultry" is only required to have 2 percent poultry.

A *drug* is *adulterated* if it contains any filthy, decomposed, poisonous, or deleterious substance, if it has been packed under unsanitary conditions, if it contains an unsafe color additive, or if it does not conform to standards of strength, quality, or purity as specified for the drug that it claims to be. *Foods* are adulterated if they contain poisonous or deleterious substances, unsafe food additives, color additives, or pesticide chemicals (in excess of prescribed levels), or if they contain filthy, putrid, or decomposed substances, or have been prepared under unsanitary conditions, or are the product of a diseased animal.

The FDA can act by seizing products, obtaining injunctions against specific activities of manufacturers, and by initiating civil or criminal prosecutions. Violations of the Food and Drug Acts are normally misdemeanors, but if there is evidence of an "intent to mislead or defraud," or if there has been a prior conviction under the acts, then violations are felonies and are punishable by up to three years imprisonment and fines of up to $10,000.

[9]A 1976 amendment further expanded the FDA's powers by allowing the agency to require that manufacturers of medical devices prove that their products are safe and effective before putting them on the market.

Evaluation

Undoubtedly, the efforts of the Food and Drug Administration have saved thousands of lives and prevented millions of days of illness. However, the FDA has not escaped its share of criticism. Most of the complaints center on the agency's drug evaluation procedures. Many believe that the delays and costs involved in new drug introductions are excessive. For example, a drug called sodium valproate was used safely in Europe for ten years before the FDA approved its use in the United States. The substance is used to control epileptic convulsions and is estimated to have the potential for controlling a million seizures per year. The so-called "beta blockers" are another illustration. Available for many years in Great Britain and Sweden, these drugs can greatly improve the prognosis for heart attack victims. But it was not until 1981 that the FDA allowed their use in the United States.

The stringent requirements of the 1962 drug amendments have increased the cost and prolonged the time required to bring new drugs to the market. During the late 1950s, about two years and $500,000 were necessary to introduce a new drug. By the early 1980s, the corresponding numbers were eight years and $50 million. A substantial portion of these time and money costs are the result of additional testing requirements imposed by the FDA. Consider the case of a recent application for approval of a muscle relaxant. Documents submitted by the manufacturer to the FDA were bound in 456 separate volumes, weighed more than a ton, and stood taller than an eight-story building.

The evidence suggests that the provisions of the 1962 drug amendments greatly reduced the rate of introduction of new drugs in the United States. Table 17.1 shows the average annual number of new drugs for selected subperiods between 1951 and

Table 17.1 AVERAGE NUMBER OF NEW DRUGS INTRODUCED: 1951–1977

Period	New chemical entities*	Other new drugs*
1951–1954	39.0	303.0
1955–1958	42.0	351.5
1959–1962	42.5	239.3
1963–1966	17.0	120.0
1967–1970	15.3	68.8
1971–1974	15.5	60.5
1975–1977	16.3	58.7
Averages		
1951–1962	41.5	297.9
1963–1970	16.1	94.4
1971–1977	15.9	59.7

New chemical entities are drugs containing a single chemical formula not previously marketed. *Other new drugs* are new combinations of previously marketed chemical entities and duplicates of chemical entities marketed under a new brand name.

Source: Peltzman, S., "An Evaluation of Consumer Protection Legislation: The 1962 Drug Amendments," *Journal of Political Economy* (September–October 1973), p. 1053 and Schnee, J. E., "Regulation and Innovation: U.S. Pharmaceutical Industry," *California Management Review* (Fall 1979), p. 25.

1977. The table indicates that introductions of chemical entities and other new drugs between 1963–1970 and 1971–1977 were much lower than during the period just prior to the 1962 amendments.

It is possible that the drop represented factors other than the impact of the legislation. An alternative hypothesis is that there was a "depletion of research opportunities." That is, all of the important drugs had already been introduced. This possibility can be examined by comparing the U.S. experience with drug introductions to that of other countries. Between 1962 and 1979 four times as many drugs were introduced in Great Britain as in the United States. Of all the drugs marketed in both Great Britain and the United States, about two-thirds were introduced in Great Britain first.[10] The argument of depleted research opportunities does not appear tenable in the face of such international comparisons.

Grabowski and Vernon contend that one of the primary effects of U.S. drug regulation has been to increase seller concentration among drug manufacturers. As costs and risks of marketing new drugs increase, smaller firms are forced out of the market. Because of opportunities to introduce drugs in other countries, the remaining firms are forced to become multinational in nature.[11] Peltzman also reached a negative conclusion about the 1962 legislation. His findings indicate that as of 1970: (1) the consumer surplus forgone from reduced innovation was $300 to $400 million annually; (2) there were few gains from FDA attempts to eliminate ineffective drugs; (3) reductions in price rivalry cost consumers about $50 million each year; and (4) the net effect of the amendments was comparable to a 5-to-10-percent tax on drug purchases.[12]

In evaluating the Food and Drug Administration, it must be recognized that regulating drugs is much more complex than dealing with other consumer products. If the sale of a bicycle is banned because of alleged safety defects, the trade-off involves reducing injuries versus restricting consumer choice. But when the FDA considers approval of a new drug or banning a substance already on the market, the choice can be much more difficult. Lives may be saved by the exercise of caution on the part of those in the agency, but there may also be lives that could be saved by accelerating the approval of the new drug or allowing the existing substance to remain on the market.

To illustrate, consider the addition of nitrites to foods. Nitrites are a valuable additive, especially in meat, because they give cured meat products their distinctive reddish color, improve the flavor, and prevent botulism. Without nitrites bacon would be white or gray in color and have a saltier taste. Storage for even short periods would require freezing, irradiation, or canning. However, preliminary studies of nitrites suggested that the additive might cause cancer in animals. Hence, any decision on allowing nitrites in meats required balancing the possibility of cancer against the threat of botulism and the economic impact on the meat-processing industry. Subsequent studies indicated that nitrites pose no threat in products such as hot dogs and ham, but that additional information is needed to determine their effects in bacon.

Officials at the Food and Drug Administration are not unaware of the controver-

[10]Wardell, W., "More Regulation or Better Therapies," *Regulation* (Sept./Oct. 1979), pp. 25–33.
[11]Grabowski, H. G., and Vernon, J. M., "Consumer Protection Regulation in Ethical Drugs," *American Economic Review* (Feb. 1977), p. 360.
[12]Peltzman, S., "An Evaluation of Consumer Protection Legislation: The 1962 Drug Amendments," *Journal of Political Economy* (Sept./Oct. 1973), pp. 1049–1091.

sies surrounding their actions. In recent years the agency has taken steps to accelerate its evaluation process, while maintaining high standards for food and drug safety. One change has been to put certain drug applications on a "fast-track" approval schedule. This approach is used when the benefits of a new drug appear great and the risks small. Although thorough tests still are required, the FDA moves much faster in evaluating the data. For example, Tagamet, a drug used in treating ulcers, was approved for limited use less than a month after the agency received the company's test data. This compares to an average review period of about two years.

Another change has been increased acceptance of foreign data. Although at least some studies in the United States usually are required, the FDA now is willing to consider data on the testing and use of a drug in other countries. Finally, the agency seems to be moving in the direction of greater post-approval surveillance. In the past, the Food and Drug Administration was limited in its ability to monitor the effects of drugs already approved for use. In spite of the voluminous testing requirements necessary to gain initial approval, some drugs currently on the market may be dangerous. The painkiller Zomax is an example. Sold in the United States and Europe for over two years, the product was removed from the market after doctors' reports suggested that it may have been responsible for several deaths. Additional resources devoted to analysis of such reports could identify potential problems sooner.

DECEPTIVE ADVERTISING AND LABELING: FEDERAL TRADE COMMISSION (FTC)
Background and Origins

Creative advertising is not an invention of the twentieth century. During the 1800s an advertisement for a popular patent medicine depicted Pope Leo XIII drinking the product. The caption claimed that the pope and the medicine were both infallible. [13] Present-day advertising suggests little improvement. Claims that toothpaste gives you "sex appeal" or that social ostracism results from having "ring around the collar" are equally suspect. Usually, such frivolous assertions do not deceive consumers, but simply call attention to the product.

However, in some cases it is difficult for consumers to differentiate between valid and deceptive advertising. A few years ago a baseball player appeared on television to promote Rise shaving cream. To demonstrate that Rise could handle even the toughest of beards, he shaved a piece of sandpaper softened with Rise. Consumers all over the nation were impressed. What they didn't know was that the sandpaper had been soaked in water for several hours before the test was conducted. About the same time, Libbey-Owens-Ford Glass Company was touting the superiority of its plate glass, which was being used in the windows of all General Motors cars. Television viewers were shown that these windows produced much less distortion than products of competitors. A Federal Trade Commission investigation revealed that L-O-F was a little less than honest. Films of G. M. cars were made with windows rolled down while the windows of other cars were streaked with vasoline. [14] The increased complexity of products and the growing sophistication of marketing techniques make it more and more difficult for

---

[13]Usborne, R., "Victorian Persuasion," *Advertising Quarterly,* No. 19 (1969), pp. 37–38.
[14]*Libbey-Owens-Ford Glass Company* v. *FTC,* 352 F 2d 415 (6th Cir. 1965).

consumers to evaluate the accuracy of the information that they receive from producers. The role of government in regulating deceptive advertising and labeling is based on the need to provide assistance to consumers in making such evaluations.

In 1914 Congress passed the Federal Trade Commission Act. Section 5 of that act gave the Federal Trade Commission the authority to prevent persons or firms from engaging in unfair methods of competition in commerce. At the time, Congress was primarily concerned with assisting consumers by improving competition between firms. There was little overt concern about protecting consumers directly. Later, the FTC did use Section 5 in the attempt to protect consumers. To remain within the intent of the law, the commission argued that firms that used unfair practices hurt not only consumers, but also honest competitors by "stealing" their sales. The difficulties that the FTC experienced in obtaining convictions with this argument suggested a need for amending the original act.

In 1938 the Wheeler-Lea Amendment to the FTC Act of 1914 was enacted. It changed Section 5 to cover "unfair or deceptive acts or practices" in addition to unfair methods of competition. By the amendment the Federal Trade Commission was given explicit responsibility for protecting consumers against fraud stemming from false or misleading advertising. As a result, unfair practices could now be prosecuted whether they injured competitors or consumers.

The authority of the FTC to protect consumers has been increased over time. The Wool Products Labeling Act of 1939 gave the commission power to regulate labeling of wool goods. The Fur Products Labeling Act of 1951 and the Textile Fiber Products Identification Act of 1958 provided similar powers with respect to fur and textile products. The Fair Packaging and Labeling Act of 1966 broadened the scope of the FTC's authority to regulate labeling. It requires informative labeling of consumer commodities so that the maker, packer, or distributor, and contents and quantities can be identified. It also prohibits deceptive labeling and packaging. The Consumer Credit Protection Act of 1968 requires complete disclosure of credit terms before a credit transaction is completed and also regulates the advertising of credit terms. The Cigarette Labeling and Advertising Act of 1965 mandated a health hazard warning on cigarette packages, while the Public Health Cigarette Smoking Act of 1969 prohibited advertising cigarettes on radio or television. Finally, the Consumer Product Warranty Act of 1975 sets minimum disclosure standards for written consumer product warranties. It also gives the FTC additional powers to deal with unfair or deceptive practices at the state and local level.

Procedures

Violations of consumer protection laws come to the attention of the FTC in two ways. First, consumers, competitors, consumer organizations, trade associations, unions, better business bureaus, or government units may complain to the commission. Second, the FTC has a staff that continually monitors radio and television commercials and printed advertising. But the task of eliminating deceptive advertising and labeling practices is a difficult one. The FTC receives thousands of complaints each year. At the same time it is monitoring hundreds of thousands of printed and electronic advertisements. However, only a small fraction can be thoroughly investigated.

When the commission encounters a practice that may violate the law, it has several possible courses of action. One approach is to seek a temporary injunction to stop the practice until a more complete investigation can be made. Originally, the right to seek temporary injunctions was restricted to a narrow range of products such as foods, drugs, and cosmetics, but subsequent legislation expanded that authority to include enforcement of any statute for which the commission has responsibility.

If additional evidence suggests that a practice should be permanently discontinued or modified, the FTC can proceed in one of three ways. First, the firm under investigation may seek to dispose of the issue informally by an *assurance of voluntary compliance* under which the firm agrees to alter its practices to conform to the desires of the commission. In return, the FTC does not disclose the names, dates, and specific details of the alleged violation. In this way, the firm is spared adverse publicity.

A second approach is the use of consent orders. In accepting a consent order a firm agrees to modify its activities to conform with the directives of the commission. By signing a consent order the firm avoids the cost, time, and uncertainty of formal proceedings. Also, while the firm agrees to the stipulations of the order, its action does not constitute an admission that it has violated the law. However, in contrast to the assurance of voluntary compliance, the FTC does publicize the details of consent orders.

Finally, if the firm and the commission are unable to agree on how a problem is to be resolved, then the case may proceed to formal adjudication. A hearing or trial is set before an administrative law judge who is a part of the commission. This judge will render an opinion, which may then be appealed to the five commissioners of the FTC. If the decision of the commissioners is against the firm, it has the right to take the issue to a United States Court of Appeals and, ultimately, to the Supreme Court.

A victory for the FTC may result in an order to cease and desist from certain practices or a requirement that the firm initiate certain actions. Sometimes the agency may require the firm to engage in *corrective advertising.* The basis for corrective advertising is the belief that simply discontinuing the deceptive advertising is not enough. There are residual effects of the earlier untruths that must be corrected if consumers are to make informed decisions. The FTC has required firms to engage in corrective advertising as part of a number of consent orders. The orders typically provide that the firm devote a substantial proportion of future advertising to correcting prior advertising claims (25 percent of all advertising for a period of one or two years is not uncommon). For example, Continental Baking Company was required to allocate one-quarter of its advertising expenditures for Profile bread for one year to correct the erroneous claim that the product was effective in weight reduction. In another action, an FTC-approved ad for Ocean Spray Cranberry Juice was to read:

If you've wondered what some of our earlier advertising meant when we said Ocean Spray Cranberry Juice Cocktail has more food energy than orange juice or tomato juice, let us make it clear: it didn't mean vitamins and minerals. Food energy means calories. Nothing more.[15]

[15]Oppenheim, S. C., and Weston, G. E., *Unfair Trade Practices and Consumer Protection: Cases and Comments* (St. Paul: West Publishing, 1974), p. 621.

Continental found that corrective advertising reduced sales by one-third and consequently stopped advertising entirely. In contrast, the sales of Ocean Spray were unaffected.

At first, the FTC used the corrective advertising approach only as part of consent orders, and there was some question as to whether the courts would accept this remedy. Faced with an order for corrective advertising, the manufacturers of Listerine, Warner-Lambert, challenged the FTC's authority. Since 1921 Listerine advertisements had claimed that the product could help prevent colds and sore throats. FTC studies found that Listerine was no more effective at battling colds than warm water. The case went all the way to the Supreme Court, which upheld the commission's order that Warner-Lambert must spend $10 million over two years to publicize that "Listerine will not help prevent sore throats or lessen their severity." [16]

Another tool of the Federal Trade Commission is its requirement that advertising claims be substantiated. One advertisement may state that an ointment will provide fast relief to hemorrhoid sufferers. Another maintains that a particular car is preferred by 90 percent of professional drivers. A third asserts that a dishwashing soap leaves less film than that of its competitors. Such claims sound impressive, but are they really true? Does the firm have data to back up its boasts, or were they just conjured up by a creative advertising agency?

Since 1971 the FTC has required that firms be ready to substantiate their advertising claims. The general philosophy is that there should be a reasonable basis for statement. For over-the-counter medical products the standard has been two clinical studies in support of a claim of efficacy. In contrast, the assertion that a brand of beer "tastes great" probably would not require any supporting evidence. Between these two extremes, the necessary amount of substantiation is less certain. However, when reference is made to tests or surveys, the source of the data must exist.

Violations of FTC orders issued under Section 5 are punishable by fines of up to $10,000 for each violation. If a firm continues to disobey or disregard a commission order, each day of violation can be defined as a separate offense. If an order has been affirmed by appeal to the federal courts, then a violation may also subject the offender to contempt of court proceedings.

Under terms of the Federal Trade Commission Improvements Act of 1975, the commission can also seek relief for consumers injured as a result of false or deceptive advertising. This relief may take the form of a court order invalidating or changing the terms of a contract, a refund to consumers, or forcing the offending firm to pay damages.

Evaluation

The Federal Trade Commission has been hindered in its pursuit of deceptive advertising and labeling by the legislation that serves as the basis for its actions. Section 5 of the Federal Trade Commission Act prohibits unfair and deceptive practices, but gives no guidance as to what such practices are. The commission is left with the difficult task of differentiating between harmless exaggeration and harmful deception. Another prob-

---

[16] *Warner-Lambert Co.* v. *FTC,* 435 U.S. 950 (1978)

lem involves the incentives for registering complaints with the FTC. Consumers receive no compensation in the form of damages for successful commission prosecutions. As a result, they have little motivation to call attention to unfair practices. On the other hand, competitors and unions have a strong incentive to point out violations. Unions may use the complaint procedure to obtain protection against products that are imported or made by nonunion labor. Firms may benefit from lodging complaints by causing their competitors to receive unfavorable publicity. The result is an imbalance, with the FTC responding to numerous and possibly frivolous complaints from firms and unions, and not receiving very much input from consumers.

Although selected activities of the FTC can be justifiably criticized, the commission performs an important function. The battle against deceptive advertising and labeling differs from most of the consumer protection regulation discussed in this chapter in that it enhances rather than restricts consumer choice. To the extent that the FTC eliminates advertising and labeling information that is inaccurate, consumers are better able to evaluate the choices with which they are confronted.

PRODUCT SAFETY: CONSUMER PRODUCT SAFETY COMMISSION (CPSC)
Background

The case for government intervention in product safety rests primarily on the claim that unaided individuals often are unable to make informed decisions about the products that they purchase. The contention is that problems of obtaining and evaluating information and possible externalities in use may cause consumers to underestimate the impacts of purchasing potentially hazardous products. As a result, dangerous products remain on the market.

The legal position of the consumer in relation to unsafe products has changed substantially in the last century. Originally, the standard was *caveat emptor,* or "let the buyer beware." Under this doctrine, purchasers assumed full responsibility for decisions and could not claim damages for faulty products. In a world where the goods purchased were few in number and relatively easy to evaluate, such a rule made sense. As goods became more complex and marketing methods more impersonal, buyers were forced to rely more heavily on the seller's honesty. The courts gave assistance by enforcing legal rules of fraud and negligence. Rules of fraud provided that consumers could recover damages where they could prove that sellers had misrepresented their products. Negligence rules allowed purchasers to be compensated for costs or injuries resulting from defects in products of which the seller was or should have been aware.

Originally, liability of manufacturers was restricted by the doctrine of *privity of contract,* which specified that a seller was legally responsible only to the immediate purchaser. Thus, General Motors would be liable to a dealer for a defective automobile, but not to the final buyer of the vehicle. This rule also has been gradually eroded. In the 1916 case of *MacPherson* v. *Buick Motor Company* the right front tire of a car collapsed, causing the vehicle to crash and injuring the occupants.[17] The court abandoned the principle of privity and held that a manufacturer could be held liable by the

---

[17]*MacPherson* v. *Buick Motor Company,* 217 N.Y. 382, 11 N.E. 1050 (1916).

final purchaser if there was evidence of negligence in the manufacture or assembly of the product.

Since the MacPherson case the courts have continued to extend the concept of producer liability. Often it was difficult to prove negligence by manufacturers, so the philosophy of "let the matter speak for itself" was applied. For example, if a sealed bottle of 7-UP was found to contain a family of cockroaches, it is unlikely that someone put the insects in after the bottling was completed. A court would probably hold that the contamination must have occurred at the bottling plant. In the 1960 case of *Henningsen* v. *Bloomfield Motors* the court seemingly abandoned the requirement for proof of negligence.[18] Mrs. Henningsen was injured when her car abruptly veered to the right and hit a wall, probably due to defective steering gear. There was no evidence of negligence, but Chrysler and the dealer were still held liable. The Henningsen precedent has been applied to a wide variety of other products in subsequent court cases. The evolution of legal precedent suggests a gradual movement from *caveat emptor* to *caveat venditor,* or "let the seller beware."

Origins

Paralleling the emergence of *caveat venditor* in the courts has been the emergence of expanding government regulatory activities to assure product safety. The Consumer Product Safety Commission represents the most ambitious attempt by government to protect consumers from shoddy and unsafe products.

In 1970 the National Commission on Product Safety reported that:

> Americans—20 million of them—are injured each year in the home as the result of incidents connected with consumer products. Of the total, 110,000 are permanently disabled, and 30,000 are killed. A significant number could have been spared if more attention had been paid to hazard reduction. The annual cost to the Nation of product-related injuries may exceed $5.5 billion.[19]

Prior to 1972 the federal government's role in product safety was based on isolated statutes intended to protect consumers from specific hazards. For example, the Flammable Fabrics Act of 1953 restricted the sale of highly flammable apparel and gave authority to the Federal Trade Commission to set rules and regulations and to enforce them. The Federal Hazardous Substances Labeling Act of 1960 authorized the Food and Drug Administration to require warnings on the labels of potentially hazardous substances. The Child Protection Act of 1966 gave the FDA power to prohibit sale of toys and other products that are potentially harmful to children. A series of laws also gave the FDA great power to regulate drugs that are marketed in the United States. There are a number of other statutes, but they have the common characteristic of being limited to a relatively narrow area of special concern.

The creation of the Consumer Product Safety Commission by the passage of the Consumer Product Safety Act of 1972 was a change in strategy. Instead of legislating

---

[18]*Henningsen* v. *Bloomfield Motors,* 32 N.J. 358, 161 A. 2d 69 (1960).

[19]National Commission on Product Safety, *Final Report of the National Commission on Product Safety* (Washington, D.C.: Government Printing Office, June 1970), p. 1.

to deal with specific problems as they occurred, the act attempted to create a comprehensive mechanism for protecting consumers against unsafe or shoddy products. Potentially, the CPSC is one of the most powerful of federal agencies. Its regulatory domain covers more than 10,000 different products and nearly 3 million firms.[20] The agency was given a broad set of tools to achieve its objective of protecting consumers. The CPSC is empowered to issue mandatory safety standards, require industry-financed testing, ban or require the recall of hazardous products, force producers to notify consumers of particular hazards, specify labeling requirements, seize and destroy dangerous products, and require manufacturers to provide performance data. The CPSC Act specifies that the commission may seek civil or criminal penalties against firms that fail to comply with its regulations.

The potential power of the CPSC is illustrated by an unfortunate experience involving the Marlin Toy Company. Marlin's main source of revenues was two children's toys. Both were transparent plastic spheres. One contained toy birds and small, plastic pellets, while the other was filled with butterflies instead of birds. At the time, the FDA had responsibility for children's toys and notified Marlin that the firm's products were considered hazardous because, if the spheres broke, children might choke on the pellets. In 15 years of marketing the products there had never been a complaint of injury. Nonetheless, Marlin complied with the FDA request and removed the pellets from the toys. The FDA indicated satisfaction with Marlin's actions and agreed to remove the toys from a list of banned products that was periodically circulated to manufacturers, distributors, retailers, and consumers. However, because the list was released only once every six weeks, Marlin lost a substantial part of its Christmas toy sales.

A year later the CPSC took over the FDA's responsibility for monitoring hazardous toys. In publishing a new list of banned products, the CPSC inadvertently included the Marlin toys. As a result, the company again lost most of its Christmas sales and was forced into bankruptcy. Although the commission's action was the result of an unfortunate error rather than poor judgment or bias, the example illustrates the tremendous influence that the CPSC can have over the fortunes of individual firms.

Procedures

The CPSC was designed to be an accessible, and yet well-insulated, government regulatory agency. The insulating provisions were intended to protect the commission from political influence. The agency is headed by five commissioners who are appointed by the president and serve for seven-year terms. The terms are staggered and no more than three of the five commissioners may be from the same political party. They do not serve at the pleasure of the president, but continue in office unless removed for neglect of duty or malfeasance. To avoid cozy relationships with industry, CPSC employees are forbidden from taking jobs with industries within the agency's jurisdiction for a period of one year.

---

[20]Certain products are excluded from the CPSC's jurisdiction. Among the specific exclusions are motor vehicles, fuels, nuclear materials, pesticides, aircraft, boats, foods and drugs, medical devices, cosmetics, tobacco products, and firearms and ammunition, all of which are regulated by other federal agencies.

Table 17.2   CPSC PRIORITY CRITERIA

Criterion	Weight
Frequency of injury	24
Severity of injury	25
Chronic illness and prospect of future injuries	16
Unforeseen nature of risk	14
Probability of exposure to the hazard	12
Vulnerability of population at risk	9

Source: Bick, T., and Kaspersen, R. E., "Pitfalls of Hazard Management," *Environment* (Oct., 1978), p. 36.

Table 17.3   CONSUMER PRODUCT SAFETY COMMISSION PRIORITIES FOR 1982

Chain saws	Indoor air quality
Cribs	Plastics flammability
Dyes and finishes	Poison prevention packaging
Formaldehyde	Upholstered furniture
House wiring and circuit breakers	Wood and coal burning heating equipment

Source: Consumer Product Safety Commission, *1982 Annual Report* (Government Printing Office: Washington, D.C.), pp. 5–9.

Accessibility to the commission is guaranteed by a provision of the original act, which specifies that "any interested person . . . may petition the commission to commence a proceeding for the issuance, amendment, or revocation of a consumer product safety rule."[21] Another section of the act gives individuals the right to bring suit against the commission if it fails to act on a petition within 120 days. Still another attempt to open the operations of the CPSC is the *offerer* process, which requires the agency to invite interested parties to submit existing standards to the commission or to offer to develop a standard.

In fulfilling its mission to upgrade product safety, the commission follows a well-defined sequence. First, the CPSC identifies the most frequent and serious product-related injuries and their causes. To do this, it uses its National Electronic Injury Surveillance System (NEISS), a network of telecommunications terminals located in emergency rooms of hospitals around the country. The hospitals are selected to provide a representative sample of injuries throughout the nation. The commission also obtains data by in-depth investigation of several thousand injuries each year by screening death certificates, evaluating consumer complaints, and by conducting laboratory experiments.

The second step is the prioritization of potential hazards. In its early days the commission dealt with problems on almost a random basis, but now it compiles product hazards into priority groupings. These priorities are based on the criteria shown in Table 17.2. The weights are determined by judgments of the commission staff and may change from time to time. Table 17.3 lists the ten CPSC priorities for 1982.

Once priorities have been established, then the commission must develop strategies for managing the high-priority hazards. The CPSC is organized into eight program

[21]Consumer Product Safety Act, Public Law 92-573.

areas: fire and thermal burns, electric shock, acute chemical and environmental hazards, chronic chemical and environmental hazards, tools and housewares, structural hazards, toys, and sports. High-priority hazards are assigned to one of the eight areas for consideration of management strategies. The strategies recommended by the program areas are reviewed by the commissioners and a particular approach is selected. If the decision is to issue a safety rule (either a standard or a ban), then rule-making procedures are initiated. If the choice is a public education campaign, then the problem is returned to the commission staff for preparation and implementation.

The offerer process previously mentioned comes into play if the decision is to set a safety standard. The commission is required by law to announce its intention publicly to issue a regulation and to invite interested parties to submit an existing standard for adoption or to offer to develop a new standard. The CPSC is required to accept one or more of these offers if the offerer is technically competent, capable of meeting the agency's deadline, and willing to comply with the commission's procedures. Only if there are no qualified offerers or if the only acceptable offerer is from the industry to be regulated may the commission develop its own standard. For standards submitted by an offerer, the CPSC has the option to accept, reject, or modify the proposal.

Once a standard is accepted by the agency it may be reviewed in the court system. The courts require that the standards be reasonable. The economic impacts of rules must be considered but are not necessarily decisive. There have been several occasions where CPSC proposed standards have been overturned by the courts, but these reversals have been primarily on procedural grounds. For example, a ban on aerosol products containing vinyl chloride was overturned because the commission failed to prepare an environmental impact statement. A ban on chemicals used in children's nightclothes was rejected because the court ruled that industry had not adequately participated in the decision-making process. Generally, however, if the CPSC adheres closely to its rule-making procedures, it has considerable power to set and enforce safety standards for consumer products.

Evaluation

In the early years of its existence, the Consumer Product Safety Commission did not meet the expectations of its advocates. An early supporter called the commission "one of his biggest disappointments" and referred to its "miserable record."[22] The primary criticism was the apparent lack of action. During its first six years, the CPSC enacted few safety standards and was not very active in banning potentially hazardous products. Further, the initial failure of the commission to set priorities for its activities caused many of its early efforts to deal with relatively inconsequential problems. For example, the first proposed regulation was concerned with swimming pool slides. The agency specified that slides should be affixed with warnings of potential injuries stemming from improper use. It also proposed that taller slides, intended for installation in deeper waters, should have chain ladders or other barriers to discourage use by young children. Undoubtedly, there was potential for injury from swimming pool slides, but the danger

[22]Representative John E. Moss as quoted in Bick, T. and Kasperson, R. E., "Pitfalls of Hazard Management," *Environment* (Oct. 1978), p. 30.

was not nearly so great as from bicycles, skateboards, or other products. To compound the problem, a federal appeals court invalidated most of the regulation on the grounds that the commission's decisions were not adequately supported by the evidence provided to the courts. A revised standard later was approved.

Although criticized by many for doing too little, the Consumer Product Safety Commission also has been criticized for doing too much. Such critics argue that the agency's charter gives it too much power to interfere with business activity. They believe that many decisions have been arbitrary and unnecessary. During the 1980 political campaign, Ronald Reagan took this position and proposed that the CPSC should be eliminated or at least reorganized. Although the agency survived this threat, it did receive a 30-percent budget cut between 1981 and 1982.

It would be inaccurate to leave the impression that the Consumer Product Safety Commission has not had its successes. The agency's system of injury surveillance is the best in the world. Based on these data, 3,173 recalls involving more than 290 million product units have been initiated since 1973. Another 181 million product units have been voluntarily recalled based on reports of possible safety defects received from manufacturers.

To date, about a dozen standards and an equal number of product bans have been mandated by the CPSC. While the total number is small, the impact on product safety is substantial. It is estimated that 100 lives are saved and 90,000 injuries prevented each year.[23] A noteworthy example is child-resistant packaging of drugs and toxic substances. It is fashionable to complain that child-proof lids are adult-proof as well, but the trade-off from this inconvenience is a 90-percent reduction in child deaths caused by accidental swallowing of poisonous substances. In addition to mandatory standards, the CPSC has negotiated over 100 voluntary standards with various industries. The estimated impact is 200 lives saved and 125,000 injuries prevented each year.

In evaluating the Consumer Product Safety Commission, the impact of the threat of regulation must not be overlooked. The possibility of action undoubtedly has caused industry to raise its standards of product safety. The availability of injury data from the commission may also have had an effect. Private attorneys use CPSC data as evidence in product liability suits. As liability judgments increase, businesses have an incentive to devote more resources to the design of safer products. It is not possible to quantify the importance of these factors, but they may be quite important in improving the safety characteristics of consumer products.

SUMMARY
Professional Competency: Occupational Licensing

Background   Every state has boards responsible for setting and enforcing standards for competency of specific professions. The rationale for licensing usually is that consumers are unqualified to differentiate between qualified practitioners and quacks. The case for licensing is particularly strong in occupations where death or injury may result from incompetent or improper service.

[23]U.S. Consumer Product Commission, *1982 Annual Report, Part One* (U.S. Government Printing Office: Washington, D.C., 1983).

Evaluation   Occupational licensing restricts entry into a profession. Often, licensing reflects the efforts and preferences of those in the profession rather than consumers. In addition to causing higher prices, licensing may limit consumer choice by excluding less-qualified individuals who could provide service at lower cost. In many fields, certification can provide most of the benefits of licensing without restricting consumer choice.

Product Safety: Food and Drug Administration (FDA)

Background   The case for government regulation of the food and drug industry is especially strong because consumers are unable to evaluate their purchases fully. Also, the consequence of an error in selection can be high—death or serious injury.

Origins and Procedures   The 1906 Food and Drugs Act prohibited the adulteration and misbranding of goods. The act also created the FDA. The legislation had limited impact, but many of the deficiencies were corrected by the 1938 Food, Drug, and Cosmetic Act. However, the FDA still was restricted in its ability to regulate the testing of proposed new drugs. The 1962 drug amendments further strengthened the agency's powers.

Evaluation   Empirical evidence suggests that the 1962 drug amendments and FDA red tape have retarded the introduction of new drugs in the United States. But food and drug regulation is a complex issue. There is a trade-off between speed and caution. While lives might be saved as a result of caution on the part of the agency, lives might also be saved if a drug were approved more quickly. Recent changes at the FDA include fast-track approval of important drugs, greater reliance on foreign data, and an increase in post-approval surveillance.

Deceptive Advertising and Labeling: Federal Trade Commission (FTC)

Background and Origins   The 1914 Federal Trade Commission Act gave the FTC authority to prohibit unfair methods of competition. The 1938 Wheeler-Lea Amendment expanded the original legislation to prohibit unfair or deceptive acts or practices.

Procedures   In acting against deceptive advertising, the FTC can (1) seek a temporary injunction pending a more complete investigation, (2) negotiate a consent order, or (3) have the matter decided before an FTC administrative law judge. The agency sometimes orders corrective advertising to remedy the lingering effects of deceptive advertising. Also, firms can be required to substantiate advertising claims.

Evaluation   Under present law, the FTC is given no guidance as to what constitutes unfair or deceptive advertising. Also, firms and unions may be able to use the agency to harass competitors and employers. Still, the FTC's efforts serve a useful purpose. In contrast to many regulatory activities, restrictions on deceptive advertising serve to enhance rather than limit consumer choice.

Product Safety: Consumer Product Safety Commission (CPSC)

Background   The courts have gradually switched from the doctrine of *caveat emptor,* or "let the buyer beware," to *caveat venditor* or, "let the seller beware." Sellers are increasingly being required to assume legal responsibility for defects in the goods and services they market.

Origins   Created in 1972, the Consumer Product Safety Commission was intended to protect consumers against unsafe and shoddy products. The agency has the power to set mandatory safety standards, ban or recall hazardous products, force producers to notify consumers of particular hazards, specify labeling requirements, and require managers to provide performance data. Civil or criminal penalties can be sought against firms that fail to comply.

Organization and Procedures   The CPSC is intended to be accessible to consumers, but isolated from political influences. Commissioners are appointed for long, staggered terms. When product safety standards are to be set, the public is involved through the offerer process, whereby interested parties are invited to offer to develop standards.

Evaluation   The early years of the CPSC were something of a disappointment. Often, the commission dealt with trivial concerns or concentrated on labeling requirements. In recent years the agency has acted more aggressively. Although the number of safety standards and product bans have been few, some have had a significant effect in reducing injuries. Also, informal negotiations have resulted in many injury-preventing product modifications.

DISCUSSION QUESTIONS

1. What effect does a move to seller liability have on product prices? On income distribution?
2. Can the offerer process ever be an effective mechanism for involving the public in product safety?
3. The CPSC has been referred to as potentially the most powerful of all federal regulatory agencies. Why?
4. Why have changes in food and drug laws generally required some tragedy as a catalyst?
5. The United States uses the rest of the world as a testing ground for new drugs. Do you agree with this statement? Explain.
6. If a drug is shown to be safe, should the FDA also require it to be proven effective?
7. Typically, licensing only affects new entrants into a profession. Why are existing practitioners seldom required to demonstrate continued proficiency?
8. Why has the accounting profession opted for certification rather than licensing?
9. When does advertising shift from being frivolous to being deceptive?
10. From society's perspective, is corrective advertising preferable to stiff fines for deceptive advertising?

chapter *18*

Social Regulation: Human and Natural Resources

Chapter Outline

The air is deadly, the water's polluted and if you try to crawl in a hole in the ground, the toxic wastes will get you. [1]

The previous chapter considered public policy with respect to unsafe products and services. This chapter examines government efforts to protect the human and natural resources necessary to produce those goods and services. The main thrust of those efforts began in 1970 with the establishment of two important federal regulatory agencies. First to be discussed is the Occupational Safety and Health Administration (OSHA), which has primary responsibility for promoting safety in the work place. The second section of the chapter focuses on the Environmental Protection Agency (EPA), which is charged with preserving natural resources.

WORKING CONDITIONS: OCCUPATIONAL SAFETY AND HEALTH ADMINISTRATION (OSHA)
Risk Premiums in Labor Markets

Risk is an integral part of modern life. Thousands of people are killed in automobile accidents each year. Hunting and boating mishaps impose a heavy toll on life and limb. Muggers practice their trade from Hawaii to Maine. People accept these risks because the enjoyment that comes from travel and recreational activities provides offsetting advantages.

Individuals in the job market make similar choices. Some jobs subject workers to considerable risk. If workers are aware of these risks, they will require extra compensation as an inducement to take and remain at such jobs. This compensation may take the form of wage premiums, additional fringe benefits, or shorter and more desirable working hours. If the total compensation package is inadequate, then the worker has the option of quitting and finding another job. The principle of compensating differentials was first recognized by Adam Smith. Writing in *The Wealth of Nations,* he observed that "The whole of the advantages and disadvantages of the different employments of labor must be either perfectly equal or continually tending to equality. The wages of labor vary with the ease or hardship, the honorableness or dishonorableness of employment." [2]

In making decisions about their workplace, managers have two choices. They can remedy health and safety problems or they can provide risk compensation to workers. If reducing risk is less costly than the additional compensation, then working conditions will be improved. However, if the marginal cost of worker compensation is less than the marginal cost of safety improvements, then the firm will choose the compensation alternative. The outcome represents an efficient allocation of resources in that the firm minimizes its total costs.

Several researchers have attempted to quantify the wage premium for risky employment. Typically, the approach has been to analyze the statistical relationship between wages and deaths or injuries in various industries. Multiple-regression tech-

---

[1]Caption from Engelhardt cartoon appearing in the St. Louis *Post-Dispatch* (Feb. 20, 1980), p. 2E.
[2]Smith, A., *The Wealth of Nations* (New York: Modern Library, reprint ed., 1937), pp. 99–100.

Table 18.1   WAGE PREMIUMS FOR HIGH-RISK OCCUPATIONS

Occupation	Annual occupational deaths per 100,000 workers	Estimated annual wage premium (1983 $)
Fishers	19	$ 100
Firefighters	44	241
Police officers	78	411
Electricians	93	492
Sailors	163	861
Bartenders	176	930
Miners	176	930
Taxicab drivers	182	960
Lumberjacks	256	1,353
Guards	267	1,410

Source: Adapted from Thaler, R., and Rosen, S., "The Value of Saving a Life: Evidence from the Labor Market," in Terleckyj, N., ed., *Household Production and Consumption* (New York: National Bureau of Economic Research, 1975), pp. 265–298.

niques are used that allow the effects of factors such as sex, education, family status, and wealth to be analyzed separately.[3] This approach is necessary because the willingness to bear risk is correlated with demographic characteristics of workers. Women, college graduates, workers with families, and those with greater net worth have been found to be more risk averse than other groups. As such, they require larger wage premiums to induce them to bear risk.

The wage premium estimates resulting from such studies exhibit substantial variation. One researcher was unable to find any risk-related adjustment, while another computed the average premium to be almost $1,000 in terms of 1983 prices.[4] Table 18.1 presents the findings of a 1973 study by Thaler and Rosen.[5] The first column of data shows the annual number of job-caused deaths per 100,000 workers in various hazardous occupations. The second column is their estimate (in 1983 dollars) of the extra annual wages paid to workers in those industries as risk compensation. Thaler and Rosen conclude that, to accept an additional one-per-thousand risk of death, the average wage premium is about $500.

Although some of the estimated risk premiums are substantial, there are reasons to believe that labor markets may not allocate sufficient resources to occupational health and safety. First is the problem of inadequate information. Data correlating job conditions and health and safety hazards are poor. In particular, many health risks appear years after the initial exposure. Radiation accidents and exposure to cancer-causing chemicals are examples. A second concern is the difficulty that workers sometimes have, even with good data, in making rational decisions. Experimental and actual experience suggests that individuals are not very adept at processing information involving small probabilities of risk. Unfortunately, the critical decisions relating to

[3]See, for example, Leigh, J. P., "Compensating Wages for Occupational Injuries and Diseases," *Social Science Quarterly* (December 1981), pp. 772–778.

[4]Chelius, J., "The Control of Industrial Accidents: Economic Theory and Empirical Evidence," *Law and Contemporary Problems,* Vol. 38 (1974), pp. 700–729, and Viscusi, K., *Employment Hazards: An Investigation of Market Performance* (Cambridge: Harvard University Press, 1979).

[5]Thaler, R., and Rosen, S., op. cit.

occupational health and safety often are characterized by events whose occurence is improbable, but very costly.

A third defect in labor market resource allocation involves the difference between private and social costs. Third parties may be adversely affected by unsafe or unhealthy working conditions. For example, exposure to dangerous substances may increase the incidence of birth defects. Although parents may be willing to assume this risk, the unborn child has no way of making its preferences known. Finally, government subsidies and insurance programs reduce the costs of accidents. To the extent that the costs of hazards are underestimated or understated, both firms and workers will underallocate resources to health and safety. All of these factors represent possible justifications for government action.

OSHA Origins and Procedures

With the age of industrialization came new occupational hazards. Power machines with moving gears and cutting blades created additional safety problems. The use of exotic materials and chemicals resulted in health issues that still are not fully understood. During the 1800s and early 1900s little was done to improve working conditions. Managers took the position that it was easier to replace injured workers than to correct hazardous situations. The view of workers was that injuries were an unfortunate, but inevitable, consequence of earning a living. Relief through the legal system was difficult because the courts frequently held that employees implicitly accepted the risks when they took a job. Relief was granted only on a clear showing of negligence on the part of the employer.

Workmen's compensation laws enacted by the states represented the first systematic efforts to improve occupational health and safety. These laws required employers to reimburse workers for injuries suffered on the job regardless of who was at fault. Later, many states enacted laws regulating working conditions, but there was considerable variation in their stringency and coverage. Also, budget limitations often resulted in weak enforcement. Annual expenditures ranged from $2.70 per worker in some states down to less than a penny in others. Further, there was little evidence that more restrictive standards or increased expenditures were closely correlated with improved safety records.

Between 1960 and 1970 the accident rate in the United States increased by over 25 percent. A 1970 government study estimated that more than 14,000 workers die and another 2.2 million are injured in job-related accidents each year. In response to a perceived "on-the-job health and safety crisis," Congress passed the Occupational Safety and Health Act of 1970. The stated purpose of the legislation was to "assure so far as possible every working man and woman in the nation safe and healthful working conditions." The act created the Occupational Safety and Health Administration and gave it the right to set and enforce mandatory health and safety standards. Within one month of its creation, OSHA adopted over 4,000 "interim standards" based on preexisting federal regulations and voluntary industry codes. Because of pressures on the agency to act quickly, few of these regulations were subjected to careful review. Years later, they still constitute the majority of OSHA standards.

OSHA regulations are enforced by unannounced inspections. Often, these inspections are the result of employee complaints or serious or fatal accidents in a particular plant. Some work places are inspected on a random basis, but recently the agency has concentrated its resources on target industries with below-average safety records. If an establishment is found to be in violation of one or more regulations, the employer may be fined. The size of the fine depends on the seriousness of the violation. There are four main categories:

> *De minimis:* A violation that has no direct or immediate relationship to job safety and health. A notice is issued but citations are not (e.g., lack of toilet partitions).
>
> *Nonserious violation:* A violation that does have a direct relationship to job safety and health but probably would not cause death or serious physical harm. A penalty of up to $1,000 is optional (e.g., tripping hazard).
>
> *Serious violation:* A violation where there is substantial probability that death or serious physical harm could result and the employer knew, or should have known, of the hazard. A penalty of up to $1,000 is mandatory. Willful and repeated violations are subject to fines of up to $10,000 (e.g., lack of guards on saws).
>
> *Imminent danger:* A violation where there is reasonable certainty that a danger exists that can be expected to cause death or serious physical harm immediately or before the danger can be eliminated through normal enforcement procedures. If the employer fails to deal with the violation immediately, OSHA can go to a federal district court for legal action as necessary (e.g., exposed high-voltage wire).

The responsibility for compliance with OSHA regulations rests with employers. In addition to maintaining safe and healthy working conditions in their establishments, they must also ensure that employees practice safe work habits. If workers are injured as a result of their own carelessness, it is possible that a penalty could still be assessed against their employers. For example, if an employee has been instructed to wear safety glasses while operating a lathe or grinder and suffers an eye injury because of her or his failure to do so, the employer may be cited and fined by OSHA.

Evaluation of OSHA

There has been a strong anti-OSHA feeling among the business community. In some cases the resentment stems from OSHA's practice of surprise inspections and the seemingly capricious manner in which they are sometimes conducted. On one occasion, an Idaho electrical and plumbing contractor refused to admit OSHA inspectors into his shop on the grounds that their actions constituted an unreasonable search in violation of the Fourth Amendment. The case went all the way to the Supreme Court, which ruled that OSHA inspectors must have a warrant if demanded by the owner of an establishment.[6] The initial reaction of businesspeople was that they had won a great victory over spreading regulation, but it now appears that the primary effect of the

[6]*Marshall* v. *Barlow's Inc.,* 436 U. S. 307 (1978).

ruling was to add yet another layer of red tape to the OSHA bureaucracy. The Court's ruling specified that to obtain a warrant, inspectors do not have to show probable cause that there is a violation in a particular working place. As a result, OSHA agents can routinely secure a warrant before conducting an inspection. Also, some employers may be reluctant to require a warrant because of the possibility of a more rigorous inspection from irritated agents. At the present time, less than 2 percent of employers are requiring OSHA inspectors to obtain a warrant before entering their premises.

Another source of opposition to OSHA has been the complex and arbitrary nature of its health and safety regulations. Some of the original standards were out of date by the time they were adopted. An infamous example was the prohibition against putting ice in drinking water. During the time when ice often was cut from polluted lakes and rivers, this restriction made sense, but changing technology has eliminated the need for protection in this area. This regulation has now been revoked. In fact, OSHA has eliminated nearly 1,000 nuisance standards. The agency also has adopted "common sense priorities," whereby 95 percent of enforcement efforts are to be concentrated on high-risk industries such as construction, manufacturing, transportation, and petrochemicals.

Another complaint against OSHA is the reluctance of the agency to give greater weight to the costs of complying with its standards. Meeting OSHA requirements can impose a financial burden on firms in a number of ways. Additional clerks may be needed to maintain the required records. Labor productivity may decrease because of mandated changes in work practices. Usually, the greatest cost involves the purchase of capital equipment or the modification of existing equipment to meet OSHA standards.

An extreme example of the high cost of meeting OSHA regulations was the agency's proposal for noise control. A standard was proposed that would have permitted a maximum noise level of 90 decibels during an eight-hour day. The noise reduction was to be achieved by extensive modifications of plant and equipment. An OSHA-commissioned study estimated that capital costs of complying with the standard would total over $10 billion, with an additional annual maintenance bill of about $1 billion. Costs per worker varied substantially by industry. In the electrical equipment industry the estimated figure was $19,000. But for textile workers the cost per worker protected was projected to be over $200,000. [7]

One of the most disquieting aspects of the noise control proposal was OSHA's unwillingness to consider meeting the standard by using earplugs instead of expensive modifications of capital equipment. It has been estimated that the annual cost of the earplug solution would be less than 5 percent of the maintenance bill alone for the OSHA proposal. OSHA administrators argue that the remedy should be at the source of the problem—earplugs treat the symptom rather than the cause. The earplug solution is also considered to be less effective and less convenient for workers. All of these arguments may be correct, but it would seem that there should be some cost differential between the capital equipment and the earplug solutions that would offset the disadvantages of the latter. Recently, OSHA officials have been more willing to consider the use of protective devices as an alternative to large capital expenditures.

The bottom line in evaluating the performance of OSHA is the agency's impact

[7]Viscusi, K., *Risk By Choice* (Cambridge: Harvard University Press, 1983), p. 127.

Table 18.2 TRENDS IN WORK PLACE SAFETY IN THE UNITED STATES

Year	Injury and illness rates per 1,000 workers	Job fatalities per 1,000 workers
1977	93	0.091
1978	94	0.082
1979	95	0.080
1980	87	0.071
1981	83	0.069

Source: Bureau of Labor Statistics, *Occupational Injuries and Illness in the United States by Industry* (Washington, D.C.: Government Printing Office, annual).

on worker safety. A preliminary assessment can be made using information collected by the Bureau of Labor Statistics. As shown in Table 18.2, annual fatalities per 1,000 workers have declined since 1977. The same is true for injury and illness rates. However, the data must be interpreted with care because there are other factors that determine safety trends. As much as anything else, accident rates seem to be the product of demographic characteristics. Older, more experienced workers have far fewer accidents than unskilled workers. During periods of high unemployment, those with job seniority usually are the last to be laid off. Thus, injuries and fatalities tend to drop. Part of the apparent trend shown in Table 18.2 may reflect the impact of a weak economy during the early 1980s.

A number of studies have attempted to assess the performance of OSHA by using statistical techniques to account for the impact of demographic characteristics. Mendeloff used multiple regression analysis to predict what injury rates in manufacturing would have been if OSHA had not existed.[8] His conclusion was that no statistically significant effect could be attributed to the agency's efforts. Studies on aggregate injury rates by Viscusi and Marlow yielded similar results.[9] Disaggregated data focusing on specific types of injuries or specific work places do provide some support for OSHA, but the estimated impacts are small.[10]

There are several explanations for OSHA's apparent lack of success. First, the evidence indicates that workers are at least partially responsible for a substantial fraction of job-related injuries. The National Safety Council estimates that only 18 percent of all workmen's compensation cases were solely the result of unsafe working conditions. The remainder were either completely the fault of the worker (19 percent) or the consequence of a combination of workplace and human factors (63 percent).[11]

A second problem is that the penalties assessed by OSHA are not sufficient to motivate a significant change in industry behavior. Although fines per violation have

[8]Mendeloff, J., *Regulating Safety: An Economic and Political Analysis of Occupational Safety and Health Policy* (Cambridge: MIT Press, 1979).

[9]Viscusi, W. K., "The Impact of Occupational Safety and Health Regulation," *Bell Journal of Economics* (Spring 1979), pp. 117–140, and Marlow, M. L., "The Economics of Enforcement: The Case of OSHA," *Journal of Economics* (1982), pp. 165–171.

[10]Mendeloff, J., op. cit. and Smith, R. S., "The Impact of OSHA Inspections on Manufacturing Injury Rates," *Journal of Human Resources* (Spring 1979), pp. 145–170.

[11]National Commission on State Workmen's Compensation Laws, *Compendium on Workmen's Compensation* (Washington, D.C.: Government Printing Office), pp. 287–288.

Table 18.3 OSHA ENFORCEMENT ACTIVITIES

	Fiscal year		
	1976	1978	1980
Inspections (thousands)	90.3	57.2	63.4
Violations (thousands)	380.3	134.5	132.4
Proportion of serious violations	.02	.25	.34
Penalty per violation (dollars)	32.6	148.0	192.6

Source: Viscusi, W. K., *Risk By Choice* (Cambridge: Harvard University Press, 1983), p. 18.

increased in the last few years, they still average out to be only $.34 per worker. [12] This compares to estimated wage premiums of several hundred dollars per worker. The implication is that OSHA efforts are dwarfed by market forces promoting occupational health and safety. Also, although OSHA conducts thousands of inspections each year, its staff is able to detect only a small fraction of all job hazards.

The "New" OSHA

Although many businesspeople advocate that OSHA be abolished, there is virtually no chance of that happening. Every government agency develops its own constituency, and OSHA is no exception. Organized labor, while often frustrated by the rigidities of OSHA procedures, would vigorously oppose abolishing or significantly weakening the agency. OSHA also has its supporters in the business community. The thousands of regulations requiring firms to purchase or modify capital equipment have spawned industries that supply the needed equipment. These industries have a critical stake in OSHA's continued health. The existence of these industries also explains the difficulties of removing or modifying current regulations. Although it may seem unnecessary to require toilet seats with open fronts (the rule was originally conceived as a means of preventing social diseases), there were firms that profitably supplied them. These firms could not be expected to allow changes in regulations without a fight. Luckily, this was a battle that the suppliers lost and the toilet seat regulation was one of the thousand rescinded in 1978.

While OSHA has managed to survive the attacks of its critics, the agency has modified its course. Table 18.3 is a summary of OSHA enforcement activities for selected years. It shows a change in emphasis over time. In 1976, 90,000 inspections were conducted. But the 1980 figure is only about two-thirds of that amount. In the intervening period, OSHA administrators decided that small-firm industries with good safety records would be exempt from random safety inspections.

While reducing the total number of inspections, OSHA administrators also directed agency personnel to devote less attention to trivial violations. The result was that the number of violations for 1980 was about one-third the 1976 total. However, the proportion of serious violations increased from 2 percent to 34 percent over the same period. There also has been a dramatic increase in penalties per violation. The 1980 average of $192.60 is about six times the 1976 level.

[12]Viscusi, *Risk by Choice*, p. 24.

OSHA also has attempted to temper the adversarial relationship that exists between the agency and the firms that it regulates. The move to eliminate harassment over trivial matters has helped. One indication is that firms now contest only about six percent of alleged violations, compared to nearly twenty-five percent of all citations in 1980. OSHA also has initiated a policy whereby individual firms would take over some of the agency's routine inspection responsibilities. Under this initiative, labor-management committees would monitor health and safety standards. OSHA's role would be to function as a consultant or to intervene when problems arise.

Although present OSHA policies are less subject to criticism than during the agency's formative years, there still are opportunities for improvement. One would be to require the agency to balance the costs and benefits of its activities. Under present policy, compliance costs are a determining factor only if it can be demonstrated that the financial health of the affected firms would be significantly impaired by a proposed regulation. The courts have upheld OSHA's position. A precedent-setting case involved textile workers and cotton dust. Prolonged exposure to cotton dust can cause chronic coughing and even death. OSHA proposed that work places should not have more than 0.2 milligrams of dust per cubic meter of air. The textile industry objected, claiming that the benefits of the proposed standard had not been compared to the cost of compliance. OSHA officials responded that they were not required to use benefit-cost analysis in establishing regulations.

The issue went all the way to the Supreme Court, which held that the 1970 legislation establishing the agency was designed to give workers maximum protection against dangerous substances. The justices argued that the use of a benefit-cost standard would result in less protection and constitute a violation of the law. [13] Although the opinion stated that OSHA was not required to balance benefits and costs, it did not forbid such calculations.

Another recommendation for OSHA is to change the nature of the standards it sets. OSHA safety regulations are usually prescriptive. This means that they specify what a firm must do to avoid violations. Most economists would suggest a switch to performance standards. Performance standards indicate the desired objective and leave the firm to decide how it can be best achieved. For example, suppose OSHA is concerned about injuries caused by clothing catching in machinery. A prescriptive standard might require that expensive guards be placed around all moving equipment parts. Typically, this standard would apply to all businesses whether they have a history of such injuries or not. For some firms the cost of compliance would be very low, while for others it might be extremely high. A performance standard would specify an objective in terms of a reduced number of injuries. It might also include a fine if a firm's injury rate exceeded the specified amount. The advantage of the performance standard is that it allows the business to decide how the requirement can best be achieved. Management may decide that the preferred solution is to require employees to wear special clothing that is designed to prevent accidents. They may determine that a system of bonuses to employees for injury-free work periods is the optimal solution. They might decide that the equipment guards mandated by the prescriptive standard are the

[13]*American Textile Manufacturers Institute, Inc.* v. *R. J. Donovon, Sec. of Labor,* 69 L. Ed 2d 185 (1981).

best approach. The point is that business is simply told what it must achieve and then left to determine preferred solutions. The judgment of management is substituted for the wisdom of bureaucrats in solving the problem.

Obviously, performance standards are not without disadvantages. How does the agency decide what the level of performance should be? How are the penalties for noncompliance to be set? These are difficult questions and may require somewhat arbitrary answers. However, the existing prescriptive standards are also highly arbitrary and do not allow firms discretion in deciding how they should be met. A switch to performance standards should result in improved resource allocation. It would also improve OSHA's image by allowing firms a larger role in the decision-making process.

POLLUTION: ENVIRONMENTAL PROTECTION AGENCY (EPA)

The human environment is a pervasive concept. It encompasses the crust of the earth, its land and water surfaces, and the surrounding atmosphere. It also includes the animals and vegetation in those regions. However, in discussing pollution it is useful to think of the environment as the places from which resources are obtained and the depository to which the residuals resulting from the use of these resources are returned.

The environment has a capability for assimilating residuals. Smoke and dust are dissipated in the atmosphere. Human and animal wastes are transformed into nourishment for plants. But the recycling capacity of the environment is finite. When the volume of discharges becomes too great, then the natural environment is changed. Pollution is said to occur when these residuals accumulate to the point that they are harmful or unpleasant. For example, early settlers of Los Angeles enjoyed blue skies and impressive views of the surrounding mountains. But as the region grew, motor vehicles and industrial processes began to spew their wastes into the air. Initially, these discharges were assimilated without perceptible change. Soon, however, the recycling capacity of the atmosphere was overwhelmed. As a result, today's residents exist under a yellow-brown dome of hydrocarbons, carbon monoxide, and soot. They endure respiratory problems and itching eyes while living in an area where mountains and large buildings only a few miles away are completely obscured.

Pollution is a distinguishing characteristic of several U.S. cities. Los Angeles is known for its foul air. Cleveland's Cuyahoga River is remembered for having spontaneously burst into flame. Prior to recent clean-up efforts, businessmen from Pittsburgh could easily be identified by their telltale "ring-around-the collar". However, pollution is not a problem unique to the United States. In Sweden, it has destroyed marine life in over 6,000 lakes. Nearly one-third of West German forests have been damaged by acid raid. India's sacred Ganges River is contaminated by millions of gallons of untreated sewage and the cremated remains of some 35,000 Hindus thrown into the river each year.

The Economics of Pollution

How much pollution should there be? If eliminating pollution was costless, then the optimal level would be zero. But anyone who has studied economics knows that there are no free lunches. Pollution levels can be reduced only by using resources that are then are unavailable for other purposes. This idea is depicted in Figure 18.1. The curve shows a trade-off between pollution and GNP. It indicates that curbing pollution requires sacrificing goods and services. The figure also implies that the terms of the trade-off are not constant. Initial levels of pollution control can be achieved with little impact on GNP, but the final increments are much more costly. The increasing marginal cost of pollution abatement is an important concept and will be discussed in greater detail later in the section.

Figure 18.1 is a production possibilities frontier. As such, it shows the choices available to society, but provides no information about the particular pollution/GNP combination that should be selected. Determining the optimal point requires an assessment of the benefits derived from reducing pollution in comparison to the value of the goods and services that must be given up. The traditional decision-rule would be to reduce pollution as long as the marginal benefit of the last unit of abatement is at least as great as the marginal value of goods and services sacrificed.

Although the marginal benefit equals marginal cost principle is a golden rule for efficient resource allocation, something seems to have gone awry in determining optimal pollution levels. Most people would agree that there is too much pollution and that there is at least some need for government action. Why has the market system failed in this area?

As just mentioned, efficient resource allocation occurs when marginal benefits are equated to marginal costs. But for some activities, the benefits to an individual may be less than the sum of benefits accruing to society. If a decision is based only on personal benefits, then too few resources may be allocated to that activity. For example, a flu shot protects the individual from the disease, but can be rather unpleasant. Comparing private costs and benefits, many persons will risk a bout with the flu. However, vaccinations also confer benefits on others by reducing the likelihood that they will become ill. If individuals ignore this external benefit, there will be too few immunizations.

In other cases, the problem is that private costs differ from the total costs imposed on society. When this happens, too many resources may be allocated to an activity. The

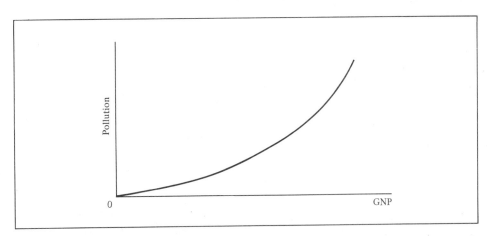

Figure 18.1. Pollution/GNP trade-off.

production of paper is a good example. A paper mill generates residuals in the form of chemicals, materials, and odors that are discharged into the environment. The excessive pollution associated with paper production occurs because the firm does not consider all of the costs of its activities. The problem is that prices of some of the inputs used by the firm do not reflect their true social cost. Specifically, the air and water used as mediums for waste discharge can be considered as free goods by the firm.

In maximizing profits, inputs that are costly are used sparingly. Managers can be less concerned about using resources that are not so expensive. Resources that are free to the firm can be used freely. Since the effective price of air and water is zero, there is no reason to conserve on their use. In fact, any attempt to reduce air and water pollution would require the substitution of other costly resources.

This result is shown in Figure 18.2. The line S_pS_p is the supply curve for paper as viewed by the firm. It is based on actual costs incurred and shows the amount of paper that will be produced at various prices. The equilibrium price and quantity are P_p and Q_p, respectively. The curve S_sS_s is the supply curve from society's perspective. It includes the private costs incorporated in S_pS_p as well as the social opportunity costs of air and water pollution. Note that S_sS_s implies that, at any given price, less paper will be produced than if S_pS_p were the basis for decision making. Using S_sS_s, the new equilibriums are Q_s and P_s. The analysis demonstrates that when the externalities involved in producing paper are included in the decision process, fewer resources are devoted to the activity and a higher price is charged.

Taking social costs into account also results in less pollution. There are two reasons for the reduction. First, since less paper is produced, fewer residuals are created. Second, if air and water no longer are considered as free mediums for waste disposal, then firms will have an incentive to economize on their use. Thus, production processes will be developed that generate less pollution.

Excess pollution occurs because of the lack of markets for some resources. Businesses that want more oil or workers must pay to obtain them. But no one can exert

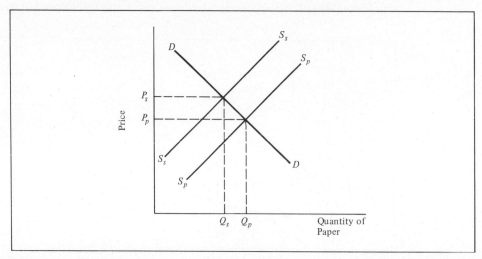

Figure 18.2.   Private and social costs of paper production.

an effective claim to ownership of the air, oceans, large lakes, or important rivers. Because there are no well-defined property rights, individuals and firms can make free use of these resources. Further, there is no mechanism to force them to take into account the social costs of their actions.

In some circumstances, those who are adversely affected by pollution may be able to negotiate with polluters. For example, consider a small community downstream from a paper mill. The residents of the town offer to compensate the firm for reducing its discharges into the river. There may be a payment that would make both the firm and the citizens better off.

Unfortunately, voluntary negotiation is not always feasible. Suppose that there are hundreds of firms and other sources polluting the river. Also assume that dozens of downstream locations are affected. Agreement between all of the involved parties would be an almost impossible task. One difficulty would be identifying the polluters and quantifying their contribution to the problem. Equally vexing is the free-rider problem. If one community pays to clean up the river, then all of the others downstream receive the same benefit without paying the cost. Knowing this, each town has an incentive to understate its willingness to contribute. The final result may be a failure to reach agreement.

The divergence between private and social costs and the impracticality of voluntary negotiations are the justifications for government intervention to protect the environment. In a free market system the absence of well-defined property rights usually makes it cheaper to pollute than not to pollute. The objective of environmental policy is to change behavior by modifying the incentive scheme so that excess pollution becomes costly. This may be accomplished by defining property rights, imposing taxes, providing subsidies, or setting limits on allowable pollution.

Major Sources of Pollution

Pollution is not a modern problem. Ancient historians wrote of garbage lining the streets of Rome. The canals of Venice have long functioned as open sewers. But widespread concern about the environment is of relatively recent origin. Two events are largely responsible for this environmental awakening. The first is urbanization. Today, over half of the people in the United States live in one percent of the land area. Where population is concentrated, there are large amounts of residuals discharged into the environment. The second event is industrialization. Huge amounts of wastes are created by power plants, refineries, slaughterhouses, and other enterprises. The aggregate result is that the regenerative powers of the environment are exceeded and excess pollution occurs.

Air Pollution   Air pollution either causes or aggravates lung cancer, respiratory disorders, diseases of the heart and blood vessels, skin diseases, allergies, and eye irritations. Although there are many contributors, the five primary sources of air pollution are:

> *Particulates.* Particulates are solid particles or liquid droplets small enough to remain suspended in the air. Included are dust, soot, and smoke, which

impair vision and breathing. Also included are various toxic substances that can poison the blood or affect vital organs.

Sulfur Oxides. Sulfur oxides are gases created by the burning of sulfer-containing fuels such as coal and oil. High levels cause a choking effect that restricts breathing. They also are the source of acid rain.

Nitrogen Oxides. High temperature burning of fuels causes nitrogen in the air to react, forming nitrogen oxides. Although these oxides are poisonous, the more important concern is that they facilitate other reactions that produce eye- and lung-irritating smog.

Hydrocarbons. Hydrocarbons are unburned fuels in gaseous or vapor form. These react in the air to form ozone, which is a principle component of smog and can aggravate various respiratory problems.

Carbon Monoxide. Carbon monoxide is a colorless, odorless poison gas resulting from incomplete combustion of fuels. Prolonged exposure reduces the amount of oxygen reaching the brain and can impair mental and physical functions.

Table 18.4 shows the amounts and sources of the five air pollutants just described. It indicates that the vast majority of carbon monoxide emissions result from motor vehicles and that industrial applications are the primary source of sulfur oxides and particulates. Responsibility for nitrogen oxides and hydrocarbons is shared by industry and transportation.

Water Pollution   Water pollution comes from point and nonpoint sources. Point sources are locations that can be clearly identified as the origin of a pollutant. Examples are sewer pipes, culverts, and other types of conduits. Pollutants flowing from locations that cannot be pinpointed are said to come from nonpoint sources. Examples are fertilizers washed from agricultural land and sediment from construction sites.

Water pollution has several harmful effects. Some substances react with dissolved oxygen. This process threatens fish and other marine life by reducing the amount of available oxygen. Other substances such as mercury and lead are highly toxic. They can affect humans directly or through their effect on the food chain. Finally, wastes and sediment can render bodies of water unfit for drinking and recreation. As with air

Table 18.4   ESTIMATES OF AIR POLLUTANTS BY TYPE AND SOURCE

Source	Millions of metric tons of pollutant				
	Particulates	Sulfer oxides	Nitrogen oxides	Hydrocarbons	Carbon monoxide
Transportation	1.4	0.8	8.5	7.7	69.5
Industry	5.8	21.7	10.7	10.7	12.5
Waste disposal	0.4	0.0	0.1	0.6	2.1
Miscellaneous	0.9	0.0	0.2	2.3	6.4
Total	8.5	22.5	19.5	21.3	90.5

Source: U.S. Environmental Protection Agency, *National Air Pollutant Emission Estimates, 1971–1981* (Washington, D.C.: U.S. Government Printing Office, September 1982).

pollution, there are many sources of water pollution. However, the most important are the following:

1. Organic wastes from sewage, farms, and industry.
2. Sediment from agriculture and construction.
3. Biological compounds such as phosphates from detergents and nitrogen from fertilizers.
4. Acid and mineral drainage from mining.
5. Toxic substances such as pesticides.

Government and the Environment

Federal legislation to protect the environment began with the Refuse Act of 1899, which required permits for discharging waste materials into navigable waters. However, enforcement was nil over the first 70 years. Additional water and air pollution legislation was passed in the 1940s and 1950s, but none of these acts had the teeth to really attack the pollution problem. Assertive federal involvement dates back only to 1970. In that year the Environmental Protection Agency was created by consolidating 15 programs administered by 5 agencies. The primary responsibility of the EPA is to control pollution by regulating discharges into the air, water, and land.

During 1970 Congress also greatly strengthened air pollution control legislation by passage of the Clean Air Act. Two years later the Water Pollution Control Act of 1972 was enacted. Subsequently, legislation such as the Toxic Substances Control Act of 1976, the Resource Conservation and Recovery Act of 1976, and the 1980 Comprehensive Environmental Response, Compensation, and Liability Act have further expanded the federal role in environmental protection.

Air Pollution and the EPA   Under provisions of the Clean Air Act of 1970, the Environmental Protection Agency established national air quality standards. These *ambient* standards specified the maximum amounts of various pollutants that should be in the air. Both primary and secondary standards were set. The primary standards focused on protecting human health, while the secondary standards were more stringent and were designed to prevent other damage such as to property, vegetation, and animals. An example is the permissible level for particulates. The primary standard specifies that the yearly average should be less than 75 micrograms per cubic meter of air. The secondary standard is 60 micrograms per cubic meter.

The primary standards were to be met by 1975. Each state was to submit a plan detailing its plans for compliance. States that did not comply or whose plan was unacceptable could be penalized by the loss of federal funds or prohibitions against industrial growth in the state. To facilitate management of the program, the EPA divided the country into 247 air quality control regions. When the 1975 deadline arrived, only 69 of the 247 regions were in compliance with all of the primary standards. Some cities, such as Los Angeles, Chicago, and Philadelphia, had not achieved the standards for any of the pollutants involved. As a result, the Clean Air Act was amended in 1977 to provide additional time. Under present law the standards were to be met by 1982, with extensions granted to 1987 for communities with special circumstances.

In addition to the national ambient standards, the Clean Air Act specified *emission* standards for both mobile and stationary sources of pollution. The standards for mobile sources were directed primarily at cars and trucks. Recall from Table 18.4 that motor vehicles are the main source of carbon monoxide and an important cause of nitrogen oxides and hydrocarbons. The Clean Air Act called for a 90-percent reduction in these emissions for 1975–6 model cars. The energy crisis of the mid-1970s and financial problems of the automobile manufacturers finally caused the deadline to be delayed to the 1981 model year. Today, manufacturers who fail to meet EPA emission standards can be fined or have their vehicles recalled.

Stationary source emission standards primarily are concerned with sulfur dioxide emissions from smokestacks. Based on local air conditions and other factors, they may require percentage reductions in emissions for specific sources of pollution. Firms that fail to comply can be fined or forced to shut down their operations. For example, an electric utility might be required to reduce its sulfur dioxide emissions by 25 percent. In response, the utility could switch to burning low-sulfur coal or it might install "scrubbers" that extract pollutants from gases as they go up its smokestacks.

Regulating thousands of stationary sources on a case-by-case basis is a complex and time-consuming task. It can also be very inefficient because costs of pollution control vary dramatically from one source to another. To illustrate, one study estimated that the cost of reducing emissions of hydrocarbons in the same region varied from $41 per ton for a gasoline terminal to $16,500 per ton in a large spray-painting operation in an automobile factory.[14] Even at a single plant there can be large variations in the cost of abatement. For example, controlling sulfur dioxide emissions from a large smokestack is much cheaper per ton of reduction than controlling emissions from a smaller stack.

Recently, the Environmental Protection Agency has begun to recognize there are alternatives to case-by-case regulation. In 1979 the agency initiated its *bubble* policy. Instead of regulating emissions on a stack-by-stack basis, this approach assumes that there is an imaginary bubble extending over an entire plant. The requirement imposed on the firm is to reduce the total emissions emanating from the bubble. The company is left to decide how to achieve the objective. This greatly reduces the total cost of compliance because resources can be allocated where they have the greatest impact. Emissions from sources that are relatively inexpensive to control will be greatly diminished. In contrast, fewer resources will be devoted to pollution sources that are costly to control.

The bubble policy shows considerable promise. By the end of 1982, the EPA had approved over 30 bubbles. The agency estimates that, in comparison to stack-by-stack regulation, the average savings to the firms involved were about $3 million. Currently, another 150 bubbles are in various stages of the approval process.[15]

An extension of the bubble concept is the use of *offsets*. Whereas bubbles promote

[14]Ginsberg, P., and Schaumburg, G., *Economic Incentive Systems for the Control of Hydrocarbons from Stationary Sources,* Report to the Council on Environmental Quality (1980).
[15]Council on Environmental Quality, *Environmental Quality, 1982 Annual Report* (Washington, D.C.: U.S. Government Printing Office, 1983), p. 8.

intrafirm efficiency, offsets perform a similar function on an interfirm basis. Essentially, they allow one firm to pollute if another firm will agree to offset the impact by reducing its emissions. If the cost of pollution control is much greater to the first firm than it is to the second, then the firms may be able to negotiate an agreement that will make both firms better off. In practice, the EPA participates in this procedure by granting "Emission Reduction Credits" to firms that reduce emissions through approved programs. These credits can then be sold to other firms or held for the firm's own expansion. In fact, the agency actually has established "banks" to facilitate the trading of Emission Reduction Credits. Currently, such banks are functioning in Oregon, Kentucky, California, Washington, and Pennsylvania.

Water Pollution and the EPA   The Water Pollution Control Act of 1972 established as its ultimate goal that "the discharge of pollutants into the navigable waters be eliminated by 1985." With respect to municipalities, the act focused on sewage systems. In 1970 almost 30 percent of the U.S. population was not served by a sewer system. The legislation increased the incentive for construction of such systems by upping the share provided by the federal government from 55 to 75 percent.

With respect to industrial sources of water pollution, the Water Pollution Control Act specified two national goals. First, by 1977 discharges into the nation's waters were to be controlled using the "Best Practical Control Technology" (BPT). This standard was to be determined by considering the performance of the most effective firms in an industry. Second, by 1983 the requirement was the use of "Best Available Control Technology" (BAT). This deadline specified the use of the best possible methods for controlling discharges.

When the 1977 deadline arrived, many firms were not in compliance with the BPT requirement. Part of the problem was that the EPA had been saddled with an unreasonable task. The legislation required the agency to set individual standards for hundreds of different industries. For example, the guidelines for canned and preserved seafood processing involved 33 subcategories. Crab alone was broken into Conventional Blue Crab, Mechanized Blue Crab, Nonremote Alaskan Crab, Remote Alaskan Crab, Nonremote Alaskan White Crab, Remote Alaskan White Crab, and Tanner Crab. Once the guidelines were established, the EPA still faced the task of issuing permits to thousands of firms. Worse, businesses that believed they had been treated unfairly could request a time-consuming hearing.

Congress responded to the problem by pushing back the deadlines. The BPT deadline was extended to 1979 and the BAT date was changed to 1984 for toxic pollutants and 1987 for others. However, the Environmental Protection Agency is on record as predicting that it is unlikely that even these relaxed deadlines will be met.[16] It seems likely that the deadlines will be extended or partially ignored.

Toxic Substances and the EPA   Pesticides have greatly improved the productivity of agriculture by reducing losses from insects and rodents. But their use involves a trade-off in that some pose a hazard to humans and animals. As amended in 1972 and 1978, the Insecticide, Fungicide, and Rodenticide Act gave the EPA power to require

[16]Ibid, p. 86.

registration and testing of compounds before they are put on the market. The Toxic Substances Control Act of 1976 extended this power to other dangerous chemicals. Products already being marketed can be removed or required to include warning labels if they are found to constitute health hazards. Perhaps the best-known action of the EPA in this area was its 1972 ban of DDT.

The most recent responsibility given to the EPA involves the disposal of hazardous wastes. Each year millions of tons of dangerous waste material are generated by industrial processes. Too often, these residuals are disposed of in an improper manner. Sometimes they are burned, spewing highly toxic substances into the atmosphere. On other occasions they are dumped in locations that allow the poisons to seep into water supplies or to contaminate urban land areas. In 1976, Congress passed the Resource Conservation and Recovery Act. This legislation requires safe disposal of hazardous wastes and empowers the Environmental Protection Agency to set up procedures for proper waste management. The Comprehensive Environmental Response, Compensation, and Liability Act of 1980 created a superfund of $1.6 billion to assist in cleaning up existing sites where hazardous wastes have been deposited. To date, over 400 priority locations have been designated. The 1980 act also specifies that, if they can be identified, individual firms can be forced to pay for clean-up efforts.

Evaluation of Public Policy

Environmental protection has been a very costly undertaking. In 1975, almost one-fifth of the total capital expenditures in the primary metals industry were for pollution abatement. By 1980 the share still was nearly 10 percent. Heavy burdens also have been imposed on producers of electricity, paper, chemicals, and petroleum. [17] Future efforts will continue to require huge amounts of resources. It is estimated that the cumulative cost between 1979 and 1988 will exceed $500 billion. [18] What are the results of these sacrifices? Is there evidence that the air and water are less polluted now than they were before the EPA was established?

Effect of Air Pollution Regulation   Trends in total emissions of various pollutants often are used to evaluate the impact of EPA air pollution control efforts. These may be misleading because they do not accurately reflect conditions in specific problem areas. As an alternative, a Pollutant Standards Index (PSI) was developed to measure air quality in specific locations on a daily basis. The index uses a scale of 0 to 500 to represent concentrations of the principal air pollutants. A value of 100 is used to designate the national ambient standard for a pollutant. A PSI value less than 100 is interpreted as good or moderate air quality with respect to that pollutant. Values from 100 to 500 are associated with unhealthful or hazardous air conditions.

Figure 18.3 is a population exposure profile for the five main air pollutants. It shows trends in the number of days per year that people in selected urban areas are exposed to high PSI values. In reporting ozone and nitrogen oxide levels, the data for

[17]U.S. Bureau of Economic Analysis, *Survey of Current Business* (Washington, D.C.: U.S. Government Printing Office, June 1982).
[18]Council on Environmental Quality, op. cit., 1980, p. 394.

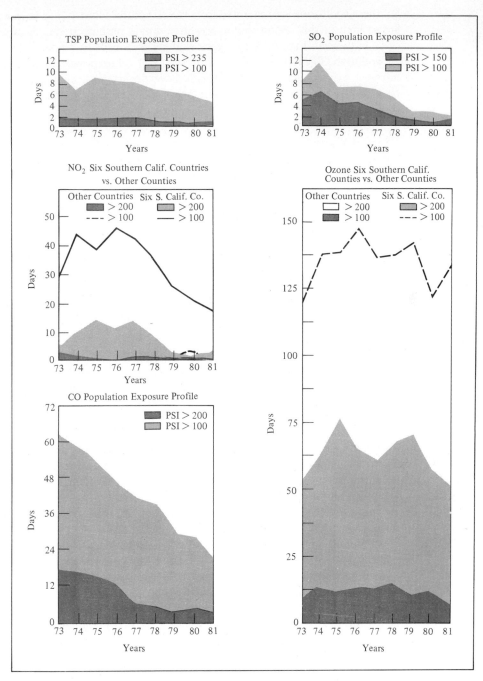

Figure 18.3. Air pollution trends. (Council on Environmental Quality, op.cit., 1980, p. 35.)

Southern California are separated from the rest of the country. The reason is that levels are so high in this region that aggregation would obscure trends in other locations.

In general, Figure 18.3 suggests that progress is being made in the battle against air pollution. The number of days with high PSI values of particulates, sulfur dioxide, nitrogen oxides, and carbon monoxide have declined substantially since 1973. The trend for ozone levels has been somewhat more erratic, but there does seem to be progress.

Effect of Water Pollution Regulation   Indices of trends in water pollution are more difficult to construct than those for air pollution. One of the problems is that each water user is sensitive to different pollution levels. Improvements in water quality for one purpose may have no effect on another. For example, dissolved oxygen in water is critical for sustaining marine life, but of no importance in water used for drinking or swimming.

One measure of changes in water quality is the assessment of individual states as to their progress in meeting the goals of the Water Pollution Control Act of 1972. In 1982, 33 states provided this information to the federal government. Of that total, 21 reported generally improving water quality and 12 indicated no change. None of the 33 states reported a statewide trend toward degradation in water quality. However, 23 states noted degradation in some localized areas.[19]

Problems and Alternatives   Until recently, the EPA has relied almost exclusively on standards as the method for regulating pollution. Such standards present a number of problems. First, when they are set on either a geographic or an industry basis it is difficult to take into account individual variations in the cost of pollution abatement. On the other hand, any attempt to tailor guidelines to individual pollution sources quickly becomes unmanageable. Second, standard setting requires a great deal of information regarding the effects of pollutants and, more importantly, about the costs of abatement. Frequently, the result is arbitrary decisions that are unrelated to the benefits and costs involved. A third problem is that standards may stifle innovation. If regulations for required emission reduction are written in terms of available technologies for control, then businesses may have little incentive to develop new techniques for abatement.

The EPA bubble and Emissions Reduction Credit programs discussed earlier in the chapter are steps in the right direction. By providing firms with flexibility in determining how pollution control expenditures can most effectively be allocated, they allow a specified reduction in emissions to be achieved at lower cost than would be possible under the conventional standards approach. The use of such policies should be expanded. A recent innovation is "netting." Usually, Emissions Reductions Credits apply only to a single pollutant. Netting is an approach whereby reductions of a pollutant below the required level can be counted or netted against another pollutant whose emissions are above the standard.

Another policy option is the use of "effluent" taxes. Under this scheme, the firm is allowed to choose the quantity of pollution, but is taxed for the privilege. By changing

[19]Council on Environmental Quality, op. cit., 1982, p. 37.

the rate of the tax the regulatory body provides varying incentives for pollution control. One advantage of effluent taxes is that they encourage efficient resource allocation. First, the externality problem is solved because the firm is forced to take into account the social costs of its actions. Second, by allowing the firm to select the optimal trade-off between emissions and taxes, variations in the cost of abatement are taken into account. Firms with high control costs will make smaller reductions and pay large amounts of tax. Revenues received can be used to compensate the victims of their pollution. Firms that can easily control pollution will make large cutbacks on discharges and avoid the tax.

Although promising, effluent taxes are not a panacea for the pollution problem. A major difficulty is determining the proper level of the tax. Theoretically, the marginal tax rate should correspond to the marginal benefit of pollution control. Thus, firms would continue to devote resources to reducing their emissions until the marginal cost exceeded the marginal benefit. In actual practice, marginal costs are difficult to determine and any assesment of marginal benefits must be highly speculative. In spite of the problems, effluent taxes have been successfully used in Europe. However, they have not been widely adopted in the United States.

SUMMARY
Working Conditions: Occupational Safety and Health Administration (OSHA)

Risk Premiums in Labor Markets   Economic theory predicts that workers who are aware of job-related risks will require wage premiums as compensation. Empirical estimates of risk premiums exhibit considerable variation. Lack of adequate information, the problem of assessing low-probability risks, and differences between private and social costs may limit the effectiveness of market forces in efficiently dealing with occupational risk.

OSHA Origins and Procedures   OSHA was established in 1970 in response to a perceived "on-the-job health and safety crisis." The agency was empowered to set and enforce mandatory standards. Employers are responsible for complying with OSHA regulations and fines can be assessed for violations.

Evaluation of OSHA   OSHA has been a particularly unpopular regulatory agency because many of its standards have been complex and arbitrary. Also, past decisions seem to have paid little attention to costs of compliance. Government figures indicate a decline in injuries and fatalities in recent years, but other factors may be partially responsible. Statistical studies provide uncertain evidence that OSHA has had much impact.

The "New" OSHA   OSHA has modified many of its most objectionable standards. The agency also has reduced inspections and citations for trivial violations. However, the agency still could improve its performance by use of benefit-cost analysis. Resource allocation might also be improved if OSHA used performance standards that allow firms to choose the manner of compliance.

Pollution: Environmental Protection Agency (EPA)

The Economics of Pollution   The opportunity cost of pollution control is reduced availability of goods and services. A market economy generates excess pollution because firms and consumers are not forced to consider the social costs of their actions. The divergence between social and private costs and difficulties in formulating voluntary agreements are the main justification for government intervention to protect the environment

Major Sources of Pollution   The five primary sources of air pollution are particulates, sulfur oxides, nitrogen oxides, hydrocarbons, and carbon monoxide. Water pollution comes from point and nonpoint sources. Pollutants include organic wastes, sediment, biological compounds, acids from mining, and toxic substances.

Government and the Environment   In 1970 the Environmental Protection Agency was established to regulate discharges into the air, water, and land. The agency is responsible for achieving national ambient standards for air quality. It also administers emission standards for mobile and stationary sources of air pollution. EPA efforts to control water pollution include federal financial assistance for sewer construction and the control of discharges into the nation's waters. The EPA also has authority to ban the use of toxic substances and to force firms to use safe practices for disposal of hazardous wastes.

Evaluation of Public Policy   Over the last decade, hundreds of billions of dollars have been spent on environmental protection. During that period there has been a general improvement in air quality and some improvement in water quality. However, the standards approach favored by the EPA is a rather inefficient way of dealing with the pollution problem. Recent innovations by the agency, such as the use of bubbles and Emission Reduction Credits, can achieve the same results at lower total costs. Effluent taxes are another policy option.

DISCUSSION QUESTIONS

1. Should employers be held responsible for employees who fail to comply with OSHA standards?
2. Should workers be allowed to waive their rights to work in an "OSHA-acceptable" work environment in return for higher wages?
3. Are performance standards always preferable to prescriptive standards?
4. Would there be a correlation between wealth and willingness to accept job-related risks? Explain.
5. Should OSHA concentrate its efforts on reducing accidents or on preventing health hazards? Which is the more difficult task?
6. How might a researcher go about estimating the benefits of pollution control? What problems would complicate the effort?

7. Does it make sense to have national standards for auto emissions? Would regional standards be a better approach?

8. How should the EPA go about limiting water pollution from nonpoint sources? What problems are involved?

9. It has been suggested that the EPA set some limit for total emissions and then auction off pollution rights to the highest bidders. What are the pros and cons of this approach?

five

SELECTED TOPICS

chapter *19*

Government Enterprise

Chapter Outline

The difference between Americans and Europeans is not that Americans have a peculiar ineptitude for operating public enterprises. The difference is that Americans have been guided by a doctrine that accords a second-rate apologetic status to such effort.

J. K. Galbraith[1]

The growth and development of regulation by administrative commission in the United States may be partially explained as a reaction to the dilemma of monopoly abuses under private control versus the distrust of public ownership. Regulation is seen as imposing constraints on the exploitive capitalist without sacrificing the virtues of capitalism. Still, there are many instances of government enterprise in the United States. Some, such as the Post Office, Amtrak, the Tennessee Valley Authority, state liquor stores, and local garbage, water, and sewage services, are highly visible. However, there are also many other types of government businesses that are less well known. For example, agencies of the federal government operate hotels, saloons, grocery stores, department stores, and printing establishments. The Department of Defense has even been in the business of manufacturing women's underwear. A comprehensive list would require many pages.

This chapter is an analysis and evaluation of government enterprise. The first section considers the circumstances and objectives that have led to public ownership. The second presents a simple model of the behavior and performance of enterprises under public versus private control. The final section of the chapter is an evaluation of selected examples of government ownership. Three case studies are considered—the Post Office as an example of public enterprise mandated by law, Amtrak to illustrate public ownership stemming from failure of private enterprise, and the electric utility industry to represent public ownership as an alternative to regulation.

OBJECTIVES AND ORIGINS OF GOVERNMENT ENTERPRISE

Examples of government enterprise date to ancient times. Athens had its state-owned mines. Rome (to the great discomfort of the early Christians) provided games and circuses for its citizens. Egypt during the time of Joseph was in the business of collecting and disbursing grain. Although the early history of state-owned enterprise is an interesting study, the remainder of this section will concentrate on government ownership in modern times.

As one looks at the scope of public ownership in other capitalist nations in comparison to the United States, the differences are significant. Figure 19.1 shows the proportion of public ownership for specific sectors in selected countries. In the United States and in all the countries shown in Figure 19.1, postal service is provided by government. In sectors such as coal mining, automobile and ship building, and steel production, the proportions in other countries vary from zero to 100 percent public ownership. In contrast, these industries are entirely in the private sector in the United States.

The energy, transportation, and communications sectors are especially interesting

[1]Galbraith, J. K., *Economics and the Public Purpose* (Boston: Houghton Mifflin, 1973), p. 281.

Percent publicly owned: ○ 0% ◔ 25%* ◑ 50%* ◕ 75%* ● all or nearly all

	Posts	Tele-commun-ications	Elec-tricity	Gas	Railways	Coal	Airlines	Motor industry	Steel	Ship-building	
Austria	●	●	●	●	●	●	●	●	◕	na	Austria
Belgium	●	●	◔	◔	●	○	●	○	○	○	Belgium
Britain	●	◑	●	●	●	●	◕	◑	◕	●	Britain
France	●	●	●	●	●	●	◕	◑	○	○	France
W. Germany	●	●	◕	◑	●	◑	●	◔	◕	◔	W. Germany
Holland	●	●	◕	◕	●	na	◕	○	◕	○	Holland
Italy	●	●	◕	●	●	na	●	◑	◑	◕	Italy
Spain	●	◔	○	◕	●	◑	●	○	●	◕	Spain
Sweden	●	●	◑	●	●	na	◑	○	◕	◕	Sweden
Switzerland	●	●	●	●	●	na	○	○	○	na	Switzerland

Figure 19.1. Public ownership in selected countries. ("Europe's Mixed Economics," *The Economist,* March 4, 1978, p. 93.)

comparisons. In the United States about one-quarter of electricity sales are made by publicly owned utilities. Most of these utilities are owned by individual communities. By way of contrast, in other capitalist countries electricity is usually sold by government-owned firms, and the degree of federal control is much greater. In the United States, natural gas is provided entirely by private industry. In other nations complete control by public enterprise is common.

Private companies operate the telephone network in the United States, while state-owned systems are the rule elsewhere. Public television in the United States has had some commendable successes, but its audience and budget are still a small fraction of the private market. Although some nations have independently owned networks, the bulk of television and radio communications outside the United States are government sponsored.

In the United States the federal government has taken over responsibility for passenger rail service, but most freight traffic still is moved by private firms over privately owned roadbeds. In other nations the railroads are typically nationalized. All intercity bus service in the United States is privately provided. In other nations public systems are the norm. The same is true for airlines. In the United States investor-owned firms such as United, Pan American, TWA, Eastern, and Delta compete for business, while most other countries have state-controlled enterprises, such as British Airways, Air France, Alitalia, and Lufthansa.

It is tempting to conclude that the differences between the United States and other nations with respect to the scope of public enterprise simply reflect differences in philosophy—that countries with more state-owned firms are those whose citizens don't have the same commitment to free enterprise as do people in the United States.

Although ideology undoubtedly has played some role in determining the scope of government ownership, it is overly simplistic to assume that there are not other, equally important, influences. In noncommunist nations the choice of public over private ownership has usually reflected specific circumstances of an industry or of the nation's economy rather than the desire to socialize per se. In the discussion that follows, some of the main forces and objectives leading to public ownership are identified. Often it has been a combination of circumstances and objectives that has precipitated government involvement.

National Objectives

Defense   During times of war, certain industries have been nationalized to mobilize their services for the defense effort. During World War I the U.S. rail system was deemed unable to meet the demands placed upon it. In their attempt to maximize profits, the individual railroads created bottlenecks and caused inefficient routings of defense materials. The government responded by assuming management of the nation's railroads from December 1917 to March 1920. Although actual operation was left to the management of the individual firms, overall allocation decisions were made by government officials. After the urgencies of the war had subsided, the railroad system was returned to its original owners.

In the case of the railroads, the government had no difficulty in transferring operations back to the private sector. At other times the task has not proved so simple. The Tennessee Valley Authority had its beginnings in 1917 as a source of electricity for production of nitrates for explosives. At the end of World War I the government put the facility up for sale, but the bids received from private companies were rejected as insufficient. After standing idle for a number of years, in the 1930s the government began selling electricity to private users. Additional facilities were constructed or purchased to form the vast public power system that exists today.

Economic Emergency   In some cases general economic conditions have been the catalyst for government enterprise. The Great Depression precipitated the formation of a number of public enterprises designed to provide assistance to ailing firms. In the United States, the Reconstruction Finance Corporation was formed to provide credit to American industry. Operating from 1933 to 1953, the RFC made nearly $50 billion in loans. In Italy the Institute for Industrial Reconstruction was established for a similar purpose in 1933. That agency has evolved into a vast holding company and presently has substantial stock interests in steel, shipbuilding, telephone service, and electricity supply in Italy. Many incursions of government into the domain of business had their genesis during the worldwide depression of the 1930s.

Multi-Use Projects   Some types of government enterprise have resulted from projects that have multiple uses. Government dam building is a good example. Dams store water to irrigate agricultural land, provide flood control, create recreational facilities, and can be used for hydroelectric generation of power. Once the government builds the dams, it normally becomes the manager of all the associated enterprises. Lease of the facilities to private entrepreneurs is a possibility, but has not been the normal practice. In particular, the government's dam-building activities have put it in the business of selling electric power.

Improved Efficiency

Standard for Evaluation   One of the bright hopes for government enterprise was that, where there were comparable private firms, the public operations could be used as a yardstick to evaluate the performance of the private sector. This concept was articulated most frequently with respect to the electric power industry. During the 1920s and 1930s problems with holding companies and cumbersome regulatory proceedings caused disillusionment with the private utilities. It was anticipated that publicly owned and operated firms, not motivated by the quest for profits, could act as a benchmark to be used by regulatory commissions and other policymaking bodies in judging the costs, rate levels, and rate structures of investor-owned firms.

It soon became apparent that the yardstick concept was better in theory than in practice. To provide a valid comparison it was necessary that public and private utilities be operating in comparable circumstances and under similar conditions. This requirement was seldom met. First, the costs faced by public enterprises were often quite different. Able to raise capital at a lower cost because of the risk-free position of the federal government or the tax-free status of interest on municipal bonds, government enterprise had a cost advantage in obtaining capital. Second, heavy taxes imposed on investor-owned utilities were not levied on public firms. Third, public distribution companies were sometimes able to obtain power at bargain rates from federal hydroelectric projects. Fourth, although publicly owned utilities are not required to satisfy the profit expectations of investors, municipal utilities are sometimes considered a source of funds for city treasuries. Where this is the case, low prices to consumers are not the only objective. Finally, if public power generation comes from a multi-use dam, then there is a problem of how the costs of the facility are allocated. It is possible that the true cost of providing electric power may be incorrectly computed, depending on the cost allocation. Although it is not possible to use the costs and prices of public power projects as a strict and precise measure of private performance, the coexistence of public and private enterprise can serve as a broad gauge of the performance of each.

Source of Competition   The existence or threat of competition from publicly owned firms may serve as a check on the practices of private firms. Once again, the electric power industry provides a good example of this possibility. In the late 1930s the Tennessee Valley Authority made drastic cuts in electricity rates. Since that time electricity rates charged by the TVA have been among the lowest in the nation. Over the years the TVA has gradually extended its market area and the possibility of further encroachment could not be ignored by private firms in the area. These utilities have responded to the TVA threat by reducing their own rates for electricity. As a result the impact of the rate experiments of the TVA has extended far beyond its marketing area. Electricity prices charged by investor-owned utilities that border the TVA are much lower than rates of companies in nearby Florida and the Northeast.

Low electricity prices of the Tennessee Valley Authority have had a significant impact on the development of that region. Prior to the TVA the area was economically stagnant. By reducing the cost of power, industry was induced into the region. The presence of new industry brought jobs and a higher standard of living. In addition, the low electric rates accelerated the electrification of the area. More homes were connected to power lines and more electricity was used in the home. Students of the TVA are in general agreement that the pricing policies of the agency have had a significant impact on the development of the enterprise's market area.[2]

Although the TVA experiment is a notable success in aggressive pricing policies by government enterprise, examples of vigorous competition between public and private businesses are not widespread. In the United States, industry has voiced consistent and effective political opposition to price cutting. Also, managers of government enterprises are often no more anxious to become involved in price competition than are their private counterparts. Outside the United States, price collusion between public and private producers is probably more common than price competition. Unless publicly owned firms are given a clear mandate to compete, there is no guarantee that their presence will have much effect on prices.

Production Efficiency   The British coal industry was nationalized in 1947 and the steel industry was taken over by the state in 1967. In both cases the goal was the improvement in the efficiency of operations. Prior to the government's intervention both of these industries had stagnated. There was a need for modernization and improved management that was not being met by the private sector. The justification for the state's involvement was that the government had the resources and the commitment to make the necessary improvements. The evidence indicates that a substantial *initial* improvement did result from these changes. Productivity increases through the early 1970s compared favorably with those in manufacturing and with similar industries under private control in other countries.[3] But union squabbles and difficult economic conditions have tarnished the record of British nationalized industries in recent years. During its first four years, the Thatcher government returned all or parts of seven large public companies to the private sector. Others are likely to follow.

Failures or Abuses in the Private Sector

High Prices   The genesis of some municipal electric utilities was the hope of the citizenry for lower prices under public ownership. In some cases price differences between private and public utilities simply represent differences in tax treatment. In moving to public ownership the taxes paid by the private firm are lost and, thus, must be made up in other ways. However, in certain circumstances the publicly owned utility can provide substantially lower electric rates. Certain federal projects can sell low-cost

[2]For a thorough study of the rate-cutting policies of the TVA, see Hellman, R., *Government Competition in the Electric Utility Industry* (New York: Praeger, 1972), pp. 115–187.

[3]See Shepherd, W. G., *Economic Performance Under Public Ownership* (New Haven: Yale University Press, 1965); and Tivey, L., ed., *The Nationalized Industries Since 1960* (Toronto: University of Toronto Press, 1973).

hydroelectric power to municipal utilities, but not to privately owned firms. Thus, by converting to public ownership, a community may become eligible for cheap energy. Obviously, there is only so much low-cost electricity available, and a wholesale rush to municipal ownership would quickly exhaust the supply. Nevertheless, there are communities that pay substantially less for power because of this arrangement.

Unprofitable Operations   The creation of Amtrak to manage rail passenger service in the United States stemmed from the large losses sustained by the railroads during the 1950s and 1960s. Had the government not assumed financial responsibility for the system, passenger service almost certainly would have been terminated on almost all routes in the United States. The origin and experience of Amtrak will be considered in detail later in the chapter. At this point it is simply pointed out as an example of a service taken over by government because it had proven unprofitable to private industry.

Another illustration of private industry's "inability to make it" is the Penn Central debacle. Faced with the bankruptcy of the Penn Central and five other Northeastern railroads, Congress authorized the formation of the Consolidated Rail Corporation (Conrail), a nonprofit government corporation, to continue the operations of these railroads. Intended as a means of helping the railroads get back on their feet, the federal government is now attempting to return Conrail to private ownership.

In some cases the problem is not that private firms could not provide the service or product, but that the price would be higher than is desired. Urban transit systems are an example. The desire for mass transit at low cost may require a subsidy of the rates that are charged. The subsidy may be justified by the attempt to reduce congestion, pollution, or fuel consumption resulting from automobile travel; the desire to provide cheap transportation for elderly or handicapped children; or as an exercise in optimal pricing that requires that price be set at marginal cost and that fixed costs be made up from other sources. Usually, there is no special reason why transit systems could not be operated privately and the subsidy paid to the firm, but the more common practice is for the city to operate the enterprise. When federal assistance has been obtained for construction of facilities, the city may be legally required to assume responsibility for operations.

Another circumstance where private industry may be unable to operate profitably in a market occurs when a firm is forced to provide service to high-cost users as part of its obligation to a regulatory commission or a governmental agency. Historically, part of the plight of the railroads was due to the difficulty of terminating service to unprofitable segments of their operations. The railroads were required to maintain and operate freight and passenger service over routes where demand was insufficient to cover even marginal costs. Because of competition from trucking, buses, and airlines, it was not possible to raise prices enough on more lucrative routes to subsidize losing operations. The desire to provide inexpensive postal services to rural areas is another example. The refusal of the government to allow private competition in the delivery of first class mail stems from the philosophy of providing universal service at uniform rates. First class mail service is maintained as a monopoly and the uniform price is kept high enough to generate a subsidy to high-cost services such as delivery to rural areas.

Size and Risk   Sometimes the costs of an endeavor are so high and the risk so great that the private sector cannot or will not provide financing. The Panama Canal, giant federal dams, and the development of satellite technology are examples. Although there were sufficient resources available in the private sector, the problems of coordination, the consequences of failure, and the very long time horizon involved in these projects made them unlikely investments for private entrepreneurs. In the case of satellites, once the delivery system had been perfected and the procedures made more reliable, industry joined with government in the launching of satellites for commercial purposes.

With respect to satellites and also peaceful use of nuclear energy, development was the result of military objectives pursued by the government. Prospects for advanced energy systems such as the breeder reactor, fusion power, or general use of photovoltaic cells for production of electricity will also be dependent on development work by the federal government. It is likely that private firms will ultimately take the lead in using whatever technologies prove technically and economically viable, but the government must first assume a large share of the risk and development cost.

Political or Philosophical Forces

Ideological Preference   In almost every case where an industry has been nationalized in the United States or in other capitalist nations, there has been a basic economic cause, such as those just identified. Although the desire for socialism has not been the fundamental force, the preferences of the prevailing political party have sometimes been the deciding factor. The British steel industry is a good example. After 30 years of problems and discussion the industry was nationalized in 1951 by the Labour Party, which was then in power. When a Conservative administration took office, it exercised its philosophical preference by putting most of the industry back into the private sector in 1953. The flip-flop occurred again in 1967, when a Labour government achieved control and steel production reverted back to public ownership. The election of a Conservative government in 1979 revived discussions of "privatization" of the industry. This step has not yet been taken. However, the Thatcher government has proposed to sell 51% of British Telecom (Britain's state-owned telephone company) to private interests.

Punishment   On some occasions nationalization has been used as a means of punishing the owners of private firms for past behavior. Before World War II Renault was a large, privately owned manufacturer of automobiles in France. The owners of the company collaborated with the Germans during the war and, in retribution, the postwar French government took over the firm. Since that time Renault has functioned as an aggressive and successful public firm. Similarly, the assets of private firms have sometimes been expropriated by leftist governments to punish capitalists for gouging consumers or exploiting workers. The action of the Allende regime in Chile in assuming ownership of the assets of U.S. copper firms in the 1970s is an example.

Nationalism   Foreign investment has been an important factor in the quest for industrialization by less-developed countries. As these nations have developed an increased sense of national identity, a resentment of what they considered to be the rape of their natural resources has often evolved. Revelations of political interference by multinational firms in their internal affairs have also aroused their displeasure. To avoid what they perceived as being a too rapid use of their resources, to retain more of the profits from industrial activities, and to rid themselves of undesirable foreign influence, some of these nations have assumed control of the assets of the multinationals. This motive differs from the punishment objective in that the incentive is the desire for a bigger share of the pie and more independence, rather than the attempt at revenge.

EFFICIENCY AND GOVERNMENT ENTERPRISE

The common perception in the United States is that public enterprise is not only ideologically inferior to private ownership, but also inherently less efficient and less responsive to consumer preferences. This judgment may be a bit hasty for at least two reasons. First, the alternatives being compared need to be made explicit. To assert that publicly owned firms aren't as aggressive or as consumer-oriented as firms in a highly competitive environment is probably true, but irrelevant. Typically, public enterprise involves activities with substantial economies of scale. As such, a large number of competing firms is not a viable alternative. On the other hand, if the comparison is between government enterprise and a private monopoly (whether regulated or unregulated), the reasons for assuming one form of ownership to be more efficient and responsive than the other are not clear. Likewise, if the alternative is an oligopolistic market structure whose firms have evolved into a pattern of collusion to avoid vigorous price competition, the choice is, again, not obvious.

Second, it is important that the criteria for comparison be specified. Typically, the economist focuses on profits, prices, and costs. However, as discussed in the previous section, public enterprises are often created for reasons other than efficiency and low prices. It is not uncommon that they be charged with achieving several, not necessarily consistant, objectives. In some cases the organization may be a means of maintaining services that private industry has or would have abandoned as unprofitable, but that are deemed to have social benefits. Other public enterprises are designed to assure equitable prices. Some government business, such as certain municipal utilities, serve an important revenue-producing function. Where there are multiple goals there must be trade-offs. Prices, profits, and costs may be higher or lower depending on the pressures exerted by other objectives. To compare a publicly owned enterprise intended to pursue multiple goals to a private firm whose primary focus is maximizing profits is to put the public firm at an inherent disadvantage.

The theory of the private firm has been developed to a high degree of specificity and sophistication. In contrast, there is no widely accepted theory of public enterprise. Most of the existing literature deals with optimal pricing and investment decisions or is directed to descriptive evaluations of performance.[4] The following discussion is an attempt at a simple theory of public enterprise and is based on previous work by

[4]One of the most useful works on pricing is Turvey, R., *Economic Analysis and Public Enterprise* (London: Allen & Unwin, 1971). For an evaluation of the British experience, see Shepherd, W. G., *Economic Performance Under Public Ownership* (New Haven: Yale University Press, 1965). An excellent book of readings is Turvey, R., ed., *Public Enterprise* (Baltimore: Penguin Books, 1968).

Lindsay.[5] It is intended to provide a partial explanation as to why government-owned firms may respond differently than would privately owned firms to identical conditions of demand.

It is assumed that managers of both public and private firms are positively motivated by the lure of higher salaries and that their actions are largely directed toward activities that increase their salaries. It is further assumed that the level of monetary compensation of managers is determined by the perceived productivity of those managers. In the case of the private firm, perceived productivity is measured by the firm's board of directors and is usually closely associated with the profit performance of the firm. For a public enterprise, perceived productivity is determined by legislatures or executive agencies and involves a subjective evaluation of the manager's contribution to the achievement of whatever goals have been set for the enterprise.

A private firm's board of directors can evaluate the performance of managers on the basis of the firm's success in the marketplace. Consumers indicate their acceptance of the firm's products by their purchases. Growing profits and a stable or improving market share are indicators of good manager performance. For public enterprise the standards of managerial excellence are not so clear-cut. If prices are not required to cover costs or if the output of the firm is difficult to quantify, then the choices of consumers may not provide the information necessary to evaluate the contribution that managers make to the enterprise. In such cases legislators or bureaucrats must find other ways of evaluating the organization's performance. Usually, this involves selecting certain aspects of the firm's operations to be monitored.

A rational manager will respond to improve his firm's performance in those areas that are most closely monitored. Conversely, for aspects of the firm's operations that are not scrutinized, there is a tendency to divert resources to the more important (i.e., closely watched) activities. This tendency leads to a conclusion about the behavior of public versus private firms. When public and private firms face the same demand conditions, variations in their behavior will be determined by differences in the standards by which their managers are evaluated. Results that are more important to a board of directors in the private sector than to legislators or bureaucrats in the public sector will be more heavily emphasized by managers of private firms. Conversely, those aspects of public enterprise that are not or cannot be monitored by public policymakers may be neglected in comparison to the behavior of a private firm.

Sometimes attributes of the performance of public firms may be monitored on a threshold basis. That is, as long as they don't drop below some minimum acceptable level, the evaluation of the enterprise will not be unfavorable. The implications of this policy are illustrated in Figure 19.2. The axes represent two attributes of some service X. Perhaps X_1 represents the number of hours each day that the service is provided and X_2 measures the courtesy of employees. The production possibility curve $F(X)$ indicates different combinations of the attributes of X that can be provided for a given expenditure.

There is a trade-off between X_1 and X_2, because providing more hours of service requires more money, and improving employee courtesy is assumed possible only by

[5]Lindsay, C. M., "A Theory of Public Enterprise," *Journal of Political Economy,* Vol. 84, No. 5 (Oct., 1976), pp. 1061–1077.

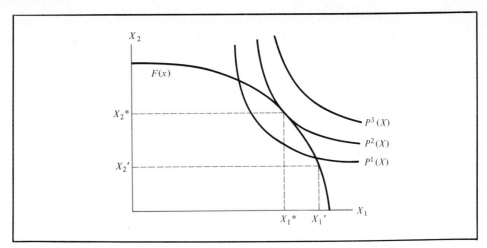

Figure 19.2. Threshold monitoring.

increasing salaries or hiring additional supervisory personnel. The $P^i(X)$ curves are isorevenue lines. Each P^i represents all combinations of the attributes X_1 and X_2 that generate equal total revenues. Because courtesy and the number of hours that the service is available are both desirable attributes from the standpoint of the consumer, a greater demand and higher level of revenues are indicated as the P^i shift to the right. (i.e., $P^3 > P^2 > P^1$). For the private firm, the profit-maximizing objective requires that the maximum revenues be obtained from any given level of expenditure. That is, the point of maximum profit is (X_1^*, X_2^*).

Now consider a government-owned firm where the courtesy attribute X_2 is monitored only on a threshold basis. That is, to avoid problems managers must make sure that at least a minimum level of courtesy, X_2', is provided, but there is no further reward for the managers' efforts to raise the level of courtesy above this level. Assume that the hours of service attribute X_1 is also monitored by the agency that evaluates the public firm's performance, but that the manager's perceived productivity is positively related to the amount of X_1 that is provided. Hence, the optimal combination of X_1 and X_2 from the manager's point of view is $(X_1', X_2'.)$ Since $X_2' < X_2^*$, the public firm is observed to be less courteous in its treatment of customers than the private firm.

For the firm in the private sector, the preferences of consumers and the drive for profits determine the optimal combination of X_1 and X_2. For the public enterprise, the desires of consumers and the quest for profits may be less important in determining the decisions of managers, because they are not the criteria that are used to evaluate management performance. As a general proposition, to the extent that the measures that are used to evaluate the performance of private firms differ from the standards used to evaluate state-owned firms, the observed behavior of the two entities will also differ.

How might the measures used to evaluate the performance of public firms differ from those used in assessing private firms? First, consumer behavior provides important information to private firms about the acceptability of their products and services. Poor quality products or inferior service usually result in diminished sales and profits. But available information on the value of outputs of public enterprise is often distinctly inferior. The enterprise may be a monopoly supplier, may not be required to cover its full costs, and/or may be charged with pursuing multiple goals. As a result, information received from markets will be inadequate or misleading, and evaluating agencies must devise other methods to assess performance. Usually these are somewhat arbitrary and mechanistic. For example, Veterans Administration hospitals are judged on dimensions such as the number of complaints that are received, the number of patient-days of care provided, and the cost per patient-day. Judgments as to the degree of patient comfort are much more difficult to measure and, hence, carry less weight in congressional evaluations at budget time. As a consequence, it is commonly accepted that VA hospitals provide fewer patient amenities than do proprietary hospitals facing competitive pressures. [6]

As a general rule, the standards by which public enterprise are evaluated are those that are relatively objective and can be quantified. More subjective and difficult-to-measure aspects of performance cannot be monitored and, consequently, may be neglected. If those who evaluate private firms were limited to the same information as public policymakers, there is no reason to believe they would be any more successful in their evaluation. Fortunately, the information generated by consumers in their purchasing decisions provides a means of quantifying additional dimensions of the firm's performance. This is a possible explanation of the alleged tendency (whose existence has not been conclusively documented) for private firms to be more responsive to consumer preferences.

Before turning to case studies of public enterprise, two qualifications need to be made about the simple theory that has been developed. First, the theory does not specify whether public enterprises will be more or less efficient than private firms in terms of cost per dollar of output. If the standards of evaluation cause public managers to stress some attributes of a product or service at the expense of others, then public enterprise costs will be lower if the monitored attributes are less costly to provide than those that are neglected and higher if the attributes are more costly. For example, VA hospitals have lower costs per patient-day than many proprietary hospitals. This reflects the stress on costs that are monitored and the neglect of patient comfort, which is monitored only at a threshold level. Second, if private firms are insulated from vigorous competition, then managers may have discretion to pursue goals that reflect their own objectives. Pursuit of these objectives may result in reduced profits, higher prices, and/or increased costs. Where competition is absent, there is no necessary reason to expect that the performance of the private firm will be superior (under any criterion) to that of the selectively monitored public enterprise.

CASE STUDIES OF GOVERNMENT ENTERPRISE
U.S. Postal Service: A Legal Monopoly

The U.S. Postal Service has a legal monopoly in first class mail service. No other organization is allowed to provide the same service. The Postal Service is a quasi-government enterprise. It is not attached to any government agency, but its directors are presidential appointees, and it does receive some financial assistance from the

[6]Ibid.

federal government. Lack of interest from the private sector is not the reason for the postal monopoly. Over the last 200 years there have been many firms willing to provide mail delivery. During the 1830s, Wells Fargo offered to take over the whole operation and guaranteed to provide service at a uniform national rate that was less than half the government's existing charge. More recently, the Independent Postal System of America offered to deliver Christmas cards for the post office at a reduced rate and on time. Both offers were rejected.

Background   Systematic delivery of letters dates back to the 1500s. [7] In Britain the right to provide postal service was originally given to favorites of the crown as a monopoly right. The monopoly grant served the patron by lining his pockets and the king by providing control over the mails—by restricting delivery to a single source it was easy to detect seditious and rebellious communications of disloyal citizens.

Not until 1692 did the British export the postal monopoly concept to their North American colonies. In fact, they never did get very involved in mail delivery in America. The British system was run by government bureaucrats who lacked the incentive to expand their operations. Laws that fixed the price of service were a major problem. The rate was sufficient to cover costs in compact England, but could not provide a fair return when applied to the sparsely populated colonies. The British government was the reluctant source of general postal service until the Revolution. Although the mails were supposed to be operated as a monopoly, when competition did spring up on a few densely populated routes, the lack of interest by the postal bureaucracy and the increasing dislike for British restrictions made prosecution impossible.

In 1775 the Continental Congress established a postal monopoly. The main purpose was to provide a reliable network for military communications. It seems to have been a monopoly more by default than design—there was no other organization in the colonies that had the ability to manage postal service. After the war the authors of the Constitution specified that Congress had the authority to establish "post offices and post roads." Nothing in the Constitution suggests that it was intended that the postal service was to be a monopoly, and a reading of the minutes of the Constitutional Conventional does not reveal much discussion on the issue. It is possible that the question did not require debate because, at the time, the possibility of competition was unlikely. It was probably assumed that there was still no other viable organization to provide nationwide mail service. Although the challenges have been few, the courts have consistently upheld the government's right to maintain a postal monopoly.

Initially, the president was given the power to decide where postal routes would be established. Although the postal system was a consistent money-loser, the service was rapidly expanded because George Washington understood its political worth. By providing routes to new areas, he gained support for the new Constitution and for his government. By 1792 Congress had realized the value of the right to make decisions on postal routes and took the responsibility from the president. Individual congressmembers gained personal favor by backing additional routes in their districts. The need

---

[7]For extended discussion of the history of the post office see Priest, G. L., "The History of the Postal Monopoly in the United States," *Journal of Law and Economics* (Apr., 1975), pp. 33–80.

to make informed decisions on each proposed route was eliminated by lumping them all together into a single bill to be passed at the end of the session.

The use of the postal system to curry political favor created the need for a government monopoly. The new routes that were being approved at the behest of (primarily) Western congressmembers were usually unprofitable. If the Post Office was not to require large sums from the general treasury, then it was necessary to charge higher prices for delivery in more dense routes to subsidize rural areas. In the absence of a monopoly, such high prices would almost certainly have spawned competitors in these populated areas. A logical question is why the representatives of the populous states would risk complaints from their constituents to help out their more rural counterparts? A reasonable conjecture is that the rural postal routes were purchased at the price of votes on other issues such as tariff measures.

By the 1830s there was a broad agitation for postal reform. The Post Office was running large and consistent deficits and the rates for mail delivery were high. On some routes it cost more to send a letter than it did to ship a barrel of flour. As a consequence, private industry attempted to enter and provide cut-rate service. The government moved to prosecute its competitors, but a technicality in the postal laws made convictions impossible. The law specified that no boat or stage could carry mail, but did not cover individuals carrying mail and riding such conveyances without the knowledge (?) of their owners. Along with the annexation of Texas, the debate over what to do about the Post Office was the hottest public issue of the 1830s.

Congressional action on the issue reflected the view that service must be maintained to rural areas even if rates on more dense routes had to remain high to provide the subsidy. It was also generally acknowledged that the Post Office could never effectively compete with private firms on those dense routes if the cross-subsidization policy was maintained. The solution adopted by the Congress was to strengthen the provisions of the law that prohibited competition in mail delivery. From the 1830s to the late 1960s the case for government monopoly of the Post Office rested primarily on the need for high prices in urban areas to assure service to rural locations.

By the late 1960s postal deficits had increased and the quality of service was deteriorating. One of the causes was believed to be the political influence on postal operations. Historically, the position of postmaster general had been a political plum awarded with little regard to background or ability. In 1970 Congress abolished the Post Office as a part of the executive branch of government and established the quasi-independent. U.S. Postal Service. The USPS is controlled by an 11-person board of governors. Nine of the board are appointed by the president of the United States and the other two are members of the USPS management who are appointed by the original nine. Revisions in postal rates are reviewed by a separate, five-person postal rate commission, which is also appointed by the president. Congressional intent was that the organization should have a degree of independence and that the degree of cross-subsidization from one class of mail to another should be reduced.

The First Class Monopoly   In 1973 the USPS board of governors completed a review of the need for the continued prohibition of competition in providing first class mail service. The report concluded that the prohibition was still necessary. Some of the main points were as follows. First, postal service has the characteristics of a natural monopoly. The declining-cost nature of the service will always give the USPS a cost advantage. Second, there are certain aspects of postal service that are beneficial to the nation but for which the public is not charged. Examples are the prosecution of mail fraud and the guarantee of letters not being opened by unauthorized individuals. Finally, the USPS is committed to serving all areas. It was argued that to allow competition would result in firms coming in the market and skimming the cream (providing service only to the most profitable areas), leaving the postal service only the sparse, money-losing routes.

Do these contentions of the board of governors constitute an acceptable defense of the continued postal monopoly? Most economists would argue that they do not. First, if the Post Office is really a natural monopoly, then there is no need for a legal prohibition against entry. The inherent advantages of size will make private firms unable to survive in the market. Second, although there may be special services that are provided by the USPS, they are not dependent on the monopoly privilege. Strict standards and a much smaller independent regulatory body could maintain the same safeguards and services. Third, the 1970 congressional mandate seemed to indicate that there should be no more cross-subsidies. Rates set in compliance with this directive would result in no cream to skim. Also, if rates are set to just cover costs (including a normal return to capital), then the USPS, by virtue of its supposed economies of scale, should be able to meet competition from any source. Most economists agree that there is little justification for USPS's continued monopoly of first class mail service.

Cross-Subsidization of Mail Classes   There are four basic classes of mail service. First class is the most expensive and is made up of business and personal correspondence. Second class mail consists of newspapers and magazines. In the case of time-urgent material such as newspapers, the quality of service may be essentially equivalent to first class. Third class comprises advertisements and books and packages sent by nonprofit organizations. Finally, fourth class mail consists of parcels and catalogues with a minimum weight of 1 pound. Delivery is usually substantially slower than for the other classes. Table 19.1 shows the volume and weight of mail in each class. Penalty and franked mail are categories reserved for governmental units. International mail consists of pieces with destinations outside the United States.

Historically, first class mail has subsidized the other three classes. Service is said to be *subsidized* if the additional revenues that are received from a class of service are less than the avoidable costs of providing the service. *Avoidable costs* are those expendi-

Table 19.1   WEIGHT AND VOLUME OF MAIL, 1982

Class	Volume (millions of pieces)	Weight (millions of lbs.)
First	62,200	2,239
Second	9,527	3,482
Third	36,719	4,296
Fourth	597	2,446
Penalty and franked	3,719	534
International	928	231

Source: U.S. Postal Service, *Annual Report of the Postmaster General, 1982* (Washington, D.C., 1983), pp. 28–29.

tures that would not have been made if the class of service were eliminated. For example, first class mail is the justification for providing multiple daily deliveries to businesses and daily service to residential areas. Without first class service it might be possible to reduce deliveries to alternate days. This would require fewer carriers. Thus, part of the avoidable costs of first class mail are the savings in labor costs. Similarly, without the bulk created by second, third, and fourth class mail, it would be possible for carriers to reduce the number of stops at relay boxes. Other avoidable costs can be identified for each class of service. In 1973, avoidable costs were estimated to be only 72 percent of revenues for first class mail. In contrast, avoidable costs were 60 percent, 36 percent, and 40 percent of revenues for second, third, and fourth class mail, respectively.[8] The excess revenues generated from first class mail, along with government subsidies, were used to finance the deficits of the other three classes. Since 1973, cross-subsidization between the four classes has been reduced, but not completely eliminated.

Cross-subsidization *within* mail classes has always been an important component of postal pricing. It costs more to provide service to those in rural areas than it does to urban residents. But the uniform pricing scheme used by the postal service does not take these cost variations into account. Thus, there is a subsidy that flows from urban to rural patrons. It is unlikely that this pattern of subsidization will ever change.

The U.S. Postal Service Today   The federal subsidy to the Postal Service was cut dramatically in the early 1980s. From 1972 to 1979, Congress appropriated $900 million each year. By 1982, the subsidy had been reduced to only $12 million. In spite of this cut, the financial position of the postal service has improved in recent years. There are at least three explanations for this improvement. First, cuts in service such as closing post offices and reducing the frequency of deliveries have generated cost savings. Second, automation has allowed mail to be sorted more efficiently. Finally, postal rates have been raised to generate additional revenues. Although the increases were rapid, present rates compare favorably with those of other nations. Table 19.2 shows letter rates for various countries. It indicates that most rates are higher than the present (1984) U.S. level of 20 cents.

Although the U.S. Postal Service has had its successes, the agency will face some formidable challenges in the future. Technological advances in telecommunications have created alternative methods of transferring information. Soon it will be possible for the average person to request information, make orders, and pay bills from a computer terminal in his or her home. These options will cut into the demand for mail service. In the future, even the traditional business letter may be transmitted electronically. For example, in 1983 MCI Communications announced a service that allows its customers to send letters over the firm's long-distance telephone network. The cost of sending a five-page letter directly to a computer terminal in any part of the country was set at $1. One of the main advantages of this method is that transmission is essentially instantaneous. MCI's intent was to compete with existing overnight couriers such as Federal Express, but the service also is a substitute for first class mail.

[8]See Wattles, G., "The Rates and Costs of the United States Postal Service," *Journal of Law and Economics* (June 1973), pp. 89–117.

Table 19.2 POSTAL RATES FOR FIRST UNIT OF DOMESTIC
LETTER POSTAGE

Nation	National currency	U.S. currency*
Federal Republic of Germany	.80 mark	34.2 cents
Norway	2.00 krona	28.7 cents
France	1.80 franc	27.1 cents
Australia	.27 A$	26.7 cents
Japan	60.00 yen	26.3 cents
Canada	.32 C$	26.0 cents
United Kingdom	.15 pound	25.2 cents
Netherlands	.65 guilder	25.0 cents
Austria	4.00 schilling	24.2 cents
Sweden	1.65 krona	22.8 cents
Italy	300.00 lira	22.2 cents
Switzerland	.40 S. franc	20.6 cents
United States	.20 US$	20.0 cents
Belgium	9.00 B. franc	19.5 cents

*Foreign exchange rates prevailing January 5, 1983, as reported in the *Washington Post,* January 6, 1983.
Source: U.S. Postal Service, *Annual Report,* 1982, p. 9.

The present postal monopoly has some of the characteristics of the old AT&T monopoly over telephone service. In both cases, the goals of universal access and uniform rates were achieved by the use of rate structures that subsidized certain classes of customers. Entry was legally prohibited to prevent cream-skimming by potential competitors. But market forces generated by technological change put pressures on the legal monopolies. In telecommunications the resolution of the problem was to open the market to competition. The same solution may be necessary for mail delivery. Ultimately, the survival of the postal service will require that it (like AT&T) expand its range of service offerings. At the same time, the enterprise may have to surrender its exclusive right for delivery of first class mail.

Amtrak: Government Enterprise by Default

Background Railroad passenger service has been rapidly reduced since World War II. In 1947 the railroads provided 415 million train-miles of service. By 1966 that figure had declined to 164 million and most operations were generating huge deficits. Losses on passenger service totaled about 30 percent of the net income of the railroads in 1968. The unprofitability of passenger service was partially the result of competition from other modes of travel. The development of a nationwide highway system allowed short trips to be made more conveniently and cheaply by automobile or bus. Only for short commuter runs did rail travel provide a time advantage in comparison to the airlines. Even without considering the value of the passenger's time, air travel was often less expensive as well. In 1929, over three-fourths of all intercity trips were made by train. By 1970 railroad passenger service was only 7 percent of the total.

By the end of the 1960s the railroads faced a dilemma. Passenger service was piling up crippling losses, but the Interstate Commerce Commission and political pressures from Congress made it difficult to abandon unprofitable routes. Equipment was outdated, but there was no money to finance the needed replacements and maintenance. In 1970 Congress acted by passing legislation to create the National Railroad Passenger Corporation, or Amtrak, as it has come to be known.

Amtrak Operations Under the new legislation, railroads experiencing substantial losses on passenger service could have their routes assumed by Amtrak on payment of an amount equal to their 1969 passenger losses. Twenty railroads put up nearly $200 million, which was used to buy existing cars and locomotives from the railroads. They were given the option of either receiving Amtrak stock as compensation for their payments or taking a tax write-off. All but four chose the write-off. The four (which included the infamous Penn Central) had such heavy losses that there was no tax liability to be reduced and, hence, they had no choice but to become Amtrak shareholders. To get things rolling, Congress also chipped in with another $200 million.

On May 1, 1971, Amtrak assumed responsibility for 23,000 miles of intercity passenger train service. Strictly speaking, it was not a pure example of government enterprise. Legislation specified that Amtrak would be governed by a 17-person board of directors. Eight of the directors were to be appointed by the president of the United States, three were to be representatives of the common stockholders, four were selected by preferred stockholders, and there were to be two ex officio directors—the secretary of transportation and the president of Amtrak. Preferred stock has never been issued by Amtrak, and so four seats have always remained vacant. It was intended that the board of directors and Amtrak management should have a considerable degree of autonomy from the other branches of the federal government, but like the Postal Service, the organization's heavy reliance on congressional appropriations has forced it to be highly responsive to political pressures.

Initially, Amtrak was just a retailer of passenger service. The railroads owned the roadbeds, maintenance facilities, and terminals. The railroads also provided all of the personnel for the operation of the system under contract with Amtrak. This arrangement continued for the first two years of the enterprise's existence. During that period it was possible for a passenger to make a reservation, buy a ticket, and complete her journey without ever encountering an Amtrak employee.

Many of the locomotives and passenger cars purchased by Amtrak were over 20 years old and frequently in poor states of repair. It had been so long since the railroads had placed orders for new cars that there was not a single supplier in the United States. Beginning in 1973, Amtrak started purchasing new cars and locomotives. By 1981 the organization was able to boast that the average age of its locomotives had been reduced to 4 years, compared with 22 years in 1971. During its first decade Amtrak spent nearly $2 billion on capital improvements. [9]

Evaluation of Amtrak Railroad passenger service in the United States is better today than it was before Amtrak. In 1982, the number of passenger-miles traveled was 60 percent greater than in 1972. The proportion of trains arriving on time rose from 63 percent to 77 percent over the same period. Another measure of improvement is the

---

[9]See National Railroad Passenger Corporation, *1982 Annual Report* (Washington, D.C.: 1983), p. 10.

decline in customer complaints. Currently, the enterprise receives one complaint for every 1,000 passengers. This ratio is less than half what was a few years ago. [10]

However, the success of Amtrak has been achieved at a substantial cost to the taxpayer. Over $5 billion in subsidies have been poured into the enterprise since its creation. Currently, the annual subsidy is nearly $700 million. Revenues are far below expenses on most routes. To illustrate, for operations between Chicago and Texas the loss was over 17 cents per passenger-mile in 1982. Between Washington and Cincinnati the average train carried 42 persons and the loss was 33 cents per passenger-mile. A study by the Congressional Budget Office reported that the average Amtrak rider travels 155 miles and pays a fare of just over $23. But the cost to Amtrak is about $61. The difference of $38 is paid by taxpayers through federal subsidies. [11] For a bus trip of the same distance the fare would be about $20. Thus, it would be possible to give each Amtrak passenger a free bus ride and still reduce the required subsidy by $18 for each trip.

Defenders have suggested a number of Amtrak advantages. First, it is argued that rail travel conserves scarce supplies of energy. While it is true that trains operating near capacity are more energy-efficient than other forms of travel, the fact is that the average passenger train operates nowhere near capacity. In terms of actual passenger-miles traveled, Amtrak trains use substantially more energy than buses and, depending on the particular route, may be no more efficient than automobiles. A second contention is that train travel is an extremely safe mode of travel. However, fatality rates for buses and airplanes also are extremely low—less than 1 per billion passenger-miles. It is also suggested that trains do less damage to the environment than other forms of travel. However, in comparison to intercity buses, Amtrak trains are actually responsible for more pollution.

A fourth argument in support of continued subsidies for rail passenger service is that transportation to and from isolated areas must be maintained. The reality is that buses serve 30 times as many cities as trains and provide service to every city in the Amtrak system. Finally, it is argued that Amtrak subsidies are justified on the grounds of equal treatment. Since billions of dollars have been provided to build the highway system and to provide airports, the relatively small sums being provided for railroad passenger service are argued to have an element of fairness. However, airlines, autos, and buses pay much of their way through user fees. For example, taxes on fuels are used for highway maintenance and construction. Also, enormous sums of government money were provided during the nineteenth and twentieth centuries for construction of the roadbeds on which the Amtrak trains operate. It is estimated that well over $1 billion was given to the railroads in the form of cash grants, right of ways, and the like, during the 1800s.

Proposals by Amtrak officials to abandon especially unprofitable routes have been met with stiff opposition by members of Congress and other politicians in the affected areas. Many of the cities slated for service termination have argued that the disappearance of rail service would significantly affect their city's economic health. In 1978, the secretary of transportation announced that his office was preparing plans for a substan-

---

[10]Ibid., p. 29.

[11]Congressional Budget Office, *Federal Subsidies for Rail Passenger Service: An Assessment of Amtrak* (Washington, D.C.: U.S. Government Printing Office, 1982), pp. 78–81.

tial reduction in the Amtrak network, which would be implemented unless Congress specifically vetoed the proposal within 90 days after it was presented. In early 1979 a plan was made public that would eliminate 43 percent of the 27,500 mile system, but still provide service to over 90 percent of the people traveling the original routes. The primary routes to be retained were through the densely populated areas along the Northeast Corridor, a number of short lines radiating from Chicago, and travel along the West Coast. The 43-percent cutback proposed by the Carter administration was pared by Congress to a much more modest reduction of about 18 percent. Figure 19.3 shows the present Amtrak network.

Municipal Electric Utilities: Government Enterprise as an Alternative to Competition

Enterprises owned and operated by city governments are the most common ownership form of electric utilities in the United States. There are over 2,000 municipal utilities, compared to fewer than 500 privately owned firms. However, most are small and many are only distributors of electricity. About 20 percent of all power sold at retail in the United States is marketed through municipal utilities.

Municipal utilities represent an alternative to private ownership. This section considers two questions in regard to such operations. First, what is the result of competition between a private and a publicly owned electric utility in a single community? Second, how do the operations of municipal and privately owned utilities compare with respect to efficiency and prices?

Competition Between Utilities   The standard view is that the production and distribution of electric power constitutes a natural monopoly. It is commonly assumed that any attempt at competition in a given market area must result in a loss of efficiency and in higher prices because of needless duplication of facilities. The reality is that there are at least 49 cities in the United States where a public and a privately owned utility compete for business of individual customers. In some cases the consumer must make a one-time choice of the utility with which he wants to do business. In other cities the customer has the right to switch at any time. In some cities the expected scenario of multiple poles carrying the wires of each enterprise is accurate. In other places the utilities share poles and certain other facilities. [12]

The origins of electric utility competition are similar for most communities. Sometime between 1900 and 1940 there was dissatisfaction over the high rates and deteriorating service being provided by the existing private firm. In some places the city fathers saw the local electric utility as a possible source of revenues to balance the budget. Sometimes the city already had a small generating facility to provide power for street lighting or other public needs. Almost always the advent of competition from the public sector had the effect of causing a reduction of rates and an improvement in the service of the private enterprise.

Primeaux reports an interesting study on the effect of competition between private

---

[12]For an extended discussion see Hellman, R., *Government Competition in the Electric Utility Industry* (New York: Praeger, 1972).

Figure 19.3. Amtrak route network as of January 1982. (Congressional Budget Office, *Federal Subsidies for Rail Passenger Service: An Assessment of Amtrak.*)

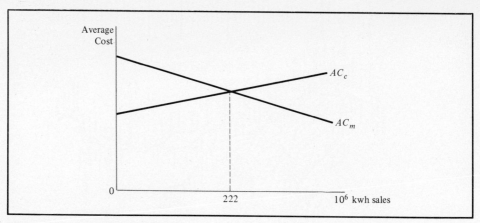

Figure 19.4. Competition and costs.

and municipally owned firms.[13] His objective was to determine whether municipal utilities had lower costs with or without the presence of competition. The approach was to collect data for 23 municipal utilities competing for business with an investor-owned firm. Each public firm was matched with a private firm that was in the same state, was about the same size, and used a similar source of power.

Primeaux used multiple regression analysis to determine how average costs are affected by size, input prices, density of market, type of customer, location, nature of the enterprise (i.e., a purchaser or a producer of electricity), and competition. Of special interest here is the relationship between costs and competition. Holding the values of the other variables constant, the average-cost curves of competing municipal utilities and monopoly investor-owned firms were found to have general characteristics as shown in Figure 19.4. AC_c represents the estimated average-cost curve for municipal utilities in competition with a privately owned utility in the same community. AC_m is the estimated average-cost curve for investor-owned utilities with exclusive market areas.

Primeaux's results indicate that small municipal utilities facing competition have average costs about 5 percent lower than small private firms without competition. However, as the size of the enterprise increases, the advantage of economies of scale seems to offset the competitive effect. Beyond an annual sales level of about 222 million kilowatt-hours the monopoly utilities were estimated to have lower average costs than the municipals competing with private firms. Primeaux notes, however, that at least 90 percent of municipal utilities in the United States fall to the left of the break-even point. He concludes that for most enterprises there would be benefits to the public if competition were present. The pressures of competition seem to be more important than the inefficiencies from duplication of facilities.

Municipal Utilities Versus Investor-owned Utilities   For electric utilities, the available evidence does not support the stereotype that government ownership is less efficient than private operation. A study by Meyer investigated the relationship between owner-

[13]Primeaux, W. J., "A Reexamination of the Monopoly Market Structure for Electric Utilities," in Phillips, A., ed., *Promoting Competition in Regulated Markets* (Washington, D.C.: Brookings Institution, 1975), pp. 175–200.

ship form and costs for seven different electric utility expense categories.[14] Using 30 municipal and 30 private electric utilities, Meyer found costs to be significantly less for the public enterprises in five of the seven categories. For the other two cost categories the difference was not statistically significant.

Research by Neuberg considered only the distribution aspect of electric operations.[15] His choice was dictated by the fact that most municipal utilities are not in the business of producing power. Using a sample of 180 utilities of both ownership forms, he analyzed the effect of sales, number of customers, market area, miles of distribution line, input prices, and ownership form on the firm's distribution costs as reported to the Federal Power Commission (now the Federal Energy Regulatory Commission). Neuberg's findings are consistent with those of Meyer and suggest that distribution costs for municipal utilities are from 6 to 25 percent lower than their private counterparts.

For the consumer, the real measure of investor-owned versus municipal utilities is the price that is charged. Meyer also considered relative prices and concluded that rates for privately owned firms were about 25 percent higher for residential customers. Private rates were computed to be higher under private ownership for all consumption categories except large commercial users. The alternative sources of power available to large users may explain this one exception.

A study by Moore focused on the effect of regulation, but also provided evidence on the public versus private ownership issue.[16] Moore attempted to compute the profit-maximizing price for 62 investor-owned and 7 municipal utilities. This price was then compared to the actual price charged by the firm. It was determined that privately owned utilities charged a price that averaged about 5 percent below the profit-maximizing rate. This was interpreted to mean that regulations have at least some effect. A similar computation for municipal enterprises estimated a cost of 10 to 22 percent below the monopoly price. Moore's findings suggest municipal utilities exercised greater restraint in pricing than their private counterparts.

The structure of rates, as well as their average level, is relevant to the evaluation of utility ownership forms. Peltzman hypothesized that the actions of managers of municipal utilities are based on the desire to maximize political support.[17] DeAlessi assumed that freedom from the quest of profits allows the public manager to pursue utility-maximizing objectives.[18] Both authors suggested similar hypotheses for a public firm in comparison to an investor-owned utility. They predict that the general level of prices should be lower (either in the attempt to gain political support or to reduce consumer complaints) and that there should be less price discrimination by the public firm (because utility-maximizing managers desire to reduce consumer complaints and limit the alienation of any particular group).

[14]Meyer, R. A., "Publicly Owned Versus Privately Owned Utilities: A Policy Change," *The Review of Economics and Statistics,* Vol. 42, No. 4 (Nov., 1975), pp. 391–399.

[15]Neuberg, L. G., "Two Issues in the Municipal Ownership of Electric Power Distribution Systems," *Bell Journal of Economics and Management Science,* Vol. 8, No. 1 (Spring, 1977), pp. 303–323.

[16]Moore, T. G., "The Effectiveness of Regulation of Electric Utility Prices," *Southern Economic Journal,* Vol. 36, No. 4 (Apr., 1979), pp. 365–375.

[17]Peltzman, S., "Pricing in Public and Private Enterprises: Electric Utilities in the United States," *Journal of Law and Economics,* Vol. 14 (Apr., 1971), pp. 109–147.

[18]DeAlessi, L., "An Economic Analysis of Government Ownership and Regulation," *Public Choice,* Vol. 19 (Fall, 1974), pp. 1–42.

The evidence provided by Peltzman and reviewed by DeAlessi is generally consistent with their suppositions. Prices were found to be lower for municipal than for privately owned utilities. There was less discrimination by government-owned firms as manifested by rates being more highly correlated between categories, rate changes showing less relation to variations in costs of providing service, and rates schedules being less complex.

Evaluation   As a general evaluation, with regard to electric utilities, the stereotype of inefficient public ownership is not supported by the evidence. Municipal utilities compare favorably with investor-owned utilities. Their prices are generally lower, they may be more efficient, and they seem to exhibit less price discrimination. In addition, it appears as though the arguments that electric power is a natural monopoly are not conclusive. In communities where public and private firms compete, cost may be lower than where there is no duplication of service.

CONCLUSIONS

Galbraith, after reviewing the extensive socialization of other market-oriented countries, argues that:

> The performance of all of these industries in Britain, Scandinavia, Germany, and Holland is categorically superior to that in the United States. In other countries— France, Italy, Japan, Switzerland—the enterprises that have been fully socialized, notably rail and urban transport, are superior. Only those that have not been socialized are deficient.[19]

Near the other end of the ideological spectrum, Friedman contends that:

> Both governmental monopoly, like the Post Office, and private monopoly, like the New York Stock Exchange or AT&T, are undesirable; but of the two evils, governmental monopoly is much the worse because it tends to be more inefficient. In Britain, both mail and telephone service are governmental monopolies; in the United States, mail is a governmental monopoly and telephone is a private monopoly. Mail service is better in Britain than in the United States (because the British civil service is more efficient than that of the United States) but phone service is much worse—a nice almost controlled experiment.[20]

Which view is correct? Does public ownership bring better results as Galbraith would contend, or is Friedman accurate in his assessment that government enterprise is even worse than the anathema, private monopoly? The best general answer would seem to be that there is no general answer. In some cases, such as municipal versus investor-owned electric utilities, performance under public ownership compares very favorably with private. In other circumstances, such as the comparison of U.S. tele-

---

[19]Galbraith, op. cit., p. 281.

[20]Friedman, M., *An Economist's Protest* (Glen Ridge, N.J.: Thomas Horton and Daughters, 1972), p. 197. The telephone monopoly in the U.S. today is more limited than when Friedman penned the above statement. It now involves only local service. See Chapter 13.

phone service with that of state-run enterprises in Britain and France, the private market seems superior.

Although it is possible to find examples to support the superiority of either private or public ownership, other factors may be at least as important. A private firm is neither efficient nor inefficient simply because it has stockholders. Its performance is determined by the people who manage it and the kind of incentives to which they must respond. Where there is strong competition from other firms or where management rewards are tied closely to performance, the firm will normally perform well. If the firm does not face competitive pressures and if management has considerable discretion, then more diverse objectives can be pursued.

Similarly, the evaluation mechanism of managers in a public enterprise rather than the firm's "publicness" per se will determine its performance. Managers respond to the criteria on which they are to be judged. If the criteria are too narrow or the methods of monitoring too simplistic, then the public enterprise's performance may be much different than its private counterpart. Many of the failures of state-owned firms can be ascribed to inadequate planning by their creators rather than some inherent defect in public ownership.

SUMMARY
Objectives and Origins of Government Enterprise

Government ownership is much less common in the United States than in other nations. In noncommunist nations, public enterprise usually reflects the specific circumstances of an industry or the nation's economy rather than a simple preference for nationalization.

National Objectives   Public enterprise may be the product of defense needs. In other cases firms have been absorbed into the public sector during economic emergencies such as the Depression of the 1930s. Multi-use projects are another source of public enterprise. For example, a dam built primarily for flood control may also put the government in the electric power business.

Improved Efficiency   The operations of government-owned enterprises may be somewhat useful as a yardstick to judge the performance of private firms. Direct competition from the public sector can also reduce prices and improve efficiency in the private sector. In some countries, sectors have been incorporated into the public domain because private industry had stagnated. The steel and coal industries in Britain are examples.

Failure or Abuses in the Private Sector   Some municipally owned electric utilities were created because their private predecessors charged excessive prices. In the case of railroads, the public sector became involved because private industry could not profitably provide the services that policymakers deemed necessary. Public projects such as fusion research were undertaken by government because cost and risk of the task made private initiation unlikely.

Political or Philosophical Forces   In Britain, the scope of nationalized industry has been somewhat a function of the ideological preference of the governing political party. In France, Renault was taken over by the government in retribution for the collaboration of its management with the Germans during World War II. In developing countries the desire to reduce foreign influences has sometimes been the catalyst for nationalization.

Efficiency and Government Enterprise

Differences in the performance of private and public enterprises may reflect differences in objectives and incentives rather than a fundamental superiority of either ownership mode. When public enterprises are charged with the achievement of multiple goals, they will perform differently than private firms pursuing profit maximization. Similarly, if managers in the public sector are monitored and rewarded on criteria dissimilar to those of their private counterparts, they will naturally guide their organizations in different directions.

Case Studies of Government Enterprise

U.S. Postal Service: A Legal Monopoly

Background   For 200 years, postal service in rural areas of the United States has been subsidized by revenues from urban areas. The government's legal monopoly over first class mail has been justified as necessary to prevent competitors from entering and skimming the profits from urban routes. In 1970, Congress established the quasi-independent United States Postal Service.

Cross-subsidization of mail classes   There are four basic classes of mail service. Historically, revenues from first class service have exceeded the avoidable costs of providing that service. In contrast, avoidable costs of second, third, and fourth class mail have been greater than the revenues received from those mail classes. The degree of cross-subsidization has been reduced, but not eliminated.

The U.S. postal service today   The financial position of the postal service has improved despite significant reductions in federal subsidies. However, technological advances involving electronic transfer of information may force the enterprise to broaden its range of services.

Amtrak: Government Enterprise by Default

Background   Railroad passenger service in the United States had deteriorated badly by the 1960s. Railroads were sustaining large losses on passenger service, but political pressures made it difficult to abandon unprofitable routes. In 1970, Congress created the National Railroad Passenger Corporation, or Amtrak.

Amtrak operations   Funding for Amtrak came from the railroads and from public funds. Originally, the corporation was forced to operate with dilapidated equipment and over poorly maintained roadbeds. In the first decade of its existence, the enterprise spent nearly $2 billion on improvements.

Evaluation of Amtrak   Railroad passenger service improved under Amtrak. But keeping the system going required $5 billion in federal subsidies over the first ten years. Currently, costs are substantially greater than revenues on almost all routes.

Municipal Electric Utilities: Government Enterprise as an Alternative to Competition

Competition between utilities   In about four dozen U.S. cities, public and privately owned electric utilities compete directly. Although the traditional view is that such competition results in wasteful duplication of facilities, the evidence indicates that small municipal utilities facing competition may actually have lower costs than their small, privately owned counterparts.

Municipal utilities versus investor-owned utilities   Several empirical studies suggest that municipal electric utilities are at least as efficient as comparable private firms. The data also indicate that their rates are lower and that price discrimination is less evident.

Conclusions

Is the performance of public enterprise inherently inferior to that of private firms? No general answer can be given to this question. Enterprises are neither efficient nor inefficient because of their form of ownership. Rather, efficiency is the result of the incentive and reward structure under which the management and employees of the firm operate.

DISCUSSION QUESTIONS

1. Once absorbed into the public sector, why is it often difficult for an enterprise to be returned to the private sector?
2. Costs of electricity generated by a government-owned dam are to be used to judge the efficiency of nearby private utilities. What problems are involved in making this comparison?
3. If the private sector cannot profitably provide a service, isn't that adequate evidence to indicate that demand is insufficient, and hence, the service should not be provided?
4. How does the threat of nationalization affect investment flowing into developing nations? Is nationalization a short-sighted policy?
5. How would the objectives or goals of the U.S. Government Printing Office differ from those of a private publisher?
6. What "threshold" or minimum standards might be used to monitor the performance of the Government Printing Office?
7. Over the last century, how has technology affected economies of scale in providing postal service?
8. What are the advantages of a subsidy from general revenues to second, third, and fourth class mail in comparison to cross-subsidization by first class mail?
9. What justification is there for government to provide assistance to failing private firms?
10. How can the superiority of European in comparison to U.S. rail passenger service be explained?
11. Should municipal electric utilities be regulated by state regulatory commissions?

chapter 20

Patents

Chapter Outline

Two centuries elapsed between the age of Copernicus and that of James Watt; one century between Watt and Michael Faraday; half a century between Faraday and the Wright Brothers; a quarter of a century between the Wright Brothers and Einstein. Since then, the intervals between major landmarks have grown even shorter. [1]

Most of the chapters in this book consider attempts by government to promote competition or to fetter monopoly. Patents run against the general flow by providing the patent holder with a legal right to exclude others from making, using, or selling a product or process for a specified period of time. The monopoly right is granted with the anticipation that the lure of supernormal profits may entice technological advance that would otherwise not be forthcoming.

Views on the patent system vary widely. Abraham Lincoln believed that the availability of patents "added the fuel of interest to the fire of genius." Speaking of the importance to "young America" of discoveries and inventions, he stated:

> I have already intimated my opinion that in the world's history, certain inventions and discoveries occurred of peculiar value on account of their great efficiency in facilitating all other inventions and discoveries. Of these were the arts of writing and printing —the discovery of America and the introduction of Patent Laws. [2]

Others see the patent system more as a tool of big business than as an incentive for the creative individual. A Ralph Nader study group report contends that "the patent today constitutes the leading instrument in our economy for the creation and maintenance of monopoly power." [3] Like most everything else, the truth probably lies somewhere between these extreme positions.

Although there is disagreement over the value of the patent system to society, there can be little doubt that the acquisition of a patent can be of immense value to an individual or a corporation. The invention of the telephone provides an interesting example of the pivotal nature of patent decisions on an industry. Daniel Drawbaugh, Elisha Gray, and Alexander Graham Bell all claimed invention of the telephone. Bell and Gray reached an out-of-court settlement, but a patent infringement suit by Bell against Drawbaugh went all the way to the Supreme Court. The evidence of the trial showed that Drawbaugh had invented the telephone several years before Bell, but had not made an immediate application for a patent. The Court's decision (two judges not voting) was four to three in favor of Bell. A switch of one vote would have altered the course of the entire industry.

The remainder of this chapter is divided into five parts. The first is a discussion of the need for some type of governmental action to stimulate technological change. The second is a short description of the history and operation of the patent system in

[1]See Mayne, R., *The Recovery of Europe: From Devastation to Unity* (London: Weidenfeld and Nicolson, 1970), p. 4.

[2]Quoted by Daddario, E. Q., "Legislative Problems in the Field of Patents and Patent Policy," in Alderson, W., Terpstra, V., and Shapiro, S., eds., *Patents and Progress* (Homewood, Ill.: Irwin, 1965), p. 88.

[3]See Till, I., "The Legal Monopoly," in Green, M. J., ed., *The Monopoly Makers* (New York: Grossman, 1973), p. 289.

the United States and in other countries. The third is a basic evaluation of the patent system, the fourth describes abuses of patent rights, and the fifth part is a consideration of proposed alternatives to the present patent system.

THE CASE FOR PATENTS

Advocates of the patent system usually make their case on one or more of the following arguments: (1) the *natural-law* thesis, which contends that a person has a right to his own ideas and that unauthorized use is a form of theft; (2) the *reward-by-monopoly* thesis, which holds that fairness requires that for his services a person receive a reward that is equivalent to their usefulness to society; (3) the *monopoly-profit incentive* thesis, which argues that adequate technological change will not occur unless special economic incentives are provided; and (4) the *exchange-for-secrets* thesis, which implies a bargain whereby the inventor surrenders his secret information in return for protection from competition.

The monopoly-profit incentive thesis is the most widely accepted basis for patent protection. It stems from the important role that technological change plays in modern society. As natural resources become increasingly scarce, the requirements of a growing population and the demand for a higher standard of living can be met only by the advance of technology. If market forces result in inadequate incentives for technological change, then government may need to act to provide the necessary stimuli. The stimuli provided by the patent system is the lure of monopoly profits stemming from the legal restriction on competition.

In order to understand patents, the process of technological change needs to be considered in greater detail. Technological change can be defined as a modification in the production function for a product that allows the same amount of product to be produced more cheaply or an improved product to be produced at the same cost. The process of technological change may be thought of as having three stages—invention, innovation, and imitation or diffusion. The invention stage involves the birth of new technological insights about a process or product. During the innovation stage an entrepreneur matches and applies the new insights to areas of practical need and introduces the resulting product or process into the market. In the imitation or diffusion stage, others recognize the success of the innovator and rush into the market in the attempt to share in the profits. The swarm of competitors has three important effects. First, the new process or product is made widely available to the general public. Second, competition erodes the monopoly profits being earned by the innovating firm. Third, many of the benefits of the innovation are transferred from the innovator to the consuming public through lower prices resulting from competition.

If inventors and innovators are motivated by economic incentives, then the amount of inventive and innovative activity will be determined by how rapidly and how completely imitators strip the original entrepreneur of his monopoly profit reward. If imitators can move in rapidly and capture a large share of the market, then the temporary profits earned by the innovator may not be sufficient compensation for the costs and risks that are borne. If there is a substantial delay between the time of innovation and the time of successful entry by competitors, then the monopoly profits earned in that interim period make invention and innovation a much more attractive activity. The patent system, by establishing a period of time during which the innovator is not subject to the threat of competition, increases the expected return to invention and innovation. By doing so, inventive and innovative efforts of economically motivated individuals may increase, and society will benefit from new processes and products that would otherwise not have been developed. The case for the patent system rests on the premise that the technological change that is stimulated will more than compensate society for the cost of the monopoly rights that are granted. This view can be found in the first formal patent law, established by the Republic of Venice in 1474:

> We have among us men of great genius, apt to invent and discover ingenious devices. . . . Now, if provision were made for the works and devices discovered by such persons, so that others who may see them could not build them and take the inventor's honor away, more men would then apply their genius, would discover, and would build devices of great utility to our commonwealth.[4]

THE PATENT SYSTEM
Background

The British followed the Venicians in granting patent rights. Unfortunately, by the early 1600s, they had strayed far from the lofty ideals of the Venician city-state. In addition to granting patent protection for inventions, the patent became a device used by the crown to reward court favorites. This was done by the granting of patents that conferred monopoly rights for the sale of existing products such as tea, sugar, and playing cards. These monopoly grants were very unpopular with the general public. Indeed, one of the catalysts of the American Revolution was the tea monopoly of the East India Company. Public dissatisfaction finally resulted in the passage of the Statute of Monopolies, which brought an end to patents "for the sole Buying, Selling, Making, Working, or Using of an Thing within this Realm." A specific exception was made in favor of patents for new discoveries. This seventeenth-century British legislation is the foundation for patent systems in the United States and throughout the world.

Several of the American colonies adopted patent laws based on the English system, but varying widely in specific provisions. The desire to establish uniformity led to the passage of the first U.S. patent law in 1790. The basis for this and subsequent patent laws is Article I, Section 8, of the Constitution, which empowers Congress "to promote the progress of Science and the useful Arts, by securing for limited Times to Authors and Inventors the exclusive Right to their respective Writings and Discoveries." The 1790 law gave the secretary of state, the secretary of war, and the attorney general the responsibility for issuing patents. Between 1790 and 1793, this committee issued 67 patents. In 1793, the Department of State was commissioned to issue patents, and in 1836 a second revision of patent laws established the Patent Office and a commissioner of patents. The present U.S. patent system rests on the basic principles of the 1836 patent law.

---

[4]Quoted by Gilgillan, S. C., *Invention and the Patent System* (Washington, D.C.: Joint Economic Committee, 1964), p. 11.

France followed the United States by adopting patent legislation in 1791. By the turn of the century, most of what are now the developed capitalist and socialist countries had patent systems of some type. Since 1900, 75 other countries have adopted patent laws. At the present time, there are few countries that do not provide some kind of patent protection. Although all patent legislation is designed to provide rewards for invention and innovation, patent systems differ with respect to the duration of patent rights, the types of inventions that can be patented, the standards for obtaining a patent, and procedures for obtaining a patent.

Duration of Patent Rights

The English Statute of Monopolies established a patent life of 14 years. This period has a historical basis, representing the time required for a craftsman to train two successive sets of apprentices. The original U.S. patent legislation provided for the same period, but has now been changed to 17 years. The present period is the product of compromise between efforts to extend the patent to 20 years and efforts to hold it at 14 years. The duration of patents in selected countries is shown in Table 20.1. In most countries, the duration is counted from the date of the patent application, but in the United States and a few other countries shown in the table, the duration is measured from the date of the patent grant.

Most of the developed capitalist countries have patent periods of 16 to 20 years. For developing countries, the table indicates much more diversity. In some countries, the duration of patent protection may vary. For example, in West Germany, full-term patents are granted for basic inventions, but "petty patents" of only three years are granted for minor inventions and improvements. In Chile and Argentina, the patent life can be set at 5, 10, 15, or even 20 years; depending on the wishes of the applicant, the merits of the invention, or both.

Table 20.1   DURATION OF PATENT RIGHTS IN SELECTED COUNTRIES

Years			
1–5	6–10	11–15	16–20
Argentina	Argentina	Argentina	Australia
Chile*	Chile*	Bulgaria	Canada*
West Germany	Colombia*	Chile*	Chile*
	Peru	Czechoslovakia	Denmark
		Egypt	East Germany
		Greece	France
		Italy	Israel
		India	Hungary
		Japan	Sweden
		Romania	Switzerland
		Spain*	United Kingdom
			United States*
			West Germany

*Duration runs from date of grant.
Source: United Nations, *The Role of the Patent System in the Transfer of Technology to Developing Countries* (New York: 1975), p. 54.

Patentable Inventions

Present patent laws in the United States allow the patenting of "any new and useful process, machine, manufacture, or composition of matter, or any new and useful improvement thereof." Excluded from the United States and most other patent systems are basic scientific principles and fundamental discoveries. Even with the best of patent attorneys, it appears that Newton could not have patented gravity, nor Einstein his theory of relativity. Newton and Einstein could, however, have patented machines making use of these discoveries.

Statutes of most countries may also exclude specific types of inventions or discoveries from patent protection. The United States has relatively liberal patent provisions, excluding only inventions pertaining to atomic energy and national defense. Other nations exclude discoveries relating to food products, plant varieties, pharmaceutical products, accounting systems, computer programs, and other areas whose patenting is "deemed contrary to public or social interest or economic development." The most common exclusion is pharmaceutical products. At least 34 nations, including Canada, Japan, East Germany, and the Soviet Union, do not provide patent protection for discoveries in this area. The basis for this exclusion is the philosophy that drugs and medicine are too important to society to allow the granting of monopoly rights and the consequent high prices. Such reasoning is curious in that, if the result of patent protection is additional inventive and innovative activity, then such activity would seem to be most necessary in the field of medicine. If researchers and entrepreneurs are motivated primarily by economic forces, then the development of new products would be slowed by removing the lure of monopoly profits. The effect of excluding drugs and medicine from patent protection will be considered later.

Standards of Patentability

The small number of patents granted during the first years (1790–1793) of the U.S. patent legislation was partially due to the very high standards that were imposed. The 1793 revision of the law was a radical departure from these first principles, authorizing the Department of State to issue patents without questioning the novelty or the usefulness of the inventions. Thomas Jefferson reacted to the change with disgust:

> I might build a stable, bring into it a cutting-knife to chop straw, a handmill to grind the grain, a curry-comb and brush to clean the horses, and, by a patent, exclude anyone from ever more using these things without paying me.[5]

Jefferson's concern was well founded. A flood of dubious patents were issued and the courts were clogged with litigants trying to press their patent claims. After four decades of ineffective patent protection, an 1836 statute required that patented inventions be new and that they be "sufficiently useful and important." Present law is based on the 1836 legislation and requires that an invention meet three criteria in order to be patentable. First, the invention must be new. Specifically, it must not have been

[5]See Jefferson, T., *Works*, Vol. 13, Liscomb ed., p. 380.

known to the public before the inventor completed it or for more than one year before the date of application for the patent. Second, it must be useful. In practice, this test is usually satisfied by any indication that the process or product can be put to practical use. Third, it must be nonobvious. This condition has proved to be the most ambiguous of the three. Some court decisions held that an invention must show the "flash of creative genius."[6] The present rule is that an invention cannot be patented if "the subject matter as a whole would have been obvious at the time the invention was made to a person having ordinary skill in the art."[7] Current legislation also provides that the patentability of an invention does not depend on the manner in which it is made.[8] An invention resulting from a flash of inspiration is no more patentable than a development resulting from tedious experimentation.

The three conditions for patentability under U.S. law are common in patent statutes of other nations. One important variation is the definition of the novelty of the invention. In the United States and most other countries, an invention cannot be patented if it is known or used any place else in the world. However, in the United Kingdom, the test of novelty is whether or not the discovery was previously known or used in the United Kingdom. Thus, it is possible to obtain a British patent on an invention already in use in another country. This provision would not seem to be consistent with the purpose of the patent system to induce new invention and innovation. All recent patent laws have adopted a test of worldwide novelty and most students of patent law would recommend a similar standard for the United Kingdom.

Procedures

A secondary purpose of granting patent rights is to provide for widespread disclosure of new ideas and techniques. Accordingly, one of the requirements for obtaining a patent in most countries is that the applicant describe his invention in sufficient detail to permit others "skilled in the art" to use it. In wording the application, the experience of the patent attorney becomes crucial. It may be that the real work of creativity is the verbal ingenuity of the attorney in describing the invention. The claims of the application must be sufficiently broad to give the inventor latitude to market his product or use his process, but, at the same time, be narrow enough to avoid conflicting with other patents. The claims must also have sufficient detail to satisfy the Patent Office, yet not disclose so much information as to allow a potential competitor to invent around the patent. The linguistic tightrope that must be walked would seem to be admirably suited for the talents of the legal profession.

The large number of patent applications and the relatively limited resources of patent offices in the United States and most other developed countries make it virtually impossible to undertake a detailed examination of each application. The U.S. Patent Office receives over 120,000 patent applications each year and may have nearly double that number pending at any given time. These are evaluated by a staff of about 100 examiners and 1,100 assistant examiners. The initial work is done by the assistant

---

[6]*Cuno Engineering Corp.* v. *Automatic Devices Corp.,* 314 U.S. 1, 18 (1966).
[7]35 U.S. Code 103.
[8]Ibid.

examiners, who are often engineers studying law at night in preparation for careers as patent attorneys.

An assistant examiner will deal with 70 or 80 applications each year. From the time the application is received until the final decision is rendered, an average of three working days will be spent on the application. In such a short time, only a cursory examination is possible. Inventions are presumed to be useful if there is no immediate evidence that they would result in harm to society. A basic search of patents already issued and related scientific publications is undertaken to assess the novelty of the invention. The question of nonobviousness is subjectively determined by the examiner. Often the patent office official will reject one or more of the claims made. The applicant then has six months to file an amended application. Of all the applications initially received by the Patent Office, about three-fifths are finally granted patents. Obtaining a patent is a lesson in patience—the average period from application to patent grant in the United States is about 24 months. From the applicant's perspective this lag is not all bad. Since the information about the invention is not made public (at least in the United States), the delay will actually lengthen the effective period of patent protection.

During the evaluation period for a U.S. patent, no opportunity is provided for third parties to oppose the granting of the patent. However, in other countries, use is made of "opposition proceedings." For example, in the United Kingdom patent applications are initially subjected to a fairly brief examination as to novelty and usefulness. On completion of this evaluation, the specifications of the application are published. For a three-month period before granting of a patent and for twelve months after, third parties may contest the application. If a challenge is made, then a more thorough examination is undertaken. The advantage of such proceedings is that the efforts of these third parties allow for more complete disclosure of controversial claims than the resources of the Patent Office alone would permit.

Once a patent is granted, its validity may be tested in the courts. Although the Patent Office grants the patent, it provides no additional support to the patent holder in court. Patentees must substantiate their claims at their own expense and effort. While the existence of a patent is considered by the courts to be prima facie evidence of a valid claim, the record of patents in the U.S. courts is not very impressive. It is estimated that nearly three-fourths of all patents that are tested in the courts are ultimately declared invalid. A major factor in the dismal courtroom performance of U.S. patents is the relative ease of obtaining a patent. The more exacting and detailed examination of patents in court cases brings out information not disclosed by the brief Patent Office evaluation.

The won-loss record of patents in court probably does not provide complete assessment of the value of patents. Most of the testing of patents is done unofficially on a day-to-day basis. Firms that have reason to doubt the validity of a patent use it without the patent holder's consent. Patent holders who believe they have strong cases, and who view the patent rights as having great value, will bring suit for patent infringement. If they have doubts about the validity of the patents or if the patent rights are of little value, they may ignore the infringement. In a way, the whole exercise is like a poker game with each player trying to gain by bluffing her or his opponent into dropping out of the hand. The value of this process is that it avoids clogging the courts

Table 20.2 MOTIVES OF INVENTORS

Motive	Percentage
Love of inventing	27.2%
Desire to improve	26.6
Financial gain	23.5
Necessity or need	16.6
Desire to achieve	10.3
Part of work	8.3
Prestige	3.8
Other or no answer	8.6

Note: The sum exceeds 100 percent because of multiple responses.
Source: Rossman, J., "The Motives of Inventors," *Quarterly Journal of Economics,* Vol. 44 (1931).

and allows the market to make the assessment rather than relying on the relatively arbitrary judgments of the judiciary. The main problem is that it provides a tremendous advantage to large firms or wealthy individuals. The adversary who can credibly threaten an opponent with extended and costly litigation may force a weaker rival to capitulate even though he or she has a good case. The same problem arises if the case actually does go to the courts. The small firm or individual inventor may not have the resources to sustain a costly legal battle. This, of course, is not a problem unique to the patent system.

EVALUATION OF THE PATENT SYSTEM
Motivation for Inventing and Innovating

The basis for the patent system is the argument that additional economic incentives are necessary to induce sufficient inventive and innovative activity. The basic assumption is that such activities are motivated primarily by economic considerations. Critics of patent rights argue that inventors are motivated as much by other factors as they are by the prospect of riches. A few years ago the Patent, Trademark, and Copyright Foundation asked inventors to assess the importance of patent protection to their inventive activity. Only one-fifth of those who replied indicated that patents made a substantial difference. Four-fifths suggested that the availability of patents made little or no difference.[9] An earlier study attempted to assess the most important motives of 710 inventors.[10] Table 20.2 shows the proportion of the sample mentioning specific motives or incentives.

To this point, patents have been discussed with respect to their effect on invention and innovation, with no particular attempt to separate these two stages of technological change. While patents are typically considered in terms of assisting in the generation of new ideas, it may be at the innovation stage that they are most crucial. Although inventors seem to have various motivations for their efforts, the innovator assumes the expense and risk in the expectation of a dollar reward. This assertion is supported by

[9]U.S. Congress, Joint Economic Committee, *Invention and the Patent System* (Washington, D.C.: Government Printing Office, 1964), p. 47.

[10]Rossman, J., "The Motives of Inventors," *Quarterly Journal of Economics,* Vol. 44 (1931), p. 524.

three examples provided by Mansfield. First, Mansfield found that for a large electrical-equipment manufacturer, more funds were budgeted to projects as the estimated profits from successful completion increased and as the probability of success went up. Second, he found that the schedule of development for 16 electronics, machinery, and chemical projects was significantly accelerated when it was believed that profits were tied to early project completion. Third, it was found that the railroad, mining, steel, and brewing industries tended to introduce new techniques more quickly as the expected profitability of those ventures increase.[11] None of the examples provided by Mansfield are particularly surprising, but they do serve to verify that innovation is dollar-sensitive. Thus, even though inventors may not be greatly influenced by patent protection, the patent system can still be justified by the stimulus that it provides for the application and market introduction of important discoveries.

Evidence of the Effects of Patents

Even if innovation does respond to the patent grant, the case for the patent system is not yet secure because of the gross nature of the instrument. Although there may be some innovations that would not occur in the absence of patent protection, in many other instances the product or process would still have been introduced. In such cases society provides the innovator with a grant of monopoly power but receives nothing that would not have been otherwise forthcoming. By continued use of patents in their present form, society grants a windfall to some in the hope of inducing innovations of great consequence from others.

As long as patents are generally available for all discoveries that meet basic standards, the evaluation of the patent system turns on whether or not the value to society of the innovations that are stimulated by the prospect of patent rights is greater than the costs of the monopoly privileges granted to innovators who would have acted without patent protection. Determining the additional innovative activity that takes place because of patent rights is an almost impossible task. Ideally, a control society without patents would be compared to an identical society with patent laws. Unfortunately, no such simple comparison can be made, and any assessment must be based on indirect and fragmentary evidence, such as the information that follows.

Presently, almost all nations have patent laws. However, The Netherlands and Switzerland did not offer patent protection during the latter part of the nineteenth century. Patent legislation in these countries was enacted in 1912 and 1907, respectively. A thorough study by Schiff concluded that the lack of a patent system did not hamper industrialization in these countries. Swiss and Dutch businesspeople were quick to import technology from other countries. Schiff also found a good deal of internal innovative activity. In Switzerland, advances were particularly dramatic. The Swiss were worldwide technical pioneers in textiles, textile machinery, steam engines, grain-milling equipment, and prepared foods during this period.[12]

A second shred of evidence can be gleaned from the fact that some nations do

---

[11]Mansfield, E., et al., *Research and Innovation in the Modern Corporation* (New York: Norton, 1971), pp. 152–155; and Mansfield, E., *Industrial Research and Technological Innovation* (New York: Norton, 1968), pp. 47–53 and 155–185.

[12]Schiff, E., *Industrialization Without Patents* (Princeton: Princeton University Press, 1971).

not allow the patenting of pharmaceutical products. Rates of introduction of new drugs in these countries can be compared to other nations, such as the United States, which do provide patent protection in this area. Such comparisons are largely inconclusive. Some of the countries without patents for pharmaceuticals rank high in the introduction of new drugs, while others rank very low. For example, the nation with the highest rate of drug introductions per dollar of GNP between 1940 and 1975 was Switzerland, which allows patents only on processes for making drugs and not the products themselves. On the other hand, Italy, which does not allow patents on either drug products or processes, ranks very low.[13] Evidently, factors other than patent protection are important determinants of the rate of innovation in the pharmaceutical industry. For example, the strict standards imposed by the Food and Drug Administration have greatly limited drug innovation in the United States.

Survey research is another source of information on the importance of patents to innovation. Scherer asked firm executives to rank the relative importance of five factors in making research and development investment decisions. The five factors were: (1) the necessity of maintaining competitive leadership, (2) the necessity of remaining competitive, (3) the desire for efficient production, (4) the desire to expand sales or diversify product lines, and (5) patent protection. Of 91 responding companies, only 7 ranked patent protection as first or second in importance. Most perceived patent protection as the least important factor and focused on the need to remain competitive or to gain competitive leadership.[14] In a United Kingdom study, Taylor and Silberston asked executives to indicate the proportion of their recent research projects in which patentability was an important factor in deciding to proceed. Of the 34 firms that responded, 7 said patentability was never important, 18 indicated it was important in a very few cases, 5 in up to 10 percent of cases, and 4 in more than 10 percent of cases. The firms were also asked to estimate the maximum proportion of their research and development expenditures that would not have been made in the absence of patent protection. Seventeen of 32 respondents indicated there would have been none or a negligible reduction, and only 6 indicated a change of as much as 20 percent. However, the importance of patents was found to differ by industry group. Patent rights were viewed as much more important in the manufacture of finished and specialty chemicals (which include pharmaceutical products) than in basic chemicals, mechanical products, and electrical products.[15]

Market Forces That Encourage Invention and Innovation

The sketchy evidence that exists does not provide strong support for the need for patent protection to stimulate innovation. Except in selected industries, it would seem that market forces are the main motivation to entrepreneurs. Evidently, the characteristics of markets that allow innovators to capture their rewards before the swarm of imitators appear are of considerable importance.

[13]Scherer, F. M., *The Economic Effects of Compulsory Patent Licensing,* monograph 1977–2 (New York University Graduate School of Business Administration, Center for the Study of Financial Institutions, 1977), pp. 37–40.
[14]Scherer, F. M., et al., *Patents and the Corporation,* 2nd ed. (Boston, 1959), pp. 117–118.
[15]Taylor, C. T., and Silberston, Z. A., *The Economic Impact of the Patent System* (London: Cambridge University Press, 1973), pp. 195–198.

Several factors may permit innovators to earn the rewards that induce them to bear the cost and risk of innovation. First, the innovator has a head start. Although imitators may appear, there is always a time lag, during which high profits may be earned. This time lag may stem from the activities of the original firm to keep its knowledge secret. A prime example is Coca-Cola, which still maintains its secret formula. It may also occur because of the accumulated know-how of the first entrant. Even with complete technical knowledge and comparable facilities, the average firm would be no match for IBM in making computers.

Second, there may be inherent advantages in being the first entrant into the market. The product may become associated in the consumer's mind with the pioneering producer. Certainly, there is a benefit to the firm when making a photocopy is commonly referred to as "xeroxing." Consumer purchasing patterns may require that new firms enter the market on disadvantageous terms that allow the innovating firm to command a premium for its product.

Finally, although the theoretical model of perfect competition in the long run predicts that no excess profits will be earned, technical barriers to entry and oligopolistic pricing practices may result in above-average profits over a long period of time. While innovators may find their profits reduced from the early period when they were able to act as monopolists, the total profit stream may still be very attractive.

Another force that encourages innovation is the requirement of remaining competitive. For example, Hewlett-Packard was first in the market with sophisticated hand calculators. For a short period of time they had a virtual monopoly in the area and offered a small number of models at prices far above production costs. The entrance of firms such as Texas Instruments and Sharp required Hewlett-Packard to cut prices and offer new versions of their calculators to meet the competition. The present market for hand calculators is characterized by low prices and a wide variety of options for the consumer. The innovative activity of Hewlett-Packard was forced on the firm. Patent protection may have enhanced the profitability of the innovations, but the survival of the firm in the calculator market was the major motivation.

The combination of competitive forces that require innovation and market imperfections that allow the innovator to be rewarded even with the ultimate emergence of imitators probably explains why the available evidence does not provide stronger support for the importance of patent laws as stimulants to innovation. However, many students of patent laws believe that the main benefit of patents is their encouragement of radical, costly, and risky departures from existing technology. Such developments are relatively infrequent, but of such great consequence that their occurrence may be worth the windfalls granted to other inventive and innovative activities. If the introduction of the telephone, radio, television, photocopier, and laser were dependent or accelerated by patent protection, then the benefits to society might be sufficient to compensate for higher prices paid for products that would have come anyway.

ABUSES OF THE PATENT SYSTEM

There may be costs of the patent system in addition to the intended monopoly position that is granted. Firms are often able to lengthen, strengthen, broaden, and coordinate the monopoly rights given by patents. This section considers these abuses of the patent system and indicates the legal status of such practices.

Lengthening of Patent Rights

The basic patent grant in the United States is 17 years. Since the average time for processing a patent is nearly two years, the actual period approaches 20 years. Sometimes, entrepreneurs can stretch the protective term even longer. A creative example comes from the early days of the automobile industry. During the 1870s, improvements in automobile technology were usually the result of basement and garage tinkerers and were often not patented. An enterprising patent attorney, George Seldon, took the initiative by filing for a patent on the *entire* automobile. For the next six years he used various delaying tactics to allow him to amend his application to include improvements as they were made. Although it was finally held to be invalid in 1911, the Seldon patent demonstrated that legal maneuvers can greatly extend patent lives.

A different approach for lengthening patent protection was taken by the drug manufacturer, Eaton Labs. The lab held a patent on Furadantin, a product used in the treatment of urinary infections. Just before the patent was to expire, a new product called Macrodantin was introduced. Macrodantin was essentially the same substance as Furadantin, but the developers were still granted a patent and, hence, protection from competition. The market for Macrodantin was guaranteed by an intensive advertising campaign by Eaton Labs. Doctors, lacking any real incentive to prescribe the lower-cost product, began to specify the "drug of choice," Macrodantin. In this way a 17-year patent was extended for a much longer time without any real benefit to the public.

Strengthening of Patent Rights

Despite the attempts of a clever patent lawyer, it may be possible for competing firms to "invent around" an important patent. Firms can make this a much more difficult prospect by obtaining patents not only on the basic product or process that they view as most promising, but also other related products or processes. For instance, the du Pont Corporation was not content to patent only the molecular composition and manufacturing process of nylon, but also filed patent applications for hundreds of related compositions. By obtaining an extensive patent portfolio in the area of synthetic fibers, the firm was able to enhance the value of its patents for nylon by making entry and competition much more difficult. Similar tactics have been pursued in the development stages of radio, television, electric lamps, shoe machinery, data processing, photo supplies, and copying equipment.

The social costs of a firm fencing off a product area depend on the products and processes involved. Presumably, the patent holder will choose from his patent holdings the product or processes that are technically and economically superior. Patent rights left unexercised will be for inferior inventions, and society will reap the benefits of the dominant technology.

If the selected process or product has clear advantages over all others, then the broad portfolio of patents held by the producing firm is of little consequence, because the alternative technologies could not be profitably used. However, in many cases the other products or processes may be only marginally inferior. They may be slightly more expensive to produce or slightly less desirable in use. If their patent rights are held by the firm producing the superior product, then these technologies may not be used at all. On the other hand, if competing firms have access to such products and processes, then such firms may be able to enter the market because of the pricing practices of the original firm. If the producer of the superior product is charging the monopoly price, then a competitor with slightly higher costs can still earn a profit. Similarly, producers of less desirable products can carve a niche in the market by selling their product at a slight discount. Pressures from these entrants will force the producers of the superior product to reduce prices and society will be benefited.

A common belief is that firms often suppress even superior technologies because of their vested interests in the status quo. For years it has been argued that the major oil companies have purchased the rights to all kinds of devices for reducing gasoline consumption and have forever hidden them from view. The modern variant is that they are retarding the advancement of solar energy in the same way. There are very few documented instances of such suppression. It is true, however, that most of the patents that are issued are never used. Estimates are that from 50 to 90 percent of all patent rights are never exercised.[16] In the vast majority of cases this is because the invention is technically or economically unsound.

In the United States, patent holders have the right to use or not use their ideas as they choose. However, use is encouraged by an increasing scale of fees. Individuals and small businesses are charged $150 to apply for a patent and another $250 if the application is approved. Keeping the patent in force beyond four years costs an additional $200. Beyond eight years requires a a fee of $400, and beyond twelve years costs $600.[17] This schedule provides some incentive for allowing marginal patents to lapse.

A second method for encouraging the use of patents is compulsory licensing. In at least 55 nations (but not the United States) a firm may be required to grant a license to make a product or use a process if the invention is not put to use. The United Kingdom and Canada have such a provision for pharmaceutical products and processes. In most cases the firm is granted a "reasonable royalty," which is set by negotiation or by the government. Although compulsory licensing is part of patent legislation in many nations, it has been used very sparingly. For example, in the United Kingdom only twenty compulsory licenses were granted between 1950 and 1971.[18]

Broadening of Patent Rights

By using the leverage that is afforded by a patent, a firm may broaden its monopoly position to include other products that are not patentable. This may be accomplished by the use of tying contracts. As discussed in Chapter 8, tying contracts are provisions that specify that a firm will be allowed to purchase or sell a product sold by a monopolist only by agreeing to purchase or sell another product that is marketed under more competitive conditions. Thus, the firm requiring the tying contracts may be able to exert

---

[16]United Nations, *The Role of the Patent System in the Transfer of Technology to Developing Nations* (New York: United Nations, 1975), pp. 40–41.

[17]U.S. Department of Commerce, Patent and Trademark Office, *General Information Concerning Patents* (Washington, D.C.: U.S. Government Printing Office, 1983), pp. 34–35. Fees are double the above amounts if the applicant or patent holder is not an individual or small business.

[18]Scherer, *The Economic Effects of Compulsory Licensing,* p. 41.

influence in the competitive market because of its strength in the monopoly market. Tied sales can occur any time that one firm has a monopoly position for a product. However, they are most common in relation to patented products because the patent is an instrument that creates a strong monopoly position. An instructive example is the IBM case decided in 1936. IBM was a seller of patented tabulating machines. The firm required purchasers of the patented tabulating machines to use only unpatented IBM tabulating cards that were available from a number of sources. The law is clear on attempts to broaden a patent monopoly through tying agreements. The Supreme Court held that IBM's practices were in violation of the Clayton Act.[19] Subsequent court decisions have taken a similarly hard stand against tied sales based on patent protection.

Coordinating of Patent Rights

The Seldon patent for the automobile was previously mentioned, but only part of the abuses indicated. Originally, the broad Seldon patent was ridiculed and ignored, but in the early 1900s patent infringement notices were issued to over 30 automobile manufacturers in the United States. Suits were initially filed against the weaker companies, which subsequently either went out of business or agreed to purchase a license under the patent. As litigation shifted to the larger firms, ten of them got together and agreed to be licensed and pay royalties in return for the right to exclude other firms from licensing. The royalties they had to pay were evidently considered a fair price for the right to deny other firms entry into the industry. An outsider, Henry Ford, applied for a license, but was refused. Ford successfully challenged the patent and the automobile industry entered a period in which the number of firms increased and competition intensified. Still, the Seldon episode is important, because it shows how patents may be used to facilitate cooperation between firms in an industry. By licensing agreements, firms can greatly restrict competition. Scherer argues that "some of the most blatant price fixing schemes in American economic history were erected on a foundation of agreements to cross license complementary and competing patents."[20]

The potential for abuse of the patent system is well illustrated by the landmark 1945 Hartford-Empire case involving patent pooling. During the early part of this century new processes were developed for making glass containers. Several groups claimed to have developed the new techniques and a rash of patent infringement suits resulted. The conflicting claims were resolved by the formation of Hartford-Empire Corporation, an amalgamation of the major competing groups. Once Hartford-Empire had established a strong position in the industry, it engaged in a program of patent purchases and litigation to gain further control. A patent pool with eight other glassware manufacturers was created. Ultimately, the pool controlled over 800 patents, and about 94 percent of all glass containers manufactured in the United States were produced on machines licensed under the pooled patents. By the late 1930s, only four manufacturers were not part of the pool and Hartford had filed suit against three of them.

The licensing agreements that the Hartford group imposed on smaller manufac-

[19] *International Business Machines Corp.* v. *U.S.,* 298 U.S. 131 (1935). See Chap. 8 for a discussion of the effects of tied sales.

[20] Scherer, F. M., *Industrial Market Structure and Economic Performance* (Chicago: Rand McNally, 1970), pp. 392–393.

turers were very restrictive and limited the quantity, price, type, color, size, and weight of the glassware that they could produce. A district court determined that price competition in the industry had been suppressed and found the defendants guilty of violating the Sherman and Clayton Acts. The companies were ordered to license outsiders under all their patents at reasonable royalties.[21]

Arrangements such as patent pools or cross-licensing are not necessarily undesirable. If they result in new technologies being more widely available, they may serve a useful social purpose. The abuse of such practices occurs when potential competitors are excluded or are required to pay excessive license fees or when the pool or licensing agreement allows the firms to restrict competition by specifying prices, territories, and/or outputs of its members. When patent agreements between firms serve to facilitate collusion rather than transfer technology, they are vulnerable to attack under the federal antitrust laws.

ALTERNATIVES TO EXISTING PATENT LAWS

It is not difficult to find ardent proponents or strident opponents of the patent system. It is, however, very difficult to assess the relative benefits and cost of the system. A fair but unsettling verdict is rendered by Machlup:

> No economist on the basis of present knowledge could possibly state with certainty that the patent system, as it now operates, confers a net benefit or a net loss upon society.
>
> If one does not know whether a system "as a whole" (in contrast to certain features of it) is good or bad, the safest "policy conclusion" is to "muddle through"—either with it, if one has lived with it, or without it, if one has lived without it. If we did not have a patent system, it would be irresponsible, on the basis of our present knowledge of its economic consequences, to recommend instituting one. But since we have had a patent system for a long time, it would be irresponsible, on the basis of our present knowledge, to recommend abolishing it.[22]

Although there are many similarities in worldwide patent legislation, there are also differences. An examination of these differences suggests ways in which the patent system in the United States may be modified to correct some of the problems identified by its critics. Among the possible changes in U.S. patent laws are the following.

Selective Areas of Patentability

Some products or processes, the most common case being in the pharmaceutical industry, are not patentable in certain countries. The philosophy behind such exclusions is that these products are so vital to the public interest that it is not permissible to allow the high prices that often follow the granting of patent rights. The curious nature of this logic has already been suggested. If the patent right is granted to induce

[21]*Hartford-Empire Co.* v. *U.S.,* 323 U.S. 386 (1945).
[22]85th Cong., 2nd Sess., Senate Subcommittee on Patents, Trademarks, and Copyrights, Senate Committee on the Judiciary, study no. 15, Machlup, F., *An Economic Review of the Patent System,* (Washington, D.C.: U.S. Senate, 1958), pp. 110–111.

innovation, then products where innovation is vital, such as drugs, are where patents are most needed.

The exclusion of pharmaceuticals may be of little practical importance, because the rate of innovation of new drugs does not seem closely connected to the presence or absence of patent privileges. However, the existing evidence is based on a world where many of the most important innovating nations do provide patent protection for pharmaceuticals. Innovations from these nations can be imported into countries that do not grant protection. The rate of innovation in a world where no country offered patents for drugs might be much different.

Variable Life of Patent Rights

Germany and other countries offer patent rights of different durations depending on the nature of the invention. Discoveries deemed to be of major importance are allowed more extended protection than less revolutionary concepts. Nordhaus, in a path-breaking study of optimal patent lives, concluded that the period of patent protection in most countries may be somewhat too long, but that there is no strong case for major changes.[23] Scherer argues that a shorter patent life would have its major effect on discouraging inventions with a relatively low benefit-cost ratio. He suggests that a standard life of three to five years be adopted, with the applicant bearing the burden of proof for a longer period of protection.[24] Although variable patent lives inject another element of uncertainty and subjectivity into the system, some flexibility would probably be desirable.

Compulsory Licensing

Some patent statues provide for compulsory licensing when an invention has not been sufficiently worked. Occasionally, remedies in U.S. antitrust cases have included provisions requiring licensing at "reasonable royalties." A possible modification of existing patent laws would require that a patent holder license all firms requesting to use the new invention. Royalties would be set by negotiation or by binding arbitration. The advantage of such a scheme is that innovators are still provided with the profit that rewards their innovation and society obtains the widespread use of the product or process.

There are several problems with compulsory licensing. A major concern is the determination of reasonable royalties. A maximum royalty that a licensee would pay is equal to the profit per unit that can be ascribed to the patent. If the patent holder is allowed to charge the maximum royalty, then the public may see little, if any, gain from the innovation. The minimum royalty is, of course, zero. In this case the innovating firm would receive no reward for its efforts. Historically, reasonable royalties have often been cost based. That is, the innovating firm has been granted enough to earn a reasonable return on its costs of research and development. Such allowances rarely approach the monopoly royalty. For example, DDSA Pharmaceuticals Ltd. applied for

[23]Nordhaus, W. D., *Invention, Growth, and Welfare: A Theoretical Treatment of Technological Change* (Cambridge, Mass.: MIT Press, 1969).
[24]Scherer, F. M., "Nordhaus' Theory of Optimal Patent Life: A Geometric Interpretation," *American Economic Review*, Vol. 62 (June, 1972), pp. 422–427.

a U.K. license to sell a drug named Librium. The license was opposed by an existing supplier, Roche Products. It was estimated that the license was worth between $800 and $1,100 per kilogram to DDSA. This value was calculated as the expected price minus the production costs of DDSA. The actual royalty that was allowed was based on estimated research, development, and promotional costs of Roche. The resulting royalty of $336 per kilogram was less than one-half of the minimum estimate of what the traffic would bear.[25]

The U.K. Patent Office was not necessarily wrong in its allowance, but the example does suggest that there may be substantial disagreements on the proper royalty. If the main criterion is the inducement for innovation, then compulsory license fees should be set near the monopoly level. If the prime concern is for lower prices to customers, then a much lower reward is called for. Like many other areas of government policy toward business, the final question is one of equity.

If royalties under compulsory licensing are below the monopoly rate, some curtailment of innovation might be expected. The desirability of a compulsory licensing provision depends on the magnitude of that reduction. There is some available evidence. Taylor and Silberston asked firms in the United Kingdom to predict the consequences of a system under which all patents were available for licensing at reasonable royalties. The estimates ranged from a reduction of 64 percent of research and development expenditures in the pharmaceutical industry to essentially no change in the manufacture of electronics.[26] The large impact in pharmaceuticals may be attributed to the riskiness and ease of imitation in that industry.

Another approach to investigating the effect of compulsory licensing is to examine the subsequent behavior of firms subject to such a requirement as a result of antitrust decrees. A 1977 study by Scherer concluded that such firms had continued research-and-development efforts as intensively as other firms of comparable size and industry origin. However, the reason for this result may be that the court decrees were largely ineffective. For example, Scherer found no changes in industry concentration beyond those that could have been predicted on the basis of trends or other factors. That is, the antitrust judgments had little effect on industry structure.[27] A survey by Hollabaugh and Wright found that in nearly half of 81 antitrust-based compulsory licensing requirements either no licenses were granted or no new licenses could be attributed to the decrees.[28] Again, the findings suggest that the antitrust remedies had little effect.

Grants for Invention

In the Soviet Union the inventor of a cost-saving technique may be granted a share of the savings. During the U.S. Constitutional Convention strong arguments were advanced for compensating inventors with cash stipends or parcels of land. It is sometimes suggested that similar practices be adopted in the United States and other market-oriented economies. The advantage of such provisions is that once the inventor has been

[25]Scherer, *The Economic Effects of Compulsory Licensing,* pp. 44–45.
[26]Taylor and Silberston, op. cit., p. 199.
[27]Scherer, *The Economic Effects of Compulsory Licensing,* pp. 67–78.
[28]Hollabaugh, M. A., and Wright, R., *Compulsory Licensing Under Antitrust Judgements,* staff report of the Subcommittee on Patents, Trademarks and Copyrights, Senate Committee on the Judiciary (Washington, D.C.: 1960), p. 14.

compensated, then the new discovery is immediately and widely made available for public use. Thus, invention is stimulated without conferring long-standing monopoly rights.

There are at least two problems with a grant system in a market economy. First, it is virtually impossible to estimate the value of a new invention. A large bureaucracy and heroic judgments would be required to make the compensation decisions. Consider the problem that the U.S. Patent Office has in just judging the patentability of inventions, let alone their value. Also, experience with public officials making assessments of reasonable royalties suggests that there is a conservative bias. Compensations would probably be low in relation to the market rewards that oculd be earned. Part of this bias stems from the political criticisms that would undoubtedly arise from an agency doling out large sums of public money. Irrefutable evidence on this point is generated by the public outcry against the puny salaries that are paid to overworked and deserving college professors in state-supported universities.

The second problem with public remuneration is that such plans typically focus on the inventive rather than the innovative stage of technological change. It has already been noted that the primary need for economic incentives seems to be as a reward for the innovator and not the inventor. Thus, the compensation of the inventor would not necessarily provide the requisite incentives to entrepreneurs. It is possible to envision a scheme of rewards for innovators, but hard to imagine much public support for a program that paid millions of dollars to General Motors for a better transmission.

CONCLUSIONS

The "Scotch verdict" of Machlup, to the effect that we should keep the patent system only because we already have it, is probably a fair recommendation. The evidence is not overwhelming that patents dramatically change the rate of technological change across the board, but most analysts would agree that there are a few very important innovations that come when they do because of the patent incentive. Although, the basic provisions of the patent system should probably be retained, some consideration might be given to changes such as a simple system of variable patent lives or compulsory licensing for nonuse. Clearly, antitrust laws should be stringently applied to prevent abuses of the patent system.

SUMMARY
The Case for Patents

If invention and innovation are spurred by economic incentives, then the amount of such activity will be affected by how rapidly and completely imitators can strip the original entrepreneurs of their rewards. Patents are a means of encouraging invention and innovation by increasing the expected returns.

The Patent System

Background Most countries offer some kind of patent protection, although the specific provisions differ. The U.S. patent system is based on the British experience and is specifically authorized by the Constitution.

Duration of Patent Rights In the United States, patent protection is granted for 17 years. In other countries the duration ranges from 3 to 20 years, sometimes depending on the importance of the invention and the wishes of the applicant.

Patentable Inventions "Any new and useful process, machine, manufacture, or composition of matter, or any new and useful improvement thereof" may be patented in the United States. However, inventions pertaining to atomic energy and national defense may not be patented.

Standards of Patentability An invention must meet three criteria to be patented in the United States. First, the invention must be new. Second, it must be useful. Finally, it must be nonobvious. Similar criteria are used to judge patentability in other countries.

Procedures Patent applications must describe the invention in sufficient detail to allow others "skilled in the art" to use it. About three-fifths of all applications are ultimately granted. The average period from application to grant is about 24 months. A large proportion of patents tested in the courts are ruled invalid.

Evaluation of the Patent System

Motivation for Inventing and Innovating Love of inventing and the desire to improve may be more important to *inventors* than the prospect of financial gain. However, profitability appears to be the most important factor encouraging *innovation*.

Evidence of the Effect of Patents Determining the effect of patent laws is a very difficult task. Fragmentary evidence does not strongly indicate the need for patent protection as a stimulus to invention and innovation. For example, businesspeople indicate that other forces, such as the need to be competitive and the desire to grow, are more important considerations in funding research and development programs than is the existence of patent protection.

Market Forces That Encourage Invention and Innovation Several factors may provide a substantial advantage to innovators, even without patent protection. First, there is a lag between innovation and competitive entry. Second, the first producer may acquire a lead in technical expertise. Third, initial sellers are often able to differentiate their products in the minds of consumers.

Abuses of the Patent System

Lengthening of Patent Rights By strategically introducing similar patented products, a firm may be able to lengthen the period of patent protection. This has been a common strategy in the pharmaceutical industry.

Strengthening of Patent Rights Firms can reduce the probability of competitors "inventing around" a patent by taking patents on related products and technologies.

Although most patent rights are never exercised, there is no evidence that superior technologies are deliberately suppressed.

Broadening of Patent Rights   By tying the sale of a patented product to the purchase of other products, firms attempt to increase the profitability of the basic patent. The courts have consistently found tied sales based on patent rights to be a violation of antitrust laws.

Coordinating of Patent Rights   Cross-licensing or patent pools can be socially useful if they serve to make new technology more widely available. However, arrangements that exclude competitors or require payment of excessive license fees represent abuses of the patent privilege and are vulnerable to antitrust attack.

Alternatives to Existing Patent Laws

Selective Areas of Patentability   In some countries, certain products are considered so important that the high prices that may accompany patent protection are not considered acceptable. But, if patent rights stimulate innovation, then these products are the very areas where innovation is most critical.

Variable Life of Patent Rights   The current patent period of 17 years in the United States may be unnecessarily long. One possibility is for a standard patent period of from 3 to 5 years, with the applicant required to justify any longer period of protection.

Compulsory Licensing   Existing U.S. patent laws could be modified to require patent holders to license firms desiring to use their inventions. However, determining reasonable royalties is not a simple task. High royalties result in high product prices, while low royalties reduce the incentives to innovate.

Grants for Innovation   Inventors of cost-saving devices in the Soviet Union may be granted a stipend for their accomplishment. Like royalties, determining the fair amount would be a very difficult task. Also, grants made to inventors may not reflect the real need, which is to give incentives to innovators.

DISCUSSION QUESTIONS

1. The duration of U.S. patents was established about 200 years ago. Have changing technological and economic conditions altered the optimum patent period? How?
2. Basic scientific principles and fundamental discoveries are not patentable under U.S. law. How can patent examiners determine which inventions fall into these categories?
3. Should pharmaceutical products be exempted from patent protection in the United States? Why?
4. Should the United States adopt the British practice of allowing third parties to contest a patent prior to its issuance?
5. Does the fact that a large proportion of court-tested patents are ruled invalid indicate that U.S. patent standards are not stringent enough?

6. For what types of inventions would market forces be most likely to provide individuals and firms with sufficient rewards to simulate innovation? Least likely?
7. How would compulsory licensing of patents in the United States affect the demand for patents?
8. Would variable patent lives with longer periods available for important inventions be an improvement of the U.S. patent system?

chapter 21

Incomes Policies and Selective Wage and Price Controls

Chapter Outline

It is our pleasure, therefore, that those prices . . . be held in attention throughout our whole domain, in such a way that all men understand that freedom to exceed them is removed.

. . . if anyone have acted with boldness against the letter of this statute, he shall be subjected to capital punishment. [1]

The term *incomes policies* is broadly defined to include a variety of schemes intended to calm inflationary expectations and to stabilize the distribution of income between capitalists and workers in the economy. Such schemes can have many different forms, but usually include three primary elements. First, there is a target or goal for wage and price changes in the economy. Second, guidelines and procedures are formulated to judge business or labor requests for changes in prices and wages. Finally, there is a mechanism for obtaining compliance with the guidelines. This mechanism may range from urgings of government to adhere to strictly voluntary guidelines for wage and price increases to formal wage and price controls enforced by fines or sanctions against firms or unions in violation.

Among the common criticisms of incomes policies are that they inevitably result in shortages and black markets, that they represent a loss of economic freedom, that they hold the potential for the abuse of political power, and that they result in an inefficient allocation of resources because prices and wages are no longer able to function as signaling devices for shifting resources. The subject of incomes policies has made some strange bedfellows as conservatives and radicals alike have joined in criticism. Friedman, for example, has argued that imposing wage and price controls on an economy is analogous to locking the rudder on a ship. Price and wage changes perform the function of guiding the economy between straits of shortage and excess. Restricting this vital function by controls or other types of incomes policies makes it impossible to steer a safe course. [2]

Radical economists oppose incomes policies for a different reason. They interpret past experience as favoring the incomes of capitalists at the expense of workers' incomes. They view this result not as an accident, but as the inevitable consequence of the alliance of big government with big business. In their view, policies are purposely designed to shift the distribution of income in the direction of the owners of capital. A typical radical perspective is that "comprehensive wage-price controls in a capitalist system combine the worst aspects of capitalism and Soviet-style socialism: a huge and inefficient bureaucracy plus private greed." [3]

Galbraith observes that there have been few questions where employers, unions, and professional economists have been as united as in opposition to wage and price regulation. Employers have viewed them as a mechanism for reducing profits. Unions interpret them as an undesirable interference with collective bargaining procedures. Economists object to the clutter and subjectivity that is imposed on otherwise "pure" models of markets. [4]

[1]The "Edict of Diocletian," as quoted in Schuettinger, R.L. and Butler, E.F., *Forty Centuries of Wage and Price Controls* (Washington, D.C.: The Heritage Foundation, 1979), p. 157.

[2]Friedman, M., "Why The Freeze Is a Mistake," *Newsweek* (Aug. 30, 1971), p. 23.

[3]Hunt, E. K., and Sherman, H. J., *Economics: An Introduction to Traditional and Radical Views* (New York: Harper & Row, 1978), p. 482.

[4]Galbraith, J. K., *The New Industrial State* (New York: New American Library, Signet, 1968), p. 261.

In spite of the chorus of objections to incomes policies by all "rational parties," they continue to tempt politicians. There is strong appeal in their apparent simplicity and high visibility. The mysteries of multipliers and the uncertainties of lags associated with monetary and fiscal policy are not required for programs of wage and price restraint. Elaborate logic and specialized jargon are not necessary to understand their operation—government simply limits wage and price increases and punishes violators. Successes are readily evident. Unfortunately, so are failures.

The first section of this chapter discusses incomes policies as a tool for dealing with cost-push versus demand-pull inflation. A theoretical analysis of the relationship between industry structure and the effectiveness of incomes policies follows. The next two sections review past use of incomes policies and suggest considerations for their implementation. Finally, rent controls and usury ceilings are considered as examples of selective price controls.

INCOMES POLICIES AND INFLATION

Most economists will (grudgingly, in some cases) admit to at least two basic kinds of inflation. The first, and most commonly accepted, is demand-pull inflation. Figure 21.1 presents a simplified version of this type of inflation.

The horizontal axis plots the real value of goods and services produced in the economy. The vertical axis represents the money value of goods and services produced or the aggregate amount of income generated from any level of production. The line Y_d represents aggregate demand by consumers, firms, and government for goods and services. The point Y_F depicts full-employment or the amount of goods and services that can be produced when there are no unemployed resources. The supply line, $0AY_s$ measures the aggregate amount of income that is generated from any given level

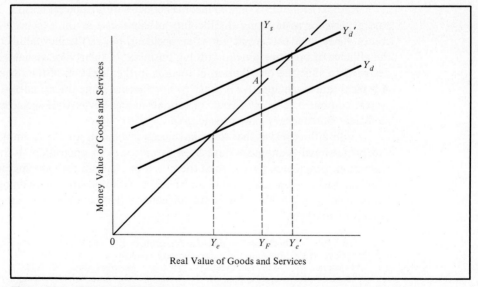

Figure 21.1. Demand-pull inflation.

of production. From 0 to A, the supply line has unitary slope, showing that the real value of goods and services produced is associated with an equivalent amount of income being generated. Beyond Y_F, the supply line becomes vertical. This is interpreted as depicting a fixed level of goods and services producing higher aggregate incomes as prices increase. The interaction of Y_d and Y_s result in an equilibrium level of economic activity at Y_e. If aggregate demand increases to Y_d', then there is excess demand in the economy. Were it not for the full-employment constraint, the level of production would increase to Y_e'. Because the extra demand cannot be realized, it manifests itself in the form of higher prices. This is represented by the intersection of Y_d' with $0AY_s$, where Y_s is vertical, indicating that a fixed real value of goods and services is generating larger amounts of money income. This phenomenon is referred to as demand-pull inflation.

Demand-pull inflation is often described as too much money chasing too few goods. The traditional remedies involve the use of monetary or fiscal policy to reduce the level of aggregate demand until the demand schedule intersects the supply schedule at point A. At this point, there is full employment of resources without inflation. Even the briefest exposure to economic history reveals that this is easier said than done.

The analysis associated with Figure 21.1 suggests that the economy may experience inflation if aggregate demand is too great, or unemployment if aggregate demand is deficient. Nowhere in the discussion is there any suggestion that high levels of unemployment and inflation could occur simultaneously. Recent experience in the United States tells quite a different story. In mid-1982, the unemployment rate was about 9.5 percent. At the same time, consumer prices were increasing at an annual rate of over 12 percent. What is the cause of rapid inflation in the face of unemployed resources? Certainly, the culprit cannot be a general excess of demand in the economy. Shortages or bottlenecks in specific sectors may be a partial answer, but the role of expectations and the existence of large firms and unions may provide additional insights.

Consider an economy with unemployed resources but stable prices. Assume that the economy is "shocked" by a large cost increase in some important sector. As a wild and improbable example, suppose that the price of imported oil is quadrupled. In the attempt to compensate for the cost increase, oligopolistic firms, producing the many products that use petroleum as an input, raise prices for those products by at least a portion of the increase in costs. The price increases set the following chain of events in motion:

Prices of products purchased by workers increase

which causes

Purchasing power of workers to be reduced

which causes

Workers to push for higher wages through collective bargaining

which causes

Wage costs of businesses to increase

which causes

Businesses to raise prices to compensate for increased costs
which causes
Purchasing power of consumers to be reduced
and on up the spiral.

The key to a continuing wage-price spiral or cost-push inflation has two parts. The first is expectations of consumers and businesses in the society. If they believe that there is going to be continued inflation, then they take actions to protect themselves against wage and price increases, and, in doing so, create additional inflationary tendencies. The original shock of higher oil prices initiated forces resulting in price increases in many other sectors, but these would have died out in a short period of time if nothing else occurred. However, when groups in the economy anticipate further inflation and act to protect themselves against further increases, their fears may be self-fulfilling. Unless something is done to change expectations of the future, wages push up prices, which push up wages, and so forth.

The second key to the wage-price spiral is the existence of firms and unions with market power. The possibility of unions successfully negotiating wage increases during times of substantial unemployment requires that they have sufficient clout in input markets to resist downward pressures on wages from unemployed workers. It is also necessary that the firms with which they negotiate have some discretion with respect to pricing policies. That is, the firms must be price makers, not price takers. If firms have market power, then they are better able to pass on wage increases. To a great extent, the willingness of economists to recognize the possibility of cost-push inflation is related to their view of the structure of the economy. Those who see competitive forces as strong and pervasive are more skeptical of the cost-push explanation than those who give greater emphasis to the importance of concentrated industries.

Proponents of wage and price controls or other forms of incomes policies argue that such policies can be used to combat cost-push inflation by changing inflation expectations. Ideally, this would occur in the following manner. Suppose that government mandates that wages and prices in all sectors of the economy will be frozen at current levels for an indefinite period of time. If (a small word hiding a great deal of uncertainty) policymakers can convince business and labor that they can make the freeze stick, then the wage-price spiral may be broken because of the change in expectations. If labor believes that its purchasing power will not be eroded by inflation, then wage demands may be more moderate. If wage demands do moderate, then business will have reduced incentives to increase prices to compensate for cost increases. As prices stabilize, labor gains additional confidence that inflation is being dealt with and further tempers its demands. If there are no pressures from excess demand when the freeze is lifted, inflation will not reappear because expectations will have been modified.

Traditional macroeconomic tools such as monetary and fiscal policy are not particularly effective in dealing with cost-push inflation. They operate on the level of aggregate demand in the economy. In periods of high inflation and high unemployment such as mid-1982, a policy that further reduces aggregate demand can alleviate inflation only at the cost of additional unemployment. Conversely, incomes policies are not considered appropriate tools during periods of demand-caused inflation. They do nothing to increase capacity or decrease demand in the economy. By holding down prices, they actually increase demand pressures and further increase the difference between demand and capacity. However, there may be one role for controls in a high-demand, low-unemployment economy. When a nation is mobilizing for war and must divert resources from consumer goods to military goods, there is a tendency for price increases as consumer products are in increasingly short supply. Combining price controls with a rationing scheme may allow the society to mobilize without a price explosion. The use of price controls in wartime will be covered later in the chapter.

INCOMES POLICIES AND INDUSTRY CONCENTRATION
Controls and Competitive Industries

Figure 21.2 depicts the supply and demand curves for a competitive industry. Each firm is considered to take as given the market price of the product as determined by the interaction of the supply and demand curves. The equilibrium price is P_e and the equilibrium quantity is Q_e. Suppose that public policy limits the price at which the product can be sold to P_c. The lower price reduces the amount that will be supplied to Q_s and induces additional consumers to enter the market so that the quantity demanded increases to Q_d. The amount that consumers desire to purchase is now greater than the available supply. There is a shortage of the price-controlled product. In the free market, prices act as a rationing device to equilibrate supply and demand. Some consumers drop out of the market as prices increase. At the same time, additional supply is called forward as production becomes more profitable. With price increases restricted, another rationing device must be found.

Historically, alternative rationing schemes have taken many forms. The most common has been the black market. If products can be purchased at low prices by consumers who value them less than others who cannot obtain them, then an opportunity for exchange exists. The "low-valuation" consumers can furtively sell the product

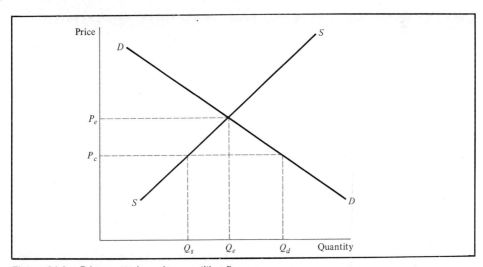

Figure 21.2. Price controls and competitive firms.

to the "high-valuation" consumers, and both will be better off than if the black-market transaction had not occurred. The existence of black markets requires that there be people who are willing to break the law and run the risk of incurring the penalties of running a black-market supply organization. It also requires that there be consumers who are willing to purchase goods illegally. It is interesting to note that there has never been a documented case of effective price ceilings that were not accompanied by some sort of black market.

Sometimes shortages associated with price controls are dealt with by government-run rationing schemes. Consumers are allotted a certain amount of a product that they can purchase. During World War II, individuals were given gas rationing stickers, which they placed on their automobiles. These stickers entitled the person to different amounts of gasoline, depending on the government's perception of his needs and the importance of his job to the war effort. During the energy crisis of the early 1970s, the government actually printed gas rationing coupons, but they were not used because the crisis abated. One of the interesting features of this scheme was that it would have allowed for "white markets." That is, consumers would be given their gas entitlements, but would be legally entitled to transfer those rights to another person for some specified price. Presumably, the allocation of resources in the economy would improve, because users who placed a high value on the incremental gallons of gasoline would be able to obtain them.

One of the serious problems with any government scheme to ration a product is that the decisions of policymakers are substituted for those of individuals. The policy-makers' decisions must be based on criteria that are simple and general enough to make them administratively feasible. This simplicity is purchased at the expense of meeting the needs of individuals. Government gasoline allocation schemes of the 1970s are a typical illustration. The government attempted to distribute a limited supply of gas equitably by giving each state a quota. This quota was based on consumption in previous years. In some cases, this decision rule produced very unfair results because of special circumstances. In Oregon in 1972, the state government had begun a campaign to conserve energy. The program had been initiated before the start of the government allocation system and had been fairly successful. Unfortunately, the federal allocation scheme gave Oregon an allotment based on its previous year's consumption. As such, Oregon was penalized for its previous conservation efforts.

Another interesting example occurred in Texas. In 1972, cotton farmers had a late harvest because of weather conditions. Hence, their fuel use for the normal harvest period was low that year. In 1973, the harvest occurred at the usual time, but the fuel allocation was based on the below-normal consumption of the previous year. Such misallocations do not reflect any lack of concern or competence on the part of bureaucrats, but simply indicate the near impossibility of decision makers performing the vital allocation function that is normally carried out by changes in relative prices.

In many countries, the common manifestation of prices artificially kept below the market level is long queues of people waiting to purchase the limited supplies of goods. Such queues are common in poor nations and have periodically occurred at gas stations in the United States. Queues are a form of rationing in the sense that only those people willing and able to stand in line get the product. The inefficiency of this type of rationing is apparent when the value of time is considered. Suppose that the price of a product as determined by market forces would be $2, but the controlled price is set at $1. If the purchaser's time is valued at, say, $5 an hour, then he has to stand in line only 12 minutes to lose the gain of being able to purchase at a lower price.

Thus far, only the short-run implications of price controls on firms in competitive markets have been considered. The long-run impacts on investment may be far more important. One of the functions of prices is to signal needs for transfer of resources from one sector of the economy to another. If prices are rising because of demand-induced pressures in one industry, then capital tends to flow to that industry to increase supply. Rising prices also generate internal investment funds for expansion by firms within the industry. If prices are restricted at artificially low levels, then the necessary signals are not provided to capital markets and the internal funds are not generated. As a result, if controls are maintained for a long period of time, shortages become more acute because of the lack of expansion in the industry. When controls are lifted, the pressures of excess demand may result in a price bulge.

Controls and Firms with Market Power

On the basis of the theoretical discussions of the previous pages, the attempt to apply controls to competitive industries is not very promising. This may explain some of the economist's disdain for such policies. However, even casual observation of business in any developed nation reveals that much of what is produced is not produced under conditions that satisfy or even approximate the competitive model. As shown in Chapter 3, much of the economic activity in the United States involves oligopolistic firms with some power to set the price at which they sell their product. This power is not complete, because such firms have rivals, but is often enhanced by formal or informal price collusion among firms.

Where firms have power to affect prices, some of the traditional objections to price controls become less compelling. For economists who express concern about the loss of freedom resulting from price controls, a relevant question in this case is, "Whose freedom?" For firms with market power, the invisible hand no longer functions as envisioned by Adam Smith. The loss of freedom is that of firms in exploiting consumers of their product. For such firms, price limitations may be viewed as controls on operations that markets can't effectively control. Here, relative prices may reflect power as much as they do scarcity.

As previously suggested, it is in these concentrated industries and their associated unions that an explanation of cost-push inflation may be found. As prices increase, unions agitate for wage increases. Because of the power of labor as a collective bargaining unit, the wage increase that is obtained is greater than if workers bargained as individuals. The firm is now faced with higher costs, but, because it has market power, it can set its price to pass on a substantial proportion of the increase. The reduction in labor purchasing power sets off another round of wage negotiations. The major difference in this process between firms in competitive and those in concentrated industries is that the latter have greater discretion in terms of pricing. Even in the face of falling demand, they may be able to resist lowering prices. Since price controls are argued as a tool for dealing with cost-push inflation, the logical place for their application is in those sectors of the economy where such inflation originates.

Theory Figure 21.3 depicts the application of price controls to a firm with market power. If left to maximize profits, the firm sets price at P_m and produces the quantity Q_m.

By setting a controlled price at the appropriate level, it is possible to constrain the price of this firm without creating shortages. If the price ceiling is set at the level where the marginal-cost curve just crosses the demand schedule, A, then this result is obtained. The profit-maximizing firm chooses a quantity such that marginal revenues and marginal costs are equal. If the maximum allowed price is P_c, then the firm has a new marginal-revenue curve out to the quantity Q_c. Since P_c is below the demand curve for all quantities less than Q_c, the firm can expand production from zero to that level by selling additional units at the same price. That is, the marginal-revenue curve is given by the horizontal straight line, P_cA. The firm should continue to expand its production as long as marginal costs are less than P_c. Thus, the profit-maximizing quantity is Q_c. If price is set at P_c, there is no shortage or excess. The firm maximizes profits by producing Q_c, and this is the same amount as consumers want to purchase at the controlled price. Prices have been reduced, monopoly profits are lower, and production has been increased. Rather than causing a misallocation of resources as they did for competitive sectors, price controls may actually improve resource allocation in concentrated industries.

The traditional objection to firms with market power is that, by setting prices too high, the quantity produced is too low and insufficient resources are utilized in that industry. Put another way, the value of the last unit purchased is greater than the opportunity cost of its production. Society would be better off if more were produced. By their effect on expanding demand and production, price controls move in this direction by channeling additional resources into the industry.

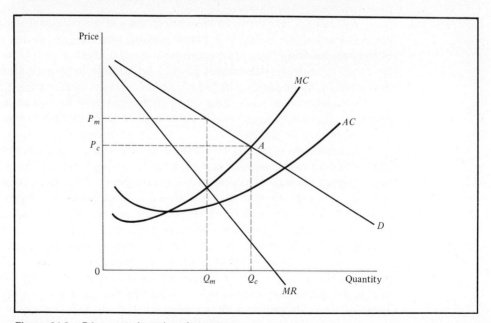

Figure 21.3. Price controls and market power.

Problems The graphs of microeconomic text books always make the solutions to problems look obvious and simple. Unfortunately, they hide the mass of administrative problems that are involved. It is one thing to instruct price controllers to specify that the controlled price will be at the intersection of the demand and marginal cost curves, but it is quite another thing to achieve that result. The firm's demand and cost curves are not known with any degree of precision even to the firm. If the policymaker mistakenly sets the controlled price below P_c, then there will be shortages in the industry because the marginal cost of the last unit produced will exceed the price and the producer will produce less than consumer's demand. If price is set above P_c, then the policymaker can avoid shortages, but is allowing higher prices than are necessary.

The results of controls also hinge on the existence of unemployed resources in other sectors of the economy. Reducing prices increases production in the industry. If resources in the economy are already fully utilized, then they can be induced into the controlled sector only by bidding up input and, ultimately, product prices. Depending on the supply elasticities of the inputs, the controls may have little or no effect on overall product prices.

Incomes Policies and Industry Concentration: Conclusion

The analysis of the preceding pages suggests that the potential success of price controls is a function of the type of industrial structure on which they are imposed and also the general economic conditions of the time. Controls will be less effective in competitive industries than for industries where there are firms with power to set prices. The long-run impacts of controls will be less adverse where the supply curve is inelastic, indicating little expansion in response to higher prices, than it will be for products for which higher prices provide a large inducement to capacity expansion.

Controls are primarily a device for changing inflationary expectations and, to a degree, reducing monopoly prices. Hence, they are expected to be most successful when there are unemployed resources in the economy and least successful when there are strong demand pressures and resources are fully employed. The next section puts the conclusions of economic theory to the test. The experience of selected nations with incomes policies is reviewed and the implications of that experience presented.

EXPERIENCE WITH INCOMES POLICIES
Pre-Twentieth Century

Experiments with incomes policies extend back nearly 4,000 years. In 1800 B.C., the ruler of Babylonia initiated restrictions on wages and prices that lasted more than a thousand years. The compliance mechanism was straightforward—violators were drowned. In 301 A.D., the Roman Emperor Diocletian fixed maximum prices for over 900 commodities and 130 different grades of labor. The relative wage rates afford an interesting glimpse as to how different skills were valued. For example, a teacher of rhetoric or public speaking was allowed over three times the wage of a math teacher. Unfortunately, there is no record of the relative value placed on economists and politicians.

The "Commanded Cheapness" edict resulted from a program of currency reform.

Diocletian had caused gold, silver, and bronze coins to be minted, but the face values of the coins badly understated the relative worth of gold and silver in relation to bronze. The inevitable result was a manifestation of Gresham's Law, with gold and silver being taken out of circulation and melted down to be resold at their true worth and bronze becoming the medium of exchange. By fixing the value of gold, silver, and many standard commodities, Diocletian intended to establish the value of the bronze coins.

Like many experiments with price controls, the edict was less than a total success. Lactantius, a fourth-century historian, writes, "There was . . . much bloodshed upon very slight and trifling accounts; and the people brought provisions no more to market since they could not get a reasonable price for them; and this increased the dearth so much that after many had died by it, the law itself was laid aside." Although it is very difficult to ascertain changes in the Roman "CPI," it is known that within four years after the edict, the value of the bronze coin in terms of gold had shrunk to 40 percent of the pegged value.[5]

Over the next 1,600 years, there were additional attempts at incomes policies: In the thirteenth century, the Mongol leader Kublai Khan fixed maximum prices. The attempt to enforce the "just price" was also a feature of medieval Europe. Wage-price restrictions came to the New World at least as early as 1636, with codes set by the Puritans. Those who violated the codes were considered to be as bad as "adulterers and whoremongers." The Continental Congress set price ceilings even before the Declaration of Independence. The problem of inflation became so severe that General Washington complained that "a wagon load of money will scarcely purchase a wagon load of provisions." Given the lack of faith in the Congress' fiat money, he may not have been exaggerating.

Wartime Policies

Most warring nations imposed some form of price controls during World War II. Germany was the first, imposing a ban on price increases in 1936. The early action by German leaders was undoubtedly associated with the nation's post-World War I experience with inflation. Between August 1922 and November 1923, prices in Germany rose at an average *monthly* rate of 322 percent. By the end of 1923, the gold mark had a value of over 15 billion paper marks. The desire to avoid another bout of hyperinflation led to strong price-restraining action.

The United States moved into World War II with a stabilization plan based on tax increases coupled with price controls on items in short supply because of the war effort. During 1941 and 1942, pressures of excess demand indicated the need for action. Between January 1941 and October 1942, hourly manufacturing wages rose by 30.7 percent and the wholesale price index rose by 24 percent. In March 1942, the General Maximum Price Regulation froze prices at their existing levels. In the fall of that year, "General Max" was replaced by policies that allowed for adjustments reflecting changing costs or conditions. This control scheme continued for the duration of the war.

Many inequities developed in the United States as firms learned that it was

---

[5]Michell, H., "The Edict of Diocletian," *Canadian Journal of Economics and Political Science* (Feb., 1947), pp. 1–12.

possible to circumvent the system. Profit margins could be improved by reducing the quality of a product, by marketing the same product in a higher quality classification, or by changing the terms of sale. The continued introduction of new products was another mechanism for increasing prices. The attempt to make the system as fair and responsive as possible required the creation of an enormous bureaucracy. By 1944, there were 350,000 volunteers and 70,000 paid employees.

Controls were more effective in some areas than in others. Where production was concentrated in a relatively small number of firms, price restrictions were quite successful. For competitive sectors of the economy, such as agriculture and rental housing, the record of controls was much less auspicious. However, the overall results of World War II wage and price controls are quite impressive. In comparison to the rapid rates of wage and price increase for 1941 and 1942, manufacturing wages and the wholesale price index increased by 14.7 percent and 5.7 percent, respectively, between March 1942 and August 1945. The successes of wartime controls were achieved in spite of strong demand pressures as the requirements for defense were superimposed on normal consumer and business needs. The commitment of the American people to the war effort was undoubtedly a major factor. Controls were viewed as a necessary part of governmental policy and group pressure was brought to bear on noncompliance. Workers were criticized for strikes with the slogan "There are no strikes in foxholes." The well-justified response of labor was that "There are no profits, either." Controls remained until the latter part of 1946, but with the common goal of winning the war now absent, they were largely ineffective after 1945. In fact, pent-up demands resulted in a price explosion with prices increasing one-third from 1945 to 1948.

With the outbreak of the Korean War, wage and price controls were reimposed in 1952. In spite of strong demand pressures, there is again evidence that citizens were willing to cooperate to assist the war effort. During 1950 and 1951, the price index for consumer durables rose by 7 percent. With wage and price controls, the 1952 increase was about 1 percent. The consumer price index rose nearly 8 percent from 1950 to 1951, but only 2.2 percent between 1951 and 1952. Controls were removed at the end of the conflict, and there was relative price stability over the next few years.

Postwar Experiences of Other Nations

Most of the nations of Western Europe have flirted with peacetime incomes policies. Almost all of the communist states fix wages and prices to some degree. Each country has implemented a policy with its own unique features and results. The experience of Great Britain and The Netherlands is reviewed briefly to provide insights into the possibilities and limitations of such schemes.

The Netherlands   The collective bargaining process in The Netherlands is fairly centralized with decisions on wages being made on a level high enough so that general economic conditions can be taken into account. In addition, a substantial portion of the nation's output is directed to exports, which means that the competitive positions of Dutch goods in international markets must be an important consideration in wage and price decisions.

In 1945, the Dutch government enacted a labor relations act providing arbitrators with authority to control wages. During the entire period from 1947 to 1953, wages increased by only 1 percent. Prices were allowed to increase only by the amount of nonwage cost increases. By most accounts, the Dutch experiment to the mid-1950s was considered a success. But over time, the competitive position of Dutch goods in international markets improved. The additional demand for goods created a labor shortage to which business responded by awarding wage increases through promotions, changes in job descriptions, and a "black" wages market. The pressures of excess demand culminated in a wage explosion in the early 1960s. During this period, the support of business and labor for incomes policies was drastically eroded. The system had effectively collapsed by the early 1970s.

Great Britain   A wage freeze in 1948 had some initial success, but culminated in a wage explosion in 1950 when labor support was lost. For the next 16 years, various types of programs of voluntary restraint had little success. One of the problems with implementing incomes policies in Great Britain is that the bargaining process is not highly centralized. There is a national Trades Union Congress, but the association has much less control over the wage determination process than does the counterpart organization in The Netherlands. Fears of devaluation of the pound led to a wage and price freeze from 1966 to 1967. This was followed by a two-year period of "moderation" similar to the Phase II program of the Nixon administration. The short freeze period was fairly effective, but the period of moderation was not, with wages rising nearly 10 percent.

   The experience of the two nations affords the opportunity for some generalizations about incomes policies. The centralized bargaining process in The Netherlands made it easier to obtain labor cooperation and more practical to limit wage agreements. A weaker labor unit in Britain impeded efforts there to carry out incomes policies. The loss of labor cooperation dealt a death blow to wage restraint in both countries. Evidently, labor support is critical to a successful incomes policy.

Wage-Price Guidelines and Jawboning

Incomes policies involve varying degrees of compulsion. In 1962, President Kennedy's Council of Economic Advisors initiated a program of voluntary wage and price guideposts tied to increases in labor productivity. The key to the program was the assumption (made somewhat arbitrarily) that the economy-wide rate of increase in labor productivity was 3.2 percent per year. As a general guide to noninflationary wage increases, settlements in each industry were expected not to exceed this average productivity gain. If productivity increases in a particular industry were greater than 3.2 percent, then it was anticipated that prices would be reduced; if the gain was less than 3.2 percent, then prices could be increased by the difference. The council defined special circumstances where the guidelines could be modified. These included labor shortages requiring higher wages to induce a movement of workers into the industry, instances where wages in an industry were lower than those earned elsewhere by similar labor, situations where industry profits were insufficient to attract capital, and circumstances where nonlabor costs rose dramatically.

   Although the guideposts were strictly voluntary, there is some evidence that they did result in some moderation of wage and price increases during 1964 and 1965. Their impact seems to have been centered in the concentrated and highly unionized sectors of the economy such as aluminum, copper, steel, and automobile industries. After 1966, excess demand pressures resulting from the Vietnam War led to the gradual abandonment of serious attempts at voluntary wage and price restraint.

The Carter administration embarked on a program of voluntary price guidelines in 1978. Businesses were asked to limit price increases to 0.5 percent less than the average increase for 1976 to 1977. Wage increases were to be limited to 7 percent. The consensus is that the guidelines had little impact. During the twelve months prior to the program, consumer prices rose by 8.3 percent. The rate of increase was 12.1 percent during the first year the guidelines were in effect and 12.7 percent the second. Wage inflation was less rapid, but hourly rates still increased at an annual rate of nearly 9 percent from 1979 to 1980.

The guidepost concept calls for voluntary action on the part of firms and unions. However, government has not been averse to assisting the process by *jawboning*—resorting to persuasion, threats, and rhetoric. The 1962 steel controversy provides an interesting example. Although operating at less than two-thirds of capacity. United States Steel and other major steel producers announced a 3.5-percent increase in steel prices. President Kennedy called a news conference for the next day and, in addition to castigating the offending companies, requested other companies to hold the line. At the same time, other sources of persuasion were marshaled. The president induced Senator Estes Kefauver, chairman of the Senate Antitrust Subcommittee, to register public dismay over the actions of the steel companies. His suggestion of the need for his subcommittee to investigate was not lost on the company executives. Later, agents of the Justice Department appeared at steel company headquarters to serve subpoenas for documents relating to the price increase. The secretary of defense announced that the government was shifting steel orders to those companies who had been obedient in holding the price line. Within 72 hours after the announcement of the price increase, the steel company front crumbled and the price hike was rescinded. For the next four years, steel prices remained relatively stable.

In March 1978, a similar confrontation occurred between President Carter and (again) U.S. Steel. Responding to the settlement of a prolonged coal-miners strike, U.S. Steel announced steel-price increases of $10.50 per ton to compensate for higher coal prices. The president and his Council on Wage and Price Stability publicly criticized the increase as excessive, the council noting that the increase in coal prices was estimated to add only $4 per ton to steel production costs. Other companies were exhorted to use restraint in announcing price increases. When Bethlehem, National, and other large companies posted increases averaging only $5.50 per ton, the council announced that it was very pleased, and U.S. Steel then reluctantly rolled back its increase to the $5.50 level. It is improbable that jawboning could be consistently effective if it was frequently used as a tool for wage and price restraint. However, used with discretion, the access of the president to the media and the extensive array of "potential threats" available to government can prove useful in selected circumstances.

Phases I, II, III, III$\frac{1}{2}$, and IV

Background and Procedures　Responding to the combination of (by pre-1970s standards) high rates of inflation and unemployment, President Nixon imposed a general

90-day freeze on wages and prices in August 1971. The freeze had a dual prupose. It was intended to check the developing wage-price spiral and also to buy time for the development of a more flexible system of wage and price controls. One of the difficulties of imposing controls is that any indication by government that they are coming results in a wage and price bulge as labor and business attempt to avoid being locked in at low levels. Hence, some kind of holding action was deemed necessary during the transition period.

During the 90-day preparation period, a 15-member pay board and a 7-member price commission were established to make decisions on wage and price increases. Ideally, the freeze period should have been used to formulate systematically well-considered policies and procedures. The evidence, particularly for the price commission, suggests that the process was rather chaotic. C. Jackson Grayson, the price commission chairman, recounts that he arrived in Washington 16 days before the end of the freeze to find no staff, no space, and no policies. The process of developing the procedures to regulate price increases for thousands of firms took place as "telephone men were making installations, carpets were being laid, furniture and files moved in, personnel streamed in with no desks, supplies, or even places to sit. One person described it as resembling a 'replacement depot for the French Foreign Legion.' "[6]

According to Grayson, the need to request an extension of the freeze was considered many times during those 16 days. The final statement of policies was the product of all-night work, an able set of cutters and pasters, a cooperative Xerox machine, and a three-hour postponement of a press conference. The pay board's activities were only slightly less frantic. At the time of the board's first meeting (18 days prior to the end of the freeze), the staff consisted of one secretary on loan and two administrative assistants.

The policies devised by the two groups were in effect from November 1971 to January 1973 and have been dubbed Phase II. The logic behind the Phase II provisions was quite simple. The pay board opted for a general policy that limited wage settlements to a 5.5-percent increase. The price commission assumed that the annual economy-wide increase in labor productivity was 3 percent. Thus, allowing for productivity gains, business could maintain its profit margins with an average price increase of 2.5 percent (5.5 percent − 3.0 percent). An annual rate of inflation of 2 to 3 percent was adopted as the goal for the price commission.

In retrospect, some of the policies adopted by the price commission appear questionable. For example, firms faced with higher costs were permitted to include a normal mark-up on the allowed increases in costs. The effect of this decision was to reduce the incentive of the firm to hold the line on costs. By allowing a mark-up on extra costs, the firm could increase its total profits by justifying a cost increase. *Term limit pricing* (TLP) *agreements* used by the price commission provide a second example. Under such agreements, a firm would agree to limit the average increase in prices for its product line to some fixed percentage (initially 2.0 percent and later 1.8 percent). In return for this concession, the firm was allowed to make individual price adjustments without obtaining commission approval. Although the TLP procedure assisted the commission by reducing its workload, it may have had adverse effects on price stability.

[6]Grayson, C. J., *Confessions of a Price Controller* (Homewood, Ill.: Irwin, Dow-Jones, 1974), p. 19.

It is generally acknowledged that the 2.0-percent overall limit was not an effective ceiling for many of the firms with which the agreements were made. In addition, it gave firms the prerogative of increasing prices in those markets where they had the greatest amount of market power. Consider a firm selling one product in a very competitive environment and another in a near-monopoly setting. The firm is constrained by its competition from increasing prices in the first market, but has considerable discretion in the second market. Under the TLP agreement, the firm holds the line in the competitive market and takes a large price increase in the market where it has market power. Because it is in the latter type of market that cost-push inflation tends to originate, the effectiveness of the control program is weakened.

Another problem faced by the price commission was that of dealing with de facto price increases resulting from changes in product quality. An alleged violation involved Mrs. Adler's Matzoh Ball Soup. AFL-CIO President George Meany accused the company of reducing the number of matzoh balls in a can of soup from four to three without a corresponding price decrease. The company insisted that it had held the line on quality. The price commission staff bought soup cans from stores all over Washington and, in opening 30 cans, found four balls in every can. There were undoubtedly many cheaters, but Mrs. Adler evidently was not among them.

In January 1973, the mandatory Phase II controls were superseded by the voluntary controls of Phase III. The provisions of the Phase III program were not greatly different from those of Phase II, except that they were to be self-administered by firms and unions. The possibility of action against noncomplying firms was used as a latent threat. It is not clear exactly what precipitated the switch from mandatory to voluntary controls. One view is that inflationary pressures in the economy had been sufficiently curtailed and that strict controls were no longer necessary. Another is that the Nixon administration had a general distaste for the controls program and attempted to scrap it after the 1972 presidential election. Regardless of the reason for adopting the Phase III voluntary controls, they proved to be a dismal failure. Shortages of raw materials in the economy put intense price pressures on important sectors of the economy. Worldwide stimulatory measures also had the effect of increasing demand. During the first quarter of 1973, the consumer price index shot up at an annual rate of 8.3 percent. Business, concerned that the failing fight against inflation might spawn another freeze, pushed up prices even more to avoid being caught with their prices down.

The anticipated freeze (dubbed Phase III$\frac{1}{2}$) came in June 1973 and lasted until August of that year. The second freeze was less successful than the first, primarily because economic conditions were much different. The environment of the Phase I freeze was an economy with significant excess capacity. The circumstance in mid-1973 was one of demand-pull inflation. The immediate consequence of the freeze was shortages in many important sectors of the economy. An interesting case is that of beef. Beef prices were actually frozen several months before the general freeze. Irate producers responded to the freeze by holding back beef from the market. Moderate shortages of beef did occur and it was predicted that, with the announced end of the freeze in August 1973, the price of beef would rise dramatically. As it turned out, the price bulge did not materialize. Producers, in their rush to get beef to market, increased supplies so much that there was little increase in prices with the end of the freeze.

The second price freeze gave way to the second round of mandatory controls

(Phase IV) in August 1973. Provisions of Phase IV were not greatly different from those of Phase II, except that firms were allowed only a dollar-for-dollar pass-through on cost increases. This was in contrast to the cost-plus mark-up rule of Phase II. This final phase was geared to get the government out of the controls business. The coverage of the program was much less extensive than before, covering only about half of the items in the consumer price index. Firms were given exemptions from controls by agreeing to use moderation in implementing future price increases.

Effects In April 1974, the final phase of the three-year control experiment was formally terminated. It is difficult to appraise the impact of controls during this period. A simplistic approach is to compare the rate of inflation before the control period to the rate during the period. A more sophisticated approach is to use empirical procedures to compare actual inflation rates during the period with those that would have been predicted in the absence of controls. A limitation of this method is the difficulty of separating the effect of controls from the effect of exogenous shocks such as weather-induced crop shortages or politically induced petroleum cartels. Another problem is the lack of precision of the empirical models. Predictions of wage and price changes are subject to considerable uncertainty.

Even if the methodology for assessing the impact of the controls program was free of defects, the results of a dozen different studies yield ambiguous results. Kraft and Roberts provide an accurate, but somewhat unsatisfying, assessment of the evidence:

> An examination of the evidence should generally result in a no-decision conclusion; the problems of measurement and specification have prevented a consensus opinion. One conclusion that can be drawn is that in Phase II, wages in general were pushed up by controls or held down to a lesser extent than prices. This evidence would indicate a redistribution of income towards workers in the form of higher real incomes. This was not true in Phase III where the balance swung back to prices.[7]

The conclusion reached by the Council of Economic Advisors in 1975 was as follows:

> Regardless of the overall effect of the program, whatever contribution it may have made was probably concentrated in its first 16 months when the economy was operating well below its potential. As various industrial sectors reached capacity operations in 1973 under the stimulus of a booming domestic and world economy, the controls system began to obstruct normal supplier-purchaser relationships and, in some cases, the controls became quite unworkable.[8]

The council's conclusion is generally accepted. During Phase I and Phase II, there was slack in the economy and some tenuous evidence of wage and price moderation. Any wage moderation involved union settlements. Price effects were most pro-

[7]Kraft, J., and Roberts, B., *Wage and Price Controls: The U.S. Experiment* (New York: Praeger, 1975), p. 148.
    [8]*1975 Annual Report of the Council of Economic Advisors* (Washington, D.C.: Government Printing Office, 1976), pp. 228–229.

nounced in concentrated sectors of the economy. In contrast, Phases III, III$\frac{1}{2}$, and IV were implemented during periods of high demand. In addition to producing no demonstrable results in reducing inflation, this period of the controls program was associated with widespread shortages and a general social unrest. Undoubtedly, the OPEC oil embargo was a major contributing factor.

Tax-Based Incomes Policies

The lack of success of traditional schemes for wage and price restraint has resulted in a search for other methods for combating the wage-price spiral. Several economists have suggested that a promising approach is to use the tax system as a carrot or a stick to induce business and labor to behave "appropriately." Such suggestions have been categorized under the general heading of *tax-based incomes policies,* or TIPS.

Several variations of TIPS have been proposed, but all have the general feature of using corporation or personal income tax credits or penalties to influence wage settlements and price increases. For example, a penalty-oriented proposal by Wallich and Weintraub would establish federal guidelines for wage settlements. Any employer granting a wage increase exceeding the guideline by more than 1 percent would be required to pay the same amount in penalty taxes. Guidelines would be set on the basis of the industry's rate of labor productivity increase and prevailing economic conditions. The penalty provision would act to stiffen management's resolve against inflationary settlements and would serve notice to labor of the upper bound.[9]

Another proposal is an incentive scheme proposed by Okun whereby a firm that held wage increases to 6 percent or less and price increases to 4 percent or less would be granted a 5-percent credit on its corporation income taxes. To induce the cooperation of workers, employees in such firms would get a yearly reduction in their personal income taxes of 1.5 percent, up to $225 per person. The exact provisions of the program could be altered to suit the needs of the time.[10]

The primary appeal of TIPS proposals is that they involve market forces rather than controls, which fetter the market in channeling resources. Firms are allowed to make whatever decisions they choose, but the relative profitability of those decisions is altered by the tax system. Firms could grant larger wage increases if they determined that the benefits of doing so were greater than the tax penalty or loss of tax credit that would result. Proponents of TIPS argue that they do not represent a new dimension of policy, but would operate similarly to the investment tax credit or accelerated depreciation provisions.

CONSIDERATIONS IN THE USE OF INCOMES POLICIES

Incomes policies have had a long and varied history. Although it is difficult to generalize, experience and theory do provide some broad conclusions about the uses and limitations of such policies under specific conditions.

[9]Wallich, H., and Weintraub, S., "A Tax-Based Incomes Policy," *Journal of Economic Issues* (June 1971), pp. 1–19.
[10]"Search for Stagflation Remedies," *Time,* Mar. 6, 1978, pp. 66–67.

Excess Demand

Incomes policies are best suited for changing expectations under conditions of simultaneous inflation and excess capacity. An almost universal conclusion is that incomes policies are not appropriate during periods of excess aggregate demand. With the exception of wartime, attempts to impose wage and price restrictions on an overheated economy have not been successful. There are many examples of controls that were imposed during periods of excess capacity that have been effectively emasculated as the economy moved into a period of excess aggregate demand.

One of the problems of incomes policies seems to be that they are viewed as a panacea and may cause policymakers to be less cautious about the use of other policy tools. Specifically, a program of wage and price controls may be viewed as license to implement expansionary monetary and fiscal policies. Unless these policy tools are used with caution, there is little hope that incomes policies can have any lasting beneficial effect.

Cooperation of Industry and Labor

Because incomes policies operate to change business and labor expectations, the cooperation of these groups is essential. Grayson observes that "no matter how many people are employed by the regulatory agency, they will never be able to check all, or even a significant percentage of, the prices in the economy. Controls can work only if the public chooses to make them work." [11]

Past experience indicates that business and labor cooperation is most easily obtained when there is some kind of a crisis. The urgencies of the war undoubtedly were a major factor in the success of price controls in World War II. The European experiments seemed to be most successful when there was a general concern with the country's position in international markets. Crises serve a useful purpose in focusing business and labor's attention on the nation's needs and mobilizing support for government policy. When the crises are resolved, there has often been a breakdown in support for incomes policies.

Another crucial factor in maintaining public support for incomes policies is the public perception of how equitably they are being administered. The term "incomes policies" denotes an attempt to maintain the real income of different groups. If one group determines, either correctly or incorrectly, that it is being discriminated against, then that group's support is quickly lost. Although there is good reason for limiting price controls to only certain segments of the economy, in practice it is difficult to avoid fairly exhaustive controls. The need for perceived equity is one of the reasons for the widespread use of rent controls after World War II. For nations desiring to impose general wage limitations, the cooperation of labor was, obviously, critical. In many cases, the price of labor cooperation was assurance of moderation in rent increases.

Competitive Versus Concentrated Industries

The theoretical analysis of price controls suggests that controls on firms in competitive industries would generally lead to shortages and the need for some form of rationing.

[11]Grayson, op. cit., p. 234.

On the other hand, industries with high degrees of producer concentration may be proper objects of well-designed price controls. The experience with price controls in the United States and other nations supports this prediction. Controls have been imposed most successfully in those industries with a relatively small number of firms. Experience with agriculture, rental housing, and other competitive industries has been very unsuccessful. In addition, the experience of European nations suggests that wage policies tend to be more effective where the collective bargaining process is more centralized. If bargaining is undertaken at a high level, then it is easier to coordinate efforts and to incorporate general economic conditions in the discussions. Wage controls have been much less effective in countries and situations where there were not strong collective bargaining units.

Galbraith suggests that one of the virtues of big business and big labor is their vulnerability to wage and price controls. He suggests that an important weapon in the arsenal of the policymaker is wage and price controls imposed on the thousand or so firms in the "planning system." [12] Few economists would be anxious to include controls as a normal part of stabilization policy. But there is general agreement that their use should be confined to oligopoly situations.

Design

Incomes policies designed to be totally fair to all concerned will tend to be difficult to administer because of the great detail required. Procedures constructed for ease of administration will tend to result in inequities to certain groups. The choice of policies and procedures must straddle the narrow line between fairness and simplicity. One of the lessons of the past is that the design of such policies is critical. The workability of incomes policies depends on how well they fit the specific institutional setting of the nation imposing them. It is virtually impossible to import designs from other nations because of differences in institutions and economic conditions. A program suitable for The Netherlands with its highly collectivized wage determination process would not be appropriate for the United States with a more federalized union organization.

Experience suggests that it is a mistake to implement policies that attempt to force business and labor to greatly modify their normal practices. For example, firms that use mark-up pricing should be controlled in ways that allow that procedure to continue. Similarly, bargaining between firms and unions should be affected only by examining the final result. The insights of the economist are critical to a well-designed incomes policy. An understanding of the forces affecting supply and demand in an industry and a knowledge of the institutional framework in which the industry operates is a necessity for a workable program.

Duration

With a few exceptions, like the Babylonian millennium of controls, successful incomes policies have not been notable for their longevity. Unless modern nations are willing to allow drowning and torture as acceptable penalties for violations, the prospects for long-lived wage and price restrictions are not good. Incomes policies are specifically

---

[12]Galbraith, J. K., *Economics and the Public Purpose* (Boston: Houghton Mifflin, 1973), pp. 312–316.

designed to break the expectations contributing to a wage-price spiral. When these expectations have been altered or when pressures of excess demand are felt, business and unions are not amenable to continue under the arbitrary restrictions of wage and price controllers. The Council of Economic Advisors observed that, "Although such controls may be unfortunately popular when they are not in effect, the appeal quickly disappears once people live under them." [13] Except in times of crisis, past experience indicates that incomes policies cannot be successfully maintained for more than a few years.

Preparation

The record of incomes policies as presented here is not particularly impressive. It is not uncommon for economists to interpret the historical record as demonstrating that there is no valid role for wage and price restrictions in a market economy. This interpretation may be a bit unfair. There is a case to be made that incomes policies have not been given an adequate test, at least in the United States.

Incomes policies have never had much intellectual standing in the economics profession. The presumption has generally been against their workability. As a result, they have not been subjected to the kind of thorough analysis given to other stabilization tools. The actual use of wage and price controls in the United States has not been preceded by adequate preparation. Grayson's account of the formulation of the Phase II procedures gives the impression of chaos. The price commission was pressed to develop a policy by the end of the freeze and learned as it operated during the control period. There was never time for the kind of industry-specific analysis required to develop a properly designed program.

The lack of preparation for incomes policies is somewhat to be expected. An announcement that government was devising a program of controls would generate a rush by labor and business to push up wages and prices to avoid being caught in the control program. Thus, the knowledge of impending controls intended to deal with inflation generates additional inflation. Countries have typically dealt with this problem by imposing a surprise freeze in preparation for controls. The freeze period has been characterized by the feverish assemblying of staff and policies to implement the controls. What is needed is for government to be able to assemble a task force to develop incomes policies, but at the same time to be able to argue effectively that they aren't really going to use them. Certainly, there must be bureaucrats whose training is admirably suited for such double-talk.

SELECTIVE PRICE CONTROLS

In some cases, nations or other governmental units have chosen to impose price controls on specific commodities or services. Common choices for selective price controls are rents and interest rates. The following discussion considers the expected and actual effects of such control programs.

---

[13] *1968 Annual Report of the Council of Economic Advisors* (Washington, D.C.: Government Printing Office, 1969), p. 119.

Usury Laws

A number of states have legislated maximum interest rates that may be charged. Such statutes are referred to as usury laws. The origin of usury laws is probably based more on ethics than economics. The lending of money for interest has not been a noble and respected profession through the ages. In ancient times, the making of money from money was considered unnatural. During the Middle Ages, the lending of money was not considered an appropriate occupation for a good Christian and was left to infidels. The attitude of the Church resulted in legislation to prevent the extortion of good people by unsavory and greedy moneylenders. The United States inherited usury laws from Great Britain, and some states still have such statutes.

The theory of price controls as developed for competitive industries is applicable to interest rate ceilings as well. In this case, the product is the amount of money that is to be borrowed or loaned. The price is the interest rate, r. Figure 21.4 depicts the expected impact of usury laws.

The demand curve is a downward-sloping function of the interest rate. As interest rates increase, there are fewer uses of money generating a return that exceeds the cost of obtaining it. On the other hand, the supply of loanable funds increases with the interest rate because, at higher rates, people are induced to divert more of their money from consumption and other uses. The interaction of supply and demand result in an equilibrium interest rate, r_e, and an equilibrium quantity of loans, Q_e. If the interest rate is controlled at a level lower than the market equilibrium, r_c, then the supply of available funds (Q_s) is exceeded by the quantity demand (Q_d).

When a lending institution has excess demand, then it must find ways of rationing the available money. The rationing schemes that are often used are not always compatible with the objective of usury laws of protecting disadvantaged groups in society. A lender assumes a certain risk in lending money. If that risk can be reduced, then his expected profit, ceteris paribus, is increased. More established, higher-income borrow-

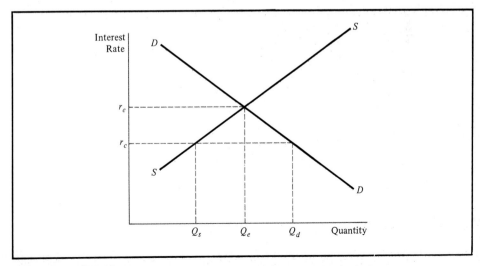

Figure 21.4. Usury laws.

ers represent a lower risk than do the poor, transient, and elderly. A rational decision by a loan officer would be to allocate the available funds to those groups with least risk. In this case, the usury law may serve to hurt those groups it was designed to assist. A low price is desirable, but not if you can't get the product or service.

Lenders also can subvert usury laws by making extra charges to raise the effective interest rate. Anyone who has taken out a home mortgage knows that there is a loan initiation fee, or "points" as they are sometimes called. In normal circumstances, a borrower may pay 2 points, or 2 percent of the loan value as an initiation fee. On a $50,000 mortgage, this handling charge would be $1,000. If there is an effective ceiling on interest rates, the lender may decide that 3 or 4 points is the appropriate amount. By increasing the number of points, the lender increases the effective interest rate and profitability of the loan. This also serves as a method of rationing loanable funds as some potential borrowers are unable or unwilling to pay the extra charges.

Statutes in Texas and Arkansas provide an interesting example of the effects of usury laws. For nearly 100 years, the Arkansas Constitution prohibited lenders from charging more than 10 percent on a loan. In addition, a ruling by the state supreme court eliminated the possibility of avoiding the ceiling by the addition of extra charges as discussed above. Business conditions in the city of Texarkana in the late 1970s vividly demonstrated the market's response to the Arkansas interest ceiling. Texarkana straddles the border between Arkansas and Texas. On one side of the street are Texas businesses and on the other, Arkansas establishments. On the more liberal Texas side were 11 new car and 23 used car dealers. The corresponding types of establishments on the Arkansas side numbered none and 3. The Texas side had 20 furniture and appliance dealers, compared to 6 on the Arkansas side. The residents of Texarkana were not unduly penalized because of the proximity of the Texas-based operations, but there was certainly a loss of business taxes for the state of Arkansas.

Rent Controls

The analysis of price controls in a competitive industry is also applicable to attempts to set rent ceilings on housing. The almost inevitable result is a shortage of available units and a deterioration of quality. In spite of the unpromising theoretical predictions for rent controls, they have been a very common practice in Europe and, to a lesser degree, in the United States. Most of the European nations experimented with some form of rent controls after World War II. Hundreds of cities in the United States have imposed rent controls at one time or another.

A dramatic example of the problems with rent controls is the experience of Paris during the first half of this century. Today in the United States it is not uncommon for rent to take 20 to 30 percent of a family's gross income. After World War II, rents in Paris were seldom more than 4 percent of income. Alas, things were not quite as good as they seemed. For those lucky enough to have rent-controlled housing, rents were ridiculously low. Unfortunately, demand far exceeded the supply. For those who did not already have a flat, there were simply none available; deaths of existing tenants were about the only possibility. The search for an apartment sometimes took the form of young couples scouring obituaries or making agreements for early notifications with undertakers. Old people were often accosted by young wives attempting to forge an agreement for the desired property. The rights to a rent-controlled apartment were as high as $1,800 to $6,000 per room (1984 dollars). As a result, many young couples were forced to live with their families.

Another consequence of rent controls in Paris was the deterioration of the housing stock. By the end of World War II, nearly 90 percent of rental housing had been built before World War I. At the low rental rates, it simply did not pay to build additional units. It also was not economical to maintain the existing housing stock. Repairs and other maintenance were sadly neglected. Between 1914 and 1948, rents increased only 6.8 times, but the cost of repairs increased by more than 120 times.[14]

Some programs have provisions designed to avoid the worst problems of rent controls. In 1978, the Los Angeles City Council passed an ordinance that limited annual rent increases to 7 percent for existing tenants. The legislation provided that new rental units and luxury units were excluded from the controls. These provisions were added to provide an incentive for new construction. The ordinance also exempts from the 7-percent-increase tenants who voluntarily vacate an apartment and those who are legally evicted. In addition, landlords are allowed to pass on the costs of capital improvements.

Rent controls in Los Angeles have provided some benefits for the tenants who are covered, but there have been many inequities. For example, while rent increases for existing tenants are limited to only 7 percent, new tenants may pay 50 or 60 percent more for the same apartment than did the previous tenants. In addition, landlords have been more prone to evict tenants over trivial matters and to let building maintenance lapse.[15]

SUMMARY
Incomes Policies and Inflation

Incomes policies are not very effective in dealing with demand-pull inflation. However, where concentrated firms and large unions contribute to a wage-price spiral, incomes policies may be useful in changing expectations.

Incomes Policies and Industry Concentration

Controls and Competitive Industries   By decreasing the quantity supplied and increasing the quantity demanded, price controls are likely to cause shortages in competitive industries. When prices are not allowed to function as a rationing device, then other mechanisms develop to deal with shortages. Queues and illegal activities such as black markets are not uncommon.

Controls and Firms with Market Power   It is possible to impose controls on firms with market power without creating shortages. If price is set equal to marginal cost, then

[14]Jouvenal, B. E., in Hayek, E. A., et al., *Rent Control—A Popular Paradox* (Vancouver, B.C.: Fraser Institute, 1976), pp. 105–112.
[15]See Hill, G. C., "As Rent Controls Spread Across the Country, Its Friends and Foes Watch Los Angeles," *Wall Street Journal* (Feb. 1, 1980), p. 38.

quantity supplied equals quantity demanded. However, many practical difficulties are associated with implementing this recommendation. For example, policymakers seldom have good information on demand and cost curves.

Experience with Incomes Policies

Pre-Twentieth Century   The use of incomes policies dates back thousands of years. In the United States, controls were implemented even before passage of the Declaration of Independence.

Wartime Policies   Most of the warring nations imposed some form of controls during World War II. The U.S. economy operated under a system of wage and price controls from 1941 to 1946. The needs of the war provided the public support necessary to make the policy effective, but a price explosion occurred as soon as controls were removed.

Postwar Experiences of Other Nations   After World War II, incomes policies were implemented in The Netherlands and Great Britain, as well as many other European nations. They proved easier to administer in the more centralized Netherlands economy than in Britain. In both cases, pressures of excess demand finally ended their effectiveness.

Wage-Price Guidelines and Jawboning   Incomes policies can involve varying degrees of compulsion. Voluntary wage-price guidelines were promoted by President Kennedy and were somewhat successful until the Vietnam War heated the economy. Voluntary guidelines proposed by the Carter administration in 1978 were not been effective. However, on some occasions, presidents have been able to moderate wage and price increases by applying political pressure.

Phases I, II, III, III$\frac{1}{2}$, and IV

Background and procedures   In 1971, President Nixon imposed a 90-day wage and price freeze (Phase I) to allow implementation of a program of controls. For the next two years (Phase II) the country operated under a policy that limited wage settlements to a 5.5 percent annual increase and prices to a 2-to-3-percent increase. Phase III had similar provisions except that compliance was voluntary. The failure of voluntary controls precipitated another freeze (Phase III$\frac{1}{2}$). Finally, a second round of controls was implemented between August 1973 and April 1974 (Phase IV).

Effects   It is very difficult to determine the effects of the Nixon wage and price controls. Although a number of studies have been made, the results are somewhat ambiguous. However, the evidence seems to indicate that any impacts in curbing inflation occurred during Phases I and II. The later phases, implemented during periods of strong demand, resulted in shortages and general social discontent.

Tax-Based Incomes Policies   Some economists have suggested that the tax system be used to induce modifications of firm and union behavior. For example, firms that hold down wage or price increases would be given a credit on their corporation income taxes.

Considerations in the Use of Incomes Policies

Past experience provides some generalizations about the use of incomes policies and selective price controls: (1) they do not work well during periods of high demand; (2) they require the cooperation of industry and labor; (3) controls work better in concentrated than in competitive industries; (4) policies and procedures must be tailored for the specific circumstances involved; (5) except during crises, incomes policies are not an effective long-term solution; (6) extensive preparation is required to formulate effective wage and price controls.

Selective Price Controls

Usury Laws   Usury laws limit the maximum interest rate that can be charged. Often, they are an attempt to help the poor. However, they may create shortages of loanable funds and require lending institutions to ration money. Rationing methods such as confining loans to low-risk customers or charging points up front may adversely affect the poor more than the high-interest rates.

Rent Controls   Rent controls are used in many European and U.S. cities. Although those who live in rent-controlled housing have very low payments, the demand for such units far exceeds the supply. Also, low rents greatly reduce the incentive to build new rental units and maintain existing units.

DISCUSSION QUESTIONS

1. When prices are held down by controls, what false signals are created for owners of resources?
2. What role do expectations regarding the future play in cost-push inflation?
3. How do the elasticities of supply and demand affect the magnitude of the shortages created by price controls imposed on competitive industries?
4. Would price controls imposed during the Vietnam War have been as effective as those used during World War II? Why?
5. Would incomes policies be more effective in a nation with a large volume of imports and exports than in a highly self-sufficient country? Why?
6. Could jawboning be used repeatedly by the president as a method of holding down wage and price increases?
7. What impact did President Nixon's political problems have on his wage and price control program?
8. If a tax-based incomes policy was to be implemented, which would be most effective, penalizing firms for failure to curb wage and price increases or rewards to firms able to moderate wage and price changes?
9. Should the federal government establish a commission to make standby preparations for implementing incomes policies? What would be the result of creating such a committee?

Index of Cases

Subject Index